THE OXFORD HANDBOOK OF

PROFESSIONAL SERVICE FIRMS

THE OXFORD HANDBOOK OF

PROFESSIONAL

SERVICE FIRMS

Edited by

LAURA EMPSON, DANIEL MUZIO,
JOSEPH P. BROSCHAK,

and

BOB HININGS

OXFORD
UNIVERSITY PRESS

OXFORD
UNIVERSITY PRESS

Great Clarendon Street, Oxford, ox2 6DP,
United Kingdom

Oxford University Press is a department of the University of Oxford.
It furthers the University's objective of excellence in research, scholarship,
and education by publishing worldwide. Oxford is a registered trade mark of
Oxford University Press in the UK and in certain other countries

Published in the United States of America by Oxford University Press
198 Madison Avenue, New York, NY 10016, United States of America

British Library Cataloguing in Publication Data
Data available

Library of Congress Control Number: 2015936759

ISBN 978–0–19–968239–3

Printed and bound by
CPI Group (UK) Ltd, Croydon, CR0 4YY

ACKNOWLEDGMENTS

LOOKING back over the acknowledgments pages of *Oxford Handbooks* in this series, a remarkable number of them begin with the same sentence. "The idea for this handbook came initially from David Musson, the Business and Management Editor at Oxford University Press." David Musson has occupied the role of Commissioning Editor at OUP for so many years now that, for most of us, we cannot imagine a time before him.

From our very first academic conference he has always been there, working quietly away over a strong coffee and a cigarette, engaged in the mysterious task of "commissioning." Sometimes he can be observed feigning mild interest as he listens courteously and carefully to an eager scholar pitching their improbable proposal for a pet project. On other occasions, it is David himself who is making the pitch, perhaps to a potential *Handbook* editor who knows the phenomenal amount of work involved in creating such a volume and is reluctant to take on that task. David plays a long game and, like a Canadian Mountie, always gets his man (or woman in my case).

So thank you David for your relentless "encouragement" to take on this task. You were right—this book did need to be written. Thank you for believing that we were the ones to write it.

LE

Contents

PART I PROFESSIONAL SERVICE FIRMS IN CONTEXT

PART II PROFESSIONAL SERVICE FIRMS: MANAGEMENT AND ORGANIZATION

PART III PROFESSIONAL SERVICE FIRMS: INDIVIDUALS AND INTERACTIONS

List of Figures

LIST OF TABLES

LIST OF CONTRIBUTORS

Mats Alvesson is Professor of Business Administration at the University of Lund, Sweden, Cass Business School, City University London, and at University of Queensland, Australia. Research interests include critical theory, gender, power, management of professional service (knowledge-intensive) organizations, leadership, identity, organizational image, organizational culture and symbolism, qualitative methods, and philosophy of science. Recent books include *The Triumph of Emptiness* (Oxford University Press 2013), *Qualitative Research and Theory Development* (Sage 2011, with Dan Kärreman), *Constructing Research Questions* (Sage 2013, with J. Sandberg), *Interpreting Interviews* (Sage 2011), *Metaphors We Lead By: Understanding Leadership in the Real World* (Routledge 2011, edited with André Spicer), *The Oxford Handbook of Critical Management Studies* (Oxford University Press 2011, edited with Todd Bridgman and Hugh Willmott), *Understanding Gender and Organizations* (Sage 2009, 2nd edn. with Yvonne Billing), *Reflexive Methodology* (Sage 2009, 2nd edn. with Kaj Skoldberg), *Changing Organizational Culture* (Routledge 2008, with Stefan Sveningsson), *Knowledge Work and Knowledge-Intensive Firms* (Oxford University Press 2004).

Louise Ashley is Lecturer in Human Resource Management and Organizational Behaviour at Royal Holloway, University of London. She specializes in researching the implementation and development of diversity and inclusion programmes in leading professional service firms, and has conducted research in the legal profession as well as occupations such as accountancy, management consulting, and investment banking. Her research encompasses a number of diversity strands although she has a particular focus on gender and social background. Louise has published articles in leading academic journals, including *Work, Employment and Society*, and *Human Relations*. She is a Fellow of the Centre for Professional Service Firms at Cass Business School.

Michael Barrett is Professor of Information Systems and Innovation Studies at Judge Business School, Cambridge University. In his research he adopts social theory and discursive approaches to understand technology-enabled change and innovation across a number of sectors including: financial services, professional service firms, and healthcare. Recent research explores processes of knowledge translation in facilitating service innovation, and the use of digital innovation to enable social innovation in emerging economies. His research has been published in journals such as *Information Systems Research, Academy of Management Journal, Organization Science*, and *MIS Quarterly*.

Mehdi Boussebaa is Associate Professor of Organization Studies at the University of Bath and an International Research Fellow at the Novak Druce Centre for Professional Service Firms, University of Oxford. His primary research investigates the institutional and political implications of economic globalization, especially in the context of global professional service firms. He has published his work in a wide range of leading management journals, including *Human Relations, Organization Studies*, and the *Journal of International Business Studies*. He serves on the editorial review boards of *Organization Studies* and the *Journal of Professions and Organization*.

Joseph P. Broschak is Associate Professor in the Department of Management and Organizations and the Interim Executive Director of the McGuire Center for Entrepreneurship at the University of Arizona, Eller College of Management. He also holds a courtesy appointment in the School of Sociology. He has a PhD in Management from the University of Texas at Austin. Joe's research revolves around two topics in organization theory. One is the structure of organizations: the demographic composition of the workforce, the employment arrangements in which workers are employed, and the system of jobs and job titles that individuals hold. The other is the dynamics of markets: the dynamics of inter-firm relationships in markets for professional services, patterns of men's and women's mobility in managerial labor markets, evolution and change of labor markets for professionals, and technological change in product markets. Joe's research has been published in a variety of management and sociology journals, including *Administrative Science Quarterly, Academy of Management Journal, American Sociological Review, Annual Review of Sociology, Decision Sciences*, and *Work and Occupations*, and in academic volumes including *Research in the Sociology of Organizations* and *Research in the Sociology of Work*. He currently serves on the editorial boards of *Administrative Science Quarterly* and the *Academy of Management Journal*.

Laurie Cohen is Professor of Organizational Behaviour at the Nottingham University Business School. Her doctoral work focused on women's transitions from employment to self-employment—an area that she has continued to work in ever since. In addition, she is interested in career-making in emerging forms of organization, and research methods in the study of career, especially interpretive approaches and the use of narrative. For many years she has also been involved in a series of studies on work and careers in professional organizations, focusing mainly on scientific research establishments and more recently engineering organizations. She has published in a wide range of journals including *Human Relations, Organization Studies*, and *Journal of Vocational Behaviour* and she is on the editorial board *of Human Relations, Journal of Vocational Behaviour, Journal of Management Inquiry*, and *Management Learning*. Her new book, *Imagining Women's Careers*, is forthcoming with Oxford University Press.

Ronit Dinovitzer is Associate Professor of Sociology at the University of Toronto, where she is cross appointed to the Institute for Management and Innovation. She is also a Faculty Fellow at the American Bar Foundation in Chicago, where she is Co-Director of the Research Group on Legal Diversity, and she is an Affiliated Faculty in Harvard's

Program on the Legal Profession. As a sociologist of the professions her research focuses on the social organization of lawyers, the role of labor markets, and the effects of culture on professional work. Recent projects include the "After the JD" study, the first national longitudinal study of law graduates in the US, the "Law and Beyond" Study, the first national study of law graduates in Canada, and a Canadian study on Ethics, the Professional Service Firm and Corporate Governance (with Hugh and Sally Gunz).

Laura Empson is Professor in the Management of Professional Service Firms at Cass Business School, London, and Director of the Cass Centre for Professional Service Firms. Her current research focuses on leadership dynamics in PSFs and is funded by a major grant from the ESRC. Her previous ESRC-funded study was of changing forms of governance in PSFs. Her research into PSFs has also covered themes such as: mergers and acquisitions, professionalization of management, organizational and individual identity, knowledge and diversity management. In 2013 she was selected to be the *Financial Times* Professor of the Week. She has published numerous articles in leading international academic journals including *Journal of Management Studies, Organization Studies, Accounting, Organizations and Society*, and *Human Relations*, as well as the Oxford University Press book, *Managing the Modern Law Firm* (ed. 2007). She is a Member of the Editorial Boards of the *Journal of Management Studies, Organization Studies*, and the *Journal of Professional Organizations*. She is also a Member of the ESRC's Peer Review College. She is an Independent Non-Executive of KPMG LLP. She was previously a Reader at the University of Oxford's Saïd Business School and has had previous careers in investment banking and strategy consulting. She has a PhD and MBA from London Business School and a BSc(Econ) from University College, London.

James Faulconbridge is Professor of Transnational Management in the Department of Organisation, Work and Technology at Lancaster University Management School. His research focuses, in particular, upon the globalization of professional and business service firms, with interest in the way knowledge is produced and circulated within global firms and the way institutions affect the organization of firms. James co-authored the books *The Globalization of Advertising* and *The Globalization of Executive Search* (both Routledge) and edited the book *International Business Travel in the Global Economy* (Ashgate). He regularly publishes in journals including *Economic Geography, Journal of Economic Geography, Organization Studies*, and *Work, Employment and Society*. He is a Fellow of the Centre for Professional Service Firms at Cass Business School.

Heidi K. Gardner is Distinguished Fellow at Harvard Law School's Program on the Legal Profession and a Lecturer on Law. Her research focuses on leadership, collaboration, and management in knowledge-based organizations, especially professional service firms. Previously she served on the faculty of Harvard Business School as an Assistant Professor of Organizational Behavior. Her research was awarded the Academy of Management's prize for Outstanding Practical Implications for Management. She has published articles in the *Academy of Management Journal, Administrative Science Quarterly, Journal of Organizational Behavior*, and *Harvard Business Review*, as well as numerous book chapters and practitioner-focused articles. She has lived and worked on four continents, including as a management consultant for McKinsey & Co., a Fulbright Fellow, and a teacher in Japan. She earned a BA in Japanese Studies from the University of Pennsylvania, a Masters from the London School of Economics, and a Doctorate from London Business School.

Hugh Gunz is Professor of Organizational Behaviour at the University of Toronto and Director of the Institute for Management and Innovation at the University of Toronto Mississauga. He has published papers on the careers of managers, professionals, and others, the management of professionals of many kinds, and management education, is the author of the book *Careers and Corporate Cultures* (1989), and the co-editor of the *Handbook of Career Studies* (2007). He serves or has served on the editorial boards of a number of journals, including *Journal of Professions and Organization, Academy of Management Journal, Journal of Managerial Psychology*, and *Emergence*, and is a former chair of the Careers Division of the Academy of Management. He has PhDs in Chemistry and Organizational Behaviour.

Sally Gunz is Professor of Business Law and Professional Ethics in the School of Accounting and Finance, University of Waterloo, Canada. Her primary research interests center around the legal and ethical responsibilities of professionals and, increasingly, how professionals make ethical decisions, and what factors impact those decisions. She has studied professionals in both employed and private practice settings. She is the author of *The New Corporate Counsel* (Carswell 1991) and several academic studies relating to in-house lawyers, lawyers in private practice, accountants, and actuaries. She is a past-President of the Academy of Legal Studies in Business and the former director of the Centre for Accounting Ethics.

Nina Katrin Hansen is Assistant Professor on the Faculty of Business Administration, Chair of Human Resource Management, University of Hamburg. Nina completed her dissertation in 2010 about the "Theoretical Foundations of the Nexus Between Strategic Human Resource Management Systems and Organizational Capabilities" at the University of Hamburg for which she received the Best PhD Thesis Award of the Faculty of Business Administration. At the beginning of 2014, she was a visiting academic at the Novak Druce Centre for Professional Service Firms, Saïd Business School, University of Oxford. Based on a multi-level approach, her research focuses on the question of how human resource management systems influence intellectual capital architectures, and how they govern the development of human capital, organizational capabilities, and organizational learning modes especially in the field of PSFs. The topic "HRM in Professional Service Firms" represents her post-doctoral research project (Habilitation) which is also reflected in her recent teaching activities for which she came in second in the Hamburg teaching prize 2012/2013. Research results have been published in national and international journals such as *The German Journal of Industrial Relations, The International Journal of Human Resource Management*, and *Human Resource Management Journal*.

William S. Harvey is Research Director and Senior Lecturer at the University of Exeter Business School, Associate Fellow in the Centre for Corporate Reputation at the University of Oxford, and Honorary Senior Lecturer at the University of Sydney. Will's research focuses on corporate reputation, talent management, leadership, and business elites. Will has published in a range of journals in business and management, sociology, geography, and industrial relations, and has recently co-edited a book on international human resource management with Cambridge University Press.

Bob Hinings is Professor Emeritus in the Faculty of Business, University of Alberta. He has received the Distinguished Scholar Award from the Organization and Management Theory Division of the US Academy of Management. He is a Fellow of the Royal Society of Canada and of the US Academy of Management as well as an Honorary Member of the European Group for Organizational Studies.

Dan Kärreman is Professor in Management and Organization Studies at Copenhagen Business School, and Professor in Management at Royal Holloway, University of London. He is also affiliated to the Lumos group at Lund University. His research interests include critical management studies, knowledge work, identity in organizations, leadership, organizational control, and research methodology, and he has published his work in *Academy of Management Review, Human Relations, Journal of Management Studies, Organization, Organization Science*, and *Organization Studies*, among others. His most recent book is *Qualitative Methodology and Theory Development: Mystery as Method* (Sage 2011, with Mats Alvesson).

Nicholas Kinnie holds the Chair of Human Resource Management in the School of Management at the University of Bath in the UK. His research interests lie in exploring the links between HR practices and business performance in a variety of organizations including professional service firms and outsourced telephone call centres. This has involved extensive empirical research in private and public sector organizations on a series of projects mostly sponsored by the Chartered Institute of Personnel and Development. Most recently this has included a research project examining the drivers and consequences of employee attitudes and behaviors in a series of professional service firms. This research has been published in a variety of academic and practitioner publications and presented at various international conferences.

Ian Kirkpatrick is Professor in Work and Organisation at Leeds University Business School and currently serves as Director of the Leeds Social Science Institute. His research interests include: management change in professional organizations, restructuring of public services, and the evolution of flexible employment patterns. Ian is co-author of two books: *The New Managerialism and Public Service Professions*, and *The Management of Children's Residential Care*, both published by Palgrave Macmillan. He has been involved in a number of large research projects including studies funded by the Department of Health and most recently, the Economic and Social Research Council and European Science Foundation. He is a co-founder of the ESRC funded Consumer Data Research Centre and Leeds Institute for Data Analytics. He has also served as a member of the editorial management team of the BSA journal, *Work, Employment and Society*.

Ann Langley is Professor of Management at HEC Montreal and Canada research chair in strategic management in pluralistic settings. Her research focuses on strategic change, leadership, identity, and the use of management tools in complex organizations with an emphasis on processual and qualitative research approaches. She has published over 70 articles and six books. She is co-editor of *Strategic Organization*, and on the editorial boards of *Academy of Management Journal* and *Organization Science*. She is also series editor with Haridimos Tsoukas of *Perspectives on Process Organization Studies* published by Oxford University Press and is currently preparing a *Sage Handbook of Process Organization Studies*. She is a member of the Board of the European Group for Organizational Studies (EGOS) and was chair of the 29th annual EGOS Colloquium held in Montreal in 2013.

Huseyin Leblebici is Merle H. and Virginia Downs Boren Professor of Business Administration at the University of Illinois at Urbana-Champaign, Department of Business Administration. He received his MBA and PhD in organizational behavior from University of Illinois. Professor Leblebici's recent research focuses on three interrelated macro organizational domains: the co-evolutionary processes in the professions and organizational fields, the sociology of professional careers, and the evolution of business models. He is currently working on the historical evolution of business models in two-faced markets such as credit cards and its implication for the development of strategic business groups and institutionalization of industry practices. He is also investigating career trajectories of US law school deans since 1900 to see how the legal profession and the academic structure of US universities have influenced their career patterns. His work has appeared in journals such as *Administrative Science Quarterly, Social Forces, Organization Studies, Strategic Organization,* and *Strategic Management Journal*. He has served on a number of editorial boards including *Administrative Science Quarterly, Academy of Management Review, Organization Science, Journal of Management, Academy of Management Review,* and *Organization Studies*. He is also one of the founding editors of *Journal of Professions and Organization*.

Namrata Malhotra is Associate Professor in Strategy in the Organization and Management Group at the Imperial College Business School. Her research interests lie in the areas of organizational change and institutional change drawing on both organizational theory and strategy. To date, her research projects have predominantly focused on examining change processes in professional service firms, especially law firms. She has also done research on internationalization strategies of engineering consulting firms. Currently, she is working on a project examining micro-processes of institutional change unfolding in law firms with the emergence of innovative career models. She is also involved in a project focused on the British nuclear industry. She is investigating how institutional complexity faced by this high risk industry has shaped key structural and strategic changes mediated by changing perceptions of risk over time. Currently, she is an International Research Fellow in the Novak Druce Centre for Professional Service Firms, Saïd Business School, University of Oxford.

John Mawdsley is a fifth-year doctoral student in Strategy & Entrepreneurship at the University of Illinois Urbana-Champaign. John's research interests reside at the intersection of cooperative strategy and strategic human capital. His research agenda seeks to understand the strategic challenges encountered by professional service firms and the firm-level outcomes of strategic choices made by these firms. In particular, John is interested in examining the implications for strategy and performance of professional service firms' investments in client relationships, how professional service firms build or acquire knowledge-based capabilities for long-run value creation, and how they organize, govern, and align knowledge workers to achieve firm goals.

Vincent-Wayne Mitchell is the Sir John E. Cohen Professor Consumer of Marketing Cass Business School, City University London. His did his PhD in Professional Services Marketing and he has published over 200 academic and practitioner papers in journals such as *Harvard Business Review*, *Journal of Consumer Psychology*, *Journal of Economic Psychology*, *Journal of Business Ethics*, and *British Journal of Management* and has won eight Best Paper Awards. He sits on the Editorial Boards of six international journals as well as being Head of the Marketing group at Cass. He has undertaken work for numerous organizations and received research funding and support from: the DTI, Cooperative Bank, British Brandowners Group, Coca-Cola, Boots, and KPMG. His book called *Real People, Real Decisions* won Financial Times/Pearson Prentice Hall Higher Education Book of the Year Award. He is a Member of the Centre for Professional Service Firms at Cass Business School.

Glenn Morgan is Professor of International Management at Cardiff Business School and Visiting Professor at the Department of Business and Politics at Copenhagen Business School. Recent book publications include *New Spirits of Capitalism? Crises, Justifications, and Dynamics* (Oxford University Press 2013, ed. with Paul DuGay), *Capitalisms and Capitalism in the Twenty-First Century* (Oxford University Press 2012, with Richard Whitley), and *The Oxford Handbook of Comparative Institutional Analysis* (Oxford University Press 2010, ed. with John Campbell and Colin Crouch). From 2004 to 2008 he was Editor of the journal *Organization*.

Timothy Morris is Professor of Management Studies at the University of Oxford. Before joining Oxford, he held faculty positions at London Business School and at Imperial College, London. His research interests are concerned with the nature and patterns of change and processes of innovation in organizations of professionals where he has studied firms in a range of sectors including law, architecture, executive search, accounting and management consulting. He has published papers in leading American and European management journals, several books, and contributions to numerous edited collections.

Daniel Muzio is a Professor of Professions and Organization at the University of Newcastle and the director of the Professions, Work and Organization research group. He has previously worked at the universities of Lancaster, Leeds, and Manchester. He has held visiting positions at Cass Business School and Luiss Guido Carli in Rome. His research interests include the organization and management of professional services firms, the sociology of the professions, and institutional theory. Daniel has published in several leading management, sociology, and law journals, including: *Organization Studies, Journal of Management Studies, Human Relations, Journal of Economic Geography*, and *Work, Employment and Society*. He is a founding Editor of the *Journal of Professions and Organization* (Oxford University Press). He is a Fellow of the Centre for Professional Service Firms at Cass Business School.

Mirko Noordegraaf is full Professor of Public Management at the Utrecht School of Governance (USG), Utrecht University, The Netherlands, and vice-head of department of the Utrecht School of Governance. He studies organization and management issues, with a particular emphasis on public organizations, public services, and professionals. He especially focuses on the reconfiguration of professionalism, inside and outside professional service organizations such as hospitals, schools, and law courts. He has published in journals such as *Organization Studies, Public Administration, Administration & Society, Public Management Review, Current Sociology*, and *Comparative Sociology*. He published/publishes books such as *Public Management: Performance, Professionalism, Politics* (Palgrave Macmillan 2014), *Professionals under Pressure* (with Bram Steijn, 2013), and *Public Professions and Professionalism: A Routledge Research Handbook* (with Justin Waring, 2016). He is editor for *Public Administration Review*, and member of the editorial board of the *Journal of Professions & Organization*.

Sigrid Quack is Professor of Comparative and Transnational Sociology at the University of Duisburg-Essen and Associated Leader of the Research Group "Institution-Building across Borders" at the Max Planck Institute for the Study of Societies in Cologne, Germany. From 2006 to 2008 she was Chair of the European Group of Organizational Studies (EGOS), and from 2011 to 2014 she served as a member of the Council of the Global and Transnational Sociology Section of the American Sociological Association. Currently, she is a coordinator of the Research Network on Professionals and Professions in a Globalizing World and a member of the Executive Committee of the Society for the Advancement of Socio-Economics (SASE). Sigrid has been extensively researching the internationalization of law firms, and the role of lawyers and accountants in transnational rule-setting. Her current research focuses on the social and political challenges posed by economic globalization for legitimate and effective transnational governance, particularly through studying standard-setting in the forest, labor, accounting, and copyright fields. She has published widely in international journals, including *Organization Theory, Organization, Theory & Society*, and *RIPE*. Her books include *Governance across Borders* (Epubli 2013), co-edited with L. Dobusch and M. Mader, *Transnational Communities* (Cambridge 2010), and *Institutions and Globalization* (Edward Elgar 2003), both co-edited with M.-L. Djelic.

Markus Reihlen is Vice-President and the Otto Group Professor of Strategic Management at Leuphana University of Lüneburg as well as Associate Fellow at the Novak Druce Centre for Professional Service Firms at the University of Oxford. His research interests are at the crossroads of professional service organizations and research in strategic management, organization theory, and international business. He is the author and co-editor of five books on innovation planning, process management, networks and alliances, internationalization of professional services, and more recently on entrepreneurship in professional services. His academic work has appeared in such journals as the *Journal of Management Studies, Research in the Sociology of Organizations, Business Research*, and the *Scandinavian Journal of Management*.

Mari Sako is Professor of Management Studies at Saïd Business School and member of the Novak Druce Centre for Professional Service Firms, University of Oxford. She is a socio-economist with expertise in global strategy, outsourcing and offshoring, and professions. Her research on the comparative political economy analysis of firms, supplier relations, employment systems, and education and training resulted in numerous publications, including *Are Skills the Answer?* (Oxford University Press 2001, with Colin Crouch and David Finegold), *Prices, Quality and Trust* (Cambridge University Press 2008), and *Shifting Boundaries of the Firm* (Oxford University Press 2006). She read PPE at Oxford, and holds an MSc and a PhD in Economics. She taught at the London School of Economics, and held visiting positions at Kyoto University, Tokyo University, Ecole Polytechnique, and MIT's Sloan School of Management. During 2011–12, she was President of the Society for the Advancement of Socio-Economics (SASE).

Elke Schüßler is Assistant Professor of Organization Theory at the Management Department at Freie Universität Berlin. Her research focuses on changing forms of value creation, transnational organizational governance, and the role of field-configuring events for institutional innovation. Her empirical focus spans from traditional manufacturing industries to creative and knowledge-intensive industries. She currently has a particular interest in the emergence of labor and environmental standards in transnational fields and their organizational underpinnings. Her work is published in journals such as the *Academy of Management Journal, Industrial and Corporate Change, Industry & Innovation, Organization Studies*, and *Economic and Industrial Democracy*.

Peter D. Sherer is Associate Professor at the Haskayne School of Business at the University of Calgary. He received his PhD from the University of Wisconsin-Madison. Prior to joining the Haskayne School, he was a faculty member at the University of Illinois, the University of Oregon, and the Wharton School. His teaching interests include strategic human resource management, organizational theory, business strategy, and research methods. He has been the recipient of six teaching awards during his years at the Haskayne School of Business, the University of Oregon, and the Wharton School. He was recognized in 2005 as one of the top MBA professors in Canada by Canadian Business. He has published a number of articles in leading journals and his work has appeared in major research volumes. Professor Sherer (along with K. Lee) was awarded the Best Paper of 2002 in the *Academy of Management Journal* by the Academy of Management for his paper on institutional change in law firms. The paper was also recognized by the editorial board of the *Academy of Management Journal* (February, 2006) as one of the most interesting academic journal articles in management over the last 100 years. Professor Sherer is on the editorial board of the *Academy of Management Journal.*

Deepak Somaya is the Steven and Christy King Faculty Fellow and Associate Professor of Strategy and Entrepreneurship at the College of Business, University of Illinois at Urbana Champaign. He also holds a courtesy appointment as Associate Professor in the College of Law and in the Institute for Genomic Biology, an interdisciplinary research center at the University of Illinois. Deepak received his PhD in Business Administration from the Walter A. Haas School of Business at the University of California at Berkeley, his MBA from the Indian Institute of Management (Calcutta), and his B.Tech. in mechanical engineering from the Indian Institute of Technology (Bombay). In his research, he studies how companies strategize about and derive competitive advantage from their knowledge assets, particularly their human capital, relational assets, and intellectual property. His research has been published in over 25 journal articles, book chapters, and conference proceedings, and he has received numerous awards including a best dissertation award (Technology and Innovation Division, Academy of Management), several conference best paper awards, and the 2012 California Management Review Best Article Award. He currently serves on the editorial boards of the *Journal of Management, Organization Science,* and *Strategic Management Journal,* and is the Associate Program Chair of the Strategic Human Capital interest group in the Strategic Management Society.

Hilary Sommerlad is Professor of Law and Research Director of the Centre for Professional Legal Education and Research at the University of Birmingham. Her research interests are access to justice, the cultural practices of the professional workplace, and diversity. Her writing on these topics includes the first full-length book on women solicitors in England and Wales and a report into the barriers to diversity in the legal profession (commissioned by the Legal Services Board). She is Articles Editor of *Legal Ethics,* and serves on the editorial boards of the *Journal of Law and Society* and the *International Journal of the Legal Profession.*

Roy Suddaby is the Winspear Professor of Management at the Peter B. Gustavson School of Business at the University of Victoria, Canada and is a Strategic Research Professor at Newcastle University Business School, United Kingdom. His research examines processes of profound change. He is the outgoing Editor of the *Academy of Management Review.* His current research examines the changing role of the corporation and the professionalization of management.

Kate Sullivan holds a PhD in Communication. She is a Lecturer in the Department of Business Administration at Lund University and a Visiting Scholar at the David Eccles School of Business at the University of Utah. Katie's research centers on issues of professionalization. Specifically, she explores how workers discursively and materially navigate (often) tense and contradictory topics such as professionalism, sexuality, and embodiment. Her work in this area is published in *Organization Studies, Gender, Work and Organization, Ephemera,* and *Management Communication Quarterly.*

Juani Swart is Professor in Human Capital Management and specializes in knowledge management and the management of knowledge workers. She is Head of the Organization Studies Group and Director of the Work and Employment Research Centre (WERC) which has centers of expertise in knowledge, change, and leadership. Her research is focused on the management of knowledge and knowledge workers, innovation, and employee attitudes and behaviors. This research aims to understand the transfer of human capital into intellectual capital, thereby linking the intellectual capital, HRM, and Performance debates. At the MBA level she teaches People Management and leads an MBA elective on Knowledge Leadership in a Global Economy where she works closely with the World Bank. Juani was Director of the MBA at Bath (2005–7) where she established the External Advisory Group of Companies and led the redesign and relaunch of the suite of MBA programmes. As a Chartered Psychologist, Juani's executive development expertise is in the areas of strategic knowledge management, leadership styles, personal effectiveness in the context of people management, and the management of professionals. She has published widely in the area of people management in knowledge-intensive firms, intellectual capital structures, innovation and knowledge sharing.

Andrew von Nordenflycht is associate Professor of Strategy at Simon Fraser University's Beedie School of Business. He received a BA in History from Stanford University and a PhD in Management from the MIT Sloan School of Management. He researches governance and management of human capital-intensive firms, especially professional services and airlines. He is the co-author of *Up In the Air: How the Airlines Can Improve Performance by Engaging Their Employees* (Cornell University Press 2013) and has published articles in leading management and industrial relations journals, including *Organization Science, Academy of Management Journal, Academy of Management Review,* and *Industrial and Labor Relations Review.*

Andreas Werr is a Professor at the Stockholm School of Economics and Head of the Center for HRM and knowledge work at the SSE Institute for Research. His research interests focus on the acquisition, application, and development of knowledge and expertise in organizations, including knowledge management and talent management. Andreas has also carried out extensive research on organizations' use of management consultants and the management of professional service firms.

CHAPTER 1

RESEARCHING PROFESSIONAL SERVICE FIRMS

An Introduction and Overview

LAURA EMPSON, DANIEL MUZIO,
JOSEPH P. BROSCHAK, AND BOB HININGS

1.1 SIGNIFICANCE OF PROFESSIONAL SERVICE FIRMS TO ECONOMICS, SOCIETY, AND SCHOLARSHIP

OVER the past three decades the Professional Service Firm (PSF) sector has emerged as one of the most rapidly growing, profitable, and significant sectors of the global economy. In 2013 the accountancy, management consulting, legal, and architectural sectors alone generated revenues of US$1.6 trillion and employed 14 million people (IBISWorld 2014a, 2014b, 2014c; MarketLine 2014). If sectors such as engineering services and advertising are included, the figure rises to US$2.5 trillion and US$18 million respectively (IBISWorld 2014d, 2014e). This is comparable in terms of revenues to the global commercial banking sector. Current reliable aggregated data for the professional services sector are not available on a global basis but in the UK this sector employs almost 12% of the workforce, accounts for 8% of output, and represents half of the trade surplus in services (HM Treasury 2009).

On an individual basis, the largest PSFs are now global giants, on a par with far more famous publicly quoted corporations. For example, PricewaterhouseCoopers (PwC), one of the "Big Four" accountancy firms, currently employs almost 200,000 people in almost 160 countries. By these measures it is significantly more global than McDonald's.

With a 2014 gross revenue of US$34 billion, PwC is also larger than Fortune 500 companies such as 3M and Time Warner. Similarly, management consultancy firm Accenture, which is itself a Fortune 500 company, has a similar market capitalization to both of these firms. By contrast, individual firms in the legal, engineering, and architectural sector are far smaller than the Big Four accountancy or global management consultancy firms, but they too are growing rapidly in terms of size, complexity, and global reach.

The significance of PSFs to the global economy extends far beyond their scale. As Sharma states (1997: 758), without PSFs "business as we know it would come to a grinding halt." This is because PSFs play an important role in developing human capital, creating innovative business services, reshaping government institutions, establishing and interpreting the rules of financial markets, and setting legal, accounting, and other professional standards. Furthermore, the high salaries they offer mean that they are able to attract a large proportion of the best qualified graduates. Indeed PSFs such as PwC, McKinsey, and consulting engineers Arup tend to dominate preferred graduate employers lists.[1] As such, PSFs, and the professions more generally, are linked through their recruitment and promotion practices to patterns of social stratification, but also potentially to social mobility (Panel on Fair Access to the Professions 2009; Sommerlad et al. 2010; Ashley and Empson 2013).

PSFs have historically acted as vehicles for the diffusion of new and often radical business practices and structures. Examples include the "M" form of business promoted by consulting firm McKinsey (Kipping 1999), the poison pill defense developed by law firm Wachtell Lipton (Starbuck 1993), and the business risk audit associated in particular with KPMG (Robson et al. 2007). More controversially, the influence of PSFs is also captured by their involvement in a string of high-profile corporate malpractice cases (Coffee 2006; Gabbioneta et al. 2013, 2014). These have highlighted the extent to which in recent years the PSF's traditional assurance role has become compromised as many have sought to become more directly involved in shaping and implementing their clients' strategies.

Importantly the influence of PSFs is not limited to the business world but stretches into broader social arenas. They are, for instance, among the top ten "corporate" donors to US presidential and congressional campaigns (Thornburg and Roberts 2008), while an extensive literature documents their role as vectors for the globalization and financialization of the economy (Arnold 2005; Suddaby et al. 2007; Faulconbridge and Muzio 2012). More specifically, they have taken the lead in the reform of public services (McDonald 2013), the administration of justice (Dezalay and Garth 1998), the structure of professional qualifications (Suddaby et al. 2007), and the operation of insolvency regimes (Halliday and Carruthers 2009). As such it is difficult to disagree with Scott's comment that professions, and within them PSFs, "have assumed leading roles in the creation and tending of institutions. They are the preeminent institutional agents of our time" (Scott 2008: 219; see also Muzio et al. 2013).

Beyond their significance as an empirical setting, PSFs are worth studying because of their theoretical significance and the insights they may generate into the contemporary challenges facing organizations within the knowledge economy. Traditional management models, which are often derived from the empirical setting of manufacturing firms, offer only limited insight into the complex interpersonal and organizational dynamics that operate within PSFs (Maister 1993; Teece 2003). Conversely, by understanding the peculiarities of PSFs and their management, scholars may in turn develop a deeper level of insight into more conventional organizations, or organizations which are attempting to move away from conventional management models to accommodate more knowledge-based forms of working. This approach, looking at PSFs for the insights they can offer into organizations more generally, is consistent with recent calls by Greenwood et al. (2014) to reintroduce comparative organizational analysis into our study of organizations and institutions.

For instance, because PSFs typically generate intangible experiential services in the form of knowledge-rich, time-sensitive advice that is tailored to a specific client's needs (Morris and Empson 1998; von Nordenflycht 2010; Brivot 2011), this implies a much higher degree of "relational embeddedness" and context sensitivity compared to many other kinds of business activities, limiting the scope for traditional strategies of standardization and commoditization. Furthermore, because people and client relationships are the main assets of the PSF, dependence on these highly mobile and highly portable assets creates significant complexities in terms of how PSFs approach their client relationship and human resource management (HRM) activities. For instance, power in PSFs tends to be highly dispersed between autonomous professionals who retain significant amounts of discretion over how their work is organized; accordingly, in these organizational settings management tends to be more consensual (Empson 2007) and mindful of individual preferences and local sensitivities (Faulconbridge and Muzio 2008). Indeed, clichés like "herding cats" or "losing one's capital every night down an elevator" capture very graphically some of this distinctiveness and its related managerial and organizational challenges.

These challenges are of course not exclusive to PSFs but they are best exemplified in this context. Accordingly, this is an area where PSFs may be leading the way in the development of new organizational forms and managerial practices and where their study may offer particular insights in the realities of the contemporary knowledge-based economy.

1.2 PROFESSIONAL SERVICE FIRMS COMING OUT OF THE SHADOWS

Despite their empirical significance and theoretical distinctiveness, for many years PSFs remained very much in the shadows of organizational research. This is evidenced by the considerable difficulty in gaining up-to-date information about the scale of the sector. A majority of PSFs are privately owned and accordingly are not legally required to disclose financial information, while national governments and supranational bodies do not gather consolidated data on this sector and only limited information is available at a disaggregated level. Perhaps because these firms disclose very little financial information and prefer to operate close to their clients and out of the public eye, they attract relatively little coverage in the mainstream business press.

Generally speaking management scholars have also been slow to recognize the scale and significance of the PSF sector; PSF scholarship represents a still small, though rapidly developing, niche in the field of management research. As one illustrative example, the UK's new Research Council Funding outputs database suggests 21 possible sectors in which research may have been conducted, but only one which relates to PSFs ("Financial services and management consulting"). UK scholars engaged in researching sectors such as accountancy and law, in which the UK is a global leader, are required to file their returns to the Research Council Funding database under the category of "Other."

Yet the last few years have marked the coming of age of PSF scholarship. A bibliometric search[2] limited to the Scopus business, management, and accounting database reveals that there are now almost 300 peer review articles explicitly referring to PSFs (this does not include the substantial number of articles referring to firms in specific professional sectors rather than PSFs more generally). Importantly, the number of entries is growing exponentially, from a couple of examples in the early 1990s, to more than 40 publications per annum in recent years. For the first two decades, the number of PSF publications tended to "spike" around a series of special issues but now there is a regular stream of new scholarship in leading management journals such as the *Academy of Management Journal, Organization Science, Journal of Management Studies, Organization Studies*, and *Human Relations*. The recent launch by Oxford University Press of a specialist journal, the *Journal of Professions and Organizations*, further signals the maturity of this field.

Against this backdrop, this volume seeks to make a timely and important contribution by bringing together and critically reflecting on the complex array of literature that has been published in recent decades on the topic of PSFs. But what exactly do we mean when we talk about PSFs?

1.3 WHAT *EXACTLY* IS A PROFESSIONAL SERVICE FIRM?

One reason it is so difficult to gain accurate aggregate data about the PSF sector is that there is very little agreement among researchers about what exactly is a PSF. Indeed von Nordenflycht (2010) shows that scholars have applied the term to organizations operating in more than 30 distinct knowledge-based sectors. This lack of clarity parallels similar long-standing debates in the sociology of the professions on the definition of professions and professionalism (Abbott 1988; Freidson 1994; Macdonald 1995; Krause 1996; Anderson-Gough et al. 1999; Kritzer 1999; Evetts 2006).

In its narrowest sense, a PSF could simply be an organization where the majority of income-generating staff are members of an established profession, i.e., von Nordenflycht's (2010) classic or regulated PSF. This definition would encompass accounting and law firms, engineering consulting firms, and architects' practices, but would also encompass medical practices which are not normally classified as PSFs. The definition of a PSF could be expanded to include a wide range of knowledge-intensive activities and aspirant professions, such as management consulting, executive search, and advertising, as the *Journal of Professions and Organizations* suggests (Brock et al. 2014). Using this approach, investment banks should be classified as PSFs, though typically they are not. Why are some types of firms unambiguously classified as PSFs while the professional status of other apparently similar ones is unclear?

It is not particularly helpful to organizational scholarship to establish narrow definitions, which exclude firms which potentially have important insights to offer in terms of comparative analysis (Greenwood et al. 2014). Equally, highly inclusive definitions undermine the credibility of the study of PSFs by making it difficult to justify the distinctiveness of the phenomenon we seek to study. We need to establish some clear boundary conditions by defining a set of characteristics which clearly identify the organizational phenomenon we are investigating while enabling us to distinguish between the different kinds of PSFs which may possess these characteristics to varying degrees. To avoid succumbing to crude generalizations we need a definition which allows for heterogeneity among the firms (von Nordenflycht et al., Chapter 7, this volume) as well as for the hybridized nature of many professional organizations (Kirkpatrick and Noordegraaf, Chapter 5, this volume).

The definition needs to encompass a small high street legal or accounting practice, and a magic circle or Big Four firm. And looking inside a Big Four firm, the ultimate multidisciplinary PSF, the definition needs to encompass the highly regulated audit function (where an auditor's first duty is to uphold the public interest) with the management consulting function (where a consultant's first duty is to his or her client). What do these various firms and distinctive parts of multidisciplinary PSFs have in common which distinguishes them from many other kinds of knowledge-intensive organizations?

In seeking to establish a definition of a PSF, it is unwise to attempt to defend phenomenologically derived boundary conditions in the rapidly changing environment in which PSFs operate. The boundaries need to be as flexible as the firms themselves, yet conceptually credible. As Zardkoohi et al. (2011) argue, the problem of defining PSFs is that changes in the context can render the definition irrelevant.

For the purposes of this volume, we define a PSF according to four key characteristics (see Figure 1.1). We recognize that many organizations will possess *some* of these characteristics. We argue that a PSF will possess *all* of them, to varying degrees. By accepting that a PSF must possess all four characteristics but can do so to varying degrees we recognize the heterogeneity that exists within the sector while drawing some conceptually defensible boundaries around the phenomenon under investigation. This makes it possible to conduct more structured comparative analysis within the sector as well as between other sectors.

These defining characteristics reflect the areas of research which have attracted the most sustained attention from PSF scholars over the years. They are consistent with previous definitions by, for example, Løwendahl (1997), Morris and Empson (1998), and

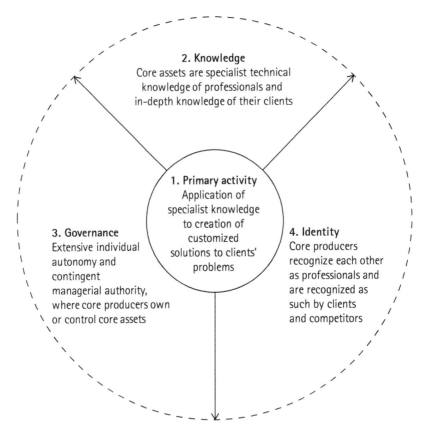

FIGURE 1.1 Defining characteristics of a Professional Service Firm.

Greenwood et al. (1990). They reflect von Nordenflycht's (2010) defining characteristics (knowledge intensity, low capital intensity, and professionalized workforce) but extend and refine his definition by bringing the themes of customization, governance, and identity to the fore.

1. Primary activity: Application of specialist knowledge to creation of customized solutions to clients' problems.

The concept of customization is central to the definition of a PSF (see Empson 2008). From this, as will be demonstrated, flow the three additional defining characteristics relating to knowledge, governance, and identity. This criterion excludes firms primarily engaged in financial services activities which are dependent on substantial capital reserves (e.g., investment banking or private equity funds) as a PSF is above all a knowledge-intensive and not a capital-intensive operation. This criterion also excludes generic knowledge-intensive firms, such as software, biotech, or "big pharma" companies, which sell packaged products. According to this criterion, a "claims farm" law firm specializing in personal injury lawsuits (employing large numbers of para-legals engaging in highly routinized processual work) will also be at the outer boundaries of the PSF definition, because its primary activity is not sufficiently customized. What distinguishes PSFs from these kinds of firms is the bespoke nature of professional work which requires an intensive interaction between professionals and their clients.

But this definition alone does not explain why hospitals and large engineering companies are typically not considered PSFs but rather as examples of the broader category of professional service organization (Scott 1965; Larson 1977). We need to refine this further, with reference to other defining characteristics of PSFs.

2. Knowledge: Core assets are specialist technical knowledge of professionals and their in-depth knowledge of clients.

The concept of knowledge (including expertise and "know-how") has been extensively researched in the PSF field but from a relatively narrow empirical base. The focus has tended to be on the professionally accredited knowledge of the established professions and on whether firms employing other forms of technical knowledge can reasonably lay claim to being professional (Abel 1988; Freidson 1994; Macdonald 1995). Other strands of research have focused on the acquisition of knowledge at the individual level and the codification and sharing of knowledge at the firm level (Morris and Empson 1998; Empson 2001). But as important, and typically neglected within the PSF literature, is the in-depth knowledge that individuals and firms develop about their clients over time, enabling them to apply their specialist technical expertise appropriately (Fincham 1999; Handley et al. 2006). In its fullest examples this leads to the co-production of knowledge whereby professionals pursue "shared learning" with their clients (Fincham 2006; see also Faulconbridge, Chapter 19, this volume).

3. Governance: Extensive individual autonomy and contingent managerial authority, where core producers own or control core assets.

Experienced professionals require, or at least expect, extensive levels of individual autonomy, legitimated by the requirement for professionals to preserve the right to make choices about how best to apply their specialist technical knowledge to the delivery of customized professional services (Freidson 1994, 2001; Empson 2007; Faulconbridge and Muzio 2008). As Derber (1982) states, in these settings professionals will enjoy high levels of both teleological (control over ends) and technical (control over means) autonomy. This extensive emphasis on individual autonomy is associated with relatively low levels of managerial authority and intervention. This is particularly so in partnerships, the prevailing form of governance within the traditional professions (Greenwood and Empson 2003) but is also common in corporate PSFs which mimic the characteristics of the partnership form of governance (Empson and Chapman 2006; von Nordenflycht 2014; see also Leblebici and Sherer, Chapter 9, this volume). This feature helps to explain why large engineering companies and hospitals, for example, are typically not considered PSFs as they are normally part of a larger corporate or public sector organization, employing a wide array of workers, and subject to more conventional bureaucratized forms of organizing (i.e., they are autonomous rather than heteronomous professional organizations; Scott 1965; Larson 1977). The relatively small number of publicly quoted PSFs are interesting aberrations yet these firms are typically still substantially owned and operated by the professionals who work within them. This emphasizes the essentially dynamic nature of the concept of the PSF.

4. Identity: Core producers recognize each other as professionals and are recognized as such by clients and competitors.

Since professionals may be only loosely bound together through their formal governance arrangements, they rely upon a shared understanding of the concept of professionalism to provide an ethically based framework to guide their actions (Grey 1998; Anderson-Gough et al. 1999; Evetts 2006; Muzio and Kirkpatrick 2011; see also Alvesson et al., Chapter 18, this volume). For PSFs within the established professions, this professional identity may have been acquired through years of education and professional training and is embodied in formal qualifications. Other kinds of PSFs rely instead upon internal socialization into professional norms of behavior. In all contexts, the firm itself is emerging as an increasingly important site where "professional identities are mediated, formed and transformed" (Cooper and Robson 2006: 416). In this context, professional identity is increasingly redefined from a matter of qualifications to a matter of displaying the appropriate attitudes and dispositions such as commitment, commercial acumen, and customer focus (Anderson-Gough et al. 1999). Above all, members of a PSF recognize each other as professionals and are perceived as such by their clients and competitors. Many knowledge workers may consider themselves to be professionals and recognize each other as such. But only if their employing organizations possess all of the other defining characteristics can they be said to work for a PSF in the fullest sense that we are deploying here.

1.4 OVERVIEW OF THE *HANDBOOK*

As the study of PSFs progresses into maturity this volume provides an opportunity for consolidation, extension, and differentiation.

1.4.1 Consolidation

The proliferation of academic studies on PSFs in recent years has created a substantial but somewhat fragmented body of literature. The chapters in this volume review and consolidate the relevant literature that stems from a range of disciplinary backgrounds, and looks beyond studies of PSFs to include a broader theoretical grounding in the relevant topics. Each chapter synthesizes what has been learnt to date from a wide range of scholarly sources and defines future research directions.

1.4.2 Extension

A major challenge in putting together this volume has been the unevenness of scholarship in this area. Certain topics have been very extensively researched (for example, identity and knowledge management). For these chapters the authors have focused on synthesizing and critiquing the literature to provide a single point of reference as a starting point for scholars new to this field. Other topics (for example, leadership or innovation) are much less developed; in this context, authors have reached outside the PSF context, to extend scholarship in this area by identifying, "importing," and adapting relevant ideas from other empirical and disciplinary contexts which speak directly to issues of particular relevance to PSFs. In so doing these authors have helped to lay the foundations for future scholarship in these areas.

1.4.3 Differentiation

Studies of firms in specific PSF sectors suffer from a tendency to claim generalizability across PSFs as a whole, without sufficient regard for the peculiarities of specific occupational or national contexts. The chapters in this volume are designed to explicitly take this specificity on board by drawing on illustrations from multiple professions and geographical settings. As such, they reflect on differences and similarities across professional sectors, markets, and national contexts, helping to distinguish findings which are more generally applicable from those which are highly sector-specific.

The volume sets out with the intention of integrating scholarship on PSFs across multiple levels of analysis. But the chapters of an *Oxford Handbook* need to be divided up into sections and, since PSF research has traditionally been contained within fairly distinct levels of analysis, the chapters of this volume fall naturally into three distinct sections: the professions, the firms, and the professionals that work within them.

Part I focuses on *Professional Service Firms in Context*. It begins with a chapter by Roy Suddaby and Daniel Muzio (Chapter 2) exploring *Theoretical Perspectives on the Professions*. They present an overview of the development of sociology-based theories of professional occupations and argue that the study of PSFs is following a similar trajectory to earlier research on professional occupations, moving away from concerns about structure and function to questions of power and privilege and, increasingly, issues of process and practice. They argue that it is time for an institutional/ecological approach to studying professions, which analyzes professions as one type of institution struggling for survival in an ecology of other, related, institutional forms. In other words, they emphasize that future research on PSFs needs to pay heed to the significance of the dynamic nature of interactions between multiple stakeholders, not just between multiple levels of analysis at the individual, firm, professional, and regulatory level, but also among competitors and PSFs, their clients, and the broader set of stakeholders upon whom they exert influence.

Chapter 3, by Sigrid Quack and Elke Schüßler, focuses on one specific aspect of PSF ecology, the *Dynamics of Regulation* in a national and international context. They examine how the changing roles and relationships between PSFs, clients, and the state have challenged traditional forms of professional regulation. Quack and Schüßler argue that the tendency for scholars to focus on self-regulation fails to do justice to the complex regulatory dynamics emerging at and across (sub-)national, regional, and global levels. Focusing on regulatory changes in the accounting and legal professions they show that, while competition, free trade, and quasi-market governance have expanded into the previously protected realms of professional organization and work, various state actors are reasserting their regulatory capacity within new and increasingly complex ecologies of actors.

Chapter 4, by Mehdi Boussebaa and Glenn Morgan, picks up on the theme of regulation in the context of their analysis of the drivers, forms, and outcomes of *Internationalization* in a PSF context. They argue that conventional internationalization theory does not apply straightforwardly to PSFs and identity three key sources of PSF distinctiveness—governance, clients, and knowledge. They show how these generate not only differences between PSFs and other types of organizations but also heterogeneity amongst PSFs themselves. They identify four different forms of PSF internationalization—network, project, federal, and transnational—and emphasize the relative dearth of research on the first two forms. In spite of the scholarly interest in the transnational form, they find little convincing evidence that it has been successfully implemented in practice and argue that, in general, PSFs are better understood as federal structures controlled by a few powerful offices than as transnational enterprises. Once again the need to develop a more subtle and nuanced understanding of the densely interwoven power dynamics within as well as between PSFs is highlighted as an important theme for future research.

Chapter 5, by Ian Kirkpatrick and Mirko Noordegraaf, on *Organizations and Occupations*, poses a challenge to deep-rooted assumptions about the mutually exclusive nature of professions and organizations, and develops the concept of hybrid professionalism in PSFs. It argues that while different traditions of research, from the sociology of professions to theories of professional organization, have emphasized conflict, they have also highlighted the interdependency and co-evolution between professional occupations and organizations. Kirkpatrick and Noordegraaf argue that, in recent years, professionalism itself has become increasingly hybridized, due not only to the encroaching demands of organizations on professionals, but also to the way professionals themselves have sought to organize themselves so as to ensure continued growth, legitimacy, and sustainability.

One of the themes underlying research on professional/occupational conflict is the theme of professional ethics. This arises from two main concerns: the fact that professionals working within corporate bureaucracies will experience a conflict with their professional norms, and that professionals working within increasingly "corporate" PSFs may be similarly compromised. These issues are addressed directly in Chapter 6, by Ronit Dinovitzer, Hugh Gunz, and Sally Gunz, who examine the origins, applications, and developments of scholarly understandings of *Professional Ethics*. In this context they examine issues such as: how ethical codes are adopted by professional bodies for complex and sometimes self-serving reasons, how professional independence is used to justify professionals' autonomy from organizational constraints, and the contested role of professional gatekeepers. Dinovitzer et al. highlight some of the ethical pressures experienced by professionals and discuss the strategies they use to cope with or adapt to these circumstances. They emphasize the power of the client to exert pressure on the professional in order to get the result they want (so-called client capture) and consider the challenges this presents for the study of ethics in PSFs.

Chapter 7, by Andrew von Nordenflycht, Namrata Malhotra, and Timothy Morris, rounds off the section on PSFs in context by examining the *Sources of Homogeneity and Heterogeneity* within PSFs. Research on PSFs has tended to emphasize similarities in how firms are organized and managed but this assumption has been challenged recently as scholars have drawn attention to organizational differences. Von Nordenflycht et al. synthesize insights from the sociology of professions literature, economics and organization theory to highlight key sources of homogeneity and heterogeneity and propose an overarching framework to better inform future empirical research on PSFs.

Part I, *Professional Service Firms in Context*, emphasizes the complex power dynamics within which PSFs are embedded and the competing claims of stakeholders with which they must contend. By contrast Part II, *Professional Service Firms: Management and Organization*, looks inside the PSF in considerable depth, and in the process examines power dynamics within these firms.

Chapter 8, by Laura Empson and Ann Langley, starts at the "top" of the PSF by examining *Leadership and Professionals*. They emphasize that PSFs present distinctive leadership challenges, given professionals' traditional expectation of autonomy from organizational constraints, and highlight the dearth of research on PSF leadership. Empson and Langley develop a framework for understanding leadership in PSFs, examining the foci, resources, and mechanisms of leadership, and the multiple manifestations of influence within these contexts. They argue that leadership in PSFs is manifested explicitly through professional expertise, discreetly through political interaction, and implicitly through personal embodiment. They suggest that these resources are rarely combined in single individuals, which gives rise to the prevalence of collective forms of leadership, supported by embedded mechanisms of social control within PSFs.

Because PSFs are often collectively owned by senior professionals working within the firm, leadership cannot be properly understood without reference to issues of governance. Yet, while PSF leadership has received very little scholarly attention, the topic of governance has been extensively researched. In Chapter 9, Huseyin Leblebici and Peter Sherer review this literature on *Governance*. They begin by presenting four foundational theoretical perspectives on governance in PSFs: the agency, the partnership/partnership ethos, the stakeholder, and the trustee perspective. They emphasize that, while these perspectives reflect well-established structural and cultural views on PSF governance, they leave unanswered several critical issues. Leblebici and Sherer suggest that future scholarship will be advanced by adopting a legal normative view of governance, defined as the legal and non-legal rules, norms, conventions, standards, and managerial practices that facilitate coordination and conflict resolution amongst the critical constituencies of PSF. In so doing, they identify a critical but unexplored issue in the study of governance: the definitions of rights and obligations among critical constituencies and how this plays into conflict resolution mechanisms.

Central to the challenge of leadership and governance in PSFs is the question of who determines a firm's strategy and how professionals are "aligned" to enable that strategy to be achieved. The theme of *Strategy and Strategic Alignment* is examined by John Mawdsley and Deepak Somaya in Chapter 10. They review the literature on the strategic management of PSFs which in turn underpins their competitive advantage and long-run performance. They focus on human capital as a critical resource for PSFs and explore different ways in which firm value is created by attracting, developing, configuring, and leveraging human capital. Further, they argue it is critical that a PSF's human capital be aligned with and harnessed to its objectives, which raises issues in relation to the motivation of professionals, the sharing of economic rents, and the overall governance of the firm. They go on to explain the corporate strategy decisions (such as service and geographic diversification) that PSFs must make, and discuss the value-creating role of client relationships—a topic explored in considerable depth in Chapter 16.

A central aspect of any PSF's strategy is the choice about whether to innovate or whether to focus on alternative means of differentiation. In the face of increasing competition and rapid technological change, service innovation is of increasing importance to PSFs. Despite these developments, there has been little discussion of innovation in the PSF literature. The emphasis has been on change and knowledge management with little recognition as to how these relate to innovation. In Chapter 11, Michael Barrett and Bob Hinings draw upon the innovation literature more generally to examine the relevant insights into the development and use of new practices by professionals. They outline an agenda for future research around a practice perspective for exploring *Service Innovation* in PSFs.

Closely associated with the practice of innovation is that of *Entrepreneurship*, a theme explored by Markus Reihlen and Andreas Werr in Chapter 12. Like Barrett and Hinings they emphasize the relative dearth of research on entrepreneurship in this context. They attribute this to scholars' assumption that there is an inherent contradiction between entrepreneurship and professionalism, as much contemporary theorizing has emphasized institutionalized isomorphism and inertia in professional fields. Reihlen and Werr adopt a broad perspective on entrepreneurship, focusing on new venture management and renewal in PSFs as well as embracing aspects such as learning, innovation, and institutional change. They examine the existing literature from three levels of analysis—the entrepreneurial team, the entrepreneurial firm, and the organizational field within which the creation and exploitation of entrepreneurial opportunities takes place.

In Chapter 13 William S. Harvey and Vincent-Wayne Mitchell focus on another area which has received very little scholarly attention, *Marketing and Reputation* in PSFs. They explore a series of problems inherent to applying traditional marketing principles and practices to PSFs and examine how PSFs seek to attract and retain clients through reputation building. They emphasize how a PSF's reputation is important to their clients as well as the firms themselves. They identify how to define and measure reputation and develop a conceptual model which highlights the antecedents and consequences of reputation in a PSF context.

A focus on marketing and reputation management leads on to another relatively neglected area of PSF research—*Client Relationships*—which is examined by Joe Broschak in Chapter 14. Broschak proposes that client relationships tend to be assumed rather than studied and focuses on three key themes in reviewing the relevant academic research. First is the different ways that PSFs/client relationships have been characterized and how this shapes researchers' attention, what aspects of client relationships researchers attend to, and the assumptions researchers make about client relationships should be studied and managed. A second theme is the life cycle of client relationships, specifically research that addresses either the formation and maintenance, or dissolution of client relationships and the factors that drive the dynamics of client relationships. Third is research that identifies how client relationships affect PSFs through the co-production of professional services, particularly in the areas of PSF strategy, structure, learning, and human resource practices.

While client relationships have always been fundamental to the success of a PSF, another set of external relationships has become increasingly important in recent years: the providers of *Outsourcing and Offshoring* services. This is the focus of Chapter 15 by Mari Sako. Once again, this important phenomenon in the PSF sector has received relatively limited scholarly attention. Sako therefore turns to broader management and economic theories to shed light on this phenomenon. She examines trends towards the disaggregation and standardization of professional work, and to digital technology, as prerequisites for outsourcing and offshoring. She explores the implications of trends in outsourcing and offshoring in terms of the ecology of professions, with particular emphasis on how non-professionals may enter into competition with professionals, and on their disruptive effect on professional jurisdictions.

Part III of the volume, *Professional Service Firms: Individuals and Interactions*, focuses on a series of issues with direct and immediate impact on individual professionals, the nature of their work lives, and their working relationships. In Chapter 16 Laurie Cohen examines *Career Forms* in PSFs. She argues that PSFs embody elements of three ideal types of career form—bureaucratic, professional, and entrepreneurial—and that these sometimes work in parallel and sometimes in competition with each other. She considers how these are institutionalized through particular career practices and highlights the importance of the client in professional career-making. Cohen then examines career enactment: the ways in which individuals engage with professional, bureaucratic, and entrepreneurial practices on a daily basis and over time. Central to her analysis is a focus on the tension between the professional career as a vehicle for the exercise of personal agency, and as a disciplinary mechanism of management control.

Cohen's chapter highlights the extent to which established notions of professional careers are being challenged by rapid changes in the professional context. Heidi K. Gardner's chapter on *Teamwork and Collaboration*, Chapter 17, highlights a similarly disruptive change to established norms. The nature of teamwork in PSFs is evolving from highly structured project teams to more fluid, open-ended, peer-to-peer collaboration, often between powerful, high-autonomy partners. Gardner emphasizes that this shift is especially challenging because senior-level collaboration requires peers from different practice groups or offices with different sub-cultures to negotiate task allocation, credit recognition, and decision-making norms, which can be difficult and politically charged. Increased partner-level collaboration is further complicated by other trends in the PSF arena such as specialization, heightened professional mobility, and increased competition. Gardner goes on to identify ways that some of these recent developments within PSFs challenge our understanding of traditional forms of teamwork.

As previously discussed, *Identity* has long been recognized as a core theme within the PSF literature and one which has significant implications for the nature of professional work and for relationships between individual professionals and the firms that employ them. In Chapter 18, Mats Alvesson, Dan Kärreman, and Kate Sullivan synthesize and extend this extensive literature to examine the relationship between individual and organizational identity in PSFs and the significant but tenuous nature of elite identity in this context. They identify four identity-related issues in PSFs: autonomy/conformity tensions, the client conundrum, ambiguity saturation, and intangibility. They explore alternative modes of identity control in PSFs (positive image, homogenization of the workforce, and anxiety regulation) and examine contemporary challenges to elite professional identities as well as the increasing critique of concepts of professionalism in this context.

Central to a knowledge worker's identity is, inevitably, the form and content of their knowledge. In Chapter 19 James Faulconbridge focuses on the central issues of *Knowledge and Learning*. He synthesizes key research in this area along three distinct themes: the organizational form, management, and governance of PSFs, the varying roles and effects of knowledge networking, and jurisdictional knowledge and contested claims about exclusive rights over a market. While acknowledging the extent to which knowledge and learning represent well-trodden paths within the scholarly literature, Faulconbridge emphasizes that the ambiguous and heterogeneous nature of knowledge ensures that these topics remain contested domains which merit considerable further scholarship.

Knowledge, of course, does not reside solely in the systems and structures of a PSF but is a product of the diverse backgrounds and experiences of its professional workforce. In theory at least, a more diverse workforce will be associated with more innovative practices, as well as bringing other associated benefits. Why then, after so much attention from both scholars and PSF leaders, are the senior ranks of most PSFs still dominated by white, heterosexual, middle-class males? In Chapter 20, on *Diversity and Inclusion,* Hilary Sommerlad and Louise Ashley examine this question in depth. A widely held belief is that meritocracy is a defining characteristic of the professions. Yet extensive research and statistical surveys have highlighted the myth of merit within PSFs. Sommerlad and Ashley examine how patterns of exclusion and inclusion have been theorized over the past four decades and explore the associated evolution of policy and practice within PSFs.

In the final chapter, Juani Swart, Nina Katrin Hansen, and Nicholas Kinnie address a core set of issues underlying all the chapters in this section. They consider how *Human Resource Management* practices are used to manage human capital (knowledge and skills) and social capital (relationships inside and outside the PSF) to generate superior performance in PSFs. They outline two models of HRM practices which are used to manage human and social capital and examine how these relate to innovation.

1.5 FUTURE RESEARCH DIRECTIONS

Handbooks are repositories of the past and present of a discipline so are well placed to comment on its future. Each of the chapters in this volume identifies directions for future research which are specific to its own topic. In the concluding section of this introductory chapter we address five broader, overarching themes that merit future research in the field of PSFs.

1.5.1 Understanding a Phenomenon in Flux

The concept of the PSF and the field within which it operates is undergoing rapid and in some cases dramatic change. For example, recent legislation relating to PSFs is introducing new ownership structures and facilitating the development of managerial hierarchies (see Leblebici and Sherer, Chapter 9, this volume; Empson and Langley, Chapter 8, this volume); technological change and deregulation are driving the outsourcing and offshoring of core processes and functions (see Sako, Chapter 15, this volume); globalization is leading to novel forms of transnational jurisdictions and practice (see Boussebaa and Morgan, Chapter 4, this volume; Quack and Schüßler, Chapter 3, this volume); new lifestyle tendencies and workforce diversity are leading to an increasing demand for salaried employment and "atypical" employment contracts (see Cohen, Chapter, 16, this volume; Sommerlad and Ashley, Chapter 20, this volume); recent scandals are eroding public confidence and undermining traditional self-regulatory arrangements (see Dinovitzer et al., Chapter 6, this volume); and developments in the economy are calling into question the sustainability of once-dominant business models and fostering new approaches to the organization and delivery of professional expertise (see Faulconbridge, Chapter 19, this volume; Barrett and Hinings, Chapter 11, this volume).

It is important to understand how these and other developments in once-stable organizational forms affect relationships between different stakeholders. For instance, could the rise of external investors as key stakeholders destabilize traditional governance regimes (see Leblebici and Sherer, Chapter 9, this volume), generate new "capture" dynamics, or compromise existing fiduciary duties (see Dinovitzer et al., Chapter 6, this volume)? Similarly, could the development of new practices and modes of organizing change affect the internal dynamics within PSFs and usher in increasing standardization, routinization, and more directive forms of leadership (see Faulconbridge, Chapter 19, this volume; Reihlen and Werr, Chapter 12, this volume; Empson and Langley, Chapter 8, this volume)? All of these organizational developments in their different ways will have real impacts for the management and performance of PSFs, the experiences of their clients, and the working lives and careers of the people who work within them. But they also raise important theoretical implications for the very concept of the PSF itself. There is much more to learn about PSFs as the firms themselves are evolving faster than scholarship in the field.

1.5.2 Broadening the Focus of Inquiry

We have emphasized the need for a definition of PSFs which covers a wider and more differentiated terrain. Existing research, and therefore this volume, has historically tended to focus on a limited set of the broader potential population. Some concepts and topics easily transcend this varied terrain; for example, strategy, client relationships, and human resource practices are all essential elements of PSFs regardless of their size, profession, or national region (see Mawdsley and Somaya, Chapter 10, this volume; Broschak, Chapter 14, this volume; Swart et al., Chapter 21, this volume). Yet most of what we know derives from studies of large firms, usually in law or accountancy and overwhelmingly in Western if not Anglo-Saxon contexts. It remains an open question to what extent which the management and application of PSF practices and client relationships transcends markets, cultures, and national boundaries. Conversely too little is known about whether distinct forms of PSFs are emerging in developing economies or about the characteristics of PSFs in new occupational contexts. This diversity needs to be more fully accounted for. In addition, more attention should be placed on the "life cycle" and stages of growth of PSFs (see Reihlen and Werr, Chapter 12, this volume; Empson and Langley, Chapter 8, this volume; Leblebici and Sherer, Chapter 9, this volume) as they move from charismatic founders to national and eventually global partnerships.

1.5.3 Extending Methods Utilized

There is considerable scope for expanding the range of research methods deployed for studying PSFs. The majority of existing research on PSFs consists of semi-structured interviews, sometimes integrated with archival sources. To date, quantitative studies of PSFs have been relatively limited, raising further questions about the generalizability of much of the "received wisdom" within this field of research. In addition, network studies could also prove particularly fruitful as a means of understanding the complex web of relationships within which professionals and PSFs must operate. Furthermore the limited number of ethnographic studies to date have pointed to their potential in generating important insights into issues such as political relationships within PSFs and the unfolding of long-term change processes. This method holds particular promise in terms of bringing back the lived experiences and everyday practices of people within PSFs which have often been neglected in existing research. Such a focus is particularly important as it is individuals within these firms that have to balance and enact the requirements of competing pressures. Indeed more sensitivity to actual tasks and activities is needed for further work in the area.

1.5.4 Examining Working Practices

While the training and accreditation processes within the professions are associated with a substantial body of theory about the technical aspects of professional work (see Faulconbridge, Chapter 19, this volume), relatively little has been written about the actual practice of professional work as it is enacted by individuals within firms. Notable exceptions include studies of accountants (Anderson-Gough et al. 2001), consultants and lawyers (Smets et al. 2012). However, these focus on very specialized aspects of professional work. As yet, organizational scholars know relatively little about what professionals actually do to deliver client service. For example, what are the precise mechanisms by which professionals work with their clients to define the "problem"? How do they identify the appropriate areas of professional expertise to address the problem? How do they co-create knowledge with their clients, and how do they adapt and use that knowledge with their new clients?

1.5.5 Analyzing Power Dynamics

To the extent that PSF research has addressed power explicitly it has focused almost exclusively on power at an institutional level; the process by which the professions have negotiated, defended, and sustained their positions of privilege (see Suddaby and Muzio, Chapter 2, this volume). At the organizational and individual levels of analysis, power is mostly treated as an implicit construct. It is taken as axiomatic that partners have greater positional power than associates in PSFs or that large PSFs have greater market power and influence than small PSFs. But the implications and dynamic nature of these power relationships remain unexamined. For instance, an individual professional's power may originate from sources other than structural position, such as relationships with prominent clients. This suggests that issues such as the profitability and prestige associated with particular client assignments may affect an individual professional's ability to accumulate and utilize power and their relationship with the leadership of their firm (see Empson and Langley, Chapter 8, this volume) but this issue has not been examined in any detail within the PSF literature. In addition, focusing on the changing balance of power between clients and PSFs (see Broschak, Chapter 14, this volume) may help researchers understand how the increasing pressures placed on individual professionals to act in the "best interests" of clients may result in ethical or legal dilemmas (see Dinovitzer et al., Chapter 6, this volume). The power relationships between PSFs and their regulators will continue to demand particular scholarly attention as these relationships are challenged and renegotiated over time.

1.6 Developing an Integrative Perspective

The space constraints and review processes of journal articles have inevitably led scholars of PSFs to focus on a relatively narrow phenomenon, the PSF itself. Yet such a narrow focus marginalizes or even neglects the complex power dynamics with which PSFs must contend. Managerialist studies of PSFs (most notably Maister 1993) have argued that PSFs are distinctive because of their need to compete effectively in two markets simultaneously: the market for clients and the market for professional staff (i.e., recognizing that both are equally important and entirely interconnected). Yet as Broschak (Chapter 14, this volume) demonstrates, although we know quite a bit about the interaction between PSFs and individual professionals, we still know relatively little about the interaction between these firms and their clients. Similarly, perhaps because of the sociology-based literatures' grounding in the professionalization project thesis (with its implicit reification of PSFs into a professional field and with it the assumption of cooperation amongst PSFs to achieve this end) very little attention has been paid to competition that occurs between PSFs in the same sectors and the different ways in which individual PSFs may interact with their professional regulators.

We argue, therefore, that researchers should adopt an integrative framework (see Figure 1.2) for analyzing PSFs, one which focuses on the dynamic interplay between the PSF and the contending, and sometimes conflicting, demands presented by the profession, professionals, clients, and competitors. This approach recognizes that PSFs are enmeshed in a complex web of relationships and subject to competing power dynamics, all of which have a significant impact on their organizational practices. PSFs simultaneously maintain employer/employee relationships with the individual professionals and market relationships with their clients and competitors, and are subject to the jurisdiction of professional or regulatory bodies that influence and limit their structure and practices. Of course, all organizations are subject to pressures from clients and competitors but PSFs are distinctive in terms of the extent to which they are also vulnerable to the actions of their professional staff and professional regulators. And it is not only the PSFs themselves that are exposed to the forces from these multiple relationships; all the

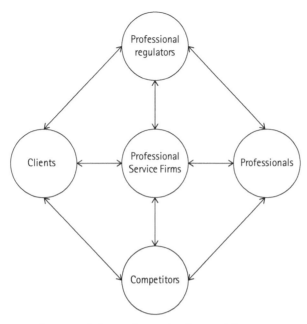

FIGURE 1.2 Integrative framework for analyzing Professional Service Firms.

actors are influenced by relationships with the other entities. Professionals, for example, are employees of particular PSFs, members of their profession and/or professional associations, and define their identity in relation to their competitor and client firms (see Alvesson et al., Chapter 18, this volume).

By neglecting to integrate the individual, organizational, and institutional levels of analysis, by ignoring or making assumptions about both the client dynamics and competitor dynamics, researchers in this field too often present a partial and even distorted perspective of the phenomenon which they are investigating. Research which is predicated on the reification of PSFs itself will inevitably neglect the fundamental role played by the individuals who enact their professional lives within them, and the clients, competitors, and professional regulators who shape the context within which these firms must operate.

As the field of PSF research has developed over the past few decades, we have learnt a great deal of significance to organizational scholarship. The scale and significance of these firms, the influence they have on the lives of their staff, their clients, and society as a whole, and the speed with which they develop and disseminate new organizational practices ensure that we have a great deal more to learn.

Notes

1. <http://www.top100graduateemployers.com>.
2. We would like to thank Luca Sabini for his help in conducting this analysis.

References

Abbott, A. (1988). *The System of Professions: An Essay on the Division of Expert Labor*. Chicago, IL: University of Chicago Press.

Abel, R. L. (1988). *The Legal Profession in England and Wales*. New York: Blackwell.

Anderson-Gough, F., Grey, C., and Robson, K. (1999). *Making Up Accountants*. Aldershot: Gower Ashgate.

Anderson-Gough, F., Grey, C., and Robson, K. (2001). "Tests of Time: Organizational Time-Reckoning and the Making of Accountants in Two Multi-National Accounting Firms," *Accounting, Organizations and Society* 26(2): 99–122.

Arnold, P. (2005). "Disciplining Domestic Regulation: The World Trade Organization and the Market for Professional Services," *Accounting, Organizations and Society* 30(4): 299–330.

Ashley, L. and Empson, L. (2013). "Differentiation and Discrimination: Understanding Social Class and Social Exclusion in the UK's Leading Law Firms," *Human Relations* 66(2): 219–244.

Brivot, M. (2011). "Controls of Knowledge Production, Sharing and Use in Bureaucratized Professional Service Firms," *Organization Studies* 32(4): 489–508.

Brock, D., Leblebici, H., and Muzio, D. (2014). "Understanding Professionals and their Workplaces: The Mission of the *Journal of Professions and Organization*," *Journal of Professions and Organization* 1(1): 1–15.

Coffee, J. C. (2006). *Gatekeepers: The Professions and Corporate Governance*. Oxford: Oxford University Press.

Cooper, D. J. and Robson, K. (2006). "Accounting, Professions and Regulation: Locating the Sites of Professionalization," *Accounting, Organizations and Society* 31(4–5): 415–444.

Derber, C. (1982). *Professionals as Workers: Mental Labor in Advanced Capitalism*. Boston, MA: G. K. Hall.

Dezalay, Y. and Garth, B. (1998). *Dealing in Virtue: International Commercial Arbitration and the Construction of a Trans-National Legal Order*. Chicago, IL: University of Chicago Press.

Empson, L. (2001). "Introduction: Knowledge Management in Professional Service Firms," *Human Relations* 54(7): 811–817.

Empson, L. (2007). *Managing the Modern Law Firm*. Oxford: Oxford University Press.

Empson, L. (2008). "Professional Service Firms," in *International Encyclopedia of Organization Studies*, ed. S. Clegg and J. Bailey. Thousand Oaks, CA: Sage.

Empson, L. and Chapman, C. (2006). "Partnership versus Corporation: Implications of Alternative Forms of Governance in Professional Service Firms," *Research in the Sociology of Organizations* 24: 139–170.

Evetts, J. (2006). Short Note: "The Sociology of Professional Groups: New Directions," *Current Sociology* 54(1): 133–143.

Faulconbridge, J. and Muzio, D. (2008). "Organizational Professionalism in Globalizing Law Firms," *Work, Employment and Society* 22(1): 7–25.

Faulconbridge, J. R. and Muzio, D. (2012). "The Rescaling of the Professions: Towards a Transnational Sociology of the Professions," *International Sociology* 27(1): 136–152.

Fincham, R. (1999). "The Consultant–Client Relationship: Critical Perspectives on the Management of Organizational Chance," *Journal of Management Studies* 36(3): 335–351.

Fincham, R. (2006). "Knowledge Work as Occupational Strategy: Comparing IT and Management Consulting," *New Technology, Work and Employment* 21(1): 16–28.

Freidson, E. (1994). *Professionalism Reborn: Theory, Prophecy and Policy*. Cambridge: Polity Press.

Freidson, E. (2001). *Professionalism: The Third Logic*. Chicago, IL: University of Chicago Press.

Gabbioneta, C., Greenwood, R., Mazzola, P., and Minoja, M. (2013). "The Influence of the Institutional Context on Corporate Illegality," *Accounting, Organizations and Society* 38(6–7): 484–504.

Gabbioneta, C., Prakash, R., and Greenwood, R. (2014). "Sustained Corporate Corruption and Processes of Institutional Ascription within Professional Networks," *Journal of Professions and Organization* 1(1): 16–32.

Greenwood, R. and Empson, L. (2003). "The Professional Partnership: Relic or Exemplary Form of Governance?" *Organization Studies* 24(6): 909–933.

Greenwood, R., Hinings, C., and Brown, J. (1990). "'P2-form' Strategic Management: Corporate Practices in Professional Partnerships," *Academy of Management Journal* 33(4): 725–755.

Greenwood, R., Hinings, C. R., and Whetten, D. (2014). "Rethinking Institutions and Organizations," *Journal of Management Studies* 51(7): 1206–1220.

Grey, C. (1998). "On Being a Professional in a 'Big Six' firm," *Accounting, Organizations and Society* 23(5–6): 569–587.

Halliday, T. C. and Carruthers, B. G. (2009). *Bankrupt: Global Lawmaking and Systemic Financial Crisis*. Stanford, CA: Stanford University Press.

Handley, K., Sturdy, A., Fincham, R., and Clark, T. (2006). "Within and Beyond Communities of Practice: Making Sense of Learning through Participation, Identity and Practice," *Journal of Management Studies* 43(3): 641–653.

HM Treasury (2009). *Professional Services Global Competitiveness Group Report*. <http://www.hm-treasury.gov.uk>.

IBISWorld (2014a). *Global Accounting Services Market Research Report*. August. <http://www.ibisworld.com/industry/global/global-accounting-services.html>.

IBISWorld (2014b). *Global Architectural Services: Market Research Report*. January. <http://www.ibisworld.com/industry/global/global-architectural-services.html>.

IBISWorld (2014c). *Global Management Consultants Market Research Report*. July. <http://www.ibisworld.com/industry/global/global-management-consultants.html>.

IBISWorld (2014d). *Global Engineering Services: Market Research Report*. June. <http://www.ibisworld.com/industry/global/global-engineering-services.html>

IBISWorld (2014e). *Global Advertising Agencies: Market Research Report*. July. <http://www.ibisworld.com/industry/global/global-advertising-agencies.html>.

Kipping, M. (1999). "American Management Consulting Companies in Western Europe, 1920 to 1990: Products, Reputation and Relationships," *Business History Review* 73(2): 190–220.

Krause, E. A. (1996). *The Death of the Guilds: Professions, States and the Advance of Capitalism, 1930 to the Present*. New Haven, CT: Yale University Press.

Kritzer, H. (1999). "The Professions are Dead, Long Live the Professions: Legal Practice in a Postprofessional World," *Law & Society Review* 33(3): 713–759.

Larson, M. S. (1977). *The Rise of Professionalism: A Sociological Analysis*. Berkeley, CA: University of California Press.

Løwendahl, B. R. (1997). *Strategic Management of Professional Service Firms*. Copenhagen Business School. Copenhagen: Handelshojskolens Forlag.

McDonald, D. (2013). *The Firm: The Story of McKinsey and its Secret Influence on American Business*. New York: Simon & Schuster.

Macdonald, K. M. (1995). *The Sociology of the Professions*. London: Sage.

Maister, D. H. (1993). *Managing the Professional Service Firm*. New York: Free Press.

MarketLine (2014). *Global Legal Services Report*. April. <http://www.marketresearch.com/MarketLine-v3883/Global-Legal-Services-8108843/>.

Morris, T. and Empson, L. (1998). "Organization and Expertise: An Exploration of Knowledge Bases and the Management of Accounting and Consulting Firms," *Accounting, Organizations and Society* 23(5–6): 609–624.

Muzio, D. and Kirkpatrick, I. (2011). "Reconnecting the Study of Professional Organizations with the Study of Professional Occupations," *Current Sociology* 59(4): 389–405.

Muzio, D., Brock, D. M., and Suddaby, R. (2013). "Professions and Institutional Change: Towards an Institutionalist Sociology of the Professions," *Journal of Management Studies* 50(5): 699–721.

Panel on Fair Access to the Professions (2009). *Unleashing Aspiration: The Final Report of the Panel on Fair Access to the Professions*. London: The Cabinet Office.

Robson, K., Humphrey, C., Khalifa, R., and Jones, J. (2007). "Transforming Audit Technologies: Business Risk Audit Methodologies and the Audit Field," *Accounting, Organizations and Society* 32(4–5): 409–438.

Scott, W. R. (1965). "Reactions to Supervision in a Heteronomous Professional Organisation," *Administrative Science Quarterly* 10(1): 65–81.

Scott, W. R. (2008). "Lords of the Dance: Professionals as Institutional Agents," *Organization Studies* 29(2): 219–238.

Sharma, A. (1997). "Professional as Agent: Knowledge Asymmetry in Agency Exchange," *Academy of Management Review* 22(3): 758–798.

Smets, M., Morris, T., and Greenwood, R. (2012). "From Practice to Field: Multi-Level Model of Practice-Driven Institutional Change," *Academy of Management Journal* 55(4): 877–904.

Sommerlad, H., Webley, L., Duff, L., Muzio, D., and Tomlinson, J. (2010). "Diversity in the Legal Profession in England and Wales: A Qualitative Study of Barriers and Individual Choices." Legal Services Board Funded Report.

Starbuck, W. H. (1993). "Keeping a Butterfly and an Elephant in a House of Cards: The Elements of Exceptional Success," *Journal of Management Studies* 30(6): 885–921.

Suddaby, R., Cooper, D., and Greenwood, R. (2007). "Transnational Regulation of Professional Services: Governance Dynamics of Field Level Organizational Change," *Accounting, Organizations and Society* 32(4–5): 333–362.

Teece, D. (2003). "Expert Talent and the Design of (Professional Service) Firms," *Industrial and Corporate Change* 12(4): 895–916.

Thornburg, S. and Roberts, R. (2008). "Money, Politics, and the Regulation of Public Accounting Services: Evidence from the Sarbanes–Oxley Act of 2002," *Accounting, Organizations and Society*, 33(2–3): 229–248.

von Nordenflycht, A. (2010). "What is a Professional Service Firm? Towards a Theory and Taxonomy of Knowledge-Intensive Firms," *Academy of Management Review* 35(1): 155–174.

von Nordenflycht, A. (2014). "Does the Emergence of Publicly Traded Professional Service Firms Undermine the Theory of the Professional Partnership? A Cross-Industry Historical Analysis," *Journal of Professions and Organizations* 1(2): 137–160.

Zardkoohi, A., Bierman, L., Panina, D., and Chakrabarty, S. (2011). "Revisiting a Proposed Definition of Professional Service Firms," *Academy of Management Review* (a dialogue) 36(1): 180–184.

PART I

PROFESSIONAL SERVICE FIRMS IN CONTEXT

CHAPTER 2

....

THEORETICAL PERSPECTIVES
ON THE PROFESSIONS

....

ROY SUDDABY AND DANIEL MUZIO

2.1 INTRODUCTION

....

THE study of professions has a long and varied intellectual history. Early theories, emanating primarily from the fields of sociology and economics, sought to understand the essential elements of professions and to explain their functional role in society. When these explanations proved inadequate, alternative accounts emerged that theorized professions based on the powerful position they occupied in both social and economic fields. As researchers identified occupational groups that lacked power but were nonetheless professions, theoretical explanations shifted yet again to focus on the micro and macro behavioral practices of professions, based on an understanding of professions not as social structures but rather as social processes or systems.

By the 1990s, just as sociologists appeared to have lost their fascination with professions, management scholars, in organization studies and accounting, became interested in understanding large professional organizations and if and how they differed from corporations. As the study of professions shifted from sociology departments to business schools, the core questions of sociology were recreated in the same sequence. Early studies sought to identify the unique characteristics of Professional Service Firms (PSFs) and explain their persistence. Later, researchers focused attention on the powerful gatekeeping role played by large professional organizations in business, commerce, and social policy. More contemporary theories of professional firms seek theoretical accounts that rely on the processes and practices that explain their internal coherence and their position in broader social systems.

This chapter offers a brief theoretical overview of the key literatures on professions and PSFs. We structure our review, both chronologically, to capture the historical movement of the study of professions from sociology to management, as well as thematically, to demonstrate how theories of professions move from questions of *structure and function* to questions of *power and privilege* to questions of *process and practice*. We conclude with a final section that raises questions about prior theories of professions, which have assumed that professions are appropriate objects of theorization in their own right. We argue, instead, for an institutional/ecological approach to studying professions, which analyzes professions as but one type of institution struggling for survival in an ecology of other, related, institutional forms.

2.2 THEORIES OF PROFESSIONS IN SOCIOLOGY

2.2.1 Structure and Function

Early studies of the professions tried to delineate how these occupational groups differed from other occupations. Considerable effort was devoted to cataloguing the unique characteristics or traits of professionals. Greenwood (1957), for example, identified five key traits: a systematic body of theory, professional authority, sanction of the community, a regulative code of ethics, and a professional culture. Goode (1957), in explaining why librarians were not a profession, pointed to the absence of prolonged special training, a formal body of abstract knowledge, a collective orientation to public service, and the absence of collective self-control. Over time a number of other traits were added to the list, including rewards based on work achievement (Barber 1963), loyalty to colleagues (Drinker 1954), a fiduciary relationship with clients (Lewis and Maude 1949), and, perhaps most importantly, a sense of social duty or "calling" (Greenwood 1957).

Trait theory grew out of earlier theoretical efforts to explain the existence of professions based on the *function* that they were thought to provide to society. Durkheim (1992 [1957]), for example, saw professions as a necessary moral foundation for society. Others argued that professions existed in order to stabilize and civilize society as they provided "centres of resistance to crude forces which threaten steady and peaceful evolution" (Carr-Saunders and Wilson 1933: 497). The existence of professions, thus, was explained by the profoundly important function they fulfilled in underpinning social structure. "It seems evident . . ." (Parsons 1939: 457) observed, ". . . that many of the most important features of our society are to a considerable extent dependent upon the smooth functioning of the professions." Professions, thus, were assumed to provide an adaptive function for the broader social system in which they were embedded.

Such structural-functional explanations of the professions ultimately succumbed to a barrage of empirical and theoretical critique (Abbott 1988; Macdonald 1995). Researchers struggled to identify occupational traits that were actually unique to professions. Early empirical research attempted to construct standardized scales as tools for measuring professionalism. Hall (1967) developed a Likert scale to measure five attitudes of professionalism. Hickson and Thomas (1969) used a Guttman scale to measure 14 professional traits. When applied to different occupational groups, however, researchers determined that the characteristics were not unique to elite professions but in fact were shared, to a greater or lesser degree, across a broad range of occupational groups. Critics suggested that perhaps professionalism was not a distinct construct uniquely tied to an identifiable social group (Johnson 1972). Others suggested that professionalism was a continuous rather than a discrete category, with quasi- or semi-professions occupying an intermediate position between "true" professions and other forms of work (Hearn 1982). Moreover, if the boundaries between professionals and non-professionals could not be clearly defined, then everyone might be considered a professional (Wilensky 1964).

Critics also noted that explanations of the stabilizing role of professions in society failed to explain how societies, and professions themselves, experience conflict and change (Benson 1975; Freidson 1986). While structural-functional accounts were based on assumptions of homogeneity and stability within the professions, empirical evidence demonstrated that professions were, themselves, highly differentiated and subject to extreme internal conflict (Bucher and Strauss 1961).

Comparative sociologists argued that claims of the moral and normative basis for professions suffered from an Anglo-Saxon cultural bias and failed to explain the function and development of professions in other societies (Torstendahl and Burrage 1990). And rather than being characterized by higher moral standards, conflicts of interest were a defining feature of many professions (Rosenberg et al. 1981). Perhaps most damaging, however, was the critique that, while professions may use the language of altruism and subordinating economic interests to a social calling, the professions were, in fact, an occupational category based on elitist power and extreme economic privilege (Johnson 1972).

2.2.2 Power and Privilege

The view that professions exist to serve their own interests, rather than those of broader society, emerged from a growing realization that, even though it was difficult to generalize the core attributes of a profession, they shared a common interest in controlling the social conditions and environment that surrounded them. Johnson (1972) argued that a key attribute shared across professions was their ability to exert control over their clients. Freidson (1973a, 1973b, 1986) extended this argument with the observation that not only do professionals wield power over their clients, they exert incredible institutional power over labor markets, constructing barriers to entry and mobility, which he termed "labor market shelters," based on their claims to expertise.

In part the power and privilege perspective of professions built on a series of ethnographic studies of elite professions (e.g., Becker et al. 1961; Freidson 1970; Daniels 1973) that contradicted many of the assumptions of altruism and collegiality described by the trait theorists. Instead of an egalitarian and communal culture of professionalism, the ethnographers observed distinct professional hierarchies characterized by intra-professional dominance (Becker et al. 1961). Similarly, the ethnographers saw professionals as motivated by elitism and domination over clients, allied occupational groups (Freidson 1970), and junior professionals (Nelson 1988; Hanlon 1994), instead of the altruistic "calling" proposed by early theorists.

The power and conflict view of professions also built on a series of historical studies that documented the capacity of some occupations to create "social closure" by constructing barriers to, and creating autonomy over, key societal stakeholders, including other occupations (Parkin 1979; Murphy 1988), the nation state (Torstendahl and Burrage 1990), and consumers (Heinz and Laumann 1982; Freidson 1989). Social closure was achieved by using key institutional strategies such as certification, licensing, credentialing, and professional associations, which gave select professions a monopoly over large sections of economic activity. Ample empirical research demonstrated that, as a result, professions were able to (and are still able to) extract economic rents for their services (Friedman and Kuznets 1954; Wright 1997; Sorenson 2000; Weeden 2002) and in many cases to translate their superior economic capital into positions of high social status (Elliot 1972). Freidson (1982: 39) described this "capacity of occupations to become organized groups independent of firms and other occupations" as a defining characteristic and competence of professions.

Larson (1977) summarized this growing dissatisfaction with early theoretical explanations of professions and professionalism with a plea to study professions not as social structures, but rather as historically situated extensions of processes of capitalism. From this perspective, early phase professions, such as medicine and law, can be characterized as projects of monopolization of knowledge, work, income, and status in a distinct market for labor or services. Larson understands professions as ongoing projects of market exchange in which expert knowledge and skill is traded for monopoly control over a labor market. Later phases of professionalism, Larson (1977) observed, are devoted to consolidating the economic control by the profession and extending it to include broader forms of political or ideological control. That is, established professions extend their control by attaching their own projects of professionalization to dominant social institutions.

While the conflict perspective of professions is still influential, the core argument—that professions are self-interested monopolies—has attracted considerable critique and contradictory empirical evidence. The challenges to the view that professions are simple expressions of social power take two distinct threads. One thread suggests that professional powers are constantly eroding—i.e., that professionalism is subject to Weberian proletarianization.

Critics point out that, while professions may provide some degree of monopolistic protection, there is as much variability in earnings and status *within* professions as *across* them (Heinz and Laumann 1982; Halliday 1987; Abel 1988). Others observe that the modern history of the professions is really one of the erosion of social barriers (Krause 1996). So, for example, when the primary mode of educating professionals shifted from the professional guilds to universities, professions lost considerable autonomy (Freidson 1984).

Similarly, critics observe that professionals are increasingly employed by large organizations, such as government and corporations. Empirical research shows that, as professional work shifts to bureaucracies, there is a concomitant loss of economic privilege and social status (Abbott 1981; Derber 1983; Burris 1993).

A second thread argues that professions, like any other occupation, are subject to deskilling pressures. The emergence of computing technology, for example, may erode the professions' control over expert knowledge (Johnson 1972; Haug 1973; Jones and Moore 1993). Similarly, the shift of professional employment from purely professional contexts to large bureaucracies encourages the commodification of professional work (Willmott 1995; Suddaby and Greenwood 2001; Covaleski et al. 2003).

Collectively, the deskilling and proletarianization arguments raised serious questions about the validity of viewing professions simply as exercises in economic self-interest. While acknowledging that professions enjoyed a degree of economic and social closure, it was neither complete nor was it the sole explanation for their existence. Professions may be powerful, but that power provided a useful check on state, corporate, and bureaucratic power (Halliday 1987) and, therefore, theories of professions should look for explanations beyond mere monopoly.

2.2.3 Process and Practice: Professions as Systems

The primary flaw with viewing professions through the theoretical lens of power, Halliday (1987) argued, was that it falsely proclaimed social closure as the primary motivation for professionalization and caused researchers to overlook alternative goals. Halliday's own research, a historical study of the Chicago Bar, showed that monopolistic pursuits constituted only a small proportion of the association's attention and resources; indeed considerably more time was devoted to broader social goals, such as creating and maintaining institutions of justice. Halliday (1987) argued that while economic closure might be an outcome of professional work, it was not its primary purpose. Instead, he suggested, researchers should try to understand the professions in their broader institutional context.

Burrage (1988; Torstendahl and Burrage 1990) echoed this fundamental concern, arguing that scholars ought to understand professions as uniquely influenced by the cultural and political context in which they evolved. His detailed comparative historical analysis of professions in the USA, France, and Germany showed considerable variation in the role, status, and operation of professions across these countries. The state, Burrage argued, is a key determinant of the role professions play in society. Burrage was supported in this position by a growing stream of research that suggested an intimate and symbiotic relationship between the emergence of the nation state, the spread of political liberalism, and modern forms of professions (Rueschemeyer 1973; Skocpol 1985; Krause 1996; Halliday and Karpik 1998).

The conceptual thread that links these writers and separates their view of professions from the power and conflict perspective is the understanding that although professions may have some unique attributes and exhibit some degree of social closure, the most effective way to study professions is not to treat them as static entities or fixed social structures. Rather, they should be understood as ongoing processes of professionaliza-tion. Thus, professions emerge from processes of negotiation, conflict, and exchange with external stakeholders, such as the state, and with internal competitors. This latter view is the primary thesis of Abbott (1988) who observed that professions are engaged in continual struggles over jurisdiction with other occupational groups. While economic monopoly and social closure may be a byproduct of this competition, it is the contest over jurisdiction and the attempt to monopolize expertise that is, for Abbott (1988), the defining characteristic of professions.

Abbott's (1988) *The System of Professions* applied a version of systems theory to the professions and encouraged studying them as ongoing and dynamic *processes* of occu-pational conflict and cooperation rather than as reified social structures. Abbott's "sys-tems" view was highly influential, virtually halting theoretical conversations on the professions in sociology for several years and, at least as measured by citations, remains a dominant voice in the sociology of the professions.

In sum, over the course of nearly eight decades of sociological research on the profes-sions, we can identify three main conceptual movements. The first, exemplified by the trait theorists and structural-functionalist approaches, sought to identify the distinctive elements of professions and professionalism as a theoretical construct. Ongoing empiri-cal inquiry, however, not only undermined the coherence of the construct, but posed serious doubt as to the theoretical validity of trying to isolate unique elements of what increasingly appeared to be an ongoing project or process.

The second movement sought to understand professions as projects of self-interested power. While this approach generated considerable empirical evidence, it was counter-manded by an equivalent army of evidence that pointed to many other possible motiva-tions for professions (Muzio et al. 2013).

Current theories of professionalism have clearly abandoned the research questions of structural-functionalism (Macdonald 1995; Leicht and Fennell 2008). However, ques-tions of elitism, power, and understanding the comparative processes by which profes-sions emerge in different social contexts (see Brint 1994; Fourcade 2006; Evetts 2011; Muzio et al. 2013), clearly continue to influence research agendas in this area.

The fascination that sociologists first expressed with the unique role of professions in society, however, seems to have waned substantially. Efforts to demonstrate the uniqueness of professions, or their special role in societal relations, have given way to a growing awareness that professions, while interesting, are but one of many social insti-tutions fighting for relevance and status in an ongoing ecology of competing institu-tions (Abbott 1995). Within this theme, one question continues to attract the interest of scholars, albeit scholars of organization and management—the inimical relationship between professions and bureaucratic organizations. A core assumption of trait theo-rists is that professional values of autonomy and independence in work would inevitably clash with bureaucratic values of hierarchy and organizational control. We elaborate this theoretical theme in the following section.

2.3 THEORIES OF PROFESSIONAL ORGANIZATIONS IN MANAGEMENT

2.3.1 Function and Structure

Early organizational researchers adopted an interest in understanding how profession-als structured their work in the context of large bureaucracies. Prior to the mid-1960s most professional work occurred within the confines of "autonomous professional orga-nizations" (Scott 1965; Hall 1967, 1968) or firms that were populated primarily by peer professionals and the goals of which were largely consistent with professional values of autonomy and independence.

As bureaucratic organizations grew in size and influence, however, they began to employ significant numbers of professionals (Montagna 1968; Buchanan 1974; Larson 1977), and even began to produce their own types of professions (Baron et al. 1986). Management researchers steeped in the trait theories of professions assumed that there would be an inherent contradiction between the core values of professionalism and the controlling organizational structures embedded in bureaucracies (Haug 1973; Oppenheimer 1973). A stream of subsequent research sought to elaborate the assumed conflict that would "naturally" occur when professionals worked in bureaucracies (Scott 1965, 1992; Sorenson and Sorenson 1974; Derber 1983; Derber and Schwartz 1991).

While early research seemed to confirm the sociological assumption of conflict-ing values and commitments between professionals and bureaucracies, later research, most of which was conducted by management scholars, offered contradictory evidence. Some research, for example, showed that professionals were often able to restructure the organization and isolate themselves within the bureaucracy in order to preserve core values of autonomy and independence by buffering their work from the bureaucratic context in which it occurs (Nelson and Trubek 1992). Indeed, some scholars (Ackroyd 1996; Reed 1996; Faulconbridge and Muzio 2008) have explicitly connected the suc-cess of the professions to their ability to take over and close off key spaces, structures, and functions in the organizations they increasingly inhabit. Others observe that large organizations offered professionals opportunities to become more specialized and their enhanced expertise and knowledge actually improved commitment to their employing organization (Nelson 1988). While this line of research persists (e.g., Aranya and Ferris 1984; Suddaby et al. 2009) the growing consensus seems to be that professionals have adapted well to work conditions within large corporate bureaucracies (Wallace 1995), thus providing further disconfirmation of trait-based theories of the professions.

A related application of structural theories of the professions by management scholars attempted to elaborate the defining characteristics, not of professionals, but rather of professional firms. Greenwood et al. (1990) thus identified a series of distin-guishing traits in governance (strategic, financial, and operating controls) that sepa-rated professional partnerships from corporate organizations. This research extended

Mintzberg's (1979) configurational approach to understanding organizations and which included one configuration that he described as the "professional bureaucracy." Von Nordenflycht (2010) and Malhotra and Morris (2009) offer a contemporary illustration of the persistent efforts to construct a taxonomy of essential characteristics of PSFs. Von Nordenflycht's key characteristics include knowledge intensity, low capital requirements, and a professional workforce while Malhotra and Morris (2009) focus on knowledge, jurisdictional control, and client relations.

An extension of the "trait" approach to theorizing professional firms seeks to identify which of these traits contributes to superior economic performance. A wide variety of potential traits have been identified in empirical research, including human capital (Hitt et al. 2001, 2006), knowledge management (Empson 2001), ownership structure (Empson and Chapman 2006; Greenwood et al. 2007; von Nordenflycht 2007), and reputation (Greenwood et al. 2005) without any particular consensus on which of these traits might be determinative.

Just as the trait theory in the sociology of professions ultimately succumbed to contradictory empirical evidence, management scholars have produced a long list of studies that demonstrate deviance from the "professional partnership" as an ideal type. Morris and Pinnington (1996), Cooper et al. (1996), Suddaby (2001), and Brock and colleagues (Brock et al. 1999, 2006; Brock 2006) each challenge the integrity of the essential traits of the professional partnership and introduce a variety of alternative configurations of traits, including the "managed professional business," the "global professional network," the "multidisciplinary professional firm," and the "star archetype" among others. Other researchers argue that the essential defining characteristic of professional firms has more to do with ownership (Empson and Chapman 2006; von Nordenflycht 2007), internal human resources practices (Lorsch and Tierney 2002), or internal decision-making practices (Tolbert and Stern 1991; Graubner 2006) than governance characteristics.

In sum, one of the problems in applying trait theory to the study of PSFs is that the assumption of unique characteristics that serve to separate them from bureaucracies and other organizational forms is simply not accurate. PSFs are increasingly adopting both the logic (Brint 1994; Leicht and Fennell 2008; Faulconbridge and Muzio 2009) and structures (Cooper et al. 1996; Brock et al. 1999, 2007) of business corporations, just as some corporations are adopting characteristics of professional firms (Starbuck 1992).

Professional identities within professional firms are often indistinguishable from those of corporate managers inasmuch as they emphasize efficiency and commerce (Anderson-Gough et al. 1999, 2000) at the expense of ethics and public service (Brint 1994; Suddaby et al. 2009). Traditional structures of professional control have migrated from the profession to large professional firms (Cooper and Robson 2006) or transnational governance structures that are dominated by professional firms (Arnold 2005; Suddaby et al. 2007), resulting in a clear erosion of the ethos of professionalism in large PSFs (Hanlon 1998, 1999; Clementi 2004; Suddaby et al. 2009).

In response to these concerns, a growing number of critics have adapted the power and privilege arguments of Freidson (1984, 1986) and Larson (1977) to argue that the real distinguishing feature of professional firms has little to do with their structure or function and much more to do with the elitist position they occupy in economic markets. We elaborate this view in the following section.

2.3.2 Power and Privilege

A growing stream of research in management adopts the view that PSFs are better understood as structures devoted to reconstructing elitist interests than as unique organizational forms. This theoretical approach adopts many of the assumptions of the power and privilege perspective in sociology, but with a specific focus on the reproduction of *economic elites*, rather than social classes.

Much of this research has occurred at the intra-organizational level of analysis and demonstrates how professional firms reproduce elite class interests internally. While early research (Auerbach 1976; Powell 1988) attempted to show that firms hired on the basis of social class rather than expertise, more recent studies (Gilson and Mnookin 1988; Galanter and Palay 1991; Hanlon 1994, 1997, 1999; Ackroyd and Muzio 2007; Faulconbridge and Muzio 2009) focus on how PSFs are increasingly turning to their own division of labor as a primary source of profitability. Marc Galanter and colleagues (Galanter and Palay 1991; Galanter and Henderson 2008) reveal how the economics of law firms are focused on the development of specific labor policies (leveraging; up or out career structure; tournament promotion systems) designed to ensure the profitable use of their human resources. Ackroyd and Muzio (2007; see also Faulconbridge and Muzio 2009), applying a labor process perspective, suggest how PSFs are becoming increasingly stratified as elites maintain their rewards by relying on the surpluses generated by expanding cohorts of subordinates lower down in the division of labor. As controlling elites (partners) tend to be predominantly male while rank and file workers tend to be predominantly female, this is also clearly a gendered process (Hagan and Kay 1995; Sommerlad and Sanderson 1998; Cooper and Taylor 2000; Tomlinson et al. 2013).

A related thread of analysis draws on the literature on identity work to show how PSFs are very effective in constructing elite professional identities that infuse the values and priorities of the firm in the individual professional (Covaleski et al. 1998; Cook et al. 2012). Similar research suggests that the creation of elitist professional identities is, in fact, the identifying characteristic of PSFs (Alvesson 1994, 2001).

Within these debates a particularly interesting stream of research has demonstrated how PSFs increasingly adopt the practices of corporations but retain the rhetoric of professionalism (Grey 1998; Anderson-Gough et al. 1999; Fournier 1999; Dent and Whitehead 2002). As professional discourse becomes disconnected from professional practice, it becomes a disciplinary tool used to manage and motivate workers but lacking any real foundation in the ethos of professionalism (Covaleski et al. 1998; Evetts 2003).

Perhaps the main thrust of the power and privilege approach to studying professions in management research, however, has occurred at the level of the organizational field. The core argument in this theoretical perspective is that PSFs are elite organizations whose primary purpose is to underpin and reproduce the global institutions of capitalism (Everett et al. 2007; Muzio et al. 2007; Neu et al. 2008; Reed 2012). Considerable research has identified the powerful "gatekeeper" function that elite PSFs play in the global economy. Perhaps unsurprisingly, law and accounting firms figure prominently in this research (Coffee 2006), but so too do executive recruitment firms (Beaverstock et al. 2010), management consulting firms (Kipping 1999; McKenna 2006), and elite business schools (Kharana 2010).

An important subtext in this research is the assertion that elite, global professional firms have allied their professional projects with the global aspirations of multinational corporations (Strange 1996; Faulconbridge and Muzio 2012). Thus Dezalay and Garth (1996) show how elite global law firms have reconstructed a parallel system of commercial arbitration that transcends both the jurisdiction and the logic of traditional commercial law. In a related project, Dezalay and Garth (2002) trace the influence of Chicago trained economists whose professionalization project of exporting neo-liberal economic policies globally became a weapon in domestic struggles for political power in countries such as Chile and Argentina. Related to this, critical accountants (Cooper et al. 1998; Arnold 2005; Suddaby et al. 2007) reveal the active role of large accountancy firms in advancing processes of globalization and deregulation, as parts of attempts to create a global market for their expertise.

Theorists who view professions from the point of view of power and privilege understand PSFs to play a critical role in the evolution of the institutions of capitalism in modernity (Reed 1996). That is, in furtherance of their own self-interested professional projects, elite PSFs have attached themselves to global projects of diffusing capitalist institutions and neo-liberal economic policies (Dezalay and Garth 1996, 2002; Hanlon 2004; Arnold 2005; Leicht and Lyman 2006; Quack 2007; Suddaby et al. 2007; Gordon 2010; Faulconbridge and Muzio 2012). Rather than seeing professions as a distinct and independent form of organizing, this theoretical perspective identifies professional firms as playing a key strategic role in disseminating neo-liberal ideology and furthering global capitalist interests.

2.3.3 Process and Practice: An Ecological Approach

An influential theoretical perspective has emerged that seeks to understand PSFs not as reified structural entities nor as naked expressions of power and privilege, but rather as ongoing processes of institutionalization (Leicht and Fennell 2008; Scott 2008; Muzio et al. 2013). In this view professions are themselves institutions, but they are also key agents of broader institutionalization processes in society. Not only are PSFs key agents "in the creation and tending of institutions" (Scott 2008: 216), their own projects of professionalization are intimately connected with the institutionalization projects of other actors such as the nation state, the large multinational corporation, or transnational governance regimes such as the WTO and the EU. Projects of professionalization, thus, carry within them projects of institutionalization (Suddaby and Viale 2011: 423).

This theoretical thread originates in research that illustrated the profoundly important role that professions play in processes of institutional change. Professional museum
curators, for example, were instrumental in shifting the control of historical collections
from wealthy individuals to public galleries (DiMaggio 1991). Even though this change
clearly benefited the professional project of curators, it was couched in the rhetoric of
public service and was legitimated by the ethos of providing public access to national
treasures. Unsurprisingly, the US government was a key ally in facilitating this change.
The curatorial profession, thus, strategically connected its project of professionalization
to the institutionalization of the nation state.

DiMaggio (1988) terms the curator's actions *institutional entrepreneurship* and considerable subsequent research has demonstrated how PSFs are often key entrepreneurs
of profound social change. Large accounting firms have been identified as key agents
in reconfiguring corporate fields (Greenwood and Suddaby 2006) and legitimating
new organizational forms (Suddaby and Greenwood 2005). Medical practices and hospitals have been shown to be key entrepreneurs in restructuring US healthcare (Scott
et al. 2000). Professionalized consultants and managers are shown to have dramatically
altered core practices of charity in the US by introducing rationalized techniques of
measurement and accountability (Hwang and Powell 2009).

More importantly, perhaps, PSFs have been shown to be significant influences in the
processes by which core practices of institutionalization, what Lawrence and Suddaby
(2006) term *institutional work*, occur in contemporary society. Power (2003), thus,
identifies the audit function, as provided by large accounting firms, as a central element
in the production of legitimacy in contemporary society. Dobbin (2009) shows how
human resource professionals are central actors in the production of equal opportunity
in North America. Edelman and colleagues (Edelman 1990; Edelman et al. 1992) analyze how the personnel profession, in conjunction with large corporations, plays a critical role in the institutionalization of affirmative action while, more recently, Daudigeos
(2013) reveals how health and safety practitioners were actively involved, as part of their
own professionalization project, in the prioritization of health and safety concerns
within organizations.

Fourcade (2006) demonstrates how economists, as a profession, engaged with global
NGOs such as the International Monetary Fund, to mutually reconstruct global economic institutions while simultaneously reinforcing the identity and jurisdiction of
economics as a globalized profession. Suddaby et al. (2007), similarly, show how large
accounting firms construct transnational institutions of regulation that are beyond the
regulatory reach of both their professional association and the nation state.

In sum, this research develops a theoretical view of the professions and PSFs that
seeks, as its core research question, to understand the role that processes of professionalization play in broader projects of institutionalization. Notably, it draws on both the
structural-functional and power perspectives in its core assumptions. The notion that
the normative value of professionalism is a persuasive element in legitimating social
change is implicit in much of this research. So too is the assumption that elite PSFs are
interested in preserving their economic and political status.

However this theoretical view differs substantially from both prior theoretical positions. For example, while it assumes that the rhetoric of professionalism is influential and persuasive, it does not adopt the essentialist view of structural-functionalists that professionalism exists in practice or that it is unique to PSFs. Similarly, while it accepts the premise of power theorists that professions are interested in perpetuating their social and economic privilege, it does not take this to be the defining characteristic of PSFs.

A critical element of this theoretical perspective, however, is that it adopts an ecological view of the professions as competing for jurisdiction and social position not only with other professions but also with other institutional forms. Moreover, it suggests that a core element of this competition is the strategic alignment of one's own professional project with a related and symbiotic project of institutionalization. That is, *projects of professionalization are embedded in a related project of institutionalization* (Suddaby and Viale 2011).

So, for example, a number of theorists of the professions point to an intimate and reciprocal connection between traditional professions, such as medicine and law, and the nation state. While these professions are highly dependent upon the nation state with respect to their professional projects in terms of accreditation and enforcing jurisdictions, so too is the nation state dependent upon them in constructing stabilizing institutions of justice, health, and accountability (Silberman 1993; Skowronek 2002; Abbott 2005; Arnold 2012). Some refer to the symbiotic relationship between traditional professions and the nation state as a "regulative bargain" (Puxty et al. 1987). As Abbott (2005: 247) observes, "[n]ot only does a jurisdictional tactic like licensing have to succeed in the system of professions, it also has to succeed in the ecology of the state, for quite other reasons."

A more expansive conceptual model, therefore, is to view the relationship between professions and other related institutions as an institutional ecology, in which successful professionalization projects are more likely to be or remain so if connected to a related institution or institutions. Moreover, these reciprocal projects of institutionalization and professionalization are effective generators of new institutional forms.

While the traditional legal profession appears to be allied with the nation state in their professionalization project, a subset of transnational lawyers appear to have allied with large corporations in constructing new systems of justice based on principles of commercial arbitration rather than common law (Dezalay and Garth 1996). Similarly, accounting firms have allied with multinational corporations to create new systems of commercial and social legitimation (Power 2003; Suddaby et al. 2007).

The strategic reciprocity between professions and adjacent institutions also tends to generate new professional forms. Thus, the ongoing relationship between global accounting firms and transnational corporations encouraged a (failed) attempt to produce multidisciplinary professional firms (Suddaby and Greenwood 2005). Similarly, the profession of human resources is a product of the military profession, the nation state, and corporations engaged in the war effort during the Second World War (Baron et al. 1986; Dobbin 2009).

Collectively, this thread of research adopts a process-oriented view of professions and professional firms in which they exist in an intimate ecological relationship with the institutions that surround them. Some of these relationships are more obvious displays of commensalism (competition) but perhaps the more interesting ones are clearly symbiotic, and involve a cooperative linkage between a profession and an institution. We term this emerging theoretical approach an *ecological-institutional theory of professions* and, in our concluding section, discuss the implications that this view might have for future research.

2.4 CONCLUSIONS: OUTLINING AN ECOLOGICAL-INSTITUTIONAL THEORY OF PROFESSIONS

Ecological reasoning has been applied to a broad range of social phenomena (Hawley 1950; Hannan and Freeman 1977; Wallerstein 1979). Abbott's (1988) view of a dynamic system of professions constantly vying for jurisdictional claims over expert knowledge is perhaps the clearest example of ecological theory applied to the study of professions. Indeed, Abbott (2005) makes this position explicit in suggesting that professions are, themselves, internal ecologies linked to other ecological systems such as governments and universities. An extension of this argument is the observation that professions are core agents of social institutions and are engaged in facilitating exchanges between institutional spheres (Scott 2008). As such, they are the key agents of institutional work (Lawrence and Suddaby 2006). That is, professions are likely to be best understood as institutional actors embedded in a complex environment of related institutions (Suddaby and Viale 2011).

Ecological theory is premised on applying the metaphor of biological ecosystems to human contexts (Hawley 1950) and has received considerable criticism as a result (e.g., Young 1989). A justifiable component of this critique is the observation that theorists selectively adopt some core assumptions of ecological theory and ignore others. So, for example, Hannan and Freeman (1977, 1984, 1989) explicitly state that while ecosystems may at times exhibit both competitive (commensalism) and cooperative (symbiotic) behaviors, they choose, somewhat arbitrarily, to focus only on the competitive elements. Similarly, they opt to emphasize elements of natural selection rather than human development and also to assume that organizational ecologies tend towards disequilibrium rather than stasis.

Adopting a broader view of ecological theory, that embraces these disparate assumptions as tensions rather than competing hypotheses, holds considerable promise for outlining a fresh research agenda for analyzing the professions as embedded institutional actors. We sketch the potential parameters of this research agenda against the backdrop of these three core tensions of ecological theory.

Commensalism and symbiosis: Prior research has established a high degree of intra-professional competition at both the level of the profession (Abbott 1988) and the professional firm (Galanter and Palay 1991). Similarly, within the functionalist vein, considerable research has sought to identify the factors that contribute to the competitive success of professional firms (Hitt et al. 2001, 2006; Greenwood et al. 2005, 2007). Some research has also been devoted to cooperative strategies used by professionals and professional firms (Faulconbridge 2006; Adler et al. 2008).

Few studies, however, seek to identify the conditions under which PSFs opt to select strategies of commensalism versus symbiosis. Moreover such research is typically undertaken at the level of the individual organization. Few analyses have studied the historical symbiosis between, for example, the corporation and the accounting profession or the large diversified hospital and the medical profession. Even more rare are studies that attempt to identify the "linked ecologies" (Abbott 1995, 2005; Mennicken 2010; Seabrooke 2014) that might exist between medicine, hospitals, and government, as institutional forms.

We need a greater understanding of the ecological relationships that develop between professions and related dominant institutional forms. Relevant questions here may include: What is the role of Professional Service Firms in linked ecologies of related institutions? What factors mediate the choice of competitive and cooperative strategies within broader professional ecologies? How do professional projects connect to broader institutional change? How do professions and Professional Service Firms favor or hinder the development of surrounding institutions?

Natural selection and human development: A central question for ecological theorists is the relative primacy of the environment or the individual organism. Critics of evolutionary theory argue that, while natural selection (i.e., the idea that some species are deselected by their environment) may play a role in non-human species, humans have an indomitable ability to adapt to or subdue the environment to human will and need.

Within the context of an ecological theory of professions, this hypothetical tension between man and nature raises the obvious question of the relative power difference that exists between professions and the institutions that surround them. One line of research discussed above, i.e., the literature on organizational professional conflict, suggests that professions are a dominant and superior institutional form that has the capacity to resist bureaucratic pressure. A competing hypothesis, aptly called the "adaptation" theory (Wallace 1995), suggests that professions have been quite skilled at adapting to the bureaucracy as an institutional form.

This research can be extended to the obvious relationships that professions have held with other institutional forms—government, not-for-profits, markets, corporations, religion, and other dominant institutions. Moreover, despite considerable research on the adaptation versus conflict issue, we still have little understanding of the contextual conditions under which professions will choose to adapt or resist. Adopting an institutional lens may offer additional insight.

Stasis or entropy: A final tension within ecological theory is the question of whether ecologies tend towards states of equilibrium or disequilibrium. Subsidiary issues within this core question attempt to understand the triggers that shift an ecosystem from one of equilibrium to disequilibrium and the activities necessary to stabilize a system that has become disrupted.

These questions are also relevant to professions and professional firms, when viewed through an ecological lens. While we have some understanding of the work needed to construct a profession (i.e., Halliday 1987; Torstendahl and Burrage 1990), or to create a new professional category (Baron et al. 1986; Dobbin 2009; Daudigeos 2013), we have little understanding of the institutional work needed to maintain stability in a linked ecology of professions and institutions. Under what circumstances do professional fields and their associated organizational forms develop or remain stable (Scott et al. 2000)? What, for example, is involved in developing the institutional linkages between universities, technology professionals, and local governments to create and maintain an innovative technological cluster (Casper 2007)? What are the institutional conditions needed to attract the new class of "creative" professionals (Florida 2001)?

In sum, we see the adoption of an ecological-institutional lens to understanding professions and professional firms as an important means of avoiding the pitfalls and culs-de-sac of prior research. While many intractable issues of how to define a profession and how professional organizations differ from corporate forms remain relevant, future research in this area should prioritize attempts to understand the dynamic interaction between professions and other social institutions and how these mutually inform, reinforce, and complement each other.

References

Abbott, A. (1981). "Status and Strain in the Professions," *American Journal of Sociology* 86(4): 819–835.

Abbott, A. (1988). *The System of Professions: An Essay on the Division of Expert Labor*. Chicago, IL: University of Chicago Press.

Abbott, A. (1995). "Things of Boundaries," *Social Research* 62(4): 857–882.

Abbott, A. (2005). "Linked Ecologies: States and Universities as Environments for Professions," *Sociological Theory* 23(3): 245–274.

Abel, R. L. (1988). *The Legal Profession in England and Wales*. New York: Blackwell.

Ackroyd, S. (1996). "Organization Contra Organizations: Professions and Organizational Change in the United Kingdom," *Organization Studies* 17(4): 599–621.

Ackroyd, S. and Muzio, D. (2007). "The Reconstructed Professional Firm: Explaining Change in English Legal Practices," *Organization Studies* 48(5): 1–19.

Adler, P., Kwon, S., and Hecksher, C. (2008). "Professional Work: The Emergence of Collaborative Community," *Organization Science* 19(2): 359–376.

Alvesson, A. (1994). "Talking in Organizations: Managing Identity and Impressions in an Advertising Agency," *Organization Studies* 15(4): 535–563.

Alvesson, M. (2001). "Knowledge Work: Ambiguity, Image and Identity," *Human Relations* 54(7): 863–886.

Anderson-Gough, F., Grey, C., and Robson, K. (1999). *Making Up Accountants*. Aldershot: Gower Ashgate.

Anderson-Gough, F., Grey, C., and Robson, K. (2000). "In the Name of the Client: The Service Ethic in Two Professional Services Firms," *Human Relations* 53(9): 1151–1174.

Aranya, N. and Ferris, K. R. (1984). "A Re-examination of Accountants' Organizational Professional Conflict," *Accounting Review* 59(1): 1–15.

Arnold, P. (2005). "Disciplining Domestic Regulation: The World Trade Organization and the Market for Professional Services," *Accounting, Organizations and Society* 30(4): 299–330.

Arnold, P. (2012). "The Political Economy of Financial Harmonization: The East Asian Financial Crisis and the Rise of International Accounting Standards," *Accounting, Organizations and Society* 37(6): 361–381.

Auerbach, J. S. (1976). *Unequal Justice: Lawyers and Social Change in Modern America*. Oxford: Oxford University Press.

Barber, B. (1963). "Some Problems in the Sociology of the Professions," *Daedalus: Journal of the American Academy of Arts and Sciences* 92(4): 669–688.

Baron, J., Dobbin, F., and Jennings, P. D. (1986). "War and Peace: The Evolution of Modern Personnel Administration in U.S. Industry," *American Journal of Sociology* 92(2): 350–383.

Beaverstock, J. V., Hall, S., and Faulconbridge, J. R. (2010). "Professionalization, legitimization and the creation of executive search markets in Europe," *Journal of Economic Geography* 10(6): 825–843.

Becker, H. S., Geer, B., Hughes, E. C., and Strauss, A. L. (1961). *Boys in White: Student Culture in Medical School*. Chicago, IL: University of Chicago Press.

Benson, J. K. (1975). "The Interorganizational Network as a Political Economy," *Administrative Science Quarterly* 20(2): 229–249.

Brint, S. G. (1994). *In an Age of Experts: The Changing Role of Professionals in Politics and Public Life*. Princeton, NJ: Princeton University Press.

Brock, D. M. (2006). "The Changing Professional Organization: A Review of Competing Archetypes," *International Journal of Management Reviews* 8(3): 157–174.

Brock, D., Powell, M., and Hinings, C. R. (1999). *Restructuring the Professional Organization: Accounting, Healthcare and Law*. London and New York: Routledge.

Brock, D. M., Powell, M., and Hinings, C. R. (2007). "Archetypal Change and the Professional Service Firm," *Research in Organizational Change and Development* 16: 221–251.

Brock, D. M., Yaffe, T., and Dembovsky, M. (2006). "International Diversification Strategies and Effectiveness: A Study of Global Law Firms," *Journal of International Management* 12(4): 473–489.

Buchanan, B. (1974). "Building Organizational Commitment: The Socialization of Managers in Work Organizations," *Administrative Science Quarterly* 19(4): 533–546.

Bucher, R. and Strauss, A. L. (1961). "Professions in Process," *American Journal of Sociology* 66(4): 325–334.

Burrage, M. (1988). "Revolution and the Collective Action of the French, American and English Legal Professions," *Law & Social Inquiry* 13(2): 225–277.

Burris, B. H. (1993). *Technocracy at Work*. Albany, NY: State University of New York Press.

Carr-Saunders, A. M. and Wilson, P. A. (1933). *The Professions*. Oxford: Clarendon Press.

Casper, S. (2007). *Creating Silicon Valley in Europe: Public Policy Towards New Technology Industries*. Oxford: Oxford University Press.

Clementi, Sir D. (2004). Report of the Review of the Regulatory Framework for Legal Services in England and Wales, Final Report. <http://www.jambar.org/clement_report.pdf>.

Coffee, J. C. (2006). *Gatekeepers: Professions and Corporate Governance*. New York: Oxford University Press.

Cook, A. C. G., Faulconbridge, J. R., and Muzio, D. (2012). "London's Legal Elite: Recruitment through Cultural Capital and the Reproduction of Social Exclusivity in City Professional Service Fields," *Environment and Planning* 44(7): 1744–1762.

Cooper, C. and Taylor, P. (2000). "From Taylorism to Mrs Taylor: The Transformation of the Accounting Craft," *Accounting, Organizations and Society* 25(6): 555–578.

Cooper, D. J. and Robson, K. (2006). "Accounting, Professions and Regulation: Locating the Sites of Professionalization," *Accounting, Organizations and Society* 31(4–5): 415–444.

Cooper, D. J., Greenwood, R., Hinings, C. R., and Brown, J. L. (1998). "Globalization and Nationalism in a Multinational Accounting Firm: The Case of Opening New Markets in Eastern Europe," *Accounting, Organizations and Society* 23(5): 531–548.

Cooper, D. J., Hinings, C. R., Greenwood, R., and Brown, J. L. (1996). "Sedimentation and Transformation in Organizational Change: The Case of Canadian Law Firms," *Organization Studies* 17(4): 623–647.

Covaleski, M. A., Dirsmith, M. L., Heian, J. B., and Samuel, S. (1998). "The Calculated and the Avowed: Techniques of Discipline and Struggles over Identity in Big Six Public Accounting Firms," *Administrative Science Quarterly* 43(2): 293–327.

Covaleski, M. A., Dirsmith, M. L. and Rittenberg, L. (2003). "Jurisdictional Disputes at Work: The Institutionalization of the Global Knowledge Expert," *Accounting, Organizations and Society* 28(4): 323–355.

Daniels, A. K. (1973). *The Professions and their Prospects.* Thousand Oaks, CA: Sage.

Daudigeos, T. (2013). " 'In Their Profession's Service': How Staff Professionals Exert Influence in Their Organization," *Journal of Management Studies* 50(5): 722–749.

Dent, M. and Whitehead, S. (eds.) (2002). *Managing Professional Identities: Knowledge, Performativity and the "New" Professional.* London: Routledge.

Derber, C. (1983). "Managing Professionals," *Theory and Society*, 12(3): 309–341.

Derber, C. and Schwartz, W. A. (1991). "New Mandarins or New Proletariat? Professional Power at Work," *Research in the Sociology of Organizations* 8: 71–96.

Dezalay, Y. and Garth, B. (1996). "Fussing about the Forum: Categories and Definitions as Stakes in a Professional Competition," *Law and Social Inquiry* 21(2): 285–312.

Dezalay, Y. and Garth, B. (2002). *The Internationalization of Palace Wars: Lawyers, Economists and the Contest to Transform Latin American States.* Chicago, IL: University of Chicago Press.

DiMaggio, P. J. (1988). "Interest and Agency in Institutional Theory," in *Institutional Patterns and Culture*, ed. L. Zucker. Cambridge, MA: Ballinger Publishing Company, 3–22.

DiMaggio, P. J. (1991). "Constructing an Organizational Field as a Professional Project: US Art Museums, 1920–1940," in *The New Institutionalism in Organizational Analysis*, ed. W. W. Powell and P. J. DiMaggio. Chicago, IL: University of Chicago Press, 267–292.

Dobbin, F. (2009). *Inventing Equal Opportunity.* Princeton, NJ: Princeton University Press.

Drinker, H. S. (1954). "The Ethical Lawyer," *University of Florida Law Review* 7(4): 375–385.

Durkheim, E. (1992 [1957]). *Professional Ethics and Civic Morals*, trans. C. Brookfield. London: Routledge.

Edelman, L. B. (1990). "Legal Environments and Organizational Governance: The Expansion of Due Process in the American Workplace," *American Journal of Sociology* 95(6): 1401–1440.

Edelman, L. B., Abraham, S. E., and Erlanger, H. S. (1992). "Professional Construction of Law: The Inflated Threat of Wrongful Discharge," *Law and Society Review* 26(1): 47–84.

Elliot, P. (1972). *The Sociology of the Professions.* London: Macmillan.

Empson, L. (2001). "Fear of Exploitation and Fear of Contamination: Impediments to Knowledge Transfer in Mergers between Professional Service Firms," *Human Relations* 54(7): 839–862.

Empson, L. and Chapman, C. (2006). "Partnership versus Corporation: Implications of Alternative Forms of Governance in Professional Service Firms," *Research in the Sociology of Organizations* 24: 139–170.

Everett, J., Neu, D., and Rahaman, D. (2007) "Accounting and the Global Fight against Corruption," *Accounting, Organizations and Society* 32(6): 513–542.

Evetts, J. (2003). "The Sociological Analysis of Professionalism: Occupational Change in the Modern World," *International Sociology* 18(2): 395–415.

Evetts, J. (2011). "A New Professionalism? Challenges and Opportunities," *Current Sociology* 59(4): 406–422.

Faulconbridge, J. (2006). "Stretching Tacit Knowledge beyond a Local Fix? Global Spaces of Learning in Advertising Professional Firms," *Journal of Economic Geography* 6(4): 517–540.

Faulconbridge, J. and Muzio, D. (2008). "Organizational Professionalism in Global Law Firms," *Work, Employment and Society* 22(1): 7–25.

Faulconbridge, J. and Muzio, D. (2009). "The Financialization of Large Law Firms: Situated Discourses and Practices of Organization," *Journal of Economic Geography* 9(5): 641–661.

Faulconbridge, J. and Muzio, D. (2012). "Professions in a Globalizing World: Toward a Transnational Sociology of the Professions," *International Sociology* 27(1): 136–152.

Florida, R. (2001). *The Rise of the Creative Class*. New York: Basic Books.

Fourcade, M. (2006). "The Construction of a Global Profession: The Transnationalization of Economics," *American Journal of Sociology* 112(1): 145–194.

Fournier, V. (1999). "The Appeal to 'Professionalism' as a Disciplinary Mechanism," *Sociological Review* 47(2): 280–307.

Freidson, E. (1970). *Profession of Medicine: A Study of the Sociology of Applied Knowledge*. New York: Dodd, Mead & Co.

Freidson, E. (1973a). "Professions and the Occupational Principle," in *Professions and their Prospects*, ed. E. Freidson. Beverly Hills, CA: Sage, 19–37.

Freidson, E. (1973b). "Professionalization and the Organization of Middle-Class Labor in Postindustrial Society," *Sociological Review Monograph* 20: 47–59.

Freidson, E. (1982). "Occupational Autonomy and Labor Market Shelters," in *Varieties of Work*, ed. P. Stewart and M. Cantor. Beverly Hills, CA: Sage, 39–54.

Freidson, E. (1984). "The Changing Nature of Professional Control," *Annual Review of Sociology* 10: 1–20.

Freidson, E. (1986). *Professional Powers: A Study of the Institutionalization of Formal Knowledge*. Chicago, Il: University of Chicago Press.

Freidson, E. (1989). "Theory and the Professions," *Indiana Law Journal* 64(3): 423–432.

Friedman, M. and Kuznets, S. (1954). "The Data on Income from Independent Professional Practice," National Bureau of Economic Research. <http://www.nber.org/chapters/c2325.pdf>.

Galanter, M. and Henderson, W. (2008). "The Elastic Tournament: The Second Transformation of the Big Law Firm," *Stanford Law Review* 60(6): 1867–1929.

Galanter, M. and Palay, T. (1991). *Tournament of Lawyers*. Chicago, IL: University of Chicago Press.

Gilson, R. J. and Mnookin, R.H. (1988). "Coming of Age in a Corporate Law Firm: The Economics of Associate Career Patterns," *Stanford Law Review* 41(3): 567–595.

Goode, W. J. (1957). "Community within a Community: The Professions," *American Sociological Review* 22(2): 194–200.

Gordon, R. W. (2010). "The Role of Lawyers in Producing the Rule of Law: Some Critical Reflections," *Theoretical Inquiries in Law* 11(1): 441–468.

Graubner, M. (2006). "Task, Firm Size, and Organizational Structure in Management Consulting: An Empirical Analysis from a Contingency Perspective," Dissertation, European Business School, Oestrich-Winkel.

Greenwood, E. (1957). "Attributes of a Profession," *Social Work* 2: 45–55.

Greenwood, R. and Suddaby, R. (2006). "Institutional Entrepreneurship in Mature Fields: The Big Five Accounting Firms," *Academy of Management Journal* 49(1) 27–48.

Greenwood, R., Deephouse, D. and Li, S. (2007). "Ownership and Performance of Professional Service Firms," *Organization Studies* 28(2): 219–238.

Greenwood, R., Hinings, C. R., and Brown, J. (1990). "P2 Form Strategic Management: Corporate Practices in Professional Partnerships," *Academy of Management Journal* 33(4): 725–755.

Greenwood, R., Li, S., Prakash, R., and Deephouse, D. (2005). "Reputation, Diversification and Organizational Explanations of Performance in Professional Service Firms," *Organization Science* 16(6): 661–673.

Grey, C. (1998). "On Being a Professional in a Big Six Firm," *Accounting, Organizations and Society* 23(5–6): 569–587.

Hagan, J. and Kay, F. (1995). *Gender in Practice: A Study of Lawyer's Lives*. New York: Oxford University Press.

Hall, R. H. (1967). "Some Organizational Considerations in the Professional-Organizational Relationship," *Administrative Science Quarterly* 12(3): 461–478.

Hall, R. H (1968). "Professionalization and Bureaucratization," *American Sociological Review* 33(1): 92–104.

Halliday, T. C. (1987). *Beyond Monopoly: Lawyers, State Crises, and Professional Empowerment.* Chicago, IL: University of Chicago Press.

Halliday, T. C. and Karpik, L. (1998). *Lawyers and the Rise of Western Political Liberalism: Europe and North America from the Eighteenth to Twentieth Centuries.* Oxford: Oxford University Press.

Hanlon, G. (1994). *The Commercialization of Accountancy: Flexible Accumulation and the Transformation of the Service Class.* Basingstoke: Macmillan.

Hanlon, G. (1997). "A Profession in Transition? Lawyers, the Market and Significant Others," *Modern Law Review* 60(6): 799–822.

Hanlon, G. (1998). "Professionalism As Enterprise: Service Class Politics and the Redefinition of Professionalism," *Sociology* 32(1): 43–63.

Hanlon, G. (1999). *Lawyers, the State and the Market: Professionalism Revisited.* Basingstoke: Macmillan.

Hanlon, G. (2004). "Institutional Forms and Organizational Structures: Homology, Trust and Reputational Capital in Professional Service Firms," *Organization* 11(2): 186–210.

Hannan, M. T. and Freeman, J. (1977). "The Population Ecology of Organizations," *American Journal of Sociology* 82(5): 929–964.

Hannan, M. T. and Freeman, J. (1984). "Structural Inertia and Organizational Change," *American Sociological Review* 49(2): 149–164.

Hannan, M. T. and Freeman, J. (1989). *Organizational Ecology*. Cambridge, MA: Harvard University Press.

Haug, M. (1973). "Deprofessionalization: An Alternative Hypothesis for the Future," *Sociological Review Monograph* 20: 195–211.

Hawley, A. (1950). *Human Ecology: A Theory of Community Structure*. New York: Ronald Press.

Hearn, J. (1982). "Notes on Patriarchy, Professionalization and the Semi-Professions," *Sociology* 16(2): 184–202.

Heinz, J. and Laumann, E. (1982). *Chicago Lawyers: The Social Structure of the Bar*. Evanston, IL: Northwestern University Press.

Hickson, D. J. and Thomas, M. W. (1969). "Professionalization in Britain: A Preliminary Measure," *Sociology* 3: 37–53.

Hitt, M. A., Bierman, L., Uhlenbruck, K., and Shimizu, K. (2006). "The Importance of Resources in the Internationalization of Professional Service Firms: The Good, the Bad and the Ugly," *Academy of Management Journal* 49(6): 1137–1157.

Hitt, M. A., Shimizu, K., and Kocher, R. (2001). "Direct and Moderating Effects of Human Capital on Strategy and Performance in Professional Service Firms: A Resource Based Perspective," *Academy of Management Journal* 44(1): 13–28.

Hwang, H. and Powell, W. W. (2009). "The Rationalization of Charity: The Influences of Professionalism in the Non-Profit Sector," *Administrative Science Quarterly* 54(2): 268–298.

Johnson, T. J. (1972). *Professions and Power*. London: Macmillan.

Jones, L. and Moore, R. (1993). "Education, Competence and the Control of Expertise," *British Journal of Sociology of Education* 14(4): 385–397.

Kharana, R. (2010). *From Higher Aims to Hired Hands: The Social Transformation of American Business Schools and the Unfulfilled Promise of Management as a Profession*. Princeton, NJ: Princeton University Press.

Kipping, M. (1999). "American Management Consulting Companies in Western Europe, 1920 to 1990: Products, Reputation and Relationships," *Business History Review* 73(2): 190–220.

Krause, E. A. (1996). *The Death of the Guilds: Professions, States and the Advance of Capitalism, 1930 to the Present*. New Haven, CT: Yale University Press.

Larson, M. S. (1977). *The Rise of Professionalism: A Sociological Analysis*. Berkeley, CA: University of California Press.

Lawrence, T. B. and Suddaby, R. (2006). "Institutions and Institutional Work," in *Handbook of Organization Studies*, ed. S. R. Clegg, C. Hardy, T. B. Lawrence, and W. R. Nord, 2nd edn. London: Sage, 215–254.

Leicht, K. T. and Fennell, M. L. (2008). "Institutionalism and the Professions," In *The Sage Handbook of Organizational Institutionalism*, ed. R. Greenwood, C. Oliver, R. Suddaby, and K. Sahlin Anderson. Thousand Oaks, CA: Sage, 431–448.

Leicht, K. T. and Lyman, E. C. W. (2006). "Markets, Institutions and the Crisis of Professional Practice," *Research in the Sociology of Organizations* 24: 17–44.

Lewis, R. and Maude, A. (1949). *The English Middle Classes*. London: Penguin.

Lorsch, J. and Tierney, T. (2002). *Aligning the Stars: How to Succeed when Professionals Drive Results*. Boston, MA: Harvard Business School Press.

Macdonald, K. M. (1995). *The Sociology of the Professions*. London: Sage.

McKenna, C. D. (2006). *The World's Newest Profession: Management Consultancy in the Twentieth Century*. New York: Cambridge University Press.

Malhotra, N. and Morris, T. (2009). "Heterogeneity in Professional Organizations," *Journal of Management Studies* 46(6): 895–922.

Mennicken, A. (2010). "From Inspection to Auditing: Audit and Markets as Linked Ecologies," *Accounting, Organizations and Society* 35(3): 334–359.

Mintzberg, H. (1979). *The Structuring of Organizations*. Englewood Cliffs, NJ: Prentice-Hall.

Montagna, P. D. (1968). "Professionalization and Socialization in Large Professional Organizations," *Administrative Science Quarterly* 74(2): 133–145.

Morris, T. and Pinnington, A. (1996). "Power and Control in Professional Partnerships," *Long Range Planning* 29(6): 842–849.

Murphy, R. (1988). *Social Closure: The Theory of Monopolization and Exclusion*. Oxford: Clarendon Press.

Muzio, D., Ackroyd, S., and Chanlat, J. F. (2007). *Re-directions in the Studies of Expertise: Doctors, Lawyers and Management Consultants*. Basingstoke: Palgrave Macmillan.

Muzio, D., Brock, D., and Suddaby, R. (2013). "Professions and Institutional Change: Towards an Institutionalist Sociology of the Professions," *Journal of Management Studies* 50(5): 699–721.

Nelson, R. L. (1988). *Partners with Power: The Social Transformation of the Large Law Firm*. Berkeley, CA: University of California Press.

Nelson, R. L. and Trubek, D. (1992). "Arenas of Professionalism: The Professional Ideologies of Lawyers in Collective and Workplace Contexts," in *Lawyers' Ideals/Lawyers' Practices*, ed. R. L. Nelson, D. M. Trubek, and R. L. Solomon. Ithaca, NY: Cornell University Press, 177–214.

Neu, D., Ocampo, E., and Leiser, S. (2008). "Diffusing Financial Practices in Latin American Higher Education," *Accounting, Auditing and Accountability Journal* 21(1): 49–77.

Oppenheimer, M. (1973). "The Proletarianization of the Professional," *Sociological Review Monograph* 20: 213–227.

Parkin, F. (1979). *Marxism and Class Theory: A Bourgeois Critique*. New York: Columbia University Press.

Parsons, T. (1939). "The Professions and Social Structure," *Social Forces* 17(4): 457–467.

Powell, M. J. (1988). *From Patrician to Professional Elite: The Transformation of the New York City Bar Association*. New York: Russell Sage Foundation.

Power, M. (2003). "Evaluating the Audit Explosion," *Law & Policy* 25(3): 185–202.

Puxty, A. G., Willmott, H. C., Cooper, D. J., and Lowe, A. E. (1987). "Modes of Regulation in Advanced Capitalism: Locating Accounting in Four Countries," *Accounting, Organizations and Society* 12(3): 273–91.

Quack, S. (2007). "Legal Professionals and Transnational Law-Making. A Case of Distributed Agency," *Organization* 14(5): 643–666.

Reed, M. I. (1996). "Expert Power and Control in Late Modernity: An Empirical Review and Theoretical Synthesis," *Organization Studies* 17(4): 573–597.

Reed, M. I. (2012). "Masters of the Universe: Power and Elites in Organization Studies," *Organization Studies* 33(2): 203–221.

Rosenberg, D., Tonkins, C., and Day, P. (1981). "A Work Role Perspective on Accountants in Local Government Departments," *Accounting, Organizations and Society* 7(2): 123–137.

Rueschemeyer, D. (1973). *Lawyers and their Society: A Comparative Study of the Legal Profession in Germany and in the United States*. Cambridge, MA: Harvard University Press.

Scott, W. R. (1965). "Reactions to Supervision in a Heteronomous Professional Organization," *Administrative Science Quarterly* 10(1): 65–81.

Scott, W. R. (1992). *Organizations: Rational, Natural and Open Systems*, 3rd edn. Newbury Park, CA: Sage.

Scott, W. R. (2008). "Lords of the Dance: Professionals as Institutional Agents," *Organization Studies* 29(2): 219–238.

Scott, W. R., Reuf, M., Mendel, P. J., and Caronna, C. A. (2000). *Institutional Change and Healthcare Organizations: From Professional Dominance to Managed Care*. Chicago, IL: University of Chicago Press.

Seabrooke, L. (2014). "Epistemic Arbitrage: Transnational Professional Knowledge in Action," *Journal of Professions and Organization* 1(1): 49–64.

Silberman, B. (1993). *Cages of Reason: The Rise of the Rational State in France, Japan, the United States and Great Britain*. Chicago, IL: University of Chicago Press.

Skocpol, T. (1985). "Bringing the State Back In: Strategies of Analysis in Current Research," in *Bringing the State Back In*, ed. P. Evans, D. Ruschmeyer, and T. Skocpol. Cambridge: Cambridge University Press, 3–37.

Skowronek, S. (2002). *The Politics Presidents Make: Leadership from John Adams to Bill Clinton*. Cambridge, MA: Belknap Press of Harvard University Press.

Sommerlad, H. and Sanderson, P. (1998). *Gender, Choice and Commitment: Women Solicitors in England and Wales and the Struggle for Equal Status*. London: Ashgate.

Sorenson, A. B. (2000). "Employment Relations and Class Structure," in *Renewing Class Analysis*, ed. R. Crompton, F. Devine, M. Savage, and J. Scott. Oxford: Blackwell, 16–42.

Sorenson, J. E. and Sorenson, T. L. (1974). "The Conflict of Professionals in Bureaucratic Organizations," *Administrative Science Quarterly* 19(1): 98–106.

Starbuck, W. H. (1992). "Learning by Knowledge Intensive Firms," *Journal of Management Studies* 29(6): 713–740.

Strange, E. (1996). *The Retreat of the State: The Diffusion of Power in the World Economy*. Cambridge: Cambridge University Press.

Suddaby, R. (2001). "Field Level Governance and New Organizational Forms: Multidisciplinary Practices in Law," PhD Dissertation, University of Alberta.

Suddaby, R. and Greenwood, R. (2001). "Colonizing Knowledge: Commodification as a Dynamic of Jurisdictional Expansion in Professional Service Firms," *Human Relations* 54(7): 933–953.

Suddaby, R. and Greenwood, R. (2005). "Rhetorical Strategies of Legitimacy," *Administrative Science Quarterly* 50(1), 35–67.

Suddaby, R. and Viale, T. (2011). "Professionals and Field-Level Change: Institutional Work and the Professional Project," *Current Sociology* 59(4): 423–41.

Suddaby, R., Cooper, D., and Greenwood, R. (2007). "Transnational Regulation of Professional Services: Governance Dynamics of Field Level Organizational Change," *Accounting, Organizations and Society* 32(4–5): 333–362.

Suddaby, R., Gendron, Y., and Lam, H. (2009). "The Organizational Context of Professionalism in Accounting," *Accounting, Organizations and Society* 34 (3–4): 409–427.

Tolbert, P. S. and Stern, R. N. (1991). "Organizations of Professionals: Governance Structures in Large Law Firms," in *Research in Sociology of Organizations*, ed. P. Tolbert and S. Barley. Greenwich, CT: JAI Press, 97–118.

Tomlinson, J., Muzio, D., Sommerlad, H., Webley, L., and Duff, L. (2013). "Structure, Agency and the Career Strategies of Women and BME Individuals in the Legal Profession," *Human Relations* 66(2): 245–269.

Torstendahl, R. and Burrage, M. (eds.) (1990). *The Formation of Professions: Knowledge, State and Strategy*. London: Sage.

von Nordenflycht, A. (2007). "Is Public Ownership Bad for Professional Service Firms? Ad Agency Ownership, Performance and Creativity," *Academy of Management Journal* 50(2): 429–445.

von Nordenflycht, A. (2010). "What is a Professional Service Firm? Toward a Theory and Taxonomy of Knowledge-Intensive Firms," *Academy of Management Review* 35(1): 155–174.

Wallace, J. E. (1995). "Organizational and Professional Commitment in Professional and Nonprofessional Organizations," *Administrative Science Quarterly* 40(2): 228–255.

Wallerstein, I. (1979). *The Capitalist World-Economy*. Cambridge: Cambridge University Press.

Weeden, K. A. (2002). "Why Do Some Occupations Pay More Than Others? Social Closure and Earnings Inequality," *American Journal of Sociology* 108(1): 55–101.

Wilensky, H. L. (1964). "The Professionalization of Everyone?" *American Journal of Sociology* 70(2): 137–158.

Willmott, H. (1995). "Managing the Academics: Commodification and Control in the Development of University Education in the UK," *Human Relations* 48(9): 993–1027.

Wright, E. O. (1997). *Class Counts: Comparative Studies in Class Analysis*. Cambridge: Cambridge University Press.

Young, R. C. (1989). "Is Population Ecology a Useful Paradigm for the Study of Organizations?" *American Journal of Sociology* 94(1): 1–24.

CHAPTER 3

DYNAMICS OF REGULATION OF PROFESSIONAL SERVICE FIRMS

National and Transnational Developments

SIGRID QUACK AND ELKE SCHÜßLER

3.1 INTRODUCTION

REGULATION of the professions has long been synonymous with strong associations controlling access and setting standards for the behavior of their members. While this picture has never been as true for professions in continental European countries as for their Anglo-Saxon counterparts, it has nevertheless been a powerful ideology there as well. Today, the professions have undergone profound transformations across the world: large Professional Service Firms (PSFs) are increasingly replacing individual practices, the expansion of mass education and civil rights movements demanding broader access have diversified the supply of professionals, and well-informed global clients are demanding integrated delivery of services and more transparency about their quality and price. Alongside these developments the regulatory environment of the professions—and PSFs—has also profoundly changed.

Over the last few decades more market competition has been permitted (Garoupa 2011), nationally restricted markets have been opened to foreign service providers (Suddaby et al. 2007), and barriers for inter-professional collaboration have been lowered. These changes go hand in hand with a process of liberalization and deregulation withdrawing national support for self-regulation by professional associations (Muzio and Ackroyd 2005: 622) and a neo-liberal political ideology accompanying the emergence of free trade agreements transnationally (Suddaby et al. 2007: 344). Many observers conclude from these developments that professional control is shifting from occupational to organizational forms. This means that social closure increasingly occurs at the firm level, intra-professional stratification grows, and global PSFs—the elite of the profession—lobby for regulatory reforms to be able to govern their own affairs (Arnold 2005; Suddaby et al. 2007).

These accounts, however, stand in tension with theoretical and empirical work on the emergence of the "new regulatory state" (Moran 2003), regulatory capitalism (Levi-Faur 2005), and transnational governance (Djelic and Quack 2003b; Djelic and Sahlin-Andersson 2006). The latter all suggest that globalization, liberalization, and privatization go hand in hand with an ever-expanding number and density of regulations, many issued by government and state agencies. Thus, the question arises whether professions are really undergoing a process of deregulation, or whether global PSFs are becoming entwined in a complex web of regulation spun by multi-scalar actor constellations.

This question is hard to answer when approaching professional regulation mainly from the perspective of PSFs without taking into account broader changes in the interests, aims, and regulatory instruments of states since the 1970s (Burrage et al. 1990). In this chapter we argue that accounts of the retreat of the state capture only half the picture. Understanding regulation as the sustained and focused attempt to shape the behavior of others with the aim of achieving a broadly defined outcome (Black 2002: 20) we suggest that new patterns of regulation catering to the specific nature of large PSFs are still highly contested and fluid. They need to be explored by studying broader transformations in the relationship between state, economy, and society in developed countries over the last few decades.

We start this chapter by characterizing the traditional regulatory bargain between the professions and the state. We then discuss how large PSFs have globalized and how a new global regulatory compact might be emerging with international trade organizations at the center. Next, we take a closer look at the changing relationship between the state and professions which reveals that various public actors at the national and regional level are reasserting their regulatory capacity in different ways and at different levels. Our review focuses on what von Nordenflycht (2010) called the "classic" PSFs in accounting and law. By comparing and contrasting regulatory changes *between* these two professions and differentiating between global, European, and selected national contexts *within* each profession we show that rather than following a universal pattern, emerging transnational regulatory regimes are characterized by a variety of actor constellations and complex processes of "uploading" and "downloading" of regulation across different geographic scales. We conclude by providing an outlook on the development of regulation of PSFs in other professional jurisdictions and outlining necessary avenues for further research.

3.2 The Traditional "Regulative Bargain" between Professions and the State

Contemporary transformations in the regulatory environment of PSFs are hard to understand without reference to the historical bargain that was struck between the professions and state authorities in most industrializing countries during the late nineteenth and early twentieth centuries. This regulatory bargain, as shown by research on the sociology of professions, consisted of state authorities granting professions control over a specific jurisdictional area of problem-solving knowledge in return for autonomy and self-regulation, provided that it served the public interest and supported state authority (Johnson 1972; Halliday 1987; Cooper et al. 1996; Suddaby et al. 2007: 337; Flood 2011: 509).

As comparative research has shown, this delegation of regulatory authority to the professions has varied considerably over time, across countries, and between professions both in extent and form, so the regulatory bargain has taken "more than a universal form of compromise" (Faulconbridge and Muzio 2012: 139). Studies of the professions in North America and the UK highlighted the autonomy of professional associations in regulating admission, education, working conditions, quality standards, and discipline of their members within the boundaries of residual control of state authorities (Larson 1977; Freidson 1986; Abbott 1988; Abel 1988). Research on professions in continental Europe (including Scandinavia), by contrast, pointed to the more active role of state authorities in shaping trajectories of professionalization, both by setting standards and by shaping demand as a main user of professional services (Burrage and Torstendahl 1990; Torstendahl and Burrage 1990). In Germany, for instance, a neo-corporatist combination of self-governance by professional chambers and state protection against excessive competition was established (Burrage et al. 1990: 219–20).

Two core dimensions of the bargain between professions and the state can nonetheless be identified across all existing historical, national, and inter-professional variation: control over access to a profession and control over the behavior of professionals. Abel (1988) referred to these two dimensions as the "production of producers" and "production by producers" (see Table 3.1), highlighting that the two are closely interlinked.

Table 3.1 Elements of the traditional regulatory bargain

Forms of market control	Forms of regulation
Production of producers	- Definition of content of education and training requirements - Influence on organizations providing professional education and training - Evaluation and screening of candidates through entry examinations, *numerus clausus* - Evaluation and screening of professionals from abroad - Informal mechanisms of social closure
Production by producers	- Restrictions on organizational forms - Regulation of inter-professional cooperation - Limitations on inter-regional competition - Price fixing, mandatory fee scales - Restrictions on advertising - Professional and ethical codes - Informal mechanisms limiting competition

Both dimensions of regulation can be administered by the state, by professional associations, or by a combination of both.

Regulation of "production of producers" has historically taken various forms (Abel 1989; Silver 2007; Garoupa 2011: 460) and revolves around: (a) defining the content of education and training requirements; (b) exerting influence over the organizations that educate and train professionals; (c) evaluating candidates after education and training by submitting them to a *numerus clausus*; (d) screening of foreign professionals aiming to practice in the domestic market; and (e) informal mechanisms of social closure operating based on race, ethnicity, gender, or other characteristics of the candidate.

The regulation of "production by producers" targets how professional services are produced, distributed, and consumed. Regulation of this type has sought to guarantee the quality of services and preserve public interests, prevent malpractice and conflicts of interests, and mediate between different interests within the profession. Among the formal policies and instruments employed to regulate "production by producers" have figured: (a) setting professional and ethical standards applied to individual members of the profession; (b) restricting organizational forms to individual practices or partnerships on the grounds that incorporation would create liability problems and invite conflicts of interests; (c) restricting or regulating inter-professional cooperation on similar grounds; and (d) limiting competition between members of the profession by restrictions on geographic areas of practice, definition of mandatory scales of fees, and bans or limits on advertising (Morgan and Quack 2005; Terry 2009; Garoupa 2011: 460–464).

Regulation of both "production of producers" and "production by producers" constitute forms of market control (Fligstein 1993), which at different times and places targeted "socially idealized occupations organized as closed associational communities" (Collins 1990: 17–18). Historically, these professional communities were constituted by individuals, and the individual professional continued to be the predominant addressee of regulation into the twentieth century, whether as a sole practitioner or as a member of a general partnership. The main actors regulating production of producers and production by producers were the state, professional associations, and educational institutions.

Both forms of regulation rest to varying degrees on coercive, normative, and cognitive foundations and often combine the force of law with socialization and ideational influences (Suddaby et al. 2007: 337). Even in Anglo-Saxon countries, professional self-regulation was typically supported by laws suppressing overt market competition for most of the twentieth century. Most professionals were prohibited from advertising, restricted in organizational form to individual practices or partnerships with personal liability, exempted from regulations prohibiting restraint of trade, protected by laws limiting outside competition, and confined in the exercise of their profession to the locality or state in which they registered. Normative professional control was exercised through the socialization of new members into occupational knowledge and ethical standards through education, training, and licensing by professional bodies. The ideational dimension refers to the ideology underpinning professional governance, such as the commitment to prioritize public concerns over narrow economic self-interest or the role of professions as trustees for social values like justice, public health, or accountability and transparency.

Three different explanations for the emergence and development of this regulative bargain between the professions and the state stand out. The first is *economic* and, starting from the assumption of information asymmetries and market imperfections, argues that markets for professional services require regulation to provide guarantees for consumers of these services, particularly those who are not repeat purchasers. Yet which form this regulation should take, whether the government should pass laws or professional bodies stipulate standards, and what the right balance is to prevent capture by private interests remains controversial among economists (Garoupa 2011: 455).

The second explanation is *sociological* and considers the bargain between the professions and the state as a response to functional requirements of modern societies (see Suddaby and Muzio, Chapter 2, this volume for a review of this literature). Parsons (1939), among others, saw the relationship between professionals and their clients as characterized by uncertainty and asymmetry of expertise, and considered the "institutionalized altruism" of professions, i.e., their orientation towards the public good, as the functional means to maintain social interactions in a modern knowledge society (see also Carr-Saunders and Wilson 1933). From this perspective, regulatory measures are needed to ensure trustworthiness and expertise and to control for commercially driven behavior of professionals (von Nordenflycht 2010). Neither of these two explanations, however, can account for the great variety of regulatory arrangements found in different countries and their evolution over time.

A third explanation, also from the sociology of professions, takes a *political* rather than a functional perspective. Building on and criticizing the research of Anglo-Saxon scholars who highlighted the autonomous bottom-up organization of professions and their struggles for autonomy from the state (Johnson 1972; Larson 1977; Freidson 1986), a group of largely continental European sociologists and social historians published a series of comparative studies in the 1980s and 1990s which had a lasting impact on our contemporary understanding of the bargain between the professions and the state (Burrage and Torstendahl 1990; Torstendahl and Burrage 1990). Specifically, Burrage and colleagues (1990: 212) demonstrated that different types of regulative bargain evolved out of historical struggles between professions, state actors, and clients in different countries. In contrast to their Anglo-Saxon colleagues, they emphasized that states had their own fiscal, electoral, and legitimacy-based motives for striking a bargain with the professions, which became even more prominent with the rise of the welfare state as third-party payer for services in medicine, law, education, and other fields. In their view, organized groups of clients had equally to be considered to understand the diversity of multilateral bargains and their transformation over time. However, in neither of these accounts did the PSF play a prominent role—a gap that Faulconbridge and Muzio (2012: 145) have recently called to overcome.

3.3 Professional Service Firms Going Global: From National Bargains towards a New Global Compact?

From the 1970s onwards, economic globalization and a wave of mergers and acquisitions have triggered significant changes in the market environment in which PSFs operate. First, the general economic climate of the 1980s pressed for deregulation, while increasing global competition placed higher demands on efficiency and bureaucratic forms of organization (e.g., Cooper et al. 1996). Second, the corporate and institutional clients of PSFs—particularly in law and accounting—have become larger and more multinational, leading to a rising demand for seamless and consistent services across national and disciplinary borders (e.g., Beaverstock 2004; Morgan and Quack 2006a, 2006b; Suddaby et al. 2007). In response to and interaction with changing demands of their clients, PSFs have grown in scale and scope, giving rise to a small number of globally operating firms as well as a whole spectrum of alternative forms of service provision such as best friends or referral networks among medium-sized service providers (Morgan and Quack 2006a, 2006b; Boussebaa 2009; Boussebaa and Morgan, Chapter 4, this volume).

The large PSFs have thereby actively promoted deregulation and free trade, shifting regulation from the national to the transnational level where some authors see professional governance being replaced with economic market-making governance (Dezalay and Garth 2010). The driving institutional force for this development is the ideology of marketization, i.e., the belief that markets are the best arrangement for allocating goods and resources (Djelic 2006). Thus regulations increasingly operate at a global level and focus on guaranteeing competitive markets. Examples are supranational trade agreements such as NAFTA, the European Union, or the General Agreement on Trade in Services (GATS) and post-Bretton Woods institutions with quasi-regulatory authority such as the IMF or the WTO (Delimatsis 2012). These institutions have been characterized as constituting a "new compact" (Suddaby et al. 2007) in which international trade organizations and NGOs are the new regulatory actors and the large PSFs act as their advisors (Cooper and Robson 2006). In order to promote this compact prioritizing free trade over other public concerns, large PSFs have become increasingly disconnected from nationally embedded professional regulation (Botzem 2012) and oppose national professional associations that want to maintain restrictions on the free movement of professionals across borders or multidisciplinary practices.

Faced with demands for greater efficiency generated by growing competition and deregulation (e.g., Cooper et al. 1996), firms introduced new layers of managerial control and identity regulation. Full-time managers increasingly replaced rotating partners in leadership positions, and firms started advertising and marketing their services more aggressively. Internationalization led to intense negotiation between partners in different regional offices about how home country practices such as remuneration or office allocation need to be modified to become compatible with host country institutions (Faulconbridge 2008). As large global PSFs moved towards a more hierarchical and specialized organization of work, they strove to gain greater control over the training and career paths of the professionals working for them in order to reproduce a unique corporate identity. This potentially undermined traditional mechanisms of socialization into a particular profession (Lane et al. 2002), diluted the normative control of professional associations over large PSFs (Wyatt 2004), and fragmented national professional labor markets, as shown by Bessy (2015) in relation to French lawyers. Within and across large globalizing PSFs, however, formal and informal transnational communities of practices (Morgan and Kubo 2010; Faulconbridge et al. 2012), often fostered by the firms' management but sometimes also supported by international professional associations (Quack 2006), established alternative mechanisms of normative and cognitive peer control affecting the socialization and career development of professionals.

While this scenario of a new global compact delineates the attempts of some PSFs and policy-makers in international trade to deregulate professional services markets, it largely neglects the difficulty of global trade negotiations on services to reach agreement on these matters (Lim and De Meester 2014). In addition, it pays too little attention to how such agreements are implemented by supranational and national authorities. Furthermore, this scenario also overlooks new forms of state regulation of PSFs that have emerged over the last decade in many jurisdictions. Thus, a closer look at the changing relationship between professions and the state is required to understand the multi-level and multi-faceted dynamics of deregulation and reregulation within professional services markets.

3.4 TRANSFORMATION OF THE STATE AND ITS REGULATORY POLICIES

Levi-Faur (2005: 22) identifies a new form of regulatory capitalism emerging since the 1980s which "rests on a new division of labor between state and society, on the proliferation of new regulatory agencies, on new technologies and instruments of regulation, and the legalization of human interactions." Within this new order, the state itself has been undergoing fundamental changes. Moran (2003: 5) identifies three images of these changes that are discussed in the literature: state withdrawal from utopian "interventionalism" of the Keynesian type, the construction of regulatory institutions for "steering" and delegation of "rowing" to business or civil society groups, and the renunciation of command-and-control regulation in favor of more interactive modes of governance. His excellent analysis of the transformation of the British state, however, portrays the state as ambitious in its own way in fostering standardization, formalization, and public reporting across policy fields. The 1970s to 1990s, according to his account, saw an increasing institutionalization of control, a codification of rules, and a level of juridification that transformed the Victorian model of club government into a "new regulatory state." This regulatory state has also fundamentally affected the regulation of the professions in that the central state began to play an increasingly active oversight role combined with professional self-governance which "could no longer establish its own terms of reference" (Moran 2003: 93). In this world, the profession has to "justify itself by externally prescribed means and externally prescribed ends. It has become an instrument for achieving wider social purposes—whether these are defined as efficient health-care provision, competent legal advice, or reasonable pricing of professional services" (Moran 2003: 94).

While different trajectories can be observed in different countries (Evetts 2002), four major changes in the goals and instruments of state regulation can be identified which challenged pre-existing regulatory bargains with the professions: the *advance of competition policy*, the *liberalization of company forms*, a *shift towards more public oversight*, and an *increasing transnational entanglement of the state*. In consequence, public authorities have shifted their focus from regulating professionals towards regulating PSFs in similar ways to those applied to other large and often multinational corporations that fulfill public or systemic functions.

3.4.1 Rise of Competition Authorities and Expansion of Competition Policy into Services

The transformation from the interventionist to the regulatory state was first and foremost signaled by the increasing independence and influence of national and European competition authorities (Majone 1994) and by the construction of an International Competition Network (Djelic 2011). From the mid-1990s onwards, the Australian and UK governments, as well as an OECD working group of national competition authorities, started to scrutinize professional regulation for restrictive access, excessive fees, bans on advertising, and other practices that were considered to exceed what could be regarded as being in the public interest (Terry 2009: 6ff.). Governments and competition authorities were not only concerned with the international competitiveness of services as a source of economic and job growth, but also responded to complaints by customers and consumer organizations that regulation was serving more the private interests of the profession than the public. In a number of countries, including the UK, governments also aimed to reduce welfare expenditure related to professional services, such as legal aid (Muzio and Ackroyd 2005; Flood 2011) or the costs of pharmaceuticals and healthcare.

Since the early 2000s, when it launched a stocktaking exercise, the European Commission has continuously asked member states to review existing rules in order to reduce unnecessary regulation (Philipsen 2010). Terry (2009), in her excellent account of European competition and professions, shows that this policy—unlike earlier rulings of the European Court of Justice—is not always based on a well-founded empirical analysis of regulatory practices in different countries and partly lacks an adequate operationalization of the public interest. While more research is still required about the actual effects of competition policy on different types of professional practitioners and PSFs, it seems safe to state that the increasing involvement of competition authorities into their regulation has been a major source of destabilization for the previously existing compact between the state and the professions.

3.4.1.1 *Liberalization of Company Forms*

Until the 1980s and 1990s, localized individual practices or professional partnerships with unlimited personal liability were the only legally permitted organizational forms for professional activities. This was justified in terms of holding professional practitioners accountable for the consequences of possible malpractice (Greenwood and Empson 2003; Empson and Chapman 2006). From the 1990s onwards, however, developments such as financial pressures for raising capital, increasing costs for indemnity premiums arising from more litigious clients, investments in the technical infrastructure connected to global organizational networks, and performance-related premiums for young cohorts of professionals have all challenged the traditional partnership structure. These requirements were then relaxed in many countries. In the late 1980s, lawyers in Germany, for example, brought cases to the Federal Court of Justice, successfully claiming that the restrictions preventing the formation of nationwide legal practices were inappropriate and should be removed (Morgan and Quack 2005).

Such changes in continental European countries were the first step in enabling consolidation of individual practitioners into larger law firms—a process that had occurred in the USA in the 1930s and in the UK in the 1970s (Faulconbridge 2008). In a second step, national regulators and legislators relaxed their opposition to the demands of PSFs to be allowed to operate under normal company law rather than being restricted to professional partnerships—though significant variations in national legislation remain. While the Australian state of New South Wales was the first worldwide allowing full incorporation of legal practices under ordinary company law in 2001 (Parker et al. 2010), such a transformation is still not possible or confined to limited liability partnerships in other countries, including Germany, Italy, and France. The move towards alternative ownership forms has been accompanied by controversies about whether non-professionals should be allowed to hold equity in the firms and how stock market listings may influence their independence in delivering professional services. In the UK, for example, where incorporation of law firms had been admitted since 1992 (Empson and Chapman 2006: 148) large law firms lobbied successfully during the debates prior to the enactment of the Legal Service Act in 2007 for non-professionals to be allowed to invest in and own law firms (Flood 2011: 514).

3.4.1.2 *Shift towards Greater Public Oversight*

In the 1990s and 2000s, national parliaments and governments in a number of countries became increasingly concerned with cases of professional malpractice by large PSFs. In the accounting industry, the US government enacted the Sarbanes-Oxley Act

(SOX) as a reaction to major corporate and accounting scandals including those affecting Enron and WorldCom. Under this act, the Securities and Exchange Commission created a new, quasi-public agency, the Public Company Accounting Oversight Board (PCAOB) charged with overseeing, regulating, inspecting, and disciplining accounting firms in their role as auditors of public companies. Among other requirements, the SOX imposed a stricter separation of auditing from consultancy and legal services provided to the same client in order to prevent conflicts of interests. Furthermore, quality control procedures and performance of audits, previously peer reviewed by other firms under the auspices of the American Institute of Certified Public Accountants (AICPA), are now subject to statutory regulation of the PCAOB implemented by public inspectors (Anantharaman 2012: 55f.). A number of other countries subsequently enacted similar acts, including Australia, France, Germany, Italy, India, Israel, Japan, South Africa, and Turkey, and a number of countries established similar new oversight agencies to control auditing firms more strictly.

In legal services, complaints about malpractice typically arose more from the small-practitioner than from the large-firm sector. In the UK, for example, consumer organizations raised complaints against restrictive practices in conveyancing and other retail legal services, which led the British government to initiate several parliamentary inquiries during the 1990s and early 2000s. The Legal Services Act passed in 2007 introduced a new system of oversight regulation modeled on its predecessors in the financial sector, as well as on the Australian regulation of legal services. Thus, the Legal Services Board, as an oversight regulator, monitors a series of frontline regulators, such as the Solicitors' Regulation Authority and the Bar Standards Board (Flood 2011: 514). In line with these observations from law and accounting, Saks (2013: 3) argues that state action in Anglo-Saxon countries was particularly targeted towards empowering citizens and customers relative to professionals.

Within this framework of stronger public oversight, different forms of firm-based risk management and ethical compliance systems were implemented. The Australian state of New South Wales, for instance, introduced new legal provisions that required "incorporated legal practices (ILPs) to implement and maintain 'appropriate management systems' to improve the management and culture of each firm as a whole and prevent ethical risks associated with multidisciplinary practices and the commercial pressures of external investment in legal practices" (Parker et al. 2010: 467). Firms report on their implementation of appropriate management systems to public oversight bodies which monitor and review the results. Under the oversight of the Solicitors' Regulation Authority in the UK, a slightly different system of Authorized Internal Regulation had to be implemented by large law firms, on which they have to report regularly (Flood 2011: 517). While some authors, such as Flood, regard management-based oversight rather skeptically, others, like Parker et al. (2010), observe a positive effect on service quality as measured by decreasing numbers of complaints and conclude that professional ethics and values are successfully enhanced through these managerial practices.

Altogether, however, the enactment of new regulation and the establishment of public oversight agencies in charge of establishing external standards and procedures by which professional self-regulation is to be monitored and reviewed on a continuous basis extends the trend towards the publicly controlled professional self-regulation regimes identified earlier by Moran (2003: 93f.). While more research is needed to assess the impact and effectiveness of the new regulatory frameworks, there can be little doubt that public authorities are taking a more active role in controlling and monitoring PSFs' operations than in the past.

3.4.1.3 *Increasing Transnational Entanglement of State Regulatory Systems and Obligations*

States and their regulatory policies are increasingly entangled in multi-level regulatory schemes fostered and institutionalized by governmental as well as non-governmental actors (Djelic and Quack 2007; Faulconbridge and Muzio 2012). They are increasingly part of simultaneously evolving "trickle-up" and "trickle-down" dynamics of transnational regulation (Djelic and Quack 2003a). At the global level, national governments, oversight bodies, and standard-setters are increasingly involved in global norm- and rule-setting. At the national level, the same actors are typically responsible for implementing, translating, and adapting globally established norms and rules to national and sub-national environments (Djelic and Sahlin-Andersson 2006). Frequently, global rule-setting and implementation in the services involves protracted bilateral and plurilateral negotiations.

A case in point is the General Agreement on Trade in Services. Since the mid-1990s, big accounting firms and some of the large law firms have been lobbying for a far-reaching liberalization of global services markets (Suddaby et al. 2007), of which the conclusion of the Disciplines on Domestic Regulation in the Accountancy Sector by the Council for Trade in Services in 1998 was considered by some authors as the successful outcome (Arnold 2005: 326). However, subsequent global trade negotiations on the services have been protracted and controversial with rather slow and only partial convergence between WTO member states (Natens 2013; Lim and De Meester 2014). At the time of writing, cross-border activities of PSFs are still subject to a complex web of bilateral and plurilateral agreements on mutual recognition of licensing requirements and procedures, qualification requirements and procedures, and technical standards, implemented by national and sub-national governments, standard-setters, and professional bodies. European Union regulation provides another example of the multi-scalar transnational embeddedness of national regulation which transforms but does not abrogate the tasks of national regulators. Both the EU Directive on the Recognition of Professional Qualifications and the EU Services Directive foresee a key role for national regulators in the administration and implementation of European regulation (Terry 2009). As a consequence, PSFs operating in different member states of the European Union continue to be confronted with a great variety of licensing and training requirements and procedures coexisting within the broader framework of common regulation (Faulconbridge and Muzio 2012 on British international law firms in Italy; Terry 2009).

Less often discussed, but equally important, is that representatives of public agencies, oversight bodies, and standard-setters increasingly form part of transnational regulatory networks, which by facilitating consensus-based cooperation expand their capacity to govern into the transnational sphere (Slaughter 2004; Verdier 2009). For accounting, Richardson (2009: 571) observes that following the Enron and WorldCom scandals, "domestic [accounting and auditing] standard-setting processes in many countries are becoming more deeply intertwined with securities regulators and various oversight bodies." Humphrey and colleagues (2009), for instance, see a growing interrelationship between the developing global financial architecture and auditing practices. Based on a network analysis, Richardson (2009) shows that Canada's accounting and auditing standard-setting processes are articulated with international and national regulatory bodies for financial regulation, producing a diffuse but dense set of rules which govern the processes, practices, and outputs of PSFs in this field.

While more developed in accounting, the emergence of transnational regulatory networks can also be observed in law. The study of Terence C. Halliday and Carruthers (2009) demonstrates how international and national professional associations together with other global actors, such as the IMF and World Bank, developed comprehensive norms for bankruptcy laws that subsequently were implemented by various national legislators. While this transnational regulatory network was targeted at substantive regulation, it also had indirect consequences for what is considered acceptable professional behavior in bankruptcy practice. At a more general level, the Council of Bars and Law Societies of Europe (CCBE) and International Bar Association (IBA) (Flood 2011: 519) have created international standards for the cross-border conduct of lawyers that intersect with national regulations. In both accounting and law, it is known that large PSFs provide significant resources for the operation of transnational regulatory networks. Yet more comparative research is required to understand better the nature and impact of their role in transnational regulatory networks (Cooper and Robson 2006; Richardson 2009).

As a consequence of these four developments, the large transnational PSF has not only become a new actor in the professional services landscape (Faulconbridge and Muzio 2012: 145), but it has also increasingly become the object and target of public regulation. In many ways, regulatory policies targeted at professional services have become more similar to those applied to manufacturing or other services: they now tend to focus on the firm rather than on the individual practitioner, regulating the management of corporate risks and conflicts of interests between different parts of the organization rather than individual liability and malpractice. Certainly, public regulators still recognize that "regulated" professions, as they are called by the European Commission, should be treated differently from other occupations even when increasingly submitted to competition law. Overall, however, regulators seem to increasingly recognize the similarities between large PSFs and large corporations in other sectors in terms of systemic risks to public order, the need to protect consumer interests, and prevention of anti-competitive practices.

Some of these changes are in line with the interests and strategies of large PSFs, others are not. Yet it is clear that the transformed regulatory state and the emergence of transnational regulatory networks are challenging the traditional (national) bargain

TABLE 3.2 Deregulation and reregulation of Professional Service Firms

	Production of producers	Production by producers
De-Regulation	*Global/regional level*	
	TRIPS, NAFTA, and EU Services Directive reduced barriers to access for professionals from other countries	TRIPS, NAFTA and EU Services Directive liberalized forms of service provision
	National/sub-national level	
	Expansion of higher education and rise of certification bodies weakened control of professional associations over access to the profession	Removal of legal limitations on competition (geographical, advertising, organizational form) Weakening of normative control of professional associations over work practices in global professional service firms

Firm level: PSFs between deregulation and reregulation

> **Global professional service firms**
> firm-based systems of managerial control and identity regulation, supported by transnational communities of practice and career networks

> **Medium and small professional service firms**
> Co-regulated by firm-based, associational and national public authorities

	Production of producers	Production by producers
Reregulation	*National/sub-national level*	
	Reregulation of formal procedures for mutual recognition of professional qualifications by public actors and/or professional associations	Introduction of entity regulation establishing firm-based risk management systems overseen by national regulators Increased oversight by public agencies and competition authorities
	Global/regional level	
	GATS, NAFTA, and EU Directive on the Recognition of Professional Qualifications establishing rules for mutual recognition	GATS and EU Services Directive recognizing authority of member states to set technical standards as long as they are not discriminatory

with the professions, while subjecting PSFs to greater degrees of scrutiny in areas where their professional behavior appears to endanger public interests. Whether this is successful or not is another question. Moran (2003), for instance, shows that ineffective regulation, if problematized by the public, triggers new attempts at reregulation rather than complete deregulation. As a result, new regulatory regimes so far seem rather fragile and fluid, characterized by overlapping dynamics of deregulation and reregulation—regulative, normative, or cognitive—across different levels (Table 3.2).

3.5 REOPENING PANDORA'S BOX: AN ALTERNATIVE SCENARIO FOR A NEW REGULATORY BARGAIN

Above, we have identified one commonly discussed scenario of the future regulation of PSFs in which traditional forms of professional regulation are being deinstitutionalized and replaced by the emergence of new transnational regulatory fields (Arnold 2005; Suddaby et al. 2007). This idea of a new global compact is mainly written from the perspective of large, Anglo-American accounting (and to a lesser degree law) firms and highlights their role as transnational institutional entrepreneurs strategically shaping regulation through intense lobbying (e.g., Greenwood and Suddaby 2006). An important precondition for such unified institutional entrepreneurship on a global scale is effective internal coordination. Greenwood and colleagues (2010) observe that the Big Four accounting firms have developed new "multiplex" organizational forms to capture the complexity of customer demands and institutional environments along different axes of expertise, multiple practice groups, and client management systems. Highly differentiated processes are balanced with a culture of reciprocity among the different partners within the transnational firms established through a strong rhetoric and different organizational practices.

Accordingly, Cooper and Robson (2006) claim that multinational service firms have become the place where professional practices are standardized and regulated, where legal rules and accounting standards are translated into practice, where professional identities are framed and transformed, and where new professional and corporate governance structures are invented and transmitted to clients and broader audiences. This organizational form could diffuse among other professional service organizations and pave the way for a further shift towards firm-based global regulation. If these firms are able to overcome collective action problems and to coordinate with their global competitors, they could support this process by lobbying for their strategic policy goals within the WTO, other international regulatory fora, and in national politics (Flood 2011).

While this scenario certainly reflects ongoing processes in a limited number of the largest transnational PSFs, it is an open question for empirical research how far this reality extends and how influential large PSFs in global negotiations really are when compared to other powerful corporate actors, countries, or international bureaucracies with often different interests. In fact, very few PSFs are truly global with offices in all continents (Beaverstock et al. 1999; Faulconbridge and Muzio 2012) and internationalized

PSFs tend to keep strong links to their home jurisdictions (Morgan and Quack 2005; Quack 2012). Additionally, not all PSFs, even when following a strategy of internationalization, are necessarily interested in global deregulation, which is often "at odds with the ethos of professionalism." This raises questions about the applicability of new regulations (Flood 2011: 521). At least some of these concerns are taken into account by an alternative scenario found in the literature.

In this second scenario, PSFs are embedded in complex multi-level regulatory arrangements with inherent tensions between national and transnational regulation, competing professional interests, and divergence between small and large firms within each profession (Saks 2013). This scenario zooms in on the managerial challenges of calibrating national regulations and professional logics with changing client and transnational regulatory demands in different countries, sectors, and firms (e.g., Morgan and Quack 2005, 2006a; Faulconbridge et al. 2012).

The second scenario does not assume a linear process of emancipation from national to global regulation, but rather perceives contemporary changes as the confluence of complex "trickle-up" and "trickle-down" dynamics (Djelic and Quack 2003a) that are taking place between multiple regulations at different scales. The traditional bargain between professions, clients, and states granting self-regulation in exchange for public trusteeship to national professional associations is being replaced by fragile settlements involving the liberalization of previously protected areas, the introduction of market mechanisms, and new forms of public oversight and risk control. The driving forces behind this development are multiple and contradictory: marketization is opposed by new forms of regulation, as well as by more articulate public demands for consumer protection and transparency.

Regulation is no longer just a bargain between professions and the state mediated by nationally embedded professional associations and, as argued by Burrage and colleagues (1990), clients and universities, but also involves firms as well as different kinds of agencies, international organizations, and transnational communities of practice. Relevant regulation is now transnational as nation states interact with supra- and sub-national agents (Faulconbridge and Muzio 2012: 141), professional firms interact with clients across different levels, and all types of actors interact across various scales.

An illustration of the second scenario can be found in the continuing struggle between members of the legal and accounting professions over acceptable forms of multidisciplinary practices. In some continental European countries, such as Germany, multidisciplinary practices between lawyers, accountants, and tax advisors have been permitted for a long time. Small firms often employed lawyers, accountants, and tax advisors as partners (Abogado 1999). In other countries, particularly the USA, multidisciplinary practices have been hotly contested by parts of the legal profession because they were seen as undermining the lawyers' professional duties (Nnona 2006; Paton 2010). Some countries with common law systems, including Australia and the UK, have now accepted multidisciplinary practices. Yet, a multinational multidisciplinary practice wanting to operate in many different countries still needs to take account of a variety of national regulations specifying liability, indemnity insurance, and conflicts of interests in ways that often differ between the two professions.

A second illustration is provided by the contemporary strategies and practices of large global law firms. Faulconbridge and colleagues (2012), for instance, show how English transnational law firms use networking through communities of practice as a "trickle-down" strategy. Specifically, communities of practices allow these firms to balance the conflicting demands and professional identities embedded in heterogeneous institutional environments. This heterogeneity originates from the significant differences separating the various national regulatory bargains struck in the past in different countries. The English common-law system, for instance, differs significantly from the German or Italian civil-law system, resulting in different attitudes, values, and behaviors (La Porta et al. 2008). In order to shape a common identity, transnational English law firms form communities of practice by organizing global events or developing diploma programs so that best practices (from the English perspective) can diffuse among the foreign lawyers working for them. These efforts can only have a partial effect, however, and create hybrid identities among members of the community.

With regards to "trickle-up" dynamics, lawyers and law firms from different national contexts contribute to shaping transnational regulatory arenas such as the EU. These do not necessarily converge on an Anglo-American model, but rather reflect the diversity of national institutional legacies (Morgan and Quack 2005). In the reverse direction, lawyers in national contexts may resist reform efforts stemming from transnational arenas. Italian lawyers, for instance, opposed government reform efforts stemming from European liberalization policies in the late 2000s by defending their right to professional self-governance vis-à-vis other regulatory bodies such as the Italian government, the antitrust authority, or the EU (Micelotta and Washington 2011). Muzio and Faulconbridge (2013) found that English global law firms which entered the Italian legal markets through loose agreements in the 1990s followed by mergers with local law firms around the turn of the millennium, failed to implement their "one-firm model" because local lawyers rejected it as a "bundle of practices" which they did not perceive as a legitimate way of organizing law firms. This result, based on in-depth study of several cases of demergers between English and Italian firms, highlights the multiplicity of tensions that global PSFs can face when expanding into countries with a rather different set of regulatory, normative, and cognitive institutions.

Finally, as a third illustration, large accounting firms, despite their global branding and integrated strategies, still use the federated organizational model (Aharoni 1999; Barrett et al. 2005), despite its limits in coping with multi-layered and fragmented transnational regulation (Empson 2010). Among the few studies that investigate their work practices in different institutional contexts, Barrett and colleagues (2005) found that auditors belonging to the same accounting firm but working in different countries tended to give different meaning and interpretations to inter-office instructions and technologies when applied to the same multinational client firm. The authors thus concur that "manifestations of convergence in audit occur alongside evidence of increased fragmentation" (Barrett et al. 2005: 21). Mennicken's (2008) study of the introduction of international auditing practices by a large post-soviet Russian firm provides a highly informative analysis of the tensions between the expectations of international financial institutions, like the IMF and World Bank, for harmonized practices and the need to appropriate and translate rules according to the requirements of the local institutional context.

3.6 CONCLUSIONS

Despite decades of struggles and negotiations about possible new regulatory solutions within and across nation states and professions, new regulatory bargains between PSFs, clients, and states are still in flux. While large global PSFs are outgrowing the traditional regulative bargain between professional associations and the state, equally comprehensive forms of regulation at a regional or global level are not in sight. Instead, large PSFs themselves have emerged as actors and arenas of regulation, alongside a plurality of transnational professional networks and professional communities with a more specialized focus. National competition and oversight agencies are forming transgovernmental networks and multi-level governance regimes. International PSFs and professional associations are active in shaping transnational regulations, but also had to adapt to regulations emanating from these transgovernmental networks or supranational organizations such as the WTO or the EU—which in turn are heavily influenced by the interests of powerful nation states. While public actors at these different levels do not always speak the same language or promote the same issues (Flood 2011), they assert their role as regulators and are likely to have more impact on PSFs than is usually recognized in the literature.

One of the reasons why little attention has been paid so far to the interaction of public and private actors in transnational professional governance is the diffuse character of the latter. Although focal actors such as PSFs, the WTO, or the EU are easy to identify, regulatory processes tend to be highly distributed and diffuse, shaped by the practices of diverse actors and different national traditions (Quack 2007). Regulatory processes also often evolve in recursive cycles (Halliday and Carruthers 2007; Quack 2007) between practice and formal rules and between national and global contexts, mediated by different actors across different scales of action. As a result, the impact of specific actors on regulatory outcomes, as well as the effectiveness of particular regulations in practice, is difficult to assess.

Our analysis should be seen as a first step towards disentangling the dynamic interplay between rules and regulations at different levels and in different contexts. Yet our study is limited because of its focus on two professions, law and accounting, and a selection of examples from a limited set of countries. In many ways, our chapter reflects the limits of our current knowledge. All too often studies focus only on a single type of PSF in a given national or transnational professional field, with a strong prevalence of large global firms from the USA and UK. This exclusive focus leads not only to a neglect of PSFs originating from continental Europe, BRICS, and developing countries, but also ignores a significant number of small and medium-sized PSFs that are equally involved in cross-border service provision but might have less opportunity to escape national regulatory regimes and to co-shape global ones. As a result, we know comparatively little about contemporary regulatory changes in countries outside the USA and UK and their interdependence with emerging transnational regimes, as well as about how regulatory changes affect medium-sized PSFs. While we have included countries such as Italy and Germany to reach beyond classical accounts of the Anglo-Saxon world, this chapter reflects in many ways the fragmented and cursory state of our knowledge of the regulation of different kinds of PSFs around the world.

There is also a scarcity of well-informed research on the role of individual and organized clients in the development of new regulatory bargains. We still know little about how clients respond to the new organizational and regulatory arrangements of professional service provision (Leicht and Fennell 1997), as well as about the role of consumers as organized interest groups in service economies (e.g., Trumbull 2010). Much more research is also needed into the role of public organizations as clients and indirect financiers of professional services, whether these are governments or international organizations. The interaction between welfare states and the provision of professional services has barely been touched upon despite its ubiquity—from legal aid to taxation and public health.

It is not surprising that comparative studies outlining regulatory developments not only across different countries, but also across professions are rare, because the complexity of such an analysis quickly exceeds the constraints of a single paper. Nonetheless, we would encourage further comparative research that includes countries from the BRICS, Asia, and the Global South and other professions such as advertising, architecture, health, or the military. There is also a need for more research on forms of networked professional governance at a transnational level—as outlined already for the field of law (e.g., Morgan and Quack 2006a; Faulconbridge et al. 2012)—in other professions, and extended to other parts of the world. We strongly suggest that these studies should conceptualize regulation as a process that unfolds across multiple levels rather than applying a unified global logic (e.g., Djelic and Quack 2010). Only then will it be possible to assess how far we can generalize from our current knowledge about certain professions and countries to PSFs elsewhere.

ACKNOWLEDGMENTS

We thank Daniel Muzio and the other editors of this volume, the participants of the Colloquium at Cass Business School on September 8–9, 2013, as well as Jonathan Zeitlin and Jörg Sydow for their helpful comments on this chapter.

REFERENCES

Abbott, A. (1988). *The System of Professions: An Essay on the Division of Expert Labor*. Chicago, IL: University of Chicago Press.

Abel, R. L. (1988). *The Legal Profession in England and Wales*. Oxford: Blackwell.

Abel, R. L. (1989). "Comparative Sociology of Legal Professions," in *Lawyers in Society, Volume 3: Comparative Theories*, ed. R. Abel and P. Lewis. Berkeley, CA: University of California Press, 80–153.

Abogado, R. M. (1999). "Report on Multidisciplinary Practices in Europe," American Bar Association—Center for Professional Responsibility. <http://www.americanbar.org/groups/professional_responsibility/commission_multidisciplinary_practice/mullerati.html> (accessed July 3, 2013).

Aharoni, Y. (1999). "Internationalization of Professional Service Firms: Implications for Accounting Firms," in *Restructuring the Professional Organization: Accounting, Health Care and Law*, ed. D. Brock, C. R. Hinings, and M. Powell. London: Routledge, 20–40.

Anantharaman, D. (2012). "Comparing Self-Regulation and Statutory Regulation: Evidence from the Accounting Profession," *Accounting, Organizations and Society* 37(2): 55–77.

Arnold, P. J. (2005). "Disciplining Domestic Regulation: The World Trade Organization and the Market for Professional Services," *Accounting, Organizations and Society* 30(4): 299–330.

Barrett, M., Cooper, D. J., and Jamal, K. (2005). "Globalization and the Coordinating of Work in Multinational Audits," *Accounting, Organizations and Society* 30(1): 1–24.

Beaverstock, J. V. (2004). "'Managing across Borders': Knowledge Management and Expatriation in Professional Service Legal Firms," *Journal of Economic Geography* 4(2): 157–179.

Beaverstock, J. V., Smith, R. G., and Taylor, P. J. (1999). "A Roster of World Cities," *Cities* 16(6): 445–458.

Bessy, C. (2015). *L'organisation des activités des avocats. Entre monopole et marché*. Paris: LGDJ lextenso éditions.

Black, J. (2002). "Critical Reflections on Regulation," *Australian Journal of Legal Philosophy* 27: 1–35.

Botzem, S. (2012). *The Politics of Accounting Regulation: Organizing Transnational Standard Setting in Financial Reporting*. Cheltenham: Edward Elgar.

Boussebaa, M. (2009). "Struggling to Organize across National Borders: The Case of Global Resource Management in Professional Service Firms," *Human Relations* 62(6): 829–850.

Burrage, M. and Torstendahl, R. (eds.) (1990). *Professions in Theory and History*. London: Sage.

Burrage, M., Jarausch, K., and Siegrist, H. (1990). "An Actor-Based Framework for the Study of the Profession," in *The Formation of Professions*, ed. R. Torstendahl and M. Burrage. London: Sage, 203–225.

Carr-Saunders, A. M. and Wilson, P. A. (1933). *The Professions*. London: Oxford University Press.

Collins, R. (1990). "Changing Conceptions in the Sociology of the Professions," in *The Formation of Professions*, ed. R. Torstendahl and M. Burrage. London: Sage, 11–23.

Cooper, D. J. and Robson, K. (2006). "Accounting, Professions and Regulation: Locating the Sites of Professionalization," *Accounting, Organizations and Society* 31(4–5): 415–444.

Cooper, D. J., Hinings, B., Greenwood, R., and Brown, J. L. (1996). "Sedimentation and Transformation in Organizational Change: The Case of Canadian Law Firms," *Organization Studies* 17(4): 623–647.

Delimatsis, P. (2012). "Transnational Private Regulation in Professional Services," paper available at SSRN. <http://papers.ssrn.com/sol3/papers.cfm?abstract_id=2140927> (accessed February 17, 2014).

Dezalay, Y. and Garth, B. G. (2010). "Marketing and Selling Transnational 'Judges' and Global 'Experts': Building the Credibility of (Quasi)Judicial Regulation," *Socio-Economic Review* 8(1): 113–130.

Djelic, M.-L. (2006). "Marketization: From Intellectual Agenda to Global Policy Making," in *Transnational Governance: Institutional Dynamics of Regulation*, ed. M.-L. Djelic and K. Sahlin-Andersson. Cambridge: Cambridge University Press, 53–73.

Djelic, M.-L. (2011). "The International Competition Network," in *The Handbook of Transnational Governance: Institutions and Innovations*, ed. T. Hale and D. Held. Cambridge: Polity Press, 80–88.

Djelic, M.-L. and Quack, S. (2003a). "Conclusion: Globalization as a Double Process of Institutional Change and Institution Building," in *Globalization and Institutions: Redefining the Rules of the Economic Game*, ed. M.-L. Djelic and S. Quack. Cheltenham: Edward Elgar, 302–333.

Djelic, M.-L. and Quack, S. (eds.) (2003b). *Globalization and Institutions: Redefining the Rules of the Economic Game*. Cheltenham: Edward Elgar.

Djelic, M.-L. and Quack, S. (2007). "Overcoming Path Dependencies: Path Generation in Open Systems," *Theory and Society* 36(2): 161–186.

Djelic, M.-L. and Quack, S. (eds.) (2010). *Transnational Communities: Shaping Global Economic Governance*. Cambridge: Cambridge University Press.

Djelic, M.-L., and Sahlin-Andersson, K. (eds.) (2006). *Transnational Governance: Institutional Dynamics of Regulation*. Cambridge: Cambridge University Press.

Empson, L. (2010). "Beyond Dichotomies: A Multi-Stage Model of Governance in Professional Service Firms," Cass Centre for Professional Service Firms, Working Paper CPSF-004, City University, London.

Empson, L. and Chapman, C. (2006). "Partnership Versus Corporation: Implications of of Alternative Forms of Governance in Professional Service Firms," in *Professional Service Firms: Research in the Sociology of Organizations*, ed. R. Greenwood and R. Suddaby. Amsterdam: Elsevier, 139–170.

Evetts, J. (2002). "New Directions in State and International Professional Occuptions: Discretionary Decision-Making and Acquired Regulation," *Work, Employment and Society* 16(2): 341–353.

Faulconbridge, J. R. (2008). "Managing the Transnational Law Firm: A Relational Analysis of Professional Systems, Embedded Actors, and Time-Space-Sensitive Governance," *Economic Geography* 84(2): 185–210.

Faulconbridge, J. R. and Muzio, D. (2012). "Professions in a Globalizing World: Towards a Transnational Sociology of the Professions," *International Sociology* 27(1): 136–152.

Faulconbridge, J., Muzio, D., and Cook, A. (2012). "Learning to Be a Lawyer in Transnational Law Firms: Communities of Practice, Institutions and Identity Regulation," *Global Networks* 12(1): 48–70.

Fligstein, N. (1993). *The Transformation of Corporate Control*. Cambridge, MA: Harvard University Press.

Flood, J. (2011). "The Re-Landscaping of the Legal Profession: Large Law Firms and Professional Re-Regulation," *Current Sociology* 59(4): 507–529.

Freidson, E. (1986). *Professional Powers: A Study of the Institutionalization of Formal Knowledge.* Chicago: University of Chicago Press.

Garoupa, N. (2011). "Regulation of Professions," in *Handbook on the Politics of Regulation*, ed. D. Levi-Faur. Cheltenham: Edward Elgar, 453–468.

Greenwood, R. and Empson, L. (2003). "The Professional Partnership: Relic or Exemplary Form of Governance?" *Organization Studies* 24(6): 909–933.

Greenwood, R. and Suddaby, R. (2006). "Institutional Entrepreneurship in Mature Fields: The Big Five Accounting Firms," *Academy of Management Journal* 49(1): 27–48.

Greenwood, R., Morris, S., Fairclough, S., and Boussebaa, M. (2010). "The Organizational Design of Transnational Professional Service Firms," *Organizational Dynamics* 39(2): 173–183.

Halliday, T. C. (1987). "Knowledge Mandates: Collective Influence by Scientific, Normative and Syncretic Professions," *British Journal of Sociology* 36(3): 421–447.

Halliday, T. C. and Carruthers, B. G. (2007). "The Recursivity of Law: Global Norm Making and National Lawmaking in the Globalization of Corporate Insolvency Regimes," *American Journal of Sociology* 112(4): 1135–1202.

Halliday, T. C. and Carruthers, B. G. (2009). *Bankrupt: Global Lawmaking and Systemic Financial Crisis.* Stanford, CA: Stanford University Press.

Humphrey, C., Loft, A., and Woods, M. (2009). "The Global Audit Profession and the International Financial Architecture: Understanding Regulatory Relationships at a Time of Financial Crisis," *Accounting, Organization and Society* 34(6–7): 810–825.

Johnson, T. (1972). *Professions and Power.* London: Macmillan.

Lane, C., Potton, M., and Littek, W. (2002). "The Professions between State and Market: A Cross-National Study of Convergence and Divergence," *European Societies* 4(2): 235–260.

La Porta, R., Lopez-de-Silanes, F., and Shleifer, A. (2008) "The Economic Consequences of Legal Origins," *Journal of Economic Literature* 46(2): 285–332.

Larson, M. (1977). *The Rise of Professionalism: A Sociological Analysis.* Berkeley, CA: University of California Press.

Leicht, K. T. and Fennell, M. L. (1997). "The Changing Organizational Context of Professional Work," *Annual Review of Sociology* 23: 215–231.

Levi-Faur, D. (2005). "The Global Diffusion of Regulatory Capitalism," *Annals of the American Academy of Political and Social Science* 598(1): 12–32.

Lim, A. H. and De Meester, B. (eds.) (2014). *WTO Domestic Regulation and Services Trade: Putting Principles into Practice.* Cambridge: Cambridge University Press.

Majone, G. (1994). "The Rise of the Regulatory State in Europe," *West European Politics* 17(3): 77–101.

Mennicken, A. (2008). "Connecting Worlds: The Translation of International Auditing Standards into Post-Soviet Audit Practice," *Accounting, Organizations and Society* 33(4): 384–414.

Micelotta, E. R. and Washington, M. (2011). "Defending Your Institution? The Case of Italian Lawyers," *Academy of Management Proceedings* 1: 1–6.

Moran, M. (2003). *The British Regulatory State: High Modernism and Hyper-Innovation.* Cambridge: Cambridge University Press.

Morgan, G. and Kubo, I. (2010). "Private Equity in Japan: Global Financial Markets and Transnational Communities," in *Transnational Communities: Shaping Global Economic Governance*, ed. M.-L. Djelic and S. Quack. Cambridge: Cambridge University Press, 130–152.

Morgan, G. and Quack, S. (2005). "Institutional Legacies and Firm Dynamics: The Growth and Internationalization of Uk and German Law Firms," *Organization Studies* 26(12): 1765–1785.

Morgan, G. and Quack, S. (2006a). "Global Networks or Global Firms? The Organizational Implications of the Internationalization of Law Firms," in *Multinationals, Institutions and the Construction of Transnational Practices: Convergence and Diversity in the Global Economy*, ed. A. Ferner, J. Quintanilla, and C. Sánchez-Runde. Basingstoke: Palgrave Macmillan, 213–238.

Morgan, G. and Quack, S. (2006b). "The Internationalisation of Professional Service Firms: Global Convergence, National Path-Dependency or Cross-Border Hybridisation?," in *Professional Service Firms: Research in the Sociology of Organizations*, ed. R. Greenwood and R. Suddaby. Amsterdam: Elsevier, 403–431.

Muzio, D. and Ackroyd, S. (2005). "On the Consequences of Defensive Professionalism: Recent Changes in the Legal Labour Process," *Journal of Law and Society* 32(4): 615–642.

Muzio, D. and Faulconbridge, J. (2013). "The Global Professional Service Firm: 'One Firm' Models Versus (Italian) Distant Institutionalized Practices," *Organization Studies* 34(7): 897–925.

Natens, B. (2013). "The Doha Round and the Future Architecture of the Multilateral Regulation of Trade in Services." Working Paper No. 110. Leuven: Leuven Center for Global Governance Studies. <https://ghum.kuleuven.be/ggs/projects/steunpunt-internationaal-vlaanderen/documenten/3-bregt-natens-report-dda-final.pdf> (accessed March 10, 2014).

Nnona, G. C. (2006). "Situating Multidisciplinary Practice within Social History: A Systemic Analysis of Inter-Professional Competition," *St. John's Law Review* 80(3): 849–922.

Parker, C., Gordon, T. R., and Mark, S. A. (2010). "Regulating Law Firm Ethics Management: An Empirical Assessment of an Innovation in Regulation of the Legal Profession in New South Wales," *Journal of Law and Society* 37(3): 466–500.

Parsons, T. (1939). "The Professions and Social Structure," *Social Forces* 17(4): 457–467.

Paton, P. D. (2010). "Multidisciplinary Practice Redux: Globalization, Core Values, and Reviving the MDP Debate in America," *Fordham Law Review* 78(5): 2193–2244.

Philipsen, N. J. (2010). "Regulation of Liberal Professions and Competition Policy: Developments in the EU and China," *Journal of Competition Law and Economics* 6(2): 203–231.

Quack, S. (2006). "Who Fills the Legal 'Black Holes' in Transnational Governance? Lawyers, Law Firms and Professional Associations as Border-Crossing Regulatory Actors," in *Global Governance and the Role of Non-State Actors*, ed. G. F. Schuppert. Baden-Baden: Nomos, 81–100.

Quack, S. (2007). "Legal Professionals and Transnational Law-Making: A Case of Distributed Agency," *Organization* 14(5): 643–666.

Quack, S. (2012). "Recombining National Variety: Internationalisation Strategies of American and European Law Firms," *Journal of Strategy and Management* 5(2): 154–174.

Ramirez, C. (2010). "Promoting Transnational Professionalism: Forays of the 'Big Firm' Accounting Community into France," in *Transnational Communities: Shaping Global Economic Governance*, ed. M.-L. Djelic and S. Quack. Cambridge: Cambridge University Press, 174–196.

Richardson, A. J. (2009). "Regulatory Networks for Accounting and Auditing Standards: A Social Network Analysis of Canadian and International Standard-Setting," *Accounting, Organizations and Society* 34(5): 571–588.

Saks, M. (2013). "Regulating the English Healthcare Professions: Zoos, Circuses or Safari Parks?" *Journal of Professions and Organization* 1(1): 84–98.

Silver, C. (2007). "Local Matters: Internationalizing Strategies for U.S. Law Firms," *Indiana Journal of Global Legal Studies* 14(1): 67–93.

Slaughter, A.-M. (2004). *A New World Order*. Princeton, NJ: Princeton University Press.

Suddaby, R., Cooper, D. J., and Greenwood, R. (2007). "Transnational Regulation of Professional Services: Governance Dynamics of Field Level Organizational Change," *Accounting, Organizations and Society* 32(4–5): 333–362.

Terry, L. S. (2009). "The European Commission Project Regarding Competition in Professional Services," *Northwestern Journal of International Law & Business* 29(1): 1–119.

Torstendahl, R. and Burrage, M. (eds.) (1990). *The Formation of Professions*. London: Sage.

Trumbull, J. G. (2010). "Consumer Policy: Business and the Politics of Consumption," in *The Oxford Handbook of Business and Government*, ed. D. Coen, W. Grant, and G. Wilson. Oxford: Oxford University Press, 622–642.

Verdier, P.-H. (2009). "Transnational Regulatory Networks and Their Limits," *Yale Journal of International Law* 34(1): 113–172.

von Nordenflycht, A. (2010). "What is a Professional Service Firm? Toward a Theory and Taxonomy of Knowledge-Intensive Firms," *Academy of Management Review* 35(1): 155–174.

Wyatt, A. (2004). "Accounting Professionism: They Just Don't Get It!," *Accounting Horizon* 18(1): 45–53.

CHAPTER 4

INTERNATIONALIZATION OF PROFESSIONAL SERVICE FIRMS

Drivers, Forms, and Outcomes

MEHDI BOUSSEBAA AND GLENN MORGAN

4.1 INTRODUCTION

In the last three decades, many Professional Service Firms (PSFs) have evolved into transnational businesses with an impressive global reach. For example, in 2014, each of the "Big Four" accountancies—Deloitte & Touche, Ernst & Young, KPMG, and PricewaterhouseCoopers—was present in more than 150 countries. Similarly, Accenture, Wipro, and Capgemini, three leading providers of consulting, technology, and outsourcing services, served clients in more than 120, 61, and 44 countries, respectively. Even smaller, elite firms such as Linklaters and Allen & Overy in the legal sector or Bain & Company and McKinsey & Company in the management consulting industry currently employ thousands in offices dotted all around the world. Few companies in non-service sectors can boast the same geographical spread and, indeed, since the 1990s manufacturing multinationals have been focused on downsizing and outsourcing their operations rather than on expanding their international footprint.

The purpose of this chapter is to present an overview of the extant literature on why PSFs have internationalized, how they have organized themselves across nations, and what difficulties they have experienced in this process. By comparison with firms in other sectors of the economy, PSFs have received little scholarly attention with regards to issues of international expansion and organization. The chapter therefore draws on multiple disciplinary domains, including accounting, economic geography, international business, and organization studies, to review, synthesize, and critique what is known about the drivers, forms, and organizational implications of PSF internationalization.

The chapter proceeds as follows. We first review general theories of internationalization and examine how they have been applied to PSFs. We argue that these theories, which are based predominantly on research into manufacturing companies, need further refinement in order to take into account the distinctive nature of PSFs. We highlight several sources of distinctiveness and, based on this discussion, identify four main forms of PSF internationalization—network, project, federal, and transnational. We then examine the organizational implications of PSF internationalization. We highlight change towards the transnational model as an underlying theme in PSF research and show that, despite much rhetoric, there is little evidence that PSFs have successfully implemented this model in practice. We argue that, in general, these organizations are better understood as federal structures controlled by a few powerful national offices than as transnational enterprises. Finally, we conclude with some suggestions for future research.

4.2 INTERNATIONALIZATION THEORY AND PROFESSIONAL SERVICE FIRMS

4.2.1 Internationalization Theory

The field of international business studies has developed a number of related approaches to understanding internationalization. Beginning with the analysis of the circumstances under which firms decide to set up overseas operations rather than export or franchise, authors such as Buckley and Casson (1976) identified the central importance of transaction costs in the internalization of production. Dunning's (1977, 1988) "eclectic paradigm" elaborated on this by identifying the relationship between ownership, location, and internalization (the OLI framework). According to this framework, firms establish foreign operations because:

- They have "ownership" advantages against firms in the host society—i.e., they have developed knowledge, skills, processes, and procedures that make them capable of producing goods and services more competitively than local companies (O).
- They require complementary assets from other countries which have "locational" advantages (L).
- The cost of internationalizing through exports, licensing, or some kind of non-equity cooperative venture is too high or too risky and, therefore, they prefer to "internalize" overseas activities (I).

From this, Dunning distinguished between four main types of multinational firm activity:

- *Market seeking*: accessing new markets for the firm's products and services;
- *Resource seeking*: ensuring access to key material resources such as oil and minerals;
- *Efficiency seeking*: reducing the costs of factors of production and maximizing economies of scale and scope by the concentration of production at appropriate locations capable of serving regional and global markets;
- *Strategic asset seeking*: searching for capital, skilled labor and ancillary services of a global quality.

Building on this work, international business scholars have also shed light on the risks involved in the internationalization process. The first risk is that associated with what has been termed "the liability of foreignness" (Zaheer 1995), i.e., the various disadvantages arising from not understanding the culture and regulations of the host context; not having the right local connections and networks; and not being known and trusted by local consumers who generally prefer home-based companies. The second and related risk is that proprietary knowledge will leak from the firm through local supply networks and local labor markets, thus diluting initial advantages. The third risk is both reputational and financial in that failure in overseas markets may lead to a broader loss of confidence in the firm and its management. The fourth risk is that of failing to adequately balance responsiveness to national markets on the one hand and global integration and centralized innovation on the other hand. The latter two capabilities represent a key source of competitive advantage because they lead to global efficiency through economies of scale and scope that increase the competitiveness of the firm locally. However, consumer expectations, local regulations, and the nature of competition in the local market can lead the firm to modify its model (its ownership advantages) so much that it can no longer achieve any scale and scope advantages.

International business scholars have shown that risk is mitigated in two main ways. One approach involves making strategic choices about the appropriate form of entry into foreign markets. Entry modes range from exports, licensing, and franchising—all of which imply limited involvement in the foreign context—to various forms of foreign direct investment (FDI), including joint ventures, mergers and acquisitions, and new start-ups. Each of these modes of entry generates specific sorts of risks and is driven by calculations of risks and returns given the specific circumstances of the firm and its market (Buckley and Casson 1985). The second way in which risk is mitigated is central in what is generally referred to as the Uppsala Internationalization Process Model (see Forsgren 2002). In this model, firms minimize risk by extending into culturally similar countries first and then gradually expanding more widely as the firm learns how to deal with more culturally distant and complex environments. In addition, Bartlett and Ghoshal (1989) suggest that firms are increasingly implementing what the authors describe as the "transnational solution," i.e., a new organizational form designed to achieve local responsiveness, global integration, and worldwide learning, simultaneously.

4.2.2 Adapting Internationalization Theory to PSFs

Is the body of theory described earlier applicable to PSFs? Early discussions of this question focused on the argument that PSFs, and service firms more generally, have distinctive characteristics which impact on how they expand across nations and organize themselves as international firms. Campbell and Verbeke (1994: 95), for instance, draw on the well-known list of characteristics that differentiate services from manufacturing—"intangibility"; "inseparability of production and consumption"; "heterogeneity"; "variability"; and "regulation"—to argue that, given these characteristics, the international expansion and organization of service firms exhibit distinctive patterns. Based on research into various service sectors, including finance (Citicorp Banking and American Express) and consulting (McKinsey, Towers Perrin, Arthur Andersen, and Ernst & Young), they for example explain that since services are intangible and generally difficult to separate from their consumption, global scale economies (and by implication global integration requirements) are "far less important" (Campbell and Verbeke 1994: 97) for service firms than they are for manufacturing ones (see also Buckley et al. 1992). In their view, what matters most to service organizations is the ability to "tailor offerings to suit local market preferences and culture" (Campbell and Verbeke 1994: 97), i.e., local responsiveness, together with the capacity to learn from, and transfer such knowledge across, the firm's various national units (i.e., economies of scope through centralized innovation).

In this respect, it is very difficult to export services, and other forms of internationalization such as licensing or franchising, while offering ways of being close to the customer, are risky because services are "intangible"—the provider–consumer interaction is key and, if this was to be under the control of a third-party licensee or franchisee, the original firm would clearly lose an element of control and be open to reputational loss in the home base or other parts of the world. In these circumstances, it might seem that internationalization through FDI is the obvious route for PSFs but, again because of the close consumer connection that is required, firms are likely to rely heavily on localization, on adaptation to the local environment, thereby reducing the potential for global economies of scale and scope. Further, the liability of foreignness is likely to be strong in services given their intangibility and inseparability, and hence consumers are more likely to trust suppliers with a local reputation, thereby placing further local-responsiveness pressures on firms.

Campbell and Verbeke (1994) argue that these problems can be overcome in part by building a global brand and in part by developing network capabilities in the host environment (i.e., trust linkages with local firms and institutions). The authors highlight a key issue in the analysis of international service firms: because of their particular need to be locally responsive, these organizations find it difficult to achieve economies of scale and scope, raising the question as to whether PSFs can ever be more than federations of relatively independent national entities. What they ignore, however, is that PSFs deal with not only local clients but also *multinational* ones who often require transnational, not just national, services; as a result, they are required to not only be locally responsive but also globally integrated, a theme that we return to later. Further, PSFs have other distinctive characteristics which Campbell and Verbeke (1994) and other international business scholars do not take into account but which also impact on processes of internationalization, as we explain next.

4.3 PSF HETEROGENEITY AND ITS IMPACT ON INTERNATIONALIZATION

The initial discussion of internationalization in the service industry highlighted not only differences between service and manufacturing companies but also "heterogeneity" among service firms themselves or rather differences in the nature of services provided by these organizations. Campbell and Verbeke (1994: 97), for example, noted that "services have the potential for considerable variation in their performance or delivery due to the labor intensity of most services production. Because services are people-centered, the marked differences between individuals result in an equivalent heterogeneity in service production." In recent years, this theme of "heterogeneity" and its impact on PSF internationalization has received increasing attention (e.g., Brock 2012; Hitt et al. 2006; Malhotra and Hinings 2010; Malhotra and Morris 2009; Morgan and Quack 2005b). In contrast to earlier writings such as those by Campbell and Verbeke, however, recent contributions emphasize the significance of three other sources of heterogeneity as influencing the internationalization of PSFs: client requirements, mode of governance, and forms of knowledge.

4.3.1 Clients

PSFs provide services across nations for a variety of different clients. In an increasingly globalized world, many companies are engaged in international business and even if they have no foreign subsidiaries, there may be occasions when they need services in other countries, e.g., legal services to sort out contract disputes. They therefore look to professional service providers to resolve their international problems. PSFs generally respond to such demand by forming networks between firms in different countries (see 4.4.2). Many clients, on the other hand, are multinational in scope and these often require integrated cross-national services. Therefore, PSFs dealing with such clients have to develop international structures able to cope with the task of transnational service provision. However, there appears to be great variability in this. As Malhotra and Morris (2009) point out, part of the variability relates to the nature of the task and the degree of face-to-face interaction in the process. In contexts such as law and advertising, for instance, the multinational client defines the problem and then the firm resolves it off-site and with its own people and practices; interaction with the client is therefore limited to senior partners or account managers. This reduces the pressure for the firm to have multiple overseas offices beyond its key marketplaces and to concentrate its key expertise in law or in creative processes of advertising in particular centers where such expertise is abundant and well-developed. In auditing, where multinational companies may require regular and standard services across the globe and where auditors have to be present within the client firm, the pressure is to have offices located in as many countries as possible. Where tasks are more likely to be one-off and to involve intensive relationships with the client as well as with other firms involved in the project (e.g., in large engineering and architectural schemes), then this requires highly experienced and valued experts drawing on abstract skills which are used to produce in consultation with the client certain customized outputs. Malhotra and Hinings (2010) argue that such PSFs internationalize frequently for specific client projects but their permanent centers of expertise are concentrated in a limited number of countries where agglomerations of skills, educational institutions, and major clients exist. The degree of physical presence across different international sites reflects the needs of the client and the project task. The result may be temporary locations embedded with other consultants subcontracted onto the contract for a fixed duration. Malhotra and Hinings discuss the transition from this sort of one-off, temporally limited entry to a foreign market (what they describe as a "bounded commitment path") to the establishment of a more permanent presence. They point out that permanent entry does not bind PSFs in the same way as it does with manufacturing firms. Unlike manufacturing firms, which invest in plants overseas and would take huge losses on withdrawing quickly, PSFs' key assets are predominantly based in people who can if necessary be moved relatively quickly in and out of countries and with little loss of value.

4.3.2 Governance

Historically, PSFs have been characterized by the partnership form, as opposed to the corporate form which is found in most sectors of the economy. The evolution of this mode of governance amongst PSFs has been subject to extended research and debate (see e.g., Brock 2006; Greenwood and Empson 2003; Greenwood et al. 1990). The partnership model was widespread before the advent in the mid-to-late nineteenth century of the joint stock corporate form which separated ownership from control and allowed limited liability. This corporate model enabled the firm to access capital for investment purposes and ensured that owners could separate their personal wealth from their investment in any particular enterprise. PSFs, on the other hand, tended not to go in this direction and to remain partnership structures. This was in part due to regulatory requirements (e.g., in law) which saw potential conflicts of interest arising if commercial considerations driven by shareholders were to supersede professional ethics and principles of best advice. PSFs have also been essentially defined by their senior members and the partnership form has been a way of binding such members (and those who wished to become such members) into the firm. In this form, the firm is basically the agglomeration of its partners, who pursue their own clients and interests subject only to review by their peers, and it is characterized by very little professional, bureaucratic management. As PSFs grew in size and scale, tensions in the partnership model arose, leading to the emergence of what researchers described as the "Managed Professional Bureaucracy" (MPB) (e.g., Cooper et al. 1996). This new PSF form is still based on a partnership mode of governance but also relies on a stronger managerial hand together with more rule-bound procedures. Since the 1990s, with regulatory structures relaxing and firms growing in size and scale, new organizational forms such as limited liability partnerships (LLP) have also emerged and some PSFs have moved towards the limited liability stock ownership model.

The result of such changes is a wide variety of different international governance structures in the professional services sector. Nevertheless, an enduring common denominator is that the PSF is highly dependent on the knowledge, networks, and expertise of its members and this has three effects on internationalization. Firstly, professionals continue to expect a degree of autonomy in the way in which they interact with clients. Therefore, integrative efforts aimed at providing standardized and consistent cross-national services can under certain circumstances meet resistance from key personnel inside PSFs and because those key personnel are essential to the firm, they cannot simply be removed in the way resisters might be elsewhere. The result is therefore that PSFs have to balance efforts to achieve global integration against the necessity to maintain not only local responsiveness but also *professional autonomy*. Secondly, the need for professional autonomy also leads to the necessity for those managing the firm to consult with professionals, particularly in partnership structures (whether these are MPB or LLP or any other version) but also in PLC structures where the loss of "star" employees is detrimental to corporate success. This means that internationalization may be a more *negotiated* process in PSFs than in other types of organizations. Thirdly, the rules on partnerships and the path-dependent effects of the particular histories of individual PSFs means that creating international governance structures linking together firms in different countries can become highly complex in comparison to manufacturing firms.

4.3.3 Knowledge

The third differentiating feature of PSFs (compared to manufacturing firms) concerns the nature of their knowledge. This has a number of dimensions. Malhotra and Morris (2009) distinguish between normative knowledge, technical knowledge, and syncretic knowledge. Normative knowledge is knowledge associated with the norms and values of a particular community. The most obvious example here is law, a form of knowledge that is deeply embedded in national contexts, especially national legal systems. Malhotra and Morris contrast normative knowledge to technical knowledge, which in their view is likely to be the same everywhere; so for example, engineering expertise is based on standardized and universal principles that are as applicable in one country as any other. They argue that other professional services such as auditing combine normative and technical aspects and this they label as syncretic. It follows that PSFs based on normative knowledge have to make substantial accommodations in order to internationalize and manage activities across different normative orders. By comparison, PSFs with a universal knowledge base do not face this sort of problem. PSFs with a syncretic mix of normative and technical knowledge have to negotiate the potential tensions.

It is important to note that other authors have pointed out that PSFs are major actors shaping the knowledge context in which they exist and are not just passive takers of the environment. For example, the "Big Four" accounting firms, which Malhotra and Morris describe as "syncretic," have been major participants in enforcing universal standards of corporate reporting through US-GAAP and International Accounting Standards (Botzem and Quack 2009; also Halliday and Carruthers 2009 on the development of global bankruptcy rules and their implementation in Asia). Thus, they have reshaped the normative environment of particular countries in order to ensure that they can offer a universal knowledge base. Similarly, law firms from the USA and the UK in particular have been instrumental in setting law from their home jurisdictions as the law of choice for major commercial and corporate transactions around the world. PSFs, therefore, have engaged strongly in a process of market making and building international and transnational standards that reflect their own specific forms of knowledge (Morgan 2009). Another example is management consulting where the largest firms, originating mainly in the USA and the UK, have exercised a huge influence on the development of firm strategy and structure across the world either directly through their role in advising large companies from different contexts or indirectly through their connections with institutionalized forms of business knowledge within dominant international business schools and their accreditation procedures (see Khurana 2010).

4.4 Forms of PSF Internationalization

The research discussed earlier shows that initial efforts to analyze the internationalization of PSFs were insufficiently sensitive both to the distinctive nature of such firms and to the degree of heterogeneity that exists among them. It also reveals how such heterogeneity gives rise to varying forms of PSF internationalization.

4.4.1 The Project Form

As described by Malhotra and Hinings (2010), this form of internationalization tends to emerge where the PSF has a limited number of large value clients with specific requirements that are spatially fixed. Thus, firms of architects tend to be located within distinctive national contexts, often drawing their reputation and expertise from the specific historical experience of their home base. However, this market has become increasingly international, with architects now being invited to design and build in many parts of the world. In order to do this, they form project teams (often with other PSFs such as consulting engineers) that are located on-site for a period of time. The home firm has to have the capability to develop such project teams by drawing together for a limited period of time individuals who can be trusted to have the skills and expertise to support the home office and maintain its reputation with clients on an ongoing basis. The temporary nature of this arrangement means that the international structure of the firm fluctuates according to the timetable of projects and engagements to which it is committed. The home office remains central in all key decisions.

4.4.2 The Network Form

Networks consist of independent firms in different national contexts that link together in order to provide international services to their clients. Networks are likely to exist where the incentive to internationalize through FDI is limited (compared to potential risks); firms want to present themselves as internationally connected in order to serve clients with occasional, not continuous needs for services involving overseas contexts. Clients are therefore generally small and medium-sized enterprises rather than large multinationals. Similarly, the tasks required are specific and limited in nature, rarely involving more than a bilateral relationship inside the network. This model is common amongst medium-sized law and accounting firms (see e.g., Morgan and Quack 2006). Such networks are mainly based on referrals between firms in different contexts where their clients require a specific service outside their home base. Referral systems are, however, almost invariably unequal in that some members of the network gain more business than others and this creates a certain tension and conflict in managing the network. Firms that believe they are providing others with more business than they are receiving may be reluctant to stay in the network without further incentives. Networks, therefore, vary on a number of dimensions:

- Degree of exclusivity: who can join the network and who controls entry?
- Degree of intensity of interaction between firms: is it simply client referrals across national boundaries or do firms join together for other purposes, e.g., developing common standards, etc.?
- Degree of formalization of the network (rules and procedures, membership fees, sanctioning and disciplining) or informality (best friends' alliances based on long-standing personal connections).

4.4.3 The Federal Form

This refers to firms that may initially have operated as networks but have now become more coordinated through the establishment of a single brand identity and an international structure responsible for providing organizational support to the constituent parts and a degree of central management. The federal form also reflects the strength of the partnership structure and provides a way of marrying the high level of local autonomy that accompanies such a structure with a degree of global integration through the gradual development of global coordination mechanisms. The "Big Four" accounting firms evolved in this way (see e.g., Cooper et al. 2000) and so have consulting firms such as McKinsey and Towers Perrin (see e.g., Campbell and Verbeke 1994). International advertising firms as constructed over the last 30 years offer a different version of this model where the identity of individual agencies (driven sometimes by individual charismatic creative talents) is retained within the structure of a financially coordinated firm such as Martin Sorrell's WPP. In the federal form, the constituent entities retain a considerable amount of independence in the running of their own business and the management of their own clients even where these clients are multinational in scope. Clients are basically "owned" by the local office which may choose to negotiate with other parts of the firm to provide support and services in different locations—but does not have to do so and may indeed manage a multinational client's project in another country without involving the office that is actually located in that country (see e.g., Boussebaa et al. 2012). Federal PSFs rely on consensual decision-making but, in practice, the largest national offices are likely to be particularly influential over decisions relating to the management of the firm and its transnational client projects and, when threatened by such management, will probably seek to resist it. However, when services are strongly standardized and commoditized, as with auditing, the degree of interconnection between the constituent parts may be stronger and the role of the international structure more important.

4.4.4 The Transnational Form

This refers to those PSFs that seek to develop the three capabilities outlined in Bartlett and Ghoshal's (1989) "transnational solution"—local responsiveness, global integration, and worldwide learning—but in keeping with the particular demands of the professional services context. Transnational PSFs are run from a strong central office that is actively engaged in determining firm-wide practices and policies and in implementing global coordination mechanisms. Clients are "owned" by the firm, not the constituent parts, as are key assets. Key assets include a strong brand that aims to reassure clients of a high level of service, a universal human resources (HR) policy in terms of recruitment, career pathways, and performance management methods, and a global knowledge management system embedded in practices and processes that are formalized in various ways and uniformly taught to new recruits around the world. In this way, the transnational firm aims to be more than the sum of its constituent parts. It is likely to be high on overheads and coordination costs and this is reflected in its pricing systems and its clientele which generally consists of Fortune Global 500 companies. Consulting firms such as Accenture and McKinsey generally portray themselves as transnationals (see e.g., Ghoshal and Bartlett 1997; Paik and Choi 2005) and, as we discuss next, a number of studies suggest that international PSFs in general are moving, or seeking to move, towards this model.

4.5 Organizational Implications

4.5.1 Federal and Transnational Models

The core question for the rest of this chapter that follows from the discussion so far concerns the specific organizational implications of the internationalization of PSFs. By "organizational implications," we refer to not only the formal structures, systems, and practices that firms put in place to coordinate work across nations but also the actual experience of such coordination mechanisms among professionals. Given that the existing PSF literature is very largely focused on what we have termed the "federal" and "transnational" forms of internationalization, we concentrate on the organizational implications of these two models.

Here, it is worth elaborating on the advantages and disadvantages of these models. The federal form offers a "local responsiveness" advantage in that it enables the firm to respond to specific local circumstances in terms of the expertise required, the cultural context of the client, and the wider institutional context in which the client is located. In organizational terms, it functions as a loosely coupled structure that resolves governance issues by maintaining a relative autonomy for partners and national partnerships. When required, transnational coordination is primarily achieved through non-hierarchical means such as lateral integrating systems (e.g., committees based on consensual negotiations particularly with the largest and most powerful national offices) and a degree of normative control (through, e.g., some shared training and inter-office networking). The federal form also provides an international brand identity that can be useful in winning clients at the local level and in recruiting top talent from across the world.

However, by virtue of being loosely coupled, the federal form is unable to achieve high levels of what may be termed "global resource integration," i.e., collaboration between, and coordination of, professionals based in different national units. It is characterized by relatively weak central control, weakly developed systems for the development of shared understandings, procedures, and processes, and an organizational structure in which careers are mainly developed within national units and national labor markets. The federal form is thus not well suited to serving the needs of multinationals given that the projects for which these companies need professional assistance often span national borders, involving multiple client subsidiaries in different countries. Such projects call for PSFs able to mobilize professionals in different geographies, to assemble global service teams, and, hence, to facilitate high levels of transnational collaboration. Cross-national projects also call for shared and consistent work methods and quality standards so as to ensure the service provided to the client is "seamless" (Rose and

Hinings 1999), a capability that is in many ways antithetical to the federal form (Ferner et al. 1995). This is a major problem for the largest PSFs given that many of the companies that they serve or seek to serve are Fortune Global 500 corporations, the projects of which are often multinational in scope (see e.g., Boussebaa 2015).

Adopting the transnational form appears to offer a solution to this problem given that it enables a greater degree of central control and more strongly developed global coordination mechanisms. The transnational form also appears to offer another advantage over the federal firm: it helps in facilitating what may be labeled "global resource transfer," i.e., the flow of professionals and their knowledge across geographic divides. This is important because international PSFs are subject to competitive pressures and, hence, required to operate efficiently and, importantly, to continually innovate and implement best practices as a way of staying ahead of rivals (Aharoni 1996; Løwendahl 2000a). As Løwendahl (2000b: 152–153) explains, "in professional service firms, the competitive advantage, if achieved, results from the ability of the firm to continuously tap into the knowledge developed in all relevant centers of the world [. . . The firm] may even gain competitive advantage from being located in a place where the market is not profitable at all, if the learning from these projects adds more value to other markets than what is lost locally." This learning process enables the firm to evolve new products and innovate in ways that can lead to new and profitable service offerings. And the key to achieving this lies in the firm's ability to develop and implement global knowledge management and employee mobility systems (Beaverstock 2004; Boussebaa 2009; Boussebaa at al. 2014b); something which the transnational form is, theoretically, more capable of achieving than the federal model.

That being said, the transnational model builds in high coordination costs associated with developing and enforcing universal standards, methods, and processes across different geographic units. It also challenges the relative autonomy of national offices and their partners. In effect, it necessitates the development of a corporate structure that can meld together different national units by evolving a "one firm" strategy and structure (Maister 1985), a process that is particularly difficult when the firm continues to operate as a federation of national partnerships (Ferner et al. 1995; Muzio and Faulconbridge 2013). Transnational PSFs are therefore likely to emerge either in contexts and sectors where the partnership form is weak or where it can be replaced by a structure of limited liability and shareholder control. Once this is established, resistance by powerful partners, though still significant, does not have a specially privileged channel for expression and is therefore weakened.

In the extant literature, it is clear that many firms are experiencing a tension between these two models, and their structures, systems, and practices tend to oscillate depending on a variety of internal and external pressures—see e.g., the discussions in studies of accounting (Aharoni 1996; Ferner et al. 1995; Rose and Hinings 1999), consulting (Boussebaa 2009, 2015; Boussebaa et al. 2012; Fenton and Pettigrew 2000; Jones 2005), and law (Faulconbridge 2008; Muzio and Faulconbridge 2013; Segal-Horn and Dean 2009). At the same time, most large international PSFs subscribe to the transnational model and, in particular, claim to have established appropriate mechanisms to achieve greater degrees of resource integration and resource transfer (see e.g., Angel 2007; Brown et al. 1996; Greenwood et al. 2010; Rose and Hinings 1999). But how exactly is this achieved in practice? And are there any differences in the ways in which different types of firms go about the problem? In section 4.6, we provide an overview of what is known on these questions.

4.6 Structures, Systems, and Practices

A review of the extant literature reveals that relatively little research is available on how PSFs achieve resource integration and transfer in practice (cf. Aharoni 1993, 1996; Baden-Fuller 1993; Boussebaa 2009; Morgan and Quack 2005b) and even less about sector effects on such processes (Malhotra and Morris 2009). Much of the existing research tends to focus on *formal* structures, systems, and practices, and typically relies on the accounts of partners as a source of evidence (see e.g., Cooper et al. 2000; Rose and Hinings 1999). For instance, scholars report on how firms have created new regional areas (e.g., America, Asia, Europe, etc.) to coordinate work at this intermediary level and introduced new roles with transnational responsibilities (e.g., global practice leader) to facilitate and manage work across geographies. The firms' international headquarters are also said to have acquired increasing responsibility and authority over time in terms of defining and implementing shared professional standards, work methodologies, training programs, and reward systems. In addition, PSFs are reported to have developed various mechanisms to facilitate global resource transfer, including centers of excellence (Moore and Birkinshaw 1998), knowledge management systems (Ambos and Schlegelmilch 2009), and new, flexible expatriation methods (Beaverstock 2004).

The literature also shows that PSFs have developed more sophisticated ways of assembling global teams of professionals in order to respond more effectively to multinational clients' demand for integrated cross-national services (Rose and Hinings 1999). The ability to assemble such teams is said to have become a major source of competitive advantage for PSFs. A former Managing Director of the law firm Linklaters explains that "competitive advantage for a global law firm lies in its ability to put together teams across practices and across offices to manage global client relationships and to undertake complex transactions more effectively than can be achieved by independent firms working alone or together" (Angel 2007: 202; see also Smets et al. 2012). In this context, global client service partners are said to have been given more authority as a way of better mobilizing and coordinating firm-wide resources (Barrett et al. 2005: 10; Rose and Hinings 1999: 58).

Furthermore, PSFs are said to be putting significant efforts into the management of their corporate cultures in ways that emphasize the importance of transnational collaboration and resource sharing (see e.g., Greenwood et al. 2010). Such efforts are supported by various international mobility systems, training programs, and networking events aimed at exposing employees to "new ways of working, different cultures, different ways of thinking" (Jones 2005: 187) and, ultimately, nurturing professionals that are able to work across national divides. New reward and recognition systems are also said to have been implemented to further stress the importance of, and incentivize, collaboration and sharing. It has even been suggested that some international PSFs have become "single integrated global partnerships with hundreds of partners sharing a single profit pool . . . across practices and offices" (Angel 2007: 201; see also Segal-Horn and Dean 2009).

4.7 THE EXPERIENCE OF INTERNATIONAL PSF ORGANIZATION

While much research has been dedicated to explicating the new mechanisms of global control and coordination that PSFs have developed to become transnational organizations, little scholarly attention has been given to the experience of such changes amongst professionals. As a consequence, the observed move towards the transnational model is not at all clearly demonstrated. The few studies that have sought to get beneath the skin of international PSFs reveal that the tension between the federal model and the transnational one has not been resolved. For instance, research in the context of some of the largest international management consultancies describes how employees, while subscribing to the idea of the transnational firm, experience a major global–local tension in relation to the staffing of client projects (Boussebaa 2009; Boussebaa et al. 2012). The research points to the importance of the national unit to employees' career prospects and financial rewards, and how this leads to priority being typically given to domestic projects and employees whatever the needs of other offices. National units operate as semi-autonomous profit centers; managers and partners at this level focus on achieving their own financial objectives and are reluctant to sacrifice these for the sake of the "one firm" ideal. So, "star" performers are kept working in their home office and only loaned out to other offices if profits made overseas can be taken back home. Such a problem is further complicated by significant fee rate differentials across offices, which makes it very difficult for smaller offices to "borrow" consultants from the larger ones without losing much of their profits. The overall result is continual inter-office struggles over staff and revenue allocations that are not consistent with the rhetoric of global resource transfer and transnational organizing more generally. Boussebaa (2015) reinforces this view and also identifies a disjuncture between the rhetoric of "global" professional standards and the reality of "local" practice in international consultancies.

Significant global–local tensions have also been identified in major international law firms (Faulconbridge 2008; Muzio and Faulconbridge 2013). Here, scholars have shown how the distinctive regulatory frameworks of different countries produce varying expectations about professional work (from both lawyers and their clients) in terms of how it should be managed, evaluated, and rewarded and, as a result, different organizational arrangements in different countries. Such "national varieties of professionalism"

(Faulconbridge and Muzio 2007), in turn, create various cross-national tensions within firms as these seek to implement firm-wide control and coordination systems (e.g., performance management and remuneration models), making collaboration on international projects particularly problematic (Morgan and Quack 2005a). For example, Muzio and Faulconbridge (2013) show how attempts by English law firms operating in Italy to implement the "one firm" model were merely attempts at reproducing home-country practices into Italian offices. This created "conditions of institutional illegitimacy in Italy" and, as a result, led to various problems, including "demergers, lawyer exoduses [and] clashes with local regulators" (Muzio and Faulconbridge 2013: 917). Such findings reveal the presence of strong national path-dependencies inside law firms and further demonstrates that the tension between federalism and transnationalism in PSFs remains unresolved (see also Morgan and Quack 2006).

Research such as this suggests that while international PSFs may present themselves as "transnational" organizations, the reality is more along the lines of a conflictual federal form. Moreover, it shows—implicitly at least—how such an organizational form tends to operate mostly in the interests of, and is broadly managed by, the most powerful national offices, which are generally those based in the UK and the USA and linked to external sources of power and prestige such as the world's major financial markets. Hanlon's (1994) study is particularly revealing here. The author shows how the (then) "Big Six" (now "Big Four") accounting firms are largely dominated, led, and shaped by offices based in England and the USA. He notes how the ideology and practices of these organizations were developed within such national contexts and how offices based in smaller and peripheral nations such as Ireland, while enjoying a degree of autonomy in relation to some business matters (e.g., partner promotion, client management, use of advertising, etc.), are required to adhere to the international standards laid down by the UK and US groups.

Boussebaa et al. (2012, 2014b) describe such processes in terms of a form of "neo-imperialism" in that a few "core" offices based in the most powerful Western economies dominate and seek greater control over smaller and "peripheral" offices based in the rest of the world (see also Boussebaa 2009, 2015; Cooper et al. 1998). Here, it is useful to note that the vast majority of the world's largest accountancies, law firms, and management consultancies are headquartered either in the UK, a former colonial power with still much influence in the global political economy, or in the USA, today's only superpower and what many refer to as an empire (see e.g., Harvey 2003). In this context, Anglo-American offices tend to dominate the rest and, in particular, have a strong influence on processes of resource integration and transfer. For example, Boussebaa et al.'s (2014b) study in the context of management consultancies reveals how UK offices portray themselves as sources of knowledge while treating peer units based in smaller nations as recipients, and how such a representation serves to naturalize and strengthen exploitative, core–periphery knowledge exchange relations within the organization. Such findings again fly in the face of the idea of the "transnational" firm and reveal how PSFs are not only characterized by an unresolved tension between federalism and transnationalism but also (re)productive of quasi-imperial power relations (see Boussebaa (2016) for a detailed examination of such power relations in the context of the Big Four).

4.8 Conclusions and Future Directions for Research

In this chapter, we examined the internationalization of PSFs and its organizational implications. We began by considering whether conventional theories of internationalization were appropriate for the study of PSFs. We highlighted how initial efforts to explore the applicability of these theories to PSFs were useful but fell short because they did not take sufficient account of governance issues, of client types and requirements, and of knowledge characteristics. Incorporating these insights, we also identified four main forms of PSF internationalization: project, network, federal, and transnational. We thus argued for the need to take into account not only the distinctive nature of PSFs in general but also the heterogeneity that exists amongst PSFs themselves.

In terms of organizational implications, we argued that scholarly interest has focused most strongly on the federal and transnational models. We highlighted how the transnational model, which implies high levels of transnational resource integration and transfer as well as a clear guiding strategic center associated with universal standards, methods, and processes, forms a core aspect of the identity of the largest international PSFs. However, we pointed out that recent research suggests that the extent to which PSFs have adopted the transnational model has been over-stated and that there in fact remain significant barriers to the implementation of such a model. These barriers reflect the interaction of various countervailing forces, including the national embeddedness of much professional knowledge, the continued influence of the partnership mode of governance, and the fragmented nature of career and reward systems inside the organization. Thus, from some perspectives, international PSFs are less "transnational" and more "federal" in form, with the constitutive entities retaining significant power and autonomy, particularly those based in the world's largest economies. We also highlighted how some parts of the firm are more powerful than others due to their embeddedness in dominant nations and, in particular, how such embeddedness leads to the (re-)production of quasi-imperial power relations within the firm.

From this analysis, several areas for further research can be suggested. The first area requiring attention is the issue of *heterogeneity*. We have identified some consistent common themes across different professional service settings but it is clear that there is also likely to be considerable variation within the professional services sector and this potentially has significant implications for research on PSF internationalization. One important source of heterogeneity we have discussed is the mode of governance. It is clear that there are now multiple modes of governance ranging from traditional partnerships through to limited liability partnerships and on to other forms of limited liability including that associated with a publicly-listed company structure where ownership is held by external shareholders, not the most powerful professionals in the business (as is the case with the partnership structure). While there has been much discussion on this issue in the PSF field, little attention has been given to its implications for the international organization of the firm. Research is much needed here. For instance, how exactly are the international boards and committees of LLPs or partnerships constituted? Who are the members of these groupings in terms of nationality, expertise, networks, etc. and what powers do they have in relation to global strategy and organization? From a comparative viewpoint, how are the varying forms of central control that are associated with different modes of governance experienced by professionals who generally operate under norms of professional autonomy and consensual decision-making?

The second area concerns the relationship between *clients* and the internationalization processes of the PSF. International expansion creates a host of different business-to-business connections as well as internal organizational issues for large PSFs. It also generates a range of activities linking the firm to individual clients in a variety of countries both through sales and through marketing and advertising efforts. Focusing on the largest global clients, how are they managed across different types of firms? Who owns and controls relationships and projects with such clients in the different firms and how does this relate to efforts to provide a seamless cross-national service or to distribute the costs and profits of such work within the firm?

A third important area needing research attention is the question of *power*. As we have shown, the international expansion and management of PSFs is neither merely a matter of organizational design nor simply one of conflicting institutional logics; it is also a question of power, especially macro-level power, i.e., relations of domination and subordination arising from the embeddedness of the firm in a hierarchical global political economy. The field of comparative and international management has begun incorporating such power in its analysis of multi-nationals and their relationships with other actors around the world (see e.g., Boussebaa and Morgan 2014; Boussebaa at al. 2014a; Ferner et al. 2012; Frenkel 2008); we believe the time has come for PSF studies to follow suit (cf. Boussebaa et al. 2012, 2014b).

A related, fourth area for research concerns the implications of the ongoing shift of political-economic power away from dominant Western nations and towards the BRIC countries and other "emerging" nations. There is very little research on how international PSFs (i.e., PSFs from the USA, the UK, and, to a lesser extent, continental Europe) are expanding into these emerging nations and how this is affecting the balance of power within the organization. Are they establishing conventional core–periphery relations with units based in emerging nations? Or might such units be resisting this process and seeking to restructure the firm in ways that are more in line with their own interests? Looking at it from a different angle, how might we understand the emergence of new international PSFs headquartered in rising powers (e.g., Wipro in India)? How will these expand into the dominant Western economies and manage their offices in those contexts?

Finally, if the study of PSF internationalization is going to be more sensitive to issues of geography and power, it is also useful to highlight the relative absence of history and time from current analyses. In this chapter, we have referred to path-dependent processes arising from national systems of professional regulation and knowledge creation. However, there is very little research that specifically examines the historical development of international PSFs. Yet this is clearly significant in a number of areas, not just to describe but to understand how various forms of internationalization and professional knowledge evolved together. Take, for example, law and the significance of UK law across the world which is in turn related to its imperial past and the transfer of the English system to cities such as Hong Kong and Singapore which have become crucial in the current period of globalization. Similarly, studies in critical accounting (e.g., Annisette 2000) have pointed out the intimate connection between the development of accounting techniques and the way in which colonial powers tried to map populations in the territories they took over, not least to determine tax liabilities to the imperial overlords. Historical studies of PSF internationalization would be very useful in shedding light on these processes and their role in the construction of present-day international PSFs.

In conclusion, the internationalization of PSFs reveals in clear view many pressing issues of global control and coordination. Initial developments in the field of international business attempted to apply a common framework to both manufacturing and PSFs. This is ultimately unsatisfactory given the distinctive nature of PSFs (cf. Boussebaa 2015) and indeed the heterogeneity that exists amongst such organizations. A greater focus on varying forms of internationalization and the driving factors behind these is required as is an appreciation of the tension between the rhetoric of the transnational PSF and the reality of more federally coordinated structures. Investigating these tensions and developments across the heterogeneous professional services sector is important as is the effort to connect this with issues of power within the firm, especially in the context of the changing geography of the global political economy (see Boussebaa 2016). This is a promising agenda for future research.

REFERENCES

Aharoni, Y. (1993). "The Internationalization Process in Professional Business Service Firms: Some Tentative Conclusions," in *Coalitions and Competition: The Globalization of Professional Business Services*, ed. Y. Aharoni. New York: Routledge, 280–285.

Aharoni, Y. (1996). "The Organization of Global Service MNEs," *International Studies of Management and Organization* 26(2): 6–23.

Ambos, T. C. and Schlegelmilch, B. B. (2009). "Managing Knowledge in International Consulting Firms," *Journal of Knowledge Management* 13(6): 491–508.

Angel, T. (2007). "Your Challenge—Sustaining Partnership in the Twenty-First Century: The Global Law Firm Experience," in *Managing the Modern Law Firm: New Challenges, New Perspectives*, ed. L. Empson. Oxford: Oxford University Press, 196–217.

Annisette, M. (2000). "Imperialism and the Professions: The Education and Certification of Accountants in Trinidad and Tobago," *Accounting, Organizations and Society* 25(7): 631–659.

Baden-Fuller, C. (1993). "Globalization of Professional Service Firms: Three Cases," in *Coalitions and Competition: The Globalization of Professional Business Services*, ed. Y. Aharoni. London: Routledge, 102–120.

Barrett, M., Cooper, D. J., and Jamal, K. (2005). "Globalization and the Coordinating of Work in Multinational Audits," *Accounting, Organizations and Society* 30(1): 1–24.

Bartlett, C. A. and Ghoshal, S. (1989). *Managing Across Borders: The Transnational Solution*. Boston, MA: Harvard Business School Press.

Beaverstock, J. V. (2004). "Managing Across Borders: Transnational Knowledge Management and Expatriation in Legal Firms," *Journal of Economic Geography* 4(2): 157–179.

Botzem, S. and Quack, S. (2009). "(No) Limits to Anglo-American Accounting? Reconstructing the History of the International Accounting Standards Committee: A Review Article," *Accounting, Organizations and Society* 34(8): 988–998.

Boussebaa, M. (2009). "Struggling to Organize Across National Borders: The Case of Global Resource Management in Professional Service Firms," *Human Relations* 62(6): 829–850.

Boussebaa, M. (2015). "Control in the Multinational Enterprise: The Polycentric Case of Global Professional Service Firms," *Journal of World Business* 50(4).

Boussebaa, M. (2016). "Professional service firms, globalization and the new imperialism," *Accounting, Auditing & Accountability Journal*, forthcoming.

Boussebaa, M. and Morgan, G. (2014). "Pushing the Frontiers of Critical International Business Studies: The Multinational as a Neo-Imperial Space," *Critical Perspectives on International Business* 10(1–2): 96–106.

Boussebaa, M., Morgan, G., and Sturdy, A. (2012). "Constructing Global Firms? National, Transnational and Neocolonial Effects in International Management Consultancies," *Organization Studies* 33(4): 465–486.

Boussebaa, M., Sinha, S., and Gabriel, Y. (2014a). "Englishization in Offshore Call Centers: A Postcolonial Perspective," *Journal of International Business Studies* 45(9): 1152–1169.

Boussebaa, M., Sturdy, A., and Morgan, G. (2014b). "Learning from the World? Horizontal Knowledge Flows and Geopolitics in International Consulting Firms," *International Journal of Human Resource Management* 25(9): 1227–1242.

Brock, D. M. (2006). "The Changing Professional Organization: Reviewing Evolving Archetypes and Typology," *International Journal of Management Reviews* 8(3): 157–174.

Brock, D. M. (2012). "Building Global Capabilities: A Study of Globalizing Professional Service Firms," *Services Industries Journal* 32(10): 1593–1607.

Brown, J. L., Cooper, D. J., Greenwood, R., and Hinings, B. (1996). "Strategic Alliances within a Big-Six Accounting Firm: A Case Study," *International Studies of Management and Organization* 26(2): 59–79.

Buckley, P. and Casson, M. (1976). *The Future of the Multinational Enterprise*. London: Holmes & Meier.

Buckley, P. and Casson, M. (1985). *The Economic Theory of the Multinational Enterprise: Selected Papers*. London: Macmillan.

Buckley, P., Pass, C. L., and Prescott, K. (1992). "The Internationalization of Service Firms: A Comparison with the Manufacturing Sector," *Scandinavian International Business Review* 1(1): 39–56.

Campbell, A. and Verbeke, A. (1994). "The Globalization of Service Multinationals," *Long Range Planning* 27(2): 95–102.

Cooper, D. J., Greenwood, R., Hinings, B., and Brown, J. L. (1998). "Globalization and Nationalism in a Multinational Accounting Firm: The Case of Opening New Markets in Eastern Europe," *Accounting, Organizations and Society* 23(5–6): 531–548.

Cooper, D. J., Hinings, B., Greenwood, R., and Brown, J. L. (1996). "Sedimentation and Transformation: The Case of Canadian Law Firms," *Organization Studies* 17(4): 623–647.

Cooper, D. J., Rose, T., Greenwood, R., and Hinings, B. (2000). "History and Contingency in International Accounting Firms," in *Globalization of Services: Some Implications for Theory and Practice*, ed. Y. Aharoni and L. Nachum. London: Routledge, 93–123.

Dunning, J. (1977). "Trade, Location of Economic Activity and the MNE: A Search for an Eclectic Approach," in *The International Allocation of Economic Activity: Proceedings of a Nobel Symposium held at Stockholm*, ed. B. Ohlin, P. Hesselborn, and P. M. Wijkman. London: Macmillan, 395–418.

Dunning, J. (1988). "The Eclectic Paradigm of International Production: A Restatement and Some Possible Extensions," *Journal of International Business Studies* 19(1): 1–31.

Faulconbridge, J. R. (2008). "Negotiating Cultures of Work in Transnational Law Firms," *Journal of Economic Geography* 8(4): 497–517.

Faulconbridge, J. and Muzio, D. (2007). "Re-inserting the Professional in the Study of Globalizing Professional Service Firms: The Case of Law," *Global Networks* 7(3): 249–270.

Fenton, E. and Pettigrew, A. M. (2000). "The Role of Social Mechanisms in an Emerging Network: The Case of the Pharmaceutical Network in Coopers & Lybrand Europe," in *The Innovating Organization*, ed. A. M. Pettigrew and E. Fenton. London: Sage, 82–116.

Ferner, A., Edwards, P., and Sisson, K. (1995). "Coming Unstuck? In Search of the 'Corporate Glue' in an International Professional Service Firm," *Human Resource Management* 34(3): 343–361.

Ferner, A., Edwards, T., and Tempel, A. (2012). "Power, Institutions and the Cross-National Transfer of Employment Practices in Multinationals," *Human Relations* 65(2): 163–187.

Forsgren, M. (2002). "The Concept of Learning in the Uppsala Internationalization Process Model: A Critical Review," *International Business Review* 11(3): 257–277.

Frenkel, M. (2008). "The Multinational Corporation as a Third Space: Rethinking International Management Discourse on Knowledge Transfer through Homi Bhabha," *Academy of Management Review* 33(4): 924–942.

Ghoshal, S. and Bartlett, C. (1997). *The Individualized Corporation*. New York: HarperBusiness.

Greenwood, R. and Empson, L. (2003). "The Professional Partnership: Relic or Exemplary Form of Governance?" *Organization Studies* 24(6): 909–933.

Greenwood. R., Hinings, B., and Brown, J. (1990). "P2 Form Strategic Management: Corporate Practice in Professional Partnerships," *Academy of Management Journal* 33(4): 725–755.

Greenwood, R., Morris, T., Fairclough, S., and Boussebaa, M. (2010). "The Organizational Design of Transnational Professional Service Firms," *Organizational Dynamics* 39(2): 173–183.

Halliday, T. C. and Carruthers, B. (2009). *Bankrupt: Global Lawmaking and Systemic Financial Crisis*. Stanford, CA: Stanford University Press.

Hanlon, G. (1994). *The Commercialization of Accountancy: Flexible Accumulation and the Transformation of the Service Class*. Basingstoke: Macmillan.

Harvey, D. (2003). *The New Imperialism*. Oxford: Oxford University Press.

Hitt, M. A., Bierman, L., Uhlenbruck, K., and Shimizu, K. (2006). "The Importance of Resources in the Internationalization of Professional Service Firms: The Good, the Bad and the Ugly," *Academy of Management Journal* 49(6): 1137–1157.

Jones, A. (2005). "Truly Global Corporations? Theorizing 'Organizational Globalization' in Advanced Business-Services," *Journal of Economic Geography* 5(2): 177–200.

Khurana, R. (2010). *From Higher Aims to Hired Hands: The Social Transformation of American Business Schools*. Princeton, NJ: Princeton University Press.

Løwendahl, B. (2000a). "The Globalization of Professional Business Service Firms: Fad or Genuine Source of Competitive Advantage?" in *Globalization of Services: Some Implications for Theory and Practice*, ed. Y. Aharoni and L. Nachum. London: Routledge, 142–162.

Løwendahl, B. (2000b). *Strategic Management in Professional Service Firms*. Copenhagen: Copenhagen Business School Press.

Maister, D. M. (1985). "The One-Firm Firm: What Makes It Successful?" *Sloan Management Review* 27(1): 3–13.

Malhotra, N. and Hinings, B. (2010). "An Organizational Model for Understanding Internationalization Processes," *Journal of International Business Studies* 41(2): 330–349.

Malhotra, N. and Morris, T. (2009). "Heterogeneity in Professional Service Firms," *Journal of Management Studies* 46(6): 895–922.

Moore, K. and Birkinshaw, J. (1998). "Managing Knowledge in Global Service Firms: Centers of Excellence," *Academy of Management Executive* 12(4): 81–92.

Morgan, G. (2009). "Globalization, Multinationals and International Diversity," *Economy and Society* 38(4): 629–654.

Morgan, G. and Quack, S. (2005a). "Institutional Legacies and Firm Dynamics: The Growth and Internationalization of UK and German Law Firms," *Organization Studies* 26(12): 1765–1785.

Morgan, G. and Quack, S. (2005b). "Internationalization and Capability Development in Professional Services Firms," in *Changing Capitalisms? Internationalization, Institutional Change, and Systems of Economic Organization*, ed. G. Morgan, R. Whitley, and E. Moen. Oxford: Oxford University Press, 277–311.

Morgan, G. and Quack, S. (2006). "Global Firms or Global Networks? The Organizational Implications of the Internationalization of Law Firms," in *Multinationals, Institutions and the Construction of Transnational Practices: Convergence and Diversity in the Global Economy*, ed. A. Ferner, J. Quintanilla, and C. Sánchez-Runde. New York: Palgrave Macmillan, 213–238.

Muzio, D. and Faulconbridge, J. (2013). "The Global Professional Service Firm: 'One Firm' Models Versus (Italian) Distant Institutionalized Practices," *Organization Studies* 34(7): 897–925.

Paik, Y. and Choi, D. Y. (2005). "The Shortcomings of a Standardized Global Knowledge Management System: The Case Study of Accenture," *Academy of Management Executive* 19(2): 81–84.

Rose, T. and Hinings, B. (1999). "Global Clients' Demands Driving Change in Global Business Advisory Firms," in *Restructuring the Professional Organization: Accounting, Health Care and Law*, ed. D. Brock, C. Hinings, and M. Powell. London: Routledge, 41–67.

Segal-Horn, S. L. and Dean, A. (2009). "Delivering 'Effortless Experience' Across Borders: Managing Internal Consistency in Professional Service Firms," *Journal of World Business* 44(1): 41–50.

Smets, M., Morris, T. and Greenwood, R. (2012). "From Practice to Field: A Multi-Level Model of Practice-Driven Institutional Change," *Academy of Management Journal* 55(4): 877–904.

Zaheer, S. (1995). "Overcoming the Liability of Foreignness," *Academy of Management Journal* 38(2): 341–363.

CHAPTER 5

ORGANIZATIONS AND OCCUPATIONS

Towards Hybrid Professionalism in Professional Service Firms?

IAN KIRKPATRICK AND MIRKO NOORDEGRAAF

5.1 INTRODUCTION

THE nature of the relationship between occupations and organizations and how it might be changing, is a topic that continues to generate controversy. A persistent image in the literature is of professionals as highly mobile sole practitioners who work independently or within particular kinds of organizations such as small firms or partnerships. According to Larson (1977: 205) this is rooted in an "ideological conception" of professions as "'communities' or as 'companies of equals' which democratically exercise mutual supervision over deeply internalized common standards." Consequently, any organizational influence over professional action is quickly seen as an "attack on professionalism" and professionals viewed as somehow "persecuted" (e.g., Farrell and Morris 2003). However, these assumptions about the mutual exclusivity of professions and organizations have always been open to question and have increasingly become more so.

Again, following Larson (1977) it is important to recognize that to a greater or lesser extent, all professionals have "structural connections" with bureaucracy. This is most apparent in the case of organizational professionals (such as managers) and expert groups located in, and formally subordinate to, *heteronomous organizations* such as public services agencies (schools, universities, hospitals) or support departments (R&D, Finance) in multinational corporations. But even in more *autonomous professional organizations*—including Professional Service Firms (PSFs) which are the main focus of our attention in this chapter—these connections are extensive. While the rhetoric of independent practice and collegial partnership remains strong in many PSFs (Kipping 2011), it is increasingly out of sync with the realities of professional work. In law, for example, a sector that has traditionally been dominated by sole practitioners, there has been a significant increase, in the UK, in the proportion of solicitors employed by larger firms (of 81 or more partners). In 2000 these firms accounted for just 0.3% of all firms, but provided employment for 18.9% of solicitors. Yet, by 2012, although the larger firms still accounted for just 0.6% of this population, they employed over one quarter (25.1%) of all solicitors (Law Society 2000, 2013). This process has gone hand in hand with the establishment of very large firms sometimes with a global presence. Today's professions are overshadowed by "mega-law" and Big Four accountancy firms (Cooper and Robson 2006; Muzio and Faulconbridge 2013), operating in dozens of jurisdictions, employing thousands if not tens of thousands of professionals and generating multi-million pound profits. In management consulting, for instance, the ten largest companies (mostly PLCs) such as Accenture, IBM, and McKinsey employ thousands of consultants globally and, while still only 2% of all companies, account for more than 50% of total fee income (O'Mahoney and Markham 2013: 50).

These changes make it more important than ever to study "professional development" in PSFs, as well as other contexts, not just in occupational terms, but "in relation to . . . the interests of organizations that employ large numbers of professionals" (Brint 1994: 11). However, while the theoretical tools needed to make sense of this changing landscape and how it impacts on the professions are available, with some exceptions (e.g., Muzio et al. 2011; Noordegraaf 2011a) there have been few attempts to bring them together systematically. In part this has been due to the emergence of separate research traditions, or sub-fields, that have focused either on occupations, or organizations such as PSFs. But, as we shall see, the division between these so-called fields is frequently over-stated.

In this chapter our aim is to address these concerns and provide a road map for how scholars may better conceptualize the changing relationship between professions and organizations. To do so we first review the available literature to draw out some of the key insights that might help to frame this topic. While it is noted that much of this work has been polarized into sub-fields, we also draw attention to the connections between these different research traditions and the potential to develop a more sophisticated understanding of how professions (as occupations) and organizations (including professionals, organizations, and firms) *co-evolve*. In the second half of the chapter we then build on these insights to explore how tendencies towards co-evolution may be becoming more pronounced. Here we look at different explanations for this process, those which focus on the encroachment of organizations on professions, and those which place more emphasis on how professionals themselves—as institutional entrepreneurs—are pushing for a stronger engagement with organizations (including management and new ways of working) to respond to wider societal pressures. In the final section we review some of the implications of this analysis for our understanding of the relationship between professions and organizations and define a number of directions for future research.

To develop these arguments this chapter will focus primarily on one kind of organizational setting, that of (autonomous) PSFs, such as law and accountancy. However, we will also make reference to more heteronomous organizations that are becoming more like PSFs, for instance, public and non-profit organizations such as trust hospitals and universities.

5.2 Organizations and Occupations: The Story So Far

5.2.1 Separate Fields and Theories

Although interest in the professions is long-standing, as noted earlier, it is possible to identify separate traditions or sub-fields focusing primarily on what Lounsbury and Kaghan (2001: 25) term the "sociology of occupations" or the "sociology of organizations." The former tradition is well documented, concerned with the broader labor market and occupational context of professions. Although the term "professional" has been hotly debated, in recent times a dominant approach has been to draw on social closure theory to understand professions as collective actors in pursuit of distinct interests in the wider socio-economic domain (Larson 1977; Abbott 1988; Macdonald 1995; Freidson 2001; see Suddaby and Muzio, Chapter 2, this volume). In this regard, the notion of the professional project has been central. Such projects are usually focused on processes of educational and legal closure whereby groups seek to control entry to and competition within labor markets, while at the same time ensuring some degree of "institutional autonomy" (Evetts 2002) to regulate their own affairs. Ultimately the objective of a professional project is to achieve degrees of regulation over a field of practice, both in terms of controlling the supply of expert labor *and* the behavior of producers (Muzio et al. 2011). Success, however, is understood to depend on the resources available to particular occupations, such as their knowledge base and wider legitimacy claims, for instance around notions of social trusteeship or serving the public good (Brint 1994).

By contrast, organizational theorists have been concerned mainly (although not exclusively) with the micro-dynamics of professional work and identity. From an early stage there has been a recurrent interest in how professionals structure their work in the context of large public and private sector bureaucracies, including "heteronomous" professional organizations (Scott 1966). A common theme in much of this work has been the idea that professional and bureaucratic logics are fundamentally in tension (Blau and Scott 1962). This tension emerges from a number of sources that are well documented, most notably from the nature of expertise, demands for self-regulation, and related value systems linked to (exogenous) professional socialization (see Raelin 1991, for a full discussion). Building on these ideas, others have sought to describe particular forms of management and leadership that are unique to professions (see Leblebici and Sherer, Chapter 9, this volume, and Empson and Langley, Chapter 8, this volume). Ackroyd et al. (1989), for instance, refer to "custodial" administration in professional work contexts, focused on buffering practice from external interference and defending the status quo.

This literature has also focused on distinct *modes of professional organization* (Montagna 1968; Bucher and Stelling 1969). Significant contributions here come from contingency and configuration theorists (Mintzberg 1983) and archetype theorists (Greenwood and Hinings 1993; Powell et al. 1999). Most recently, this has been linked to a growing interest in PSFs as an increasingly important category of organizations which are distinctive in terms of their knowledge intensity (expert human capital), low capital intensity, and professionalized workforce (von Nordenflycht 2010). As outlined in Chapter 1 of this volume, although PSFs are often associated with canonical examples of law and accounting firms, this label also now seems relevant to a host of other organizations associated with knowledge work, the provision of business services, or the privatization of public services. Hospitals, schools, and universities, for example, increasingly resemble professional firms, with strategic apexes, management functions, and divisional structures (e.g., Zardkoohi et al. 2011).

As suggested earlier, it is argued that these two sub-fields of organizations and occupations have become increasingly fragmented. On the one hand Lounsbury (2007: 300) comments on "the relative neglect" within the sociology of professions literature "of how professionalization is fundamentally intertwined with broader organizational dynamics." Hinings (2005: 407) also notes that accounts of professional development tend to "dislocate" the "relationship between professionals and organizations, shifting the locus of debate to power and labour markets." A classic example of this is the work of Burrage and Torstendahl (1990) who identify four key "actors" in the development of professions—practicing members, users, the state, and universities—but say little when it comes to the distinctive role of employing organizations. By contrast, organizational theorists have focused primarily on the evolution of organizations "but have spent little energy investigating the role of professionalisation projects" (Lounsbury 2007: 300). If anything, this latter tendency has been exaggerated recently by what von Nordenflycht (2010: 158) refers to as the "managerial turn" in the literature on PSFs, making it "less anchored to the professions, in the classic sociological sense." Indeed, in recent years business schools have emerged as an important production site for work and research on professionalism, leading to the growth of a practitioner-focused literature concerned with issues such effective leadership, organizational performance, and strategic development (Maister 1997; Løwendahl 2005; Empson 2007).

5.2.2 Combining Occupational and Organizational Insights

Notwithstanding the above concerns it is easy to over-state the significance of differences between organizational and occupational strands in the literature on professions and ignore the very important synergies that exist between them. Indeed, one has only to scratch below the surface of the sociology of professions (SOP) to see how the organizational dimension might be theorized. Johnson (1972) for example, differentiates between "state mediated" and "corporate patronage" professionals. The former essentially rely on public organizations to underwrite a monopoly of service and guarantee income, while the latter, even if self-employed, are nevertheless entirely dependent on large corporate clients (read organizations) for their livelihood. As we noted earlier Larson (1977) also questions the idea that professionals and bureaucracy (organization) necessarily represent opposing forces, locked in tension. Rather, she explains, "all professions are ... bureaucratized to a greater or lesser extent" (Larson 1977: 179), with "underlying structural affinities between profession and bureaucracy" (1977: 199). Formalization serves as a source of control over clients, offering the possibility of access to resources and by reinforcing hierarchical distinctions between professionals, opportunities for career advancement. Hence, one can argue that the idea that professional projects may be significantly bound up with organizations is present in much of the SOP literature, even if not always fully developed.

In a similar vein one can see how many organization theorists have embraced the notion of professional strategies/projects, especially in recent times. A well-cited example is Reed's (1996) attempt to theorize different forms of expert knowledge and how these translate into what he terms "occupational strategies." Whereas so-called "liberal" professions (law and medicine) might follow a classic professionalization model, groups such as general managers have pursued their interests directly through organizations, seeking to dominate "relatively powerful and privileged positions within technical and status hierarchies" (Reed 1996: 585). Occupations such as managers or administrators may therefore prosper from their ability to control the bureaucratic machinery they inhabit and to resolve central problems of their organization (Leicht and Fennell 2001).

The importance of organizations as sites for professional colonization is also central to Ackroyd's (1996: 606) notion of double closure, whereby groups seek to retain "some form of corporate identity outside the organisation that employs them." This means that professional strategies are not just pursued in the wider arena of labor markets and education systems, but within organizations as well, as these occupations seek to mold work tasks and the division of labor. This may also have implications for the composition of management as different professions—such as accountancy, engineering, and HR management—engage in competing "collective mobility projects" aimed at colonizing key positions, roles, and decision-making processes within large firms (Armstrong 1985).

More recently, this kind of analysis has been advanced by neo-institutional theorists. Emphasized here is the way professions not just colonize organizations, shaping practice within them, but are frequently instrumental in the very design (or theorization) of organizational fields more generally (DiMaggio and Powell 1991; Thornton 2002). Scott (2008: 219), for example, refers to the professions as "the pre-eminent institutional agents of our time," active in the process of "creating, testing, conveying and applying cultural-cognitive, normative and/or regulative frameworks that govern one or another social role" (2008: 233). Others have also stressed this formative role, suggesting that professions may be viewed as institutional entrepreneurs in theorizing and legitimating the particular models of service delivery or organization that are permissible in a specific field (DiMaggio 1988; Barley and Tolbert 1991). Hence, Suddaby and Viale (2011) argue that professional projects are inseparable from wider institutional projects, this having obvious implications for the design and behavior of organizations. Similarly, Muzio et al. (2013) draw on the notion of institutional work to describe the practice of professions, as agents in opening up spaces for their expertise, populating existing social spaces with new actors, and redrawing the boundaries and rules governing fields.

5.2.3 Taking Stock

From the discussion so far it is clear that the sociology of professions and organization theory do not represent two mutually exclusive sub-schools. A closer inspection of the literature reveals numerous potential synergies between these two strands, highlighting, as Lounsbury (2007: 303) puts it, the "complex interplay of professional development and organizational evolution."

Specifically, what this implies is a more inclusive approach towards understanding professional development in which organizations (including those owned and run by professionals themselves) are assigned a central role (Kirkpatrick and Ackroyd 2003). This means acknowledging how organizations may be important contexts that shape the way professional projects unfold. As noted earlier, there are many instances where occupational closure is underwritten by organizations which provide access to employment opportunities, clients, and other resources.

A further implication is that professional activity in the wider arena (or field) may have a powerful influence on how organizations (that employ or host professionals) are managed and structured (Kipping and Kirkpatrick 2013). This, of course, is most apparent in highly regulated fields, such as law and accounting, where PSFs are substantially "penetrated by institutional templates," which limit choices regarding staff recruitment, career development, reward systems, and the organization of work more generally (Suddaby et al. 2007). Greenwood and Hinings (1996: 1027), for example, note in relation to accounting how "the values of professional partnership became reinforced by professional associations that worked closely with universities and state agencies to promulgate and protect the self-regulating independence and autonomy of accountancy firms." However, even when professional bodies are less well established and where PSFs are more loosely regulated they may play a crucial role in the development, legitimization, and dissemination of specialist knowledge and quality standards (Muzio et al. 2011). Either way the focus shifts from viewing professional and organizational formation as separate themes to a focus on their co-evolution.

Where PSFs are concerned, these ideas mean paying greater attention to how aspects of organizational design, culture, human resources, and working practices are, to a greater or lesser extent, influenced by the strategies of professions in the wider (occupational or field) domain. Such an approach has already found its way into the PSF literature (see for example, Pinnington and Morris 2002; Malhotra et al. 2006; Malhotra and Morris 2009) and is central to ongoing efforts to better connect insights from institutional theory and the sociology of professions (Muzio et al. 2013).

5.3 THE GROWING IMPORTANCE OF ORGANIZATIONS FOR PROFESSIONS

Thus far we have drawn attention to the ways in which it is possible, conceptually, to understand the relationship between organizations and professions. Less, however, has been said about *how* that relationship might be changing, *why* it is changing, and what this means for theory and the meaning of professionalism. In the literature, opinions on this topic are widely divergent (especially regarding the extent of change), although it is useful to differentiate between two broad perspectives. First are more established accounts which focus on how organizations are *encroaching* on professional autonomy at a number of levels, not just within the workplace, but also at the institutional level (Evetts 2012). The emphasis here is very much on how professionals are being forced to change in response to (largely unwelcome) organizational demands. By contrast, a more recent strand of thinking has begun to stress more the way in which professionals themselves are actively *engaging and aligning* themselves with organizations and organizing principles, in order to better respond to wider changes in their environment (Noordegraaf 2007, 2011b; Adler et al. 2008). Both perspectives are about the hybridization of professionalism, but they sketch different routes and reasons, which we now explore in the following sections.

5.3.1 The Encroaching Organization

Descriptions of the shifting balance of power and influence between professions and organizations are numerous and long-standing. Historically, a substantial body of literature has emphasized the underlying dynamics of proletarianization, highlighting the progressive subordination of professionals—as employees of organizations—to bureaucratic controls (Oppenheimer 1973; Derber and Schwartz 1991). This idea is also picked up in "labor process" theory and neo-Weberian accounts, which emphasize the systematic deskilling of professionals as a result of new technology and changing human resource practices that routinize and delegate tasks to non-professionals (Braverman 1974; Ritzer and Walczak 1988). In this context, professionals may ultimately lose their autonomy and independence not only with regards to the terms and conditions of work but also to the definition, execution, and evaluation of their own occupational activities.

As hinted earlier, these tendencies may be most pronounced in heteronomous professional organizations, especially in the public sector (Kirkpatrick et al. 2005; Ackroyd et al. 2007). It is clear though that even in more autonomous PSFs the work of professionals is becoming increasingly subject to (self-imposed) bureaucratic controls. Until recently the dominant assumption has been that these firms are best described as adhocracies or "entrepreneurial" forms which "deviate heavily from bureaucratic principles" (Starbuck 1992; Alvesson 2000: 1102). There is, however, a growing body of research and opinion that questions this assumption in a range of different PSF settings (Morris and Empson 1998; Hansen et al. 1999; Alvesson and Thompson 2004; Kipping and Kirkpatrick 2007). Kärreman and Alvesson (2004), for example, note how in large management consulting firms strong cultural norms are increasingly combined with a system of bureaucratic controls aimed at ensuring "behavioral uniformity." These large firms, they suggest, are a far cry from the ideal adhocracy. Work is governed by standardized rules and methodologies, differences in power and status within the hierarchy are marked, while individual performance is closely monitored. Similar findings come from a study of PSFs in the high tech scientific consulting sector (Robertson and Swan 2004). Here too the trend is away from weak controls to more formalized hierarchy, clearly defined career structures, and the use of detailed performance metrics. According to the authors, this is "paradoxical in the face of findings which suggest that, in order to promote organizational innovation and creativity, highly autonomous working conditions need to be provided" (Robertson and Swan 2004: 145).

With the rise of global PSFs these tendencies may also be relevant even to established professions such as law, architecture, and accountancy (Brock et al. 1999, 2007). Indeed, one finds a broad consensus in this literature that PSFs are increasingly adopting "more corporate and managerial modes of operation" that are "less distinctive from for-profit business corporations" (Hinings 2005: 414, 419). In law and accounting, for instance, the trend is said to be towards a managed professional business (MPB) archetype, in which the "range of corporate involvement" in professional work escalates, while "standards become increasingly bureaucratized" (Cooper et al. 1996: 632).

A further and more recent dimension of change concerns the way in which PSFs are increasingly shaping the *context* in which professional projects develop sometimes even promoting their own, distinctively *corporate*, versions of professionalism. Important here is the role of employing organizations both as "significant actors *and* sites for professional regulation" (Suddaby et al. 2007: 333). Large accounting and law firms, for example, are said to have become increasingly immune to the normative and coercive influence of their respective professional associations at the national level (Suddaby and Greenwood 2006; Faulconbridge and Muzio 2008, 2012). This in turn has allowed these firms to act as institutional entrepreneurs playing a bigger role in shaping the rules and priorities of professional regulation. Hence, in law Malhotra et al. (2006: 194) note how in the UK the largest firms have "initiated their own training of associates with different content and standards of assessment" abandoning the broad programme of education championed by the Law Society in favor of new curricula which emphasize narrow corporate specialisms.

This dimension is also highlighted in an emerging body of research that explores PSFs as sites "where professional identities are mediated, formed and transformed" (Cooper and Robson 2006: 416). In accounting, for example, a number of studies have shown how large firms have become more instrumental in shaping the way new trainees enact professionalism, setting out behavioral rules relating to presentation, appropriate dealings with clients, and even traits associated with social interaction and time keeping (Grey 1994; Covaleski et al. 1998; Anderson-Gough et al. 2000; Mueller et al. 2011). The emphasis therefore is on how organizations have become increasingly prominent actors in the socialization of professions as a means of control to promote their own commercial priorities and how this may be undermining a wider, collective, sense of professional identity. This process in turn, may be reshaping the priorities of professionals, eroding older commitments to social trusteeship in favor of logics that stress more the values of technical expertise and commercial objectives (Hanlon 1998; Reed 2007; Suddaby et al. 2007).

A further extension of this is the attempt by firms, in new knowledge-intensive fields such as advertising, management consulting, or financial services, to hijack notions of professionalism to enhance their own legitimacy or brand reputation. Empson and Chapman (2006: 165) note how some management consulting firms have "mimicked the practices and language of partnership in order to assume the mantle of professionalism that it conveyed." Kipping (2011) and Kipping and Kirkpatrick (2013) also show how consulting firms have sought to exploit images and discourses of professionalism to promote their own brands and enhance their reputational capital in competitive markets. Indeed, they suggest that this has engendered new forms of "corporate professionalism" in which even professional associations have adopted their strategies to accommodate the interests of firms (Kipping et al. 2006). Elements of this corporate professionalism include firm-level membership of associations, a focus on organizational specific skills and certification, and reduced emphasis on ethical standards that highlight public trusteeship over and above technical competencies.

5.3.2 Reconfiguring Professionalism

While much of the literature referred to has stressed exogenous pressures that are forcing professionals (largely against their will) to acquire new identities and ways of working, a slightly different perspective has emerged which places more emphasis on the "entrepreneurial role" (Powell et al. 1999) of professionals themselves. Here the focus is on professionals as agents of change, actively seeking new forms of accommodation with organizations (at the micro and macro levels) as a strategy of modernization and—ultimately—survival. This literature challenges the old dualisms that have characterized much of the thinking on the so-called unhappy relationship between professions and organizations (Gleeson and Knights 2006). Instead it points to how professionals, especially in professional organizations and firms, including hospitals and universities, may be actively reinventing themselves to find more effective ways of using organizations and working with them to achieve wider goals.

Elements of this approach can be found in much of the recent literature on institutional theory described earlier. As we saw, this has explored the role of professions as institutional entrepreneurs in theorizing new organizational templates and reshaping organizational fields (Greenwood et al. 2002; Scott 2008; Muzio et al. 2013). Others, however, have taken this idea much further.

A notable case in point is the work of Paul Adler and colleagues (Adler et al. 2008). Here it is recognized that established models of professional community are being challenged by competing principles of hierarchy and markets. This, however, is not necessarily leading to the destruction of professional community, but rather to its reformulation as "collaborative community" which is better equipped for responding to contemporary demands. Importantly, this notion of collaborative community incorporates elements of hierarchy, standardization, and competition, but merges them with professional organizational principles. The results are new organizational forms which stress the need for teamwork, the balancing of individual and collective interests, and which rely on value rationality (and evidence-based practice) over and above authority based on position. To illustrate these developments Adler et al. (2008) focus primarily on the case of medicine, although clearly their arguments have wider relevance, including to more traditional PSFs.

A growing body of European literature has also focused on how professions, in a variety of settings, are now rethinking their relationship with organizations in response to the wider societal challenges they face (Kurunmäki 2004; Noordegraaf 2007, 2011b; Kurunmäki and Miller 2011; Dent et al. 2012). In particular Noordegraaf (2011b) has drawn attention to how professionals are becoming "hybridized" to the extent that traditional taxonomies have become increasingly redundant. Specifically, Noordegraaf identifies three pressures that are driving this process: the emergence of *wicked cases, changing risk perceptions*, and *demographic shifts*. Each of these pressures, he argues, fragments professional fields and makes them more open to "outside" influences. This, in turn, has required professionals to focus more on actively managing and organizing their own practices in order to make them more effective, legitimate, and sustainable. In what follows we describe this approach in more detail given its potential to transform the way we think about organizations and professions.

Where the emergence of *wicked cases* is concerned, the main spur for change, according to Noordegraaf, is the need to develop more effective inter-professional working which, in turn, is only achievable if professionals become better organized. Traditionally, professional knowledge has been highly specialized and focused on individual case treatment: curing patients, teaching pupils, balancing the books, and giving sound advice. The emergence of wicked cases, however, requires a greater pooling of knowledge and expertise. This is especially pronounced in areas such as healthcare, where there is now a "growing number of patients [who] suffer from chronic and over-lapping health problems (multi-morbidity)" (e.g., Plochg et al. 2009: 1), who can no longer be treated by specialized and segmented medical professionals (also Plochg et al. 2011). The need for more joined-up service provision is also apparent in many PSFs, for example, consulting, law, and accountancy (Robertson et al. 2003). As Malhotra and

Morris (2009: 895) suggest, when knowledge is contested and when clients are difficult to treat, "organizational form, team-working and pricing systems" need to be adjusted. Professionalism can no longer be seen as merely treating cases in isolation. Rather, dealing with complex cases has turned into a collaborative affair that needs to be organized and financed.

According to Noordegraaf (2011b) the desire of professionals to become better organized also has much to do with the need to ensure the continued *legitimacy* in light of growing public perceptions of risk and failure. In domains like accountancy, public confidence in professionals has been shaken by high-profile events such as the Enron affair (Carnegie and Napier 2010) and more recently by the post-2008 financial crises (e.g., Arnold 2009; Humphrey et al. 2009). Accountants should have helped private companies and financial institutions to mitigate risks, but instead have fueled the spread of risky practices (Mala and Chand 2012). Again, however, to deal with this, accountants are becoming more organized, pushing for greater transparency and an "international convergence in accounting practices" (Humphrey et al. 2009: 822). The "production of legitimacy" (Power 2003) increasingly depends on improving regulations, rules, and standards (Cooper and Robson 2006) backed by professional management. Similar tendencies can be noted in other professional sectors where there has been mounting public concern about risks and failures (Miller et al. 2008; Kurunmäki and Miller 2011).

Finally, Noordegraaf (2011b) highlights how processes of hybridization are being driven by changing demographics, such as aging and the gender mix within professional labor markets. These factors mean that work preferences, motivations, and careers of professional groups and members will change in nature and that the composition of professional fields might also be transformed. Many scholars, for example, point towards the growing influx of women in professional fields, including previously male-dominated areas such as medicine (Kuhlmann and Bourgeault 2008; Adams 2010) and law (Bolton and Muzio 2007, 2008). One possible consequence of this feminization might be restratification, renewed inequalities, and the loss of status (Witz 1990; Chiu and Leicht 1999; Wrede 2008; Evetts 2012). Feminization might also have consequences for professional motivation, commitment, and devotion. Instead of 24/7 professionalism, recomposed professional workforces seek work/life balance and keep a stricter eye on working times. In this regard Heiligers and Hingstman (2000) stress the "decreasing centrality of work" for physicians, while others have identified similar trends where groups such as management consultants are concerned (O'Mahoney and Markham 2013). Demographic changes in the professions, in particular with regard to greater female participation (Leicht and Fennell 1997), are therefore having important implications for how work is organized. For Noordegraaf these tendencies require more effective modes of organization to deal with shifting career patterns, flexible working regimes, and preferences (Briscoe 2007, 2009).

Turning to the more specific issue of how these pressures for hybridization will translate into new forms of organization and practices, Noordegraaf (2011b) highlights a few key developments. First, are changes in professional socialization and identity (see Alvesson et al., Chapter 18, this volume). Instead of merely stressing traditional professional values in relation to individual clients, it is becoming more common for professionals to focus on the bigger picture, which is not only about treating cases well, but also about treating multiple cases and dealing with workloads in demanding service environments. This means professionals will acknowledge the importance of setting priorities, dealing with cases in an efficient manner, making acts transparent, and improving professional accountabilities. Second, and closely related to this, is the acquisition of new skills and capabilities, for example, around managing, accounting, organizing, leadership, and networking. Kurunmäki (2004), for example, has shown how Finnish medical professionals were hybridized in the 1990s by teaching them management accounting skills, a trend which has also been noted in legal services (Francis and Sommerlad 2009). Finally, it may be the case that these processes will further accelerate the growth of newer organizational professionals such as managers, controllers, and procurement experts (e.g., Leicht and Fennell 2001; Empson et al. 2013). This will be both to enhance the status of these aspirant groups and also in response to demands for increased support from more established professions as they seem to become better organized.

Hence it is argued that professionals are seeking a closer accommodation with organizations (and *organizing*), not just because they are forced to, but because this represents a more appropriate way of responding to positively to wider societal challenges. In this respect the work of Noordegraaf (2011b, 2014) and others (including Adler et al. 2008) seeks to move beyond established dualisms (such as professional versus organization). The focus instead shifts to how professionals may be actively embracing ideas about management and leadership, and seeking new ways to become more organized to ensure legitimacy and sustainability. What this also implies is that professionalism itself is being "reconfigured" (cf. Noordegraaf 2014). Instead of representing a set of self-regulatory mechanisms that enable groups of people (professionals) to operate in isolated silos, the implication is that in order to become effective and legitimate, present-day professionalism will need to become much more open and *connective*. This requires sets of regulatory mechanisms that enable fragmented groups of people (groups of professionals) to form collaborative networks of experts, clients, and stakeholders and new ways to build effective and legitimate professional action.

5.4 Conclusions

In this chapter our aim has been to draw attention to and challenge certain deep-rooted assumptions regarding the mutually exclusive nature of professions and organizations and relate this back to the literature on PSFs. Specifically we have identified strands in both the sociology of professions and organizational theory literature which move beyond this dualism and, following Lounsbury (2007: 303), highlight instead the "complex interplay of professional development and organizational evolution." From this perspective, professional interests are not (and arguably never have been) separate from organizations which provide important resources, employment, and work contexts where they apply their knowledge. Establishing control over these organizational settings and fields has therefore been as important to the professions as has control over labor markets and the provision of education.

However, what this perspective also suggests is that organizations are important in reshaping professional work and values and that, if anything, this tendency has accelerated in recent years. As we saw, accounts of this change fall into two broad schools. First are those who emphasize the way in which the demands of organizations to ensure control in pursuit of specific objectives are forcing change in professional work, identities, and even the nature of professional projects more generally. Quite often this process is conceptualized as an assault on professionalism. By contrast, a more recent strand of work has looked at how professions themselves are actively seeking a different accommodation with organizations. Here it is argued that due to a variety of economic and societal forces, professional work is being reconfigured and is becoming more open and organized. Instead of viewing professionalism as narrowly specialized, focused on the treatment of individual cases, acting professionally increasingly becomes a matter of handling many complex and risky cases in demanding environments. This calls for well-organized working relations and the ability to deal with technical, moral, and political dimensions of service delivery.

Yet, while these arguments hold out the possibility for a closer synthesis between understandings of professional action (in the wider arena) and developments within organizations (specifically PSFs), they clearly raise almost as many questions as they answer. To start with are concerns about how relationships between organizations and professions play out in an international context and whether we can generalize. Useful here is Collins's (1990: 98) distinction between "Continental" and "Anglo-Saxon" modes of professionalism. While the latter emphasizes "the freedom of self-employed-practitioners to control work conditions," in the former the state represented the main actor in professional development. Hence in the French case, greater emphasis on ensuring that key actors participated through the political process effectively "restricted the autonomy of the institutions of civil society," with education through *grandes écoles* carrying greater status/cachet than membership of professional associations. As a result, in France "knowledge based services have remained in the ambit of the state, restricting the success of the professional project" (Macdonald 1995: 97). The importance of these distinctions is that they raise the possibility that in some European (and other national) contexts professional formation followed a different trajectory, one that from the outset was much more closely aligned to organizational interests. To be sure, this applies mainly to those professionals employed within the state (or public sector), but may also be relevant to PSFs, especially if these sectors (such as law and accountancy) have been more heavily state regulated historically (Krause 1996). Indeed, the latter is suggested by a recent study focusing on global law firms where "one firm" management practices are shaped by host country institutions in the context of the UK and Italy (Muzio and Faulconbridge 2013).

More specifically, there are questions about the validity of some of the predictions made in the literature about the *nature and consequences* of changing relationships between professions and organizations. This applies especially to studies focusing on how organizations are encroaching on professional domains, threatening their autonomy and distinct identity. More research is needed here to determine the extent to which professional institutions are being challenged, the extent of resistance, and whether the changes are radical or convergent. Where PSFs are concerned this topic has already been hotly debated for some time (Powell et al. 1999; Brock et al. 2007; Muzio et al. 2007). While some highlight a gradual trend towards new organizational models—the MPB—which depart from professional norms (Hinings 2005), others have depicted a more contested, sedimented process of change (Cooper et al. 1996; Faulconbridge and Muzio 2008).

A similar concern applies to predictions regarding the impact of PSFs on professional regulation more generally, as to whether tendencies towards "corporate professionalism" are that clear cut (Muzio et al. 2011). It may well be that professional associations are now becoming more attentive to the needs of PSFs (especially global firms) as businesses and employers. However, has this also completely undermined the prospects for more conventional professional regulation (independently of PSFs) at the national or even supra-national level? On the one hand it might be argued that these prospects are somewhat bleak, as professional associations become subservient to the interests of large firms embracing the values of the marketplace (Leicht and Lyman 2006). Against this is the suggestion that, in the post-Enron era, consultants (and other groups) may face growing pressure from governments and clients to reinvent third-party regulation to moderate their "power without responsibility" (McKenna 2007: 212).

A perhaps even bigger question regards the more recent accounts that are starting to emphasize a professionally led process of accommodation with organizations and the emergence of new forms of "reconfigured professionalism" or "collaborative community" (Noordegraaf 2011b, 2014; Adler et al. 2008). While these accounts are able to produce numerous examples—from a variety of public and private sector professional services—there is clearly a need for more empirical research to validate some of the predictions about trends towards hybridization. More work is also needed here specifically on what reconfigured professionalism might mean in different types of PSF. For example, following von Nordenflycht (2010), are we likely to see any differences between so-called classic and neo-PSFs? These two organizational forms are subject to variations "in the existence and strength of regulatory mechanisms and professional codes for that occupation or field" (von Nordenflycht 2010: 164). This means that there are likely to be marked differences in the extent to which professionals in these contexts have already embraced (and identified with) organizational principles, historically. But will this have any bearing on how we understand future tendencies towards hybridization?

In addition to this are questions about the likely consequences of any future trend towards a greater accommodation between professions and organizations. On the one hand, hybridization could enhance the effectiveness and (trustworthy) performance of professional services. There could be more innovation in service delivery and more emphasis on co-production with users, including multi- and inter-disciplinarity where the tackling of wicked problems and safety issues are concerned. Hybridization could also contribute to reinforcing public trust and confidence in (reconfigured) professional services.

On the other hand, there are also risks. First is the question of whether professionals will be overburdened if they are expected to participate in leadership work and start acquiring new organizational skills. Are the new demands aimed at making professional work effective and legitimate too excessive? Such questions clearly give cause for concern. Yet it may be argued that over time, the acquisition of organizational skills will increasingly occur within work settings as part of the normal socialization and development of professionals. Learning about appropriate ways to handle cases might also alleviate burdens, as many aspects of rendering services become easier to manage. This could call for new educational programs and learning processes, including a greater focus on "contextual" and "situated learning" that is integrated, as opposed to being separate from professional practice (Koens et al. 2005; Ten Cate et al. 2010).

Lastly there are questions about the orientation and priorities of professionals. Will hybrid professionalism lead to a more technocratic, individualistic, commercial orientation at the expense of public or social trusteeship and wider public good models of professionalism (Brint 1994)? Can the latter be maintained, when professionals start to focus more on efficiency and profitability? As before, these questions give cause for concern, although one might argue that they are also misleading. In medicine for example, instead of focusing on opposing, mutually exclusive values, such as quality of care or efficiency, hybrid professionalism implies that producing healthcare is now a matter of combining multiple logics simultaneously. In this regard, the trend towards more hybrid forms of organized professionalism may not necessarily lead to the dominance of a single logic (say efficiency) over another (social trusteeship). Rather it implies a new, more dynamic form of professional practice that incorporates multiple priorities simultaneously, although precisely how this change will be played out and with what consequences remains to be seen.

References

Abbott, A. (1988). *The System of Professions: An Essay on the Division of Expert Labour*. Chicago, IL: University of Chicago Press.

Ackroyd, S. (1996). "Organisation contra Organisation: Professions and Organisational Change in the United Kingdom," *Organization Studies* 17(4): 599–621.

Ackroyd, S., Hughes, J. A., and Soothill, K. (1989). "Public Sector Services and their Management," *Journal of Management Studies* 26(6): 603–619.

Ackroyd, S., Kirkpatrick, I., and Walker, R. (2007). "Public Management Reform and Its Consequences for Professional Organisation: A Comparative Analysis," *Public Administration* 85(1): 9–26.

Adams, T. L. (2010). "Gender and Feminization in Health Care Professions," *Sociology Compass* 4(7): 454–465.

Adler, P., Kwon, S., and Hecksher, C. (2008). "Professional Work: The Emergence of Collaborative Community," *Organization Science* 19(2): 359–376.

Alvesson, M. (2000). "Social Identity and the Problem of Loyalty in Knowledge Intensive Companies," *Journal of Management Studies* 37(8): 1101–1123.

Alvesson, M. and Thompson, P. (2004). "Post-Bureaucracy?" in *The Oxford Handbook of Work and Organization*, ed. S. Ackroyd, R. Batt, P. Thompson, and P. S. Tolbert. Oxford: Oxford University Press, 485–507.

Anderson-Gough, F., Grey, C., and Robson, K. (2000). "In the Name of the Client: The Service Ethic in Professional Service Firms," *Human Relations* 53(9): 1151–1174.

Armstrong, P. (1985). "Changing Management Control Strategies: The Role of Competition between Accountancy and Other Organizational Professions," *Accounting, Organization and Society* 10(2): 129–148.

Arnold, P. J. (2009). "Global Financial Crisis: The Challenge to Accounting Research," *Accounting, Organizations and Society* 34(6): 803–809.

Barley, S. R. and Tolbert, P .S. (1991). "Introduction: At the Intersection of Organizations and Occupations," *Research in the Sociology of Organizations* 8: 1–16.

Blau, P. and Scott, W. R. (1962). *Formal Organizations: A Comparative Approach*. Stanford, CA: Stanford University Press.

Bolton, S. C. and Muzio, D. (2007). "Can't Live With 'em, Can't Live Without 'em: Gendered Segmentation in the Legal Profession," *Sociology* 41(1): 47–64.

Bolton, S. C. and Muzio, D. (2008). "The Paradoxical Processes of Feminization in the Professions: The Case of Established, Aspiring and Semi-Professions," *Work, Employment & Society* 22(2): 281–299.

Braverman, H. (1974). *Labor and Monopoly Capital: The Organization of Work in the Twentieth Century*. New York: Monthly Review Press.

Brint, S. G. (1994). *In an Age of Experts: The Changing Role of Professionals in Politics and Public Life*. Princeton, NJ: Princeton University Press.

Briscoe, F. (2007). "From Iron Cage to Iron Shield? How Bureaucracy Enables Temporal Flexibility for Professional Service Workers," *Organization Science* 18(2): 297–314.

Briscoe, F. (2009). "The Design of Work as a Key Driver of Work-Life Flexibility for Professionals," in *Work-Life Policies*, ed. A. C. Crouter and A. Booth. Washington, DC: The Urban Institute, 83–93.

Brock, D. M., Powell, M. J., and Hinings, C. R. (eds.) (1999). *Restructuring the Professional Organization: Accounting, Healthcare, and Law*. London: Routledge.

Brock, D. M., Powell, M. J., and Hinings, C. R. (2007). "Archetypal Change and the Professional Service Firm," in *Research in Organizational Change and Development*, 16, ed. W. A. Passmore and R. W. Woodman. Oxford: Elsevier, 221–251.

Bucher, R. and Stelling, J. (1969). "Characteristics of Professional Organizations," *Journal of Health and Social Behavior* 10(1): 3–15.

Burrage, M. and Torstendahl, R. (eds.) (1990). *Professions in Theory and History: Rethinking the Study of the Professions*. London: Sage.

Carnegie, G. D. and Napier, C. J. (2010). "Traditional Accountants and Business Professionals: Portraying the Accounting Profession after Enron," *Accounting, Organizations and Society* 35(3): 360–376.

Chiu, C. and Leicht, K. T. (1999). "When Does Feminization Increase Equality? The Case of Lawyers," *Law and Society Review* 33(3): 557–593.

Collins, R. (1990). "Changing Conceptions in the Sociology of the Professions," in *Knowledge, State and Strategy: The Formation of Professions in Europe and North America*, ed. M. Burrage and R. Torstendahl. London: Sage, 11–23.

Cooper, D. J. and Robson, K. (2006). "Accounting, Professions and Regulation: Locating the Sites of Professionalization," *Accounting, Organizations and Society*, 31(4–5): 415–444.

Cooper, D. J., Hinings, C. R., Greenwood, R., and Brown, J. L. (1996). "Sedimentation and Transformation in Organizational Change: The Case of Canadian Law Firms," *Organization Studies* 17(4): 623–647.

Covaleski, M., Dirsmith, W., and Heian, J. B. (1998). "The Calculated and the Avowed: Techniques of Discipline and Struggles Over Identity in Big Six Public Accounting Firms," *Administrative Science Quarterly* 43(2): 293–327.

Dent, M., Kirkpatrick, I., and Neogy, I. (2012). "Medical Leadership and Management Reforms in Hospitals," in *Leadership in the Public Sector: Promises and Pitfalls*, ed. C. Teelken, E. Ferlie, and M. Dent. London: Routledge, 105–125.

Derber, C. and Schwartz, W. A. (1991). "New Mandarins or New Proletariat? Professional Power at Work," in *Research in the Sociology of Organizations: Organizations and Professions*, ed. P. S. Tolbert and S. R. Barley. Greenwich, CT: JAI Press, 71–96.

DiMaggio, P. (1988). "Interest and Agency in Institutional Theory," in *Institutional Patterns and Organization: Culture and Environment*, ed. L. Zucker. Cambridge: Ballinger Publishing, 3–21.

DiMaggio, P. and Powell, W. W. (1991). "The Iron Cage Revisited: Institutional Isomorphism and Collective Rationality," in *The New Institutionalism in Organizational Analysis*, ed. W. W. Powell and P. DiMaggio. Chicago, IL and London: University of Chicago Press, 63–82.

Empson, L. (2007). *Managing the Modern Law Firm*. Oxford: Oxford University Press.

Empson, L. and Chapman, C. S. (2006). "Partnership versus Corporation: Implications of Alternative Forms of Governance for Managerial Authority and Organizational Priorities in Professional Service Firms," *Research in the Sociology of Organizations* 24: 145–176.

Empson, L., Cleaver, I., and Allen, J. (2013). "Managing Partners and Management Professionals: Institutional Work Dyads in Professional Partnerships," *Journal of Management Studies* 50(5): 808–844.

Evetts, J. (2002). "New Directions in State and International Professional Occupations: Discretionary Decision Making and Acquired Regulation," *Work, Employment and Society* 16(2): 341–353.

Evetts, J. (2012). "Similarities in Contexts and Theorizing: Professionalism and Inequality," *Professions and Professionalism*, 2(2): 1–15. <http://dx.doi.org/10.7577/pp.322>.

Farrell, C. and Morris, J. (2003). "The Neo-Bureaucratic State: Professionals, Managers and Professional Managers in Schools, General Practices and Social Work," *Organization* 10(1): 129–156.

Faulconbridge, J. and Muzio, D. (2008). "Organizational Professionalism in Globalizing Law Firms," *Work, Employment and Society* 22(1): 7–25.

Faulconbridge, J. and Muzio, D. (2012). "Professions in a Globalizing World: Towards a Transnational Sociology of the Professions," *International Sociology* 27(1): 136–152.

Francis, A. and Sommerlad, H. (2009). "Access to Legal Work Experience and Its Role in the (Re)Production of Legal Professional Identity," *International Journal of the Legal Profession* 16(1): 63–86.

Freidson, E. (2001). *Professionalism: The Third Logic*. Cambridge: Polity Press.

Gleeson, D. and Knights, D. (2006). "Challenging Dualism: Public Professionalism in 'Troubled' Times," *Sociology* 40(2): 277–295.

Greenwood, R. and Hinings, C. R. (1993). "Understanding Strategic Change: The Contribution of Archetypes," *Academy of Management Journal* 36(5): 1052–1081.

Greenwood, R. and Hinings, C. R. (1996). "Understanding Radical Organizational Change: Bringing Together the Old and New Institutionalism," *Academy of Management Review* 21(4): 1022–1054.

Greenwood, R., Suddaby, R., and Hinings, C. R. (2002). "Theorizing Change: The Role of Professional Associations in the Transformation of Institutionalized Fields," *Academy of Management Journal* 45(1): 58–80.

Grey, C. (1994). "Career as a Project of the Self and Labour Process Discipline," *Sociology* 28(2): 479–497.

Hanlon, G. (1998). "Professionalism as Enterprise: Service Class Politics and the Redefinition of Professionalism," *Sociology* 32(1): 43–63.

Hansen, M. T., Nohria, N., and Tierney T. (1999). "What's Your Strategy for Managing Knowledge?" *Harvard Business Review* 77(2): 106–116.

Heiligers, P. and Hingstman, L. (2000). "Career Preferences and the Work–Family Balance in Medicine: Gender Differences among Medical Specialists," *Social Science & Medicine* 50(9): 1235–1246.

Hinings, C. R. (2005). "The Changing Nature of Professional Organizations," in *The Oxford Handbook of Work and Organisation*, ed. S. Ackroyd, R. Batt, P. Thompson, and P. S. Tolbert. Oxford: Oxford University Press, 404–424.

Humphrey, C., Loft, A., and Woods, M. (2009). "The Global Audit Profession and the International Financial Architecture: Understanding Regulatory Relationships at a Time of Financial Crisis," *Accounting, Organizations and Society* 34(6): 810–825.

Johnson, T. J. (1972). *Professions and Power*. London: Macmillan.

Kärreman, D. and Alvesson, M. (2004). "Cages In Tandem: Management Control, Social Identity, and Identification in a Knowledge-Intensive Firm," *Organization* 11(1): 149–175.

Kipping, M. (2011). "Hollow from the Start? Image Professionalism in Management Consulting," *Current Sociology* 59(4): 530–550.

Kipping, M. and Kirkpatrick, I. (2007). "From Taylor as Product to Taylorism as Process: Knowledge Intensive Firms in a Historical Perspective," in *Redirections in the Study of Expert Labour: Law, Medicine and Management Consultancy*, ed. D. Muzio, S. Ackroyd, and F. Chalant. Basingstoke: Palgrave Macmillan, 777–807.

Kipping, M. and Kirkpatrick, I. (2013). "Alternative Pathways of Change in Professional Services Firms: The Case of Management Consulting," *Journal of Management Studies* 50(5): 777–807.

Kipping, M., Kirkpatrick, I., and Muzio, D. (2006). "Overly Controlled or Out of Control? Management Consultants and the New Corporate Professionalism," in *Production Values: Futures for Professionalism*, ed. J. Craig. London: Demos, 153–165.

Kirkpatrick, I. and Ackroyd, S. (2003). "Archetype Theory and the Changing Professional Organization: A Critique and Alternative," *Organization* 10(4): 739–758.

Kirkpatrick, I., Ackroyd, S., and Walker, R. (2005). *The New Managerialism and Public Service Professions*. Basingstoke: Palgrave Macmillan.

Koens, F., Mann, K. V., Custers, E. J., and Ten Cate, O. T. (2005). "Analysing the Concept of Context in Medical Education," *Medical Education* 39(12): 1243–1249.

Krause, E. A. (1996). *The Death of the Guilds: Professions, States and the Advance of Capitalism: 1930 to the Present*. New Haven, CT: Yale University Press.

Kuhlman, E. and Bourgeault, I. L. (2008). "Gender, Professions and Public Policy: New Directions," *Equal Opportunities International* 27(1): 5–18.

Kurunmäki, L. (2004). "A Hybrid Profession: The Acquisition of Management Accounting Expertise by Medical Professionals," *Accounting, Organizations and Society* 29(3–4): 327–347.

Kurunmäki, L. and Miller, P. (2011). "Regulatory Hybrids: Partnerships, Budgeting and Modernising Government," *Management Accounting Research* 22(4): 220–241.

Larson, M. S. (1977). *The Rise of Professionalism: A Sociological Analysis*. Berkeley, CA: University of California Press.

Law Society (2000). *Trends in the Solicitors' Profession: Annual Statistics Reports 2000*. London: Law Society Research Unit.

Law Society (2013). *Trends in the Solicitors' Profession: Annual Statistics Reports 2012*. London: Law Society Research Unit.

Leicht, K. T. and Fennell, M. L. (1997). "The Changing Organizational Context of Professional Work," *Annual Review of Sociology* 23: 215–231.

Leicht, K. T. and Fennell, M. L. (2001). *Professional Work: A Sociological Approach*. Oxford: Blackwell.

Leicht, K. T. and Lyman, E. C. W. (2006). "Markets, Institutions and the Crisis of Professional Practice," *Research in the Sociology of Organizations* 24: 17–44.

Lounsbury, M. (2007). "A Tale of Two Cities: Competing Logics and Practice Variation in the Professionalizing of Mutual Funds," *Academy of Management Journal* 50(2): 289–307.

Lounsbury, M. and Kaghan, W. N. (2001). "Organizations, Occupations and the Structuration of Work," *Research in the Sociology of Work* 10: 25–50.

Løwendahl, B. (2005). *Strategic Management of Professional Service Firms*. Copenhagen: Copenhagen Business School Press.

Macdonald, K. M. (1995). *The Sociology of the Professions*. London: Sage.

McKenna, C. D. (2007). "Give Professionalization a Chance! Why Management Consulting May Yet Become a Full Profession," in *Redirections in the Study of Expert Labour: Established Professions and New Expert Occupations*, ed. D. Muzio, S. Ackroyd, and J.-F. Chalant. Basingstoke: Palgrave Macmillan, 204–16.

Maister, D. H. (1997). *Managing the Professional Service Firm*. New York: Free Press.

Mala, R. and Chand, P. (2012). "Effect of the Global Financial Crisis on Accounting Convergence," *Accounting and Finance* 52(1): 21–46.

Malhotra, N. and Morris, T. (2009). "Heterogeneity in Professional Service Firms," *Journal of Management Studies* 46(6): 895–922.

Malhotra, N., Morris, T., and Hinings, C. R. (2006). "Variations in Organization Form among Professional Service Organizations," in *Research in the Sociology of Organizations: Professional Firms*, ed. R. Greenwood, R. Suddaby, and M. McDougald. Oxford: JAI Press, 171–202.

Miller, P., Kurunmäki, L., and O'Leary, T. (2008). "Accounting, Hybrids and the Management of Risk," *Accounting, Organizations and Society* 33(7): 942–967.

Mintzberg, H. (1983). *Structure in Fives: Designing Effective Organizations*. Englewood Cliffs, NJ: Prentice-Hall.

Montagna, P. D. (1968). "Professionalization and Bureaucratization in Large Professional Organizations," *American Journal of Sociology* 74(2): 138–145.

Morris, T. and Empson, L. (1998). "Organisation and Expertise: An Exploration of knowledge bases and the Management of Accounting and Consulting Firms," *Accounting, Organizations and Society* 23(5–6): 609–624.

Mueller, F., Carter, C., and Ross-Smith, A. (2011). "Making Sense of Career in a Big Four Accounting Firm," *Current Sociology* 59(6): 551–567.

Muzio, D. and Faulconbridge, J. (2013). "The Global Professional Service Firm: 'One Firm' Models versus (Italian) Distant Institutionalized Practices," *Organization Studies* 34(7): 897–925.

Muzio, D., Ackroyd, S., and Chanlat, J. F. (eds.) (2007). *Redirections in the Study of Expert Labour: Established Professions and New Expert Occupations*. Basingstoke: Palgrave Macmillan.

Muzio, D., Brock, D. M., and Suddaby, R. (2013). "Professions and Institutional Change: Towards an Institutionalist Sociology of the Professions," *Journal of Management Studies* 50(5): 699–721.

Muzio, D., Kirkpatrick, I., and Kipping, M. (2011). "Professions, Organizations and the State: Applying the Sociology of the Professions to the Case of Management Consultancy," *Current Sociology* 59(6): 805–824.

Noordegraaf, M. (2007). "From Pure to Hybrid Professionalism: Present-Day Professionalism in Ambiguous Public Domains," *Administration & Society* 39(6): 761–785.

Noordegraaf, M. (2011a). "Remaking Professionals? How Associations and Professional Education Connect Professionalism and Organizations," *Current Sociology* 59(4): 465–488.

Noordegraaf, M. (2011b). "Risky Business: How Professionals and Professionals Fields (Must) Deal with Organizational Issues," *Organization Studies* 32(10): 1349–1371.

Noordegraaf, M. (2014). "Reconfiguring Professional Work: Changing Forms of Professionalism in Public Services," *Administration & Society* (forthcoming).

O'Mahoney, J. and Markham, C. (2013). *Management Consultancy*. Oxford: Oxford University Press.

Oppenheimer, M. (1973). "Proletarianization of the Professional," in *Professionalization and Social Change*, ed. P. Halmos. Keele: Keele University Press, 213–227.

Pinnington, A. and Morris, T. (2002). "Transforming the Architect: Ownership Form and Archetype Change," *Organization Studies* 23(2): 182–210.

Plochg, T., Klazinga, N., and Starfield, B. (2009). "Transforming Medical Professionalism to Fit Changing Health Needs," *BMC Medicine* 7(64): 1–7 (doi: 10.1186/1741-7015-7-64).

Plochg, T., Klazinga, N. S., Schönstein, M., and Starfield, B. (2011). "Reconfiguring Health Professions in Times of Multimorbidity: Eight Recommendations for Change," in *Health Reform: Meeting the Challenge of Ageing and Multiple Morbidities*. Paris: OECD Publishing, 109–136.

Powell, M. J., Brock, D. M., and Hinings, C. (1999). "The Changing Professional Organization," in *Restructuring the Professional Organization: Accounting, Health Care and Law*, ed. D. Brock, M. Powell and C. R. Hinings. London: Routledge, 1–19.

Power, M. (2003). "Auditing and the Production of Legitimacy," *Accounting, Organizations and Society* 28(4): 379–394.

Raelin, J. A. (1991). *The Clash of Cultures: Managers and Professionals*. Boston, MA: Harvard Business School Press.

Reed, M. (1996). "Expert Power and Control in Late Modernity: An Empirical Review and Theoretical Synthesis," *Organization Studies* 17(4): 573–597.

Reed, M. (2007). "Engineers of Human Souls, Faceless Technocrats or Merchants of Morality? Changing Professional Forms and Identities in the Face of the Neo-Liberal Challenge," in *Human Resource Management: Ethics and Employment*, ed. A. Pinnington, R. Macklin, and T. Campbell. Oxford: Oxford University Press, 171–189.

Ritzer, G. and Walczak, D. (1988). "Rationalization and the De-professionalization of Physicians," *Social Forces* 67(1): 1–22.

Robertson, M. and Swan, J. (2004) "Going Public: The Emergence and Effects of Soft Bureaucracy within a Knowledge Intensive Firm," *Organization* 11(1): 123–148.

Robertson, M., Scarborough, H., and Swan, J. (2003). "Knowledge Creation in Professional Service Firms: Institutional Effects," *Organization Studies* 24(6): 831–858.

Scott, W. R. (1966). "Professionals in Bureaucracies: Areas of Conflict," in *Professionalization*, ed. H. M. Vollmer and D. L. Mills. Englewood Cliffs, NJ: Prentice-Hall, 265–275.

Scott, W. R. (2008). "Lords of the Dance: Professionals as Institutional Agents," *Organization Studies* 29(2): 219–238.

Starbuck, W. (1992). "Learning by Knowledge-Intensive Firms," *Journal of Management Studies* 29(6): 713–740.

Suddaby, R. and Greenwood, R. (2006). "Institutional Entrepreneurship in Mature Fields: The Big Five Accounting Firms," *Academy of Management Journal* 49(1): 27–48.

Suddaby, R. and Viale, T. (2011). "Professionals and Field-Level Change: Institutional Work and the Professional Project," *Current Sociology* 59(4): 423–442.

Suddaby, R., Cooper, D., and Greenwood, R. (2007). "Transnational Regulation of Professional Services: Governance Dynamics of Field Level Organizational Change," *Accounting, Organizations and Society* 32(4): 333–362.

Ten Cate, O., Snell, L., and Carraccio, C. (2010). "Medical Competence: The Interplay between Individual Ability and the Health Care Environment," *Medical Teacher* 32(8): 669–675.

Thornton, P. H. (2002). "The Rise of the Corporation in a Craft Industry: Conflict and Conformity in Institutional Logics," *Academy of Management Journal* 45(1): 81–101.

von Nordenflycht, A. (2010). "What is a Professional Service Firm? Toward a Theory and Taxonomy of Knowledge-Intensive Firms," *Academy of Management Review* 35(1): 155–174.

Witz, A. (1990). "Patriarchy and Professions: The Gendered Politics of Occupational Closure," *Sociology* 24(4): 675–690.

Wrede, S. (2008). "Unpacking Gendered Professional Power in the Welfare State," *Equal Opportunities International* 27(1): 19–33.

Zardkoohi, A., Bierman, A., and Panina, D. (2011). "Revisiting a Proposed Definition of Professional Service Firms," *Academy of Management Review* 36(1): 180–187.

CHAPTER 6

PROFESSIONAL ETHICS
Origins, Applications, and Developments

RONIT DINOVITZER, HUGH GUNZ, AND
SALLY GUNZ

6.1 INTRODUCTION

THE professions and ethics have had an ambiguous relationship with each other since professions were acknowledged as an identifiable occupational group (Carr-Saunders and Wilson 1933). In this chapter we shall review the arguments and evidence surrounding professions and ethics, with particular reference to Professional Service Firms (PSFs). Research on ethics in the professions highlights a long-standing tension between formal and popular understandings of professionals. On the one hand, what we shall describe below as the classical model of the professions is premised on the concept of ethical codes of behavior that are used to reassure the professions' clients that the arcane (to the layperson) arts of professionals are exercised in the public interest (Carr-Saunders and Wilson 1933; Smigel 1964). On the other hand, there is abundant evidence that the public views the concept of the ethical behavior of professionals and their professional bodies with great skepticism; take for example the large body of lawyer jokes that focus on lawyers' unethical behavior (Galanter 2005). Professionals, in this latter view, are seen as no different from any other occupation, subject to the same self-serving pressures as anyone else, and as likely as anyone else to give in to them (Heinz and Laumann 1982; Leicht and Fennell 2001). Of course ethical failures are, for the layperson, easier to identify than other failures in professional practice because professional work typically depends on a lengthy education and a certification process. So while it may be hard to know whether, for example, a lawyer has drafted a contract competently, it may be easier to observe that a lawyer has failed to inform a client adequately of risk, breached confidentiality inappropriately, acted in a conflict of interest, or lacked independence.

The ethical behavior of professionals demands even more attention when the scale of the problem is larger, as in the case of major economic failures or crises. Questions are asked about the behavior of the management of the organizations that play key roles in these crises (Langevoort 2012). This was the case, for example, following the 2008 financial crisis when the financial service industries of the Western economies were held up to close scrutiny. But executives do not develop final versions of formal business agreements, nor do they prepare reports mandated by authorities. Any examination of corporate misbehavior inevitably turns to the role of the professionals and asks: "where were the accountants [or lawyers, or actuaries]?" (Langevoort 2012). The audit opinion may only be provided by an accountant. Lawyers draft securities compliance documents. The actuary certifies the adequacy of pension funds to cover future liabilities. Managers in these situations are unable to undertake any significant action, proper or improper, without the work of the professional advisor who is mandated by law, or has the requisite skill set, to document the action. The focus thus turns to the ethical role of the professional when asked to facilitate actions that are illegal, border-line illegal ("gray"), or simply questionable in the sense that no laws are being broken, but the actions transgress the profession's ethical code. The discipline of ethics, and applied ethics in particular, asks the questions that go beyond the bounds of what the law might prescribe.

It is useful to expand upon the distinction between legal and ethical obligations. Professionals at times act with willful negligence or actual fraud, actions that may have criminal or civil consequences.[1] The auditor for Madoff was charged with (and subsequently pleaded guilty to) securities fraud for his failure to apply any due diligence to the audits he provided (US Securities and Exchange Commission 2009). While these events undoubtedly raise ethical questions, they are primarily concerned with the factors that might lead a highly skilled professional to turn, quite simply, "bad." We focus here on the more subtle questions of unethical behavior; behavior where professionals comply with the technical constraints of the law, but for reasons that are not immediately obvious, ignore their broader ethical responsibilities.

As a first step in our analysis of ethics as applied to the PSF we turn to the literature on theoretical and applied ethics for some basic concepts, in order to trace the origins of the area of applied ethics known as professional ethics. We then consider three practical aspects of professional ethics: ethical codes, the significance of professional autonomy to the ability of the professional to behave in accord with ethical codes, and the controversial role of professional as gatekeeper. Next, we examine the ethical pressures faced by professionals first in the context of non-professional organizations, and then in professional service organizations. Finally, we consider the implications of these observations for future research on professional ethics.

6.2 THEORETICAL AND APPLIED ETHICS

The study of ethical theory is largely beyond the scope of this chapter. It would be disrespectful to perhaps the most ancient of intellectual disciplines to summarize millennia of thought in a matter of two to three pages. Nonetheless, it is important to place current debates within the framework of ethical theory so that we may then understand how ethics in the PSF relates to the broader context of ethical thought.

To begin, we distinguish between two fields of ethics: metaethics and normative ethics. Metaethics examines the nature of ethics, asking questions such as what is it actually to be good? In contrast, normative ethical theories are about how people *ought* to act. Another description of metaethics helps clarify the distinction:

> the range of issues, puzzles and questions that fall within metaethics' purview are consistently abstract. They reflect the fact that metaethics involves an attempt to step back from particular substantive debates within morality to ask about the views, assumptions, and commitments that are shared by those who engage in the debate. By and large, the metaethical issues that emerge as a result of this process of stepping back can be addressed without taking a particular stand on substantive moral issues that started the process. In fact, metaethics has seemed to many to offer a crucial neutral background against which competing moral views need to be seen if they are to be assessed properly. (Sayre-McCord 2012)

The three best-known normative ethics theories are virtue ethics, deontology, and consequentialism (Chappell 2012; Moore 1903; Rawls 1971). Virtue ethics has ancient roots in Western culture going back to Plato and Aristotle and focuses upon moral character (virtues). Virtues are entrenched in a person's character. Most people do not possess perfect virtues (e.g., courage, honesty) but tend towards them. The study of virtue ethics declined in comparison to the other forms of normative ethics from the nineteenth century until the 1950s (Hursthouse 2013). While all three theories remain important to the study of professional ethics (see Cheffers and Pakaluk 2005), virtue ethics became a particularly popular basis for examining professional ethical obligations from at least the 1980s (e.g., Libby and Thorne 2004).

Deontology emphasizes duties or rules and owes much of its origins to the works of Immanuel Kant (1724–1804). In its most general sense it describes morally good behavior in terms of compliance with good moral norms. Again, very generally, deontological theories can be divided between those that are (a) agent-centered (the norms or rules which relate to each individual agent) or (b) victim- or patient-centered (theories presuming individuals' rights) (Alexander and Moore 2013).

If deontology assesses moral choices by compliance with prior established norms, consequentialist theories evaluate them in terms of, as the name suggests, outcomes or consequences of action (Simnott-Armstrong 2013). Indeed, it is argued that the consequences or outcomes are the only measure by which the morality of choices should be assessed. While there are various forms of consequentialism, the classic presentation takes the form of utilitarianism as derived from the work of Jeremy Bentham and John Stewart Mill. Generally, utilitarianism talks in terms of assessing choices by what yields the greater good or pleasure over bad or pain ("the greatest good for the greatest number").

A summary of the three approaches can be expressed in this manner:

> [Virtue ethics] may, initially, be identified as the one that emphasizes the virtues, or moral character, in contrast to the approach which emphasizes duties or rules (deontology) or that which emphasizes the consequences of actions (consequentialism). Suppose it is obvious that someone in need should be helped. A utilitarian [one consequentialist approach] will point to the fact that the consequences of doing so will maximize well-being, a deontologist to the fact that, in doing so the agent will be acting in accordance with a moral rule such as "Do unto others as you would be done by" and a virtue ethicist to the fact that helping the person would be charitable or benevolent. (Hursthouse 2013)

Within the practical context of professional ethics, take the example of a lawyer who is assessing whether she should step down from an engagement because she believes that the client is not making adequate public disclosure of what she considers to be a material event even though the issue is not clear-cut (a "gray" area). A virtue ethics approach might have the lawyer assess her choice in terms of the qualities of her self-perception as a "good" lawyer. A deontological approach might seek guidance from general principles for the profession such as refusing to be associated with misleading reports. A utilitarian approach could include an assessment of the outcomes or consequences of staying versus stepping down as lawyer: for example, might greater good be derived from having a cautious lawyer remain in place should more serious challenges arise?

This short discussion introduces the complexity of normative theory. We now turn to applied ethics, or, as it is increasingly becoming known, practical ethics. As we noted above, this approach allows us to examine the practical ethical issues that face professionals and members of PSFs in particular. We have so far used the term "applied ethics" as if it is a subset of normative ethics, although this is subject to debate. Those opposed to its use do so because it implies that this is a sub-discipline that literally applies existing theoretical principles to practical circumstances (LaFollette 2003). "[P]hilosophical principles cannot be applied in any straightforward way to particular problems and policies. In the face of concrete dilemmas, we need to revise philosophical principles as much as we rely on them for justification" (Thompson 2007). For pure convenience here we use the more common expression "applied ethics" but we will return to the discussion of the relationship to ethical theory shortly. We first consider the modern origins of applied ethics.

While many philosophers, ancient and modern, have applied ethical thought to practical problems, applied ethics as a distinct field of inquiry owes its modern roots to the social movements of the 1960s and 1970s. Put formally, "[a]pplied ethics is a general field of study that includes all systematic efforts to understand and to resolve moral problems that arise in some domain of practical life" (Winkler 2012: 174). Alternatively, applied ethics addresses everyday problems in real-life contexts. It has grown as a field of study around particular areas of interest. While early work in applied ethics dealt with issues such as the Vietnam War or abortion, today, medical/bioethics, business and professional ethics, and environmental ethics are the largest categories of applied ethics. Yet the many monographs or journals about applied (or practical) ethics demonstrate a lengthy collection of social problems or contexts to which ethicists turn their attention.

As applied ethics evolved so too did the debate about its connection to ethical theory. Initially it was popular to reject traditional theory (Winkler 2012), which is perhaps not surprising given the modern origins of applied ethics in a time of social turbulence. Increasingly, however, it became an accepted position that it would be improbable that a generalized normative theory could provide the basis for more applied discussion (Winkler and Coombs 1993). Instead, LaFollette (2003) talks of its theoretical basis in a different manner: how thinking about practical issues leads to reflection that "reveals the connections between particular cases, isolates the contrasts between competing theoretical perspectives, and [makes us become] aware of tensions between what we were taught and what experience and reflection reveal. These require us to step back from our preconceptions to examine an issue more abstractly" (LaFollette 2003: 8). Included among the examples he gives are those of corporate responsibility and whistle blowing, evaluation of which also require thinking about the "moral status of corporations" (LaFollette 2003: 8). In the context of the professions, medical and bioethics have attracted the most attention. In accounting or law, issues of independence and conflict of interest have also generated considerable debate.

Professional ethics is one form of applied ethics. Within the scope of professional ethics is the further application of ethics in the context of the PSF. The organizational context of the professional matters, of course, because it sets up a particular type of relationship between professionals and those with whom they interact, with resulting implications for their ethical behavior.

6.3 Professional Ethics: Codes, Autonomy, and Gatekeepers

Professional ethics—"the ethics of the professionals who are members of a given profession" (Airaksinen 2012: 616)—is a form of applied or practical ethics. In Thompson's (2007) view, "[p]ractical ethics tries to relate professional rules and clinical experience to the broader social context in which professionals practice, and to the deeper moral assumptions on which professions depend." Further, professional ethics must be considered not only in terms of individual professional–client/patient relationships but also the institution in which decisions are made: "the moral life that dwells among the structures of society" (ibid.). The discussion of professional ethics that follows is centered on three key interrelated concepts: codes, autonomy, and gatekeepers. As the discussion will show, codes are an expression of the profession's own values; autonomy underlies many of the assumptions regarding ethics in practice; and the role of gatekeeper challenges the extent of the ethical responsibility.

Koehn (1994) provides a helpful starting point to this discussion by focusing on the notion of the trust that users of professional services are required to place in the individual members of the profession:

> We should not forget that professions represent the only mechanism we have for collectively providing ourselves with the goods of health, legal justice, and spiritual peace. If professionals are not trustworthy, whom should we trust? This question must be confronted. We cannot simply hope that the sick, the accused or the injured, and the spiritually needy will provide adequately for themselves. Clients grant, or at least permit, professionals access to something of value (e.g., their bodies) precisely because they are unable to secure or promote a desired state of affairs (e.g., a return to health) by themselves or are better able to do so with assistance. Given that the critics are not proposing any alternative source of help, we will be left without recourse if we cease to believe that professionals merit trust under some conditions. (Koehn 1994: 5–6)

This is a familiar description. Suddaby and Muzio (Chapter 2, this volume) introduce the historic significance of ethics both to how the term "profession" is defined and to the role of professions in society. In seeking a definition of profession that captures its unique qualities vis-à-vis occupations in general, the trait or attribute approach—identifying the unique characteristics of a profession—typically included some sense of a higher calling or unique talent and identified the code of ethics as a common feature across professions (Greenwood 1957). The social bargain (Suddaby and Muzio, Chapter 2, this volume) implicit in professions being given monopoly power over their activities, as often happens for professions in Anglo-Saxon societies, typically results in obligations being imposed on them to act in the manner described above by Koehn: "The rationale behind such an arrangement is that if it is a good bargain, then both society and those in the occupation will benefit from it; society, by obtaining expert service in these learned occupations, and the practitioners by gaining status, control, and some protection against political scrutiny" (Barker 1992: 92).

6.3.1 Codes of Ethics

Codes may be interpreted as the means by which the professions themselves define their ideal of professional conduct (or, to return to the earlier metaphor, their "contractual obligations"). It is not that codes equate to professional ethics, but rather that they help explain the common agreement amongst members of professions as to their collective standards of appropriate behavior (Adler and Kwon 2013). If codes reflect the agreed values, from an individual perspective they should ideally encourage self-reflection: "The ethic of the professional is to be found in the dialectical interaction between the conscience of the individual professional and the collective conclusions of the profession as a whole, and the formulations of the 'Professional Code,' always provisional and continually being revised, are the medium of that dialectical process" (Newton 1982: 40). This is the ideal.

The ethics literature addresses the issues of codes and economic self-interest. For example, "[p]rofessional associations serve many functions, but they always look after their power base." (Airaksinen 2012: 617). Codes are certainly the means by which the self-interest of the professions is maintained and boundaries are established against "imposters" (Fisher et al. 2001), a particularly important perspective when considering professions in terms of their power in society (Newton 1982). Barker challenges this position by focusing on the "ethical ideal of service to society" as a means of "curb[ing] their selfish impulses" (Barker 1992: 89) and defends this position in normative terms. This is the position to which members of the profession *ought* to aspire, and that they do not is a matter for self-discipline within the profession and not a reason to throw away such an ethical ideal (Barker 1992). Indeed he goes further by arguing that such an aspiration is a way of understanding professions themselves. Similarly:

> At the heart of the career concept is a certain attitude toward work which is peculiarly professional. A career is essentially a calling, a life devoted to "good works." Professional work is never viewed solely as a means to an end; it is the end itself. (Greenwood 1957: 53)

While trait approaches have, for many years, had their critics (e.g., Cogan 1953), there remains intact the notion that there is an ethical ideal to which we expect professionals to aspire.

Further, codes are, of course, there to be enforced and there is mixed evidence as to how this process enhances overall ethical standards. Enforcement of ethical obligations is most often in terms of violations of relatively technical provisions in the code (e.g., failure to maintain competence, committing a criminal act, or bringing the profession into disrepute) or neglect of clients (Levin and Mather 2012) and seldom in terms of violations of the more aspirational goals such as placing client or public interest ahead of that of the individual professional. Large firm lawyers often escape disciplinary sanctions (Wilkins 1992). Rarely, if ever, is there serious examination by the professions of the more subtle ethical issues that will be the focus later in this chapter. It turns out that it takes particularly egregious behavior for a case to be made, such as that against David Duncan of the accounting firm, Arthur Andersen.

This approach to enforcement is not a new phenomenon. Abel (1989: Chapter 7) examines a broad range of research on the way that the American legal profession regulates itself. He demonstrates that the profession has proven itself over the years to be reluctant to take complaints against its members seriously. First, lawyers themselves demonstrate remarkably poor understanding of their profession's ethical code. For example, Abel (2008: 349) recounts the case of a lawyer who did not have a written retainer agreement with his client, even though written agreements are part of the rules of professional conduct. The lawyer in question retained a client's tax refund as payment for his services. While the lawyer was indeed entitled to substantial fees he was ultimately suspended.

Had he only understood the rules and implemented a retainer agreement, he would have received his fees and avoided suspension. Second, "[d]isciplinary procedures still dismiss more than 90% of complaints with little or no investigation. There is reason to believe that this expresses the solicitude practicing lawyers feel for each other" (Abel 1989: 147). Abel also finds prosecution uneven across types of practitioners. For example, complaints against inexperienced solo practitioners were significantly more likely than others to be prosecuted (Arnold and Hagan 1992). The lawyers and judges dealing with these cases were "extremely solicitous of excuses for misbehavior" (Abel 1989: 148), and those who were convicted were typically dealt with leniently. Finally, of the very small proportion of those who were actually disbarred, most were subsequently readmitted either to the bar that sanctioned them or to another one (Abel 1989). A similar pattern is found within accounting. Fisher et al. (2001) identify instances of enforcement apparently solely in defense of the private interests of the (accounting) profession and not the more expected interests of both the profession and the public interest.

A discussion of codes of ethics must also reference their relationship with the fiduciary, a key quality of all professions (Suddaby and Muzio, Chapter 2, this volume) The legal concept of the fiduciary in common law jurisdictions, "[t]he relationship of one person to another, where the former is bound to exercise rights and powers in good faith for the benefit of the latter" (Osborn 1964), imposes broad responsibilities that might also generally be described as ethical and which exist over and above the strictly contractual (in civil law jurisdictions equivalent provisions for specific contexts may be found in the Code). Generally, fiduciary duties cannot be avoided and arise in all cases where a member of a specific profession is acting in that capacity in exchanges with others. The duties require the professional to put client interests ahead of their own; they must avoid conflicts of interest, avoid abuse of power, not use confidential information for personal advancement, etc. In practical terms, this is perhaps the closest example of the law imposing ethical responsibilities on the professional (Suddaby and Muzio, Chapter 2, this volume) and in interpreting the requisite standards to which individual professions must adhere in order to fulfill their fiduciary responsibilities, courts are most commonly influenced by the rules of the profession itself as expressed in its particular code of ethics (e.g., *Hodgkinson v. Simms*, 1994).

The purpose of this discussion is not to equate fiduciary duties with the ethical responsibilities of the professional; at best there is a partial overlap. Nor is it to suggest that a trait approach allows for an adequate definition of profession or professional ethics. It does not, and its critics abound (Abbott 1988; Macdonald 1995). As Koehn (1994) suggests, such an approach is purely descriptive and avoids examination of what the norms of a profession *should* be:

> We must also bear in mind that it is a normative matter to assert that a profession has no inner meaning but rather consists of the sum total of what a majority of its members happen to be doing at a certain time. Taken at its extreme, this position will yield mind-boggling claims of the sort that Adolf Eichmann's lawyer offered in defense of that war criminal's actions: Eichmann was innocent of the killings by gas because

gassing "was indeed a medical matter, since it was prepared by physicians; it was a matter of killing, and killing too, is a medical matter." Unless one is willing to say that doctors and mass murderers belong to the same profession and are equally good and worthy of respect, our practice of holding persons responsible for their actions will eventually force us to confront the question with which I propose to begin: what do professionals do, and what, if anything, legitimates their practice? (Koehn 1994: 7)

The purpose of the above accounts is instead to raise questions about the appropriateness of the self-regulating nature of professions—that is, professional bodies being assigned the role of protecting clients through enforcement of codes and justifying the trust placed in professionals. Functionalist accounts of the professions argue that such rights are justified because of the need to ensure that clients receive uniformly high levels of service (Sutton 2001). The Weberian view, by contrast, regards professions as occupations that are particularly successful at fending off competition, and sees ethical codes as part of their armory intended to demonstrate to the world that their professional monopoly is being operated in the interests of the clients (Sutton 2001). As Sutton (2001) points out, the evidence that we briefly reviewed above supports the Weberian view; if it were otherwise, then one would expect a great deal more interest in the professions in dealing with transgressors. From this perspective, ethical codes allow a profession to show, so long as nobody inquires too closely into how things happen in practice, that it has a well-constructed code of behavior designed to ensure that its practitioners act in the interests of their clients and the broader public, and that if they do not the profession will protect the client (public).

6.3.2 Autonomy

The self-regulating nature of professions and the enforcement of their ethical codes is in fact one instance of the expression of the broader concept of autonomy (see Empson and Langley, Chapter 8, this volume) as it relates to professions and professional ethics. Within self-regulating professions, the expression "autonomous" implies that the individual or firm practice their art in a manner that is independent of both self-interest and partisan client interest. It also references the fact that the state (the regulator) has delegated jurisdiction over the rules of practice and the conditions of membership of the profession to the professional body. In order to determine why such a condition may be deemed to be necessary we must return to the notions of service and trust discussed earlier.

For each profession, there exists a broader social responsibility that again varies by context. These responsibilities are a condition of their regulated authority to practice and, using the contractual analogy, the quid pro quo for the monopoly rights provided by self-regulation. For example, in the case of the auditor, the values imposed are expressed as objectivity and independence: "The principle of objectivity imposes the obligation to be impartial, intellectually honest, and free of conflicts of interest.

Independence precludes relationships that may appear to impair a member's objectivity in rendering attestation services" (American Institute of Certified Public Accountants 2014). For the actuary, although most rules of conduct relate directly to the protection of the client, there is also a residual obligation to society: "An actuary shall perform professional services with integrity, skill and care. He [*sic*] shall fulfil his professional responsibility to his client or employer and shall not act against the public interest" (GCAAPCE 2014). For lawyers, there is some version of the following rule that imposes overriding responsibility not to the client but to society: the lawyer must maintain "respect for the rule of law and the fair administration of justice" (CCBE 2013) even where to do so runs counter to the interests of their own client (duty as "officer of the court" or as "minister of justice").

The notion of the autonomous professional in practical terms is derived from the traditional model of the self-employed professional or the professional in the PSF who might maintain independence through a large portfolio of clients. No one individual client could then be significant enough to compromise the duty of the professional to wider social (professional) obligations. This, of course, is not always a safe assumption for much of professional practice, for example that of corporate law, and we return to it in section 6.4. Before doing so, we examine the third of the three concepts underpinning professional ethics: the role of the professional as gatekeeper.

6.3.3 Gatekeepers

The legal profession uses the term "gatekeeper" in a sense that is somewhat different from that found in the organizational literature. Coffee (2006: 2) defines it as "an agent who acts as a reputational intermediary to assure investors as to the quality of the 'signal' sent by the corporate issuer. The reputational intermediary does so by lending or 'pledging' its reputational capital to the corporation, thus enabling investors or the market to rely on the corporation's own disclosures or assurances where they otherwise might not." Coffee is writing post-Enron and the language of this definition clearly fits that of the auditor in particular.

In terms of the ethical duties of professionals, the issue implied by imposing a gatekeeper duty is whether ethical responsibilities extend to intervention when the client is perceived to be acting improperly. From the perspective of users of such services—for example, those who might rely on the audit assurance for investment decisions—it is often assumed that this is the case. If professionals are not responsible for preventing their clients from embarking on a harmful course of action, why are they there? The response from professions has been largely a reluctance to extend responsibility to this territory. The audit profession, for example, once talked of an expectations gap, a divergence between the expectations of the profession and the public as to the responsibility, say, to identify management fraud (e.g., McEnroe and Martens 2001). This "gap" is to be narrowed, not by extending the auditor's responsibility but by better educating the public and lowering its expectations.

In fairness to accountants, these issues were overshadowed by ever-present threats of litigation. Further, the corporate failures of the turn of the century led in the USA to significantly increased responsibilities imposed by the Sarbanes-Oxley Act. The legal profession has resisted the notion of gatekeeper vigorously. For example, they successfully defended against an extension of responsibility in the Sarbanes-Oxley Act that would have required what is known as a "noisy withdrawal" where they were unable to prevent a client from engaging in significant violations of the law; that is, they would have been required not only to resign from the engagement but also report the events to regulators as auditors in the USA are obliged to do (Kim 2011). Kim (2011) explores the arguments against the lawyer-gatekeeper and carefully documents the solid resistance from the profession to such an approach:

> Official comments in the SEC administrative rulemaking process complained that the proposed rules could "eviscerate the attorney's traditional role as advocate, confidant and advisor" and "risk destroying the trust and confidence many issuers have up to now placed in their legal counsel." They worried that the proposals would "drive a wedge between client and the counsel who advised it on a matter" and decried that "the Commission would be using the attorney as the Commission's eyes and ears to build a case against the client." Lawyers maintained that by "requiring attorneys to police and pass judgment on their clients," lawyers for corporations would slide down the slippery slope from trusted counselor to policeman. (Kim 2011: 132–133)

Kim concludes, however, that it is in the best interests both of the profession and public for lawyers to assume such a role.

Coffee (2006: 3–4) notes that "one problem overshadows all others": even where the professionals are acting as gatekeeper, they are also paid by the entity that hires them. And the term "pay" can be used broadly to include any form of economic dependency. The securities lawyer who allows a generous interpretation of a corporate event being below the threshold for disclosure may be influenced not only by the fees for this particular service but also the promise of a continued revenue stream to come. The logical response to this concern is to return to the concept of autonomy (Adler and Kwon 2013: 935–936). It is an ethical obligation to retain independence from client pressure, economic self-interest, or firm revenue demands, and it is that that allows the public to retain trust that the professional will act in its best interests rather than their own.

We have hinted at more than one point in this chapter that there are exigencies in professional practice which affect the way in which professionals interpret their ethical responsibilities. We now examine this issue in greater depth, beginning with situations in which it has been posited that professionals are under inherent stress because of their structural position (Gunz and Gunz 1994b), namely where they are employees of non-professional organizations. This section will lay an important foundation for the following discussion of the role of professionals within PSFs.

6.4 The Autonomous Professional in Non-Professional Organizations

If the ideal of the autonomous professional evolved from the notion of the wise counselor operating unfettered by messy commercial pressures, it is one we would be hard pressed to find in today's society. A very high proportion of professionals are employed in non-professional organizations (NPOs: business or public corporations that are not PSFs; Leicht and Fennell 1997). Discussion of employed professionals provides a useful context for introducing influences that affect the way in which ethical matters are handled by professionals, influences that can also, as we show later, be identified in the PSF. More importantly, it may well be that as PSFs have become larger and more bureaucratic, there is more in common between the world of employed professionals in the NPO and that of their counterparts in the PSF than was traditionally assumed.

Suddaby and Muzio (Chapter 2, this volume) discuss the literature on organizational professional conflict from the perspective of the theory of professions (see also Kirkpatrick and Noordegraaf, Chapter 5, this volume). There are, however, also important ethical concerns. If, as many researchers have found, there is little evidence amongst professionals of perceived organizational professional conflict (Adler and Aranya 1984; Bamber and Iyer 2002; Benson 1973; Davies 1983; Gunz and Gunz 1994a; Shafer 2002; Wallace 1993), what are the inferences that should be drawn about professional ethical decision-making? Several possible explanations suggest themselves (Gunz and Gunz 1994b): (1) managers in NPOs may side-step professionals when considering difficult ethical issues; (2) the professional simply does not recognize an ethical conflict when presented with it; or (3) professionals may find a means of resolving issues without great effort thereby, for them, downgrading the intensity of the dilemma (Zohar 2005).

The first option—that managers may routinely avoid involving employed professionals when something occurs about which they know the professionals will raise a problem—is beyond the scope of this chapter. The second and third options imply that the issue either lacks, for the professional, the necessary salience or vividness for it to be recognized as an ethical dilemma (Jones 1991; Rest 1986), or, if it is, the judgment process invoked (May and Pauli 2002) does not give the professional great difficulty. Why might these be the case; what might they tell us about how the professional resolves ethical dilemmas?

The proletarianization literature on professionals (Bourgeault et al. 2011; Derber 1982; Murphy 1990; Oppenheimer 1973), based on the precept that "professionals have become subject to new forms of control that are eroding their status as professionals" (Wallace 1995: 229), provides a useful entry point. Wallace (1995) shows that professionals' organizational commitment—an indication of the extent to which this proletarianization might be taking effect—"is highly dependent on perceived opportunities for career advancements and the criteria used in the distribution of rewards" (Wallace 1995: 228). The key here is that organizational commitment may in fact have implications for ethical decision-making. Evidence supporting this interpretation comes from a study of Canadian corporate lawyers (Gunz and Gunz 2007), which showed that the more salient an organizational identity was to these counsel, the more likely it was that they would adopt an approach to an ethical dilemma in a manner consistent with that of a non-professional employee, as opposed to that of a lawyer (for a discussion of professional identity conflict see Alvesson et al., Chapter 18, this volume).

The NPO literature, then, provides evidence to suggest that the orientation of professionals to the organization in which they practice, and consequentially their approach to handling ethical dilemmas, is contingent on the way that the organization rewards and promotes them. PSFs are, of course, different from NPOs in the sense that their dominant cultures tend more to the professional (Faulconbridge and Muzio 2008). But they, too, are subject to strong commercial pressures, and we address the implications for ethical decision-making in such organizations next.

6.5 PROFESSIONAL ETHICS IN PROFESSIONAL SERVICE FIRMS

PSFs have, as has been widely observed, increasingly become large bureaucracies, and many authors have commented on the impact of this trend on the manner in which their members practice (Brock 2006; Malhotra and Morris 2009; Muzio and Faulconbridge 2013). It could be argued that the professional ethos of the PSF (Faulconbridge and Muzio 2008) will be more supportive of an approach to professional ethics aligned with that prescribed by the profession itself. Indeed there is evidence that lawyers working in law firms feel a greater commitment to their profession than do solo practitioners, perhaps because the latter are under greater pressure to run their businesses (Wallace and Kay 2008). Yet many writers have pointed to the commercial pressures faced by professionals (Brint 1994; Hanlon 1998; Malhotra and Morris 2009; Rittenberg and Covaleski 2001). More specifically, recent work on client capture (Leicht and Fennell 2001) suggests that professionals working in PSFs can be subject to pressures that do have implications for ethical decision-making.

The greater the (usually economic) power of clients over professionals, the greater the potential challenge to professional autonomy. Professionals find it harder to defend their ethical position when being pressed by their client to act expediently. Furthermore the shift to expert (Brint 1994) or commercialistic (Hanlon 1998) professionalism implies that professionals with such orientations are more likely to be in sympathy with the client's aims (Dinovitzer et al. 2014a). In the 1990s the key professional services (audit in particular) in the major accounting firms were subsumed to the interests of business interests (e.g., consulting). The argument was made (e.g., Boyd 2004; Wyart 2004) that as a consequence individuals were not always able or willing to defend their professional values when faced with the enormous economic power of the client and firm. Arguably, that trend continues today at least in some of the very large international professional partnerships. By way of illustration, take the following example from the "About Us" page of one of the largest law firms in the world:

> Baker and McKenzie defined the global law firm in the 20th century, and we are redefining it to meet the challenges of the global economy in the 21st . . . Ours is a passionately collaborative community of 60 nationalities. We have the deep roots and knowledge of the language and culture of business required to address the nuances of local markets worldwide. And our culture of friendship and broad scope of practice enable us to navigate complexity across issues, practices and borders with ease. (Baker and McKenzie 2015)

Much as with the major international accounting firms at least in the 1990s, the average reader would be hard pressed to catch that these highly skilled members of a "passionately collaborative community" are actually professionals, let alone autonomous professionals, and indeed lawyers. On the "Our People" page is found: "Every day our more than 4,000 lawyers, economists, tax advisors and other professionals share insights and best practices across borders and practices" (Baker and McKenzie 2015), a practice world far removed from that in which the traditional professional ideal evolved.

Baker and McKenzie appears to have chosen to define itself at one extreme of the range of business-focused law firms. However, all major commercial law practices share common characteristics with major accounting firms: they are large, they have complex bureaucratic structures, their focus is upon the needs of commerce, and individuals usually succeed or fail on their individual ability to generate revenue. So while a partnership's legal structure retains the focus on the individual for performance measurement purposes, the individual must be influenced by both the structure of the firm and others within it and in a manner not envisaged in Brint's (1994) model of social trustee professionalism.

How do these pressures towards a commercial approach manifest themselves in the ethical behavior of professionals? At the core of the issue of ethics in PSFs is that of the power of the client. Professionals working in NPOs can be used as a limiting case, in which the power of the client, as the professional's employer, is perhaps at its greatest. Leicht and Fennell (2001) introduce the label "client capture" in the PSF to describe this:

> some professional groups have faced a situation whereby the consumers (clients) or new ways of performing work (technologies) will undermine professional prerogatives and status. We refer to these trends under the heading of professions "captured" by clients or technologies. Under client capture the consumers of professional work gain the ability to control the activities, timing, and costs of professional work. In effect the "consumer becomes sovereign" much as consumers search for (and price) other consumer goods and services. (Leicht and Fennell 2001: 105–106)

Evidence for client capture comes from the accounting profession. Macey and his co-authors have persuasively argued that client capture is more commonly found among accounting firms than, for example, legal firms because, although a large firm may have many clients, often individual partners have only one, giving that client great power over the partner in question (Macey and Sale 2003). Furthermore, the size of client firm makes a difference as well. In a sample of large US firms it was shown that the larger the client firm, the more likely it was to restate its financial results (an indication of accounting error), suggesting that larger firms have greater power to persuade their auditors to approve erroneous or misleading financial statements (Eisenberg and Macey 2004). Similar evidence comes from the actuarial profession (Armstrong et al. 2012).

Client capture and its consequent impact on ethical decision-making is complex (Dinovitzer et al. 2014b). In its most obvious form it is the direct demand of a client exerting economic power over the professional; arguably the case of Enron pressuring David Duncan, its auditor. It may, however, also be indirect and more subtle. Dinovitzer et al. (2014b) point out that commercial law typically involves a relationship not between two individuals, professional and client, but between two organizations, meaning that client capture may be a far more complex phenomenon than a simple matter of one actor exerting influence over another. Indirect client capture might occur when a powerful member of the PSF (perhaps the partner responsible for the client relationship) imposes pressure on the individual professional to please the client in contravention to their own beliefs. It is also well documented (Gunz and Gunz 2008) that others in the firm with an economic interest in the client may exert pressure in defense of their own economic interests. The professional may have no direct client contact at all—they may, for example, be brought in solely for a specific task (finance or tax expertise)—but the pressure to compromise integrity and satisfy the client may occur through peers. Finally and not uncommonly is what has been described as "misdirected" client capture (Dinovitzer et al. 2014b). As noted above, the actual client to which a professional owes their ethical responsibility is, most often, a person in law only; it is a corporation. The professional interacts with, is hired by, paid, and pressured by, a human manager (Coffee 2006). The potential then exists for the professional to meet the desires of that manager at the expense of their ethical responsibilities to the actual client (the corporation). A particularly egregious example of this effect was described by the Enron bankruptcy examiner, referencing the actions of those in the outside law firms. As he noted, Enron's outside counsel were given instructions from certain Enron officers that "if carried out, constituted a breach of a legal duty to Enron (such as a breach of fiduciary duty) or a violation of law (such as inadequate disclosure)" (Batson 2003: 28).

The organizational complexity of PSFs not only leads to varied forms of client capture, it is also related to the ways in which lawyers construct their own identities that in turn impact the manner in which ethical dilemmas might be resolved. As we have seen in the previous section, much of this work has been conducted in the context of the NPO, although recently there have been extensions to the PSF (e.g., Dinovitzer et al. 2014a). The Dinovitzer et al. study found evidence not only of distinct identities, but also some evidence of the impact of certain of those identities on the way ethical dilemmas are resolved. For example, lawyers whose identity was more strongly influenced by the law than by their personal experience and who showed little tendency to regard themselves as members of a collectivity (even though they were partners in large law firms) were found to be more likely to bend to the pressure of a client manager, even when to do so compromised an ethical responsibility to elevate an issue within the true client (the corporation and not the manager; that is, the misdirected client capture referenced above).

Understanding ethics within the PSF thus requires attention, first and foremost, to the organizational context of the professional. While at first glance professionals in the PSF are thought to be technically independent of their client, as our discussion shows, this independence is fraught with commercial and collegial pressures. The issues raised earlier—of codes, gatekeeping, and autonomy—take on a particular valence when analyzed within the PSF, and demonstrate that scholars must take into account the exigencies in professional practice in order to understand the ethical responsibilities of professionals.

6.6 Conclusions

The study of ethics in the PSF is today largely empirical. While there is an extensive and continuing literature on professional ethics in general and a lively debate about the normative elements of professional ethics in particular, for the most part these are based on a generic understanding of the professional—for example a lawyer, an actuary, or an accountant who is understood to perform certain highly skilled tasks—without consideration of the context in which their art is practiced. For example, Martin (2000: 4) talks of the dominant perspective as focusing upon "the moral requirements attached to a profession and imposed on all its members, together with the ethical dilemmas created when the requirements conflict or are too vague to provide guidance."

Yet this ignores the very real pressures experienced by professionals in PSFs resulting from phenomena such as the client capture we describe above and the overriding commercial pressures and increasingly competitive environment faced by PSFs more generally that are responsible for much of these pressures. It is, in other words, naïve to assume that professionals are able to maintain a level of autonomy that places them above the temptations of the commercial world, particularly since PSFs themselves are increasingly—and probably always were—deeply embedded in and an integral part of that world. Autonomy is encroached on from many directions: from the client, who may want the professional to act in a way convenient to them but not in accord with the ethical standards of the profession; and from colleagues and senior management in the firm who also have an interest, for their own reasons, in the same client. The complexity of relationships between PSFs and their large corporate clients can mean that professionals fail to recognize who the real client is (the client corporation), potentially leading to a form of goal displacement in which the professionals' actions are focused on the needs of their contact within the client firm rather than the interests of the actual client, sometimes with disastrous results (*vide* Enron).

Indeed the tensions between what users expect of professionals and what professionals are willing and able to deliver have threatened, and may continue to threaten, the continued existence of professions if the extent of the ethical lapses that result destroy the trust of the public in the profession in question. This was the case with accountants in 2002. More importantly, a continued drip of ethical failures will feed a popular cynicism about the worth of professionals. What then are the challenges for the study of ethics in the PSF?

First, it is evident that in order to understand the ethical pressures at work on professionals in PSFs we need to know more about the PSFs themselves. Are some professions more vulnerable than others to pressures like the various forms of client capture that we describe above? How might variation in the organizational form and governance of PSFs (Leblebici and Sherer, Chapter 9, this volume) affect the relationship between the professionals and their client? To what extent is professionals' ethical judgment protected, in the sense that they feel able to act strictly in accord with their profession's code, by the professional culture (Faulconbridge and Muzio 2008), or lack thereof, of the firm? How might different kinds of careers affect ethical judgment (see Cohen, Chapter 16, this volume)? For example, something as simple as increased evidence of lateral moves by professionals (Henderson 2014) may well have a profound impact on ethical decision-making, because newcomers to the firm may well be more concerned about the need to establish themselves with their colleagues and thus be more vulnerable to phenomena such as client capture. The classic perspectives on the influence of the firm as guardian of ethical mores (Smigel 1964) may be moot if we no longer assume that the individual professional is committed to the PSF itself but is instead more focused on personal career advancement and job (in)security (e.g. Clay and Seeger 2012; Galanter and Henderson 2008). Such changes might impact all aspects of the firm and increase competitive pressures between and within PSFs, which in turn can increase ethical pressures (Dinovitzer et al. 2014a).

Further, the focus of the study of ethics in the PSF has been mostly limited in its context to large firms and, in particular, large accounting and law firms (but see Levin and Mather 2012). However, the largest proportions of lawyers in the USA, for example, practice in small firms or as sole practitioners (Harvard Law School 2007), and it is known that ethical challenges are not only just as rife there but may be more difficult to resolve than in larger firms that have conflicts or opinion committees to provide an internal check against unethical behavior (Gunz et al. 2002; Levin and Mather 2012). In addition, this discussion has largely been confined to the legal and accounting professions, especially the former, which reflects the attention these two have received in the literature. There is plenty of scope for extending this work to other professions, for example engineering, the actuarial profession, or indeed the investment advising industry, the work of all of which can destroy the lives of their clients, sometimes literally.

Cross-cultural ethical issues form yet another area into which this work could be extended. As PSFs increasingly operate internationally either as firms themselves or through the offshoring of aspects of professional work (Boussebaa and Morgan,

Chapter 4, this volume), a broad range of critical ethical issues arise. For example, is there common agreement as to ethical obligations between countries in which firms operate? What is the effectiveness of international ethical codes, and should they exist? Ought clients in one jurisdiction be made aware that their work is being conducted in quite a different jurisdiction? These raise complex ethical issues and there is little evidence of any rigorous approach to date as to how they should be addressed.

There is, evidently, a large and rich potential for scholarly work devoted to ethics in the PSF. One important caution should be noted: empirical ethical work is difficult, which no doubt explains why there is such a dearth of existing work in this field. Traditional social science methodologies such as those of self-report or direct observation are problematic for many reasons. Ethical problems are comparatively rare events, making observational studies largely impractical: the researcher has no way of knowing when such an event may happen, and therefore has little, if any, chance of being there to observe it. Retrospective studies are complicated by issues of confidentiality: it is not easy to persuade people to tell you about things they have done which might, if revealed, get them into trouble. Self-report hypothetical studies are affected by social desirability bias, and instead of providing a "true" answer (that might indicate an lapse in ethical judgment for example), respondents will instead provide one which is socially acceptable (King and Bruner 2000); and so on.

Ethical issues are (fortunately) rare for professionals, and even when encountered, probably fall into the category described by Zohar (2005) as low intensity, in other words the minor, everyday issues that involve minor ethical judgments which do not, on the whole, have the potential to land a transgressor in court or before a professional disciplinary tribunal. But every so often ethical lapses become large enough that they hit society hard, and the more we can understand the pressures leading to these lapses, the greater our chance of preventing their recurrence. This research, in other words, may be difficult, but its potential payoff makes it exceedingly worthwhile.

NOTE

1. The terminology here is kept deliberately generic: descriptive rather than necessarily legally precise—while the authors work in a common law jurisdiction, the same issues apply to all legal systems.

REFERENCES

Abbott, A. (1988). *The System of Professions: An Essay on the Division of Expert Labor*. Chicago, IL: University of Chicago Press.

Abel, R. L. (1989). *American Lawyers*. New York: Oxford University Press.

Abel, R. L. (2008). *Lawyers in the Dock: Learning from Attorney Disciplinary Proceedings*. New York: Oxford University Press.

Adler, P. S. and Kwon, S.-W. (2013). "The Mutation of Professionalism as a Contested Diffusion Process: Clinical Guidelines as Carriers of Institutional Change in Medicine", *Journal of Management Studies* 50(5): 930–962.

Adler, S. and Aranya, N. A. (1984). "A Comparison of the Work Needs, Attitudes and Preferences of Professional Accountants at Different Career Stages," *Journal of Vocational Behavior* 25(1): 45–57.

Airaksinen, T. (2012). "Professional Ethics," in *The Encyclopedia of Applied Ethics*, ed. R. F. Chadwick. San Diego: Academic Press, 616–623.

Alexander, L. and Moore, M. (2013). "Deontological Ethics," *The Stanford Encyclopedia of Philosophy*. <http://plato.stanford.edu/entries/ethics-deontological>.

American Institute of Certified Public Accountants (2014). "Objectivity and Independence, Principles of Professional Conduct."

Armstrong, C., Ittner, C., and Larcker, D. F. (2012). "Corporate Governance, Compensation Consultants, and CEO Pay Levels," *Review of Accounting Studies* 17(2): 322–351.

Arnold, B. L. and Hagan, J. (1992). "Careers of Misconduct: The Structure of Prosecuted Professional Deviance Among Lawyers," *American Sociological Review* 57(6): 771–780.

Baker and McKenzie (2015). "About Us." <http://www.bakermckenzie.com/aboutus/>.

Bamber, E. M. and Iyer, V. M. (2002). "Big 5 Auditors' Professional and Organizational Identification: Consistency or Conflict?" *Auditing: A Journal of Practice & Theory* 21(2): 21–38.

Barker, S. F. (1992). "What is a Profession?" *Professional Ethics: A Multidisciplinary Journal* 1(1–2): 73–99.

Batson, N. (2003). "Final Report of Neal Batson, Court-Appointed Examiner." United States Bankruptcy Court, Southern District of New York, Case No. 01-16034 (AJG), November 4, 2003.

Benson, J. K. (1973). "The Analysis of Bureaucratic-Professional Conflict: Functional Versus Dialectic Approaches," *Sociological Quarterly* 14(3): 376–394.

Bourgeault, I. L., Hirschkorn, K., and Sainsaulieu, I. (2011). "Relations between Professions and Organizations: More Fully Considering the Role of the Client," *Professions & Professionalism* 1(1): 67–86.

Boyd, C. (2004). "The Structural Origins of Conflict of Interest in the Accounting Profession," *Business Ethics Quarterly* 14(3): 377–398.

Brint, S. (1994). *In an Age of Experts: The Changing Role of Professionals in Politics and Public Life*. Princeton, NJ: Princeton University Press.

Brock, D. M. (2006). "The Changing Professional Organization: A Review of Competing Archetypes," *International Journal of Management Reviews* 8(3): 157–174.

Carr-Saunders, A. M. and Wilson, P. A. (1933). *The Professions*. Oxford: Clarendon Press.

CCBE (2013). "Charter of Core Principles of the European Legal Profession and Code of Conduct for European Lawyers." <http://www.ccbe.eu/fileadmin/user_upload/NTCdocument/EN_CCBE_CoCpdf1_1382973057.pdf>.

Chappell, T. (2012). "Theories of Ethics, Overview," in *The Encyclopedia of Applied Ethics*, ed. R. Chadwick. San Diego: Academic Press, 343–353.

Cheffers, M. and Pakaluk, M. (2005). *A New Approach to Understanding Accounting Ethics*, 2nd edn. Sutton, MA: Allen David Press.

Clay, T. S. and Seeger, E. A. (2012). "Law Firms in Transition: An Altman Weil Flash Survey." <http://www.altmanweil.com/dir_docs/resource/1667e5c8-b99e-4557-93ac-73174118ea29_document.pdf>.

Coffee, J. C. Jr. (2006). *Gatekeepers: The Professions and Corporate Governance.* Oxford and New York: Oxford University Press.

Cogan, M. L. (1953). "Toward a Definition of Profession," *Harvard Educational Review* 23(1): 33–50.

Davies, C. (1983). "Professionals in Bureaucracies: The Conflict Thesis Revisited," in *The Sociology of the Professions: Lawyers, Doctors and Others,* ed. R. Dingwall and P. Lewis. London: Macmillan, 177–194.

Derber, C. (1982). "The Proletarianization of the Professional: A Review Essay," in *Professionals as Workers: Mental Labour in Advanced Capitalism,* ed. C. Derber. Boston: G. K. Hall, 13–33.

Dinovitzer, R., Gunz, H., and Gunz, S. (2014a). "Corporate Lawyers and their Clients: Walking the Line between Law and Business," *International Journal of the Legal Profession* 21(1): 3–21.

Dinovitzer, R., Gunz, H., and Gunz, S. (2014b). "Unpacking Client Capture: Evidence from Corporate Law Firms," *Journal of Professions and Organization* 1(2): 90–117.

Eisenberg, T. and Macey, J. R. (2004). "Was Arthur Andersen Different? An Empirical Examination of Major Accounting Firm Audits of Large Clients," *Journal of Empirical Legal Studies* 1(2): 263–300.

Faulconbridge, J. R. and Muzio, D. (2008). "Organizational Professionalism in Globalizing Law Firms," *Work, Employment & Society* 22(1): 7–25.

Fisher, J., Gunz, S., and McCutcheon, J. (2001). "Private/Public Interest and the Enforcement of a Code of Professional Conduct," *Journal of Business Ethics* 31(3): 191–207.

Galanter, M. (2005). *Lowering the Bar: Lawyer Jokes and Legal Culture.* Madison, WI: University of Wisconsin Press.

Galanter, M. and Henderson, W. (2008). "The Elastic Tournament: A Second Transformation of the Big Law Firm," *Stanford Law Review* 60(6): 1867–1929.

GCAAPCE (2014). "Code of Professional Conduct for Actuaries in EC Countries." <http://www.aktuarioak.org/res/ethicsCode_en.pdf>.

Greenwood, E. (1957). "Attributes of a Profession," *Social Work* 2(3): 45–55.

Gunz, H. P. and Gunz, S. P. (1994a). "Professional/Organizational Commitment and Job Satisfaction for Employed Lawyers," *Human Relations* 47(7): 801–828.

Gunz, H. P. and Gunz, S. P. (1994b). "Ethical Implications of the Employment Relationship for Professional Lawyers," *University of British Columbia Law Review* 28(1): 123–139.

Gunz, H. P. and Gunz, S. P. (2007). "Hired Professional to Hired Gun: An Identity Theory Approach to Understanding the Ethical Behaviour of Professionals in Non-Professional Organizations," *Human Relations* 60(6): 851–887.

Gunz, H. P. and Gunz, S. P. (2008). "Client Capture and the Professional Service Firm," *American Business Law Journal* 45(3): 685–721.

Gunz, H. P., Gunz, S. P., and McCutcheon, J. C. (2002). "Organizational Influences on Approaches to Ethical Decisions by Professionals: The Case of Public Accountants," *Canadian Journal of Administrative Sciences* 19(1): 76–91.

Hanlon, G. (1998). "Professionalism as Enterprise: Service Class Politics and the Redefinition of Professionalism," *Sociology* 32(1): 43–63.

Harvard Law School (2007). "Harvard Law School Program on the Legal Profession and Law Firms." <www.law.harvard.edu/programs/plp/pages/statistics.php#wlw>.

Heinz, J. P. and Laumann, E. O. (1982). *Chicago Lawyers: The Social Structure of the Bar.* New York: Russell Sage Foundation/American Bar Association.

Henderson, W. D. (2014). "From Big Law to Lean Law," *International Review of Law and Economics* 38 (Supplement): 5–16.

Hodgkinson v. Simms (1994). *S.C.R.*, 3, 377.

Hursthouse, R. (2013). "Virtue Ethics," in *The Stanford Encyclopedia of Philosophy*, ed. E. N. Zalta. <http://plato.stanford.edu/entries/ethics-virtue/>.

Jones, T. M. (1991). "Ethical Decision Making by Individuals in Organizations: An Issue-Contingent Model," *Academy of Management Review* 16(2): 366–395.

Kim, S. H. (2011). "Naked Self-Interest? Why the Legal Profession Resists Gatekeeping," *Florida Law Review* 63(1): 129–162.

King, M. F. and Bruner, G. C. (2000). "Social Desirability Bias: A Neglected Aspect of Validity Testing," *Psychology and Marketing* 17(2): 79–103.

Koehn, D. (1994). *The Ground of Professional Ethics*. New York: Routledge.

LaFollette, H. (ed.) (2003). *The Oxford Handbook of Practical Ethics*. Oxford: Oxford University Press.

Langevoort, D. C. (2012). "Getting (Too) Comfortable: In-House Lawyers, Enterprise Risk, and the Financial Crisis," *Wisconsin Law Review* 2: 495–519.

Leicht, K. T. and Fennell, M. L. (1997). "The Changing Organizational Context of Professional Work," *Annual Review of Sociology* 23: 215–231.

Leicht, K. T. and Fennell, M. L. (2001). *Professional Work: A Sociological Approach*. Malden, MA: Blackwell.

Levin, L. C. and Mather, L. (2012). *Lawyers in Practice: Ethical Decision Making in Context*. Chicago, IL: University of Chicago Press.

Libby, T. and Thorne, L. (2004). "The Identification and Categorization of Auditors' Virtues," *Business Ethics Quarterly* 14(3): 479–498.

Macdonald, K. M. (1995). *The Sociology of the Professions*. London: Sage.

McEnroe, J. E. and Martens, S. C. (2001). "Auditors' and Investors' Perceptions of the 'Expectations Gap'," *Accounting Horizons* 15: 345–358.

Macey, J. R. and Sale, H. A. (2003). "Observations on the Role of Commodification, Independence, and Governance in the Accounting Industry," *Villanova Law Review* 48(4): 1167–1187.

Malhotra, N. and Morris, T. (2009). "Heterogeneity in Professional Service Firms," *Journal of Management Studies* 46(6): 895–922.

Martin, M. W. (2000). *Meaningful Work: Rethinking Professional Ethics*. New York: Oxford University Press.

May, D. R. and Pauli, K. P. (2002). "The Role of Moral Intensity in Ethical Decision Making," *Business and Society* 41(1): 84–117.

Moore, G. E. (1903). *Principia Ethica*. London: Cambridge University Press.

Murphy, R. (1990). "Proletarianization or Bureaucratization: The Fall of the Professional?," in *The Formation of Professions: Knowledge, State and Strategy*, ed. M. Burrage and R. Torstendahl. London: Sage, 71–96.

Muzio, D. and Faulconbridge, J. R. (2013). "The Global Professional Service Firm: 'One firm' Models versus (Italian) Distant Institutionalized Practices," *Organization Studies* 34(7): 897–925.

Newton, L. (1982). "The Origins of Professionalism: Sociological Conclusions and Ethical Implications," *Business and Professional Ethics Journal* 1(4): 33–43.

Oppenheimer, M. (1973). "The Proletarianization of the Professional," in *Professionalization and Social Change*, ed. P. Halmos. Staffordshire: J. H. Books, 145–173.

Osborn, P. J. (1964). *A Concise Law Dictionary*. London: Sweet & Maxwell.

Rawls, J. (1971). *A Theory of Justice*. Cambridge, MA: Harvard University Press.

Rest, J. R. (1986). *Moral Development: Advances in Research and Theory*. New York: Praeger.

Rittenberg, L. and Covaleski, M. A. (2001). "Internalization versus Externalization of the Internal Audit Function: An Examination of Professional and Organizational Imperatives," *Accounting, Organizations and Society* 26 (7–8): 617–641.

Sayre-McCord, G. (2012). "Metaethics," in *The Stanford Encyclopedia of Philosophy*, ed. E. N. Zalta. <http://plato.stanford.edu/entries/metaethics/>.

Shafer, W. E. (2002). "Ethical Pressure, Organizational-Professional Conflict, and Related Work Outcomes among Management Accountants," *Journal of Business Ethics* 38(3): 263–275.

Simnott-Armstrong, W. (2013). "Consequentialism," in *The Stanford Encyclopedia of Philosophy*, ed. E. N. Zalta. <http://plato.stanford.edu/entries/consequentialism/>.

Smigel, E. (1964). *The Wall Street Lawyer*. New York: Free Press.

Sutton, J. (2001) *Law/Society: Origins, Interactions, and Change*. Thousand Oaks, CA: Sage.

Thompson, D. F. (2007). "What is Practical Ethics?" *Ethics at Harvard, 1987–2007*. <http://ethics.harvard.edu/what-practical-ethics>.

US Securities and Exchange Commission (2009). "Securities and Exchange Commission v. David G. Fiehling, C. P. A. and Friehling & Horowitz, C. P. A.'s, P. C., (S.D.N.Y. Civ. 09 CV 2467): SEC charges Madoff auditors with fraud. Litigation Release No. 20959 / March 18, 2009. Accounting and Auditing Enforcement Release No. 2992 / March 18, 2009." <http://www.sec.gov/litigation/litreleases/2009/lr20959.htm>.

Wallace, J. E. (1993). "Professional and Organizational Commitment: Compatible or Incompatible," *Journal of Vocational Behavior* 42(3): 333–349.

Wallace, J. E. (1995). "Organizational and Professional Commitment in Professional and Nonprofessional Organizations," *Administative Science Quarterly* 40(2): 228–255.

Wallace, J. E. and Kay, F. M. (2008). "The Professionalism of Practising Law: A Comparison Across Work Contexts," *Journal of Organizational Behavior* 29(8): 1021–1047.

Wilkins, D. B. (1992). "Who Should Regulate Lawyers?," *Harvard Law Review* 105(4): 799–887.

Winkler, E. R. (2012). "Applied Ethics Overview," in *The Encyclopedia of Applied Ethics*, ed. R. Chadwick. San Diego: Academic Press, 191–196.

Winkler, E. R. and Coombs, J. R. (eds.) (1993). *Applied Ethics: A Reader*. Cambridge, MA: Blackwell.

Wyart, A. R. (2004). "Accounting Professionalism: They Just Don't Get It!" *Accounting Horizons* 18(1): 45–53.

Zohar, D. (2005). "Safety as a Marker of Corporate Ethics," paper presented at the Nova Scotia Safety Council Conference, Halifax, Nova Scotia.

CHAPTER 7

SOURCES OF HOMOGENEITY AND HETEROGENEITY ACROSS PROFESSIONAL SERVICES

ANDREW VON NORDENFLYCHT, NAMRATA MALHOTRA, AND TIMOTHY MORRIS

7.1 INTRODUCTION

THERE is growing interest in Professional Service Firms (PSFs) among organization theorists (Empson 2001; Greenwood et al. 2006; Hinings and Leblebici 2003). PSFs are of interest because they are presumed to have characteristics that set them apart from other firms and hence demand distinctive theories of management (Greenwood et al. 2005; Hinings and Leblebici 2003; Løwendahl 2005; Maister 1993; Malhotra et al. 2006; Malhotra and Morris 2009; von Nordenflycht 2010). In the past decade, interest in PSFs has been further fueled by the notion that they are distinct in ways that will be increasingly relevant to non-PSFs. Often described as extreme examples of knowledge intensity, PSFs are seen as models for an increasingly knowledge-based economy (Empson 2007; Gardner et al. 2008; Gilson and Mnookin 1989; Greenwood et al. 2006; Hinings and Leblebici 2003; Løwendahl 2005; Maister 1982; Scott 1998; Teece 2003; Winch and Schneider 1993).

A common question that this growing field of research faces is definitional: what *is* a PSF? More specifically, what characteristics make them distinct from other types of organizations? Implicit to the existence of a field of research on professional services is an assumption that PSFs share some characteristic (or characteristics) that distinguish them from firms that are not professional services. In other words, there must be at least one important source of *homogeneity* that links all the organizations that might be considered professional services. Clearly articulating this source or sources is necessary to be able to empirically test any theories about PSFs. As von Nordenflycht (2010) pointed out, ambiguity about what these sources of homogeneity are has led to a constricted range of empirical research that focuses overwhelmingly on only two or three professional services and contains almost no cross-industry comparisons.

Of course, even as PSFs are homogeneous on some dimensions that may lead to similarities in how they are organized and managed, they vary along other dimensions that also shape how they are organized and managed. In other words, even though PSFs face a common set of characteristics that impose certain managerial challenges, the organizational outcomes that stem from those shared challenges may be quite different depending on *other* characteristics that *vary* from one industry or firm to the next—i.e., there are important sources of *heterogeneity* as well. At one level this is obvious. Nevertheless, as noted above, there is a strong tendency in the existing literature on professional services to theorize and develop research findings by studying one particular profession or industry and then to assume that such findings will necessarily hold for any other professional service. This is based on an assumption that any distinctive organizational or managerial features of a given professional service necessarily stem from the characteristics it shares with other professional services—the sources of homogeneity. But they could stem instead from features that vary across professional services—from sources of heterogeneity.

To enable more rigorous theorizing about the organization and management of PSFs we need to identify explicitly important sources of both homogeneity and heterogeneity among these firms and grasp fully how these sources impact upon the organization and management of these firms.

The purpose of this chapter is to identify key sources of homogeneity and heterogeneity among PSFs, drawing on several recent publications, including von Nordenflycht (2010) and Malhotra and Morris (2009). Von Nordenflycht (2010) synthesizes literature from the sociology of the professions as well as from economics and organization theory to identify several sources of homogeneity and heterogeneity across PSFs. Malhotra and Morris (2009) identify key sources of heterogeneity across PSFs by drawing particularly from the sociology of the professions literature.

Synthesizing these two works in addition to recent work by Zardkoohi et al. (2011), we discuss eight characteristics. We first propose that there are two principal sources of homogeneity across all PSFs: knowledge intensity and customization. Second, we identify two characteristics of professions—jurisdiction and ideology—which are core to the definition of a PSF, but whose strength varies across the broad set of PSFs. In other words, greater strength of these characteristics makes an organization "more" of a PSF (or gives it greater professional service intensity). We refer to these characteristics as sources of "definitional heterogeneity."

Third, we identify several sources of non-definitional heterogeneity—i.e., characteristics that vary across PSFs but do not define more or less professional service intensity. We first discuss two that stem from the sociology of the professions literature: the nature of knowledge (normative vs. technical) and the degree of client capture. And then we discuss two more from the management and organization theory literature: degree of face-to-face client interaction and capital intensity. For each of the eight characteristics, we define the construct, provide examples of how it varies (in the case of sources of heterogeneity), and theorize the organizational implications of the characteristic.

Variation in these characteristics—in the nature of knowledge, the degree of professionalization and/or professional social closure, capital intensity, customization, and client characteristics—is typically conceptualized as stemming from the nature of the profession itself or from the nature of its work or its regulation. Thus the variation is assumed to occur across professions or professional service industries. However, there is also important heterogeneity across firms *within* a particular professional service. We thus identify two firm-level characteristics that may drive this heterogeneity: firm *size* and firm *strategy*.

Finally, we discuss the likely influence of deregulation—such as is occurring in law in various jurisdictions around the world—on increasing heterogeneity by allowing more variation in organizational forms and providing opportunity for more variation in strategies. Our resulting framework—the characteristics and their organizational implications—is summarized in Figure 7.1.

The framework of sources of homogeneity and heterogeneity we propose should help both to interpret the generalizability of existing research and to define future research opportunities. By defining sources of homogeneity, we can more clearly define the set of firms to which our theories of PSFs should be applicable. And by defining key sources of heterogeneity, we can theorize whether and how the findings from one industry might apply to others, as well as better theorize why some professional service organizations are organized quite differently than others, despite sharing the challenges of knowledge intensity and customization. Our framework also reiterates the need for empirical work that *compares* across multiple professional service settings, especially comparing beyond law and accounting. And it points out that intra-industry variation may be as important a source of empirical variation as inter-industry variation.

7.2 SOURCES OF HOMOGENEITY: DEFINITION AND IMPLICATIONS

7.2.1 Knowledge Intensity

We define knowledge intensity as a condition in which the production of an organization's output relies on frontline workers who possess a substantial body of complex knowledge (Alvesson 2000; Starbuck 1992; von Nordenflycht 2010; Winch and Schneider 1993). To be the basis of a sustainable claim to professional status, this knowledge usually relates to some form of skill that is difficult enough to require training and reliable enough to produce results (Collins 1979: 132). Freidson (2001) calls this

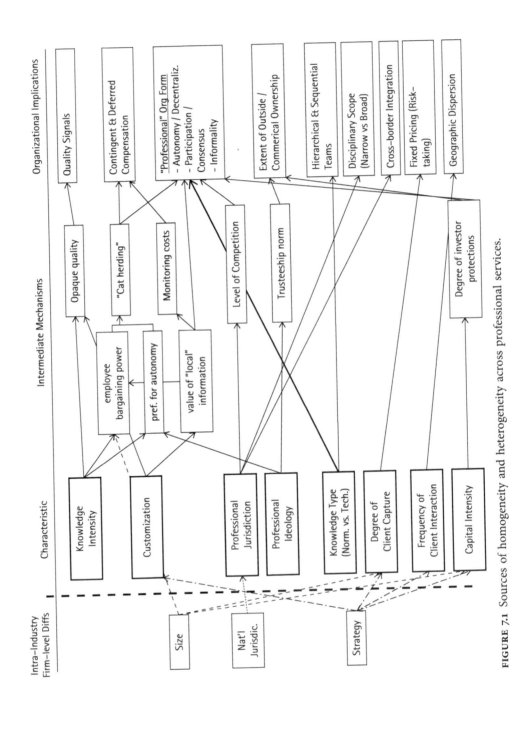

FIGURE 7.1 Sources of homogeneity and heterogeneity across professional services.

discretionary intangible skill. So a knowledge-intensive firm is one that relies on an intellectually skilled workforce, not just among its executive or support functions (e.g., R&D), but among its "frontline workers" (Alvesson 2000; Starbuck 1992).

We argue that knowledge intensity is the central or overarching characteristic of PSFs, as reflected in both the sociology of professions and management literatures. Of the explicit definitions of PSFs reviewed by von Nordenflycht (2010), 86% include some construct related to knowledge intensity. The sociological literature on professions starts from the implications of knowledge claims made by occupational groups. In other words, the ability to lay exclusive claim to an area of knowledge is a prerequisite for a sustainable claim to professional status. As Malhotra and Morris (2009: 895) note at the very outset of their analysis: Inherent to the work of all professionals is a claim over some area of expert knowledge applied in work settings (Abbott 1988; Freidson 2001; Larson 1977; Sharma 1997).

This general proposition has been the basis for developing generic frameworks applicable to the organization of PSFs across many sectors or professions, especially distinguishing from manufacturing firms (e.g., Greenwood et al. 1990).

Since knowledge in PSFs is embodied in people, knowledge intensity raises interesting managerial challenges. Maister (1982) describes a PSF as the ultimate embodiment of that familiar phrase "our assets are our people." PSFs often sell to their clients the experience and services of particular individuals and, in fact, clients often demand names of people who would be involved in delivering the service (Løwendahl 2005). Therefore, PSFs build their competencies on people, but the risk is that people can walk out of the door. Managing people as the embodiment of knowledge presents significant managerial challenges to do with hiring, training, but most importantly retaining people. Von Nordenflycht (2010) appropriately describes this as a "cat herding" challenge for PSFs.

Another related challenge that arises on account of knowledge intensity and, consequently, the high reliance on human capital, is the natural variability in quality that can occur both in the quality of the final outcome and the process of delivery of service (e.g., Campbell and Verbeke 1994). Part of what clients purchase is the process of interaction which means there is a significant intangible component involved which makes the assessment of quality very difficult for clients. As Campbell and Verbeke (1994: 96) succinctly described, "since services are performances rather than objects, they cannot be touched or seen in the same manner as goods."

This creates uncertainty in the minds of clients about the quality of the final outcome. Quality transparency and measurement problems are aggravated, especially in more process-oriented services such as engineering consulting and management consulting, where it is difficult to negotiate all parts of a contract *ex ante* and difficult to anticipate all contingencies in advance—von Nordenflycht (2010) labels this challenge as "opaque quality." We discuss below how PSFs respond to the challenges of "cat herding" and "opaque quality" organizationally.

Cat herding. By "cat herding," we refer to the challenge of retaining and directing highly skilled employees. Employees with substantial human capital (such as complex knowledge) are in a strong bargaining position relative to the firm, since their skills are scarce and, in many instances, transferable across firms (Teece 2003). Thus, employees have strong outside options, which make them hard to retain. They are also hard to direct, as scholars often argue that highly skilled individuals have strong preferences for autonomy and a consequent distaste for direction, supervision, and formal organizational processes (DeLong and Nanda 2003; Greenwood and Empson 2003; Lorsch and Tierney 2002; Starbuck 1992; Winch and Schneider 1993). Løwendahl (2005) has referred to this challenge as "herding cats." Knowledge-intensive firms may thus need to do more "guiding, nudging, and persuading," rather than commanding (Malhotra et al. 2006: 175), and find that traditional authority and compensation systems are less effective (Eccles and Crane 1988; Gilson and Mnookin 1985; Greenwood and Empson 2003; Lorsch and Tierney 2002; Maister 1993; Teece 2003).

Coff (1997) identifies a number of organizational responses to the "cat herding" challenge which fall under the broad heading of "alternative incentive mechanisms." One is *contingent compensation*: where traditional authority is problematic, various forms of contingent compensation, which link employee pay to performance outcomes, might induce employees to direct their efforts towards the interests of the firm (Coff 1997). A second is *deferred compensation*: where retention is problematic, forms of deferred compensation which induce employees to stay with the firm, such as stock options, restricted stock grants, and pensions, might be more prevalent (Roberts 2004). In this way, knowledge-intensive firms might be characterized by the broad application of compensation techniques usually reserved for senior managers at traditional firms.

Knowledge-intensive firms may also display more autonomy for employees and more informality in organizational processes, as a way to satisfy employees' preferences for autonomy (Greenwood and Empson 2003; Greenwood et al. 1990; Hinings et al. 1991; Malhotra et al. 2006; see also Leblebici and Sherer, Chapter 9, this volume). Specific manifestations of autonomy may include greater decentralization of decision-making to employees and/or greater participation of employees in firm-level decisions, which has been consistently linked to greater employee satisfaction (Coff 1997). Specific manifestations of informality include fewer formal rules and looser reporting relationships (Greenwood et al. 1990).

Opaque quality. Service quality is difficult to guarantee as it is impossible to "test-drive" a service, nor can a service be stored (Løwendahl 2005). The issue of opaqueness in quality is further compounded by the information asymmetry that exists between a professional service provider and the client. Clients perceive a lawyer or an architect or engineer with the expertise and superior knowledge, but the more specialized that expertise the more it exacerbates the gap in knowledge, making it more difficult for the client to evaluate quality. In a nutshell, the quality of an expert's output is hard for non-experts (i.e., clients) to evaluate, even after the output is produced and delivered (Løwendahl 2005).

PSFs deal with the challenge of opaque quality through mechanisms that may proxy for or signal quality. We briefly illustrate four such mechanisms: reputation; organizational routines; ethical codes, and bonding. One powerful mechanism to compensate for opaque quality of what PSFs produce and deliver is *reputation*—both the reputation of the firm and the professional reputation of the professionals in the firm. The track record and brand name of a PSF matter. Further, reputation of individual professionals, for example, the "star" engineer; the "highly regarded" partner in a law firm, etc. can allay doubts in the mind of clients. Importantly, the prevalence of autonomy, particularly to senior professionals in the conduct of client relationships, is likely to reinforce the importance of individual-level reputations of professionals. Having said that, while individual professionals first build their reputation through their personal rapport with the client, the firm acquires a reputation of its own through the people that comprise it (Malhotra 2003).

Eventually, a well-established reputation of the firm as a whole can override or at least mitigate reliance upon reputations of individual professionals. Malhotra (2003) argues that it is a PSF's history of experience and exposure to the variety of client problems and interactions with clients that serve to enhance clients' trust in the firm. These are the building blocks of reputation that signals high quality in the eyes of the clients (Greenwood et al. 2005; Løwendahl 2005; Nanda 2003). Firm reputation also has the positive effect of overcoming opportunistic behavior of individual professionals as clients eventually come to the "firm" because they trust in the brand (Malhotra 2003). In a sense, the role of firm reputation not only helps counter the challenges of opaque quality but also to an extent mitigates the problem of cat herding by reducing reliance on individual professionals. For example, an engineering design consultant notes, "They [engineers] can certainly leverage on their association with a brand name firm but cannot match the greater history of experience of the firm" (Malhotra 2003: 953).

A second mechanism is the development of *organizational routines* that help mitigate variability in quality or ensure consistency. Knowledge embodied in individual professionals over time accumulates to become a part of the firm's repertoire of knowledge. Individual creativity contributes to the growth of collective knowledge (Nonaka and Takeuchi 1995). At this point firms develop organizational routines and coordinating mechanisms which lend stability and provide a structure that ensures greater predictability in quality of the service outcome and process of delivery. These routines capture the experiential knowledge of organizing, managing, and coordinating expertise to produce and deliver a client solution (Malhotra 2003). Again the development of organizational routines not only deals with the challenge of opaque quality but also mitigates the cat herding problem. When a firm as a collective accumulates knowledge, and learns and develops routines as an entity, the line blurs between the individual professional and the professional firm. Over time clients come back to the "firm" even if the people change (Malhotra 2003).

Third, scholars have also suggested that *ethical codes* are a way to signal quality (Leicht and Lyman 2006; Nanda 2003; see also Dinovitzer et al., Chapter 6, this volume). Experts pledge to uphold a code of conduct whose goal is to protect clients' interests, and their adherence to this code is enforced by the experts' professional association. Since ethical codes are one of the core features of a profession (Nanda 2003), the professionalization of an occupation (described in more detail later) may be a response to opaque quality, as implied by the asymmetry of expertise argument in the professions literature (Abbott 1988; Gross and Kieser 2006; Parsons 1939).

Lastly, *bonding* mechanisms include organizational features that guarantee quality by creating penalties for producing low quality. For example, scholars have argued that quality might be ensured by organizing as an unlimited liability partnership which induces partners to monitor and pressure each other to provide quality service, since each is at risk for any actions of the others that expose the firm to financial or legal liability (Greenwood and Empson 2003; see also Leblebici and Sherer, Chapter 9, this volume).

In summary, knowledge intensity is the primary source of homogeneity across professional services. It raises several managerial challenges that may be linked to a range of distinctive organizational outcomes, including high levels of contingent compensation, deferred compensation, autonomy and informality, as well as field- or industry-level outcomes, including particularly important roles for status and for ethical codes.

7.3 CUSTOMIZATION

Customization refers to the idea that PSFs generally apply their human capital to a client's specific situation, rather than producing the same standardized outputs for multiple clients. Customization is also frequently proposed as a defining characteristic of PSFs (Løwendahl 2005). It was the second most mentioned characteristic, behind knowledge intensity, in the definitions of PSFs reviewed by von Nordenflycht (2010). Zardkoohi et al. (2011) in fact imply that customization is a critical omission in von Nordenflycht's (2010) framework for defining PSFs.

We argue that customization, like knowledge intensity, is a defining source of homogeneity across PSFs. Customization entails bundling knowledge, held by individual professionals and collectively in the firm, in myriad ways to address different clients' unique problems (Jones et al. 1998; Morris and Empson 1998). All PSFs produce customized output to some degree (and not customizing would, in fact, suggest that a firm is not a PSF). That said, we also acknowledge that the level of customization vs. standardization of a firm's output is a common dimension of differentiation in several professional service contexts (Hansen et al. 1999; Maister 1993).

Maister (1982) notes that PSFs can sell three things and a firm may specialize in any one of these three Es: expertise, experience, or their execution capability. On one end of the continuum are services that are highly customized based on creativity and innovativeness to solve non-routine problems; and on the other end are services that involve more standard procedures to solve routine problems. For example, auditing is relatively more standardized than engineering and architectural designs for buildings. So customization can also be a source of heterogeneity *among* PSFs. It is also important to note that what may look like a standard solution in terms of the application of expertise may involve greater customization on the execution front depending on specific circumstances of the client.

The primary organizational implications of customized output are actually the same as those of knowledge intensity. In fact, customization in some ways exacerbates the challenges posed by knowledge intensity. It increases the cat herding challenge by increasing employees' bargaining power vis-à-vis the organization for several reasons. One, it reduces the amount of alienable assets that the firm can own, since there is no standardized product whose rights or inventories are owned by the firm. Two, the more customized the output, the more important employees' judgment and discretion is in producing and tailoring that output (Løwendahl 2005)—i.e., the organization is even more tightly tied to the skills and efforts of employees when output is customized. Three, customization increases the value of local, idiosyncratic information, especially about specific clients, which makes employees' work harder to monitor (Zardkoohi et al. 2011). All of these conditions may increase the value of—and hence organizations' use of—contingent and deferred compensation as well as individual autonomy. Zardkoohi et al. (2011) argue that customization may also drive high levels of employee autonomy not just as an incentive mechanism (i.e., satisfying skilled employees' preferences for autonomy) but also to allow organizations to exploit the local, idiosyncratic information that employees have, which is more valuable the more that output is customized.

Customized output also increases the opaqueness of quality. A high degree of customization suggests that there is a greater element of innovativeness to respond to different clients' idiosyncratic needs. This only aggravates the problem of assessing and measuring quality as there are no clear benchmarks. Since there is no product produced in advance, customers cannot inspect the final product before buying it and experiencing it. It also creates more ambiguity, further widening the information asymmetry between the professional service provider and the client. What's more, Løwendahl (2005) points out that customization can often require high-quality inputs from the customers themselves, such as accurate information and appropriate usage, which further complicates the ability to assess the quality of what the firm produced.

Thus, customization amplifies the challenges and organizational responses induced by knowledge intensity.

7.4 Professionalization as a Source of "Definitional Heterogeneity": Jurisdictional Control and Professional Ideology

Given that our central construct, PSF, contains the term "professional," one might be surprised that "professionalization" is listed as a source of heterogeneity, rather than homogeneity. In fact, the sociological literature identifies three characteristics of professions relevant to our discussion: a distinct base of knowledge or expertise; social control or claims over the use of that knowledge, aka "jurisdiction"; and an ideology that embodies norms that are central to what professionals do and how they conduct themselves. So the knowledge intensity construct, which we identified as the central source of homogeneity—the foundational characteristic of PSFs—in fact derives from one essential feature of professions. Our discussion of professionalization as a source of heterogeneity focuses on the latter two characteristics: the degree of a profession's control and the strength of its ideology.

We describe these two sources of heterogeneity as "definitional heterogeneity." We use this term to describe characteristics that clearly vary across the set of organizations considered PSFs but that nonetheless are often considered to define or distinguish PSFs. For instance, the jurisdictional control over a defined body of knowledge may be considered a defining feature of professions, and hence, of PSFs. But at the same time, many industries with very low or non-existent jurisdictional control are often considered professional services, such as management consulting and advertising. Von Nordenflycht (2010) suggests a useful way to interpret these characteristics: that they define increasing *degrees of professional service intensity*. In other words, firms that have high levels of the "definitional heterogeneity" factors are the "most" professional service-like, whereas firms that face lower levels of them are "less" professional service-like, though can still reasonably be considered professional services as long as knowledge intensity applies. By contrast, sources of "non-definitional heterogeneity," which we discuss in later sections, do not define more or less degrees of professional service intensity. Variation in those characteristics is simply theorized to lead to different types of organizational responses, but not to define stronger vs. weaker forms of PSF.

7.5 PROFESSIONAL JURISDICTION

As noted above, a central feature of a profession is exclusive control over the application of an area of knowledge in a domain of work activities, what Abbott (1988) labeled a jurisdiction. Jurisdictional control is a form of social closure that allows a profession to exclude rivals, protect their privileges, and defend against incursions into their territory (Macdonald 1985, 1995). Jurisdiction entails the formation of professional institutions that accredit members, establish and monitor standards of professional behavior, and have some degree of disciplinary control over members. And in the archetypal profession, this certification is backed by the state, such that no one can legally practice the profession without certification by the association (Gross and Kieser 2006). In essence this means that a profession has a self-regulated monopoly (Freidson 1970; Larson 1977).

However, jurisdictional control does not automatically follow from the possession of a knowledge base. Success in maintaining a jurisdiction requires that the profession withstands challenges from other occupations and, where necessary, mobilizes to confront new problems in its domain of work. Larson (1977) calls this the professional mobility project. Such a project is a continuing process in which a collective actor, a profession, seeks to secure a monopoly of a market, both by restricting supply and legitimizing status inequality. Heterogeneity across expert occupations may emerge on account of both the nature of the occupations' work as well as idiosyncratic historical contingencies. For example, engineering, while being strongly grounded in a technical knowledge base, has not been able to preserve its social closure, partly because it needed relatively large capital infusions which were more amenable to corporate funding and partly because of its fragmented origins across different specializations.

By contrast, law has generally been seen as a strong profession because it has been able to establish tight jurisdictional control over the areas of work associated with legal knowledge and to define what work can be undertaken by other occupations, usually in subordinate roles and in lower status areas of law (Abel 1989). And on the other end of the spectrum of jurisdictional control, management consulting has no dominant professional association and no association controls the ability to practice consulting or stipulates how consultancies can be organized. So the extent of social closure and jurisdictional control can and does vary across knowledge-intensive fields.

Variations in the degree of jurisdictional control, or social closure, may lead to different organizational characteristics. First, professions with strong social closure will be more likely to limit the range of specialties within the firm to the core profession and resist diversification; conversely, firms in professions with weaker social closure will tend to be multidisciplinary, expanding beyond the core profession (Malhotra and Morris 2009).

Second, jurisdictional control may vary in terms of how constrained it is geographically. For instance, law tends to be regulated at a national level, such that lawyers of a given nationality are not automatically permitted to practice law in other countries. This relates to the fact that laws tend to be nation-specific. By contrast, technical knowledge is more or less universal, being based on scientific laws. The degree to which jurisdictions permeate geographic boundaries will shape the degree of geographic centralization of multinational organizations. Where jurisdiction extends across national boundaries, firms can adopt global structures in which national offices collaborate closely using standardized methodologies. So, for instance, as accounting standards have been increasingly harmonized around the world, greater geographic permeability has been possible which has been conducive to the global expansion of the largest accounting firms. In contrast, where jurisdiction is constrained within specific geographies, as in law, firms cannot adopt such tight organizational structures and are more likely to use networks to deliver transnational services. Recent studies also suggest that large law firms try to respond to limitations on account of jurisdictional boundaries by adopting integrative mechanisms at the work practice level (e.g., Muzio and Faulconbridge 2013; Smets et al. 2012).

Third, the strength of a jurisdiction influences the degree of competition within a profession. First, control over certification erects significant entry barriers into the occupation or industry. Second, control over behavior and conduct codes is employed to mute competition *among* professionals. Unfettered competition among providers of professional services is often seen as a threat to the trustworthiness of professionals in the eyes of clients, as it is argued to encourage deterioration in the quality of service provided (Torres 1991). So in the name of preserving the profession's trustworthiness, professional codes tend to prohibit a range of commercially competitive behavior, including soliciting competitors' clients, any advertising (Cox et al. 1982; Torres 1991), and even competing on price (Morrison and Wilhelm 2008; Torres 1991).

In turn, the degree of competition shapes the degree of organizational slack (Cyert and March 1963) or inefficiency (Tirole 1988) that firms can operate with: the lower the competition, the higher the slack (i.e., the lower the need for efficiency). More slack provides an opportunity to address the challenges of cat herding in ways that would not be possible in more competitive environments. For example, firms may be better able to satisfy employee preferences for autonomy by adopting highly informal structures, whose consequent lack of internal coordination might be too inefficient in more competitive environments. Thus, the third organizational implication of strong jurisdictional control may further increase the amount of autonomy and informality (which was already theorized to stem from both knowledge intensity and customization).

7.6 PROFESSIONAL IDEOLOGY

A professional ideology consists of a set of norms, manifested both in explicit ethical codes enforced by professional associations and in internalized preferences often developed during professional training (Leicht and Lyman 2006). One of the central professional norms is a strong preference for autonomy (Alvesson and Kärreman 2006; Bailyn 1985; Briscoe 2007; Freidson 1970; Hall 1968; Lipartito and Miranti 1998; Scott 1965). Thus, one organizational implication of variation in the strength of professional ideology should be variation in the degree of employee autonomy within organizations.

A second core professional norm is the idea that professionals have a responsibility to protect the interests of clients and/or society in general. This norm—described with various labels such as "conflict of interest" (Nanda 2003), "altruistic service" (Løwendahl 2005), or "trusteeship" (Brint 1994; Greenwood and Suddaby 2005)—is at the core of professional codes of ethics and is often contrasted against a "commercial" or "economic" ethos which allows unfettered pursuit of self-interest (Greenwood et al. 2006; Lipartito and Miranti 1998).

One managerial implication of this *trusteeship norm* is the existence of normative and coercive prohibitions against organizational forms that are perceived to threaten trusteeship behavior. A primary example is a resistance to having non-professionals, especially commercially-oriented non-professionals (such as investors), involved in the ownership and governance of professional firms (von Nordenflycht 2014). This is intended to prevent the introduction of pressures that might compromise the interests of clients. In some cases, the professional code expressly prohibits non-professionals from sharing ownership in professional firms. In other cases, such as hospitals, organizing as a non-profit is another way to minimize commercially-oriented governance (Hansmann 1996).

Thus, heterogeneity across occupations or industries in the strength of the professional ideology could be expected to drive differences in the degree of employee autonomy inside organizations and in the presence and/or extent of commercially-oriented, non-professional ownership of organizations.

7.7 Sources of "Non-Definitional Heterogeneity" from the Sociology of Professions

7.7.1 Nature of Knowledge Base

While we propose that knowledge intensity is the central source of homogeneity across PSFs, we also note that differences in the nature of a profession's knowledge may be a key source of organizational heterogeneity.

Halliday (1987) proposed that the different epistemological bases of professional knowledge were key to understanding differences among professions. Building on Halliday's typology, Malhotra and Morris (2009) show how these differences in nature of knowledge affect the conduct of professional work and, in turn, the organization of PSFs.

The starting point is to differentiate two different kinds of knowledge: *normative* and *technical*. Normative knowledge is primarily concerned with matters of value (what ought to be the value) while technical knowledge, as deployed by scientific professions, is concerned with matters of fact (what is the case) (Halliday 1987). A third category—syncretic knowledge—describes knowledge bases that utilize both normative and technical knowledge.

Malhotra and Morris (2009) outline how differences in the nature of knowledge, that is, normative, technical, or syncretic, influence the internal organizational structure of PSFs. Specifically, firms in professions with a normative knowledge base, such as law, are more likely to use the professional partnership form, with its high levels of individual autonomy and wide participation in firm-level decision-making. Firms within a profession with a technical knowledge base, such as engineering consulting, are more likely to have a bureaucratic organization form. They argue that this is because technical knowledge is more amenable to analyzability and has well-understood formulae and processes. Firms in those professions with syncretic knowledge bases, such as accounting, are likely to operate with a hybrid professional-bureaucratic form because they combine elements of highly codified formal audit processes with a need for some exercise of judgment within ambiguous contexts (Malhotra and Morris 2009: 904).

Further, the knowledge base influences the nature of team production in PSFs: normative underpinnings tend to lead to more hierarchically and sequentially organized team structures because of the need for senior professional judgment. Conversely, more technical knowledge predicts more lateral and consensual processes at the team level because of the project-based nature of work involving multiple specialties and closely interdependent tasks in which the consequences of a change in one area of work have to be calculated across the other specialties. Thus, firms within professions with a technical knowledge base combine bureaucratic features with strong lateral work processes and flexible structures.

7.8 CLIENT CAPTURE

It is generally argued that the expert knowledge of the professional creates a dependency relationship with the consumer or client (Greenwood et al. 2005; Starbuck 1992). However, an inversion of this argument in the sociological literature is that powerful clients can control professions (Johnson 1972). This has been called client capture and refers to the degree to which clients can control or influence the process of production of a professional service, including its costs, timing, and delivery (Leicht and Fennell 2001; Dinovitzer et al., Chapter 6, this volume). Client capture is most likely to occur where the professional works for large corporate clients or important brokers in a network and is either dependent on maintaining good relations to secure further work or finds that the resource expertise of the client matches that of the professional advisor.

Client capture will influence pricing models. Where the degree of client capture is high, the client is more likely to be able to determine the pricing method for the professional's work. In engineering consulting, while the client is dependent on the high technical expertise of the engineer in determining important risk factors, such as the stress loads on a bridge, the client is in a powerful market position in relation to the advisor. In this situation the client is likely to be able to impose their preferred method of pricing, by fixing a fee for work *ex ante*. The advantage to the client of doing this is that it reduces the risk to the client in buying a service which is complex and often delivered over a long period of time and therefore contains inherent uncertainties (Sharma 1997). The fixed pricing system has also likely been reinforced by the unavoidable structural overlap that has occurred as engineering firms have been continuously exposed to structures and systems of other contracting and non-professional firms in the course of organizing their service (e.g., Thornton et al. 2005).

Where client capture is lower, the client cannot so easily impose control over the risks inherent in buying a complex service over a period of time. This means that the professional is more likely to be able to sustain a pricing model in which the uncertainties inherent to production are absorbed by the client by a variable pricing system. In such cases, the typical pricing system is based on the input of professionals' time, either in hourly rates or some other time division.

7.9 SOURCES OF "NON-DEFINITIONAL HETEROGENEITY" FROM THE MANAGEMENT AND ORGANIZATIONS LITERATURE

7.9.1 Extent of Face-to-Face Client Interaction

We identified customization as a shared distinctive characteristic of PSFs: that PSFs apply their knowledge base to the specific circumstances of a given client. The process of customizing application of expertise to different clients' problems requires interaction between the client and service provider. *Interaction* is thus an important part of the whole package of delivering a customized service. Malhotra and Morris (2009) argue that there is variation across professional services in the importance of *face-to-face* interaction with clients, or at least variation in the frequency with which this interaction is needed to complete a professional task. For example, in the case of law firms face-to-face interaction between the client and lawyers is relatively limited. Lawyers' technical skills are based on the ability to make sense of large amounts of written documentation, to draft with great attention to detail and legal precision, and to assess the logic and implications of legal propositions and develop arguments (e.g., Halpin 2000). Thus, lawyers can perform these activities spatially separated from the client, needing to engage in face-to-face interaction relatively infrequently. In contrast, engineering consulting firms require a much greater degree of interaction with their clients. Much of their work is project-based which typically comprises several phases including pre-bidding, bidding, conceptual design, detailed engineering, and supervision and management of construction. The design phase and the supervision and management of construction especially require frequent face-to-face interaction with clients. Also, firms that go through a bidding process often prefer to do some preliminary ground work to build a rapport with the client before bidding for the project and some firms prefer not to engage in a bidding process at all, as a senior engineer in a design services firm notes: "a lot of our success has been because we don't get into bids, rather we get the work handed to us on a relationship basis" (Malhotra 2003: 943). An important facilitator of relationship building is face-to-face interaction with the client. Importantly, projects are not static but dynamic and unfolding, requiring deliberations with the client as unanticipated contingencies arise. The more knowledgeable client expects a higher degree of consultation and participation while the client who is less knowledgeable expects hand-holding and continuous assurances (Malhotra and Hinings 2010: 342).

Overall, engineering consulting firms require more face-to-face interaction with clients than law firms do. Accounting firms present yet another variation. When we consider the delivery of auditing services in particular, there are well-defined rules that require the service provider to minimize the role of the client in the delivery of that service, even though the process of conducting an audit task occurs on the client's premises.

Over time, however, collaboration and interaction with the client has become important in delivering audit services (e.g., Barrett et al. 2005). Auditing firms have to continuously balance the need to maintain a distance from the client while being on the premises in the course of an audit task and the need to interact with the client outside of the audit task. In summary, the frequency of face-to-face interaction is likely to be higher in the conduct of their professional work compared to lawyers but less than engineering consultants (Malhotra and Morris 2009).

Organizationally, variation in the extent of face-to-face interaction required has implications for physical presence required to enable proximity to the client. Physical presence takes the form of the number and geographical dispersion of offices in each sector. Law firms, for example, have a limited number of offices concentrated in a few locations. Engineering consulting firms cater to a spatially dispersed distribution of projects through a network of temporary project-based and permanent regional offices (e.g., Fenton and Pettigrew 2000). The structure is relatively fluid and fluctuating as the configuration of project-based offices changes as projects are completed and new ones begin (Malhotra and Hinings 2010). Accounting firms have a widely dispersed network of permanent offices at client locations along with regional offices and headquarters. The structure is relatively permanent due to the repetitive nature of client tasks.

7.10 CAPITAL INTENSITY

Capital intensity refers to the extent to which an organization's production involves significant amounts of non-human assets, such as inventory, factories, and equipment.

Capital intensity is independent of knowledge intensity: one can imagine firms whose production requires *both* an intellectually skilled workforce *and* significant non-human assets (e.g., hospitals, where a large fraction of the workforce has advanced degrees, but non-human capital, such as medical equipment and a large, specialized building, is also critical). Thus, within the universe of knowledge-intensive organizations, there can be (and is) heterogeneity in the degree of capital intensity. For example, as alluded to in the earlier discussions of jurisdictional control and types of knowledge, the engineering occupation has tended to require substantial amounts of capital investment to complete its production process, in contrast to law and accounting. This in turn has been theorized to help explain the lower degree of social closure in engineering.

For knowledge-intensive firms, capital intensity has two important implications. First, like knowledge intensity and customization, it influences employee bargaining power for three reasons. If production does not require much capital, employees' skills become even more important. Employees' outside options also increase as they can more easily start up their own firms. And without non-human capital to specialize to, there is less likelihood of generating firm-specific human capital which would reduce employee mobility (Teece 2003). Where knowledge intensity creates the cat herding problem, low capital intensity turns it into a situation where *the assets go down the elevator each night* (Coff 1997; Lorsch and Tierney 2002; Scott 1998) and the organization can't control whether they come back.

Capital intensity also drives the need for raising investment funds. And the need to raise investment has organizational implications because of the need to protect outside investors. For example, attracting outside investment likely requires allocating a substantial share of equity to outside investors. It may also require firms to be more centralized and formalized, in order to maintain greater control over the firm so as to assuage investors' concerns about having their funds expropriated (Masten 2006). By contrast, an absence of outside investment would allow *all* of the firm's equity to be allocated to employees to maximize the effect of contingent and deferred compensation. And it would allow firms to adopt more autonomy and informality, to better satisfy employee preferences. Thus, among knowledge-intensive firms, variation in their level of capital intensity is hypothesized to affect the intensity of their use of alternative incentive mechanisms, including contingent and deferred compensation and autonomy and informality, as well as the likelihood or extent of outside ownership.

7.11 HETEROGENEITY WITHIN AN INDUSTRY: FIRM SIZE AND STRATEGY

We now discuss heterogeneity *within* industries or settings. In general, the heterogeneity identified above—in the degree of jurisdictional control, strength of professional ideology, nature of knowledge, degree of client capture, degree of client interaction, and capital intensity—is conceptualized as stemming from the nature of the profession itself, either from its work or its regulation. Thus the variation is assumed to occur across professions or professional service industries. However, there is also important heterogeneity on these dimensions across firms within a particular professional service. We identify two firm-level characteristics that may drive this heterogeneity: firm *size* and firm *strategy*. Finally, we discuss the likely influence of deregulation—such as is occurring in law in various jurisdictions around the world—in increasing heterogeneity by allowing more variation in organizational forms and providing opportunity for more variation in strategies.

7.11.1 Firm Size

Variations in the size of PSFs may drive variations in at least two of the aforementioned characteristics: the degree of client capture and capital intensity. Client capture occurs where PSFs are highly dependent on a few large clients. Larger PSFs are likely to be less dependent on a few clients than smaller firms, simply because the larger firms are closer in size to the large clients. Thus, pricing models that shift risk to the clients are more likely to be observed among larger PSFs. It should be noted, however, that this may not be the case in professional service contexts where there is "size differentiation," as described by von Nordenflycht (2011). In some professional service markets, clients tend to seek service providers whose relative size is similar to their own size, relative to other clients: they want providers that are large enough to have the capability to service their size and scope, but not so large that the client is a small fish who won't get any attention. Thus, firms and their clients "match" on size. In such contexts, the degree of dependence on a few clients may not actually vary across the size of the PSFs.

Firm size may also influence the degree of capital intensity. As size increases, firms tend to need to adapt to changes in scale and scope. Larger firms are likely to adopt more managerial modes with greater emphasis on strategic planning and control of professionals' activities that displace the limited control over strategic direction and day-to-day activities of individual partners, characteristic of the traditional professional partnership model (Greenwood et al. 1990). In adding scope (e.g., more office locations; more practices) and managerial processes, firms will tend to increase the amount of "non-producing" overheads—office expenses and personnel that do not directly generate client revenue. This increases the requirements for working capital and investment—thus, the larger firm tends to be more capital intensive than the smaller firm. As noted earlier, greater capital intensity reduces employee bargaining power—as human capital contributions represent a smaller fraction of the firm's productive inputs—and thus reduces the cat herding problem.

Larger firm size may also reduce the cat herding problem directly, as a given individual professional is, arguably, less important to a larger firm than to a smaller firm. Finally, as noted above, larger firm size tends to be accompanied by greater managerial routines, further reducing the bargaining power of individual employees. Overall, then, larger firms may face a less intense cat herding problem, ultimately leading to less frequent and/or less intensive use of the various managerial responses to the cat herding problem, e.g., contingent compensation, deferred compensation, informality, etc.

There is an interesting irony around the size and growth of PSFs. PSFs pursue growth partly to satisfy the demands of junior professionals for promotion to partner (Galanter and Palay 1991; Gilson and Mnookin 1989; Malos and Campion 2000; Morris and Pinnington 1998; see also Cohen, Chapter 16, this volume). Yet, where size leads to greater managerial control, this is likely to impact upon the desire for autonomy which underlies the cat herding problem outlined above. Stronger control may lead to tighter coordination of activities between partners but at the price of some loss of motivation.

7.11.2 Firm Strategy

Like variation in firm size, variation in strategic positions can also lead to variations in some of the eight characteristics identified earlier, as well as to variation in other outcomes. Strategy in the PSF context has two primary aspects. First, PSFs make strategic choices about the nature of work they pursue; and second, they make choices about their geographic and functional scope.

Maister (1993) categorizes the nature of professional work along three Es: more procedural type of work in a firm requires good Execution capabilities; work entailing creativity requires Expertise as the key capability; and work that requires "gray hair" reflects breadth of Experience of professionals. Firms within the same sector may focus predominantly on one type of work or another; while some may pursue some complex mix of work. Variation in the nature of the work should have implications for the degree of knowledge intensity, customization, and capital intensity. For instance, firms pursuing procedural work will likely adopt more managerial routines and administrative overheads, relative to those relying on expertise or experience of individual professionals. Thus, the former firms will likely face lower knowledge intensity and customization, and higher capital intensity. This in turn means the procedural/execution-based firms will feature fewer of the alternative incentive arrangements that we identified as responding to the cat herding challenge central to professional services.

In addition, strategic differences in the choice of type of work to pursue will lead to differences in firms' internal architectures, specifically the relative mix of seniors (finders), managers (minders), and juniors (grinders) (Maister 1982). In partnership structures, the ratio between associates and partners—referred to as leverage—needs to be aligned (e.g., Galanter and Palay 1991). Firms pursuing more expertise-based work are likely to maintain low leverage structures, while those pursuing more efficiency-based work will have highly leveraged structures (e.g., Maister 1993).

The second aspect of strategy is concerned with the extent to which firms pursue a diversification strategy, expanding into new services and into new geographic areas (e.g., Nayyar 1993; Nelson 1988). We have noted that some professions, such as law, tend not to move outside their core professional base but others, such as accounting, have moved into contiguous areas. Law strategy has therefore largely been concerned with the scope of practices within the legal field and with geographic diversification. Large accounting firms have pursued service diversification into tax, consulting, and advisory work, areas that are not traditionally staffed by professionalized workforces.

Diversifying into new geographic areas can serve as a trigger for adding new services important in that area, thus expanding the portfolio of services generating economies of scope. Similarly, new services can serve as a launching pad for entering new geographic areas, creating economies of scale (e.g., Hitt et al. 2001). The two forms of diversification require specific managerial skills and structures to adequately manage the diversity (e.g., Markides and Williamson 1996) and in a PSF the extent of diversification is likely to have ramifications for the composition of human capital in terms of skills or capabilities and the organization of human capital (e.g., Hitt et al. 2001; Løwendahl 2005; Samuelson and Jaffe 1990). Firms with a higher degree of diversification (service and geographic) require a greater pool of experiential firm-specific tacit knowledge usually held by senior managers or partners, high social capital and prestige, as well as elite networks of these professionals derived from the quality of the schools/universities they attended (Hitt et al. 2001). This implies greater knowledge intensity.

In addition to differences in the degree of relational and managerial capabilities there are other organizational implications. Hitt et al. (2001) note in a study investigating the effect of human capital on diversification strategy of law firms, that achieving the benefits of economies of scope and scale through the simultaneous pursuit of service and geographic diversification, requires significant coordination across specialized service teams (units of specialized legal services) and across geographic locations. There is evidence from accounting and engineering design firms as well of how pursuing diversification, geographic and service, involves a continuous balancing of centralizing certain functions, making knowledge held by human capital accessible, and maintaining the flexibility to personalize the service (e.g., Malhotra and Hinings 2010; Rose and Hinings 1999). Hence, there is likely to be a high degree of variation in structural complexity among firms within the same sector depending on the extent of diversification they pursue.

Further, in highly diversified firms senior professionals are likely to be relatively more motivated to leverage their capabilities and have elaborate mentoring and training for juniors to continuously build and sustain the necessary capabilities. At the same time, a greater scale and scope also means greater managerial controls in the firm. So while the greater importance of experienced senior professionals in a diversified firm increases the employee bargaining power and the cat herding problem, this greater need for managerial controls to coordinate across broad geographic and functional scope implies a reduction in the bargaining power of individual professionals. The net effect of these countervailing influences on the organizational features on more diversified PSFs is an open empirical question.

It is important to note that the two aspects of PSF strategy—type of work and diversification—are not mutually exclusive. As a firm diversifies, it is also likely to take on a more complex mix of different types of work. Thus, firms within the same professional services sector will exhibit heterogeneity in their configuration and composition of resources and capabilities, which are essentially centered on human capital, and their structural complexity depending on the extent of diversification and the mix of types of work (expertise-based, experience-based, or efficiency-based) that dominates the strategy of each firm.

7.12 DEREGULATION

One trend that is likely to increase intra-industry variation among firms is greater deregulation of professions. For instance in some countries such as the UK and parts of Australia, legal controls on ownership of law firms have been relaxed thereby permitting external ownership and funding. As we have argued above, the relatively low capital intensity of many PSFs means that external capital injections are not required for day-to-day operations, but these changes in the regulatory framework may well mean that firms take advantage by bringing in outside investors. These new owners are likely to be a source of innovation in several ways, such as introducing forms of management that address the cat herding/incentive design issue, using novel templates that take different approaches to the autonomy preference of incumbent professionals, and, strategically, seeking out entry into different jurisdictions; that is, diversifying across professions as well as geographies, as well as looking at different ways of organizing professional work. Deregulation and new sources of capital may also mean that the growth opportunities of firms change so that existing patterns of size differences within particular professions change, perhaps through industry consolidation or by the hiring of teams of professionals to grow existing or new practices. Thus, exogenous factors such as deregulation are likely to have a substantial impact on intra-industry variation among PSFs by affecting their strategic ambitions as well as their management and organization.

7.13 CONCLUSIONS

The purpose of this chapter is to provide definitional clarity to the term Professional Service Firm in order to understand what exactly makes this group of organizations distinct from others and to aid further theorizing about the implications of this distinctiveness. As we noted at the outset, the existing literature has tended not to address this problem properly, even though it is frequently recognized that there are obvious differences between firms that are commonly included within the definition of a PSF such as whether the members of the firm belong to a formal profession. Further, much scholarship has compounded this problem either by implicitly or explicitly generalizing from organizations within a limited group of professions, such as law or consulting, and by failing to undertake comparative analysis across firms in different occupations. A fundamental challenge for fruitful theorizing about PSFs is therefore that we establish clearly the basis on which a set of firms can properly be included within the scope of professional services as well as the nature of differences between them. We did this by systematically outlining the sources of homogeneity and heterogeneity across PSFs and their implications for the way these firms are organized. Our framework is summarized in Figure 7.1.

By drawing on and synthesizing several recent papers in the professional service literature, this chapter has proposed an enhanced framework that identifies sources of homogeneity and heterogeneity across the universe of professional service organizations, as well as the organizational and managerial implications of these factors. This enhanced framework of sources of homogeneity and heterogeneity makes several key contributions, both to interpreting the generalizability of existing research and to guiding future research.

First, it defines what exactly is distinctive about the PSF as an organizational form from other types of organization. Doing this means we can define more clearly the set of firms which are included in this broad term and where the boundary conditions of theories of the PSF can be established. We can also predict where likely differences, that is heterogeneity, among PSFs are likely to lie and explain why these occur.

Second, the framework has several implications for the design of future research. We note that many of the eight characteristics discussed here have overlapping organizational implications. For instance, as can be seen in Figure 7.1, five of the eight characteristics—knowledge intensity, customization, jurisdiction, type of knowledge, and capital intensity—are hypothesized to influence the extent to which organizations use the "professional partnership" form, especially autonomy and informality. Thus, the archetypal distinctive organizational features of PSFs are over-determined: *ex ante*, we cannot link them to one specific characteristic. This analysis, then, reiterates the need for empirical comparisons across these dimensions of heterogeneity—especially beyond just law, accounting, and consulting—to help assess the various theoretical propositions embodied in this framework.

Furthermore, by focusing the definition of PSFs on characteristics, rather than on lists of specific industries, the framework may help explain within-industry variation in organizational structures—such as the fact that some two-thirds of UK law firms do not use the up-or-out promotion system so commonly associated with law firms (Morris and Pinnington 1998). At the very least, this framework points to such intra-industry variation as another important source for comparative empirical work. We have therefore identified two sources of intra-industry variation, firm size and strategy, and proposed that these factors need to be considered in future studies when seeking to understand differences and similarities between PSFs.

Finally, we note that exogenous factors will also influence both strategy and size considerations and we discuss how one such factor, the deregulation of ownership that is starting to occur in certain professions, is likely to play out by increasing the variation between firms. Using this framework and showing the dynamic interactions between its components can provide the means by which scholars can undertake systematic comparisons across firms and professions to build more theoretically robust propositions about the nature and distinctiveness of the PSF.

REFERENCES

Abbott, A. (1988). *The System of Professions: An Essay on the Division of Expert Labor.* Chicago, IL: University of Chicago Press.

Abel, R. (1989). "Comparative Sociology of Legal Professions," in *Lawyers in Society, Volume 3: Comparative Theories*, ed. R. Abel and P. Lewis. Berkeley, CA: University of California Press, 80–153.

Alvesson, M. (2000). "Social Identity and the Problem of Loyalty in Knowledge-Intensive Companies," *Journal of Management Studies* 37(8): 1101–1123.

Alvesson, M. and Kärreman, D. (2006). "Professional Service Firms as Collectivities," in *Research in the Sociology of Organizations: Professional Service Firms, Vol. 24*, ed. R. Greenwood and R. Suddaby. Oxford: JAI Press, 203–230.

Bailyn, L. (1985). "Autonomy in the Industrial R&D Lab," *Human Resource Management* 24(2): 129–146.

Barrett, M., Cooper, D. J., and Jamal, K. (2005). "Globalization and the Coordinating of Work in Multinational Audits," *Accounting, Organizations and Society* 30(1): 1–24.

Brint, S. (1994). *In an Age of Experts: The Changing Role of Professions in Politics and Public Life.* Princeton, NJ: Princeton University Press.

Briscoe, F. (2007). "From Iron Cage to Iron Shield? How Bureaucracy Enables Temporal Flexibility for Professional Service Workers," *Organization Science* 18(2): 297–314.

Campbell, A. and Verbeke, A. (1994). "The Globalization of Service Multinationals," *Long Range Planning* 27(2): 95–102.

Coff, R. (1997). "Human Assets and Managerial Dilemmas . . ." *Academy of Management Review* 22(2): 374–402.

Collins, R. (1979). *The Credential Society: An Historical Sociology of Education and Stratification.* New York: Academic Press.

Cox, S. R., DeSerpa, A. C., and Canby Jr., W. C. (1982). "Consumer Information and the Pricing of Legal Services," *Journal of Industrial Economics* 30(3): 305–318.

Cyert, R. M. and March, J. G. (1963). *A Behavioral Theory of the Firm.* New York: Prentice-Hall.

DeLong, T. and Nanda, A. (2003). *Professional Services: Text and Cases.* Boston, MA: McGraw-Hill Irwin.

Eccles, R. G. and Crane, D. B. (1988). *Doing Deals: Investment Banks at Work.* Boston, MA: Harvard Business School Press.

Empson, L. (2001). "Knowledge Management in Professional Service Firms," *Human Relations* 54(7): 811–817.

Empson, L. (2007). "Professional Service Firms," in *International Encyclopedia of Organization Studies*, ed. S. Clegg and J. Bailey. Thousand Oaks, CA: Sage, 1311–1315.

Fenton, E. and Pettigrew, A. (2000). "Integrating a Global Professional Services Organization: The Case of Ove Arup Partnership," in *The Innovating Organization*, ed. A. Pettigrew and E. Fenton. London: Sage, 47–81.

Freidson, E. (1970). *Professional Dominance: The Social Structure of Medical Care.* New York: Atherton Press.

Freidson, E. (2001). *Professionalism: The Third Logic.* Chicago, IL: University of Chicago Press.

Galanter, M. and Palay, T. (1991). *Tournament of Lawyers: The Transformation of the Big Law Firm.* Chicago, IL: University of Chicago Press.

Gardner, H. K., Anand, N., and Morris, T. (2008). "Chartering New Territory: Diversification, Legitimacy, and Practice Area Creation in Professional Service Firms," *Journal of Organizational Behavior* 29(8): 1101–1121.

Gilson, R. J. and Mnookin, R. H. (1985). "Sharing Among the Human Capitalists: An Economic Inquiry into The Corporate Law Firm and How Partners Split Profits," *Stanford Law Review* 37(2): 313–397.

Gilson, R. J. and Mnookin, R. H. (1989). "Coming of Age in a Corporate Law Firm: The Economics of Associate Career Patterns," *Stanford Law Review* 41(3): 567–595.

Greenwood, R. and Empson, L. (2003). "The Professional Partnership: Relic or Exemplary Form of Governance?" *Organization Studies* 24(6): 909–933.

Greenwood, R. and Suddaby, R. (2005). "Rhetorical Strategies of Legitimacy," *Administrative Science Quarterly* 50(1): 35–67.

Greenwood, R., Hinings, C. R., and Brown, J. (1990). "'P2-Form' Strategic Management: Corporate Practices in Professional Service Firms," *Academy of Management Journal* 33(4): 725–755.

Greenwood, R., Li, S. X., Prakash, R., and Deephouse, D. L. (2005). "Reputation, Diversification, and Organizational Explanations of Performance in Professional Service Firms," *Organization Science* 16(6): 661–673.

Greenwood, R., Suddaby, R., and McDougald, M. (2006). "Introduction," in *Research in the Sociology of Organizations: Professional Service Firms, Vol. 24*, ed. R. Greenwood and R. Suddaby. Oxford: JAI Press, 1–16.

Gross, C. and Kieser, A. (2006). "Are Consultants Moving Towards Professionalization?" in *Research in the Sociology of Organizations: Professional Service Firms, Vol. 24*, ed. R. Greenwood and R. Suddaby. Oxford: JAI Press, 69–100.

Hall, R. H. (1968). "Professionalization and Bureaucratization," *American Sociological Review* 33(1): 92–104.

Halliday, T. (1987). "Knowledge Mandates: Collective Influence by Scientific, Normative and Syncretic Professions," *British Journal of Sociology* 36(3): 421–447.

Halpin, A. (2000). "Law, Theory and Practice: Conflicting Perspectives?" *International Journal of the Legal Profession* 7: 205–223.

Hansen, M., Nohria, N., and Tierney, T. (1999). "What's Your Strategy for Managing Knowledge?" *Harvard Business Review* 77(2): 106–118.

Hansmann, H. (1996). *The Ownership of Enterprise*. Cambridge, MA: Belknap Press of Harvard University Press.

Hinings, B. and Leblebici, H. (2003). "Introduction: Knowledge and Professional Organizations," *Organization Studies* 24(6): 827–830.

Hinings, C. R., Brown, J. L., and Greenwood, R. (1991). "Change in an Autonomous Professional Organization," *Journal of Management Studies* 28(4): 375–393.

Hitt, M., Bierman, L., Shimizu, K., and Kochhar, R. (2001). "Direct and Moderating Effects of Human Capital on Strategy and Performance in Professional Service Firms: A Resource-Based Perspective," *Academy of Management Journal* 44(1): 13–28.

Johnson, T. (1972). *Professions and Power*. London: Macmillan.

Jones, C., Hesterly, W. S., Fladmoe-Lindquist, K., and Borgatti, S. P. (1998). "Professional Service Constellations: How Strategies and Capabilities Influence Collaborative Stability and Change," *Organization Science* 9(3): 396–410.

Larson, M. S. (1977). *The Rise of Professionalism: A Sociological Analysis*. Berkeley, CA: University of California Press.

Leicht, K. and Fennell, M. (2001). *Professional Work: A Sociological Approach*. Malden, MA: Blackwell.

Leicht, K. and Lyman, E. C. W. (2006). "Markets, Institutions, and the Crisis of Professional Practice," in *Research in the Sociology of Organizations: Professional Service Firms, Vol. 24*, ed. R. Greenwood and R. Suddaby. Oxford: JAI Press, 17–44.

Lipartito, K. J. and Miranti, P. J. (1998). "Professions and Organizations in Twentieth-Century America," *Social Science Quarterly* 79(2): 301–320.

Lorsch, J. and Tierney, T. (2002). *Aligning the Stars: How to Succeed when Professionals Drive Results*. Boston, MA: Harvard Business School Press.

Løwendahl, B. (2005). *Strategic Management of Professional Service Firms*. Copenhagen: Copenhagen Business School Press.

Macdonald, K. M. (1985). "Social Closure and Occupational Registration," *Sociology* 19(4): 541–556.

Macdonald, K. M. (1995). *The Sociology of the Professions*. London: Sage.

Maister, D. (1982). "Balancing the Professional Service Firm," *Sloan Management Review* 24(1): 15–29.

Maister, D. (1993). *Managing the Professional Service Firm*. New York: Free Press.

Malhotra, N. (2003). "The Nature of Knowledge and the Entry Mode Decision," *Organization Studies* 24(6): 935–959.

Malhotra, N. and Hinings, C. B. (2010). "An Organizational Model for Understanding Internationalization Processes," *Journal of International Business Studies* 41(2): 330–349.

Malhotra, N. and Morris, T. (2009). "Heterogeneity in Professional Service Firms," *Journal of Management Studies* 46(6): 895–922.

Malhotra, N., Morris, T., and Hinings, C. R. (2006). "Variation in Organizational Form among Professional Service Organizations," in *Research in the Sociology of Organizations: Professional Service Firms, Vol. 24*, ed. R. Greenwood and R. Suddaby. Oxford: JAI Press, 171–202.

Malos, S. B. and Campion, M. A. (2000). "Human Resource Strategy and Career Mobility in Professional Service Firms: A Test of an Options-Based Model," *Academy of Management Journal* 43(4): 749–760.

Markides, C. C. and Williamson, P. J. (1996). "Corporate Diversification and Organizational Structure: A Resource-Based View," *Academy of Management Journal* 39(2): 340–367.

Masten, S. (2006). "Authority and Commitment: Why Universities, like Legislatures, are not Organized like Firms," *Journal of Economics and Management Strategy* 15(3): 649–684.

Morris, T. and Empson, L. (1998). "Organization and Expertise: An Exploration of Knowledge Management in Accounting and Consulting Firms," *Accounting, Organizations and Society* 23(5–6): 609–624.

Morris, T. and Pinnington, A. (1998). "Promotion to Partner in Professional Service Firms," *Human Relations* 51(1): 3–23.

Morrison, A. D. and Wilhelm, W. J., Jr. (2008). "The Demise of Investment Banking Partnerships: Theory and Evidence," *Journal of Finance* 63(1): 311–350.

Muzio, D. and Faulconbridge, J. 2013. "The Global Professional Service Firm: 'One Firm' Models versus (Italian) Distant Institutionalized Practices," *Organization Studies* 34(7): 897–925.

Nanda, A. (2003). *The Essence of Professionalism: Managing Conflict of Interest*. Boston, MA: Harvard Business School.

Nayyar, P.R. (1993). "Performance Effects of Information Asymmetry and Economies of Scope in Diversified Service Firms," *Academy of Management Journal* 36(1): 28–57.

Nelson, R. L. (1988). *Partners with Power: The Social Transformation of the Large Law Firm*. Berkeley, CA: University of California Press.

Nonaka, I. and Takeuchi, H. (1995). *The Knowledge-Creating Company: How Japanese Companies Create the Dynamics of Innovation*. New York: Oxford University Press.

Parsons, T. (1939). "The Professions and Social Structure," *Social Forces* 17(4): 457–467.

Roberts, J. (2004). *The Modern Firm: Organizational Design for Performance and Growth*. Oxford: Oxford University Press.

Rose, T. and Hinings, C. R. (1999). "Global Clients' Demands Driving Change in Global Business Advisory Firms," in *Restructuring the Professional Organization: Accounting, Health Care, and Law*, ed. D. M. Brock, M. J. Powell, and C. R. Hinings. London: Routledge, 41–67.

Samuelson, S. S. and Jaffe, L. J. (1990). "A Statistical Analysis of Law Firm Profitability," *Boston University Law Review* 70: 185–211.

Scott, W. R. (1965). "Reactions to Supervision in a Heteronomous Professional Organization," *Administrative Science Quarterly* 10(1): 65–81.

Scott, M. C. (1998). *The Intellect Industry: Profiting and Learning from Professional Services Firms*. New York: John Wiley.

Sharma, A. (1997). "Professional as Agent: Knowledge Asymmetry in Agency Exchange," *Academy of Management Review* 22(3): 758–798.

Smets, M., Morris, T., and Greenwood, R. (2012). "From Practice to Field: A Multilevel Model of Practice-Driven Institutional Change," *Academy of Management Journal* 55(4): 877–904.

Starbuck, W. (1992). "Learning by Knowledge-Intensive Firms," *Journal of Management Studies* 29(6): 713–740.

Teece, D. J. (2003). "Expert Talent and the Design of (Professional Services) Firms," *Industrial and Corporate Change* 12(4): 895–916.

Thornton, P., Jones, C., and Kury, K. (2005). "Institutional Logics and Institutional Change in Organizations: Transformation in Accounting, Architecture, and Publishing," in *Research in the Sociology of Organizations: Transformation in Cultural Industries*, ed. C. Jones and P. Thornton. London: Elsevier, 125–170.

Tirole, J. (1988). *The Theory of Industrial Organization.* Cambridge, MA: MIT Press.

Torres, D. (1991). "What, If Anything, is Professionalism? Institutions and the Problem of Change," in *Research in the Sociology of Organizations: Organizations and Occupations, Vol. 8*, ed. P. S. Tolbert and S. R. Barley. Oxford: JAI Press, 43–68.

von Nordenflycht, A. (2010). "What is a Professional Service Firm? Toward a Theory and Taxonomy of Knowledge Intensive Firms," *Academy of Management Review* 35(1): 155–174.

von Nordenflycht, A. (2011). "Firm Size and Industry Structure under Human Capital Intensity: Insights from the Evolution of the Global Advertising Industry," *Organization Science* 22(1): 141–157.

von Nordenflycht, A. (2014). "Does the Emergence of Publicly Traded Professional Service Firms Undermine the Theory of the Professional Partnership? A Cross-Industry Historical Analysis," *Journal of Professions and Organizations* 1(2): 137–160.

Winch, G. and Schneider, E. (1993). "Managing the Knowledge-Based Organization: The Case of Architectural Practice," *Journal of Management Studies* 30(6): 923–937.

Zardkoohi, A., Bierman, L., Panina, D., and Chakrabarty, S. (2011). "Revisiting a Proposed Definition of Professional Service Firms," *Academy of Management Review* 36(1): 180–184.

PART II

PROFESSIONAL SERVICE FIRMS: MANAGEMENT AND ORGANIZATION

CHAPTER 8

....

LEADERSHIP AND PROFESSIONALS

Multiple Manifestations of Influence in Professional Service Firms

....

LAURA EMPSON AND ANN LANGLEY

8.1 INTRODUCTION

....

CONVENTIONAL models of leadership are predicated on the assumption that leaders, by definition, must have followers (Avolio et al. 2009; Howell and Shamir 2005). In a Professional Service Firm (PSF), the distinction between "leaders" and "followers" is problematic as traditional hierarchical dyadic relationships are replaced by more ambiguous and negotiated relationships amongst professional peers (Adler et al. 2008). As a result "leadership is a matter of guiding, nudging, and persuading" (Greenwood et al. 1990: 748). According to Fenton and Pettigrew (2006: 102), therefore, "there is not much to be gained from taking existing theories of leadership as a lens for interpretation" of leadership in PSFs. The distinctive challenges of PSF leadership derive from two interrelated organizational characteristics: extensive individual autonomy and contingent managerial authority (Mintzberg 1979, 1983). Experienced professionals require, or at least expect, extensive individual autonomy (Miner et al. 1994; von Glinow 1988). This autonomy is legitimated by the requirement for professionals to preserve the right to make choices about how best to apply their specialist technical expertise to the delivery of customized professional services; it is perpetuated by the fact that the core value-creating resources of a PSF—the technical knowledge and client relationships—are often proprietary to specific professionals (Empson 2001a).

This emphasis on relatively extensive individual autonomy is associated with contingent managerial authority (Greenwood et al. 1990). In organizations of professionals, authority is "collegial and fragile" (Hinings et al. 1991) and deemed to rest with the professional peer group rather than the individual (Marcson 1962). Clan control, i.e., behavior controlled through common values, traditions, and commitment to the organization (Ouchi 1980) is the norm and power rests with professionals in the operating core (Mintzberg 1983). PSFs' senior executives are selected, and often elected, by their peers to formal leadership roles for a fixed term of office and can be deposed if they fail to retain the support of their peers (Empson 2007). As Mintzberg (1989: 181) states, a senior executive in a PSF "maintains power only as long as the professionals perceive him or her to be serving their interests effectively." This is particularly so in partnerships, the prevailing form of governance within the traditional professions such as law and accounting (Greenwood and Empson 2003), but is also common in corporate PSFs which mimic the characteristics of professional partnership governance (Empson and Chapman 2006). As a result, the formal authority of senior executives in PSFs is contingent. They can only lead by consent. As we will argue in this chapter, they need to be acutely aware of the implicit power structures and shifting networks of influence among their colleagues and have highly developed political skills in order to navigate and negotiate these networks of influence.

In spite of their distinctiveness, PSFs have received very little direct attention from leadership scholars, perhaps because of the difficulty of isolating notions of leadership and followership in settings where they tend to converge. Conversely, despite some recognition of the influence of the professions in macro-level institutional change (O'Reilly and Reed 2011; Scott 2008), scholars of PSFs have generally neglected the theme of leadership within the firms themselves. This may reflect the fact that such scholars tend to be oriented towards organizational theory or strategy and "the domains of strategy and organizational theory have been ignoring the critical role of leadership" (Miller and Sardais 2011: 175). Alternatively it could be, as Alvesson (2004: 137) states, that "apart from at certain stages such as the foundation and early expansion of a firm and during crises calling for conflict-ridden changes, leadership is probably a less important aspect of [PSFs] than of many other organizations."

We dispute this final assertion. In this chapter we will demonstrate that, while leadership in the conventional sense may not be immediately apparent within a PSF, *it permeates all aspects of professional work and all levels of the firm but needs to be conceptualized in such a way as to recognize how it is distinctive from leadership in conventional hierarchical organizations.*

In this chapter we seek to rectify management scholars' apparent neglect of the topic of leadership in PSFs. Specifically, we seek to emphasize the subtle and distinctive characteristics of leading professionals that are present to varying degrees within any organization of knowledge workers, where individual autonomy is enshrined within the work processes. We begin by establishing a "working definition" of leadership in PSFs which emphasizes the centrality of influencing in the process of leadership in this context. We develop a conceptual framework of leadership in PSFs by drawing upon studies which shed light on the topic of leadership, together with studies of leadership in other contexts, focusing on professionals in settings such as healthcare, academia, and the arts, where similar leadership dynamics are likely to apply (e.g., Cohen and March 1986;

Denis et al. 1996, 2001; Reid and Karambayya 2009). Our conceptual framework identifies nine manifestations of leadership in PSFs and highlights the multiple foci of influence that leadership of PSFs encompasses and the multiple resources and mechanisms for influencing at leaders' disposal. We argue that a single individual is unlikely to perform these multiple and distinctive leadership roles equally effectively and suggest this helps explain the prevalence of plural forms of leadership in PSFs, where multiple individuals perform distinctive leadership roles and negotiate their shared roles space on an ongoing basis (Denis et al. 2012). We conclude by refining our definition of leadership, re-emphasizing the dearth of empirically rigorous and theoretically informed studies of leadership in PSFs, and outlining important areas for future research.

8.2 CONCEPTUALIZING LEADERSHIP IN PROFESSIONAL SERVICE FIRMS

8.2.1 A Working Definition

Many authors have deplored the confusion that surrounds the definition of leadership (Alvesson and Spicer 2011; Barker 1997; Miller and Sardais 2011; Yukl 1989). Within the literature on PSFs, the term leadership rarely appears but, when it does, it is often used interchangeably with, or in place of, various other terms including: strategic management (Løwendahl 2005); administration (Mintzberg 1989); decision-making (Morris et al. 2010); and entrepreneurship (Strannegård 2012). For example, the title of Mintzberg's (1998) article, "Covert Leadership: Notes on *Managing* Professionals" (emphasis added) exemplifies a terminological ambiguity concerning the concepts of leadership and management which is often present within PSFs themselves. The leadership literature more generally is replete with definitions. Yukl (1989) argues that the multitude of definitions have little more in common beyond an agreement that leadership involves *influencing*. Alvesson and Spicer (2011: 9) caution that, by defining the term so broadly "leadership can easily become everything and nothing." As Miller and Sardais (2011: 175) argue, "we need a concept of leadership that is neither too broad to be useful nor too narrow to be applicable." As a starting point for this chapter, we adopt a broad working definition to enable us to draw upon a wide range of studies that can shed light on the phenomenon of leadership in PSFs. Following Yukl's classic and heavily cited overview of the leadership literature (1989: 253) we begin by defining leadership as: "influencing task objectives and strategies, influencing commitment and compliance in task behavior to achieve these objectives, influencing group maintenance and identification, and influencing the culture of an organization."

Yukl's definition highlights how the activity of leadership permeates multiple aspects of work and multiple levels within a firm. Influence can be exercised at the individual and group level as well as the organizational and strategic level. As we will demonstrate, these multiple foci of influence underpin the conceptual framework of leadership in PSFs which we have developed.

8.2.2 Developing the Conceptual Framework

We began by identifying studies of PSFs which shed light on the topic of leadership, exploring themes such as governance and organizational change. We also drew upon studies of leadership more generally which we deemed most relevant to the PSF context, particularly those which emphasize leadership as processual and plural. We sought to make explicit and synthesize the insights these studies offered into leadership in PSFs.

Unusually for an academic literature review, we also drew on practitioner studies. We did this for two reasons. First, while there has been very little rigorous scholarly research into leadership in PSFs, the topic has attracted considerable attention from practitioner-oriented writers (Broderick 2011; DeLong et al. 2007; Lorsch and Tierney 2002; Maister 1981, 1993). The plethora of practitioner texts reflects the fact that there is a substantial market for advice and executive education programs about PSF leadership among senior executives who find themselves struggling to perform these roles. Second, the most popular practitioner-oriented texts have inevitably influenced how leaders of PSFs construct and interpret their roles and will inevitably shape how they report their activities to researchers. While practitioner texts may lack a systematic empirical basis or rigorous methodological and theoretical underpinnings, they can help to identify what we intuitively "understand" about PSF leadership and, by making this explicit, help us to develop an empirically grounded critique of taken-for-granted assumptions.

As we read these various bodies of literature, we accumulated sets of keywords used to characterize the phenomenon of leadership. We then organized these keywords into separate clusters and groupings, seeking to identify points of similarity and difference and searching for the key dimensions underlying these distinctions. We then returned to the literature in order to refine and amplify our emerging conceptual framework. This process ultimately culminated in our development of a conception of leadership in PSFs as constituted through two dimensions: focus of influence and resources for influencing.

8.2.3 Manifestations of Leadership in Professional Service Firms

The first dimension of our conceptual framework (see Table 8.1) concerns the *focus of influence*, which encompasses the *individual and group* as well as the *organizational and strategic* level. This emphasis on influence is implicit in Yukl's (1989) definition of leadership (see section 8.2.1), which also encompasses the multiple foci of influence we have highlighted. The second dimension concerns *resources for influencing*. We classify these as *professional, political*, and *personal*. We also identify three *mechanisms for influencing*

Table 8.1 Manifestations of Leadership in Professional Service Firms

Mechanisms for influencing	Resources for influencing		
	Professional Expertise	Political Interaction	Personal Embodiment
Focus of influence			
Individual/Group	Coaching	Nurturing	Role-modeling
Organizational	Balancing	Enabling	Meaning-making
Strategic	Championing	Consensus-building	Visioning

associated with these resources: *expertise, interaction*, and *embodiment*. Together these represent three ways in which senior executives in PSFs can enact their multiple manifestations of leadership: by "having" professional expertise, by "doing" political interaction, and by "being" a personal embodiment of the values which professionals are supposed to enact in this context. Our triad of resources and mechanisms for influencing can be related to three key systems of influence identified by Mintzberg (1983) in his book *Power In and Around Organizations*: the systems of expertise, politics, and ideology.

In the following sections, we examine each of the cells shown in Table 8.1 in turn, identifying and synthesizing the relevant literature. We structure the discussion around each of the three resources and mechanisms for influencing.

8.2.4 Leadership Grounded in Professional Expertise

The emphasis on *professional expertise* as a core resource and mechanism for influencing reflects the notion of professional organizations as "meritocracies" (Mintzberg 1983), where the central system of influence is expertise rather than bureaucratic authority. Multiple authors have suggested that, while professional organizations may explicitly espouse egalitarian values and commitment to autonomy, they are nevertheless characterized by informal hierarchies that may be more or less explicit and are often related to recognized technical expertise and professional seniority (Brown et al. 2010; Diefenbach and Sillince 2011; Robertson and Swan 2003). In other words, leadership and professional expertise in PSFs are often intimately related.

Professional expertise can be a resource for influencing in multiple ways. At an individual and group level it is embedded in the apprenticeship model of skills transfer through *coaching* which is fundamental to the professional socialization and training process in PSFs (Anderson-Gough et al. 2000, 2001, 2002). At an organizational level, professional expertise is deployed in *balancing* the PSF through the careful alignment of the firm's economic and organizational models. Professional expertise also represents a resource for influencing at a strategic level, specifically when it is mobilized by entrepreneurial professionals *championing* new initiatives (Strannegård 2012). We now explore the literature on each of these in more depth.

8.2.5 Coaching

The apprenticeship model, which is a fundamental element of the professional development process, enables trainee professionals (as well as more senior professionals) to learn both the technical and interpersonal skills required in their job through close observation of, and detailed discussions with, their more experienced colleagues (Anderson-Gough et al. 2000, 2001, 2002; Faulconbridge 2006). See Faulconbridge's chapter in this volume for a more detailed discussion of this process. In the accredited professions, professional qualifications provide a mechanism for transferring explicit knowledge. Within firms, formalized knowledge management systems can also play a role in knowledge transfer. The most valuable professional expertise, however, is tacit (Empson 2001b) and transferred via one-to-one coaching. Werr and Stjernberg (2003) show for example how the codified methods and case histories that form part of generic knowledge management systems in major consulting firms such as Accenture and Cap Gemini Ernst & Young are complemented by individualized and group-level coaching based on tacit knowledge and experience. The coaching process goes beyond a simple transfer of technical expertise to encompass more personalized coaching in interpersonal skills. Leaders in this context manifest their influence by helping to shape the identity of their juniors (Ibarra 1999) and by helping them develop the professional judgment they need to apply this appropriately to deliver a customized service to their clients and to manage their teams. Leaders in this context need to apply their finely tuned professional expertise to decide which professionals need more or less coaching and what form that coaching should take.

Coaching represents a key theme in the practitioner literature on leading professionals. For example, Maister (1993) devotes only one brief section to leadership in his entire book and this is presented as coaching. Maister emphasizes the need for "highly individualized closed door counseling" where the practice leader can act as the professional's "chief cheerleader" and "chief critic." Similarly, Lorsch and Tierney (2002) refer to "starmaking" as even more critical than "rainmaking" to the development and survival of the PSF, and argue that it is an often under-recognized area of leadership activity in these firms.

8.2.6 Balancing

The concept of "balancing" in a PSF context was coined by Maister (1981) who argued that leaders of PSFs must struggle at all times to align the economic and organizational models of the firm in order to compete simultaneously in the market for professional services and professional staff. Balancing concerns issues such as: how many train-ees to hire, what proportion of managers to promote to partner, what level of attri-tion to embed within the up-or-out model, how to trade off income-generating with reputation-building work, and how to split profits. Balancing can therefore be seen as representing the core management activities of the firm but is about more than that. Balancing a PSF also requires leadership; leaders of a PSF must make use of their exper-tise in order to achieve the requisite balance.

For example, decisions about which professionals to make up to partner and how to split profits among the partner group are at one level about quality control of pro-fessional work but also encompass cultural issues, as they demonstrate which behav-iors are appropriate and which are penalized among professional staff. As Empson et al. (2013) have shown, such decisions cannot be taken by management professionals on the basis of their *management* expertise because of the difficulty in evaluating the deliv-ery of highly customized, specialized, and intangible services. Instead they remain the preserve of the senior executives who utilize the experience and legitimacy they have acquired through the development of their *professional* expertise over many years of fee-earning activity. Senior executives must also have the professional credibility among their peers to persuade them to accept the decisions that are required to "balance" the firm. In a PSF such decisions cannot simply be imposed by management fiat but require subtle leadership to persuade influential professionals to accept constraints.

8.2.7 Championing

The entrepreneurial ethos is deeply embedded in the founding myth of many PSFs. The largest PSFs were typically established by entrepreneurial individuals who identi-fied and exploited market opportunities, i.e., who championed innovations within their professional domain. For example, Kiechel's (2010) popular book *The Lords of Strategy* focuses on the emergence of specialized strategy consultants and the entrepreneurs that invented this new domain of expertise (including Bruce Henderson of BCG; Bill Bain of Bain & Company, and Michael Porter of Monitor Corporation). Starbuck (1993) describes the key role that the founders of law firm Wachtell, Lipton, Rosen & Katz (and more particularly Marty Lipton—the inventor of the "poison pill defense") played in creating a distinctive strategic niche. In so doing these entrepreneurs were applying their specialist professional expertise to define and implement the strategic direction of the firm, as well as (at least in these examples) championing innovations that signifi-cantly changed the shape of business practices beyond the firm's boundaries (Suddaby and Viale 2011).

Looking at relatively recently established PSFs, even Alvesson (2004), who with Sveningsson (Alvesson and Sveningsson 2003c) articulated the concept of "non-leadership" in PSFs, acknowledges that "in some cases ... there are one or two central actors, often the founders of the firm, who have guru status and these people may have considerable influence" (Alvesson 2004: 123). These individuals may belie the traditional view of PSF leadership as peer-based and consensual; evolving beyond these founder-champions can represent an intensely risky stage in the development of a PSF (Empson 2012). If these firms are able to survive and grow beyond the retirement of the founders, the entrepreneurial ethos must remain embedded within them. Indeed, professional expertise is the basis for entrepreneurial leadership in larger PSFs as individuals identify and champion opportunities through their professional practice (see Reihlen and Werr in this volume and Strannegård 2012). In this context, entrepreneurial professionals may be dispersed across the firm but may have an influence at the strategic level as their "pet projects" gain traction and become organizationally embedded. Anand et al. (2007) studied the processes underlying new practice development in PSFs, whereby entrepreneurial professionals drew upon their in-depth understanding of existing professional practices to extend and apply existing frameworks and develop differentiated service offerings. In so doing, they demonstrated "socialized agency" and "differentiated expertise." These two elements illustrate the key role of professional expertise as a resource for this championing in the context of strategic leadership. In order for practice development to be successful, leaders also need to embed their initiatives externally with clients and internally with colleagues through a process of legitimation (see also Gardner et al. 2008; Heusinkveld and Benders 2005). Thus while expertise, and the autonomy that accompanies it, lies at the root of entrepreneurial professional leadership, it is not enough. Champions also need political skill to win support for their innovative initiatives more generally across the firm.

8.3 LEADERSHIP GROUNDED IN POLITICAL INTERACTION

Because PSFs bring together multiple experts protective of their autonomy and disinclined towards followership, *political interaction* represents another key mechanism for influencing professionals (see Cohen and March 1986; Denis et al. 2007 for academic and healthcare professionals, respectively). As Morris et al. (2010: 297) state, PSFs are "uniquely political environments ... many traditional professional partnerships are consensus-based democracies but as such they are subject to the lobbying, scheming, and bargaining which occurs in any other political arena to achieve agreement on decisions among diverse individuals and interest groups." At an individual level this political interaction may take the form of *nurturing*. Through their nurturing activities leaders exercise influence through careful and sustained one-to-one interaction with key professionals, seeking to understand better their colleagues' concerns and motivations and attempting to respond appropriately to win their support (Alvesson and Sveningsson 2003c). At an organizational level this political interaction may take the form of *enabling*, whereby the leaders of a PSF facilitate the initiatives of their entrepreneurial colleagues by encouraging them to take action and removing impediments to action

(Empson 2001a). At a strategic level, political interaction becomes manifested through the process of *consensus-building*, whereby leaders negotiate with their colleagues to achieve a degree of strategic alignment across the partnership as a whole (Adler et al. 2008; Denis et al. 2007).

8.3.1 Nurturing

Coaching implies a transfer of professional expertise to influence the way that individuals and groups sell and deliver professional services and manage themselves and colleagues. By contrast, nurturing focuses on the more interpersonal and ultimately political interactions by which leaders seek to influence their fellow professionals. The professionals experiencing this nurturing may not be aware it is taking place as the process is subtle. Mintzberg (1998) emphasizes that, since senior professionals are highly trained and highly motivated individuals who know what to do, they require little direction and supervision from their formal leaders. Professionals need protection and support. Leaders, he argues, should focus on encouraging professionals and removing obstacles to getting their work done. In this context, Mintzberg says, "covert leadership may be far more important than overt leadership" (1998: 144). The leader determines what the professional should be motivated to do and which obstacles to remove and which to retain. As such, this nurturing activity encompasses a political subtext.

Alvesson and Sveningsson take this idea further in three articles about leadership in PSFs: "The Great Disappearing Act: Difficulties of Doing 'Leadership'" (Alvesson and Sveningsson 2003a), "Managers Doing Leadership: The Extra-Ordinarization of the Mundane" (Alvesson and Sveningsson 2003b), and "Good Visions, Bad Micro-Management and Ugly Ambiguity: Contradictions of (Non-) Leadership in a Knowledge Intensive Organization" (Alvesson and Sveningsson 2003c). These studies emphasize that, while senior managers in PSFs may make substantial claims about their role and significance as leaders, the activities they describe are often "passive, vague, and fragmented" (Alvesson and Sveningsson 2003a: 376). When asked how they spend their time, these individuals stress three activities: "listening, chatting, and being cheerful" (Alvesson and Sveningsson 2003b: 1436). Senior managers believe these are important activities in their own right, not simply a means of building consensus. These interactions enable key professionals to feel valued, supported, and cared for; helping to ensure that they remain in the firm and motivated to do their best work. Similarly, in his description of an exceptionally successful law firm, Wachtell, Lipton, Rosen & Katz, Starbuck (1993: 908) quotes a respondent lauding the style of one of the founding partners, "George Katz . . . embodied [the] family style. He visited all the offices almost every day, bringing encouragement or news or gossip . . . Always optimistic, George would report on current matters and ask for advice from everyone on thorny legal questions, giving even the new junior associates the sense that their participation was valuable." Leadership influence through nurturing is hard to pin down, to the point where Alvesson and Sveningsson wonder if what is claimed to be leadership really deserves the label. Yet, to the extent that such activities contribute to building trust, loyalty, and cohesion in a workforce inclined towards autonomy (and, by extension, individualism), nurturing can be interpreted as fundamental to the evolution and development of PSFs.

8.3.2 Enabling

Mintzberg's articulation of covert leadership among professionals applies at the organizational as well as the individual level. Cohen and March's (1986) study of university presidents emphasizes that these leaders seem to have little formal power, but they can sometimes achieve considerable influence through unobtrusive action and even self-effacement. In the highly political and status-conscious setting of a PSF, drawing glory towards oneself may be counterproductive. However, acting behind the scenes to remove roadblocks and allow colleagues to take credit for substantive initiatives aligned with the strategic goals of the firm may be highly effective. Cohen and March (1986: 208) call this "exchanging status for substance." For example, in a study of the development of healthcare networks, Martin et al. (2009) noted the effectiveness of a "quiet" form of leadership on the part of senior physicians in relation to their colleagues, as compared with a directive style.

Similarly, studies of successful change processes in PSFs have highlighted the significance of apparent leadership inaction in influencing organizational outcomes. Leaders of PSFs cannot drive change in the conventional top-down sense (Greenwood et al. 1994) but they can enable it. Some of their fellow professionals, at least the most entrepreneurial among them, will use their expertise to take the initiative themselves (Empson 2000), a form of individual-level leadership discussed earlier under "championing." In such an environment, an important role of senior leaders may be to enable others' initiatives by removing impediments and facilitating their colleagues' entrepreneurialism (Anand et al. 2007).

For example, the senior leadership in Empson's (2000, 2001a, 2001b) studies of mergers in the consulting and accounting sectors appeared to be abrogating responsibility to their more entrepreneurial colleagues. In all of the mergers studied, the senior leaders did very little during the first year post-merger in order to reassure professional staff that their autonomy would not be impinged upon. The more entrepreneurial professionals sought out like-minded colleagues in the merger partner firm and began to explore ways of working together. In time, the facilitative passivity of the senior leadership group came to be seen by their colleagues as a "leadership vacuum," who began demanding that they take action to resolve impediments to integration. These demands gave the senior leadership the authority they needed to move away from an essentially passive enabling role to take directive action.

Empson finds no evidence that this delayed reaction was deliberately orchestrated. Instead she finds an "undirected process of integration" where the selective intervention was forced upon them by their colleagues. This contrasts with Empson's (2011) study of post-recession partner restructuring in a law firm where selective intervention was a deliberate strategy. In this case the managing and senior partner delegated responsibility for decision-making to an increasingly large group of professionals but intervened regularly. Empson argues that the combination of progressive cooption and selective intervention requires sophisticated political skills and an acute understanding of the power dynamics within the firm.

This enabling approach to leadership, accompanied by selective intervention, is consistent with Uhl-Bien et al.'s (2007) concept of complexity leadership, which they argue is particularly relevant to knowledge-based organizations. They describe complexity leadership as "emergent, interactive . . . a complex interplay from which a collective impetus for action and change emerges" (Uhl-Bien et al. 2007: 299). Leadership activity is dispersed among networks throughout the organization and the role of the senior leader is to enable these leadership activities to emerge. Notions of "servant leadership" (Greenleaf and Spears 2002) or "empowering leadership" (Chuang et al. 2013), in which leaders are primarily motivated to provide support and encouragement for the led, also resonates with both the enabling and nurturing forms of leadership, though scholars of servant and empowering leadership sometimes overlook the strongly political dimension inherent in these leadership activities.

8.3.3 Consensus-Building

It is through political interaction at the strategic level and the process of consensus-building that senior executives manifest leadership in a manner particularly characteristic of PSFs (Broderick 2011; Denis et al. 2007; Lorsch and Tierney 2002). Lorsch and Tierney (2002) portray leadership in PSFs as about channeling the activities of senior professionals, a potentially disparate group of individuals pursuing a pluralistic agenda, towards a common strategic goal. They term this process "achieving alignment." This perspective is consistent with the focus on consensus-building articulated within the academic literature on PSF governance (see Leblebici and Sherer, Chapter 9, this volume).

Perhaps the most influential of these studies is by Greenwood et al. (1990) who identify and describe an organizational archetype which they call the P^2, or professional partnership. Although this study focuses on the systems, structures, and interpretive scheme which embody the traditional partnership, it does refer to leadership in passing. "Dispersed power, coupled with professionals' inclination to resist autocratic actions, and the territorial jealousies that arise in geographically dispersed firms, militates against personalized, directive leadership" (Greenwood et al. 1990: 736). In this context, Greenwood et al. (1990) argue, the role of senior leaders is to build consensus among their peers within the partnership. Greenwood et al. (1990: 748) emphasize that "consensual decision making does not imply an absence of strategic leadership" but that the structural and ideological context within which managing partners have to operate "constrains the style they have to adopt and the pace at which they can advance change." As Hinings et al.'s (1991) subsequent study of abortive change in an accounting firm demonstrates, in PSFs the authority structure can be too fragile to deal with substantial strategic change initiatives. Hinings et al. suggest that, because of the diffuse and collegial nature of the authority structure, "a high degree of leadership (is) required, linking the collegial authority (structure) to a vision and rationale for change" (Hinings et al. 1991: 390). Their study points to the need to ensure that powerful actors are part of the implementation team and for leaders to devote considerable time to building consensus among them.

Greenwood et al.'s (1994) study of an accounting firm merger is characterized by just such an absence of consensus-building leadership. It demonstrates how the senior leadership group struggled to impose any degree of direction; its members essentially abrogated responsibility for coordinating or directing post-merger integration. While notionally adopting an enabling approach (i.e., by not attempting to control the process, they created a space for entrepreneurial colleagues to step forward), they failed fundamentally at consensus-building (i.e., so that their colleagues failed to take action in support of the initiative).

Whereas the concept of achieving alignment outlined by Lorsch and Tierney (2002) implies that PSF leaders should develop a strategic vision for the firm and then persuade their colleagues to adopt it, the concept of consensus-building is less directive. According to this approach, the role of the leader is to identify the collective will of the partnership and to develop and pursue a strategy which is consistent with that. This creating consensus approach to leadership is implicit in Empson's (2007) study of partner dynamics which argues that the role of the managing and senior partners of the firm is to resolve the inherent tension within the partnership between the needs of the individual and the needs of the collective. Leadership in this context is about managing the delicate balance between preserving each individual partner's individualistic desire to self-actualize and the collective partnership's desire to profit maximize. The election of individuals to these roles is a manifestation of the partnership's collective will. It is their responsibility, within the delegated authority structure of the partnership, to build the consensus they need to implement that collective will.

8.4 LEADERSHIP GROUNDED IN PERSONAL EMBODIMENT

In pluralistic settings such as PSFs there may be a tendency towards fragmenting interests among autonomous professionals. In this context individuals may acquire considerable influence by embodying overarching values with which organization members can positively identify (Denis et al. 2007; Gioia and Chittipeddi 1991; Thompson 1967). We highlight this resource for influencing under the category of *personal embodiment* of organizational values and identity. At the individual/group level this may take the form of *role-modeling*, where leaders exercise influence by explicating and embodying the beliefs and behaviors required of a partner and leader in a PSF (DeLong et al. 2007). At the organizational level, personal embodiment can represent a resource for influencing through the *management of meaning*. Leaders shape the organizational identity and provide professionals with an organizationally sanctioned vocabulary of motives (Alvesson and Willmott 2002), thus enabling them to exercise a degree of informal control over autonomous professionals. At a strategic level, certain leaders may exercise influence through their personal embodiment of the organization's strategic objectives, i.e., *visioning* (Gioia and Chittipeddi 1991).

8.4.1 Role-Modeling

Role-modeling is a manifestation of leadership at the individual level whereby individuals influence their professional colleagues by "being" a personal embodiment of what is expected of professionals, rather than by "having" professional expertise (coaching), or by "doing" political interaction (nurturing). Role-modeling is fundamentally concerned with identity, and can represent an implicit form of identity regulation (Alvesson and Willmott 2002). As Alvesson, Kärreman, and Sullivan demonstrate in this volume (see Chapter 18), the interaction of high levels of ambiguity and insecurity in PSFs causes them to become "identity-intensive" environments. As Ibarra (1999) recognizes, young professionals prepare themselves for partnership by observing their successful senior colleagues closely and experimenting with provisional professional selves. When senior professionals deliberately use these role-modeling behaviors in an attempt to shape the beliefs and values of their colleagues, the emphasis shifts from informal identity development to more systematic identity regulation. Being seen as a role model within a PSF confers power on a professional among their peers.

Lorsch and Tierney (2002) emphasize that senior leaders of PSFs require personal credibility to influence their star performers as well as their more junior colleagues. They argue that, in the absence of formal power, leaders of PSFs rely upon informal power derived from simply being better than most of their colleagues at performing their professional work. Similarly, DeLong et al. (2007: 38) emphasize what they call "personal example" as the cornerstone of their proposed "integrated leadership model" for PSFs, referring to qualities such as "unswerving commitment to market leadership, demonstrating passion and belief, treating everyone with dignity and respect, demonstrating the highest integrity, giving credit to others and taking responsibility for failure" as elements contributing to influence through inspiration. The concept of leadership as role-modeling is observed empirically in Muhr's (2011) study of two professionals in leadership roles in their organizations. Muhr draws on the metaphor of the leader as a "cyborg" and highlights the influence of leaders with "exceptional work capacity ... almost inhuman in (their) extraordinary accomplishments" (Muhr 2011: 142). These individuals set an example to their teams through tireless energy, performing their professional work to an exemplary standard. The cyborg PSF leader is "rational, calculative, competitive, and focused"

(Muhr 2011: 138), with an unshakeable confidence in their ability so that they "appear almost mechanistic and robot-like" (Muhr 2011: 138). While they set exceptionally demanding standards for the professionals who work with them, they attract a considerable following within their firms. This may in part be due to their success at winning new business which enables them to "feed" their followers with work, but may also be because they inspire confidence and create a focus that helps their followers to perform better.

Professionals' attachment to what could be perceived as unrealistically demanding managers, rather than admirable role model leaders, needs to be understood in the context of the insecure environment in which professionals work. It can be inferred that, in PSFs, where professionals must accommodate high levels of ambiguity (Alvesson 1993) and compete in an up-or-out tournament (Anderson-Gough et al. 1998), individuals will be drawn to leaders who can protect them by keeping them in work, inspire them by setting demanding goals, and reassure them by giving them the confidence to believe they can achieve these goals.

8.4.2 Meaning Making

In the context described above, the role of leadership at the organizational level is more akin to the management of meaning described by Smircich and Morgan (1982: 258). This approach suggests that leaders may attempt to "frame and define the reality" of their fellow partners, seeking to forge a unified pattern of meaning which may provide a point of reference against which a "*feeling* of organization and direction can emerge" (emphasis added). The importance of culture, and the role of leaders in sustaining it through the management of meaning, is explicit in much of the practitioner literature on PSFs. For example, Broderick (2011: 24–28) identifies several tactics PSF leaders claim to use to "embed values and culture" including "telling the firm's story" through orientation programs and videos, mixing people on teams, and engaging in retreats and other rituals that rehearse and reaffirm firm values.

The role of leadership in managing meaning is also revealed in more academic (and sometimes critically oriented) empirical studies. For example, in their account of power relations in an architectural firm, Brown et al. (2010: 534) describe how the directors framed work as democratic and open, with a distinctive emergent design philosophy, though most creative work was in fact performed by the senior architects. The emphasis on creativity and belief in a noble and superior mission had a powerful motivating effect on employees, even when they were required to perform mundane technical work. As Brown et al. (2010: 537) report, "Many people said that they 'work 80, 90 hour weeks a lot of the time', but did so 'quite happily' . . . because they felt pride in being part of a high-performing team that made them . . . feel 'like a unified force'." Robertson and colleagues (Robertson and Swan 2003; Robertson et al. 2003) provide similar accounts of how PSFs were able to gain commitment from employees by maintaining ambiguity about consulting roles while offering a "corporate identity premised on 'elitism'" (Robertson and Swan 2003: 831). This rhetoric of elitism was promulgated and perpetuated by the senior leadership group.

The role of meaning-making is also addressed by Lawrence et al.'s (2012) study of three law firms undergoing change towards more corporate structures. The authors showed that the new management systems tended not to be institutionalized within the fabric of the firm unless the systems were "legitimated by key actors through the skilled use of language to create supportive frames for interpreting their value in the day-to-day working of the firm" (Lawrence et al. 2012: 133). Moreover, leaders were more effective in initiating radical change when they drew on more centralized authority structures that were seen as legitimate with respect to "traditional values" (Lawrence et al. 2012: 134)—in other words, when these particular leaders embodied qualities that were valued by the firm, such as their commercial reputation and professional competence, and when they embedded the attempts at change in participative and collegial processes.

Finally, linking with the previous notion of "covert leadership," e Cunha (2002: 493) describes a successful information technology services firm as having a "low-profile leadership style" in association with "high-profile culture." "Organizational culture, by emphasizing initiative and loyalty, substitutes the leader's role. Low-profile leaders, in turn, make the organizational culture more salient and provide personal support and opportunities for sense making" (e Cunha (2002: 493).

8.4.3 Visioning

As the final manifestation of leadership in our conceptual framework, we come to personal embodiment at a strategic level, whereby senior professionals articulate and enact their vision for the firm. Mintzberg (1979) refers to strategy in a professional setting as emergent, composed essentially of the cumulative autonomous decisions made by its operating professionals. Therefore the creation of an overarching and integrative strategic direction or "vision" does not seem likely at first sight. If it exists, it will tend to be a flexible negotiated consensus and constructed through political processes (Greenwood et al. 1990). And yet, as Thompson (1967) notes, lack of clarity about goals and diffuse power within an organization can create a sense of fragmentation and even "anomie"—leaving room, especially in times of crisis and dispute, for the emergence of "charisma." This can be viewed as a form of leadership which bridges differences and mobilizes energy, projecting an overarching strategic vision that reaches beyond a simple amalgam of current emergent orientations, and imbued with values to which others may be drawn. This visioning is in fact an extension of the meaning-making role from sustaining an existing culture at the organizational level to redirecting the firm at a strategic level.

The literature provides a number of examples of strategic leadership as visioning in professional service contexts that illustrate its potential and limitations. For instance, Carlsen (2006) describes how a new leader arriving in a failing technology consulting firm managed to identify a potential strategic niche that had some initial successes, and then engaged in what Carlsen calls "imagination by dramatizing," building commitment and enthusiasm among employees through "evangelist visioning" that involved the "celebration of proprietary frameworks and concepts" and the use of metaphor to describe the firm. Similarly, Gioia and Chittipeddi (1991) describe the efforts by a new principal in a university to develop a new vision and strategic plan whose central metaphor involved becoming a "top ten university." Similarly, while not strictly in a PSF context but certainly in a knowledge-intensive setting, Abdallah and Langley (2014) describe how a new top manager in an arts organization was able to re-energize a demoralized workforce through the development of a vision that drew strongly on the organization's foundational values associated with social engagement and innovation, and offered hope for the future.

The incidents of visioning in these examples have a number of elements in common. First the strategic visions were mobilizing in part because they drew on a foundation of common values, promoted excellence and promised success, with the potential to enhance the identity of those who might be associated with them. Second, they were generated by individuals whose credibility and reputation tended to be well-established—these leaders embodied the values they were promoting (Abdallah and Langley 2014; Lawrence et al. 2012). Third, while visions were clearly leader-driven, they passed through processes of back and forth consultation and consensus-building before acquiring certain legitimacy (Abdallah and Langley 2014; Gioia and Chittipeddi 1991; Lawrence et al. 2012).Visions generated in this manner are often characterized by ambiguity. Gioia et al. (2012) laud the "virtues of vagueness" in such settings, arguing that it is ambiguity that enables people to buy into proposed strategic directions while providing multiple ways to interpret them, thus leaving opportunities for creativity and autonomy (see also Gioia and Chittipeddi 1991; Robertson and Swan 2003; Sillince et al. 2012). Abdallah and Langley (2014) underline, however, the double-edged nature of ambiguity. They argue that, while ambiguous visions can initially enable mobilization, the multiplicity of initiatives they accommodate, combined with the potential for contradiction, can ultimately generate incoherence, overstretching, and disillusionment.

Leadership in the form of strategic visioning in PSFs is thus likely to be a sporadic and fragile enterprise. It may be needed to bridge diversity and generate some form of coherence where this seems to be absent. However, such visions are likely to be fluid, value-based, and ambiguous, designed to accommodate multiple possibilities and ad hoc initiatives of star professionals, rather than being sharp, clean, and exclusionary as described by Broderick (2011: 18), "a somewhat vague destination that [PSF leaders] continually strive for but, in fact, never really achieve."

8.5 Bringing It All Together: Leadership in the Plural

An overworked cliché about leadership and management in PSFs is that it is like "herding cats" (von Nordenflycht 2010). As we noted at the beginning of this chapter, professionals tend to expect (and even need) autonomy to accomplish their work and therefore resist forms of management authority. As we have also shown, however, there are a variety of alternative resources and mechanisms by which professionals can lead and influence others. These may be grounded in professional expertise, political interaction, and personal embodiment. PSFs may not have the formalized command and control hierarchies found in other types of organizations, but they do have explicit and implicit meritocratic hierarchies in which seniority and professional expertise constitute bases for influence (Brown et al. 2010; Diefenbach and Sillince 2011), and are manifested in leadership practices such as one-to-one coaching at the individual level, balancing the economic and organizational structures at the firm level, and championing entrepreneurial activity at the strategic level. Moreover the distributed nature of authority ensures that PSFs are fertile environments for political forms of leadership that may involve nurturing, enabling, and consensus-building through the development of coalitions. Finally, the fragmentation and individualism of PSFs may be overcome to a degree through the personal embodiment of value-based leadership, where individuals acquire influence not by giving orders but by exemplifying valued behavior (role-modeling), through meaning-making that sustains a valued firm identity, and by offering inspirational visions that are broad enough to bridge divergent perspectives.

Yet, while leadership in PSFs appears clearly in multiple forms of behavior, it seems unlikely that all of these behaviors will be manifested by a single individual, whatever their position in the firm. Leadership in PSFs (at least those of any size) is necessarily distributed. Moreover, because of their fluid power dynamics, integrated direction seems unlikely to develop unless multiple individuals coalesce to form a coalition combining professional expertise and political skill, and if these individuals are also able to personally embody the relevant values. Effective strategic leadership in professional organizations is therefore typically a *collective* endeavor (Currie and Lockett 2011; Denis et al. 2010, 2012; Empson et al. 2013; Fitzgerald et al. 2013; Greenwood et al. 1990; Reid and Karambayya 2009) in which different individuals may play different roles.

To the extent that leadership roles among individuals are specialized, differentiated, and complementary (i.e., fit together and cover the full range of issues), it may be possible to speak of a "leadership constellation" that effectively drives the direction of the firm (Denis et al. 2001, 2012; Hodgson et al. 1965). Indeed, several authors have noted how knowledge-based organizations often have formally defined pooled leadership at the top (e.g., dyads or triads of leaders working in concert), as in the case of senior and managing partners in law firms (Empson 2007, 2012; Empson and Chapman 2006), professional/managerial hybrids in healthcare (Fitzgerald et al. 2013), administrative and artistic directors in the performing arts (Reid and Karambayya 2009), and co-leadership among high technology ventures (Google, Research in Motion), as well as financial service firms such as Goldman-Sachs (Alvarez and Svejenova 2005).

Beyond notions of pooled leadership at the top (Denis et al. 2012), leadership influence is also likely to be "distributed" throughout levels and areas within the firm. This is manifested for example in the ability of professionals to champion new entrepreneurial initiatives based on their specific areas of expertise, as well as the propensity for PSFs to rely on teamwork in which leadership is typically distributed among those who have the most valuable expertise relating to a particular project (Gardner et al. 2012).

In summary, rather than being absent as Alvesson and Sveningsson (2003c) suggest, we argue that *in PSFs, leadership is potentially everywhere*. The challenge appears to lie in rendering it coherent and sustainable in situations of diffuse power where people are often elected to leadership positions by their peers. Yet, many firms appear to have achieved coherent and effective leadership over time, with some growing to giant organizations operating in multiple countries. This suggests that PSFs hold valuable lessons for other kinds of organizations struggling to adopt more plural forms of leadership (Denis et al. 2012), in areas such as education (Gronn 1999), healthcare (Denis et al. 2001), and in knowledge-based organizations more generally (Uhl-Bien et al. 2007). It is tempting to conclude from the preceding discussion that leadership in PSFs is infinitely complex, representing distinctive and sometimes even insurmountable challenges. As stated earlier, however, Alvesson (2004: 137) argues that "leadership is probably a less important aspect of [PSFs] than of many other organizations."

How can these apparently opposing perspectives on PSF leadership be reconciled? The key may be to recognize the presence of an additional, disembodied, player in the complex power dynamics within PSFs, the extensive social control systems, which serve as a "substitute" for leadership (Gronn 1999; Kerr and Jermier 1978) or, put differently, contribute to leadership plurality (Spillane 2006). It is this aspect of leadership in PSFs which perhaps holds the greatest potential for insights into plural leadership in organizations more generally.

Leaders may struggle to exert influence and to knit together an apparently disparate group of self-directed and highly autonomous professionals but they have a powerful ally: the extensive social control systems which are deeply embedded within PSFs, from the elaborate and protracted selection and promotion processes, to the less formalized but equally powerful socialization processes and all-pervasive practices of peer control. Taken together, these constitute an elaborate system of control which preserves the perception among professionals that they are acting autonomously while in fact ensuring a high degree of compliance. As an accounting firm partner in Empson's (2004: 767) study put it: "I do what I want, but the things I want are likely to help the firm because that is the way I have been trained. At one level we (partners) are completely independent, but we all march to the same tune without even thinking about it." Such a statement clearly nuances considerably the simplistic assertion that leadership in a PSF is like "herding cats." Instead it suggests that a key role for leaders in a PSF is to assist their professional peers in constructing, reproducing, and adapting their own collective "iron cages" (Barker 1993; DiMaggio and Powell 1983) that mutually orient behavior in subtle but important ways. This insight potentially applies to plural leadership of any organization of highly skilled knowledge workers, not just PSFs.

8.6 Conclusions: Towards a Refined Conception of Leadership in Professional Service Firms

We began this chapter by adopting Yukl's classic and all-encompassing definition of leadership as: "influencing task objectives and strategies, influencing commitment and compliance in task behavior to achieve these objectives, influencing group maintenance and identification, and influencing the culture of an organization" (Yukl 1989: 253). We were conscious of Fenton and Pettigrew's (2006: 102) assertion that, in the context of PSFs, "there is not much to be gained from taking existing theories of leadership as a lens for interpretation." Through our analysis and synthesis of a broad range of studies with implications for leadership in professional contexts, we have developed a more nuanced, detailed, and context-specific definition of leadership in PSFs.

We argue that leadership in PSFs is, above all, *a process of interaction* among professionals seeking to influence each other. It is *manifested explicitly through professional expertise, discretely through political interaction, and implicitly through personal embodiment*. These influencing processes simultaneously encompass multiple foci, from the individual and group, to the organizational and strategic. Each are of equal significance since, ultimately in a PSF, strategy can only be realized in the actions and interactions of individual professionals.

We have identified nine distinctive manifestations of leadership in this context and argue that an effective leader in a PSF is one who is able to *understand and navigate the complex power dynamics among senior professionals and to encompass multiple manifestations of leadership*: from coaching to consensus-building, from championing to meaning-making, from nurturing to visioning, from balancing to enabling and role-modeling. Because individual professionals may struggle to manifest these multiple behaviors, leadership in PSFs is often more effectively carried out by a plural leadership group, or leadership constellation.

Looking to the future, since so little systematic empirical research has been conducted into leadership in PSFs, the field is "wide open" to future opportunities for contribution. Below we highlight various topics that build on the conceptualization developed here and that merit further research attention. The preceding analysis has sought to knit together an extensive yet fragmented set of studies to develop a coherent overview of leadership in PSFs. Yet this approach inevitably imposes an erroneous impression of homogeneity. There is of course considerable variation within the professional services sector and this potentially has significant implications for leadership and leadership research. One significant source of heterogeneity is the life stage of the PSF (Empson 2012). For example, how does leadership in founder-managed firms vary from that in more established PSFs? How might leadership practices in these firms evolve as the firm grows and develops (e.g., from more emphasis on personal embodiment towards more political and bureaucratic processes)? As firms grow, does the importance of leadership become less or more significant? How do the power dynamics of leaders in relation to their professional colleagues change as a professional partnership becomes a publicly owned corporation?

Another significant source of heterogeneity is the type of business in which a PSF is engaged. Previous studies have suggested that there is a consistent set of individual-level characteristics common across all professions (von Glinow 1988). Even if this is the case, there is considerable variation in the kind of work professionals do and the organizational and regulatory context in which they do it (Brock et al. 1999; Malhotra and Morris 2009; von Nordenflycht 2010). The preceding analysis has brought together studies of the established traditional professionals (e.g., accountants and lawyers) with more creative regulated professionals (e.g., architects and engineers) with aspirant professionals (e.g., management and technology consultants), and public sector professionals (e.g., healthcare workers and academics). We have identified some consistent leadership themes across these contexts but we can infer that there is also likely to be considerable divergence, associated with different patterns of socialization, different ownership structure, and the varying significance of professional and state regulation.

Given the dearth of research and the significance of the professional service sector to the global economy, leadership in PSFs is worth studying in its own right. But research in such a context also has the potential to make important contribution to organizational theory more generally, particularly around the themes of power and politics. Denis et al.'s (2012) examination of leadership in the plural highlighted the neglect of discussions of power within this literature. A study of leadership in PSFs, which is most typically "plural," is a fertile context in which to explore the theme of power and power dynamics more fully. For example, there is much to be learnt about the power dynamics within the leadership dyad of senior and managing partner and how this dyad engages with the powerful "barons" who serve as practice leaders, and "rainmakers" within the firm. Empson et al. (2013) have highlighted the increasing significance of management professionals (with managerial expertise but not professional expertise) in these firms. How can they establish the authority they require to lead without the requisite professional expertise which the fee-earning professionals require of their leaders? How are they able to personally embody the firm when they themselves are not a product of it? It can be inferred that they must rely predominantly on political skill but, if so, how do they develop and deploy these skills in the distinctive context of the PSF?

And how do the power dynamics of an extended leadership group shift in response to external and internal disruption? For example, what is the impact of contested leadership elections on carefully constructed coalitions among professional peers? And under conditions of crisis, are leaders of PSFs able to assume a greater degree of power vis-à-vis their professional colleagues? Would crisis conditions lead to a fundamental and lasting shift in the nature of power relations between leaders and their professional colleagues, or must leaders revert to their protracted political processes of influencing and coalitional building once these conditions are past?

As stated at the start of this chapter, scholars of PSFs have generally neglected the theme of leadership, focusing their analysis at the level of the organization and individual professional but neglecting the role of leadership in integrating individual actions with organizational intentions. Similarly, PSFs have received very little direct attention from leadership scholars. Yet PSFs can be seen as pioneering organizational responses to leadership challenges which are becoming increasingly relevant to organizations more generally within the knowledge economy—specifically how to persuade highly educated, relatively autonomous knowledge workers to work collaboratively to serve the needs of their organization. PSFs have therefore grappled with, and to a significant extent resolved, one of the most challenging power dynamics at the heart of contemporary organizational life (Clegg et al. 2006). Heckscher and Adler (2006) have gone so far as to suggest that organizations of professionals are pioneering a new organizational form, the collaborative community, where the apparently oppositional organizing principles of market, hierarchy, and community, are reconciled and accommodated in a dynamic tension which reconciles the competing values of individualism and collectivism. If this is indeed the case, it implies a significant role for leadership, in exercising influence at the individual, organizational, and strategic level. Yet, Heckscher and Adler are silent on the topic of leadership in this context.

It is time, therefore, for scholars of both leadership *and* PSFs to turn their attention to leadership *in* PSFs, to develop a deeper understanding of this significant but neglected phenomenon.

Acknowledgments

Some of the ideas outlined in this chapter were developed as part of work funded by the UK's Economic and Social Research Council through grant RES-062-23-2269, "Understanding the dynamics of leadership in Professional Service Firms."

References

Abdallah, C. and Langley, A. (2014). "The Double Edge of Ambiguity in Strategic Planning," *Journal of Management Studies* 51(2): 235–264.

Adler, P. S., Kwon, S. W., and Heckscher, C. (2008). "Perspective—Professional Work: The Emergence of Collaborative Community," *Organization Science* 19(2): 359–376.

Alvarez, J. L. and Svejenova, S. (2005). *Sharing Executive Power: Roles and Relationships at the Top*. Cambridge: Cambridge University Press.

Alvesson, M. (1993). "Organizations as Rhetoric: Knowledge-Intensive Firms and the Struggle with Ambiguity," *Journal of Management Studies* 30(6): 997–1015.

Alvesson, M. (2004). *Knowledge Work and Knowledge-Intensive Firms*. Oxford: Oxford University Press.

Alvesson, M. and Spicer, A. (2011). *Metaphors We Lead By: Leadership in the Real World.* London: Routledge.

Alvesson, M. and Sveningsson, S. (2003a). "The Great Disappearing Act: Difficulties in Doing 'Leadership,'" *Leadership Quarterly* 14(3): 359–381.

Alvesson, M. and Sveningsson, S. (2003b). "Managers Doing Leadership: The Extra-Ordinarization of the Mundane," *Human Relations* 56(12): 1435–1459.

Alvesson, M. and Sveningsson, S. (2003c). "Good Visions, Bad Micro-Management and Ugly Ambiguity: Contradictions of (Non-) Leadership in a Knowledge-Intensive Organization," *Organization Studies* 24(6): 961–988.

Alvesson, M. and Willmott, H. (2002). "Identity Regulation as Organizational Control: Producing the Appropriate Individual," *Journal of Management Studies* 39(5): 619–644.

Anand, N., Gardner, H. K., and Morris, T. (2007). "Knowledge-Based Innovation: Emergence and Embedding of New Practice Areas in Management Consulting Firms," *Academy of Management Journal* 50(2): 406–428.

Anderson-Gough, F., Grey, C., and Robson, K. (1998). " 'Work Hard, Play Hard': An Analysis of Organizational Cliche in Two Accountancy Practices," *Organization* 5(4): 565–592.

Anderson-Gough, F., Grey, C., and Robson, K. (2000). "In the Name of the Client: The Service Ethic in Two Professional Services Firms," *Human Relations* 53(9): 1151–1174.

Anderson-Gough, F., Grey, C., and Robson, K. (2001). "Tests of Time: Organizational Time-Reckoning and the Making of Accountants in Two Multi-National Accounting Firms," *Accounting, Organizations and Society* 26(2): 99–122.

Anderson-Gough, F., Grey, C., and Robson, K. (2002). "Accounting Professionals and the Accounting Profession: Linking Conduct and Context," *Accounting and Business Research* 32(1): 41–56.

Avolio, B. J., Walumbwa, F. O., and Weber, T. J. (2009). "Leadership: Current Theories, Research, and Future Directions," *Annual Review of Psychology* 60: 421–449.

Barker, J. R. (1993). "Tightening the Iron Cage: Concertive Control in Self-Managing Teams," *Administrative Science Quarterly* 38(3): 408–437.

Barker, R. A. (1997). "How Can We Train Leaders If We Do Not Know What Leadership Is?" *Human Relations* 50(4): 343–362.

Brock, D., Powell, M. J., and Hinings, C. R. (1999). "The Restructured Professional Organization: Corporates, Cobwebs and Cowboys," in *Restructuring the Professional Organization: Accounting, Health Care and Law*, ed. D. Brock, M. J. Powell, and C. R. Hinings. London: Routledge, 215–229.

Broderick, M. (2011). *The Art of Managing Professional Services: Insights from Leaders of the World's Top Firms.* Upper Saddle River, NJ: Prentice-Hall.

Brown, A. D., Kornberger, M., Clegg, S. R., and Carter, C. (2010). " 'Invisible Walls' and 'Silent Hierarchies': A Case Study of Power Relations in an Architecture Firm," *Human Relations* 63(4): 525–549.

Carlsen, A. (2006). "Organizational Becoming as Dialogic Imagination of Practice: The Case of the Indomitable Gauls," *Organization Science* 17(1): 132–149.

Chuang, C. H., Jackson, S. E., and Jiang, Y. (2013). "Can Knowledge-Intensive Teamwork be Managed? Examining the Roles of HRM Systems, Leadership, and Tacit Knowledge," *Journal of Management* (forthcoming).

Clegg, S. R., Courpasson, D., and Phillips, N. (2006). *Power and Organizations: Foundations for Organizational Science.* London: Sage.

Cohen, M. D. and March, J. G. (1986). *Leadership and Ambiguity: The American College President.* Cambridge, MA: Harvard Business School Press.

Currie, G. and Lockett, A. (2011). "Distributing Leadership in Health and Social Care: Concertive, Conjoint or Collective?" *International Journal of Management Reviews* 13(3): 286–300.

DeLong, T. J., Gabarro, J. J., and Lees, R. J. (2007). *When Professionals Have to Lead: A New Model for High Performance*. Cambridge, MA: Harvard Business School Press.

Denis, J. L., Lamothe, L., and Langley, A. (2001). "The Dynamics of Collective Leadership and Strategic Change in Pluralistic Organizations," *Academy of Management Journal* 44(4): 809–837.

Denis, J. L., Langley, A., and Cazale, L. (1996). "Leadership and Strategic Change Under Ambiguity," *Organization Studies* 17(4): 673–699.

Denis, J. L., Langley, A., and Rouleau, L. (2007). "Strategizing in Pluralistic Contexts: Rethinking Theoretical Frames," *Human Relations* 60(1): 179–215.

Denis, J. L., Langley, A., and Rouleau, L. (2010). "The Practice of Leadership in the Messy World of Organizations," *Leadership* 6(1): 67–88.

Denis, J. L., Langley, A., and Sergi, V. (2012). "Leadership in the Plural," *Academy of Management Annals* 6(1): 211–283.

Diefenbach, T. and Sillince, J. A. A. (2011). "Formal and Informal Hierarchy in Different Types of Organization," *Organization Studies* 32(11): 1515–1537.

DiMaggio, P. J. and Powell, W. W. (1983). "The Iron Cage Revisited: Institutional Isomorphism and Collective Rationality in Organizational Fields," *American Sociological Review* 48(2): 147–160.

e Cunha, M. P. (2002). "'The Best Place to Be': Managing Control and Employee Loyalty in a Knowledge-Intensive Company," *Journal of Applied Behavioral Science* 38(4): 481–495.

Empson, L. (2000). "Merging Professional Service Firms," *Business Strategy Review* 11(2): 39–46.

Empson, L. (2001a). "Fear of Exploitation and Fear of Contamination: Impediments to Knowledge Transfer in Mergers Between Professional Service Firms," *Human Relations* 54(7): 839–862.

Empson, L. (2001b). "Introduction: Knowledge Management in Professional Service Firms," *Human Relations* 54(7): 811–817.

Empson, L. (2004). "Organizational Identity Change: Managerial Regulation and Member Identification in an Accounting Firm Acquisition," *Accounting, Organizations and Society* 29(8): 759–781.

Empson, L. (2007). *Managing the Modern Law Firm: New Challenges, New Perspectives*. Oxford: Oxford University Press.

Empson, L. (2011). "Navigating Ambiguity: Collective Leadership Processes in Professional Service Firms," paper presented at the Academy of Management Annual Meeting, San Antonio, Texas.

Empson, L. (2012). "Beyond Dichotomies: A Multi-Stage Model of Governance in Professional Service Firms," in *Handbook of Research on Entrepreneurship in Professional Services*, ed. M. R. Reihlen and A. Werr. Cheltenham: Edward Elgar, 274–296.

Empson, L. and Chapman, C. (2006). "Partnership Versus Corporation: Implications of Alternative Forms of Governance in Professional Service Firms," *Research in the Sociology of Organizations* 24: 139–170.

Empson, L., Cleaver, I., and Allen, J. (2013). "Managing Partners and Management Professionals: Institutional Work Dyads in Professional Partnerships," *Journal of Management Studies* 50(5): 808–844.

Faulconbridge, J. R. (2006). "Stretching Tacit Knowledge Beyond a Local Fix? Global Spaces of Learning in Advertising Professional Service Firms," *Journal of Economic Geography* 6(4): 517–540.

Fenton, E. and Pettigrew, A. (2006). "Leading Change in the New Professional Service Firm: Characterizing Strategic Leadership in a Global Context," *Research in the Sociology of Organizations* 24: 101–137.

Fitzgerald, L., Ferlie, E., McGivern, G., and Buchanan, D. (2013). "Distributed Leadership Patterns and Service Improvement: Evidence and Argument from English Healthcare," *Leadership Quarterly* 24(1): 227–239.

Gardner, H. K., Anand, N., and Morris, T. (2008). "Chartering New Territory: Diversification, Legitimacy, and Practice Area Creation in Professional Service Firms," *Journal of Organizational Behavior* 29(8): 1101–1121.

Gardner, H. K., Gino, F., and Staats, B. R. (2012). "Dynamically Integrating Knowledge in Teams: Transforming Resources into Performance," *Academy of Management Journal* 55(4): 998–1022.

Gioia, D. A. and Chittipeddi, K. (1991). "Sensemaking and Sensegiving in Strategic Change Initiation," *Strategic Management Journal* 12(6): 433–448.

Gioia, D. A., Nag, R., and Corley, K. G. (2012). "Visionary Ambiguity and Strategic Change: The Virtue of Vagueness in Launching Major Organizational Change," *Journal of Management Inquiry* 21(4): 364–375.

Greenleaf, R. K. and Spears, L. C. (2002). *Servant Leadership: A Journey into the Nature of Legitimate Power and Greatness.* Mahwah, NJ: Paulist Press.

Greenwood, R. and Empson, L. (2003). "The Professional Partnership: Relic or Exemplary form of Governance?" *Organization Studies* 24(6): 909–933.

Greenwood, R., Hinings, C. R., and Brown, J. (1990). "'P²-Form' Strategic Management: Corporate Practices in Professional Partnerships," *Academy of Management Journal* 33(4): 725–755.

Greenwood, R., Hinings, C. R., and Brown, J. (1994). "Merging Professional Service Firms," *Organization Science* 5(2): 239–257.

Gronn, P. (1999). "Substituting for Leadership: The Neglected Role of the Leadership Couple," *Leadership Quarterly* 10(1): 41–62.

Heckscher, C. and Adler, P. S., (2006). *The Firm as a Collaborative Community: Reconstructing Trust in the Knowledge Economy.* Oxford: Oxford University Press.

Heusinkveld, S. and Benders, J. (2005). "Contested Commodification: Consultancies and their Struggle with New Concept Development," *Human Relations* 58(3): 283–310.

Hinings, C. R., Brown, J., and Greenwood, R. (1991). "Change in an Autonomous Professional Organization," *Journal of Management Studies* 28(4): 376–393.

Hodgson, R. C., Levinson, D. J., and Zaleznik, A. (1965). *The Executive Role Constellation.* Cambridge, MA: Harvard Business School Press.

Howell, J. M. and Shamir, B. (2005). "The Role of Followers in the Charismatic Leadership Process: Relationships and Their Consequences," *Academy of Management Review* 30(1): 96–112.

Ibarra, H. (1999). "Provisional Selves: Experimenting with Image and Identity in Professional Adaptation," *Administrative Science Quarterly* 44(4): 764–791.

Kerr, S. and Jermier, J. M. (1978). "Substitutes for Leadership: Their Meaning and Measurement," *Organizational Behavior and Human Performance* 22(3): 375–403.

Kiechel, W. (2010). *The Lords of Strategy.* Cambridge, MA: Harvard Business School Press.

Lawrence, T. B., Malhotra, N., and Morris, T. (2012). "Episodic and Systemic Power in the Transformation of Professional Service Firms," *Journal of Management Studies* 49(1): 102–143.

Lorsch, J. W. and Tierney, T. J. (2002). *Aligning the Stars*. Cambridge, MA: Harvard Business School Press.

Løwendahl, B. R. (2005). *Strategic Management of Professional Service Firms*. Copenhagen: Copenhagen Business School Press.

Maister, D. H. (1981). *Balancing the Professional Service Firm*. Cambridge, MA: Harvard Business School Press.

Maister, D. H. (1993). *Managing the Professional Service Firm*. New York: Free Press.

Malhotra, N. and Morris, T. (2009). "Heterogeneity in Professional Service Firms," *Journal of Management Studies* 46(6): 895–922.

Marcson, S. (1962). "Decision-Making in a University Physics Department," *American Behavioral Scientist* 6(4): 37–39.

Martin, G. P., Currie, G., and Finn, R. (2009). "Leadership, Service Reform, and Public-Service Networks: The Case of Cancer-Genetics Pilots in the English NHS," *Journal of Public Administration Research and Theory* 19(4): 769–794.

Miller, D. and Sardais, C. (2011). "A Concept of Leadership for Strategic Organization," *Strategic Organization* 9(2): 174–183.

Miner, J. B., Crane, D. P., and Vandenberg, R. J. (1994). "Congruence and Fit in Professional Role Motivation Theory," *Organization Science* 5(1): 86–97.

Mintzberg, H. (1979). *The Structuring of Organizations*. Englewood Cliffs, NJ: Prentice-Hall.

Mintzberg, H. (1983). *Power In and Around Organizations*. Englewood Cliffs, NJ: Prentice-Hall.

Mintzberg, H. (1989). *Mintzberg on Management: Inside our Strange World of Organizations*. New York: Free Press.

Mintzberg, H. (1998). "Covert Leadership: Notes on Managing Professionals," *Harvard Business Review* 76(6): 140–148.

Morris, T., Greenwood, R., and Fairclough, S. (2010). "Decision Making in Professional Service Firms," in *Handbook of Decision Making*, ed. P. Nutt and D. Wilson. Chichester: John Wiley, 275–306.

Muhr, S. L. (2011). "The Leader as Cyborg: Norm-Setting, Intimidation and Mechanistic Superiority," in *Understanding Leadership in the Real World: Metaphors We Lead By*, ed. M. Alvesson, and A. Spicer. London: Routledge, 138–161.

O'Reilly, D. and Reed, M. (2011). "The Grit in the Oyster: Professionalism, Managerialism and Leaderism as Discourses of UK Public Services Modernization," *Organization Studies* 32(8): 1079–1101.

Ouchi, W. G. (1980). "Markets, Bureaucracies, and Clans," *Administrative Science Quarterly* 25(1): 129–141.

Reid, W. and Karambayya, R. (2009). "Impact of Dual Executive Leadership Dynamics in Creative Organizations," *Human Relations* 62(7): 1073–1112.

Robertson, M. and Swan, J. (2003). "'Control–What Control?' Culture and Ambiguity Within a Knowledge Intensive Firm," *Journal of Management Studies* 40(4): 831–858.

Robertson, M., Scarbrough, H., and Swan, J. (2003). "Knowledge Creation in Professional Service Firms: Institutional Effects," *Organization Studies* 24(6): 831–857.

Scott, W. R. (2008). "Lords of the Dance: Professionals as Institutional Agents," *Organization Studies* 29(2): 219–238.

Sillince, J., Jarzabkowski, P., and Shaw, D. (2012). "Shaping Strategic Action Through the Rhetorical Construction and Exploitation of Ambiguity," *Organization Science* 23(3): 630–650.

Smircich, L. and Morgan, G. (1982). "Leadership: The Management of Meaning," *Journal of Applied Behavioral Science* 18(3): 257–273.

Spillane, J. P. (2006). *Distributed Leadership.* San Francisco, CA: Jossey-Bass.

Starbuck, W. H. (1993). "Keeping a Butterfly and an Elephant in a House of Cards: The Elements of Exceptional Success," *Journal of Management Studies* 30(6): 885–921.

Strannegård, L. (2012). "Leadership in Entrepreneurial Professional Service Firms," in *Handbook of Research on Entrepreneurship in Professional Services*, ed. M. R. Reihlen and A. Werr. Cheltenham: Edward Elgar, 170–180.

Suddaby, R. and Viale, T. (2011). "Professionals and Field-Level Change: Institutional Work and the Professional Project," *Current Sociology* 59(4): 423–442.

Thompson, J. D. (1967). *Organizations in Action: Social Science Bases of Administrative Theory.* New Brunswick, NJ: Transaction Publishing.

Uhl-Bien, M., Marion, R., and McKelvey, B. (2007). "Complexity Leadership Theory: Shifting Leadership from the Industrial Age to the Knowledge Era," *Leadership Quarterly* 18(4): 298–318.

von Glinow, M. A. (1988). *The New Professionals: Managing Today's High-Tech Employees.* Cambridge, MA: Ballinger Publishing.

von Nordenflycht, A. (2010). "What is a Professional Service Firm? Toward a Theory and Taxonomy of Knowledge-Intensive Firms," *Academy of Management Review* 35(1): 155–174.

Werr, A. and Stjernberg, T. (2003). "Exploring Management Consulting Firms as Knowledge Systems," *Organization Studies* 24(6): 881–908.

Yukl, G. (1989). "Managerial Leadership: A Review of Theory and Research," *Journal of Management* 15(2): 251–289.

CHAPTER 9

....

GOVERNANCE IN PROFESSIONAL SERVICE FIRMS

From Structural and Cultural to Legal Normative Views

....

HUSEYIN LEBLEBICI AND PETER D. SHERER

9.1 INTRODUCTION

....

CONSIDER governance in a fairly typical larger Professional Service Firm (PSF).[1] While the firm was once governed like a partnership in which partners all had a say in firm matters, it now behaves more like a corporation in the way that it carries on business. Firm-wide committees, acting as senior management, wield significant decision-making powers that allow them to act without consulting professionals on any number of business matters. These committees, among other things, provide strategic direction for the firm, determine which professionals at senior levels will be terminated, and make decisions on whether to acquire other PSFs. Furthermore, many of these committees' decisions are weighted towards what clients want, and several conflicts have had to be resolved over the years in dealings with clients. Even so, the firm still has key features of a partnership, with an ethos of "being there for one another," and individuals referring to themselves as "partners." At the same time, certain individuals have been entrusted with the firm's reputation and its continuance into the future, and these individuals see themselves as the firm's guardians, although not everyone in the firm sees it that way.

Reflective of this scenario, governance has taken a number of perspectives in the PSF literature. The dominant view has been that of a "partnership model" in which the focus is on how partners govern among themselves through a legal structure and/or the ethos of a partnership irrespective of whether there legally is a partnership (Empson and Chapman 2006; Greenwood and Empson 2003; Greenwood et al. 1990). The alternative dominant view has focused on the fact that many PSFs today are legally organized as limited liability firms (LLP, LLC, or C Corporation). Even though their managers use the titles that are traditionally identified with partnerships (e.g., managing partner), officially they are CEOs or other officers of the top management teams (Delong et al. 2007). In other words, the distinctions that are taken for granted in traditional corporate settings where the CEO is a professional manager and the board of directors represent the shareholders' interests are no different within PSF governance. These two views represent the tension within PSF governance in which PSF management and conflict resolution among critical players require more complex mechanisms of governance and greater political skills.

What this suggests is that there is a complexity and variation to governance in PSFs that has not been sufficiently addressed in the governance literature on PSFs. Therefore, with this chapter, we start with a review of four foundational perspectives in order to help define what we mean by governance and highlight the theoretical debates in the field. We then focus on the issues of governance that are most relevant to PSFs in order to untangle the tension highlighted above. In so doing, we take a legal normative view of governance, defined as the legal and non-legal rules, norms, conventions, standards, and managerial practices that facilitate the coordination and conflict resolution among the critical constituencies of PSF for the firm as an institution. With that in mind, we identify a major unexplored issue that can broaden our understanding of governance in PSFs: the definitions of rights and obligations among critical constituencies and how that plays into the nature of conflict resolution mechanisms built into PSF governance.

9.2 WHAT IS GOVERNANCE?

Governance is one of the critical building blocks of PSFs. Therefore, before going into the details of the four perspectives on PSF governance, it is important to specify what is meant by governance. We define governance as: *the management of the relationships between a firm's management and its critical transacting constituencies*. It is composed of a complex set of legal, organizational, and institutional practices that allocates the rights and obligations of the firm's constituencies to each other for the maintenance of the firm as a going concern. As such, governance defines the nature of financial and professional relationship among partners; it structures the career progressions of associates as they move towards partnership and clarifies the compensation practices; it provides the guidelines on how various participants within the firm should interact with each other and with clients; it shapes the incentives for developing and protecting the intellectual capital of these firms; and it provides oversight in succession planning. All of these topics are potential sources of conflict and contention for organizational members as well as the clients of the firm.

Corporate governance is a well-discussed subject within the economic and the strategic management literature; still the concept of governance is a less understood and less organized terrain. Academic research on governance has been truly interdisciplinary, with much work being undertaken by researchers not only from economics and finance but also from law, management, sociology, and accounting. Even though the ongoing debates on corporate governance seem to be complex and sometimes esoteric, they are the products of how researchers define "the firm" and what/who needs to be governed. When the firm is traditionally defined as only constituting the shareholders as owners, and the ownership of financial assets is separated from top management action, corporate governance focuses on the allocation of risk between the shareholders and the management. In their influential survey of corporate governance literature, Shleifer and Vishny (1997: 737) argue that corporate governance deals with the "ways in which suppliers of finance to corporations assure themselves of getting a return on their investments." Within such a view, governance is assumed to be accomplished through the structure of incentives, administrative controls, and the contract law regime (Williamson 2005).

But when the definition of "the firm" is relaxed to include other parties in addition to the shareholders, especially the holders of human and other intellectual capital, the focus of governance shifts to organizational aspects (Aoki 2010), wherein a variety of interdependent actors (employees, clients, and even the creditors) interact within the firm and alternative governance structures mediate the distribution of rights and obligations among these different class of participants. In contrast to economics and finance, other fields such as sociology, management (Daily et al. 2003), and international business (Aguilera and Jackson 2003), have been more inclusive by taking into account legal, cultural, and institutional arrangements through which control over organizations is established, decisions are made, and rewards are allocated (Davis 2005).

9.3 GOVERNANCE IN PROFESSIONAL SERVICE FIRMS: A REVIEW OF THE FOUNDATIONAL LITERATURE

As highlighted in the previous section, theoretical debates on governance hinge on the way a PSF is defined and how the critical constituencies of the firm are identified. In addition to the partnership/partnership ethos perspective, it is possible to identify three other perspectives on governance: the agency perspective, the stakeholder perspective, and the trusteeship perspective. As summarized in Table 9.1, each perspective attempts to address the fundamental issues of governance by taking a structural (legal-contractual) or a cultural view and defining the relationship between the firm and its critical constituencies either in the traditional principal–agent or in the beneficiary–trustee framework. The importance of these two dimensions has been critical in the

Table 9.1 A typology of governance perspectives

Emphasis is on	Principal–Agent	Beneficiary–Trustee
Structure	The Agency Perspective	Trusteeship Perspective
Culture	Stakeholders' Perspective	Partnership Perspective

evolution of governance debate within the PSF literature. As Empson and Chapman (2006: 139) have argued succinctly, "there is a need to develop a more nuanced understanding of the relationship between governance as a legal form and governance as an interpretive scheme."

We begin with the agency perspective, a structural view, in which stockholders as the owners and boards acting as the principals on behalf of the owners oversee managers acting as the agents of the shareholders. The ground-breaking work of Fama and Jensen (1983a, 1983b) in an agency perspective had a particularly strong influence on the PSF literature on governance, in part because it distinguished between open corporations (which are open in the sense that ownership can be freely traded in outside stock markets) and partnerships (wherein ownership is internally allocated among individuals and the transfer of ownership typically involves restrictions). Fama and Jensen argue that small professional partnerships "solve" the agency problem that occurs when risk bearing by owners is separated from decision management, but create their own additional problems. Just as importantly, they argue that as professional partnerships increased in scale and scope they came to have similar agency problems and needed solutions as the large open corporation did. Subsequent work in the agency perspective for the most part did not specifically address PSFs but looked to how to best structure the principal–agent relationship through incentives, how to deal with incomplete contracting, and what was the significance of property rights.

We then look at the partnership/partnership ethos perspective. This perspective, which was influenced early on by the Cravath Model of partnership, looked to how partners legally govern among themselves as professionals through such practices as up-or-out partnership promotion and share systems of compensation. Subsequent work, such as Empson (2007), sought to understand partnership beyond these practices and its legal form by providing a cultural perspective and looking to the ethos that partners or like-minded professionals in a firm had.

We then look to the work of Freeman and others that followed (Donaldson and Preston 1995; Freeman 1984; Freeman and Reed 1983) in the stakeholder perspective. This perspective on governance takes the view that many different parties have a stake in the organization, like customers, and, as such, these parties are critical players in a firm's governance. The stakeholder model has not, for the most part, been explicitly addressed in the governance literature on PSFs, but it is implicit in much of the PSF literature on governance, no doubt because of the critical role played by clients of PSFs. We view the stakeholder model as a cultural perspective that provides a normative extension of the simple two-party model of agency to a multi-party model of agency. We suggest its influence on the governance literature on PSFs has been underestimated, and it is, therefore, important to recognize and address what it says specifically about and implies for governance in the PSF.

We see additionally in the PSF literature on governance elements of an alternative structural view that we refer to as a "trustee model." In this perspective, governance has to do with how leadership in a PSF governs by acting as guardians or keepers of the firm's past, present, and future. Legal scholars in the past (Dodd 1932) suggested such a perspective and in recent years we see a revival of such arguments (Lan and Heracleous 2010). In the trustee model, the board is not so much the agent for stockholders but instead is the guardian of the firm as an institution.

We argue that each of these four foundational perspectives has something to say about governance in PSFs. For it is clear that the practice of governance in many firms is something of an amalgam of these different perspectives and that there are differences in governance across firms. However, we argue subsequently that there are a number of key issues that have not been addressed or are in need of much more discussion and that take us beyond the cultural and structural views that these four perspectives embody to that of a legal normative view of governance.

9.3.1 The Agency Perspective

The starting point for our review of the literature on governance in PSFs is the agency theory perspective of Fama and Jensen (1983a, 1983b). In their work, they returned to the issue of the separation of ownership from control in the modern corporation that was identified by Berle and Means (1932). The modern corporation meant that the principals or owners in publicly held companies came to be equated with stockholders (Berle and Means 1932). Management acted as agents that had a control function. With the separation of ownership from control, the argument went, managers as agents acted as a class unto themselves and not necessarily in the interests of the principals. Hence, the agency problem was that of managers acting as agents for their own self-interest and not acting in the interests of their principals.

Fama and Jensen argued that governance via the board of directors was the means to address the agency problem. The role of the board was to be the advocates for the principals. The board took the control role of ratifying key issues facing the firm that had been generated by management as well as monitoring and incentivizing senior management in its performance. In this way, the agency problem was "solved."

Small professional partnerships avoided the agency problem, just as proprietorships did, as there was no separation of ownership from control. Partners in such a PSF have ownership in the firm, and have voice and vote in the firm's matters. The additional factor in the PSF is that partners also provide their human capital as professionals, which means that they operate as *both* principals and agents. Fama and Jensen argued that professional partnerships limit free riding and quality issues with their partners through mutual monitoring and consulting among one another. In this way, the small professional partnership provides an ethos among partners who are bound together, particularly because they share unlimited liability (Empson 2007). Moreover, in such professional partnerships, governance often (although not always) takes the form of a pure form of democracy in which each individual partner has voice and vote in firm matters (to be more complete, we need to mention that there are other instances, where founding or more wealth-producing partners have disproportionate decision-making power).

Fama and Jensen (1983b: 332) suggested that the professional partnership avoided the agency problem associated with risk bearing being separated from key decision-making, but had its own costs tied to its decision-making: "The decision process suffers efficiency losses because decision agents must be chosen on the basis of wealth and willingness to bear risk as well as for decision skills. Residual claimants forgo optimal diversification so that residual claims can be combined into a small number of agents." More generally, partnership limits who can be risk bearers and restricts who can act as managers and internal committee members to those who have human capital in that specific profession, not that of a manager. The result is that the firm might not have the best managers or internal committee members; it has to settle for who it has internally and who is in the profession. Thus, in Fama and Jensen's view, there are management problems linked to professional partnership, but they are largely limited to issues concerning selection of the managers and internal boards, not the problems of governing partners.

As Fama and Jensen additionally specify, small and large professional partnerships have different problems because of their scale and scope. Large professional partnerships, numbering into the thousands of partners and operating in many different professional practices and geographical locations, have what Fama and Jensen (1983a: 316) say are "diffuse residual claimants." As such, governance moves from the mutual monitoring and pure form of democracy (or autocracy) of the small professional partnership to representative government with internal committees, which Fama and Jensen equate to boards of directors. On this point, Fama and Jensen (1983a: 316) state:

> The board is involved in decisions with respect to the management of the partnership, for example, where new offices should be opened, who should be admitted to the partnership, and who should be dismissed. The board is also involved in renegotiating the shares of the partners . . . The role of the board is to develop acceptable consensus decisions from this information. Thus, the boards of large professional partnerships are generally called committees of managing partners rather than boards.

These committees are comprised of internal partners, many of whom are quite senior, and who are experts in the ongoing activities of the firm. It is to these committees that the firm turns over the larger part of the governance of the firm.

But once the critical steps in decision-making of initiation, ratification, implementation, and monitoring (Fama and Jensen 1983a), are allocated to different parties as a result of organizational size or geographical dispersion, basic agency problems become inevitable and must be resolved through governance mechanisms. The solutions offered by the agency perspective are usually based on structural (or contractual) mechanisms that focus on managerial incentives, asymmetric information, or the property rights of diverse parties involved with the firm.

The incentive perspective assumes that the right incentives such as compensation based on firm performance or direct monitoring of managerial decisions could motivate the managers in the right direction to solve the agency problem. The incomplete contracting perspective, on the other hand, defines the agency problem in terms of asymmetric information that is built into managerial decision-making. It highlights the complex interactions among decision-making stages and decision types. Who actually makes which decision and the nature of communication among various parties are not really incorporated into the traditional agency models. The decision-makers' private information as well as the other parties' information about a given decision would directly influence what kind of governance structure would be optimal. Following the seminal work of Holmström (Holmström 1999; Holmström and Milgrom 1994), a vast literature on organizational incentives has incorporated the informational aspects of managerial action.

Contracting under incomplete information requires additional governance mechanisms to resolve the agency problem. Given transaction costs associated with contracts such as negotiation, information gathering, and monitoring, the parties could not or would not write comprehensive contracts. Incomplete contracts would necessitate renegotiations as new information becomes available. Governance structure acts as the mechanism for making decisions that have not been specified in the initial contract (Hart 1995: 680).

The property rights approach, as another alternative reformulation of the agency problem, focuses on the question of who controls the specialized physical and especially intangible assets of the firm. In contrast to the traditional agency perspective where the corporate assets are all owned by the shareholders, it acknowledges that employees have ownership rights over their human capital and corporate governance must incorporate the employees' investment in firm-specific knowledge. Recent theoretical as well as empirical research points out that intellectual property, technological investments, and firm-specific assets all require a new understanding of incomplete contracts and governance. Wang et al. (2009) show that traditional governance mechanisms must incorporate some forms of shared governance in order to motivate employees to make firm-specific investments. Such an approach requires a more systematic analysis of shared governance mechanisms.

We believe the agency perspective has had a very influential effect on the PSF literature on governance. Nonetheless, even given its many advances, we do not find the agency literature to be sufficient for understanding the complexity and diversity of governance in PSFs. That is where the partnership model/partnership ethos perspective comes in. This perspective provides insight into how firms are governed when firms are sufficiently large and diverse.

9.3.2 The Partnership/Partnership Ethos Perspective

The early literature on governance in PSFs was influenced by the Cravath Model that was developed by Paul Cravath of the law firm Cravath, Swaine and Moore (Swaine 1948). The most well-known aspect of the Cravath Model was the up-or-out system in which young, junior lawyers spent an apprenticeship of approximately seven years at the firm before a decision was made for them to go up to partner or out of the firm. Admittance to partnership was, in fact, a part of governance because the individual was being selected to be one of the partners. Additional issues, such as compensation, were meaningful to governance in that they involved shares in the organization, and, reflecting that, were called "share systems."

The Cravath Model had important implications for how partners governed among themselves. Swaine (1948: 12) discussed how, in fact, the Cravath firm evolved to a more democratic form from the tight control that founding partner, Paul Cravath, early on exercised over the firm:

> Cravath believed that a law firm, like any other successful organization, must have strong executive direction, and until the mid-1930s his firm was under a dictatorship in his person ... Cravath never completely delegated to anyone ultimate determination of office policy or evaluation of associates and partners. However ... [as the firm grew] rapidly after World War I, he relied more on the judgement of his partners. Weekly firm meetings started about 1923, where matters of general policy and of management, as well as current law problems, are discussed. Today every partner has a voice in the decision of every important question, as well as the benefit of the views of all his partners.

Greenwood et al. (1990) extend the logic of the Cravath Model in their discussion of the P^2 model of PSFs. Greenwood et al. (1990: 733) suggest that with the P^2 form: "The distinctive mark of a professional partnership is the nature of the authority system that emanates from its primary task and becomes enshrined in the structure of governance." To illustrate their argument, Greenwood et al. (1990: 730) detail the structure of a large accounting firm:

> The structure's dominant feature is that of the national office of a firm ... the formal equivalent of a corporate headquarters, is controlled through a form of representative democracy. At the strategic apex (Mintzberg, 1979) is a partnership body, which generally meets at least twice a year and which elects an executive policy committee. The executive policy committee, drawn from the ranks of the partnership, is typically constituted to represent major functional areas, such as audit and taxation, and major geographical areas. . . . committees, moreover, are ultimately accountable to the

full body of a partnership: individual partners thus figure at both the base and the apex of these organizations.

What is critical here is that the structure captures a representative democracy in which: (1) decision-making occurs where operating expertise lies, (2) there is necessary centralization on, for example, professional training and expertise, and (3) there are checks and balances to ensure that the partnership as a whole has a say in the major ongoing matters of the firm.

Greenwood et al.'s (1990) characterization of governance in a large accounting firm in 1990 as compared to today might only differ in shades of gray. Accounting and law firms have arguably had the most limited shift from the P^2 model. However, even in law firms, there has been a significant shift from this model. In a number of firms, there has been a break from partnership and a shift to incorporation. And, in other firms that have remained as partnerships, there has been an erosion from what might be called the "partner primacy model" that Greenwood et al. (1990) characterize. Checks and balances and the role of the partnership as a whole to make decisions have given way to more "streamlined" decision-making, with much less say by the partnership as a whole in firm matters. Cooper et al. (1996) referred to the shift away from the P^2 model and towards a model that acts on business matters more like a corporation as the MPB, the Managerial Professional Business.

Empson (2007), recognizing the shift away from the legal mode of partnership towards a model like the MPB, broadens the argument by suggesting that partnership either in its legal form *or* as an ethos is what underlies the governance of the PSF. Empson (2007: 13) argues that partnership per se is not what is most critical; what is most critical is the partnership ethos. Empson (2007: 19) states: "when professionals talked about what partnership meant to them, they were not referring to the legal form of partnership but to its 'ethos' (i.e., the characteristic beliefs and behaviours of a community: *Oxford English Dictionary*). It was this ethos of partnership that inspired strong sentiments."

Recognizing the partnership ethos as distinct from partnership as the legal form opens up two possibilities. The first is that partnership can continue to operate as a legal form after the partnership ethos has ceased to exist in a meaningful sense. The second is that publicly traded corporations can embody the most meaningful and valuable aspects of the partnership ethos without having to be a legal form of partnership.

Empson (2007) suggests that in a professional partnership individualism versus collectivism are at a fundamental and continual tension. Individualism involves professionals acting as they individually see fit; collectivism involves individuals being part of a larger entity and having, if not unlimited personal liability for one another, shared responsibility for the reputation of the firm. Empson (2007: 20) argues that governance, through the partnership ethos, is used to address this tension: "This tension between individualism and collectivism is fundamental to understanding the dynamics of partnership. The legal form of partnership creates the tension—the ethos of partnership resolves that tension." Moreover, governance involves determining whether there is a weighting towards individualism or the collective: Empson (2007: 20) notes:

> In some partnerships, the balance may be tipped strongly towards individualism—partners are free to pursue their personal priorities, whether it is income maximization or self-actualization ... In other partnerships, the balance may be tipped strongly towards the interests of the collective (i.e., the firm). Senior management will have a clear mandate from the partners to manage the firm on their behalf.

Thus, Empson (2007: 21) suggests that in the governance of PSFs: "The management of the partnerships are in effect engaged in a constant struggle to identify and resolve the tension between the individual and the collective. In this context, a commonly understood partnership ethos represents a powerful unifying force which serves to counteract the potentially self-serving impulses that drive each partner individually."

Managerial research in PSFs that has been based on the partnership ethos attempts to resolve this tension between the individual and the collective by explicitly focusing on leadership and internal management. The role of the top management and specifically the board is to coordinate the activities of the firm's members, help develop necessary firm-specific human capital, allocate the benefits of the collective production, and mediate disputes among team members over the allocation decisions. The team production theory of corporate law calls this a "mediating hierarch" where team members give up important property rights to the firm that they belong to (Blair and Stout 1999: 753) in order to protect the collective. Three different but related streams of research have provided various solutions to fundamental tensions between the individual and the collective.

One stream of research has specifically focused on the role of the top management or the managing partner in protecting the integrity of the firm itself rather than simply a specific group of participants such as partners. In a PSF, a diverse set of participants including associates and the clients enter into an implicit agreement to cooperate involving inputs of time, intellectual knowledge, and information. The role of the management is to keep these participants engaged with the firm by making sure that conflicts are resolved and the engagements with clients are conflict free. As shown by Empson (2012), the role of the top management focus changes as the firm goes through the evolutionary stages of its life cycle which requires different approaches of governance. Moreover, the successful maintenance of the coalition within the firm for successful team production requires investment in firm reputation. As Greenwood and his colleagues (Greenwood et al. 2005) demonstrate, the success of large accounting firms depends on both firm reputation and careful diversification strategies involving human capital.

The second stream, which can be described as governance through leadership, has looked into the unique relationship between the firms' leaders and the professionals in PSFs. Within a knowledge-intensive setting where team production takes place, leadership represents more than simply a relationship between a manager and a subordinate. It is usually described in terms of teaching, mentoring, and guiding where the focus is on learning, socialization, and career development (Empson and Langley, Chapter 8, this volume). In other words, exercising leadership requires the development of senior managers in developing knowledge, teams, and clients (Alvesson 2004; Alvesson and Robertson 2006; Løwendahl et al. 2001). One of the unique concerns of PSFs is how to recruit talented managers with sufficient professional authority and respect, who are willing to spend time and energy in internal matters and capable of maintaining the professional reputation and prestige of the firm both internally and externally (Løwendahl 1997). When the most critical resources of team production and value creation are under the control of the professionals within the firm, simple hierarchical structures and incentives that are based on traditional employment contracts are not sufficient to govern the firm. Additional extra-contractual tools must be available to the top managers of the firm and they need to learn how to use them. These extra contractual tools include the conscious development of firm culture that involves the development of firm-specific routines in formal and informal reporting structures, talent development processes, and coordination systems. Research on these micro-level governance mechanisms emphasizes the critical role leadership plays in managing PSFs.

The third stream of research, which can be described as governance through professional norms, emphasizes self-regulation, professional codes of ethics, and loyalty to the profession and clients. Professional norms within each professional setting provide unique governance mechanisms involving competition in the marketplace, responsibility to the client, and loyalty to the firm. In other words, the differences among professions influence directly the ways these firms are organized, governed, and managed. This literature, even though limited in volume, focuses on the differences among professions and how these differences lead to differences in firms' governance. The sources of these differences are related to the nature of knowledge in a given profession, the jurisdictional control over this knowledge, and the nature of client relations (Malhotra and Morris 2009). Studies looking into firms operating within accounting, law, or medical professions demonstrate why these differences occur and how they influence the structure as well as the management of these firms (Brock et al. 1999; Malhotra et al. 2010; Suddaby et al. 2009). These studies point out the importance of professional norms in establishing governance structures.

These diverse attempts to address the governance problems within PSFs challenge the traditional agency views of governance (Klein et al. 2012) and are in line with Empson's (2007) argument that governance entails identifying and resolving tensions. As Daily et al. (2003: 371) argue, governance has to do with: "the determination of the broad uses to which organizational resources will be deployed and the resolution of conflicts among the myriad participants in organizations." In this vein, we also see underlying tensions and potentially competing interests and conflicts with the autonomy of the local and national offices versus the partnership as a whole as described in Greenwood et al. (1990).

We suggest there are other tensions that the firm faces and that are resolved through governance. The stakeholder approach suggests additional parties, particularly clients and the profession in the case of PSFs, through which such tensions arise and are addressed.

9.3.3 The Stakeholder Perspective

Stakeholder models became influential through the work of Freeman and others that followed (Donaldson 1999, 2012; Donaldson and Preston 1995; Freeman 1984; Freeman and Evan 1990; Freeman and Reed 1983) and, as we have suggested, have found their way into the governance literature on PSFs, if not explicitly, certainly implicitly. Freeman and Reed (1983: 89) argued the stakeholder approach: "is indeed a deceptively simple one. It says that there are other groups to whom the corporation is responsible in addition to stockholders: those groups who have a stake in the actions of the corporation." Freeman and Reed went on to propose both a wider and narrower definition of the stakeholder. Freeman and Reed (1983: 91) proposed as the wider view: "Any identifiable group or individual who can affect the achievement of an organization's objectives or who is affected by the achievement of an organization's objectives." Freeman and Reed (1983: 91) also proposed as the narrower view: "Any identifiable group or individual on which the organization is dependent for its continued survival." The wider view of a stakeholder meant that even competitors might constitute stakeholders to the degree a firm's objectives were affected by other firms or could affect those other firms.

We view stakeholder arguments to be a multi-party extension of the two-party agency model (Hill and Jones 1992). Stakeholder theory extends the agency argument, by suggesting that shareholders are not the only "principals" that are affected or affect the organization. Hence, those other parties should be attended to.

We certainly agree that the firm should attend to *all* the parties that have the potential to affect it and its survival. That is good strategy. Recent research specifically links leadership with explicit recognition of stakeholders in formulating strategic priorities for their firm (Doh and Quigley 2014). But whether that constitutes governance is in our view questionable. Governance has to do with how a firm governs in regards to those parties for whom it has a contractual obligation or it otherwise transacts with. Particularly important stakeholders in this regard are clients. PSFs rely on their reputations to provide quality services to clients especially since what they provide often is something of an intangible asset.

We see value too in a stakeholder perspective when it comes to the role of the profession in PSFs. Governance in a PSF has an additional layer to that of firms that are not professional based, as there are times when the profession is a party to the governance of the firm. Thus, we believe it is important to avoid blankly suggesting there are or are not stakeholders to the firm external to the firm, but to very clearly pinpoint them and identify their role.

Another way in which to think about stakeholders prioritizes them in terms of which parties invest in or share a common fate with the firm (Freeman and Evan 1990; Lan and Heracleous 2010). Lan and Heracleous (2010) argue that the greater the asset specificity of an individual, group, or unit to the organization, the higher the priority of that entity in terms of stakeholders. Regardless if one thinks that asset specificity is the key way in which to prioritize, it is clear that the profession and clients weigh heavily in how governance plays out. Moreover, the significant role that the profession and clients play in the PSF suggests another arena in which conflict and conflict resolution needs to be addressed.

9.3.4 The Trusteeship Perspective

The trusteeship perspective suggests that those tasked with governing (be it via internal committees, boards of directors, or senior leadership), are entrusted with ensuring the legacy and continuity of the firm. This perspective is in a sense more novel for the literature on governance in our view, but yet we see aspects of it in prior work (Davis et al. 1997; Dodd 1932; Greenwood 2007; Mayer 2013). Lan and Heracleous (2010: 29) additionally argue that case law, at least in the USA, has taken the view that boards are not agents but "autonomous fidiciaries," as they act independently as trustees of the organization.

Elements of the trusteeship perspective were foreshadowed in Davis et al.'s (1997: 24–25) stewardship theory of management and governance. They argue:

> According to stewardship theory, the behavior of the steward is collective, because the steward seeks to attain the objectives of the organization (e.g., sales growth or profitability). This behavior in turn will benefit principals such as outside owners (through positive effects of profits on dividends and share prices) and also principals who are managerial superordinates, because their objectives are furthered by the steward.

Davis et al. (1997: 25) further state: "a steward's behavior can be considered organizationally centered. Stewards . . . are motivated to make decisions that they perceive are in the best interests of the group."

Stewardship theory has an underlying assumption that agents such as managers have at heart the good of the organization. It is intended as an antidote to agency theoretic arguments that are premised on the view that governance is needed to ensure that self-seeking agents are kept in check. Neither of these views has to be subscribed to fully. Instead, individuals can be seen at times as acting with self-interest for themselves or the groups that they are attached to and other times acting in the benefit of a larger collective good. Part of what governance involves is to "get above" these individual differences and find ways to govern the self-interested and those that act as stewards.

Greenwood (2007) suggests a social trusteeship perspective of PSFs, which looks to professions and codes of behavior as the basis for governance. Greenwood (2007: 191) states:

> Fundamental to this perspective is the belief that the complexities of modern society require expertise for the pursuance of some occupations, creating an asymmetry of knowledge between practitioner and client. This asymmetry opens up a serious opportunity for the former to exploit the latter. Professionals refrain from doing so because they are guided by an ethical code of behavior, embodying values such as

peer vocation, public service, self-regulation, and autonomy. Brint (1994) suggests that this perspective embodies a *social trustee* ideal of professional behavior.

The social trustee model highlights that at the population level of firms in a profession there is an additional governance mechanism, the profession.

Lan and Heracleous (2010) use case law and the writings of legal scholars to provide a legal perspective on the notion of trustee. Their aim is to counter the notion of governance as a principal–agent relationship. Lan and Heracleous (2010: 300) argue: "courts in the US have on several occasions clearly stated that directors are not agents of the shareholders but fiduciaries of the corporation." Lan and Heracleous (2010: 300) conclude: "The board's main task here as a mediating hierarch is to balance team members' competing interests in a fashion that keeps everyone content enough so that the productive coalition holds together (Blair and Stout 1999)." Thus, in their view, what boards are entrusted with and where they get their autonomy is that they act on behalf of the corporation itself to balance the interests of those parties that constitute the team and make the firm a going concern.

Mayer (2013: 199) specifies what a trustee model entails by distinguishing between a trustee and an agency relationship:

> In trust law, the property of one party (the settlor) is managed by a second (the trustee) on behalf of a third (the beneficiary). The trustee owes a fiduciary duty to the beneficiary, who is the beneficial owner of the trust property. *It differs from the agency relation of a director to a shareholder in a company, by which the director owes a fiduciary responsibility to the shareholder as the owner as well as beneficiary of the property, i.e. the settlor and the beneficiary are one and the same.* [Our emphasis]

Mayer (2013: 196) also says: "What the trusts do . . . is to lay down the values of the business and the principles by which the individual businesses operate. They are therefore the guardians of the company's philosophy . . ." The trust firm, Mayer (2013: 201) states, acts as: "a corporation that has a board of trustees who are the guardians of the corporation's stated values and principles . . . they do not interfere in the day-to-day running of the firm, but do ensure that the firm has clearly articulated values and principles and abides by them."

Mayer argues that organizations face the problem of the commons, which he suggests has to do with finding ways through governance to ensure that present generations do not allocate resources in such a way as to deny future generations of their benefits. The trustee model, he argues, does that by having those tasked with governance operating with a longer-term horizon about the firm as an institution. The actual and potential conflicts that arise with those of shorter and longer-term horizons are at the heart of what governance entails.

The trusteeship perspective requires the managers to be responsible for the survival and prosperity of their firm. As a legal and economic institution, the firm, including PSFs, is not simply an asset owned by shareholders, but a trust that enables productive cooperation and facilitates human investments that would benefit its direct beneficiaries.

9.4 FUTURE DIRECTIONS

In its broadest definition, governance involves the management of the relationship between the firm represented by its management and the firm's critical constituencies. The four perspectives presented in this chapter provide structural or cultural views and are based on unique definitions of what a firm is and who the critical constituencies are. The solutions to the governance problems are directly tied to how these constituencies are identified and what is meant by the "firm."

The structural solutions offered by the agency perspective, whether they are based on organizing incentives (Holmström 1999), incomplete contacting, or property rights (Hart and Moore 1990), focused on developing contracts that are designed to take into account the differing interest and motivation of the parties (Reve 1990). Similarly, the trusteeship perspective (Blair and Stout 2001; Lan and Heracleous 2010; Mayer 2013) provided a contractual/structural view of the firm and its relation to various beneficiaries.

The cultural views of governance, on the other hand, argue that simple reliance on contractual terms undermines the importance of firm's history, its relations to larger society including its obligations to its clients prescribed by professional norms. The long-term contractual arrangements that govern professional partnerships must be designed with an understanding that contract completion is *not* the objective but that the continuity of the contract is. Such a perspective necessitates a cultural view where the interpretive scheme of governance defines managerial action through professional norms and organizational expectations. The stakeholder theory takes an ethical bent (Donaldson and Dunfee 1994) and the trustee and partnership/partnership ethos perspectives emphasize the importance of governance through leadership and firm culture.

In PSFs, the leaders of the firm such as managing partners are the trustees whose responsibility is to represent the interest of all the team members including the firm itself. Within a knowledge-intensive setting where team production takes place, leadership is more than simply a relationship between a manager and a subordinate. It is usually described in terms of teaching, mentoring, and guiding where the focus is on learning, socialization, and career development (see Empson and Langley, Chapter 8, this volume). In other words, exercising leadership requires the development of senior managers in developing knowledge, teams, and clients (Alvesson 2004; Alvesson and Robertson 2006; Løwendahl et al. 2001).

Each of these perspectives offers distinct understanding on two critical components of governance: (a) what a firm is and how the critical constituencies of the firm must be determined; and (b) what needs to be governed, in other words, how the rights and obligations of various parties are allocated, in order to allocate the collective benefits of the going concern and to resolve potential conflicts. In section 9.4.1, we address these issues and argue that future research on governance in PSFs must focus on each of these elements in a more detailed fashion.

9.4.1 Governance, Rights, and Obligations and the Nature of Conflict Resolution

What is explicitly and implicitly embedded in the governance debate is alternative theories of what the firm is. As our understanding of the notion of the firm changes, the critical aspects of governance also change (Rajan and Zingales 2000). Alternative theories of the firm define who owns the firm (e.g., shareholders) and what the role of senior managers is towards them. For instance, while the agency perspective has argued that principals are the owners of the firm, recent legal scholarship has gone so far as to argue that no one owns the firm (Chassagnon and Hollandts 2014).

Within the traditional governance literature the question of what needs to be managed is usually answered by referring to the rights of various categories of constituencies, such as the shareholders, partners, employees, or even clients in relation to the obligations of the management. What is not directly addressed in either the structural or cultural views of governance is the ambiguity of some of the critical terms such as rights, power, authority, and control within each governance perspective. For instance, within the property rights view of the firm discussed earlier, Hart and Moore (1990) argue that power is a unique right but is not contractible. Power is simply a way to encourage and protect relationship specific investments that are not valuable outside of that relationship. Inside the firm managers use power by giving differential access to firm's unique physical and human assets. Similarly Rajan and Zingales (2001) argue that through authority managers are able to coordinate and enhance the overall performance of the firm.

From a structural point of view, especially in the case of traditional agency theory, all rights and obligations, such as decision-making rights (initiation, ratification, implementation, and monitoring) are assumed to be explicitly included in governance. Recent research on agency theory and economic theories of the firm, on the other hand, argue that firms are governed by implicit contracts that are informal agreements and unwritten codes of conduct (Baker et al. 2002: 39). In other words, rights and obligations of the parties are not explicitly included in a contract. These non-contractible rights produce unclear obligations. For instance, Hart and Moore (1990) argue that power is a unique right but is not contractible. Power is a way to encourage and protect relationship-specific investments that are not valuable outside of that relationship. Inside the firm, managers use power by giving differential access to firm's unique physical and human assets. But they never specify the obligations of the other side. Similarly Rajan and Zingales (2001) argue that through authority, managers are able to coordinate and enhance the overall performance of the firm. Such lack of specificity limits our ability to provide a clear picture of how these implicit/relational contracts could be used in developing governance structures.

We propose that Hohfeldian jurisprudence (Hohfeld 1913) can be used to produce a feasible set of rights and obligations that are relevant for understanding relational contracts and governance structures. The Hohfeldian schema specifies four alternative categories of rights with their corresponding obligations. As shown in Table 9.2, each pair of the relationship specifies what each part must, may, can, and cannot do with respect to specific claims included in a contract (Leblebici 2000). Furthermore, each of these pairs of rights and corresponding obligations can be grouped into two distinct legal relations: discrete contracts that are mostly observed in the market settings and relational contracts that are usually associated with organizational settings (Baker et al. 2002; Macneil 1980).

Most of the discrete contracts in the marketplace are composed of Right–Duty (you must) and Liberty–Exposure (I may) pairs. Beyond specific duties of performance, each party is free to carry on other activities as they wish. It is assumed that there is no other expectation or relationship between the parties outside of the contract and the identities of the parties are irrelevant. This is usually what is implied by "contract" in within the agency/property rights views of governance. In other words, what is important for internal governance, such as authority and hierarchy, other than asset ownership do not matter. What complicates the situation in governance is the realization that most contracts are incomplete and non-contractible rights must be utilized to coordinate collective action.

The Power–Liability (I can) and Immunity–Disability (you cannot) pairs, on the other hand, are relational and represent internal contractual arrangements within a hierarchy. Power gives one party the ability to choose among alternative acts on behalf

Table 9.2 Types of rights and their corresponding obligations in discrete and relational contracts

Contractual Relationship	RIGHTS	DEFINITION	OBLIGATIONS
Discrete Contracts (Market-like)	RIGHT	one's specific affirmative claim against another party in a contract (MUST)	DUTY
	LIBERTY	one's freedom from specific claims of another party in a contract (MAY)	EXPOSURE
Relational Contracts (Organization-like)	POWER	one's affirmative control over a given contractual relationship and to affect a particular legal change (CAN)	LIABILITY
	IMMUNITY	one's freedom from the control of another in some aspect of their contractual relation (CANNOT)	DISABILITY

Adapted from Leblebici (2000: 163).

of another party to produce certain results (such as a manager assigning subordinates to various tasks). Power in this sense has no correlative duty but liability. For instance, an employer, in an employment contract, has the power to assign an employee to a certain set of tasks and allocate specific resources from a set of permissible alternatives. This ability (or authority), however, does not create a direct duty (must) but a liability on the part of an employee. But this authority must be balanced with certain immunities given to the employees in terms of which tasks they have the right to refuse to do (March and Simon 1958).

All of these rights and obligations are part of governance but the relational rights are especially relevant for the PSF. Relational rights provide the means by which cooperative norms and mutual dispute resolution mechanisms could be easily embedded into the governance structure. Relational governance that integrates professional norms and the norms of cooperation creates future expectations and the initial contracts simply play the role of a reference point for future actions (Hart and Moore 2008) similar to the ones described in behavioral economics. In other words, an effective governance structure creates expectations that future exchanges will occur in a relatively predictable manner and the preservation of the relationship in a collective sense becomes part of the contract (Macneil 1980). Expectations of a long-term relationship produce internal governance rules, which are not part of the initial explicit/discrete contracts, facilitate the development of customs that shape the behavior of participants, and help develop unwritten rules about promotion policies, task assignments, and norms of conduct. In other words, cultural norms of governance are produced through relational rights.

In addition to the collective preservation of the ongoing relationship, governance structures require harmonization of conflicts (Macneil 1980). Conflict in intense joint production settings is inevitable, especially when conditions change. In addition to good faith and trust, it is vital for a relational contract to develop conflict resolution mechanisms internal to the group. As contractual relations expand and become permanent, such as in complex partnerships or corporations, supra contractual norms such as equality, fairness, procedural justice, and professional identity become part of the collective. This is where power becomes critical to resolve conflicts, produce institutionalize change, and maintain the integrity of the collective (Lawrence et al. 2012)

Effective governance structures that are instituted on relational contracts provide alternative courses of action to various participants when disagreements arise. Three alternatives—exit, voice, and loyalty—are the most common. Agency theory has traditionally assumed that "exit" would send the necessary message through the market mechanism to correct the situation and the court system that is built into the contract would sort out the claims of the parties towards each other. In a world of relational contracts where rights and obligations are non-contractible, however, such governance mechanisms are not very feasible and other two alternatives—voice and loyalty—must be considered (Hirschman 1970).

Most governance structures, especially within the context of PSFs, do and must include all these three alternatives. Hirschman (1980: 431) argued that "the proper balance of institutional incentives ought to be adjusted so as to strengthen voice in relation to exit." What is ironic is that the whole debate on establishing corporate governance structures to protect the residual claims of shareholders neglects the fact that shareholders arguably have the easiest option to exit by selling their shares in an active stock market. In the case of PSFs where there is no active market to exchange ownership, other means must be utilized. Internal hierarchy within PSFs can be considered as a structural arrangement not for suppressing voice but rather for its institutionalization and routinization (Hirschman 1980).

Within a relational contractual view of the firm, where informal agreements are formed around non-contractible rights and unwritten codes of conduct define the relationships among various constituencies of the firm, governance is a part of the evolutionary process of the firm. This is what makes each governance structure unique and tied to the culture of a specific professional firm. As the identities and reputations of the parties become important, norms such as reciprocity, professional and organizational identity become critical in creating better governance structures emphasizing voice rather than exit (Alvesson 2000).

9.5 Conclusions

The debate in the governance literature that started with the separation of decision rights of the managers and the control rights of the shareholders as residual claimants evolved into a much more nuanced understanding of who should be in charge and who should be involved in decision-making. The insight herein is especially true in the case of PSFs. Traditional agency perspectives' focus on the partners is predicated on the definition of what a firm is and who the firm's owners are. Diverse groups of participants, however, directly or indirectly invest in organizations. As partners, we have shares; as associates, we invest our human capital and careers; as clients, we buy their services and enter into long-term contracts. And in return, we expect to receive benefits that are commensurate with our investments. These relationships become problematic when these investors are not directly involved in decisions involving organizations' action. Lack of direct control makes all investing parties vulnerable "to mismanagement of the organization, misallocation of its resources and even misappropriation of its returns" (Hermalin 2012: 732). The potential loss explains why governance in PSFs is more than a set of by-laws that specify the voting rights of its partners and the selection of its officers. Effective governance addresses this loss by bringing together partners', employees', clients', and professionals' expectations.

Governance in PSFs is a product of a specific profession's expectations and specific legal regimes of partnership contracts. With the emergence of alternative partnership arrangements, for instance, partners have new alternative associational forms which will require new governance structures (Hillman 2003). Professional governance must take into account the relationship among various intellectual property owners (present and future), the unique professional norms associated with professional reputation and ethics, and the career expectations of individuals within these firms. Professional expectations regulate not only the relationship among various participants inside the firm but also the relationships with the clients of these firms as well as the nature of competition among professional firms in the market (Hillman 2001). Thus, governance regimes within different professions and their organizational forms are the products of the endogenous evolution rather than simply exogenous market forces.

Rethinking governance in PSFs has become more urgent because of two recent interrelated developments. The first has to do with the increasing movement towards the corporate model of governance and away from traditional partnerships (von Nordenflycht 2007). As a result of rapid growth, many mid-size PSFs needed additional resources to facilitate growth, and were either acquired by corporations (e.g., Mercer HR Consulting or A. T. Kearney) or became corporate entities. Firms such as Bain and Company, Boston Consulting Group, and McKinsey, which have been legally incorporated for many years, manage themselves as if they were partnerships and refer to their senior-level professionals as "partners," even though their actual titles are vice president, officer, principal, or director (Broderick 2011). These new arrangements create different types of demands on the management of these organizations and a new way of looking at governance becomes necessary.

The second development is the recent series of scandals involving PSFs in consulting, law, and investment banks. The traditional assumption was that for these firms reputation is the most critical asset in their business and the partnership form assures the clients that their interests are protected (Greenwood and Empson 2003). But recent experiences with Goldman Sachs, which profited from selling investment advice to their clients during the financial crisis, Morgan Stanley, which selectively provided valuable information about the Facebook IPO, or McKinsey whose managing partner was convicted of providing insider information to hedge funds firms, have eroded the public's and clients' confidence in these firms. As some critics point out, failures of governance systems have produced damaging reputational outcomes (Macey 2013).

These developments indicate that governance in PSFs must be reconsidered in terms of its function, objectives, and operational mechanisms. Recognizing that PSFs are themselves highly diverse and do not lend themselves to a monolithic application of any one perspective, the objective of this chapter was to bring together different strands of literature on governance in order to focus on governance in PSFs. Our ultimate aim is to clarify how management scholars should think about governance in PSFs and to suggest where future research might be most beneficial.

What we learn from each of these perspectives is that governance is not only a complex phenomenon but also that there is an understudied heterogeneity among firms that is not sufficiently explored in the literature (see von Nordenflycht et al., Chapter 7, this volume). In order to understand the heterogeneous choices made by individual PSFs in forming their governance structures, it is not enough to simply look at organizational form choices each firm makes but also how these forms are implemented given each firm's history, the professional setting they operate in, and the competitive forces they face.

What the previous sections of this chapter reveal is that the existing debates on governance in the academic literature fail to account for the ongoing changes within PSFs. As in the mainstream corporate governance research, which has traditionally focused on the relationship between management and shareholders, PSF governance research has also focused on the partnership forms, regularly ignoring critical third parties such as clients, employees (partners as well as associates), and professional expectations.

Most larger PSFs work with clients who are themselves trained in the professions or are sophisticated customers of the services offered. Across every professional sector, clients attempt to hire the best PSFs. Consultants, lawyers, investment bankers, accountants, and advertising professionals constantly work with other similar professionals, who are not only knowledgeable about their trade but also operate within relational contracts where reputations, informal agreements, and professional codes of conduct are critical. In other words, the ongoing engagements are not arm's-length with short-term expectations involving discrete contracts. Thus, management of PSFs as the trustees of their firms must incorporate all transactional parties, who are the beneficiaries of the firm, into the dynamic and evolving governance of their going concern.

NOTE

1. The description of this firm is a composite of a number of larger PSFs.

REFERENCES

Aguilera, R. V. and Jackson, G. (2003). "The Cross-National Diversity of Corporate Governance: Dimensions and Determinants," *Academy of Management Review* 28(3): 447–465.

Alvesson, M. (2000). "Social Identity and the Problem of Loyalty in Knowledge-Intensive Companies," *Journal of Management Studies* 37(8): 1101–1123.

Alvesson, M. (2004). *Knowledge Work and Knowledge-Intensive Firms*. Oxford: Oxford University Press.

Alvesson, M. and Robertson, M. (2006). "The Best and the Brightest: The Construction, Significance and Effects of Elite Identities in Consulting Firms," *Organization* 13(2): 195–224.

Aoki, M. (2010). *Corporations in Evolving Diversity: Cognition, Governance, and Institutions*. Clarendon Lectures in Management Studies. Oxford: Oxford University Press.

Baker, G., Gibbons, R., and Murphy, K. J. (2002). "Relational Contracts and the Theory of the Firm," *Quarterly Journal of Economics* 117(1): 39–84.

Berle, A. A. and Means, G. C. (1932). *The Modern Corporation and Private Property*. New York: Macmillan.

Blair, M. M. and Stout, L. A. (1999). "A Team Production Theory of Corporate Law?" *Journal of Corporation Law* 24(4): 751–806.

Blair, M. M. and Stout, L. A. (2001). "Trust, Trustworthiness, and the Behavioral Foundations of Corporate Law," *University of Pennsylvania Law Review* 149(6): 1735–1810.

Brint, S. (1994). *In an Age of Experts: The Changing Role of Professionals in Politics and Public Life*. Princeton, NJ: Princeton University Press.

Brock, D. M., Powell, M. J., and Hinings, C. R. (eds.) (1999). *Restructuring the Professional Organization: Accounting, Health Care and Law*. New York: Routledge.

Broderick, N. (2011). *The Art of Managing Professional Services: Insights from Leaders of the World's Top Firms*. Upper Saddle River, NJ: Prentice-Hall.

Chassagnon, V. and Hollandts, X. (2014). "Who Are the Owners of the Firm?: Shareholders, Employees or No One?" *Journal of Institutional Economics* 10(1): 47–69.

Cooper, D. J., Hinings, B., Greenwood, R., and Brown, J. L. (1996). "Sedimentation and Transformation in Organizational Change: The Case of Canadian Law Firms," *Organizational Studies* 17(4): 623–647.

Daily, C. M., Dalton, D. R., and Cannella Jr., A. A. (2003). "Corporate Governance: Decades of Dialogue and Data," *Academy of Management Review* 28(3): 371–382.

Davis, G. F. (2005). "New Directions in Corporate Governance," *Annual Review of Sociology* 31(1): 143–162.

Davis, J. H., Schoorman, F. D., and Donaldson, L. (1997). "Toward a Stewardship Theory of Management," *Academy of Management Review* 22(1): 20–47.

DeLong, T. J., Gabarro, J. J., and Lees, R. J. (2007). *When Professionals Have to Lead: A New Model for High Performance*. Boston, MA: Harvard Business School Press.

Dodd, M. E. (1932). "For Whom Are Corporate Managers Trustees?" *Harvard Law Review* 45(7): 1145–1163.

Doh, J. P. and Quigley, N. R. (2014). "Responsible Leadership and Stakeholder Management: Influence Pathways and Organizational Outcomes," *Academy of Management Perspectives* 28(3): 255–274.

Donaldson, T. (1999). "Making Stakeholder Theory Whole," *Academy of Management Review* 24(2): 237–241.

Donaldson, T. (2012). "The Epistemic Fault Line in Corporate Governance," *Academy of Management Review* 37(2): 256–271.

Donaldson, T. and Dunfee, T. W. (1994). "Toward a Unified Conception of Business Ethics: Integrative Social Contracts Theory," *Academy of Management Review* 19(2): 252–284.

Donaldson, T. and Preston, L. E. (1995). "The Stakeholder Theory of the Corporation: Concepts, Evidence, and Implications," *Academy of Management Review* 20(1): 65–91.

Empson, L. (2007). "Surviving and Thriving in a Changing World: The Special Nature of Partnership," in *Managing the Modern Law Firm: New Challenges and New Perspectives*, ed. L. Empson. Oxford: Oxford University Press, 10–36.

Empson, L. (2012). "Beyond Dichotomies: A Multi-Stage Model of Governance in Professional Service Firms," in *Handbook of Research on Entrepreneurship in Professional Services*, ed. M. Reihlen and A. Werr. Cheltenham: Edward Elgar, 274–294.

Empson, L. and Chapman, C. (2006). "Partnership Versus Corporation: Implications of Alternative Forms of Governance in Professional Service Firms," *Research in the Sociology of Organizations* 24: 139–170.

Fama, E. E. and Jensen, M. C. (1983a). "Separation of Ownership and Control," *Journal of Law and Economics* 26(2): 301–325.

Fama, E. F. and Jensen, M. C. (1983b). "Agency Problems and Residual Claims," *Journal of Law and Economics* 26(2): 327–349.

Freeman, R. E. (1984). *Strategic Management: A Stakeholder Approach*. Boston, MA: Pitman.

Freeman, R. E. and Evan, W. M. (1990). "Corporate Governance: A Stakeholder Interpretation," *Journal of Behavioral Economics* 19(4): 337–359.

Freeman, R. E. and Reed, D. L. (1983). "Stockholders and Stakeholders: A New Perspective on Corporate Governance," *California Management Review* 25(3): 88–106.

Greenwood, R. (2007). "Redefining Professionalism? The Impact of Management Change," in *Managing the Modern Law Firm: New Challenges and New Perspectives*, ed. L. Empson. Oxford: Oxford University Press, 186–195.

Greenwood, R. and Empson, L. (2003). "The Professional Partnership: Relic or Exemplary Form of Governance?" *Organization Studies* 24(6): 909–933.

Greenwood, R., Hinings, C. R., and Brown, J. (1990). "'P2-Form' Strategic Management: Corporate Practices in Professional Partnerships," *Academy of Management Journal* 33(4): 725–755.

Greenwood, R., Li, S. X., Prakash, R., and Deephouse, D. L. (2005). "Reputation, Diversification and Organizational Explanations of Performance in Professional Service Firms," *Organization Science* 16(6): 661–676.

Hart, O. (1995). "Corporate Governance: Some Theory and Implications," *Economic Journal* 105(430): 678–689.

Hart, O. and Moore, J. (1990). "Property Rights and the Nature of the Firm," *Journal of Political Economy* 98(6): 1119–1158.

Hart, O. and Moore, J. (2008). "Contracts as Reference Points," *Quarterly Journal of Economics* 123(1): 1–48.

Hermalin, B. E. (2012). "Corporate Governance: A Critical Assessment," in *Handbook of Organizational Economics*, ed. R. Gibbons and J. Roberts. Princeton, NJ: Princeton University Press, 732–763.

Hill, C. W. L. and Jones, T. M. (1992). "Stakeholder-Agency Theory," *Journal of Management Studies* 29(2): 131–154.

Hillman, R. W. (2001). "Professional Partnerships, Competition, and the Evolution of Firm Culture: The Case of Law Firms," *Journal of Corporation Law* 26(4): 1061–1067.

Hillman, R. W. (2003). "Organizational Choices of Professional Service Firms: An Empirical Study," *Business Lawyer* 58(4): 1387–1411.

Hirschman, A. O. (1970). *Exit, Voice, and Loyalty: Responses to Decline in Firms, Organizations, and States*. Cambridge, MA: Harvard University Press.

Hirschman, A. O. (1980). "Exit, Voice, and Loyalty: Further Reflections and a Survey of Recent Contributions," *The Milbank Memorial Fund Quarterly. Health and Society* 58(3): 430–453.

Hohfeld, W. N. (1913). "Fundamental Legal Conceptions as Applied in Judicial Reasoning," *Yale Law Journal* 23: 16–29.

Holmström, B. (1999). "Managerial Incentive Problems: A Dynamic Perspective," *Review of Economic Studies* 66(226): 169–182.

Holmström, B. and Milgrom, P. (1994). "The Firm as an Incentive System," *American Economic Review* 84(4): 972–991.

Klein, P. G., Mahoney, J. T., McGahan, A. M., and Pitelis, C. N. (2012). "Who is in Charge? A Property Rights Perspective on Stakeholder Governance," *Strategic Organization* 10(3): 304–315.

Lan, L. L. and Heracleous, L. (2010). "Rethinking Agency Theory: The View from Law," *Academy of Management Review* 35(2): 294–314.

Lawrence, T. B., Malhotra, N., and Morris, T. (2012). "Episodic and Systemic Power in the Transformation of Professional Service Firms," *Journal of Management Studies* 49(1): 102–143.

Leblebici, H. (2000). "Allocation of Rights and the Organization of Transactions: Elements of a Generative Approach to Organizing," *Journal of Management & Governance* 4(1–2): 149–168.

Løwendahl, B. R. (1997). *Strategic Management of Professional Service Firms*. Copenhagen: Copenhagen Business School Press.

Løwendahl, B. R., Revang, O., and Fosstenløkken, S. M. (2001). "Knowledge and Value Creation in Professional Service Firms: A Framework for Analysis," *Human Relations* 54(7): 911–931.

Macey, J. R. (2013). *The Death of Corporate Reputation: How Integrity Has Been Destroyed on Wall Street*. Upper Saddle River, NJ: FT Press.

Macneil, I. R. (1980). *The New Social Contract: An Inquiry into Modern Contractual Relations*. New Haven, CT: Yale University Press.

Malhotra, N. and Morris, T. (2009). "Heterogeneity in Professional Service Firms," *Journal of Management Studies* 46(6): 895–922.

Malhotra, N., Morris, T., and Smets, M. (2010). "New Career Models in UK Professional Service Firms: From Up-or-Out to Up-and-Going-Nowhere?" *International Journal of Human Resource Management* 21(9): 1396–1413.

March, J. G. and Simon, H. A. (1958). *Organizations*. New York: John Wiley.

Mayer, C. (2013). *Firm Commitment: How the Corporation is Failing Us and How to Restore Trust in It*. Oxford: Oxford University Press.

Mintzberg, H. (1979). *The Structuring of Organizations*. Englewood Cliffs, NJ: Prentice-Hall.

Rajan, R. G. and Zingales, L. (2000). "The Governance of the New Enterprise," in *Corporate Governance: Theoretical and Empirical Perspectives*, ed. X. Vives. Cambridge: Cambridge University Press, 201–232.

Rajan, R. G. and Zingales, L. (2001). "The Firm as a Dedicated Hierarchy: A Theory of the Origins and Growth of Firms," *Quarterly Journal of Economics* 116(3): 805–851.

Reve, T. (1990). "The Firm as a Nexus of Internal and External Contracts," in *The Firm as a Nexus of Treaties*, ed. M. Aoki, B. Gustafsson, and O. E. Williamson. Newbury Park, CA: Sage, 133–161.

Shleifer, A. and Vishny, R. W. (1997). "A Survey of Corporate Governance," *Journal of Finance* 52(2): 737–783.

Suddaby, R., Gendron, Y., and Lam, H. (2009). "The Organizational Context of Professionalism in Accounting," *Accounting, Organizations and Society* 34(3–4): 409–427.

Swaine, R. T. (1948). *The Cravath Firm and Its Predecessors, 1819–1948*. New York: Privately Published.

von Nordenflycht, A. (2007). "Is Public Ownership Bad for Professional Service Firms? Ad Agency Ownership, Performance, and Creativity," *Academy of Management Journal* 50(2): 429–445.

Wang, H. C., He, J., and Mahoney, J. T. (2009). "Firm-Specific Knowledge Resources and Competitive Advantage: The Roles of Economic- and Relationship-Based Employee Governance Mechanisms," *Strategic Management Journal* 30(12): 1265–1285.

Williamson, O. E. (2005). "The Economics of Governance," *American Economic Review* 95(2): 1–18.

CHAPTER 10

STRATEGY AND STRATEGIC ALIGNMENT IN PROFESSIONAL SERVICE FIRMS

JOHN MAWDSLEY AND DEEPAK SOMAYA

10.1 INTRODUCTION

PROFESSIONAL Service Firms (PSFs) that provide services in such areas as law, accounting, management consulting, and advertising have become a vital sector in modern developed economies, and continue to increase in economic importance. In 2011, according to the US Bureau of Economic Analysis, the professional and business services (PBS) sector contributed approximately 9% *more* to US Gross Domestic Product (GDP) than the entire manufacturing sector, and these estimates are likely quite conservative because they exclude PSFs in industries like real estate, financial services, and medical services.[1] Moreover, GDP value added by the US PBS sector—as defined above—grew by 260% in the two decades between 1991 and 2011, compared to only a 77% growth for US manufacturing. Similarly, US employment in the PBS sector was 49% more than manufacturing in 2011, and grew by 49% between 1991 and 2011 whereas employment in manufacturing actually fell by 31% during this time period.

Despite the significant and growing importance of PSFs in the economy at large, academic research on the *strategic management* of PSFs has been somewhat sparse. For this review, we undertook a comprehensive search of academic databases to identify research pertaining to the strategic management of PSFs and found fewer than 100 relevant articles, many of which were published in specialized journals or profession-specific journals such as law reviews. In searching for relevant research, we followed von Nordenflycht (2010) in defining PSFs as firms that have *high knowledge intensity, low capital intensity*, and *comprising a professionalized workforce*.[2] Despite the limited research conducted so far, PSFs have piqued the interest of strategy scholars because, unlike other types of firms, PSFs are built almost entirely from knowledge-intensive assets that are highly mobile and not amenable to secure property rights (Coff 1997, 1999; Teece 2003), conditions which run counter to those that the strategy literature has identified as necessary for sustaining competitive advantage (Barney 1991; Peteraf 1993).

Systematic thinking about the strategic management of PSFs goes back at least to Maister who noted that "Management of a professional firm requires a delicate balancing act between the demands of the client marketplace, the realities of the people marketplace . . . and the firm's economic ambitions" (1993: 3). In our extensive review of strategy research on PSFs, we identified several core themes in the literature, namely, how PSFs create value from human capital, the alignment of the professional workforce with the firm's goals, and how value is created from client relationships. The remaining theme builds on these foundations to examine research explaining various corporate-level strategies on PSFs. We conclude our review by identifying potential directions for future strategy research on PSFs.

10.2 STRATEGIC MANAGEMENT AND VALUE CREATION FROM THE PROFESSIONAL WORKFORCE

Perhaps the most salient characteristic of PSFs related to strategic management is the extent to which their critical knowledge assets and core drivers of competitive advantage come from human capital. Therefore, as a starting point for our review we examine the core mechanisms through which PSFs create and capture value from their human assets. *Inter alia*, we review the role of knowledge management in PSFs, which is intimately connected to the organization and management (including training, development, and deployment) of human assets. Elsewhere in this volume knowledge management in PSFs is examined in the context of variation in PSF characteristics across firms and professional service industries. Our review focuses on how PSFs strategically *organize and align* their professional workforce, and examines the competitive impacts. *Seriatim*, we review the roles played by the organizational infrastructure for human capital, knowledge hierarchies and leverage, "star" and expert talent, and mechanisms adopted by PSFs to ensure the goals of the professional workforce align with those of the firm.

10.2.1 Infrastructure for Organizing Human Capital

One stream of strategic management research—the knowledge-based view—describes firms as repositories and organizers of multiple strands of knowledge that underlie a firm's capabilities and performance (Grant 1996; Kogut and Zander 1992).

A knowledge-based view of PSFs considers how PSFs can create value from their organizational infrastructure for managing knowledge and by using various mechanisms to organize, transfer, integrate, and protect knowledge across different individuals and groups within the firm (Jensen et al. 2010; Morris 2001).

PSFs may organize by codifying their knowledge and deploying technology to enable fast and reliable access to this codified knowledge repository. Here, value can be created from economies of scale generated by the reuse and dissemination of knowledge *as an organizationally owned asset*, while direct access to codified core information can reduce internal costs to communication and enable consistency in delivering client services (Hansen et al. 1999). However, critical knowledge within PSFs may be largely tacit and difficult to codify. For example, the experience and skills of expert professionals may only be effectively communicated through personal interactions with others. However, tacit knowledge forms part of an employee's human capital and thus is *not* an organizationally owned asset, though organizations may seek to employ and appropriate some of this knowledge. Moreover, in some PSF industries, client needs may be highly complex and non-standard, limiting the benefits of codified knowledge.

A central challenge for PSFs in deriving value from human capital is therefore devising ways to encourage professionals to share their tacit knowledge that can also give those professionals a personal competitive advantage (Empson 2001; Morris 2001). At the same time, knowledge that is well understood or codified is at greater risk of replication by competitors or clients, while mobile professionals are also more likely to transfer codified knowledge when they migrate between firms (Phillips 2002; Wezel et al. 2006). Thus, one strategic concern for PSFs is to balance value creation from codifying the tacit knowledge held by their human capital on the one hand against potential value erosion from the easier expropriation of codified knowledge on the other.

Extant research literature provides numerous examples of how PSFs generate value through codified knowledge management. For example, bureaucratic procedures developed to organize the PSF's knowledge may create value by transferring externally sourced knowledge, such as that gained from clients, across the firm's internal stakeholders (Briscoe 2007). Indeed, in modern-day PSFs that increasingly follow a more "corporate-style" organizational model (Cooper et al. 1996), systems that codify best-practice solutions to recurring client problems and monitor the productivity and fee income generated from these solutions often support value-creating strategies (Brivot 2011; Forstenlechner et al. 2009). Finally, Morris (2001) shows in a case study of a large UK management consulting firm that the firm's codified knowledge largely consisted of a "knowledge architecture" that supported a technically consistent methodological approach across projects, which effectively gave the consultancy a "brand."

At the other end, PSFs may adopt strategies that draw primarily on individual and collective tacit expertise—developed through repeated internal and client interactions—to provide solutions for very complex and high-level strategic problems (Hansen et al. 1999). Thus, while this feature varies in degree across professional services, value is created through the ability of expert professionals to address unique problems by using tacit knowledge, where codified knowledge resources are largely used to support the delivery of professionals' tacit expertise (Hansen et al. 1999). Even in Morris's (2001) case study, the codified knowledge architecture described above provided a consistent process template but left individual consultants with sufficient autonomy to deliver value from their tacit professional expertise, which was instrumental in identifying client problems and constructing complex solutions for them.

In sum, we see that PSFs may adopt an internal infrastructure that harnesses, deploys, and in some cases stores the critical knowledge that drives PSF performance. We turn next to specific ways in which value created and captured by PSFs is driven by how they manage knowledge and develop the expertise of employees.

10.2.2 Knowledge Hierarchies and Leverage

The dominant PSF model, particularly in legal, consulting, and accounting services, is the vertical differentiation of human capital, which lends itself to a top-down knowledge management structure that has been labeled as a "knowledge hierarchy" (Garicano and Hubbard 2007). In the typical PSF partnership model, the largely tacit human capital of senior PSF members (experts) is "leveraged" by junior members (novices)[3] through a hierarchical structure that generates economies of scale to the experts' experience and expertise while simultaneously building the knowledge, skills, and experience of novices through learning-by-doing (Garicano and Hubbard 2007; Gilson and Mnookin 1989). Through this knowledge-management process, novices gain industry (and firm-specific) knowledge under the supervision of experienced and often high caliber professionals in their field.

Leverage is typically operationalized in research as the PSF's "leverage ratio," which is the number of novices per expert (partner) in a firm. A higher leverage ratio allows experts to delegate higher volumes of routine work to novices, enabling PSFs to take on more new business as the productive time of experts is reserved for higher value-added client services and strategic management of the firm (Kor and Leblebici 2005; Kordana 1995). Accordingly, a key knowledge management strategy for many PSFs is the dynamic adjustment of their leverage ratio according to the scale of demand for services (Garicano and Hubbard 2007, 2009). For example, research has shown that as market demand for PSF services increases, PSFs may capitalize on this demand by employing more novices and intensively leveraging expert human capital (Garicano and Hubbard 2007; Sherer 1995). Building on this logic, studies have generally found a positive relationship between a PSF's leverage ratio and PSF profitability (Greenwood et al. 2005; Hitt et al. 2001; Kor and Leblebici 2005; Sherer 1995), while corroborating anecdotal evidence states that when demand for PSF services is high, increasing the firm's leverage ratio is akin to "printing money" (Heinz 2009).

Implicitly, knowledge management and the corresponding management of human assets for value creation reflect both the nature of underlying professional knowledge and the type of client service (Malhotra and Morris 2009). As such, not all PSFs are organized as partnerships; rather, many PSFs are private or public corporates, and some start as private or partnership firms before going public through an initial public offering (IPO) (for example, investment banking giant Goldman Sachs and global business advisory and consulting firms KPMG and Accenture). Moreover, extant research reveals that ownership and governance form may be related to the particular professional service industry; legal services, accounting, and management consultancy dominate the partnership form of ownership, while advertising and architecture are most notable as being corporations (Greenwood and Empson 2003; von Nordenflycht 2007). However, despite these important differences between PSFs, very little research has been conducted on knowledge management in *non*-partnership PSFs (i.e., public or private corporations). There are, therefore, research opportunities available to gain a deeper understanding of knowledge management within PSF corporations, such as uncovering the particular knowledge management mechanisms and their impacts on PSF performance. Another line of inquiry may be to compare knowledge hierarchies between PSFs in the same industry that are governed differently. Von Nordenflycht (2007) finds differences in financial performance and productivity between public and privately owned advertising agencies and future studies could build on these findings to understand if systematic knowledge-based differences occur as a result of different ownership and governance form. However, it may be that, rather than in knowledge management per se, the impacts of differences between partnerships and private and public corporations manifest most strongly in the strategic concerns of appropriation, and incentives and motivation of the professional workforce, which we turn to next.

10.2.3 Strategic Alignment of the Professional Workforce

As noted earlier, for PSFs, human assets are *the* critical resource for generating firm performance. However, professional workers are highly mobile and can often quit their employer at will or withhold effort (Coff 1997, 1999). Arguably, employee exit or reductions in employee productivity are most likely when the goals of the firm and goals of employees diverge. Incentives for behavior and motivation have a significant bearing on both the ability of PSFs to retain professionals and to enhance their productivity (Castanias and Helfat 1991, 2001; Coff 1999, 2010), and indeed, economic rents generated from human assets will be diminished if effort and motivation are misdirected (Coff 1999; Coff and Kryscynski 2011). Thus, *an important strategic concern for PSFs is aligning the personal interests and goals of professionals with those of the firm* (Coff 1997, 1999; Coff and Kryscynski 2011; Teece 2003).

Prior research shows that PSF ownership and governance form can have a significant bearing on PSF performance (Greenwood and Empson 2003; Greenwood et al. 2007; von Nordenflycht 2007). Differences in PSF performance across ownership and governance form have been associated with differences in the incentives and motivation of professionals, and the level of "agency costs" for PSFs. In PSFs, agency costs occur when conduct of a professional employee deviates from that which is best for the firm. Agency costs are particularly high when there is a clear separation of ownership and control, or where the behavior of professionals may be largely undetected without the PSFs incurring significant costs for monitoring the behavior of its professional employees (for an overview of agency theory and its contributions to organizational theory see: Alchian and Demsetz 1972; Eisenhardt 1989; Fama and Jensen 1983; Jensen and Meckling 1979). However, agency theory maintains that firms can circumvent high monitoring costs by ensuring appropriate incentives are in place to motivate and align employees. For example, research suggests that the partnership form of ownership is particularly effective at aligning managers because shared firm ownership (and thus profits), and personal liability for firm debt and misconduct of other managers both provide incentives for acting in the interests of the firm and increase peer monitoring (Greenwood and Empson 2003). However, as partnerships become very large, with hundreds or even thousands of partners, significant principal–principal agency problems may surface and pose a novel set of challenges that has not yet been systematically studied.

In aligning the professional workforce to the goals of the firm, PSFs need to devise mechanisms to motivate and reward employees at both expert and novice levels. While incentives in PSFs are closely linked to rent division and appropriation there are also important non-pecuniary motivators of professional workers, and as such, the core motivators include money, power, status, autonomy, learning opportunities, and alignment to professional norms (Gottschalg and Zollo 2007). This section reviews how the strategy literature has discussed the challenges for PSFs in devising systems and processes that guide, integrate, and make more productive the autonomous but interconnected work of highly skilled workers, who may also have divergent interests (Teece 2003).

10.2.3.1 *Appropriation of Economic Rents*

The production of value in PSFs is often socially complex and as such PSFs may not hold clear property rights over many critical value-generating assets; therefore numerous stakeholders can arguably claim a share of the economic rents (profits) of the firm (Coff 1997, 1999; Teece 2003). Drawing on Coff's insightful comment that "Organizations don't appropriate rent, people do" (1999: 120), we note that division of rents in PSFs is largely within and between the ranks of senior managers (who are also typically the shareholders) and junior members (or associates).

Research on PSFs has equated rent appropriation to the relative bargaining power of employees vis-à-vis the firm (Campbell et al. 2012; Coff 1999). Employees are often in an advantageous bargaining power position due to the portability of human capital that enables them to capture a larger share of value generated from their knowledge and expertise (Coff 1999). Moreover, professional workers are more than ever aware of their own brand and value (Teece 2003) and in turn, expert professionals can exploit low barriers to mobility to maximize their personal compensation (Henderson 2006; Henderson and Bierman 2009). In PSFs organized as partnerships, and where professionals hold a higher degree of autonomy (such as legal services), the compensation structure of the firm may be highly dispersed in order to retain the most value-creating talent (Campbell et al. 2012; Carnahan et al. 2012); in effect, PSFs contain extreme earners who may be compensated several times more than a peer employee.

The degree to which firm value is generated from human capital alone has been shown to have a significant bearing on employee rent appropriation (Bowman and Swart 2007). Indeed, when firm value is derived from the combination or embedding of human capital with complementary firm assets (such as firm brand or reputation), combinations of human capital (such as teams) professionals, or from firm-specific knowledge of the firms routines and processes, professionals may have less legitimate claims that their human capital is *the* critical value-generating asset (Bowman and Swart 2007; Coff 1999; Malos and Campion 2000). Research dating back to the origin of human capital theory (e.g., Becker 1964) posits that the higher the proportion of firm-specific human capital an employee holds, then the lower his or her bargaining power over the rents created, in part, because the threat of exit is less credible. In order to maximize bargaining power (and mobility), professionals may resist making substantial investments in firm-specific human capital, and therefore PSFs may still be at risk of unproductive workers if professionals feel that their personal contributions to firm value are not being rewarded. In these instances, PSFs may need to build effective non-pecuniary reward structures to ensure the ongoing satisfaction of employees, maintain higher levels of productivity, and drive firm performance (Coff and Kryscynski 2011), which we turn to in section 10.2.3.2 on incentives and motivation.

Finally, as is explored in more detail in other chapters in this volume, there is variation in the ownership and governance form of PSFs which has implications for rent appropriation, and in turn for employee incentives and motivation. In non-partnership PSFs (i.e., corporations), firm profits are *not* distributed exclusively to manager-owners (partners), but instead are concentrated in a smaller group of firm owners (private corporation) or widely dispersed among external shareholders (public corporation). The key implication that is highlighted in the literature for non-partnership PSFs is a weakening of the link between human capital and financial reward, which can delink incentives of the firm's human capital from the overall performance of the firm (Greenwood and Empson 2003; Greenwood et al. 2007). We explore these incentive and motivation issues next.

10.2.3.2 *Incentives and Motivation of the Professional Workforce: Partnership Model*

When organized as a hierarchy (typically the "partnership model"), the vertical division of labor creates different incentive mechanisms between the levels—or tiers—of professional talent. Until recently, the dominant incentive mechanism adopted by these PSFs was a profit-sharing model. In this model, the level of compensation and strategic authority is allocated according to seniority in the firm (Gilson and Mnookin 1985), where the strategic emphasis is on *collective* (i.e., firm) rather than individualistic performance. In this model, managers (partners) typically remained at the same firm for most of their career and thus had incentives to invest deeply in the development and long-term success of the *firm*. However, the modern-day focus on production and profit-maximization targets, allied to increased mobility of professional workers, has increased the relative bargaining power of key talent. In turn, PSFs began to incentivize partners by directing the distribution of profits and authority to individuals who contributed most significantly to firm performance (Campbell et al. 2012; Carnahan et al. 2012). Moreover, because these PSFs are driven primarily by the individualistic motivations of financial reward and personal reputations, partners in these PSFs face an ongoing incentive to maximize billing hours (and achieve high reward) or see their compensation drop due to under-performance, and potentially being forced out of the firm.

In the partnership model, PSFs incentivize and motivate novice workers using different mechanisms than those used for partners. Primarily, PSFs use expert mentoring from partners and the chance of partnership which confers participation in profit sharing (thus creating a "tournament model") to drive associates to align with the goals of the firm (Galanter and Palay 1990; Gilson and Mnookin 1989; Malos and Campion 1995, 2000). However, PSFs which derive competitive advantages from *firm-specific* human capital may find it more challenging to motivate novices to invest in accumulating less transferable skills as this can constrain alternative employment opportunities and reduce employee bargaining power vis-à-vis the firm (Becker 1964; Coff 1999). Research has shown that when PSFs rely on greater levels of firm-specific human capital, the use of non-pecuniary mechanisms to motivate novice employees may increase (Malos and Campion 1995, 2000). For example, these PSFs may have a lower leverage ratio which enables closer mentoring from experts and reduced competition between novices for promotion to partner. In addition, the length of time required before becoming eligible for promotion to partner may be shorter, which may also be a spillover effect from closer mentoring and broader work experiences during novice training (Malos and Campion 2000).

In sum, while partners and associates are incentivized using different mechanisms, at a fundamental level the levers are similar. One set of motivating mechanisms is based on firm-specificity and collegiality, whereas the other is based on incentivizing individual performance through higher levels of compensation and transferable skills. However, this discussion is in the context of PSFs organized as partnerships. We discuss next the incentive and motivation implications in PSFs not organized as partnerships.

10.2.3.3 *Non-Partnership PSF Model: Public and Private Corporation*

Although the research literature that pertains to strategy in PSFs is largely in the context of the partnership model and in specific industries (notably the legal industry), our review would not be complete without discussing how research in the non-partnership model context explains incentives and motivation of professionals as drivers of firm performance.

As noted earlier, important differences in the incentives and motivation of the professional workforce may result from the type of ownership and governance form, and these differences may be reflected in the overall performance of the PSF (Greenwood and Empson 2003; Greenwood et al. 2007; von Nordenflycht 2007). For example, while publicly owned PSFs may benefit from market discipline such as a more formal strategic direction and clearer accountability (Greenwood et al. 2007), the separation of ownership and control increases internal agency costs. Moreover, while public ownership gives greater access to capital, often this capital is not required as the investment needs of PSFs (for such things as physical assets and R&D) are generally low (von Nordenflycht 2010). Thus, the benefits of public ownership may be minimal, while the incentive and motivation costs can be substantial. Indeed, research in management consulting has found that, on average, publicly owned PSFs have the lowest financial performance when compared to partnerships and private PSF corporations. On the other hand, von Nordenflycht (2007) shows that when PSFs (in this case advertising agencies) are publicly listed companies, the expected negative impact on performance due to lower financial incentives for professional workers *does not* automatically materialize. Rather, the size of the PSF is an important moderator of the relationship between ownership form and PSF performance. The key finding of von Nordenflycht (2007) is that for smaller advertising agencies, public ownership was associated with inferior performance, but not for larger advertising agencies. One explanation put forward is that as PSFs grow larger, fixed capital expenditures are greater and this increases the need for access to capital, while employee incentives may be less important considerations (von Nordenflycht 2007).

Nevertheless, in non-partnership PSFs, the weakening of the link between ownership and control, and distribution of firm profits away from managers can reduce the incentives of professionals to align with the strategic goals of the firm. The dilemma for PSFs is how to motivate these individuals to work in the interests of the firm, especially as extant research in both legal services and advertising has found clients to have often stronger bonds with PSF employees than the firm itself (Broschak 2004; Somaya et al. 2008). One possible motivator for employees to align with the firm may stem not from any firm-specific mechanism but from the internal motivations of the professional herself. Consistent with Gottschalg and Zollo (2007), professional workers may be motivated by an intrinsic desire to produce high quality client services within the institutional norms of their profession, regardless of their employer. Thus, while professionals in non-partnership PSFs may not share in the profits of the firm or have ownership control, professionals in general pay a significant amount of attention to developing their personal brand and building social capital (Teece 2003). Such intrinsic motivation may substitute, to some extent (and more so in professional service industries than others) pure financial reward. In terms of developing and reaping advantages from their own brand, we turn next to a particular type of professional—star or expert talent.

10.2.4 Stars and Expert Talent

A notable characteristic of the professional service industries and knowledge-intensive work generally is the presence of "star" or "expert" human capital. Stars are individuals who are disproportionally productive relative to average performers in their profession due to the superior education, skills, motivation, and/or experience they hold as human capital. Allied to being expert service providers, they may also have superior strategic and general management abilities (Teece 2003). Furthermore, as stars represent a small fraction of the labor market and their human capital is only imperfectly imitable (Barney 1991), they typically also have a high replacement cost to the firm (Coff 1999). PSFs with star talent should, holding everything else equal, be able to generate competitive advantages over PSFs lacking such talent. In addition to their human capital, stars typically also hold valuable social capital embedded in their extensive professional networks, client relationships, and perceived high status (Teece 2003). The value can manifest itself through access to additional competencies through professional contacts, while the personal reputation of expert human capital can attract high caliber clients and other professional talent. Human capital and social capital are thus two important complementary, yet distinct, mechanisms through which stars generate value for the PSF.

While PSFs are naturally drawn to star individuals to provide a strong foundation for the firm, it is important to underscore that there may be important firm-specific contributions to the value that stars produce. Stars do not work in a vacuum; rather the organizational contexts of PSFs may make firm-specific contributions to value creation that "enhance the star's brightness" (Groysberg et al. 2008). Examples of firm-specific contributions to value creation include administrative or structural processes that support and mobilize stars' human and social capital, routines shared with team members, and firm-level resources such as superior financial or reputational strength. Indeed, research from the mutual fund industry shows expert fund managers who are responsible for investment decisions may only contribute between 10 and 50% to fund performance (Baks 2003), while Groysberg et al. (2008) show that stars can suffer a deep and prolonged performance decline if removed from their work environment to a new firm. Moreover, Groysberg et al. (2011) find that while building project teams with multiple experts can initially increase team performance, there are decreasing marginal returns after a certain point (especially if the individuals have similar expertise) as clashes of status and ego coupled with the lack of functional hierarchical arrangements impede team effectiveness. Taken together, the research literature suggests that while expert talent can deliver substantial value to PSFs, it is important for PSFs to understand that stars require significant organizational supports (Teece 2003) and that having too many stars working together may not be an effective use of human resources.

10.3 STRATEGIC OPPORTUNITY

Strategic concerns in PSFs extend beyond the purely human capital and human resource related aspects discussed thus far. Indeed, a key central concern of PSFs is the creation of "opportunity space." In this section on strategic opportunity we examine a set of distinct, but interrelated, strategic factors that PSFs implement at the corporate level—i.e., corporate strategy. We also examine how PSFs strategize in terms of client relationships and how value is derived from these relationships.

Corporate strategy is fundamentally about the ways in which firms create value and derive competitive advantages from the configuration of multi-market activities (Porter 1985). Thus, it is essentially concerned with strategies related to the scope of the firm. For PSFs, this entails a set of issues pertaining to the range of client services (including multi-profession PSFs) and geographic footprint, and also the degree of integration across these different operations. Relatedly, an important dimension of corporate strategy is the extent to which PSFs use mechanisms such as mergers and acquisitions (M&A) and network alliances to implement choices related to corporate scope. Critically, the viability and performance of specific corporate strategies may depend on the quality of human capital and degree to which human capital is leveraged (Hitt et al. 2001; Kor and Leblebici 2005), expertise in particular specializations (Garicano and Hubbard 2007, 2009; Sherer 1995), and relational assets with clients (Chatain and Zemsky 2007; McKee and Garner 1992; Rose and Hinings 1999). Thus, corporate strategy in PSFs cannot be considered in isolation of the professional workforce.

10.3.1 Service Scope of PSFs

Professional service industries are characterized by PSFs of varying size and scope of services. The service scope of PSFs pertains to the array of services it offers clients, either within the same industry (e.g., law or advertising) or across industries, such as the "Big Four"[4] global business advisory PSFs who dominate across the fields of accounting services and management consulting.

PSFs may undertake a specialist "boutique" strategy, operating in a narrow range of closely related areas underpinned by tightly aligned organizational structures, processes, and human capital that enables them to provide of best-of-market services (Garicano and Hubbard 2007). In contrast, other PSFs prefer to function as multi-service providers that create value from operating in numerous client markets, offering clients "one-stop shopping" (Siggelkow 2002) and at the same time strengthening client ties and building relational benefits (Chatain and Zemsky 2007). Other PSFs implement "hybrid" strategies (Greenwood et al. 2005) that provide multiple client services but are more dominant in a single service or profession. However, hybrid multi-service PSFs (in accounting) have been shown to not perform as well as specialist or broader-based PSFs, ostensibly because the "lesser" services are not deemed "creditworthy" (Greenwood et al. 2005).[5] However although Greenwood et al. (2005) find a balanced, broad service portfolio is associated with better performance, von Nordenflycht (2010) suggests PSFs may remain specialized to signal the quality of their expertise in a narrow area.

The corporate strategy of PSFs is likely to be intimately linked to prevailing market conditions. For instance, research has found that with greater market demand, PSFs may become more narrowly specialized in order to differentiate from the market based on quality, where, in turn, deep expert knowledge is often more highly leveraged

(Garicano and Hubbard 2007; Sherer 1995). Greater market demand is presumed to give PSFs greater confidence in making sunk-cost investments in highly specialized expert knowledge; and markets with higher demand also have deeper labor markets that enable firms to find higher quality professional talent. Further, as market demand increases, so too does the number of PSFs looking to capture a share of this demand, which encourages firms to differentiate their services based on quality and specialization (thereby attracting high caliber talent, and clients who want best-of-market services). The consequences of specialization for human capital leverage stem from a smaller set of highly coordinated organizational processes that allow some knowledge to be codified into common repositories that novice workers can access directly, while managers themselves may find it easier to train novices within a narrower and more tightly aligned knowledge domain (Garicano and Hubbard 2007, 2009; Sherer 1995).

Other studies have noted the influence of the relational dimension of client and industry ties for PSFs corporate strategy. Indeed, when opportunities to cross-sell services to clients exist, a multi-service as opposed to specialized strategy may become increasingly valuable (Chatain and Zemsky 2007). For example, Rose and Hinings (1999) and McKee and Garner (1992) suggest that the overall design of global accounting and business advisory PSFs is in direct response to the specific service needs of their clients, whereby these PSFs have extended both geographically and in services (beyond audit) to leverage client relationships by meeting new (e.g., business advisory) needs of their clients. Similarly, in a study of the Canadian investment banking industry, Shipilov (2006) found clients place high value on the superior sector expertise of specialist banks but also on accessing the broader-based investor networks of multi-service banks. Indeed, broad-based banks in large networks that provide significant opportunities to connect clients to investor groups outperformed specialists in this context (Shipilov 2006). While these studies have made some initial forays into assessing the relative tradeoffs between service specialization and diversification in PSFs, in the concluding section we outline additional research opportunities in this area.

10.3.2 Geographic Scope of PSFs

While many large PSFs compete in multiple distinct geographic markets, the geographic scope strategy of PSFs (which is arguably quite unique when compared with the corporate strategies of manufacturing firms) has been relatively understudied, with one exception—global expansion. Global commerce requires PSFs to be able to facilitate transactions and solve disputes that span national borders and institutions, and global multinational clients may desire to deal with PSFs that can provide seamless and reliable services across multiple jurisdictions. Indeed, in 2012, the top five global law firms by gross revenue operated in a total of 127 overseas countries that accounted for almost 54% of attorney headcount,[6] while the behemoth "Big Four" business advisory PSFs have grown into global entities. Yet, the drivers of international corporate scope in PSFs mirror service scope in many ways. Research in the accounting industry informs us that accounting and business advisory firms went global to leverage and maintain relationships with clients who themselves were internationalizing (Rose and Hinings 1999). Thus, client relational assets and client pressures can be an important driver of global expansion in PSFs. From a human capital perspective, Hitt et al. (2006) found that US legal firms, whose expert talent held higher levels of firm and occupation-specific human capital, were more likely to expand overseas; however, after a certain level of overseas expansion these firms faced diminishing economic returns to further expansion. For UK law firms, the opposite relationship has been found, whereby international expansion is loss making until a certain threshold level of expansion is reached (Brock et al. 2006), again highlighting the potential for further research to understand the tradeoffs inherent in the geographic and international expansion of PSFs.

Moreover, Hitt et al. (2006) indicate the importance of human capital, not only as a key resource whose development might be affected by corporate scope choices, but also as a critical *enabling* resource for changes in PSF scope. In PSFs, senior managerial human capital is a critical resource for both running the day-to-day service operations of the firm, as well as managing the expansion into new service and geographical areas (Hitt et al. 2001, 2006; Kor and Leblebici 2005). Drawing on the Penrosean theory of firm growth (Penrose 1959), Kor and Leblebici (2005) note the limited capacity of managers to simultaneously manage a significant strategic move, while also mentoring large numbers of junior colleagues and responding to client needs. Indeed, Hitt et al. (2001) find that PSFs with superior expert talent can increase profits when undertaking *either* higher levels of service or geographic expansion, but not both at the same time. Kor and Leblebici (2005) extend Hitt et al. (2001) by also investigating the effect of human capital *leverage* on the diversification–performance relationship, and show highly leveraged PSFs suffer a drop in performance when undertaking *either* high levels of service or geographic diversification, or when recruiting higher numbers of expert talent. Taken together, these results show that when embarking on strategies to expand the scope of their organization, PSFs need to pay careful attention to the strains placed on their managerial human capital and understand the competing demands faced by them. In addition, expansion of firm scope inherently implies a need for human capital in new areas—e.g., a new location, or a new service—and raises questions about how such human capital can be efficaciously acquired or developed, to which we now turn.

10.3.3 Mergers and Acquisitions, Alliance Networks, and Global Expansion

PSFs typically do not begin life as multi-service firms. For example, in the accounting and business advisory industry, the firms who globally dominate both the accounting and management consulting industries operated initially as more focused accounting, audit, and tax PSFs. While PSFs can grow organically by hiring and training new talent, accessing and acquiring competencies of other PSFs (through M&A or alliance) is generally the preferred mechanism for PSFs to quickly and substantially alter their corporate scope.

M&A is a pervasive corporate strategy across professional services, as exemplified by legal services where the top 200 law firms alone have been involved in over 350 M&A transactions between 2000 and 2012.[7] The potential benefits of M&A are well documented in the broader strategy literature (but empirical studies are lacking in PSFs), which include scale and scope economies, acquiring new competencies, and access to new markets and clients. However, while achieving synergies between strategic and operational elements is fundamental to any M&A, the human aspects of integration—particularly, the fusing of disparate human capital and organizational infrastructures—are also critical for acquisition success, especially when human capital is the key asset. Extant strategy literature (e.g., Greenwood et al. 1994; Larsson and Finkelstein 1999) highlights differences in management styles (such as differences in managerial problem solving, risk preferences, formal governance, and communications) as key integration challenges, which may not be apparent ex ante and only be realized during the integration process (Greenwood et al. 1994). Pertinent to PSFs, clashes about professional ethics, performance measures, rewards and compensation, and paths to promotion can all contribute to undermining successful integration (Greenwood et al. 1994) or even result in a deal collapsing (Wootton et al. 2003), while other significant issues may be related to newly acquired individuals resisting their new employers' attempts to impose "property rights" over their knowledge and client relationships (Empson 2001). At the same time, the *non*-integration of incoming talent, for example due to path-dependency of existing relationships, distrust of new people, or the initial unwillingness to share resources (e.g., clients) may result in the preservation of separate cultures and management styles, which can also be value destroying (Briscoe and Tsai 2011).

Research also investigates the influence of client relationships as important antecedents to M&A, which can also have a significant impact on the efficacy of M&A (Rogan 2014b; Rogan and Sorenson 2014). Clients can serve as bridging ties between PSFs, leading to more interactions between firms. Research shows that an M&A event is more likely to occur between those PSFs who have a common client (Rogan and Sorenson 2014) as PSFs can use that client as a source of reliable information on potential acquisition targets. However, PSFs who use common clients as part of the M&A search process may suffer post-acquisition loss of clients, and of those clients it retains, the PSF may receive less new business (Rogan and Sorenson 2014).

This research highlights the risk that a PSF incurs when increasing the "competitive overlap" of its portfolio of clients by acquiring another. An important concern for PSFs in general is that "competitive frictions" can materialize when serving multiple clients. Typically, clients prefer to not use a PSF that also represents key market competitors due to the risks of knowledge leakage, while conflicts of interest often prevent the same PSF from representing clients who may be engaged in aggressive competition (e.g., litigation) against each other. Following an M&A between PSFs, the merging of the respective client portfolios can result in the competitive frictions described above, and thus result in the dissolution of client relationships (Rogan 2014b; Rogan and Sorenson 2014). Moreover, Rogan shows in a study of M&As between advertising agencies that the decision of the advertising agency to merge with a firm that serves the competitor of a long-standing client can increase the likelihood that the long-standing client relationship will terminate due to "a violation of norms governing behavior in embedded exchange" (2014b: 6).

In general, however, corporate strategy research on PSFs would benefit from more systematic investigation into the drivers and performance effects of M&A; despite the high volume of M&A undertaken by PSFs and recent work examining client-based impacts of M&A, our understanding of this phenomenon is lacking compared to other industrial contexts.

As an alternative to M&A (or greenfield expansion), specifically for global expansion, a significant proportion of PSFs operate as members of global alliance networks (Koza and Lewin 1999; Lenz and James 2007), which may in turn differ in their strategic objectives. In accounting and business advisory services, the largest networks are operated (and branded) by the "Big Four" (e.g., "KPMG International"). Member firms operate independently but are required to adhere to standardized processes in return for access to common resources, knowledge, expertise, and the use of the brand name of the host firm (Lenz and James 2007). Value is generated for the host firm (e.g., KPMG) by having a truly global reach, while smaller member firms reap the membership and spillover advantages of alliancing with global leaders (Baskerville and Hay 2010). A second form of alliance network is structured for referral purposes only, where each member is a separate firm in the truest sense and no costs or profits are shared for accounting purposes; e.g., Nexia International in accounting and business advisory services, and Lex Mundi in legal services. Value for PSFs following this alliance network strategy is generated through cross-referrals between members. However, tensions can often occur due to strict restrictions on one network member serving clients in another member's territory (Koza and Lewin 1999). In the case of Nexia International, asymmetries in the volume of referrals ultimately resulted in a Middle Eastern member exiting the network and opening a New York office (Koza and Lewin 1999). Other network risks include damage to reputations from the behavior of other member firms, or opportunistic behavior arising from members who follow their own interests rather than that of the network (Jones et al. 1998; Lenz and James 2007). Strategy research on the drivers and impacts of PSFs' network memberships has also been quite limited, and presents a unique opportunity for future studies.

10.3.4 Client Value and Client Relationships

In our final review section we discuss the importance of client relationships as a source of value for PSFs. As noted above, one way client relationships impact value creation in PSFs is in the efficacy of corporate strategy, specifically, the negative impact of M&A on client relationships. However, the discussion of client relationships within extant research literature is wider reaching. Notably, research considers that *relational assets* between PSFs and their clients can be a source of *strategic advantage* for PSFs, particularly in the capture of new business (Chatain 2011; Levinthal and Fichman 1988; Mayer et al. 2012; Moeen et al. 2013). Accordingly, PSFs may dedicate substantial firm resources towards identifying and meeting the emerging needs of *existing* clients, leading some scholars to describe PSFs as often having a more relational or more transactional strategic orientation (e.g., Baker 1990; Baker et al. 1998). Although client relationships are addressed in more depth in a separate chapter in this volume, we focus here on the strategic implications of the different types of value added in these relationships (Chatain 2011).

In his seminal text on managing PSFs, Maister (1993) stated a critical strategic concern for PSFs is balancing the firm's economic ambitions with the client marketplace. PSFs often leverage client relationships in formulating new strategies, in particular because existing clients represent a profitable source of new business. For example, the entry into management consulting of the "Big Four" accounting and business advisory PSFs has been noted to be a result, at least in part, of value-adding strategies of firms who recognized the opportunities to serve more needs of their clients by increasing their portfolio of business services. Similarly, the globalization of the "Big Four" has also been described in the context of these firms paralleling their clients' international expansion. By following the expansion of clients, those PSFs can provide a seamless global service to international clients, strengthening the bond with clients and increasing the likelihood of future new business. Drawing on these palpable implications of client relationships for PSF corporate scope choices, recent academic research has found that PSFs may diversify in response to demand from clients and are more likely to do so when they share valuable relational assets with their clients (Mawdsley and Somaya 2014).

Separately, building on ideas regarding the specificity or specialization of knowledge held by PSFs' human capital, research has shown that clients may outsource work to PSFs in order to access their superior (industry) domain-specific and/or occupational (professional) knowledge (Mayer et al. 2012). Thus, the PSF's expertise in a specific professional area or industry domain may be an important source of value in its relationship with clients. In the current environment where clients shift their work more frequently between PSFs (Heinz 2009) and have become more sophisticated in assessing PSF capabilities, the ability of PSFs to develop unique expertise and adapt their expertise to changing market conditions is central to value-addition in servicing clients (Chatain 2011). Thus, evolving client needs and the resulting divergence in client–supplier fit may be associated with supplier switching (Baker et al. 1998), and thus poses a counter-balance to the value of relational assets embedded in client relationships.

Nonetheless, the stock of client-specific knowledge that a PSF may acquire through past outsourced projects is a relationship-sustaining source of value, which can give the PSF a privileged position in obtaining subsequent related business from the client (Mayer et al. 2012). Additionally, client relationships may also embed other relational assets—such as inter-firm coordination routines and informal trust and governance—that can help the transacting firms overcome market frictions and work more effectively across organizational boundaries (Dyer and Singh 1998). PSFs that develop client-specific knowledge and other relational assets are therefore likely to cement PSF–client relationships and break away from a more transactional model of service provision. Prior research on US patent legal services has attributed increased PSF business from clients to the strengthening of such client relational assets through employee mobility (Carnahan and Somaya 2013; Somaya et al. 2008), and suggested that clients may increase the "concentration" of their outsourced business to PSFs with whom they share such relational assets (Moeen et al. 2013). Similarly, in the UK legal services industry, law firms holding higher levels of client-specific knowledge were more likely to be chosen to fulfill the emerging needs of existing clients (Chatain 2011). Furthermore, research in advertising also shows that clients respond favorably to suppliers that actively nurture client relationships (LaBahn and Kohli 1997).

An important tension regarding client relationships, and one that is yet to be fully investigated in the literature, concerns the locus of control over the relationship—in other words, who effectively "owns" the relational value: the firm or key "boundary spanning" professionals? Several research papers in the literature indicate that clients' ties to professionals may be stronger than to the firm. In the advertising industry, clients have been found to dissolve ties when key relationship managers exit the PSF (Baker et al. 1998; Biong and Ulvnes 2011; Broschak 2004), while Seabright et al. (1992) show in accounting that the likelihood of client tie dissolution is attenuated by longer tenure of senior human capital. On the other hand, Rogan (2014a) finds in the advertising industry that PSFs can in some cases mitigate the effects of employee departure when the firm has multiple ties to the same client. Moreover, research in (patent) law has also shown that professionals can port client relationships when they switch firms (Somaya et al. 2008). It is interesting to note, however, that Biong and Ulvnes (2011) also find that clients are less likely to follow the professional (even when she has valuable human capital) when the PSF has a greater level of structural (relational) capital with the client. Therefore, there do appear to be important firm-level contributions to the client relationship even when the client derives significant value from individual-level talent. Future research should further elucidate where the locus of client–relationships resides, and how PSFs may strategically influence its location.

10.4 CONCLUSIONS AND FUTURE DIRECTIONS

In this chapter we have reviewed the extant literature on the strategic management of PSFs. Given the importance of human capital for PSFs, it is only natural that the strategy literature on PSFs is built significantly on a human capital foundation. In particular, we have reviewed the different ways in which PSFs seek to create value from human capital, which includes the vertical differentiation of talent (e.g., within knowledge hierarchies) as well as the organizational infrastructures to support, develop, combine, and co-specialize human capital. In turn, PSFs seek to align their talent with the firms' overall objectives through a delicate balance of motivational tools, rent division with professionals, and governance structures for the firm. Another important resource for virtually all PSFs is their relationship with clients, although ownership over these relationships may be shared with professionals and thus raises similar concerns regarding rent division and motivation as human capital. Lastly, we reviewed the literature on corporate strategies pursued by PSFs, which include both decisions about firm (service and geographic scope) as well as specific strategic actions such as M&A and alliances that can be used to support these corporate scope choices.

Within each of the reviewed streams of research, we have described a number of fruitful avenues for future research in the strategic management of PSFs. For instance, we note the need to develop a deeper understanding of the limits of leveraging, tradeoffs between different types of human capital specialization, performance implications of PSF governance, the ownership locus of client relationships, geographic scope choices, and the use of M&A and alliance networks. Additionally, research on strategy in professional services may benefit from exploring additional measures of firm performance besides profitability. While most research on PSF performance focuses on profits per partner as the dependent variable, many industry sources (e.g., published law firm rankings) base their rankings on gross revenue or number of professionals, rather than average partner profits. Performance measures such as growth, revenues, billing rates, and survival may also have theoretical appeal in the context of PSFs, in addition to their practical real-world significance. Indeed, in recent times we have witnessed the dissolution of large and seemingly financially strong PSFs, but we are yet to fully understand the reasons or triggers for collapse. While each of these areas (and others besides) are certainly promising areas for research, we are particularly struck by the need for integration and reconciliation between the different research streams within our review.

Consider for example the interactions between human capital building through leveraged knowledge hierarchies, its specificity to firm, industry, or occupation, and the organizational infrastructures within which it is built and deployed. While prior research has explored each of these aspects in significant detail, significant gaps remain in our understanding of the connections and tradeoffs between them. Similarly, the relationships between different human capital building strategies (Chauradia 2014) and the motivation and governance of human capital are quite underdeveloped, although recent work on compensation dispersion has begun to fill this lacuna (Campbell et al. 2012; Carnahan et al. 2012). Another significant research opportunity lies in connecting client relationships with the development and maintenance of important human capital-based expertise within both PSF and client organizations (e.g., Mayer et al. 2012). Last but not least, while research on corporate strategy has incorporated considerations of human capital (Hitt et al. 2001, 2006; Kor and Leblebici 2005) corporate strategies related to firm governance and client relationships remain under-research areas (for an exception, see Mawdsley and Somaya 2014).

Furthermore, the strategic landscape of professional services has been undergoing significant changes. A globalized economy created by advances in telecommunications and transportation has led to the significant growth and consolidation of national and multinational corporate clients for professional services. PSFs have in turn become more "corporate orientated" and moved away from traditional, collegial partnerships towards target-driven Managed Professional Businesses (Cooper et al. 1996). This shift has brought with it increasing levels of employee mobility as PSFs seek to attract the highest caliber talent and dispose of under-performers, while professionals have been able to develop highly specialist domain capital which they can leverage as bargaining power when negotiating for economic returns to their human capital. However, as global growth has tapered and this model of professional services has matured, PSFs are poised for yet another strategic shift. Their clients have become increasingly more sophisticated, demanding, cost sensitive, and capable of handling more work internally. The next generation of research on strategy in professional services will also need to reflect these important shifts in PSFs' strategic environment.

Naturally, this review makes no claim to being comprehensive in covering all pertinent issues related to strategic management of PSFs. One area that deserves mention, and is lacking within strategy research in PSFs, is the wider institutional framework within which PSFs operate. Our review has presented strategic management concerns based on PSFs being in a position to *make* important choices. However, institutional theorists often challenge the assumption that firms can freely make choices, arguing instead that firms are constrained by institutional pressures, such as being required to operate in a certain way in order to conform and maintain legitimacy (DiMaggio and Powell 1991). Future research should investigate the different institutional pressures that PSFs face and how these may impact important strategic decisions (such as the scope of the firm). Another avenue for future research in this area could be to contrast the performance of PSFs who maintain conformity to institutional expectations with those who diverge. We also know little about how PSFs themselves influence and shape the institutional environment, such as public policy. For instance, to what extent can PSFs navigate or influence government regulation that defines the competitive environment? What role can PSFs play in the aftermath of a crisis, such as the most recent recession, and how would this impact the strategic issues described throughout this chapter? This is a nascent area of PSF research where many opportunities lie. Given the increasing economic importance of professional services and professional work more generally, we expect research in these areas (and in the study of PSFs' strategies generally) to grow rapidly in the near future.

Notes

1. <http://www.bea.gov/industry/index.htm> (accessed April 7, 2013). Statistics are taken from the industry tables compiled and published by the Bureau of Economic Analysis (US Department of Commerce). Industries such as Real Estate, Financial and Insurance

Services, and Healthcare, which are also significantly comprised of PSFs, were excluded from our computations because the statistics on PSFs within these industries are not separately reported. By the same token, the Professional and Business Services sector also includes some industry segments—Management of Companies and Enterprises and Administrative and Waste Management Services—that may not fit the PSF mold. Excluding these segments, the residual "Professional, Scientific, and Technical Services" segment is still about 67% the size of manufacturing in GDP value-added, and grew by 260% in the two decades to 2011.

2. Specifically, we searched the Proquest, ABI-Inform Complete, EBSCO and Econ-Lit databases using a number of search algorithms that combined the search terms "strategy" or "compete" or "competitive advantage" or "performance" or "competition" AND "professional service" or "PSF" or "law firm" or "accounting" or "advertising" or "investment bank" or "consulting" or "human capital." We complemented this search with relevant articles and reports from focused professional services journals, and finally we also incorporated research from the reference sections of articles we found in this manner and from the authors' personal knowledge.

3. We adopt the language of "experts" and "novices" to distinguish between senior and junior employees. These terms may be used interchangeably with, respectively, "partners" and "associates." However, because many PSFs are not organized as partnerships (especially those outside of law, accounting, and consulting) for consistency we use "experts" and "novices" to reflect a generalizable difference in human capital expertise across all professional service sectors.

4. The "Big Four" consists of KPMG, Ernst & Young, PricewaterhouseCoopers, and Deloitte.

5. Greenwood et al. (2005) cite the example of accounting firm Arthur Anderson being unable to merge with elite law firms in the UK, and the separation of its consulting arm to form Accenture because its managers grew tired of their secondary status.

6. Statistics from the Global 100 published by *American Lawyer*. <http://www.americanlawyer.com/index.jsp>.

7. Statistics from *American Lawyer*. <http://www.americanlawyer.com/index.jsp>.

References

Alchian, A. A. and Demsetz, H. (1972). "Production, Information Costs, and Economic Organization," *American Economic Review* 62(5): 777–795.

Baker, W. E. (1990). "Market Networks and Corporate Behavior," *American Journal of Sociology* 96(3): 589–625.

Baker, W. E., Faulkner, R. R., and Fisher, G. A. (1998). "Hazards of the Market: The Continuity and Dissolution of Interorganizational Market Relationships," *American Sociological Review* 63(2): 147–177.

Baks, K. P. (2003). "On the Performance of Mutual Fund Managers," Working Paper (Emory University).

Barney, J. (1991). "Firm Resources and Sustained Competitive Advantage," *Journal of Management* 17(1): 99–120.

Baskerville, R. F. and Hay, D. (2010). "The Impact of Globalization on Professional Accounting Firms: Evidence from New Zealand," *Accounting History* 15(3): 285–308.

Becker, G. S. (1964). *Human Capital: A Theoretical Analysis with Special Reference to Education*. New York and London: Columbia University Press.

Biong, H. and Ulvnes, A. M. (2011). "If the Supplier's Human Capital Walks Away, Where Would the Customer Go?" *Journal of Business-to-Business Marketing* 18(3): 223–252.

Bowman, C. and Swart, J. (2007). "Whose Human Capital? The Challenge of Value Capture When Capital is Embedded," *Journal of Management Studies* 44(4): 488–505.

Briscoe, F. (2007). "From Iron Cage to Iron Shield? How Bureaucracy Enables Temporal Flexibility for Professional Service Workers," *Organization Science* 18(2): 297–314.

Briscoe, F. and Tsai, W. (2011). "Overcoming Relational Inertia: How Organizational Members Respond to Acquisition Events in a Law Firm," *Administrative Science Quarterly* 56(3): 408–440.

Brivot, M. (2011). "Controls of Knowledge Production: Sharing and Use in Bureaucratized Professional Service Firms," *Organization Studies* 32(4): 489–508.

Brock, D. M., Yaffe, T., and Dembovsky, M. (2006). "International Diversification and Performance: A Study of Global Law Firms," *Journal of International Management* 12(4): 473–489.

Broschak, J. P. (2004). "Managers' Mobility and Market Interface: The Effect of Managers' Career Mobility on the Dissolution of Market Ties," *Administrative Science Quarterly* 49(4): 608–640.

Campbell, B. A., Ganco, M., Franco, A. M., and Agarwal, R. (2012). "Who Leaves, Where To, and Why Worry? Employee Mobility, Entrepreneurship and Effects on Source Firm Performance," *Strategic Management Journal* 33(1): 65–87.

Carnahan, S., Agarwal, R., and Campbell, B. A. (2012). "Heterogeneity in Turnover: The Effect of Relative Compensation Dispersion of Firms on the Mobility and Entrepreneurship of Extreme Performers," *Strategic Management Journal* 33(12): 1411–1430.

Carnahan, S. and Somaya, D. (2013). "Alumni Effects and Relational Advantage: The Impact on Outsourcing When a Buyer Hires Employees from a Supplier's Competitors," *Academy of Management Journal* 56(6): 1578–1600.

Castanias, R. P. and Helfat, C. E. (2001). "The Managerial Rents Model: Theory and Empirical Analysis," *Journal of Management* 27(6): 661–678.

Castanias, R. P. and Helfat, C. E. (1991). "Managerial Resources and Rents," *Journal of Management* 17(1): 155–171.

Chatain, O. (2011). "Value Creation, Competition, and Performance in Buyer–Supplier Relationships," *Strategic Management Journal* 32(1): 76–102.

Chatain, O. and Zemsky, P. (2007). "The Horizontal Scope of the Firm: Organizational Tradeoffs vs. Buyer–Supplier Relationships," *Management Science* 53(4): 550–565.

Chauradia, A. J. (2014). "Three Essays on the Strategies of Human Capital Building and Acquiring," PhD Dissertation, University of Illinois at Urbana Champaign, Illinois.

Coff, R. W. (1997). "Human Assets and Management Dilemmas: Coping With Hazards on the Road to Resource-Based Theory," *Academy of Management Review* 22(2): 374–402.

Coff, R. W. (1999). "When Competitive Advantage Doesn't Lead to Performance: The Resource-Based View and Stakeholder Bargaining Power," *Organization Science* 10(2): 119–133.

Coff, R. W. (2010). "The Coevolution of Rent Appropriation and Capability Development," *Strategic Management Journal* 31(7): 711–733.

Coff, R. W. and Kryscynski, D. (2011). "Invited Editorial: Drilling for Micro-Foundations of Human Capital-Based Competitive Advantages," *Journal of Management* 37(5): 1429–1443.

Cooper, D. J., Hinings, B., Greenwood, R., and Brown, J. L. (1996). "Sedimentation and Transformation in Organizational Change: The Case of Canadian Law Firms," *Organization Studies* 17(4): 623–647.

DiMaggio, P. J. and Powell, W. W. (1991). "Introduction," in *The New Institutionalism in Organizational Analysis*, ed. W. W. Powell and P. J. DiMaggio. Chicago, IL: University of Chicago Press, 1–40.

Dyer, J. H. and Singh, H. (1998). "The Relational View: Cooperative Strategy and Sources of Interorganizational Competitive Advantage," *Academy of Management Review* 23(4): 660–679.

Eisenhardt, K. M. (1989). "Agency Theory: An Assessment and Review," *Academy of Management Review* 14(1): 57–74.

Empson, L. (2001). "Fear of Exploitation and Fear of Contamination: Impediments to Knowledge Transfer in Mergers between Professional Service Firms," *Human Relations* 54(7): 839–862.

Fama, E. F. and Jensen, M. C. (1983). "Separation of Ownership and Control," *Journal of Law and Economics* 26(2): 301–325.

Forstenlechner, I., Lettice, F., and Bourne, M. (2009). "Knowledge Pays: Evidence from a Law Firm," *Journal of Knowledge Management* 13(1): 56–68.

Galanter, M. and Palay, T. M. (1990). "Why the Big Get Bigger: The Promotion-to-Partner Tournament and the Growth of Large Law Firms," *Virginia Law Review* 76(4): 747–811.

Garicano, L. and Hubbard, T. N. (2007). "Managerial Leverage is Limited by the Extent of the Market: Hierarchies, Specialization, and the Utilization of Lawyers' Human Capital," *Journal of Law and Economics* 50(1): 1–43.

Garicano, L. and Hubbard, T. N. (2009). "Specialization, Firms, and Markets: The Division of Labor Within and Between Law Firms," *Journal of Law, Economics, and Organization* 25(2): 339–371.

Gilson, R. J. and Mnookin, R. H. (1985). "Sharing Among the Human Capitalists: An Economic Inquiry into the Corporate Law Firm and How Partners Split Profits," *Stanford Law Review* 37(2): 313–392.

Gilson, R. J. and Mnookin, R. H. (1989). "Coming of Age in a Corporate Law Firm: The Economics of Associate Career Patterns," *Stanford Law Review* 41(3): 567–595.

Gottschalg, O. and Zollo, M. (2007). "Interest Alignment and Competitive Advantage," *Academy of Management Review* 32(2): 418–437.

Grant, R. M. (1996). "Toward a Knowledge-Based Theory of the Firm," *Strategic Management Journal* 17(Winter Special Issue): 109–122.

Greenwood, R. and Empson, L. (2003). "The Professional Partnership: Relic or Exemplary Form of Governance?" *Organization Studies* 24(6): 909–933.

Greenwood, R., Deephouse, D. L., and Li, S. X. (2007). "Ownership and Performance of Professional Service Firms," *Organization Studies* 28(2): 219–238.

Greenwood, R., Hinings, C., and Brown, J. (1994). "Merging Professional Service Firms," *Organization Science* 5(2): 239–257.

Greenwood, R., Li, S. X., Prakash, R., and Deephouse, D. L. (2005). "Reputation, Diversification, and Organizational Explanations of Performance in Professional Service Firms," *Organization Science* 16(6): 661–673.

Groysberg, B., Lee, L., and Nanda, A. (2008). "Can They Take It With Them? The Portability of Star Knowledge Workers' Performance," *Management Science* 54(7): 1213–1230.

Groysberg, B., Polzer, J. T., and Elfenbein, H. A. (2011). "Too Many Cooks Spoil the Broth: How High-Status Individuals Decrease Group Effectiveness," *Organization Science* 22(3): 722–737.

Hansen, M. T., Nohria, N., and Tierney, T. (1999). "What's Your Strategy for Managing Knowledge?" *Harvard Business Review* 77(2): 106–116.

Heinz, J. P. (2009). "When Law Firms Fail," *Suffolk University Law Review* 43(1): 67–78.

Henderson, W. D. (2006). "An Empirical Study of Single-Tier versus Two-Tier Partnerships in the Am Law 200," *North Carolina Law Review* 84: 1691–1750.

Henderson, W. D. and Bierman, L. (2009). "Empirical Analysis of Lateral Lawyer Trends from 2000 to 2007: The Emerging Equilibrium for Corporate Law Firms," *Georgetown Journal of Legal Ethics* 22: 1395–1430.

Hitt, M. A., Bierman, L., Shimizu, K., and Kochhar, R. (2001). "Direct and Moderating Effects of Human Capital on Strategy and Performance in Professional Service Firms: A Resource-Based Perspective," *Academy of Management Journal* 44(1): 13–28.

Hitt, M. A., Bierman, L., Uhlenbruck, K., and Shimizu, K. (2006). "The Importance of Resources in the Internationalization of Professional Service Firms: The Good, the Bad, and the Ugly," *Academy of Management Journal* 49(6): 1137–1157.

Jensen, M. C. and Meckling, W. H. (1979). "Rights and Production Functions: An Application to Labor-Managed Firms and Codetermination," *Journal of Business* 52(2): 469–506.

Jensen, S. H., Poulfelt, F., and Kraus, S. (2010). "Managerial Routines in Professional Service Firms: Transforming Knowledge into Competitive Advantages," *Service Industries Journal* 30(12): 2045–2062.

Jones, C., Hesterly, W. S., Fladmoe-Lindquist, K., and Borgatti, S. P. (1998). "Professional Service Constellations: How Strategies and Capabilities Influence Collaborative Stability and Change," *Organization Science* 9(3): 396–410.

Kogut, B. and Zander, U. (1992). "Knowledge of the Firm, Combinative Capabilities, and the Replication of Technology," *Organization Science* 3(3): 383–397.

Kor, Y. Y. and Leblebici, H. (2005). "How do Interdependences among Human-Capital Deployment, Development, and Diversification Strategies Affect Firms' Financial Performance?" *Strategic Management Journal* 26(10): 967–985.

Kordana, K. A. (1995). "Law Firms and Associate Careers: Tournament Theory versus the Production-Imperative Model," *Yale Law Journal* 104(7): 1907–1934.

Koza, M. P. and Lewin, A. Y. (1999). "The Coevolution of Network Alliances: A Longitudinal Analysis of an International Professional Service Network," *Organization Science* 10(5): 638–653.

LaBahn, D. W. and Kohli, C. (1997). "Maintaining Client Commitment in Advertising Agency–Client Relationships," *Industrial Marketing Management* 26(6): 497–508.

Larsson, R. and Finkelstein, S. (1999). "Integrating Strategic, Organizational, and Human Resource Perspectives on Mergers and Acquisitions: A Case Survey of Synergy Realization," *Organization Science* 10(1): 1–26.

Lenz, H. and James, M. (2007). "International Audit Firms as Strategic Networks: The Evolution of Global Professional Service Firms," in *Economics and Management of Networks*, ed. G. Cliquet, M. Tuunanen, G. Hendrikse, and J. Windsperger. Heidelberg and New York: Physica-Verlag, 367–392.

Levinthal, D. A. and Fichman, M. (1988). "Dynamics of Interorganizational Attachments: Auditor–Client Relationships," *Administrative Science Quarterly* 33(3): 345–369.

McKee, D. L. and Garner, D. E. (1992). *Accounting Services, the International Economy, and Third World Development*. Westport, CT: Praeger.

Maister, D. H. (1993). *Managing the Professional Service Firm*. New York: Free Press.

Malhotra, N. and Morris, T. (2009). "Heterogeneity in Professional Service Firms," *Journal of Management Studies* 46(6): 895–922.

Malos, S. B. and Campion, M. A. (1995). "An Options-Based Model of Career Mobility in Professional Service Firms," *Academy of Management Review* 20(3): 611–644.

Malos, S. B. and Campion, M. A. (2000). "Human Resource Strategy and Career Mobility in Professional Service Firms: A Test of an Options-Based Model," *Academy of Management Journal* 43(4): 749–760.

Mawdsley, J. and Somaya, D. (2014). "Relational Advantage and Partner-Driven Corporate Scope: The Case for Client-Led Diversification," Working Paper (University of Illinois at Urbana Champaign, Illinois).

Mayer, K. J., Somaya, D., and Williamson, I. O. (2012). "Firm-Specific, Industry-Specific, and Occupational Human Capital and the Sourcing of Knowledge Work," *Organization Science* 23(5): 1311–1329.

Moeen, M., Somaya, D., and Mahoney, J. T. (2013). "Supply Portfolio Concentration in Outsourced Knowledge-Based Services," *Organization Science* 24(1): 262–279.

Morris, T. (2001). "Asserting Property Rights: Knowledge Codification in the Professional Service Firm," *Human Relations* 54(7): 819–838.

Penrose, E. T. (1959). *The Theory of the Growth of the Firm.* New York: John Wiley.

Peteraf, M. A. (1993). "The Cornerstones of Competitive Advantage: A Resource-Based View," *Strategic Management Journal* 14(3): 179–191.

Phillips, D. J. (2002). "A Genealogical Approach to Organizational Life Chances: The Parent–Progeny Transfer among Silicon Valley Law Firms, 1946–1996," *Administrative Science Quarterly* 47(3): 474–506.

Porter, M. E. (1985). *Competitive Advantage: Creating and Sustaining Superior Performance.* New York: Free Press.

Rogan, M. (2014a). "Executive Departures Without Client Losses: The Role of Multiplex Ties in Exchange Partner Retention," *Academy of Management Journal* 57(2): 563–584.

Rogan, M. (2014b). "Too Close for Comfort? The Effect of Embeddedness and Competitive Overlap on Client Retention Post-Acquisition," *Organization Science* 25(1): 185–203.

Rogan, M. and Sorenson, O. (2014). "Picking a (Poor) Partner: A Relational Perspective on Acquisitions," *Administrative Science Quarterly* 59(2): 301–329.

Rose, T. and Hinings, C. (1999). "Global Clients' Demands Driving Change in Global Business Advisory Firms," in *Restructuring the Professional Organization: Accounting, Health Care and Law*, ed. D. Brock, M. Powell, M., and C.R. Hinings. London: Routledge, 41–67.

Seabright, M. A., Levinthal, D. A., and Fichman, M. (1992). "Role of Individual Attachments in the Dissolution of Interorganizational Relationships," *Academy of Management Journal* 35(1): 122–160.

Sherer, P. D. (1995). "Leveraging Human Assets in Law Firms: Human Capital Structures and Organizational Capabilities," *Industrial and Labor Relations Review* 48(4): 671–691.

Shipilov, A. V. (2006). "Network Strategies and Performance of Canadian Investment Banks," *Academy of Management Journal* 49(3): 590–604.

Siggelkow, N. (2002). "Evolution toward Fit," *Administrative Science Quarterly* 47(1): 125–159.

Somaya, D., Williamson, I. O., and Lorinkova, N. (2008). "Gone but Not Lost: The Different Performance Impacts of Employee Mobility between Cooperators versus Competitors," *Academy of Management Journal* 51(5): 936–953.

Teece, D. J. (2003). "Expert Talent and the Design of (Professional Services) Firms," *Industrial and Corporate Change* 12(4): 895–916.

von Nordenflycht, A. (2007). "Is Public Ownership Bad for Professional Service Firms? Ad Agency Ownership, Performance, and Creativity," *Academy of Management Journal* 50(2): 429–445.

von Nordenflycht, A. (2010). "What is a Professional Service Firm? Toward a Theory and Taxonomy of Knowledge-Intensive Firms," *Academy of Management Review* 35(1): 155–174.

Wezel, F. C., Cattani, G., and Pennings, J. M. (2006). "Competitive Implications of Interfirm Mobility," *Organization Science* 17(6): 691–709.

Wootton, C. W., Wolk, C. M., and Normand, C. (2003). "An Historical Perspective on Mergers and Acquisitions by Major US Accounting Firms," *Accounting History* 8(1): 25–60.

CHAPTER 11

SERVICE INNOVATION IN PROFESSIONAL SERVICE FIRMS

A Review and Future Research Directions

MICHAEL BARRETT AND BOB HININGS

11.1 INTRODUCTION

WHILE the study of service innovation in organizations as a key source of growth and competitive advantage has been widely recognized (Christensen et al. 2004; Damanpour et al. 2009), its explicit development in the literature on Professional Service Firms (PSFs) has been less evident. This is particularly surprising given the significant development of the wider and related area of innovation in services (Salter and Tether 2006), as we move increasingly towards what some have termed a service economy (Chesbrough and Spohrer 2006). In PSFs such as accounting, law, architecture, and management consulting firms, service provision often requires a high degree of interaction and co-production of knowledge with clients and other business partners for both diagnosis and delivery of service (Gann and Salter 2000; Dougherty 2004), with multiple actors involved in innovating within these service organizations.

Over the past two decades there have been wide-ranging studies of change in PSFs (Malhotra et al. 2006; Malhotra and Morris 2009; von Nordenflycht 2010), but there have been few that deal with innovation in a direct way, despite the fact that innovation involves implementation of new ideas (Greenwood et al. 2002) which inevitably require the managing of change in the process (Damanpour and Gopalakrishnan 2001; Birkinshaw et al. 2008). Similarly, despite knowledge management and information systems being recognized as strategic resources of value creation (Ofek and Sarvary 2001; Fosstenløkken et al. 2003; Anand et al. 2007) in the PSF literature, there has been surprisingly less incorporation of conceptual developments of innovation.

The main purpose of this chapter is to open up the discussion of service innovation in PSFs, which has been largely neglected, despite being an important and emerging area of research more generally (Miles 2001, 2008; Adner 2012; Lusch and Vargo 2014). The limited PSF work that exists around the theme of service innovation has focused on the introduction of new practice areas, often through diversification (Gardner et al. 2008), and the development of new organizational structures and systems (Empson and Chapman 2006). Other literature has emphasized how practice-based knowledge is necessary for service innovation, particularly in organizing practice for strategic ends (Dougherty 2004). For example, recent research adopting a practice approach has sought to better understand how the production of "seamless" cross-border services emerges from improvisations in everyday work (Smets et al. 2012) while also enabling the dynamics of institutional change at the field level. We build on these recent developments in practice theory to further our understanding of service innovation in PSFs. In particular, our practice perspective recognizes relationality across professionals and between these professionals and other communities (Styhre 2011) while also highlighting the materiality in the (social) practice in what has been termed a sociomaterial practice (Scott and Orlikowski 2013). Such an approach highlights the entanglement of tools, technologies, and methodologies (Orlikowski and Scott 2008) in the practice of development and delivery of service innovation in PSFs.

This chapter is structured as follows. We start by taking stock of the literature that deals directly with innovation in service firms and PSFs. In doing so, we review studies of organizational change in PSFs with the purpose of showing the links between innovation and change. We also review the role of knowledge and knowledge management and suggest links with the development of innovation in PSFs. We subsequently discuss the literature developing around service and service innovation, and the implications for service innovation in PSFs. We subsequently propose the further development and use of practice theory in examining service innovation within PSFs and briefly illustrate these ideas through examples of service innovation in the PSF literature.

11.2 INNOVATION IN PROFESSIONAL SERVICE FIRMS

An overview of the literature on innovation in PSFs produces a number of observations. First, there is very little mention of service innovation, per se. Exceptions discussed below include Hinings et al. (1991), Dougherty (2004), Anand et al. (2007), and Gardner et al. (2008). So, it would seem that innovation is not part of the lexicon in the study of PSFs. However, a second observation is that there has been substantial concern with change in PSFs, and this is related to the concept of innovation. Indeed the revival of interest in PSFs that occurred in the 1990s was driven by an interest in the changes that were said to be happening (Hinings 2004). This latter research stream actually reflects a concern with service innovation even though this term was not used. Thirdly, there is a literature centered on knowledge management as something central to PSFs (see Faulconbridge, Chapter 19, this volume), which is understood to be critical for value creation in the literature on innovation (Fosstenløkken et al. 2003; Anand et al. 2007). The next sections look at each of these key points in turn to better understand the connections and disconnects between these related literatures.

11.2.1 PSFs and Service Innovation

There are a small number of PSF studies that do examine service innovation (Dougherty 2004; Anand et al. 2007). Dougherty (2004) studied professional services in IT, civil engineering, and training and sought to examine "how work in service organizations can be organized to capture and exploit the knowledge that is necessary to create new services" (Dougherty 2004: 35). In professionally-based organizations knowledge is highly practice-based and the challenge for service innovation is how to capture that knowledge in the practice of everyday activities across the organization, including how to strategically organize practice for value creation between clients and the firm in redesigning work. What we see here is a theme which is evident in much work on PSFs, that knowledge rests primarily with the individual professional and is based on the set of practices pursued at the level of the individual (see Faulconbridge, Chapter 19, this volume). In Dougherty's (2004) work we also see a strong interconnection of service innovation with managing knowledge as well as the recognition that knowledge is embedded in the actual practice of innovation. However, while practice theorists recognize knowledge as situated in collective action, they often focus on clearly bounded occupations or disciplines which presuppose established activities which is not the case in PSFs (Dougherty 2004). It is this recognition that professional service work is inextricably bound up with collective knowledge sharing that emphasizes that professionals need to be able constantly to collaborate and interact with peers and with other (non-) professional communities in their daily practice.

Service innovation in PSFs therefore depends on knowledge as an important strategic resource (Løwendahl et al. 2001), in particular how these firms can improve their knowledge development processes for value creation through client interaction (Fosstenløkken et al. 2003). Further, service provision and innovation require a high degree of interaction and co-production of knowledge with clients and other business partners for both diagnosis and delivery of service (Gann and Salter 2000; Dougherty 2004). Articles by Anand et al. (2007) and Gardner et al. (2008) also deal with service innovation; diversification by creating new practice areas in management consulting and law firms. They also point out that innovation in PSFs is inherently knowledge-based but, due to the ambiguous nature of knowledge, innovation in such circumstances is challenging. In this work there is an emphasis on the agency of the individual professional (although within both a firm and regulatory body context which we will take up later), and the professional networks and communities of practice of

which they are a part. We will return to this relationship of knowledge and service innovation in a later sub-section.

There are other studies that concern service innovation in PSFs though they do not
use the language of innovation per se, but that of new markets, new services, diversification, etc. One such study is that of WebTrust (Gendron and Barrett 2004; Barrett and
Gendron 2006) in which the authors argue, along with others (Power 1997; Hinings et al.
1999), that the accounting profession "had to further expand and diversify its services
into e-commerce if it wanted to prevent its decline" (Gendron and Barrett 2004: 568).
WebTrust was meant to be a seal of assurance issued by a professional accountant for
online consumers certifying that the client followed best practice. As such it was to
be a new service that built upon the expertise of accountants in providing assurance
through financial audits. In a somewhat different professional setting (legal services),
Sako (2009, 2010) also examines service innovation, again without framing the issue as
one of innovation. For her, the innovation is one of making decisions about which services to retain within the firm and which to outsource or offshore in legal services, such
as "make or buy" or legal process outsourcing (LPO). Sako's work (see Sako, Chapter 15,
this volume) highlights a number of elements that go into such decisions, but of particular importance to our argument is the emphasis on strategic decision-making and
business models and the importance of a professional setting. In particular, Sako has
noted the influence of professional expertise and identity on organizational design and
industry structure in law firms on the decision about which service to supply.

These studies emphasize several important issues for service innovation in PSFs.
First, PSFs are knowledge-based organizations and innovation depends on new or
expanded knowledge for value creation. Because that knowledge is based in the professional, legitimacy is conferred, at least initially, through acceptance by those professionals. Second, obtaining and establishing legitimacy is critical because professionals
are central and, primarily, operate within a relatively non-hierarchical organization
(Empson and Chapman 2006). Individual professionals are the location of knowledge
and practices; it is one of the things that defines them as professionals. And PSFs are
organized to recognize that centrality by giving those individuals considerable autonomy through organizing around a non-hierarchical authority system (Hinings 2004).
A third element is the existence of multiple actors in the innovation process, both as a
source of innovative practices and as having an important role in legitimizing such practices. Fourth, and very significantly, these studies all point to an important link between
service innovation and changes in organizational structure, systems, and practices.
Service innovations arise from the ideas and practices of individual professionals who
then redesign (innovate) new structures and authority systems "on the hoof." Indeed,
there is a two-way interaction between service innovation and change. On the one hand,
introducing service innovations requires organizational change. On the other hand,
prior changes in organizational structure are a way to generate and exploit new forms of
knowledge, and such changes allow innovative knowledge-based structures to emerge
and become embedded in organizations. We now examine in more depth the PSF literature on organizational change.

11.2.2 Organizational Change in PSFs

The regeneration of interest in PSFs in the 1990s came from a substantive concern with both contextual and organizational change in these organizations. For the past 20 years there have been two significant and interrelated theoretical framings for the study of PSFs. The first was to be concerned with the changes in organization, as a reaction to changes in markets, competition, deregulation, and globalization (Greenwood and Lachman 1996; Malhotra et al. 2006). While innovation is not dealt with, this literature is about service innovation both in terms of new practice areas and the development of new service business models. The argument is that with the deregulation of professional markets and the increased competition that it brings, cost pressures, changes in government policy, globalization, increasingly sophisticated clients, and technological change, there is substantial pressure on PSFs to review their service profiles and change their organizational systems (Brock 2007) to deliver new forms of value as service innovation.

The second framing, within institutional theory, is very much connected to the general interest in change, but with an emphasis on archetypes and organizational fields (Greenwood et al. 2002; Pinnington and Morris 2003). It adds a very important dimension, that of interpretive schemes or institutional logics (Greenwood and Hinings 1993; Thornton et al. 2012); in doing that it also emphasizes the important dimension of professional logics and the professional field. The emphasis has primarily been on the professional logic underlying one organizational form (P^2) and the more corporate logic of the Managed Professional Business (see Leblebici and Sherer, Chapter 9, this volume). There are two important points from these approaches.

First, the centrality of the professional logic and how it affects service innovation in PSFs (see Sako, Chapter 15, this volume). Much of the work on innovation of services in PSFs shows that there are clashes between the logic of professionalism and the logic of corporatism. Such clashes are based around issues of legitimacy of the new models and practices because of their perceived distance from professional ways of providing service. In their analysis of a failed innovation, Hinings et al. (1991: 390) say, "The nature of the organizational change challenged the concept of partnership and ran counter to professional values," so, in the terms of Gardner et al. (2008), anything that challenges the professional logic is a radical innovation. A particular organizational element, changing the distribution of authority, was more than a "technical" innovation: it was seen by partners in the firm as striking at the heart of what it meant to operate with professionalism, collegiality, peer evaluation, autonomy, and informality of management. Similarly, Pinnington and Morris (2002), in studying architectural firms, suggested that while there were elements of a managerial form of organization, the core elements of the traditional form of professional organization were not transformed. Thus, there was protection of central elements of the professional logic.

Second, more recent work (Smets et al. 2012) shows how there is practice-driven institutional change. Bottom-up improvisation of new practices leads to field-level change in professional logics with innovation taking place through professional and new practice development originating in the everyday work of professionals. We will return and build on this work later in the chapter when we develop further a practice approach to service innovation.

11.2.3 Knowledge Management and Value Creation in PSFs

At the heart of value creation for new services in PSFs is how practice-based knowledge (Dougherty 2004) can be effectively captured and exploited. However, developing service innovation can be a difficult challenge for PSFs as professionals may be fearful of losing control of their knowledge claims. As Malhotra and Morris (2009: 895) put it: "Inherent to the work of all professionals is a claim over some area of expert knowledge applied in work settings." It is this claim to expert knowledge that distinguishes professionals from other occupations. But knowledge comes in different forms and Malhotra and Morris (2009) use these differences as one basis for distinguishing between professions and PSFs. Expert knowledge can be normative (for example, law), syncretic (for example, accounting), or technical (for example, engineering) and these differences have implications for organizational forms. Similarly, von Nordenflycht (2010: 159) states that "Knowledge intensity is perhaps the most fundamental distinctive characteristic of PSFs."

There are two issues that arise in examining innovation through knowledge in PSFs. Firstly, the focus is on the location of knowledge in a professional, protected by the professional logic of a profession (Empson 2001). Further, it is the interaction of the expert professional (knowledge worker) with clients, ongoing work, and organizational structure that produces knowledge-based innovation. As part of service innovation, PSFs manage their proprietary professional knowledge. That knowledge, itself, may be a service innovation, as in management consulting firms systematizing knowledge to produce a strategic planning process for organizations. However, any new knowledge comes from both interactions with clients, and transfer between firm members who, in a global firm, may be anywhere in the world. Moore and Birkinshaw (1998) have elaborated the notion of various kinds of centers of excellence within global service firms as a way of systematically capturing knowledge of best practice and future possibilities and also moving to codify that knowledge in some way. However, attempts to codify knowledge for purposes of service innovation run into the problems of the professional logic together with the nature of professional knowledge residing in individual practitioners.

The professional emphasis on both individuality and collegiality (Alvesson 2001) means that schemes for organizational systems of knowledge codification are likely to be resisted. Empson (2001) shows that individual professionals fear "exploitation" and "contamination" when asked to share knowledge. Morris (2001) argues that, when faced with a knowledge codification project, professionals may actually cooperate, but this is because they understand the real limits to the codification of their knowledge.

"Professionals perceive that their true value to their clients (and their source of power within their PSF) derives from their unique combination of experiences and intuition. They recognize that this knowledge is not susceptible to codification" (Empson 2001: 814).

Secondly, innovation in PSFs is carried out in a formal regulatory context. Part of the working out of the collegiality aspect of a professional logic is the existence of associations which regulate the actions of individual professionals, and sometimes, PSFs. Thus, those associations have an impact on service innovation. Swan and Newell (1995) examined the role of professional associations in technology diffusion, pointing out that such associations see themselves as key agents in the diffusion of new knowledge. When examining the introduction of production and inventory control, the professional association was an important network for learning about new developments. Similarly, Greenwood et al. (2002) and Suddaby and Greenwood (2005) show that service innovation around the development of multidisciplinary practice involves acceptance and legitimizing by a professional association. The promotion of such changes in business models within accounting firms involves interaction between those PSFs that wish to introduce it (in this case the large accounting firms), and the professional associations who are the regulators and guardians of the professional logic and of what constitutes knowledge.

In summary, we can draw and restate a number of conclusions from these literature streams. Firstly, somewhat surprisingly, there has been relatively little engagement with the innovation literature despite the considerable amount of work on change which covers service innovation without framing the studies in those terms. Secondly, PSFs, as knowledge-based organizations, innovate through new and expanded knowledge which rests in the hands of individual professionals. Both the individual professionals and the firm are defined through a professional logic which legitimizes particular ways of delivering services and organizing for such services. Because of that strongly legitimized organizational archetype, and the role of external regulators, innovation is likely to be contested. Finally, service innovation involves multiple actors and interactions amongst multiple practices in the development of new service models across the institutional field. We now examine how the emerging literature on service logic and service innovation provides insights for the PSF literature.

11.3 SERVICES AND SERVICE MODEL INNOVATION IN PSFs

Given the primacy of services in today's knowledge economy (Den Hertog 2000), there has been, understandably, an increasing focus on innovation in services (Barras 1986, 1990; Miles 2001, 2008) as an important innovation type that influences organizational performance (Damanpour et al. 2009). There is also a recognition that new approaches are needed to explain the adoption of innovations in service organizations (Damanpour et al. 2009) including PSFs. Service innovations are primarily market driven, and their introduction results in differentiation of the firm's output (often products) for its customers or clients (Abernathy and Utterback 1978; Damanpour and Gopalakrishnan 2001). In this way, services offered by organizations in the service sector are conceptualized to be similar to products introduced by organizations in the manufacturing sector (Sirilli and Evangelista 1998; Miles 2001, 2005). Hence, like product innovations, the drivers of services innovations are mainly clients' demand for new services and executives' desire to create new services for existing markets or find new market niches for existing services (Matthews and Shulman 2005; Damanpour et al. 2009). This notion fits very well with what we have described in studies of PSFs, with the emphasis on clients and new markets (Greenwood and Lachman 1996).

From this viewpoint, service innovation is understood through its relationship to the service user involving the introduction of new services to existing or new clients and the offer of existing services to new clients. Models of service innovation built on this logic (Den Hertog 2000) often recognize four dimensions of novelty, namely service concept, client interface, service delivery system, and technology, with many service innovations involving some combination of these four dimensions (Miles 2008). For example, a new service will often require a new service delivery system and changes to the client interface, and it is often the case that a service innovation mainly involving one dimension may trigger the need for changes in other dimensions, sometimes to the extent of what we see in PSFs with service innovations requiring innovations in the form of organization structures, knowledge management systems, and information systems (Cooper et al. 1996).

For example, digital innovation enables modularity (Simon 1996) in PSFs for service innovation. Sako (2010, 2012) has examined the disintegration of the global value chain for law firms being enabled by digital innovation, and examined how these PSFs apply modularity or break down their value chain. Such strategic decision-making has been a key influence on the rapid growth of third-party LPO providers, who have grown from a $440 million business in 2007 to an $860 million business in 2011 (Sako 2012). However, despite the current and projected growth in this business, the trajectory for this innovation bears significant uncertainty. The potential for information technology to facilitate modularity and distanced delivery through vehicles such as LPO vendors (Sako 2012) may be adversely influenced by the professional logic in PSFs.

These developments of LPO providers in law firms described above focus on "services" and alternative modes of their delivery. Recent literature has called for a shift in conceptualization from "services" to a focus on *service*. A service logic is seen as emphasizing customers and clients and the process of co-creation through client interactions. A service logic therefore represents a shift from providing "services" to focusing on "service" to the client (Vargo et al. 2008); it is the needs of the client that determine service innovation. Focusing on service therefore centers on the use of one's resources for the benefit of another entity through a process of co-creation, jointly and reciprocally, between providers and beneficiaries.

The PSF literature, while not explicitly connecting to the service innovation litera-ture, highlights the way in which changing contextual pressures are leading to chang-ing client needs and are motivating a shift in services (Greenwood and Lachman 1996; Greenwood et al. 2002; Greenwood and Suddaby 2006). The relationships between clients and PSFs are, in general, an understudied area, and there is a real lack of stud-ies that deal with service innovation as a co-creation of PSFs and their clients. This has implications for future PSF research on service innovation as will be discussed in the last section.

Increasingly, value creation involves effective resource integration between actors in actor-to-actor networks (Chandler and Vargo 2011) which does not privilege one set of actors as "producers" distinct from more passive "customers." Value co-creation takes place in actor-to-actor configurations referred to as service systems or ecosystems which can be *either* customers and/or producers, and this conceptualization affords the potential to recognize multiple actors adopting different roles and working within and across multiple service ecosystems to develop new practices for service innovation in service ecosystems. For example, in healthcare, citizens and patients are being given more responsibility and accountability for their healthcare and personal health budgets in choosing their health service providers. These changes in the regulatory and busi-ness landscape have implications for service innovation and who in the ecosystem pro-vides leadership (Adner 2012) whether it be healthcare providers or other partners such as pharmacos, IT vendors, medical device companies, the national health service, and the like.

Information technology is a critical enabler of service innovation enabling the estab-lishment of such value ecosystems and allowing the sharing and integrating of resources and knowledge in that ecosystem. Additionally with IT becoming increasingly a part of new offerings through digitization, this allows it to be an actor that triggers the innova-tion (Lusch and Nambisan 2013). This is possible as IT plays a key role in the resource integration within actor-actor networks in service ecosystems (Vargo and Lusch 2011) through the recombining or rebundling of existing resources (Normann 2001) for value. Recent research on business models (Baden-Fuller and Haefliger 2013) has highlighted the importance of their interconnection with technological innovation which has also significant implications for service innovation. For example, technological innovations such as Big Data infrastructures allow the collection of granular information and the use of tools for analyzing patterns across large volume data sets to enable the creation and capture of value for service model innovation across the business ecosystem (George et al. 2014). The potential and capability for professionals to leverage this increasingly complex practice-based knowledge is a significant challenge and opportunity for PSFs in developing service innovation in today's business landscape.

In addition to dramatic change in how a firm may develop its service line through wrapping its business model innovation around disruptive technologies, firms are responding to pressures of globalization by adopting business model innovation as a strategy of internationalization that goes beyond simply offering services as part of a global expansion. By innovating their service business models internationally across different countries, firms will be in a better position to deliver new services as they are closer to the clients, and can both listen to their needs and co-create solutions. In addition to service development, business model innovation can include new forms of service delivery in delivering these customer value propositions and this has important implications for the organization of the firm. For example, LPO organizations (Sako 2009) are using information and communication technologies to deliver services through new service models, and these are having important implications for the structure and culture of law firms influenced by their professional identity and institutional practices (Sako 2010). An implication may be that the traditional pyramidal organizational structure of the law firms in a partnership model may gradually transition to a more diamond-shaped structure. Work commodification could lead to a new structure involving fewer junior lawyers as some legal work may now be outsourced to a new category of "para-legal worker" who may likely not share in the socialization or professional identity of lawyers.

11.4 CONCLUSIONS AND FUTURE RESEARCH DIRECTIONS: TOWARDS A PRACTICE APPROACH TO SERVICE INNOVATION

In this final section we synthesize key insights from our review and suggest some implications for future research. We subsequently propose a practice approach which we believe can be usefully drawn on to study service innovation in PSFs.

Our review of the PSF literature has highlighted that there have been few studies that deal with innovation in a direct way. This would seem to suggest that the concept of innovation is not one that sits well within current discussions of professionalism in the field. One of our aims is to open up this discussion to critically examine whether and in what way PSFs are innovating or may innovate. Our discussion of the legal services ecosystem highlighted the future possibilities of new occupational categories (e.g., para-legal worker) and new actors such as LPOs in the legal services ecosystem. However, we have noted that where the professional logic is strong, professionals can be highly risk averse, and in other cases clients may not even want innovation, or be willing to pay for such innovation, in service delivery. In other cases, however, opportunities for innovation may be embraced by PSFs who adopt a service logic and set up innovative practices and mechanisms for the development of new services across their ecosystem. Future research on service innovation could examine both the dynamics of innovation by actors across the ecosystem and study the relationship between emerging service logics and professional logics in PSFs.

The literature on service and service innovation also highlighted the importance of co-creation in value creation for new services and service innovation. As a professional logic is central to PSFs, future research could usefully examine the implications for developing service innovation through co-creation strategies. How may co-creation be adopted and used to facilitate service innovation in PSFs? Professionals and PSFs have typically relied on their expertise, professional knowledge, and asymmetrical control in the client relationship to create and capture (premium) value for their service. With significant changes towards a commercial logic across different professional areas (Barrett and Gendron 2006; Picard et al. 2014), this has implications for shifts in expectations of clients, their knowledge, and the involvement of clients in the client relationship.

As such, future research on service innovation therefore could fruitfully examine the relationship between emerging service logics and professional logics in PSFs. Do they support each other or how might they be in conflict? Is a professional logic something that encourages service innovation or discourages it, why, how, and when? Logics are institutionally embedded (Thornton et al. 2012) and PSFs are part of the institutional field of professions which Thornton et al. (2012) following Friedland and Alford (1991), define as a basic institutional order of society. As such, innovation is liable to be difficult and take considerable time (Greenwood et al. 2002). Introducing service innovation which cannot be firmly connected to the professional logic can therefore be expected to be met with resistance (Hinings et al. 1991). As service logics are not located in any one institutional field their transfer into a professional field will likely be problematic.

In addition to institutional logics, a practice perspective to service innovation would examine how the overarching institutional logic (Lounsbury and Crumley 2007; Jarzabkowski 2008) informs and is informed by the doing of work at a local level. In recent PSF research, Smets et al. (2012) used a practice approach to study English and German banking lawyers in a newly formed international law firm who sought to produce "seamless" cross-border services. They developed a multi-level model of practice-driven institutional change to examine the dynamics of change which emerged from improvisations in everyday work, which was consolidated within an organization, and then radiated to the level of the field. Their approach focused on practices viewed as enactments of institutional logics (Sahlin and Wedlin 2008) anchored in field-level institutional logics. As the focus is on how institutional phenomena are constituted in people's everyday activities and in turn how everyday activities are shaped by institutional influences (Orlikowski and Scott 2014), practice perspectives do not require a choice between a macro or a micro level of analysis, or a conflation between the two (Feldman and Orlikowski 2011).

In studying service innovation from a practice perspective a particular emphasis is on how services are constituted in practice. What is distinctive in PSFs is the emphasis on individual professionals as being the location of knowledge which is necessarily practice based. At the same time, professional groups in these firms are working in large organizations or networks of organizations. As such, knowledge is situated in collective action which needs to go beyond clearly bounded professional disciplines to involve multiple actors including peers, clients, professional associations, and non-professional communities. The performativity of professional work in which professionals accomplish their work therefore depends on everyday practices based on joint collaborations in which know-how and experiences are shared (Styhre 2011). The emphasis of service innovation is therefore increasingly involving a wider set of intersecting practices involving a network of organizations.

At the same time, professional practice is being increasingly exposed to new managerial ideologies and institutions penetrating their day-to-day work. The subsequent shift in practice over time is influenced, however, by the extent to which their rhetorical strategies can be found to be legitimate (Green Jr. 2004; Suddaby and Greenwood 2005; Barrett et al. 2013) to different agents across the ecosystem. This raises new challenges for accounting institutes and professional associations as to whether they can effectively promote service innovation through traditional roles as guardians in controlling or legitimating the development of new practices which are no longer the sole province of the professional logic, or where professionals seek to expand beyond their jurisdiction of knowledge claims. Further, as it is not only professionals but a range of different actors who are able to innovate in the business ecosystem there is increasing negotiation of competences of practitioners and a challenge to the role they play in the new practice. Further, with practices being increasingly infused with technologies and other materiality the processes by which material configurations are enacted and entangled is likely to involve adapting materiality (Bjorkeng et al. 2009).

This suggests a focus on services as sociomaterial practices, in which services are materially constituted. As such, they necessarily entail a range of activities, bodies, and artifacts to be produced and consumed. What the service is at any given time and place reflects the materiality in its constitution in practice. Drawing on the entertainment service of viewing a movie in a theater (Barrett and Davidson 2008), Orlikowski and Scott (2014) highlight how the specific materialization of films, cameras, and VCRs matters as to how the service is developed and delivered. In sum, a practice approach to service innovation could usefully adopt a relational epistemology to sociomaterial practices (Orlikowski 2007) by considering the materiality of the relations that are woven together as a practice unfolds (Gherardi 2012).

We suggest that future research on service innovation in PSFs could usefully adopt a practice approach which is sensitive both to the enactment of institutional logics as well as to the material constitution of activities, bodies, and artifacts engaged in developing and delivery of the service. Returning to our earlier example of WebTrust (Gendron and Barrett 2004), we would examine these reciprocal relationships in understanding this as a professionalization project to develop a new market in e-commerce assurance. As the WebTrust case shows (Gendron and Barrett 2004; Barrett and Gendron 2006) online consumers and managers did not readily adopt this service innovation or realize its value as yet another "performance" of an audit in providing assurance. Rather, it highlighted that the performativity or the outcomes produced "by the doing" depends on the specific materialization of the service in how it is developed and delivered. So, it matters who is involved in relation to which practices. Accounting partners are authoritative in relation to audit service performed with their CFO clients, and which is legitimized by regulators as a mandatory financial requirement, and widely used by financial analysts in the marketplace. However, the same could not be said for accountants' relations with marketing managers and technology security specialists in charge of e-commerce assurance within these firms nor was it the case in relation to e-Joe Public in recogniz-ing the value of these online services for providing online trust (Barrett and Gendron 2006). Materiality of the icon was also viewed as important in how these services were delivered in time and space. For example, the seal's icon changed significantly in its design with the word "WebTrust" and the name of the accountancy firm carrying out the audit replaced the previously designed icon for the seal which bore the account-ing institute's acronyms (e.g., CICA). Finally, deciding on the appropriate development and delivery of the service would mean experimenting with service models involving different audiences over time. While the initial materialization of a B2C service model was largely unsuccessful, the subsequent redevelopment of WebTrust as a set of crite-ria, best-practice guidelines to give advice on organization systems and to provide B2B assurance between organizations, was more successful. It placed accountants in a more traditional role, making recommendations to increase internal control systems with corporate managers who had more of a financial orientation.

This brief exposition to include sociomaterial practices in understanding WebTrust as a failed service innovation suggests great promise for a practice approach to study service innovation in PSFs. We believe that the timing of research in this area is at an important crossroads theoretically with potentially valuable benefits made possible by bringing related themes of practice for understanding service innovation as the development and use of new practices develops within a wider institutional context. Additionally, through the WebTrust case we are alerted to fruitful synergies in con-ceptual development around the interconnected set of practices, how materiality is constituted in the practice, and the way in which practices are anchored in field-level institutional logics.

References

Abernathy, W. J. and Utterback, J. M. (1978). "Patterns of Industrial Innovation," *Technology Review* 80(7): 40–47.

Adner, R. (2012). *The Wide Lens: A New Strategy for Innovation*. London: Penguin.

Alvesson, M. (2001). "Knowledge Work: Ambiguity, Image and Identity," *Human Relations* 54(7): 863–886.

Anand, N., Gardner, H. K., and Morris, T. (2007). "Knowledge-Based Innovation: Emergence and Embedding of New Practice Areas in Management Consulting Firms," *Academy of Management Journal* 50(2): 406–428.

Baden-Fuller, C. and Haefliger, S. (2013). "Business Models and Technological Innovation," *Long Range Planning* 46(6): 419–426.

Barras, R. (1986). "Towards a Theory of Innovation in Services," *Research Policy* 15: 161–173.

Barras, R. (1990). "Interactive Innovation in Financial and Business Services: The Vanguard of the Service Revolution," *Research Policy* 19: 215–237.

Barrett, M. and Davidson, E. (2008). "Exploring the Diversity of Service Worlds in the Service Economy," in *Information Technology in the Service Economy: Challenges and Possibilities for the 21st Century*, ed. M. Barrett, E. Davidson, C. Middleton, and J. de Gross. Boston, MA: Springer, 1–10.

Barrett, M. and Gendron, Y. (2006). "WebTrust and the 'Commercialistic Auditor': The Unrealized Vision of Developing Auditor Trustworthiness in Cyberspace," *Accounting, Auditing and Accountability Journal* 19(5): 631–662.

Barrett, M., Heracleous, L., and Walsham, G. (2013). "A Rhetorical Approach to IT Diffusion: Reconceptualizing the Ideology-Framing Relationship in Computerization Movements," *MIS Quarterly* 37(1): 201–220.

Birkinshaw, J., Hamel, G., and Mol, M. J. (2008). "Management Innovation," *Academy of Management Review* 33(4): 825–845.

Bjorkeng, K., Clegg, S., and Pistis, T. (2009). "Becoming a Practice," *Management Learning* 40(2): 145–159.

Brock, D. M. (2007). "Health Care Resource Prioritization and Rationing: Why is it so Difficult?" *Social Research* 74(1): 125–148.

Chandler, J. D. and Vargo, S. L. (2011). "Contextualization and Value-in-Context: How Context Frames Exchange," *Marketing Theory* 11(1): 35–49.

Chesbrough, H. and Spohrer, J. (2006). "A Research Manifesto for Services Science," *Communications of the ACM* 49(7): 35–40.

Christensen, C. M., Anthony, S. D., and Roth. E. A. (2004). *Seeing What's Next: Using the Theories of Innovation to Predict Industry Change.* Cambridge, MA: Harvard Business School Press.

Cooper, D. J., Hinings, C. R., Greenwood, R., and Brown, J. (1996). "Sedimentation and Transformation in Organizational Change: The Case of Canadian Law Firms," *Organization Studies* 17(4): 623–647.

Damanpour, F. and Gopalakrishnan, S. (2001). "The Dynamics of the Adoption of Product and Process Innovations in Organizations," *Journal of Management Studies* 38(1): 45–65.

Damanpour, F., Walker, R. M., and Avellaneda, C. N. (2009). "Combinative Effects of Innovation Types and Organizational Performance: A Longitudinal Study of Service Organizations," *Journal of Management Studies* 46(4): 650–675.

Den Hertog, P. (2000). "Knowledge-Intensive Business Services as Co-Producers of Innovation," *International Journal of Innovation Management* 4(4): 491–528.

Dougherty, D. (2004). "Organizing Practices in Services: Capturing Practice-Based Knowledge for Innovation," *Strategic Organization* 2(1): 35–64.

Empson, L. (2001). "Fear of Exploitation and Fear of Contamination: Impediments to Knowledge Transfer in Mergers between Professional Service Firms," *Human Relations* 54(7): 839–863.

Empson, L. and Chapman, C. (2006). "Partnership versus Corporation: Implications of Alternative Forms of Governance in Professional Service Firms," *Research in the Sociology of Organizations* 24: 139–170.

Feldman, M. S. and Orlikowski, W. J. (2011). "Theorizing Practice and Practicing Theory," *Organization Science* 22(5): 1240–1253.

Fosstenløkken, S. M., Løwendahl, B. R., and Revang, Ø. (2003). "Knowledge Development through Client Interaction: A Comparative Study," *Organization Studies* 24(6): 859–879.

Friedland, R. and Alford, R. R. (1991). "Bringing Society Back In: Symbols, Practices and Institutional Contradictions," in *The New Institutionalism in Organizational Analysis*, ed. W. W. Powell and P. J. DiMaggio. Chicago, IL: University of Chicago Press, 232–263.

Gann, D. and Salter, A. (2000). "Innovation In Project-Based, Service-Enhanced Firms: The Construction of Complex Products and Systems," *Research Policy* 29(7–8): 955–972.

Gardner, H., Anand, N. and Morris, T. (2008). "Chartering New Territory: Diversification, Legitimacy and Practice Area Creation in Professional Service Firms," *Journal of Organizational Behavior* 29(8): 1101–1121.

Gendron, Y. and Barrett, M. (2004). "Professionalization in Action: Accountants' Attempt at Building a Network of Support for the WebTrust Seal of Assurance," *Contemporary Accounting Research* 21(3): 563–602.

George, G., Haas, M., and Pentland, A. (2014). " Big Data and Management," *Academy of Management Journal* 57(2): 321–326.

Gherardi, S. (2012). *How to Conduct a Practice-Based Study*. Cheltenham: Edward Elgar.

Green Jr., S. E. (2004). "A Rhetorical Theory of Diffusion," *Academy of Management Review* 29(4): 653–669.

Greenwood, R. and Hinings, C. R. (1993). "Understanding Strategic Change: The Contribution of Archetypes," *Academy of Management Journal* 36: 1052–1081.

Greenwood, R. and Lachman, R. (1996). "Change as an Underlying Theme in Professional Service Organizations: An Introduction," *Organization Studies* 17(4): 563–572.

Greenwood, R. and Suddaby, R. (2006). "Institutional Entrepreneurship in Mature Fields: The Five Big Accounting Firms," *Academy of Management Journal* 49(1): 27–48.

Greenwood, R., Suddaby, R., and Hinings, C. R. (2002). "Theorizing Change: The Role of Professional Associations in the Transformation of Institutionalized Fields," *Academy of Management Journal* 45(1): 58–80.

Hinings, C. R. (2004). "The Changing Nature of Professional Organizations," in *The Oxford Handbook of Work and Organization*, ed. S. Ackroyd, R. Batt, P. Thompson, and P. Tolbert. Oxford: Oxford University Press, 404–424.

Hinings, C. R., Brown, J. L., and Greenwood, R. (1991). "Change in an Autonomous Professional Organization," *Journal of Management Studies* 28(4): 375–394.

Hinings, C. R., Greenwood, R., and Cooper, D. J. (1999). "The Dynamics of Change in Large Accounting Firms," in *Restructuring the Professional Organization: Accounting, Healthcare and Law*, ed. D. Brock, M. Powell, and C. R. Hinings. London: Routledge, 131–153.

Jarzabkowski, P. (2008). "Shaping Strategy as a Structuration Process," *Academy of Management Journal* 51(4): 621–650.

Lounsbury, M. and Crumley, E. T. (2007). "New Practice Creation: An Institutional Perspective on Innovation," *Organization Studies* 28(7): 993–1012.

Løwendahl, B. R., Revang, Ø., and Fosstenløkken, S. M. (2001). "Knowledge and Value Creation in Professional Service Firms: A Framework for Analysis," *Human Relations* 54(7): 911–931.

Lusch, R. F. and Nambisan, S. (2013). "Service Innovation: A Service-Dominant (S-D) Logic Perspective," *MIS Quarterly* (forthcoming).

Lusch, R. F. and Vargo, S. L. (2014). *Service Dominant Logic: Premises, Perspectives, Possibilities*. Cambridge: Cambridge University Press.

Malhotra, N. and Morris, T. (2009). "Heterogeneity in Professional Service Firms," *Journal of Management Studies* 46(6): 895–922.

Malhotra, N., Morris, T., and Hinings, C. R. (2006). "Variations in Organizations from among Professional Service Organizations," in *Research in the Sociology of Organizations: Professional Firms*, ed. R. Greenwood, R. Suddaby, and M. McDougald. Oxford: JAI Press, 171–202.

Matthews, J. H. and Shulman, A. D. (2005). "Competitive Advantage in Public Sector Organizations: Explaining the Public Good/Sustainable Competitive Advantage Paradox," *Journal of Business Research* 58(2): 232–240.

Miles, I. (2001). *Services Innovation: A Reconfiguration of Innovation Studies*. Manchester: PREST.

Miles, I. (2005). "Innovation in Services," in *The Oxford Handbook of Innovation*, ed. J. Fagerberg, D. C. Mowery, and R. R. Nelson. Oxford: Oxford University Press, 433–458.

Miles, I. (2008). "Patterns of Innovation in Service Industries," *IBM Systems Journal* 47(1–2): 115–128.

Moore, K. and Birkinshaw. J. M. (1998). "Managing Knowledge In Global Service Firms: Centres of Excellence," *Academy of Management Executive* 12(4): 81–92.

Morris, T. (2001). "Asserting Property Rights: Knowledge Codificiation in the Professional Service Firm," *Human Relations* 54(1): 54–71.

Normann, R. (2001). *Reframing Business: When the Map Changes the Landscape.* Chichester: John Wiley.

Ofek, E. and Sarvary, M. (2001). "Leveraging the Customer Base: Creating Competitive Advantage Through Knowledge Management," *Management Science* 47(11): 1441–1456.

Orlikowski, W. J. (2007). "Sociomaterial Practices: Exploring Technology at Work," *Organization Studies* 28(9): 1435–1448.

Orlikowski, W. J. and Scott, S. V. (2008). "Sociomateriality: Challenging the Separation of Technology, Work and Organization," *Annals of the Academy of Management* 2(1): 433–474.

Orlikowski, W. J. and Scott, S. V. (2014). "The Algorithm and the Crowd: Considering the Materiality of Service Innovation," *MIS Quarterly* (forthcoming).

Picard, C. F., Durocher, S., and Gendron, Y. (2014). "From Meticulous Professionals to Superheroes of the Business World: A Historical Portrait of a Cultural Change in the Field of Accountancy," *Accounting, Auditing & Accountability Journal* 27(1): 73–118.

Pinnington, A. and Morris, T. (2002). "Transforming the Architect: Ownership Form and Archetype Change," *Organization Studies* 23(2): 189–210.

Pinnington, A. and Morris, T. (2003). "Archetype Change in Professional Organizations: Survey Evidence from Large Law Firms," *British Journal of Management* 14(1): 85–99.

Power, M. (1997). "Expertise and the Construction of Relevance: Accountants and Environmental Audit," *Accounting, Organizations and Society* 22(2): 123–146.

Sahlin, K. and Wedlin, L. (2008). "Circulating Ideas: Imitation, Translation and Editing," in *The Sage Handbook of Organizational Institutionalism*, ed. R. Greenwood, C. Oliver, K. Sahlin and R. Suddaby. London: Sage, 218–242.

Sako, M. (2009). "Globalization of Knowledge-Intensive Professional Services," *Communications of the ACM* 52(7): 31–33.

Sako, M. (2010). "Outsourcing Versus Shared Services," *Communications of the ACM* 53(7): 27–29.

Sako, M. (2012). "Business Models for Strategy and Innovation," *Communications of the ACM* 55(7): 22–24.

Salter, A. and Tether, B. S. (2006). "Innovation in Services: Through the Looking Glass of Innovation Studies," *Advanced Institute of Management (AIM) Research's Grand Challenge on Service Science* 1–38.

Scott, S. V. and Orlikowski, W. J. (2013). "Sociomateriality: Taking the Wrong Turning? A Response to Mutch," *Information & Organization* 23(2): 77–80.

Simon, J. M. (1996). "SPICE: Overview for Software Process Improvement," *Journal of Systems Architecture* 42(8): 633–641.

Sirilli, G. and Evangelista, R. (1998). "Technological Innovation in Services and Manufacturing; Results from an Italian Study," *Research Policy* 27: 881–899.

Smets, M., Morris, T., and Greenwood, R. (2012). "From Practice to Field: A Multilevel Model of Practice-Driven Institutional Change," *Academy of Management Journal* 55(4): 877–904.

Styhre, A. (2011). "The Architect's Gaze: The Maintenance of Collective Professional Vision in the Work of the Architect," *Culture & Organization* 17(4): 253–269.

Suddaby, R. and Greenwood, R. (2005). "Rhetorical Strategies of Legitimacy," *Administrative Science Quarterly* 50(1): 35–67.

Swan, J. A. and Newell, S. (1995). "The Role of Professional Associations in Technology Diffusion," *Organization Studies* 16(5): 847–874.

Thornton, P. H., Ocasio, W., and Lounsbury, M. (2012). *The Institutional Logics Perspective: A New Approach to Culture, Structure and Process*. Oxford: Oxford University Press.

Vargo, S. L. and Lusch, R. F. (2008). "A Service Logic for Service Science," in *Service Science, Management and Engineering Education for the 21st Century*, ed. B. Hefley and W. Murphy. Berlin: Springer, 83–88.

Vargo, S. L. and Lusch, R. F. (2011). "It's all B2B . . . and Beyond: Toward a Systems Perspective of the Market," *Industrial Marketing Management* 40(2): 181–187.

Vargo, S. L., Maglio, P. P., and Akaka, M. A. (2008). "On Value and Value Co-Creation: A Service Systems and Service Logic Perspective," *European Management Journal* 26(3): 145–152.

von Nordenflycht, A. (2010). "What is a Professional Service Firm? Towards a Theory and Taxonomy of Knowledge-Intensive Firms," *Academy of Management Review* 35(1): 155–174.

CHAPTER 12

....

ENTREPRENEURSHIP AND PROFESSIONAL SERVICE FIRMS

....

MARKUS REIHLEN AND ANDREAS WERR

12.1 INTRODUCTION

ALTHOUGH professional services have been among the fastest growing sectors in the past decades and described as "innovative by their nature" (Hargadon and Bechky 2006; Nikolova 2012), research on entrepreneurship and entrepreneurial renewal in Professional Service Firms (PSFs) has been rather limited. This may be understood in terms of opposing values of entrepreneurialism and professionalism where entrepreneurialism is founded on ideals such as cultural individualism and change, while professionalism is based on ideals of a stable and protected knowledge base. Professional work may involve judgment, discretion, and advanced problem-solving, but it is not typically a novelty-creating entrepreneurial enterprise (Freidson 2001: 17).

This chapter sets out to investigate the specific conditions of entrepreneurship in PSFs and reviews the extant research at the intersection of entrepreneurship and PSFs. Entrepreneurship is here defined as how opportunities are discovered, created, and exploited to bring "future" goods and services into existence (see Venkataraman 1997) and thus goes beyond narrow definitions of entrepreneurship focusing on new firm creation. In line with recent developments, we view entrepreneurship as closely linked to the opportunity concept, describing entrepreneurship as opportunity-seeking and opportunity-exploiting behavior (Eckhardt and Shane 2003; Hitt et al. 2011; Shane and Eckhardt 2003; Shane and Venkataraman 2000). This may be manifested in the establishment of new firms but often takes place within existing firms, where it is observable through the creation of new services, markets, and processes (traditionally referred to as intrapreneurship or corporate entrepreneurship).

Following Wood and McKinley (2010), we argue from a constructivist view which understands the subjectivity of entrepreneurs and their interaction with their socio-cultural environment as an integral component of the opportunity creation process. Entrepreneurial processes couple the expanding business with new interactive socio-economic milieus as represented by new regional markets, new client industries, or new segments of the talent market. Therefore the necessary learning and innovation processes of an entrepreneurial PSF embrace not only the discovery of industry-specific facts and skills, but also the firm's "embedding" itself into and "shaping" the "new" social context with its own local regulations and institutional practices (Greenwood and Suddaby 2006; Reihlen and Apel 2007; Reihlen et al. 2010). Entrepreneurship therefore involves the emergence of conceptualizations and evaluations of opportunities and how these entrepreneurial cognitions are subsequently linked with social processes of influence through the use of cultural (e.g., rhetoric, impression management), economic (e.g., scarce technology), or political resources (e.g., positional authority, lobbying) through which opportunities are socially created in the market.

Framing the concept of opportunity and entrepreneurship within a constructivist perspective allows us to connect dispersed research streams in the entrepreneurship field as well as in the professional service field that have been published under various headings. In the following review we will first discuss the tension between the concepts of professionalism and entrepreneurship and then we turn to the specific characteristics of professional service work and PSFs and their consequences for opportunity creation and exploitation. These sections are followed by a review of extant research structured along three levels of analysis—the team, the organization, and the organizational field. In a final section future research opportunities are identified.

12.2 ENTREPRENEURSHIP AND PROFESSIONALISM: OPPOSING CONCEPTS?

Entrepreneurship as an institution is founded on ideals such as cultural individualism and change (Brandl and Bullinger 2009). Cultural individualism encourages individuals who are considered as autonomous and uncontrolled to engage in creative and innovative activities. This autonomy of the free-willed entrepreneur reflected in cultural individualism is regarded as a necessary social condition for entrepreneurship to emerge. Change is then seen as the consequence of opportunity seeking entrepreneurs. Through processes of creative destruction (Schumpeter 1942) entrepreneurs engage in rule-breaking behavior, and demonstrate their capacity to control the external world. The entrepreneurial organization or society is one in which change becomes the norm and stability the exception.

Professionalism, on the other hand, is something quite different. Abbott (1988), for instance, emphasizes that a key distinguishing feature of professional work lies in its reliance on academic knowledge that formalizes and standardizes the skills on which professional work proceeds. Professionalization can be conceived as a process of cognitive standardization. This permits, as Larson (1977: 40) points out, "a measure of uniformity and homogeneity in the 'production of producers.'" Professionalism therefore is a method of how exclusive knowledge is controlled by the professional occupation through mechanisms of recruitment, training, socialization, and peer monitoring. While professional work involves fresh judgment and discretion, it is not typically a rule-breaking entrepreneurial practice (Freidson 2001: 17).

To resolve some of the contradictions between entrepreneurialism and professionalism, we argue to differentiate different types of professional organizations. In particular, we distinguish between classic or regulated PSFs such as accounting, law, or architectural firms and neo-PSFs such as consulting firms or advertising agencies (von Nordenflycht 2010). While in the former case firms belong to a classic profession with well-developed institutions of professionalism, in the latter case at least some of these institutions are missing. Especially, neo-PSFs lack a clearly confined academic knowledge base. In management consultancy, for instance, very little, if any, commonly accepted knowledge standards and good professional practices exist (Gross and Kieser 2006). On the contrary, in classic PSFs these standards are well-defined by professional associations and mediated through teaching programs and credentials as a reference point for assessing professional practice. Consequently, the more the professional knowledge base is confined, the less discretionary freedom and creativity is left to the professional. Innovation is then caged within professional boundaries. This explains why management consultancy, lacking a clearly defined body of knowledge, can engage in more "creative" problem-solving, while their counterparts from accounting become accused of "cooking the books" when interpreting accounting rules in novel ways. Yet, as studies on entrepreneurship in the regulated professions show, classic PSFs do innovate beyond professional boundaries. However, they do so by taking institutional leadership roles in professional associations, and thereby get actively involved in setting standards of their own profession (Greenwood and Suddaby 2006).

12.3 SPECIFIC CONDITIONS FOR ENTREPRENEURSHIP IN PROFESSIONAL SERVICE FIRMS

Professional work and firms are by previous research attributed certain characteristics that shape the context for entrepreneurial initiatives in important ways. Central characteristics identified in previous research are the motivational disposition of the professional, service delivery as the main locus of innovation, and a relationship-based marketplace.

12.3.1 Motivational Disposition of the Professional

Professionals strive for challenging assignments providing opportunities to learn (Fosstenløkken et al. 2003; Maister 1993; Teece 2003). Challenging tasks are generally presented as more important for motivation and retention of personnel than financial and other kinds of rewards (Alvesson 2004; Løwendahl 2005). This provides a fertile ground for continuous learning and innovation and individual entrepreneurial initiatives (cf. Heusinkveld and Benders 2002).

The organizational and commercial exploitation of these opportunities generated by individual and local experiments is, however, challenged by several countervailing forces. One of these is professionals' preference for autonomy. Directing and coordinating professionals during entrepreneurial ventures is considered a special challenge and has been described as the "herding cats" (e.g., Løwendahl 2005) or "aligning stars" (Lorsch and Tierney 2002) problem. Professionals cherish their autonomy dearly and resist efforts to curtail it through managerial interventions telling them, for example, what services to deliver and in what way (Maister 1993).

Such a focus on the sovereignty of the individual expert may also hamper the dissemination of innovations within PSFs and thus the exploitation of entrepreneurial opportunities. In individualistic expert cultures, sharing as well as seeking knowledge outside of one's professional domain may easily be perceived as an illegitimate invasion of other experts' domains or the admittance of professional weakness (Hargadon and Bechky 2006). The institutionalization of new services in PSFs (often taking the form of new practices) has also been found to be a highly politicized process (Anand et al. 2007; Heusinkveld and Benders 2005).

Finally, the often claimed primary loyalty of professionals to a profession or knowledge domain rather than a specific employing organization (Freidson 2001; Løwendahl 2005) creates challenges in relation to retention, since professionals are highly mobile, and the firm's commercial orientation. Professionals need to be given challenging work to maintain their motivation, but this work generally has to be balanced with less stimulating (but economically more rewarding) work which exploits existing competencies.

12.3.2 Service Delivery as the Locus of Innovation

New ideas are typically developed in interaction with colleagues and clients, and triggered by challenges experienced by clients (Fosstenløkken et al. 2003; Heusinkveld and Benders 2002; Skjølsvik et al. 2007). The exploration of such opportunities is supported both by the search for new challenges by professionals, and also by the reward and career systems of PSFs, where the ability to generate business (which to some extent involves the creation of new service offerings in order to stay at par with clients) is an important prerequisite for individual success. In the larger organizations the building up of a new service offer (practice) is often seen as a prerequisite for promotion to partner (Anand et al. 2007).

Given that innovation is intimately linked to client assignments, the choice and design of these assignments shapes both the content and character of emerging opportunities, thus making the stock of existing and potential clients an important asset. Expansion into new service areas involves the acquisition of assignments in that area both to develop and validate the service offerings as well as the competencies necessary for their delivery. Acquiring such projects in novel areas is often easier with established clients than with entirely new ones (Fosstenløkken et al. 2003; Liedtka and Haskins 1997). Client assignments that support knowledge creation and innovation share a number of characteristics, including novel tasks demanding customization, delivery in multidisciplinary assignment teams, time pressure, a certain size involving both many people and an extended duration, and finally opportunities for face-to-face interaction with the client (Skjølsvik et al. 2007).

12.3.3 A Relationship-Based Marketplace

The entrepreneurship literature has shown that nascent entrepreneurs' personal networks play a crucial role in creating new business opportunities (Aldrich and Ruef 2006). Since the market for professional services is to a large extent based on personal relationships and reputation (Glückler and Armbrüster 2003; Hanlon 2004), it is a prime example how network structures in which professional entrepreneurs or PSFs are embedded represent a significant portion of their opportunity space. A majority of new business in most professional service sectors is derived from existing clients (Armbrüster 2006; Maister 1993). This relationship- or network-based character of the professional service industry both enables and restricts the creation and exploitation of entrepreneurial opportunities. Established client relationships are a common basis of entrepreneurial activity, such as geographical expansion and expansion into new service areas. Within management consulting, for example, the internationalization process has to a large extent been driven by the needs of increasingly internationalized clients desiring the support of consultants in a growing number of locations (Glückler 2006; Kubr 2002; Maister 1993; Spar 1997). In a similar vein, responding to client needs for support in related service areas is a common driver for diversification in the professional service industry (Greiner and Malernee 2005; Løwendahl 2005). This way of leveraging existing customer relations has been a key driver of, for example, the diversification of accounting firms into legal services and management consulting (Hanlon 2004). Such diversifications of PSFs illustrate another important characteristic of the professional services sector, namely the rather fluid boundaries of especially the neo-professions, which open up a considerable entrepreneurial space.

12.4 THE ENTREPRENEURIAL TEAM

PSFs create new entrepreneurial opportunities by bringing together the knowledge and expertise of individuals, often across discipline and organizational boundaries (Hargadon 1998). This is typically realized in project-based work forms, in which professionals, often together with client representatives, form an engagement team with the sole focus of solving a client's problem (Handley et al. 2012).

Previous research on the ability of teams to make use of their members' knowledge and experience in processes of learning, knowledge creation, or knowledge integration is extensive. However, only a rather limited portion of it is conducted in the specific context of PSFs that through their specific organizational context (e.g., highly competitive career structures) and inter-organizational nature (involvement of the client) represent unique challenges. We review some of these challenges and the attributes and processes of teams that facilitate entrepreneurship.

12.4.1 Challenges to Opportunity Creation in Engagement Teams

To exploit the creativity of collectives and potential of professionals, there must be active engagement by professionals in seeking others' knowledge as well as sharing their own knowledge. Professionals must also engage in the reflective reframing—joint exploitation of this diverse knowledge in social interactions—in which they "make new sense of what they already know" (Hargadon and Bechky 2006: 491). These processes presume that professionals are willing and able to engage in these kinds of activities, something that previous research provides several reasons to question.

First, we may question professionals' willingness to share and seek knowledge. Professionals' identity and "value" in organizations is to a large extent linked to their possession of a unique set of expertise and experience (Morris 2001). Against this background, it has been argued that professionals may be reluctant to share their knowledge, as that may reduce their power in relation to the organization (Morris 2001). In a similar vein, seeking help in highly competitive organizations may risk being perceived as an admittance of ignorance providing a threat to professionals' career chances and self-confidence (Hargadon and Bechky 2006). In addition, psychological barriers, such as fear of being ridiculed or criticized, may limit the extent to which professionals share or seek knowledge (Argyris and Schön 1978; Edmondson 1999; Hargadon and Bechky 2006). Research has thus found that there is a strong tendency in groups to focus on widely shared knowledge among the participants rather than bringing up their unique knowledge, which is the knowledge that has the largest potential to contribute to innovative solutions (Edmondson 2002).

Second, research provides reason to question professionals' ability to share and seek knowledge. Previous research has shown that the differences in knowledge underlying the idea of innovation through knowledge complementarities may create communication boundaries (Carlile 2002; Ringberg and Reihlen 2008). A focus on homogeneity of people and strong personal bonds—both within PSFs and in relations with clients—are thus common. While they may limit the innovative capacity of PSFs they increase efficiency in communication (Nikolova 2012).

Third, research questions professionals' willingness and ability to engage in reflective reframing as this may be related to considerable psychological risks. These are especially salient in the relationship between the professional and their clients. As argued by Schön (1983), this relationship is often carried out within an "expert framework" where any doubts and uncertainties by the professional are suppressed in order not to compromise the client's confidence in the professional or threaten the professional's self-esteem (Schön 1983). It has also been argued that the asymmetry of the relation may be the other way around (Niewiem and Richter 2004), with the client dictating what the professional should do or think, which equally limits the potential for innovation in the engagement team (Nikolova 2012; Skjølsvik et al. 2007).

12.4.2 Attributes and Processes of the Opportunity-Creating Engagement Team

While realizing the entrepreneurial opportunities of the engagement team may be challenging, previous research has looked extensively at how these barriers may be overcome. Research on knowledge sharing and knowledge integration in teams highlights the importance of the possibility for direct interaction between individuals as it enables the sharing of tacit and experience-based knowledge as well as the dynamic reflective reframing through which existing knowledge may be revaluated and made relevant (or irrelevant) and new solutions may be found (Hargadon 1998; Hargadon and Bechky 2006). However, as noted above, opportunities for direct interaction will not necessarily create entrepreneurial opportunities. In order for these to emerge, interaction needs to take place in a climate that encourages knowledge sharing and reflection.

In order for individuals to engage in knowledge sharing and reflection, the social environment needs to be perceived as safe by those acting in it. Edmondson (1999) shows that what she calls "psychological safety" is related to a group's ability to reflect and learn. She defines psychological safety as "a shared belief that the team is safe for interpersonal risk taking . . . a sense of confidence that the team will not embarrass, reject or punish someone for speaking up" (Edmondson 1999: 354). This is supported by clear and shared understandings of the task. Additional characteristics of groups in which knowledge sharing is enabled include having fun (Dougherty and Takacs 2004) and communicating in terms of approving rather than disapproving terms (Losada and Heaphy 2004). The interactive climate is further linked to patterns of power and influence, where research has shown that knowledge sharing and innovation in groups is supported by relatively egalitarian power structures (Edmondson 2002; Hargadon and Bechky 2006; von Krogh 1998).

Furthermore, previous research has emphasized the importance of professionals' understandings of their roles and responsibilities in performing the joint task. These, it has been argued, shape the extent to which knowledge is actively shared and exploited in joint reflection as they set the boundaries of which individuals may have relevant competence and to what extent they may legitimately seek or contribute to this knowledge and which aspects of the task are open for reflection and reframing and which are not

(Dougherty and Takacs 2004; Hargadon and Bechky 2006). Broad representations, creating redundancy and overlap between individual professionals' perceived responsibilities, support knowledge integration as they make it legitimate for actors to step into each other's domains (Dougherty and Takacs 2004; Swan et al. 1999; Swart and Kinnie 2003; Werr 2012; Werr and Runsten 2013).

12.5 The Entrepreneurial Firm

As the size and importance of PSFs have grown, interest in the entrepreneurial strategies these firms may employ to update and develop their service portfolios and thus market position has increased. Still, research on the entrepreneurial strategies of PSFs is rather limited, as the PSF has been attributed a less important role in entrepreneurial activity than either the profession or the professional. Four main approaches to investigating the entrepreneurial PSF may be identified; new venture management process, identifying different entrepreneurial strategies in different types of PSFs, the development and embedding of new practices in PSFs, and governance of entrepreneurial firms.

12.5.1 New Venture Management

One of the core research areas in entrepreneurship is new venture creation or start-up management (Cooper 1981; Gartner 1985). There are a number of general factors influencing the start-up management from its foundation to its early growth such as active entrepreneurial cognitions (Mitchell et al. 2007), actions (Frese 2009), personal networks (Ostgaard and Birley 1996), and venture team dynamics (Ensley et al. 2002) as well as environmental conditions including industry competition (Sandberg and Hofer 1987), capital availability (Cooper et al. 1994), legitimacy (Zimmerman and Zeitz 2002), and regulation (Capelleras et al. 2008). We can assume these factors also play an important role for venture creation of PSFs, but it is surprising how little empirical research has been conducted in this field.

The little empirical work that exists is mainly based on qualitative case studies. In a study of a small consulting firm, for instance, Ram (1999) explores the emergence of the firm and analyzes three related processes: the hiring process of consultants, the client relationship management, and the dynamics of project management. Ram's findings suggest that small PSFs operate under unstable cooperation conditions among their key constituencies, making it particularly challenging to manage the tension between the need to increase organizational efficiency and the pressure for continuous entrepreneurialism. The study of Clarysse and Moray (2004) investigates the constitution of the entrepreneurial team of a university spin-off and explores how the team deals with and learns from a crisis situation during the start-up phase. The authors argue that the crisis in the entrepreneurial team co-evolves with disturbances in the development of the business. More recently, Günther (2012) studied the start-up and early growth stages of two successful corporate law firm spin-offs. He shows that these firms orchestrated a number of different strategies that helped them to mimic standards of large corporate law firms by high involvement service delivery and distinctive people development and to create a degree of uniqueness by particular client strategies and a strong cultural alignment. Furthermore, in a longitudinal study of law firms in Silicon Valley, California, Phillips (2002, 2005) analyzed the consequences of "organizational life chances when a member of an existing firm leaves to found a new firm" (Phillips 2002: 474). His study highlights a number of consequences when resources and routines are transferred from the parent firm to the newly founded spin-off. As he shows, resource transfer increases life chances for off-springs, but decreases life chances for parents (Phillips 2002). Furthermore, he shows that in the newly founded firm gender inequality is likely to be reproduced (Phillips 2005). Overall, existing studies on new ventures provided scattered evidence. So far, they emphasize that venture success rests on a number of factors such as the firm's ability to learn quickly, including learning from crisis and learning through new hires, the creation of legitimacy and reputation, and leveraging social capital for new venture management.

12.5.2 Different Entrepreneurial Strategies in Different PSFs

A recurrent theme in the literature on PSFs is the recognition that PSFs may adhere to different configurations, internally consistent patterns, of strategy, structure, service delivery, and HR processes (Greenwood et al. 1990; Løwendahl 2005; Maister 1993). This approach has led to the creation of a number of ideal type PSFs such as the Brain, Grey Hair or procedure PSF (Maister 1993), the P^2 vs. MPB (managed professional business) firm (Pinnington and Morris 2003), the P^2, Star and Global professional network (GPN) (Brock 2006), or the A, B and C form PSF (Løwendahl 2005). In spite of the differences in label, the different configurations identified show considerable similarities in abstracting empirical phenomena.

While seldom explicitly discussed, the different configurations offer different opportunities for opportunity recognition and exploitation. Løwendahl (2012) provides a rare explicit discussion of entrepreneurial strategies in different kinds of PSFs and argues that entrepreneurial strategies in PSFs may relate to one or several of three key areas—the resource base (the development of new competencies and skills), the domain (kinds of clients targeted), and the service delivery process (organization and procedures). She discusses three different configurations, type A, B, and C firms, with type A firms offering generalist services to a select group of clients, based on the expertise of individual consultants and type B firms offering specialized services to a broad range of clients based on "organizational" knowledge. Type C firms represent a position between these extremes.

A first entrepreneurial strategy, mainly associated with type A firms, may be labeled an organic strategy, where extensions in the resource base through recruitment may lead to new services and extended client relations. Type A firms are typically rather small, characterized by a strong reliance on the expertise of individual consultants, and new solutions are developed in the work of individual consultants. The lack of formal knowledge management and other kinds of formalization strategies, however, inhibits the organizational spread of such innovations. Over time, the knowledge base of the firm is mainly developed through the recruitment of new experienced consultants, which will typically have similar expertise to those already employed. At times, however, professionals with different expertise and client relations may be recruited which provide a potential for entrepreneurial opportunities. These may emerge both in the interaction between existing and new professionals that may create new services and in relation to the client base that may be broadened.

A second entrepreneurial strategy may, following Heusinkveld and Benders (2002), be labeled a corporate driven entrepreneurial strategy and was dominant in type B firms. These focus on the delivery of specialized services to a broader set of clients and to a larger extent than type A firms rely on structural capital in terms of coordinated procedures and routines to ensure reliant and efficient service delivery. Type B firms are more tightly and hierarchically controlled and mainly hire juniors rather than experienced professionals. While entrepreneurial opportunities in the type A firm mainly occurred serendipitously, type B firms had experts assigned to the development of entrepreneurial opportunities in their domains of expertise and dedicated R&D initiatives. A large part of these developments would be directed towards more efficient service delivery processes or incremental developments of the service offering, thus making these the main source of opportunities in the type B firm. Given that these firms mainly recruited juniors, opportunity creation in the resource base was rare. A strong focus on a rather narrow service range also created potential challenges in relation to broadening the domain (client base). This was, however, sometimes overcome through acquisitions of firms offering complementary services.

A third strategy, labeled professional driven (Heusinkveld and Benders 2002), was finally central to type C firms. These focused on delivering highly specialized services, with a reputation of excellence and innovativeness. Innovation in each client project is thus an integrated part of the strategy of the type C PSF. However, the exploitation of these opportunities requires a strong entrepreneurial mind-set among professionals in the firm. Opportunities in the type C firms could also emerge in the resource base through the hiring of new expertise or in the domain through the acquisition of new clients with new demands.

12.5.3 The Process of New Practice Creation

Recent research has further investigated the process of new practice development, which is typically the outcome of exploiting new opportunities, leading to new service offerings. Exploiting new knowledge areas and opportunities is highly contested in PSFs and new ideas for service offerings are not necessarily welcomed by managers or professionals (Anand et al. 2007; Gardner et al. 2008; Heusinkveld and Benders 2005;

Heusinkveld et al. 2009). While new practice areas may originate from new client needs, lateral hires, or from within the pool of professionals, they can also challenge individual and departmental interests and power positions as well as established client relations and reputation (Heusinkveld and Benders 2005). This highlights the need to not only identify entrepreneurial opportunities but to create legitimacy around them internally as an important aspect of entrepreneurship in PSFs (Gardner et al. 2008). Anand et al. (2007) identify four prerequisites for the successful establishment of a new practice area. The first prerequisite is *agency*—the existence of a champion with a desire to create and develop a new practice area. This desire is in large PSFs driven by the career system and its focus on reputation and the establishment of a distinct area of expertise. Second, new practice areas are built on an *expertise* which is sufficiently differentiated from existing practice areas to be perceived as distinct but similar enough not to become too alien. Nevertheless, new expertise areas were often highly contested by representatives of existing core areas of expertise which felt their individual and organizational positions to be threatened (Gardner et al. 2008; Heusinkveld and Benders 2005). Third, new practice areas required the establishment of a *defensible turf*, i.e., the establishment of clear territorial boundaries around the new practice area both internally towards other practice areas in the organization and externally in relation to clients. The development of a client pool was identified as an important resource in establishing internal legitimacy and thus a defensible turf. Fourth, *organizational support* in terms of resources and political sponsorship was required to establish a new practice area.

12.5.4 Entrepreneurial Governance

The question of governance of the entrepreneurial PSF has been a largely neglected area of research. Previous research has focused on a dichotomous view on governance of PSFs, in which firms choose between professional partnerships versus corporations (Empson 2007; Empson and Chapman 2006; Greenwood and Empson 2003), between collegial clan control (Greenwood et al. 1990; Starbuck 1993) versus corporate hierarchy (Brown et al. 1996), or between professional bureaucracy versus adhocracy (Mintzberg 1979). As Empson (2012) argues, a good deal of governance systems and practices cannot be captured by these dichotomized models. We argue that especially the specific type of entrepreneurial governance has been overlooked by mainstream governance research of PSFs. This is surprising since prominent empirical examples such as Greenberg Traurig LLP, a fast-growing Miami-based law firm (Kolz 2007), or the large advertising conglomerate WPP (Grabher 2001), do not seem to be explained well by either partnership or corporate models of governance.

Following some more recent work that builds upon configuration theory (Harlacher 2010; Harlacher and Reihlen 2014), we suggest that entrepreneurial governance is a distinctive form that attempts to maximize entrepreneurial opportunity seeking of organizational members by expanding individual autonomy. Contrary to managerial governance that strives to create firm-wide consistency in approaches, services, and markets, or partnership governance that attempts to reach consensus on strategic matters, entrepreneurial governance captures the benefits of market opportunities by encouraging its members to engage in entrepreneurship—seeking out new market opportunities in services, industries, and/or regional locations. This governance form is reflected in its structure, culture, and systems to manage professionals. The governance structure is more decentralized and its culture favors entrepreneurial values emphasizing personal autonomy (for their individual commercial gain) and thus opposing the formalization and standardization usually associated with becoming more "corporate" (Empson and Chapman 2006). Furthermore, remuneration incentivizes individual performance (e.g., eat-what-you-kill) and de-emphasizes seniority-based (e.g., lockstep) remuneration more commonly found in partnerships.

12.6 INSTITUTIONAL ENTREPRENEURSHIP

Institutional entrepreneurship has become an emerging and increasingly important research area in the field of professional services. Institutionalists initially focused on explaining convergent change in response to isomorphic pressures within organizational fields (e.g., DiMaggio and Powell 1983; Meyer and Rowan 1977; Scott 1987; Tolbert and Zucker 1983; Zucker 1977, 1983). Their over-emphasis on the social environment imposing upon—rather than also emerging from—human interaction, however, produced increasing dissatisfaction with their inability to conceptualize divergent change (e.g., Barley and Tolbert 1997; DiMaggio and Powell 1991; Greenwood and Hinings 1996; Hirsch and Lounsbury 1997; Oliver 1991, 1992). In response, institutionalist scholars refocused on explaining the role of interest and agency in divergent institutional change and, following DiMaggio's (1988) early lead, subsumed their efforts under the concept of "institutional entrepreneurship." This initial framing informed subsequent research in two ways. First, it pointed to the centrality of interest, agency, and resources for explaining institutionalization as a process rather than a state (e.g., Barley and Tolbert 1997; Greenwood and Hinings 1996). Second, it opened institutional arguments to ideas from the co-evolving entrepreneurship literature (e.g., Aldrich and Fiol 1994; Aldrich and Martinez 2001). The core argument of the institutional entrepreneurship literature, hence, centers on the conditions and mechanisms that enable entrepreneurs to actively shape their institutional environment from within.

Initially, institutional entrepreneurship was associated with disadvantaged actors located in the periphery of mature fields or within emerging fields trying to gain a more central (privileged) position. More recently, entrepreneurial action by central, elite participants in mature fields has been conceptualized as "the toughest example of embedded action" (Greenwood and Suddaby 2006: 43). In the following we review major streams and show how different empirical foci correspond to different phases of theory development, and explain how this correspondence shaped our understanding of institutional entrepreneurship in PSFs.

12.6.1 Institutional Entrepreneurship in Emerging Fields

Emerging fields are still relatively under-organized domains, characterized by weakly entrenched, relatively localized "proto-institutions" (Lawrence et al. 2002). Actors within emerging fields recognize some degree of mutual interest, but interact sporadically rather than through a structured system of social positions. Hence, actors lack clearly delineated reference groups of dominant or peer organizations whose isomorphic demands they would have to observe. This ambiguity provides considerable opportunity and motivation for institutional entrepreneurs to act strategically, shape emerging institutional arrangements or standards to their interests, and secure for themselves a central and resourceful position in the emerging field (e.g., Fligstein and Mara-Drita 1996; Garud et al. 2002; Hargadon and Douglas 2001; Maguire et al. 2004). Previous studies have investigated institutional entrepreneurship in emerging technological fields such as sponsorship strategies in setting common technological standards (Garud et al. 2002) or HIV/AIDS treatment advocacy in Canada (Maguire et al. 2004). These examples deal with specific types of knowledge-intensive organizational fields composed of technology developers that, however, are not considered yet to have gained full professional status.

Previous research primarily attended to peripheral actors and emerging fields. As a consequence, this strand of research has greatly advanced the notion of agency in institutional theory. Emerging fields are characterized by low institutionalization and weak isomorphic constraints on human agency. Consequently, the image that is often painted is one of a single organization acting innovatively (Greenwood and Suddaby 2006; Hargrave and Van de Ven 2006; Lounsbury and Crumley 2007) or a heroic or "hypermuscular" (Lawrence et al. 2009) activist driving change.

This empirical one-sidedness has been reflected in theory development as critics note that the resultant understanding of agency is overly voluntaristic, individualistic, and disembedded (e.g., Lawrence et al. 2009; Leca and Naccache 2006; Lounsbury and Crumley 2007; Seo and Creed 2002). Accounts of institutional entrepreneurship are based on a model of planned change with institutional entrepreneurs engaging in actions that are "purposive" (Lawrence and Suddaby 2006), or "directed toward" (Lawrence 1999) realizing a preferred institutional arrangement.

However, to address the criticisms discussed above and take seriously the embeddedness of agency in stable institutional structures, institutional entrepreneurship research reoriented its empirical focus and attended to instances of institutional change initiated by privileged, central actors in mature fields who so far had been assumed to be strongly embedded and unmotivated to challenge the institutional status quo.

12.6.2 Institutional Entrepreneurship in Mature Fields

Searching for strong cases of embedded action, empirical work in this stream of research rediscovers classic professions such as accounting, healthcare, and law as fruitful research settings, exemplifying highly institutionalized fields. The apparent stability and strength of institutional structures in professional contexts as well as the recognized role of professionals as institutionalized and institutionalizing actors (DiMaggio and Powell 1983; Scott 2008) make professional contexts an appropriate empirical setting for studying embedded motivated action. Instead of the professions per se, however, institutionalists now attend to PSFs as elite actors in mature fields. For instance, Greenwood and colleagues publish a series of papers on the efforts of the "Big Five" global accounting firms to legitimize multidisciplinary practice as an appropriate organizational form (Greenwood et al. 2002; Greenwood and Suddaby 2006; Suddaby and Greenwood 2005). Covaleski and colleagues (2003) attend to the same set of elite organizations and their interactions with professional and regulatory bodies in legitimizing new work practices. Sherer and Lee (2002) choose elite US law firms to document the demise of the highly institutionalized "Cravath"-style promotion system. Reay and colleagues (2006) focus on the critical role of professional associations and managers in shaping the micro-political moves of introducing a new work role in healthcare.

12.6.3 Institutional Entrepreneurship in Maturing Fields

What has remained surprisingly underexplored in this extreme swing from emerging to mature fields, however, are those proto-professions and proto-professional firms whose institutional projects have made some progress, but whose organizational forms, practices, and logics cannot yet be considered fully institutionalized. These arenas, which can be described as "maturing" fields (Smets and Reihlen 2012), combining characteristics of emerging and mature fields, may hold particular conditions for institutional entrepreneurship. Typical cases of maturing fields are advertising or management consulting. Drawing on illustrative data from the German management consulting field Reihlen et al. (2010) explore those conditions and identify a portfolio of strategies such as co-option, lobbyism, membership, standardization, and influence that institutional entrepreneurs in the consulting industry employ and show how these strategies serve a dual purpose: creating individual competitive advantage and enhancing individual or collective institutional capital. This interplay of competitive and institutional strategy has previously received little attention.

12.7 CONCLUSIONS AND OUTLOOK

Based on the review of the literature a number of opportunities for further research may be identified on different levels of analysis. An *individual* level of analysis has not been part of our review, as research on this is largely missing in the PSF context. It has, however, been a strong focus of entrepreneurship research in general which has extensively investigated the individual entrepreneur and his or her drivers, characteristics, and strategies in creating and exploiting entrepreneurial opportunities (Frese 2009; Rauch and Frese 2007). Given that large parts of professional service sectors are traditionally dominated by single practitioners or small, entrepreneurial ventures (Brock et al. 1999, 2007), this lack of research provides large opportunities for research initiatives, especially as we may assume that the drivers for entrepreneurial activity among professionals, given their often claimed unique motivational structure, may be different from those of other kinds of entrepreneurs (Løwendahl 2012).

On a *team* level of analysis, extant research has highlighted the role of client projects and the engagement team as a locus for the creation and exploitation of entrepreneurial opportunities in PSFs. The nature and quality of communication and interaction in this setting is found to be an important enabler of opportunity creation, and aspects such as the interactive climate and actors' understandings of the situation and their roles in it have been identified as shaping the conditions of this interaction. Further research is needed to investigate these aspects in the specific context of different kinds of PSFs. Unique features in this context include the often highly competitive career structures in PSFs and how this may facilitate opportunity creation and learning from, for example, failures (Handley et al. 2012; Smets et al. 2012; Stollfuss et al. 2012) as well as the challenges involved in interacting with clients across organizational and contractual boundaries (e.g., Handley et al. 2012; Nikolova 2012). Previous research has highlighted the embedded nature of entrepreneurial processes in PSFs in multiple networks of discourse, cognition, and power (Reihlen and Nikolova 2010). Future research may investigate in more detail how this embeddedness is played out in concrete client–professional teams. Especially the highly ambiguous role of power that may be both a barrier as well as an enabler of the creation of entrepreneurial opportunities in engagement teams is an issue deserving of further research. Which are the processes by which certain ideas gain "interpretive dominance" and how do they affect the number and innovativeness of the ideas considered? (Nikolova 2012).

Moving to the *firm* level of analysis, research has highlighted the activities aimed at opportunity creation and exploitation on the firm level, although they are generally not labeled as entrepreneurial activities. Especially firms in the less bounded professions, such as management- or PR-consulting may have considerable opportunities for entrepreneurial action. This research points at the importance of attentiveness towards different kinds of PSFs and the different contexts for entrepreneurship they offer. Different kinds of firms (e.g., size, strategy, client relationships) and professions (e.g., the level of institutionalization) may provide very different conditions for entrepreneurial activities and thus display different kinds of entrepreneurial processes. Firm level research has also demonstrated the contested nature of the establishment of new services in PSFs. While entrepreneurial opportunities are repeatedly created in ongoing client work, their exploitation through new institutionalized service offerings is challenged by a need to gain both internal and external legitimacy and support for these new services. A limited amount of research has also been identified in the area of entrepreneurial governance structures for PSFs.

Opportunities for further research on the firm level also emerge in relation to research on the creation of new PSF ventures, the entrepreneurial strategies of PSFs, and the development of new services within the context of PSFs. Additional research is needed both on the conceptualization of these processes as well as how they play out in different contexts. Previous work has provided us with scattered evidence of why new professional service ventures are created and how they are managed through different stages of development. Following Malhotra and Morris's (2009) earlier call, we suggest that future research on entrepreneurship should also focus on differences and heterogeneity of professional service sectors as they create unique institutional conditions for firms, teams, and professionals shaping particular opportunity spaces and constraints. Some contextualized studies on entrepreneurship in particular professions have been conducted, for instance, in healthcare (Scott et al. 2000), higher education (Clark 1998), or law (Muzio and Flood 2012). Despite these scattered accounts, there is need for more systematic comparisons across professional fields that will allow for refined theoretical explanations as to why different entrepreneurial strategies emerge in different professions and PSF configurations (Løwendahl 2012).

Extant research on the challenges involved in new practice creation also highlights the socially constructed nature of entrepreneurial opportunities in PSFs. Further research may pay special attention to the distribution of power in this process of opportunity construction and the consequences of different power distributions. How does the distribution of power among actors interact with the identification and realization of entrepreneurial opportunities (Nikolova 2012)? More research is, further, needed at the intersection between the governance structures of PSFs and the identification and exploitation of entrepreneurial opportunities. While empirically the entrepreneurial governance type (Harlacher 2010; Harlacher and Reihlen 2014) seems to proliferate in different industries such as advertising (Grabher 2001), law (Kolz 2007), or even universities (Clark 1998), research has just started to take notice of this trend. We see great need to develop theoretical and empirical accounts that help to understand design parameters, conditions, and limitations of the entrepreneurial governance forms.

Finally, there is a need on the firm level of analysis for research about the management of the entrepreneurial PSF in relation to which Løwendahl (2012: 199) concludes: "It is not obvious that firm growth, size, formal structure, globalization and the like are positive for the firm and all its stakeholders, nor that they are indicators of PSF success. We need a lot more research into what are the true key success factors of such firms of different kinds, what are the challenges, and what firms can do in order to overcome them."

The review of current research reported in this chapter reveals that the term "entrepreneurship" in relation to PSFs has almost exclusively been applied to the organizational field level, where research on "*institutional* entrepreneurship" to a large extent has been carried out within the context of professional services. This may be explained by the institutional embeddedness of especially the classical professional services such as law and accounting and the ongoing struggles of the neo-professions such as management and PR-consulting to institutionalize. Entrepreneurship under these conditions requires changes not only of individual firm practices but of institutionalized rules of the game, thus making especially the classical professional services suitable objects of study of this interplay between firm and institutional environment.

While this aspect of entrepreneurship in the context of professional services has attracted considerable attention recently, future research in this area is needed to investigate maturing fields like management consulting or advertising. These offer potential for further insights on organizational field formation, disruption, and reconstruction. Since institutional entrepreneurship has traditionally been investigated in emerging or mature fields, maturing organizational fields that are caught in limbo between structurally unconfined and highly embedded agents would further inform research on the entrepreneurial opportunities of PSFs as well as institutional theory. In this context, there is a need for research on institutional entrepreneurship to go beyond either overly individualistic approaches that portray entrepreneurship as a mainly voluntaristic endeavor or overly collectivist approaches that regard entrepreneurship as a surrogate of collective meaning systems. Alternatively, a systemic approach to institutional entrepreneurship promises a meta-theoretical perspective that allows researchers to integrate agency and structure and blends the micro- and macro-foundations of institutional entrepreneurship (Reihlen et al. 2007).

References

Abbott, A. (1988). *The System of Professions*. Chicago, IL: University of Chicago Press.

Aldrich, H. E. and Fiol, C. M. (1994). "Fools Rush In? The Institutional Context of Industry Creation," *Academy of Management Review* 19(4): 645–670.

Aldrich, H. E., and Martinez, M. A. (2001). "Many are Called, But Few are Chosen: An Evolutionary Perspective for the Study of Entrepreneurship," *Entrepreneurship Theory and Practice* 25(4): 41–57.

Aldrich, H. E. and Ruef, M. (2006). *Organizations Evolving*, 2nd edn. Los Angeles, CA: Sage.

Alvesson, M. (2004). *Knowledge Work and Knowledge-Intensive Firms*. Oxford: Oxford University Press.

Anand, N., Gardner, H. K., and Morris, T. (2007). "Knowledge-Based Innovation: Emergence and Embedding of New Practice Areas in Management Consulting Firms," *Academy of Management Journal* 50(2): 406–428.

Argyris, C. and Schön, D. (1978). *Organizational Learning: A Theory of Action Perspective*. Reading, MA: Addison-Wesley.

Armbrüster, T. (2006). *The Economics and Sociology of Management Consulting* Cambridge: Cambridge University Press.

Barley, S. R. and Tolbert, P. S. (1997). "Institutionalization and Structuration: Studying the Links between Action and Institution," *Organization Studies* 18(1): 93–117.

Brandl, J. and Bullinger, B. (2009). "Reflections on the Societal Conditions for the Pervasiveness of Entrepreneurial Behavior in Western Societies," *Journal of Management Inquiry* 18(2): 159–173.

Brock, D. M. (2006). "The Changing Professional Organization: A Review of Competing Archetypes," *International Journal of Management Reviews* 8(3): 157–174.

Brock, D. M., Powell, M. J., and Hinings, C. R. (eds.) (1999). *Restructuring the Professional Organization: Accounting, Health Care and Law.* London and New York: Routledge.

Brock, D. M., Powell, M. J., and Hinings, C. R. (2007). "Archetypal Change and the Professional Service Firm," in *Research in Organizational Change and Development*, ed. W. A. Pasmore and R. W. Woodman. Amsterdam: Elsevier, 221–251.

Brown, J. L., Cooper, D. J., Greenwood, R., and Hinings, C. R. (1996). "Strategic Alliances within a Big Six Accounting Firm: A Case Study," *International Studies of Management & Organization* 26(2): 59–79.

Capelleras, J.-L., Mole, K. F., Greene, F. J., and Storey, D. J. (2008). "Do More Heavily Regulated Economies Have Poorer Performing New Ventures? Evidence from Britain and Spain," *Journal of International Business Studies* 39: 688–704.

Carlile, P. R. (2002). "A Pragmatic View of Knowledge and Boundaries: Boundary Objects in New Product Development," *Organization Science* 13(4): 442–455.

Clark, B. R. (1998). *Creating Entrepreneurial Universities: Organizational Pathways of Transformation.* Oxford and New York: Published for the IAU Press by Pergamon Press.

Clarysse, B. and Moray, N. (2004). "A Process Study of Entrepreneurial Team Formation: The Case of a Research-Based Spin-Off," *Journal of Business Venturing* 19(1): 55–79.

Cooper, A. C. (1981). "Strategic Management: New Ventures and Small Business," *Long Range Planning* 14(5): 39–45.

Cooper, A. C., Gimeno-Gascon, F. J., and Woo, C. Y. (1994). "Initial Human and Financial Capital as Predictors of New Venture Performance," *Journal of Business Venturing* 9(5): 371–395.

Covaleski, M. A., Dirsmith, M. W., and Rittenberg, L. (2003). "Jurisdictional Disputes over Professional Work: The Institutionalization of the Global Knowledge Expert," *Accounting, Organizations & Society* 28(4): 323–355.

DiMaggio, P. J. (1988). "Interest and Agency in Institutional Theory," in *Institutional Patterns and Organizations: Culture and Environment*, ed. L. G. Zucker. Cambridge, MA: Ballinger, 3–21.

DiMaggio, P. J. and Powell, W. W. (1983). "The Iron Cage Revisited: Institutional Isomorphism and Collective Rationality in Organizational Fields," *American Sociological Review* 48(2): 147–160.

DiMaggio, P. J. and Powell, W. W. (1991). "Introduction," in *The New Institutionalism in Organizational Analysis*, ed. W. W. Powell and P. DiMaggio. Chicago, IL: University of Chicago Press, 1–38.

Dougherty, D. and Takacs, C. H. (2004). "Team Play: Heedful Interrelating as the Boundary for Innovation," *Long Range Planning* 37(6): 569–590.

Eckhardt, J. T. and Shane, S. A. (2003). "Opportunities and Entrepreneurship," *Journal of Management* 29(3): 333–349.

Edmondson, A. C. (1999). "Psychological Safety and Learning Behaviour in Work Teams," *Administrative Science Quarterly* 44(2): 350–383.

Edmondson, A. C. (2002). "The Local and Variegated Nature of Learning in Organizations: A Group Level Perspective," *Organization Science* 13(2): 128–146.

Empson, L. (2007). "Your Partnership—Surviving and Thriving in a Changing World: The Special Nature of Partnership," in *Managing the Modern Law Firm: New Challenges, New Perspectives*, ed. L. Empson. Oxford: Oxford University Press, 10–36.

Empson, L. (2012). "Beyond Dichotomies: A Multi-Stage Model of Governance in Professional Service Firms," *Handbook of Research on Entrepreneurship in Professional Services*, ed. M. Reihlen and A. Werr. Cheltenham: Edward Elgar, 274–294.

Empson, L. and Chapman, C. (2006). "Partnership versus Corporation: Implications of Alternative Forms of Governance in Professional Service Firms," *Research in the Sociology of Organizations* 24: 139–170.

Ensley, M. D., Pearson, A. W., and Amason, A. C. (2002). "Understanding the Dynamics of New Venture Top Management Teams: Cohesion, Conflict, and New Venture Performance," *Journal of Business Venturing* 17(4): 365–386.

Fligstein, N. and Mara-Drita, I. (1996). "How to Make a Market: Reflections on the Attempt to Create A Single Market in the European Union," *American Journal of Sociology* 102(1): 1–33.

Fosstenløkken, S. M., Løwendahl, B. R., and Revang, Ö. (2003). "Knowledge Development through Client Interaction: A Comparative Study," *Organization Studies* 24(6): 859–879.

Freidson, E. (2001). *Professionalism: The Third Logic*. Cambridge: Polity Press.

Frese, M. (2009). "Toward a Psychology of Entrepreneurship: An Action Theory Perspective," *Foundations and Trends in Entrepreneurship* 5(6): 437–496.

Gardner, H. K., Anand, N., and Morris, T. (2008). "Chartering New Territory: Diversification, Legitimacy, and Practice Area Creation in Professional Service Firms," *Journal of Organizational Behavior* 29(8): 1101–1121.

Gartner, W. B. (1985). "A Conceptual Framework for Describing the Phenomenon of New Venture Creation," *Academy of Management Review* 10(4): 696–706.

Garud, R., Jain, S., and Kumaraswamy, A. (2002). "Institutional Entrepreneurship in the Sponsorship of Common Technological Standards: The Case of Sun Microsystems and Java," *Academy of Management Journal* 45(1): 196–214.

Glückler, J. (2006). "A Relational Assessment of International Market Entry in Management Consulting," *Journal of Economic Geography* 6(3): 369–393.

Glückler, J. and Armbrüster, T. (2003). "Bridging Uncertainty in Management Consulting: The Mechanisms of Trust and Networked Reputation," *Organization Studies* 24(2): 269–297.

Grabher, G. (2001). "Ecologies of Creativity: The Village, the Group, and the Heterarchic Organisation of the British Advertising Industry," *Environment and Planning A* 33(2): 351–374.

Greenwood, R. and Empson, L. (2003). "The Professional Partnership: Relic or Exemplary Form of Governance?" *Organization Studies* 24(6): 909–933.

Greenwood, R. and Hinings, C. R. (1996). "Understanding Radical Organizational Change: Bringing Together the Old and the New Institutionalism," *Academy of Management Review* 21(4): 1022–1054.

Greenwood, R. and Suddaby, R. (2006). "Institutional Entrepreneurship in Mature Fields: The Big Five Accounting Firms," *Academy of Management Journal* 49(1): 27–48.

Greenwood, R., Hinings, C. R., and Brown, J. (1990). "'P2-Form' Strategic Managment: Corporate Practices in Professional Partnerships," *Academy of Management Journal* 33(4): 725–755.

Greenwood, R., Suddaby, R., and Hinings, C. R. (2002). "Theorizing Change: The Role of Professional Associations in the Transformation of Institutionalized Fields," *Academy of Management Journal* 45(1): 58–80.

Greiner, L. and Malernee, J. K. (2005). "Managing Growth Stages in Consulting Firms," in *The Contemporary Consultant*, ed. L. Greiner and F. Poulfelt. Mason, OH: Thomson South-Western, 3–22.

Gross, C. and Kieser, A. (2006). "Consultants on the Way to Professionalization?" *Research in the Sociology of Organizations* 24: 69–100.

Günther, A. (2012). *Entrepreneurial Strategies of Professional Service Firms: An Analysis of Commercial Law Firm Spin-Offs in Germany*. Cologne: Kölner Wissenschaftsverlag.

Handley, K., Sturdy, A., Fincham, R., and Clark, T. (2012). "A Space for Learning? Physical, Relational and Agential Space in a Strategy Consultancy Project," in *Handbook of Research on Entrepreneurship in Professional Services*, ed. M. Reihlen and A. Werr. Cheltenham: Edward Elgar, 65–85.

Hanlon, G. (2004). "Institutional Forms and Orgainzational Structures: Homology, Trust and Reputational Capital in Professional Service Firms," *Organization* 11(2): 187–210.

Hargadon, A. B. (1998). "Firms as Knowledge Brokers: Lessons in Pursuing Continuous Innovation," *California Management Review* 40(3): 209–227.

Hargadon, A. B. and Bechky, B. A. (2006). "When Collections of Creatives Become Creative Collectives: A Field Study of Problem Solving at Work," *Organization Science* 17(4): 484–500.

Hargadon, A. B. and Douglas, Y. (2001). "When Innovations Meet Institutions: Edison and the Design of the Electric Light," *Administrative Science Quarterly* 46(3): 476–502.

Hargrave, T. J. and Van de Ven, A. H. (2006). "A Collective Action Model of Institutional Innovation," *Academy of Management Review* 31(4): 864–888.

Harlacher, D. (2010). *The Governance of Professional Service Firms*. Cologne: Kölner Wissenschaftsverlag.

Harlacher, D. and Reihlen, M. (2014). "Governance of professional Service Firms: A Configurational Approach," *Business Research* 7(1): 125–160.

Heusinkveld, S. and Benders, J. (2002). "Between Professional Dedication and Corporate Design: Exploring Forms of New Concept Development in Consultancies," *International Studies of Management and Organization* 32(4): 104–122.

Heusinkveld, S. and Benders, J. (2005). "Contested Commodification: Consultancies and their Struggle with New Concept Development," *Human Relations* 58(3): 283–310.

Heusinkveld, S., Benders, J., and van den Berg, R.-J. (2009). "From Market Sensing to New Concept Development in Consultancies: The Role of Information Processing and Organizational Capabilities," *Technovation* 29(8): 509–516.

Hirsch, P. M. and Lounsbury, M. (1997). "Ending the Family Quarrel: Toward a Reconciliation of 'Old' and 'New' Institutionalisms," *American Behavioral Scientist* 40(4): 406–418.

Hitt, M. A., Ireland, R. D., Sirmon, D. G., and Trahms, C. A. (2011). "Strategic Entrepreneurship: Creating Value for Individuals, Organizations, and Society," *Academy of Management Perspectives* 25(2): 57–75.

Kolz, A. (2007). "To Miami's Greenberg Traurig, Culture is No Vice," *Legal Times*, March 5.

Kubr, M. (2002). *Management Consulting: A Guide to the Profession*, 4th edn. Geneva: International Labour Office.

Larson, M. S. (1977). *The Rise of Professionalism*. Berkeley, CA: University of California Press.

Lawrence, T. B. (1999). "Institutional Strategy," *Journal of Management* 25(2): 161–188.

Lawrence, T. B. and Suddaby, R. (2006). "Institutions and Institutional Work," in *The Sage Handbook of Organization Studies*, ed. S. Clegg, C. Hardy, T. Lawrence, and W. Nord. London: Sage, 215–253.

Lawrence, T. B., Hardy, C., and Phillips, N. (2002). "Institutional Effects of Interorganizational Collaboration: The Emergence of Proto-Institutions," *Academy of Management Journal* 45(1): 281–290.

Lawrence, T. B., Suddaby, R., and Leca, B. (2009). "Introduction: Theorizing and Studying Institutional Work," in *Institutional Work: Actors and Agency in Institutional Studies of Organizations*, ed. T. Lawrence, R. Suddaby, and B. Leca. Cambridge: Cambridge University Press, 1–28.

Leca, B. and Naccache, P. (2006). "A Critical Realist Approach to Institutional Entrepreneurship," *Organization* 13(5): 627–651.

Liedtka, J. M. and Haskins, M. E. (1997). "The Generative Cycle: Linking Knowledge and Relationships," *Sloan Management Review* 39: 47.

Lorsch, J. and Tierney, T. (2002). *Aligning the Stars: How to Succeed when Professionals Drive Results*. Boston, MA: Harvard Business School Press.

Losada, M. and Heaphy, E. (2004). "The Role of Positivity and Connectivity in the Performance of Business Teams: A Nonlinear Dynamics Model," *American Behavioral Scientist* 47(6): 740–764.

Lounsbury, M. and Crumley, E. T. (2007). "New Practice Creation: An Institutional Perspective on Innovation," *Organization Studies* 28(7): 993–1012.

Løwendahl, B. R. (2005). *Strategic Management of Professional Service Firms*, 3rd edn. Copenhagen: Copenhagen Business School Press.

Løwendahl, B. R. (2012). "Entrepreneurial Strategies for Professional Service Firms," in *Handbook of Research on Entrepreneurship in Professional Services*, ed. M. Reihlen and A. Werr. Cheltenham: Edward Elgar, 183–201.

Maguire, S., Hardy, C., and Lawrence, T. B. (2004). "Institutional Entrepreneurship in Emerging Fields: HIV/AIDS Treatment Advocacy in Canada," *Academy of Management Journal* 47(5): 657–679.

Maister, D. (1993). *Managing the Professional Service Firm*. New York: Free Press.

Malhotra, N. and Morris, T. (2009). "Heterogeneity in Professional Service Firms," *Journal of Management Studies* 46(6): 895–922.

Meyer, J. W. and Rowan, B. (1977). "Institutionalized Organizations: Formal Structure as Myth and Ceremony," *American Journal of Sociology* 83(2): 340–363.

Mintzberg, H. (1979). *The Structuring of Organizations*. Englewood Cliffs, NJ: Prentice-Hall.

Mitchell, R. K., Busenitz, L. W., Bird, B., Gaglio, C. M., McMullen, J. S., Morse, E. A., and Smith, J. B. (2007). "The Central Question in Entrepreneurial Cognition Research 2007," *Entrepreneurship Theory and Practice* 31(1): 1–27.

Morris, T. (2001). "Asserting Property Rights: Knowledge Codification in the Professional Service Firm," *Human Relations* 54(7): 819–838.

Muzio, D., and Flood, J. (2012). "Entrepreneurship, Managerialism and Professionalism in Action: The Case of the Legal Profession in England and Wales," in *Handbook of Research on Entrepreneurship in Professional Service Firms*, ed. M. Reihlen and A. Werr. Cheltenham: Edward Elgar, 369–386.

Niewiem, S. and Richter, A. (2004). "The Changing Balance of Power in the Consulting Market," *Business Strategy Review* 15(1): 8–13.

Nikolova, N. (2012). "Innovating through Clients," in *Handbook of Research on Entrepreneurship in Professional Service Firms*, ed. M. Reihlen and A. Werr. Cheltenham: Edward Elgar, 86–106.

Oliver, C. (1991). "Strategic Responses to Institutional Processes," *Academy of Management Review* 16(1): 145–179.

Oliver, C. (1992). "The Antecedents of Deinstitutionalization," *Organization Studies* 13(4): 563–588.

Ostgaard, T. A. and Birley, S. (1996). "New Venture Growth and Personal Networks," *Journal of Business Research* 36: 37–50.

Phillips, D. J. (2002). "A Genealogical Approach to Organizational Life Chances: The Parent–Progeny Transfer among Silicon Valley Law Firms, 1946–1996," *Administrative Science Quarterly* 47(3): 474–506.

Phillips, D. J. (2005). "Organizational Genealogies and the Persistence of Gender Inequality: The Case of Silicon Valley Law Firms," *Administrative Science Quarterly* 50(3): 440–472.

Pinnington, A. and Morris, T. (2003). "Archetype Change in Professional Organizations: Survey Evidence from Large Law Firms," *British Journal of Management* 14(1): 85–99.

Ram, M. (1999). "Managing Consultants in a Small Firm: A Case Study," *Journal of Management Studies* 36(6): 875–897.

Rauch, A. and Frese, M. (2007). "Let's Put the Person Back Into Entrepreneurship Research: A Meta-Analysis on the Relationship between Business Owners' Personality Traits, Business Creation, and Success," *European Journal of Work and Organizational Psychology* 16(4): 353–385.

Reay, T., Golden-Biddle, K., and Germann, K. (2006). "Legitimizing a New Role: Small Wins and Microprocesses of Change," *Academy of Management Journal* 49(5): 977–998.

Reihlen, M. and Apel, B. A. (2007). "Internationalization of Professional Service Firms as Learning: A Constructivist Approach," *International Journal of Service Industry Management* 18(2): 140–151.

Reihlen, M. and Nikolova, N. (2010). "Knowledge Production in Consulting Teams," *Scandinavian Journal of Management* 26(3): 279–289.

Reihlen, M. and Werr, A. (2012). "Towards a Multi-Level Approach to Studying Entrepreneurship in Professional Services," in *Handbook of Research on Entrepreneurship in Professional Service Firms*, ed. M. Reihlen and A. Werr. Cheltenham: Edward Elgar, 3–20.

Reihlen, M., Klaas-Wissing, T., and Ringberg, T. (2007). "Metatheories in Management Studies: Reflections upon Individualism, Holism, and Systemism," *M@n@gement* 10(3): 49–69.

Reihlen, M., Smets, M., and Veit, A. (2010). "Management Consultancies as Institutional Agents: Strategies for Creating and Sustaining Institutional Capital," *Schmalenbach Business Review (SBR)* 62(3): 318–340.

Ringberg, T. and Reihlen, M. (2008). "Towards a Socio-Cognitive Approach to Knowledge Transfer," *Journal of Management Studies* 45(5): 912–935.

Sandberg, W. R. and Hofer, C. (1987). "Improving New Venture Performance: The Role of Strategy, Industry Structure, and the Entrepreneur," *Journal of Business Venturing* 2(1): 5–28.

Schön, D. (1983). *The Reflective Practitioner: How Professionals Think in Action*. Aldershot: Avebury.

Schumpeter, J. A. (1942). *Capitalism, Socialism and Democracy*. New York: Harper & Brothers.

Scott, W. R. (1987). "The Adolescence of Institutional Theory," *Administrative Science Quarterly* 32(4): 493–512.

Scott, W. R. (2008). "Lords of the Dance: Professionals as Institutional Agents," *Organization Studies* 29(2): 219–238.

Scott, W. R., Ruef, M., Mendel, P. J., and Caronna, C. A. (2000). *Institutional Change and Healthcare Organizations: From Professional Dominance to Managed Care*. Chicago, IL: University of Chicago Press.

Seo, M.-G. and Creed, W. E. D. (2002). "Institutional Contradictions, Praxis, and Institutional Change: A Dialectical Perspective," *Academy of Management Review* 27(2): 222–247.

Shane, S. and Eckhardt, J. (2003). "The Individual-Opportunity Nexus," in *Handbook of Entrepreneurship Research*, ed. Z. J. Acs and D. B. Audresch. Dordrecht: Kluwer, 161–191.

Shane, S. and Venkataraman, S. (2000). "The Promise of Entrepreneurship as a Field of Research," *Academy of Management Review* 25(1): 217–226.

Sherer, P. D. and Lee, K. (2002). "Institutional Change in Large Law Firms: A Resource Dependency and Institutional Perspective," *Academy of Management Journal* 45(1): 102–130.

Skjølsvik, T., Løwendahl, B. R., Kvålshaugen, R., and Fosstenløkken, S. M. (2007). "Choosing to Learn and Learning to Choose: Strategies for Client Co-Production and Knowledge Development," *California Management Review* 49(3): 110–127.

Smets, M. and Reihlen, M. (2012). "Institutional Entrepreneurship: A Literature Review and Analysis of the Maturing Consulting Field," in *Handbook of Research on Entrepreneurship in Professional Service Firms*, ed. M. Reihlen and A. Werr. Cheltenham: Edward Elgar, 297–317.

Smets, M., Morris, T., and Malhotra, N. (2012). "Changing Career Models and Capacity for Innovation in Professional Services," in *Handbook of Research on Entrepreneurship in Professional Service Firms*, ed. M. Reihlen and A. Werr. Cheltenham: Edward Elagar, 148–169.

Spar, D. L. (1997). "Lawyers Abroad: The Internationalization of Legal Practice," *California Management Review* 39(3): 8–28.

Starbuck, W. H. (1993). "Keeping a Butterfly and an Elephant in a House of Cards: The Elements of Exceptional Success," *Journal of Management Studies* 30(6): 885–897.

Stollfuss, M., Sieweke, J., Mohe, M., and Gruber, H. (2012). "Dealing with Errors in Professional Service Firms," in *Handbook of Research on Entrepreneurship in Professional Service Firms*, ed. M. Reihlen and A. Werr. Cheltenham: Edward Elgar, 42–64.

Suddaby, R. and Greenwood, R. (2005). "Rhetorical Strategies of Legitimacy," *Administrative Science Quarterly* 50(1): 35–67.

Swan, J., Newell, S., Scarbrough, H., and Hislop, D. (1999). "Knowledge Management and Innovation: Networks and Networking," *Journal of Knowledge Management* 3(4): 262–275.

Swart, J. and Kinnie, N. (2003). "Sharing Knowledge in Knowledge-Intensive Firms," *Human Resource Management Journal* 13(2): 60–75.

Teece, D. J. (2003). "Expert Talent and the Design of (Professional Services) Firms," *Industrial & Corporate Change* 12: 895–916.

Tolbert, P. S. and Zucker, L. G. (1983). "Institutional Sources of Change in the Formal Structure of Organizations: The Diffusion of Civil Service Reform, 1880–1935," *Administrative Science Quarterly* 28(1): 22–39.

Venkataraman, S. (1997). "The Distinctive Domain of Entrepreneurship Research: An Editor's Perspective," in *Advances in Entrepreneurship, Firm Emergence and Growth: Vol. 3*, ed. J. A. Katz and R. Brockhaus. Greenwich, CT: JAI Press, 119–138.

von Krogh, G. (1998). "Care in Knowledge Creation," *California Management Review* 40(3): 133–153.

von Nordenflycht, A. (2010). "What is a Professional Service Firm? Towards a Theory and Taxonomy of Knowledge-Intensive Firms," *Academy of Management Review* 35(1): 155–174.

Werr, A. (2012). "Knowledge Integration as Heedful Interrelating: Towards a Behavioral Approach to Knowledge Management in Professional Service Firms," in *Handbook of*

Research on Entrepreneurship in Professional Service Firms, ed. M. Reihlen and A. Werr. Cheltenham: Edward Elgar, 23–41.

Werr, A. and Runsten, P. (2013). "Understanding the Role of Representation in Interorganizational Knowledge Integration: A Case Study of an IT Outsourcing Project," *The Learning Organization* 20(2): 118–133.

Wood, M. S. and McKinley, W. (2010). "The Production of Entrepreneurial Opportunity: A Constructivist Perspective," *Strategic Entrepreneurship* 4(1): 66–84.

Zimmerman, M. A. and Zeitz, G. J. (2002). "Beyond Survival: Achieving Vew Venture Growth by Building Legitimacy," *Academy of Management Review* 27(3): 414–431.

Zucker, L. G. (1977). "The Role of Institutionalization in Cultural Persistence," *American Sociological Review* 42(5): 726–743.

Zucker, L. G. (1983). "Organizations as Institutions," in *Research in the Sociology of Organizations*, ed. S. B. Bacharach. Greenwich, CT: JAI Press, 1–42.

....

CHAPTER 13

MARKETING AND REPUTATION WITHIN PROFESSIONAL SERVICE FIRMS

....

WILLIAM S. HARVEY AND
VINCENT-WAYNE MITCHELL

13.1 INTRODUCTION

DESPITE their importance to the economy and people's lives, Professional Service Firms (PSFs) have received relatively little attention from marketing scholars. One problem is that there are multiple definitions of what marketing is and little consistency about how these definitions apply to PSF marketing in particular. Since few PSF theorists or practitioners have reflected on this, marketing has often been defined by what is being done, rather than what PSFs could or should be. To begin with, the American Marketing Association (2013) suggests that "Marketing is the activity, set of institutions, and processes for creating, communicating, delivering, and exchanging offerings that have value for customers, clients, partners, and society at large." The exchange which takes place is largely knowledge for money, although in some cases, such as management consultancy, there is distinct reciprocity in the transfer of knowledge as well as money. We might also replace "offerings" with knowledge-based services and remove society at large since few PSFs have a corporate social responsibility (CSR) agenda and the definition of marketing says nothing about building relationships. The way PSFs can create value for clients is via the seven Ps of services marketing, namely: Product/Service, Price, Place, Promotion, Physical Evidence, People, and Process. Productivity is sometimes added as an eighth P. Of course, professionals are and have been creating and exchanging value for clients on a personal level for years, and thus what is left as they often perceive, is just promotion. Hence marketing can be pigeon-holed as only dealing with the communications of the firm.

Increasingly professionals have to market themselves, partly because there is more supply than demand and partly because clients are more demanding of value for money due in part to the increased involvement of professional procurement personnel in the PSF selection process. Better procurement is needed as many factors contribute to increasing the risk for clients with choosing PSFs, including: the characteristics of services; the high financial risk; the conflict of interest; the length of purchase commitment; organizational risks; the inexperience of decision-makers; the conspicuousness of the decision and extent of linked decisions. In addition, making quality comparisons across PSFs is significantly more difficult because clients seldom have like-for-like comparisons across projects and their experience with a given project is carefully managed by the PSF. This means that creating differentiation and communicating the differences between PSFs competitive offerings becomes more significant. Further, many PSFs operate on a global scale under a single brand, which gives the impression of a consistent and uniform reputation. But the quality of service a PSF delivers will vary across countries and offices due to different employees as well the expectations of different clients. These factors together with the fact that clients cannot inspect, compare, or control for quality before purchase, means that potential clients experience "transactional uncertainty" (Glückler and Armbrüster 2003: 1728). In other words, there is a high degree of risk involved in purchasing professional services. This has implications for how professional services need to be communicated and the nature of the buying process which becomes more complex to try and reduce the transactional uncertainty. PSFs therefore present distinctive marketing challenges as a result of the extensive individual autonomy professionals have within firms, highly contingent managerial authority, and the need to build consensus among producer/owners. As a consequence, certain assumptions which operate in circumstances where companies make marketing decisions centrally and deliver on them fully, are problematic in PSFs. Marketing expertise within PSFs is in growing demand with reports of top law firms, for example, paying high salaries and bonuses to the heads of marketing departments, in certain cases at levels similar to some of their partners (Stanton 2014).

Here we review the extant literature on PSF marketing and in particular how these firms seek to attract and retain clients through reputation building. We begin by introducing the concept of reputation within PSFs and demonstrate how and why it is important for clients as well as PSFs. We organize this literature around two themes: defining and measuring reputation and the antecedents and consequences of reputation. We must note, however, that the conceptual model of reputation we create, which provides a framework for organizing the work in this area, is by no means exhaustive; other important antecedents and consequences may exist. Finally, we synthesize and critique this literature and identify future research directions for both marketing and reputation within PSFs.

13.2 REPUTATION WITHIN PSFs

Reputation is an important area of marketing research that is critical for PSFs because clients will use this to make determinations of potential PSF quality. When clients do not have a prior exchange relationship then PSF reputation acts as an important criterion for potential quality (Podolny 1994). Fombrun (1996: 62) argues that the effect of reputation on customers is strongest within the service sector because judgments of quality are particularly difficult to make. Therefore, customer firms rely heavily on reputation as a proxy for quality. Similarly, Rindova et al. (2005) argue that the more difficult it is for customers to assess product quality prior to purchase, the more likely they are to rely on signals of quality such as reputation. However, to date, there has been scant research on reputation within PSFs (Greenwood et al. 2005; von Nordenflycht 2010), despite the fact that reputation is arguably particularly difficult to judge in this sector owing to "information asymmetries" when certain stakeholders hold more reliable information than others (Fombrun and Shanley 1990; Kärreman and Rylander 2008; Podolny 1994; Rindova et al. 2010). Reputation can be viewed as the brand of a PSF and therefore employees are encouraged to "live the brand" to help create and sustain a positive corporate reputation (Gotsi and Wilson 2001). We outline below how reputation is defined and measured (see Table 13.1 for a summary) before providing a conceptual

Table 13.1 Summary of defining and measuring reputation

Defining reputation	Reference
Reputation is often confused with other related concepts such as identity, image, prestige, goodwill, esteem, and standing	Wartick 2002; Brown et al. 2006; Chun 2005; Jøsang et al. 2007
Reputation can be a state of awareness, an assessment of an organization or an asset	Barnett et al. 2006
Three approaches to defining reputation are the evaluative school, the impressional school, and the relational school	Chun 2005
Definition used in this chapter	
A collective assessment of a company's attractiveness to a specific group of stakeholders made with reference to companies with which it competes	Fombrun 2012
Measuring reputation	
The five main ways of measuring reputation are: first, ranking measures such as FMAC; second, brand equity scales; third, image measures; fourth, identity measures; fifth, multiple stakeholder measures	Chun 2005
A single reputation score simplifies the complexities of multiple client perceptions	Bromley 2002; Helm 2007
Measurement used in this chapter	
Should be tied to definitions and incorporate five attributes: first, perceived reputation; second, issue-specific and an aggregated perception; third, comparative; fourth, positive and negative; fifth, stable and enduring	Walker 2010

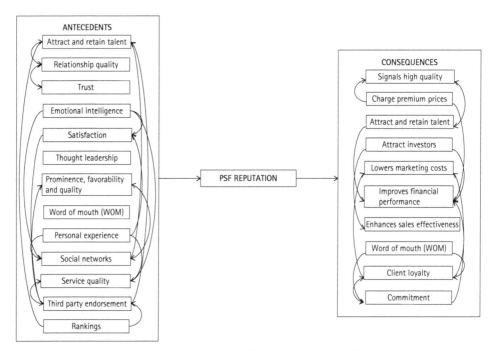

FIGURE 13.1 Antecedents and consequences of Professional Service Firm reputation.

model of the antecedents and consequences of reputation within PSFs (see Figure 13.1 for a summary), with a particular focus on marketing. Our focus is predominantly on the positive aspects of reputation, but as we discuss below there are also significant factors to consider related to negative reputations.

13.2.1 Defining Reputation

Many concepts have been used almost synonymously with corporate reputation such as identity, image, prestige, goodwill, esteem, and standing, and their use varies by discipline (Wartick 2002). For instance, Brown et al. (2006: 102) distinguish between identity, intended image, construed image, and reputation. Identity is the mental associations about an organization held by organizational members. Intended image is the mental associations about the organization that leaders of that organization want key stakeholders to hold. Construed image is the mental associations that organizational members believe others outside of the organization hold about the organization. Reputation is the mental associations about the organization actually held by others outside of the organization. Similarly, Chun (2005) has suggested that reputation is similar to the other related concepts in that it is based on aggregating individual mental associations, but it is different in orientation because it tends to be based on the perceptions of both internal and external stakeholders. To date, scholars have used different definitions for each of the related terms, which has made it problematic for comparative purposes.

Even the term reputation itself has complex dimensions. Fombrun (1996) suggests that reputation has three important attributes. First, it is based on the perception of stakeholders towards organizations; second, it is the aggregate perception of all internal and external stakeholders, and third, it is a comparative measurement which is made in relation to competitors. Walker (2010) extends this definition, arguing that reputation can be positive or negative, and it is generally stable and enduring. Barnett et al. (2006: 32) argue that stakeholders have three levels of engagement with reputation: a state of awareness, an assessment, and an asset. Awareness is when actors know of a company's name or logo, but are not in a position to make a judgment about its activities. Assessment is when stakeholders have a better understanding of the company's activities and therefore are able to make more informed judgments. Asset is when stakeholders believe that reputation holds a particular value for the company.

There are three approaches to defining reputation, according to Chun (2005: 94). First, the Evaluative School understands reputation as the evaluation of an organization's financial performance from the perspective of a single stakeholder. Second, the Impressional School understands reputation as the overall impression of an organization from the perspective of a single stakeholder. Third, the Relational School understands reputation as involving gaps between the views of internal and external stakeholders from the perspective of multiple stakeholders. The conceptual fuzziness of reputation has meant that there have been numerous definitions such as: "what is generally said or believed about a person's or thing's character or standing" (Jøsang et al. 2007: 3) and "the set of beliefs shared by top managers and stakeholders about the central, enduring, and distinctive characteristics of an organization" (Scott and Lane 2000: 44, drawing on Albert and Whetten 1985). In the context of this chapter, we follow Fombrun's (2012: 100) definition: "a collective assessment of a company's attractiveness to a specific group of stakeholders relative to a reference group of companies with which the company competes for resources" (Fombrun 2012: 100). Here, the emphasis is on the perceptions of a group of stakeholders (e.g., clients and employees) and how their perceptions of a firm compare to their perceptions of the firm's competitors.

13.2.2 Measuring Reputation

The multiple definitions of reputation, and the related terms, have meant that there have been various approaches to understanding and measuring reputation depending upon the disciplinary and methodological backgrounds of scholars. Chun (2005) argues that scholars have tended to focus on five measurements of reputation. First, some scholars utilize ranking measures such as Fortune's Most Admired Companies (FMAC) to assess firm reputation. Second, others use brand equity scales that focus on dimensions such as corporate credibility, expertise, trustworthiness, and likability. Third, some researchers use image measures which look at satisfaction and perceptions of quality. Fourth, other researchers focus on identity measures which analyze how companies see themselves or want others to see them. Fifth, multiple stakeholder reputation is sometimes utilized which measures firm reputation from the perspective of a range of internal and external actors.

Some scholars have criticized measures of reputation which aggregate multiple perceptions of a firm into a single reputation score because it can mask data variation across individuals (Bromley 2002; Helm 2007). The "single" reputation approach, for example, can overlook the multiple identities of individuals within PSFs which are independent, but overlap with that of the entire organization (see Table 13.1). In addition, many PSFs operate on a national and global scale and may hold very distinct office and team reputations and identities from one another, based on the individual reputations of particular partners and individuals at specific offices. This suggests that a single reputation at the firm level, compared to the business unit level, may be particularly problematic for many PSFs which are structured to operate multiple offices to service the needs of clients in varied locations. Some researchers argue that significant differences between the various stakeholder groups' perceptions indicate weaknesses in reputation (Whetten 1997). Partly acknowledging this, Fombrun (2012: 100) argues that reputation "should reflect the collective assessments of a specific stakeholder group towards a given firm, which are benchmarked in relation to the firm's competitors."

It is important that any operationalization of reputation such as measurement reflects how it is defined (Wartick 2002). Following Walker's (2010) comprehensive review of the definitions, measurements, and theories of reputation, we argue in the context of this chapter that reputation measurements should incorporate the following five attributes that he identifies (Walker 2010: 372–375). First, it is a perception of stakeholders as opposed to a factual representation of reality such as market share. Second, it is issue-specific and an aggregated perception. Although definitions recognize that reputation should be an aggregated representation of stakeholder perceptions, measurements tend to lose important information for each stakeholder. Third, reputation is comparative not only to competitors, but also to the firm's prior reputation as well as to the industry's reputation. Fourth, reputation is both positive and negative with most studies tending to focus only on positive reputations, whereas measuring both may provide more insight into reputation. Fifth, it is stable and enduring rather than constantly changing, which lends itself more to longitudinal studies, although cross-sectional measurements of reputation can provide valuable insights.

13.3 A CONCEPTUAL MODEL OF THE ANTECEDENTS AND CONSEQUENCES OF REPUTATION

Having identified the importance of reputation within PSFs and some of the challenges of defining and measuring reputation, this section discusses the antecedents and consequences of reputation. This is important for understanding how reputation can be built within PSFs as well as for understanding what the outcomes of reputation are.

13.3.1 Antecedents

Antecedents are the conditions that help to build reputation, both directly and indirectly through their affect on other antecedents. We provide a conceptual model in Figure 13.1 of the direct and indirect effects of building reputation. Because PSFs are people intensive, *attracting and retaining talent* is a vital building block of reputation because the caliber of the workforce determines the quality of the services that can be delivered. This closely relates to the McKinsey & Company term "war for talent" which indicates that attracting and retaining talent is critical for the competitiveness of organizations and has subsequently been adopted in the talent management literature (Chambers et al. 1998; Michaels et al. 2001; Tarique and Schuler 2010). Mawdsley and Somaya (Chapter 10, this volume) emphasize the role of stars and expert human capital for the competitiveness of PSFs because they provide confidence among clients that PSFs can deliver a high quality service. PSFs sometimes transfer talent from one project or office to another as both a resourcing strategy as well as to ensure reputational consistency across different geographic regions, which can otherwise vary. Talented employees are not only important for building reputation, but also significant for other antecedents such as building *relationship quality* with the client, which can affect the reputation of individuals and the firm. People are in a relationship when they have impact on others and they are interdependent, meaning that change in one person causes change in another, and vice versa (Berscheid and Peplau 1983: 12). A significant body of research within PSFs has focused on the value of social networks for building commitment, trust, and quality, which are also important antecedents of reputation (Harste and Richter 2009; Rosenbaum et al. 2006). This highlights that the antecedents of reputation do not exist individually in a vacuum, but interact with other antecedents to build reputation.

An extreme example of the effects of talent is the celebrity CEO who can both benefit and damage organizational reputation because analysts place a strong attribution on the competencies of leaders when evaluating the performance of organizations, such as their financial performance (Hayward et al. 2004). Although a celebrity CEO, such as Richard Branson of Virgin and Warren Buffett of Berkshire Hathaway, can increase an organization's reputation in the short term, their effect on reputation can be fleeting. For instance, a staggering 28% of elite CEOs who had won five or more awards from major business periodicals "fell from grace," which the authors defined as "voluntary terminations, being indicted within two years of leaving the job, and/or being a CEO while leading the company into bankruptcy" (Graffin et al. 2013: 316).

Trust is a major factor in building organizational reputation among clients, particularly when operating in conjunction with other related antecedents discussed before such as relationship quality. It is particularly important in PSFs because clients rely on professionals to treat information confidentially. Added to which, difficult decisions often need to be made which can have significant implications for the client firm and therefore for the reputation of the PSF. Trust can be seen as a multidimensional concept which includes: dependability/reliability (confidence, consistency, faith, loyalty, predictability, respect, and security), honesty (fairness, motivation to lie, and openness of management), buyer/seller orientation (altruism, business sense and judgment, congruence, intention and motives), and friendliness (acceptance, benevolence, and liking (Swan et al. 1985). Nooteboom (2000) argues that clients tend to hold high levels of trust towards their service providers, despite the potential for the latter to act opportunistically. Bagdoniene and Jakstaite (2009) note that trust has been related to other concepts such as: hope, faith, confidence, assurance, initiative (Lewicki et al. 1998), ability and congruence (Sitkin and Roth 1993), benevolence (Mayer et al. 1995), predictability (Coleman 1990; Dasgupta 1988), common values (Eriksson and Lindvall 2000; Gillespie and Mann 2004), consistency, commitment, and capability (Hacker et al. 2001). Trust has also been categorized in three ways: first, access trust, which describes trust in principals for the purpose of accessing resources owned by or under the responsibility of the relying party. Second, delegation trust describes trust in an agent (the delegate) that acts and makes decisions on behalf of the relying party. Third, identity trust describes the belief that an agent's identity is as claimed (Grandison and Sloman 2000). In all three cases, trust is an important antecedent of reputation because clients believe that PSFs will operate ethically, in their best interests and deliver as they have claimed. If a PSF demonstrates trustworthiness then it will build its reputation among clients, but if it does not meet the client's expectations in terms of trust then it will likely damage its reputation.

Emotional intelligence (EI) is another important antecedent of reputation within PSFs because employees need to have a strong awareness of their own emotions, recognize different emotions in others, and manage social relationships with clients at all stages of the professional engagement (Goleman 1995). These soft skills of professionals are important for impression management with clients. EI in marketing exchanges can be grouped under the dimension of: perceiving, facilitating, understanding, and managing. EI has been found to be positively related to service quality in certain PSFs such as real estate and insurance agents, even when controlling for the effects of domain-general EI, self-report EI, cognitive ability, and several control variables. The reason for this is that high levels of emotional intelligence enable professionals to better understand the context of their business relationships and respond to the various signals and cues from clients to ensure that they are highly satisfied. Sales professionals with higher EI are not only superior revenue generators, but also better at satisfying clients. In addition, EI interacts with key marketing exchange variables—customer orientation and manifest influence—to heighten performance such that high-EI salespeople more effectively employ customer-oriented selling and influence customer decisions (Kidwell et al. 2011). This is because EI is something which clients can evaluate and therefore put more weight on when evaluating individual service providers.

A further factor that has been shown to affect reputation is client *satisfaction* because satisfied clients want to work with PSFs on future projects and are also willing to refer them to others (Patterson et al. 1997). Satisfaction can be managed through communication effectiveness, for example displaying empathy and listening skills, accurately explaining fees and charges, and setting realistic expectations about risk and returns as well as educating clients along the way so they can make more informed decisions (Sharma and Patterson 1999). Interestingly, firms with good prior service levels experience greater reputation suffering when customers perceive that they have undergone a loss arising from a service encounter—due to the existence of a contrast effect (Bolton 1998). Other research has shown different levels of client expertise affect how certain characteristics, such as experience and qualifications, influence satisfaction judgments and therefore reputation within a professional service context (Garry 2007). In short, client satisfaction is important for building reputation, but it is critical that PSFs show consistency in their service delivery to avoid sending ambiguous messages about their reputation.

One strategy for reputation enhancement which McKinsey & Company has adopted since the 1960s, is publishing *thought leadership* work in the management domain under the banner of its *McKinsey Quarterly* journal. This signals to clients that the firm is not only working with client challenges, but is continually producing new knowledge which forms the basis of what it advises to clients. Other management consulting firms have followed suit, for example: *bcg perspectives*, *Bain Insights*, and Roland Berger's *think:act*. Accountancy firms such as PwC and Deloitte are providing similar material, much of which is publicly available and often used as a marketing and PR exercise to strengthen the company's reputation. Clients assume that PSFs that are consistently producing high quality knowledge which is well recognized and highly publicized have the capacity to deliver high quality service work.

Three important ways that people form perceptions of reputation are: *word of mouth* (WOM) from different sources, through their own personal experiences and through various forms of social networks. WOM is powerful for clients both during the pre-purchase process (ex ante or input) and post-purchase during the output stage (ex post or output). Input WOM increases the data that clients draw upon to make an informed evaluation of the quality of the PSF's work. Input WOM can help confirm or challenge their existing impressions of a PSF and can affect the decision criteria clients use during the tendering process. Input WOM also affects the importance attached to decision criteria when purchasing PSFs for skills training in sales (Sonmez and Moorhouse 2010) because it provides additional information to clients from trusted sources, giving them greater confidence to make their decision. Crucially, WOM provides either experience information as to how other clients viewed the professionals' work or credence information from other professionals qualified to pass expert judgment on the work of the PSF.

Research has also found that *personal experience* carries more weight with clients than referrals and that client satisfaction with the quality of previous projects likely influences purchasing decisions more than does personal networks (Jøsang et al. 2007). Depending on their prior experience and engagement with PSFs, clients will change their expectations and their judgments (Shapiro 1982; Sharma and Patterson 2000). If expected quality is different from experienced quality then clients need to make sense of this difference (Pfarrer et al. 2010). It is assumed that previous quality, which will often be related to a different service, will be a good predictor of future quality. Clients who experience a high quality of service over time will form positive reputations of the PSF, particularly if personal experiences have been consistently high across a range of projects.

Social networks are also significant for influencing perceptions of reputation, particularly in the context of PSFs where quality is hard for potential and existing clients to assess. Capitalizing on this, many ex-consultants attain executive positions in corporations and are likely to subsequently contract external consulting services within their network of trusted relations (Amorim and Kipping 1999; Glückler and Armbrüster 2003; Kipping 1999). In addition, some PSFs such as law, accounting, and management consulting firms have "up or out" policies whereby many employees are encouraged to move outside of their firm to become future clients (Gilson and Mnookin 1989). Some firms have realized this potential acquisition effect by documenting alumni careers and institutionalizing networks of post-employment relations in order to extend their webs of reference into client corporations (Kaas and Schade 1995). Although this has the potential advantage of alumni favoring the services of their former employer, it also arguably places greater demand on PSFs because former employees are sophisticated and experienced buyers who know what to expect (Somaya et al. 2008) and who also hold strong impressions about the reputations of different firms. It is not only alumni whose social networks are important for the reputation of PSFs. Employees of PSFs, and particularly partners, are expected to build and maintain strong social networks with their clients to help build their own personal reputations for particular functions as well as to build the reputation of the PSF. Employees are also expected to build social networks with other stakeholders such as public relations professionals and journalists. This helps to generate positive stories and news on behalf of their PSF, which in turn may help to attract and retain high quality employees and clients and further enable the building of the firm's reputation.

The emerging literature on celebrity firms argues that the positive reputational benefits a celebrity firm can provide include: enhanced performance and survival rates, lower chances of bankruptcy, better ability to secure exchange partners, and higher bargaining power (Graffin et al. 2013). However, celebrity status can also attract unwanted attention from a broader group of stakeholders, highlighting the general importance of *prominence, favorability*, and *quality* as antecedents of reputation within PSFs. Prominence is when a firm achieves a high degree of attention among a broader group of stakeholders and they understand who the firm is and what work it does. Favorability is when a firm is generally well regarded by particular clients in relation to its competitors in specific industries. Quality is when a firm is known in the client universe (potential, existing, and former clients) for having expertise in certain areas (Harvey et al. 2013: 227). Lange et al. (2011) provide a conceptual model which shows the interaction of the three dimensions of prominence, favorability, and quality are important for building corporate reputation. Harvey et al. (2015) test this model empirically within a global management consulting firm and find that the interaction of these three dimensions is important for building reputation, but certain pathway and institutional and market conditions are needed to enable the building of reputation. In terms of pathways, PSFs need legitimated expertise, relevant celebrity, and strong relationships. In terms of institutional and market conditions, PSFs need to understand the context of the industry as a whole, the knowledge of clients, and the competitiveness of the market as well as the firm's history and path dependency.

Most services are almost impossible to evaluate until they have been "experienced" (Kärreman and Rylander 2008; Shapiro 1982), but judging quality even after a professional service has been delivered is highly complex and problematic for clients (Sharma and Patterson 1999). Evaluating professional services is difficult for clients because they are unable to evaluate the technical aspects of the advice, known as credence qualities. Because clients cannot evaluate whether these technical service aspects are the best quality, they place emphasis on the things they can evaluate such as experiential qualities like the responsiveness, empathy, and confidence of the professional when they evaluate their service. Some assessment of these can be gleaned prior to purchase via the interview and the tendering process to complement search characteristics, such as who they have worked for, what projects they have done and reputation to date, which are used as surrogates for future performance (Shostack 1977).

Service quality is considered an important building block of reputation. Perceived service quality (SERVQUAL) is viewed as the degree and direction of discrepancy between consumers' perceptions and expectations (Parasuraman et al. 1988) on five dimensions, namely: Tangibles: physical facilities, equipment, and appearance of personnel; Reliability: ability to perform the promised service dependably and accurately; Responsiveness: willingness to help customers and provide prompt service; Assurance: knowledge and courtesy of employees and their ability to inspire trust and confidence; Empathy: caring, individualized attention the firm provides to its customers (Parasuraman et al. 1988). However this one-dimensional view of expectations and the gap formation for service quality has been challenged by the finding that service quality is directly influenced only by perceptions (of performance) (Cronin, Jr. and Taylor 1994), the serious problems in conceptualizing service quality as a difference score (Brown et al. 1993), and the finding that the service performance (SERVPERF) scale exhibits the same factor instability inherent in the SERVQUAL difference scores across service industries (Cronin, Jr. and Taylor 1994). If quality is being used as an overall assessment of an organization, then it is similar to reputation. But if it is being used to assess how good a particular aspect of the organization is, then it is an antecedent of reputation (e.g., quality).

Another way of building reputation is the use of *third-party endorsements*, which works for several reasons. First, clients presume that a quality third party would not be associated with a second-rate PSF. Therefore, the quality of third-party endorsers reflects the quality of PSFs. Second, some of these third parties are able to judge the credence qualities of PSF and therefore are signaling that the quality of these difficult-to-evaluate aspects is high. Third, clients often assume that reputable PSFs attract high quality employees and high quality potential employees want to work for reputable PSFs. Thus PSFs who hold strong reputations in the client and labor market presumably hold a double competitive advantage over PSFs who hold weaker reputations in both markets. Investment banks have adopted similar principles of exclusivity in selecting exchange partners, engaging in exchange relations with those with whom they have transacted in the past and engaging in transactions with those of similar status (Podolny 1994). Results for business schools also provide empirical support for the theoretical argument that the prominence dimension of reputation depends on support and endorsement by influential third parties, such as institutional intermediaries and high-status actors. But it is not clear how true this is for other PSFs (Rindova et al. 2005).

Performing well in high profile *rankings* has a positive effect on reputation and sends important quality signals to potential clients and potential employees about the reputation of PSFs. Such rankings may focus on the quality of the service, as Kennedy Consulting Research & Advisory does for potential clients of management consulting firms, or which firms are the most reputable to work for, as Vault does for potential employees (Gardner, Chapter 17, this volume).

13.3.2 Consequences of Reputation

The outcomes of reputation can be both positive and negative (Walker 2010). Here, we focus on the positive outcomes of a strong reputation (see Figure 13.1), although negative or no outcomes is likely for organizations who hold weak or mediocre reputations. It is also important to highlight that these consequences are a direct outcome of reputation and in some cases also an indirect outcome via other consequences. A positive reputation, for example, directly signals high quality and indirectly signals high quality through a PSF charging premium prices. The literature argues that corporate reputation is a vital "intangible asset" that can provide firms with a competitive advantage within stock, consumer, client, and labor markets, with the last three being pertinent for PSFs (Fombrun 1996, 2012; Rindova and Fombrun 1999; Rindova et al. 2006; Roberts and Dowling 2002). A strong reputation among clients is important within PSFs because it is easier to gain new business projects through marketing to existing clients, making it difficult for new competitors to enter the market (Amonini et al. 2010; Bolton 1998; Chiou and Droge 2006; Kitay and Wright 2004; Maister 1997).

So why is reputation so important for the marketing of PSFs? Although judging quality within PSFs is highly challenging for clients, a positive reputation provides PSFs with a number of benefits. First, it *signals high quality* to clients and potential clients because it is assumed that firms with positive reputations deliver high quality services to their clients (Lange et al. 2011). Second, it enables firms to *charge premium prices* (Beatty and Ritter 1986; Klein and Leffler 1981; Milgram and Roberts 1986). For example, in the context of business schools, prominence had the largest total effect on price premium and clients are willing to pay higher costs for what they perceive to be a higher quality of service from reputable firms (Rindova et al. 2005). Third, it improves a firm's ability to *attract and retain talent* (Fang 2005; Harvey and Morris 2012; Stigler 1962). As mentioned earlier, attracting and retaining talent is an important antecedent of reputation, but it is also an important consequence of reputation. Firms with strong reputations receive a higher number of applications from potential employees (Harvey and Morris 2012) and existing employees are less likely to move to other organizations with lower reputations if their current employer is highly reputable. Employee loyalty is integral to the competitiveness of PSFs because of the high demands within the sector for knowledge creation, providing innovative solutions, and building and maintaining strong relationships with clients (Hitt et al. 2001; Malos and Campion 1995, Morris and Empson 1998).

Fourth, reputation *attracts investors* and a broader group of stakeholders because PSFs with positive reputations send strong signals to the capital markets about their ability to create and sustain value (Milgram and Roberts 1986). Fifth, it *lowers marketing costs* because clients actively seek higher status firms (Podolny 1993, 1994). Sixth, it leads to *improved financial performance* (Greenwood et al. 2005) because firms with good reputations achieve higher profits owing to their reduced learning costs, their ability to charge premium prices for services (see before), and the tendency for clients to commission more services from current advisors (Greenwood et al. 2005) and *ceteris paribus*, employees prefer to work for high-reputation firms, and should therefore work harder, or for lower remuneration (Roberts and Dowling 2002). Highly reputable banks, for instance, obtain lower yields and charge higher fees, but issuers' net proceeds are higher (Fang 2005). Seventh, it *enhances sales force effectiveness* because clients assume that reputable PSFs deliver high quality services and therefore selling is easier compared to PSFs with a lower reputation. Reputable firms are also able to introduce new products and expand into different markets (Roberts and Dowling 2002), as has been demonstrated by the large accounting firms who now offer extensive management consulting services. Finally, salespeople are likely to be more motivated and proud to work for a reputable organization and therefore work harder.

Eighth, improved output WOM is also likely as a post-purchase behavior and varies across services being affected by input WOM, company size, prior experience in contracting for professional services, type of company ownership, and satisfaction (Maru et al. 1994). In particular, once a PSF has a strong reputation then it becomes more prominent which provides clients with greater confidence in its services. This is because stakeholders have more reasons to talk as they know more about the organization and are more favorably disposed to it. Ninth, the greater a PSF's reputation, the greater is *client loyalty*. Research on client loyalty in terms of professional consulting services found that non-economic factors played a significant role, while client dependence was found to have a relatively modest effect on client loyalty (Harste and Richter 2009). Clients may not be loyal to a PSF, but can be in a long-term relationship with their PSF for other reasons such as inertia or ignorance. Some evidence suggests that customers' willingness to recommend the firm to relatives or friends is a key driver of customer commitment to the organization (Eisingerich and Bell 2007). Other research suggests professional service customers utilize both satisfaction and commitment (rather than trust or service quality) to determine repurchase intentions (Rosenbaum et al. 2006).

Commitment is one of the most frequently studied variables in business-to-business relationships and it is an important consequence of reputation because strong reputations are indicators of quality and reliability which stimulate trust. Very strong reputations invariably mean that the PSF has had some direct prior working relationship with the client organization and commitment is therefore increased due to social networks and social capital built up over time. It is also reinforced by other consequences of reputation such as output WOM, because PSFs will want to demonstrate that they have the commitment to client problems that other referrers have suggested, and client loyalty because PSFs will want to show that they are able and willing to reciprocate their professional relationship with clients. Commitment has been defined as "an implicit or explicit pledge of relational continuity between exchange partners" (Dwyer et al. 1987: 19). It comprises three components: affective, calculative, and normative (Geyskens et al. 1996; Kumar et al. 1995). Affective commitment means that clients want to stay in the relationship because they like their PSF partner, enjoy the partnership, and feel a sense of belongingness. This will affect the reputation of PSFs because it will lead to positive esteem, referrals, and client loyalty. Calculative commitment is the extent to which partners perceive the need to maintain a relationship due to the significant anticipated switching costs or lack of alternatives. Normative commitment means that partners stay in the relationship because they feel they ought to (Geyskens et al. 1996; Kumar et al. 1995). Higher levels of calculative and normative commitment mean that PSFs can reduce their marketing costs, but they should also be aware of the need to improve the quality of their service delivery. Of the three forms of commitment, affective commitment, which is positively dependent on both trust and social networks, has been found to be the strongest motivator for customer loyalty (Cater and Cater 2009; Cater and Zabkar 2009; De Ruyter et al. 2001; Gounaris 2005; Kumar et al. 1995; Wetzels et al. 1998), while client dependence or calculative commitment has a relatively modest effect on client loyalty, particularly in the long term (Harste and Richter 2009). For example, a management consultant might understand the business and be able to give technical advice, but if they are unable to produce a report at short notice to save the client from some internal repercussion, then trust and affective commitment will be reduced. Trust and social networks have no significant relation either to normative or to calculative commitment, while the relationship of overall satisfaction with normative and calculative commitment is negative (Cater and Zabkar 2009).

13.4 FUTURE RESEARCH AGENDA DERIVED FROM OUR CONCEPTUAL MODEL OF REPUTATION

There are a series of research questions and issues which stem from our conceptual model of reputation. With many antecedents and consequences of reputation as well as direct and indirect effects to consider (see Figure 13.1), important questions arise about which of these are more important, in what ways, and how they overlap, interrelate, and support each other.

The literature on corporate reputation argues that reputation is based on perceptions of different stakeholders, which can be a source of competitive advantage (Fombrun 2012; Pfarrer et al. 2010; Rindova and Fombrun 1999; Walker 2010). An interesting observation can be made that PSFs often seek to develop their reputation within the profession, rather than within a target set of customers. In doing so, they often focus on convincing other PSFs of their worth by being better on the technical and credence aspects of their activities which other professionals can assess, but which clients cannot. Therein lies a mismatch between how PSFs often see reputation (or their own identity) and how clients perceive it.

In general, reputation is an overall judgment based on numerous perceptions of which quality is one. What is less clear is whether clients aggregate reputation into a single impression from which they make purchasing and re-purchasing decisions, or whether they hold a series of impressions, from which they tailor purchasing decisions, depending upon the context. The lack of clarity surrounding the parameters of reputation opens up some interesting research questions such as: can or do reputable firms under-deliver to clients, particularly to those clients who are seen as less prestigious? Do less reputable firms have to over-deliver to clients in order to ensure that they are considered by future clients? Also, if we conceive of reputation as brand equity of the firm, we can use existing marketing models to define what it is. Branding plays a special role in service companies because strong brands increase customers' trust of the invisible purchase (Berry 2000). Differentiation is a problem for many PSFs where the branding literature can help and brand equity can be a key differentiator (Sharp 1996). How and in what ways brand equity is formed and transformed in PSFs seems a key research question. For example, should it contain aspects of: brand awareness, uniqueness and favorability of associations, perceived quality, brand loyalty, and brand personality (Aaker 1996)?

We can deconstruct reputation or brand by unit of analysis where the reputation can reside. For example, this can be at the individual professional level, the group practice level, the service offering level, the "office" level either by region or country, and the overall firm level. At the service offering level, some PSFs may have a positive reputation for something (e.g., producing feasible solutions for clients), but a negative reputation for something else (e.g., high-end strategy work). At the firm level, they may have a reputation for being expensive or cheap. It is likely that internal and external actors play a critical role in shaping the reputation of PSFs, but as yet our understanding of how they do this and the extent of their success remains highly limited. This is important because individual social relationships are critical for building trust (Putnam 1995), but to what extent can individual-level trust be scaled up to firm-level trust? In other words, in what ways can key stakeholders transform "trust in me" into "trust in us"? There are thus important research questions around the brand architecture of PSFs and in terms of which unit of reputation a firm should separate and promote, if any.

Managing brand or reputation, whatever the unit of analysis, is difficult because it is highly people-based and it can change quickly as people join and leave the firm. This can present a major communications problem for firms and an inevitable lag in client

perceptions. In addition, there is the issue of reconciling multiple and possibly conflicting reputations. For example, can clients hold multiple reputations for something (e.g.,
producing high quality work), with someone (e.g., a particular stakeholder), in some-
place (e.g., UK versus the US), and over time (e.g., 2010 compared to 2013)? A further
complexity is the "collaborative imperative" (Gardner, Chapter 17, this volume). When
PSFs may be required to work with each other on large client projects it can become
unclear who is accountable in reputation terms for the outcome of a client project or
who owns the reputation when clients co-produce knowledge with their professional
service providers.

We have discussed the importance of satisfying clients as well as building trust and
loyalty. However, there are increasing external challenges to these endeavors such
as: the needs of clients are continually changing, there are fewer inexperienced clients,

the need for auditor rotation and procurement departments who refuse to work from
preferred supplier lists, the influence of professional bodies which are about promoting professional standards of knowledge and skills, and rather less about what clients
want or need. Additional internal factors make pursuing client loyalty more challenging, such as the pressure on professionals to earn high fees for personal gain and the
benefit of the partnership, the "prestige of partner" effect which makes them focused on
how to achieve partnership as opposed to how to best serve clients, and the issue of professionals marketing themselves internally to the firm to make partner. All these make
whatever can be done by PSFs to increase client loyalty all the more important to reduce
the tension between more demanding clients and less client-focused professionals. This
raises questions around the sustainability of this arrangement, both from the client perspective in terms of their choices of PSFs and from the PSF perspective in terms of their
loyalty to clients.

Furthering the cause of getting closer to clients, client participation is on the increase,
but research suggests it could be a double-edged sword for PSFs (Chan et al. 2010). On
the one hand, it can enhance the satisfaction of clients and therefore increase their social
capital with PSFs. But at the same time it can increase the workload, stress, and dissatisfaction of PSF employees because of the greater client demands placed on them. This in
turn could affect long-term quality delivery because PSFs are likely to either lose people
if client demands increase or they will take shortcuts in their delivery. This is likely to
occur if clients cannot differentiate quality across PSFs (leading to higher demands),
or if PSFs take on more work than they can deliver effectively (leading to lower quality
delivery). Yet surprisingly little research has been conducted on how the nature of client
engagement can shape their judgments of service quality (Sharma and Patterson 1999).
Moreover, the effects of client participation in value creation are contingent on individual cultural value orientations: customers and employees within higher collectivist
and less power distance cultures may value co-creation more than low collectivist high
power distance cultures. They might also perceive less economic value and more relational value from customer participation.

Within the client context, EI is a key driver of affective loyalty discussed earlier. Since
people can learn EI (Mayer and Salovey 1995), training could help sales professionals

improve their performance (Kumar et al. 2008), but low cognitive ability does not seem to benefit from training for greater EI (Kidwell et al. 2011). There is significant work needed to explore how EI in PSFs affects perceptions from both the PSF and client perspective. This raises the issue of the relative importance of how a service is experienced and delivered versus the technical substance of what is delivered. We would suggest that there are likely to be marked differences on this issue both within and between different PSF sectors.

It is important to consider that although the focus of our review of reputation has been on its positive antecedents and consequences, Walker (2010) reminds us that reputation can also be negative and therefore have a series of negative outcomes such as a fall in client demand, lowering prices, a loss of potential and existing talent, and greater media and public scrutiny (Harvey 2014). Relatively little research has been conducted on ethical failures within PSFs, which is surprising given the proliferation of corporate scandals in the sector such as Enron, Arthur Anderson, Fannie Mae, Société Générale, and Northern Rock, to name only a few examples. However, despite these markedly different experiences, there is little support for any significant differences among the various types of professional services in customers' propensity to switch services when there is service failure (Olorunniw and Hsu 2007).

From a reputation perspective, it is less clear at what stage a "tipping point" occurs whereby the PSF's reputation is affected in light of its goals no longer aligning close enough to those of its clients, or when the actions of PSFs significantly changes the attitudes of clients, either positively or negatively. This raises an important question that is discussed elsewhere in this handbook (Broschak, Chapter 14, this volume), namely under what conditions do clients switch to different providers? Other research has investigated customers' reasons for switching property service providers within a business-to-business context using the services of credit rating agencies, valuers, real estate agents, architects, and lawyers. Researchers have uncovered several key reasons for switching across different types of service providers and clients within the context of property markets: core service failures, external requirements, relationships, changes in client requirements, attraction by competitors and pricing (Levy and Lee 2009). It is thus important for any service provider to ascertain the reasons for their clients' decisions to leave them for their competitors. Finally, what are the success and failure rates across different PSFs and what do we know about clients switching service providers in different types of PSFs?

13.5 Future Research Agenda from Relevant Marketing Studies

With regard to organizing the marketing function, the general consensus among scholars is that marketing should continue to exist as a functional group (Greyser 1997; Varadarajan 1992; Webster 1997; Workman, Jr. et al. 1998). The *functional group perspective* focuses on marketing as a distinct organizational entity, while the *activity-based perspective* emphasizes things traditionally considered as marketing and sales activities (Workman, Jr. et al. 1998). For example, more than 30 years after the call to integrate sales and marketing activities, one study found no firms had adopted this recommendation (Workman, Jr. et al. 1998). Part of the reason is that: "if marketing is everybody's responsibility, it ends up being nobody's responsibility and the marketing skills of the organization atrophy" (Webster 1997: 66). This is particularly problematic for PSFs because professionals need to market themselves individually and some marketing needs to be devolved to the practice level. This devolution of marketing activity is necessary, yet does not replace the need to promote at a firm level and to take strategic marketing decisions at the firm level. Therefore, the hierarchical level at which marketing decisions and marketing activities are best made and executed is not clear.

Some research has developed a contingency approach to the structure and performance of marketing activities using the theoretical implications of traditional organization theory and transaction cost economics to explain the effectiveness, efficiency, and adaptiveness of various marketing organizational structures (Ruekert et al. 1985). Three basic propositions from the system-structural perspective emerge (Hage 1965; Pugh et al. 1968). First, centralization leads to greater effectiveness due to the ability of the decision-maker to plan, coordinate, and control activities. Second, formalization leads to greater efficiency because such rules serve to routinize repetitive activities and transactions. Formalization and centralization tend to be positively related, and they both vary inversely with specialization/differentiation (Hage 1965). Third, greater specialization/differentiation leads to increased adaptiveness, because specialists understand problems more clearly, adapt more readily to change, and discover new ways of doing things (Ruekert et al. 1985). From these considerations, four archetypal organizational forms for the marketing function can be identified: organic, relational, bureaucratic, and transactional (Ruekert et al. 1985), of which the latter seems best suited to PSFs. However, many questions still remain unanswered such as: how this might vary by type of professional service such as law firm versus management consultancy or health professionals and between small, medium, and large firms where the ability and need to formalize, centralize, and specialize can be very different.

Of the eight Ps of services marketing, the PSF literature has little to say on many and nothing to say on some. For example, Place, or availability of PSFs and how to innovate in that sphere remains largely unexplored. Although there is anecdotal evidence that practically PSFs manage the element of physical evidence well, there is little research into the whys and wherefores of the selection of physical evidence to represent their services. The element of people is dealt with extensively elsewhere in this volume (Mawdsley and Somaya, Chapter 10), but very little work has considered how services are delivered and the processes behind their delivery. The literature also has little to say on productivity of service providers and how PSFs could address this issue. In addition, as Peter Drucker explains, the purpose of marketing is to make selling superfluous, which means getting the service right in the first place, so that the persuasive art of personal selling is not required. Thus, there is a need to understand that marketing is more than promotion and adoption of marketing philosophy; practice is more of a change management issue, rather than a marketing issue.

Traditionally, the marketing literature has shown the effect of the price/quality relationship which shows the higher the price, the higher the perceived quality *ceteris paribus* (Suk et al. 2012) and this has implications for reputation management. However, pricing decisions in PSFs often fall into the category of what is called "cost-plus" pricing (Scardino et al. 2005). While this is a feasible way to price service goods, it is not necessarily the most effective way, with respect to overall profit, to approach the pricing problem. The capacity and value based pricing (CVBP) model for professional services was derived out of a need for a new way to think about how professional service "products" should be priced in a competitive marketplace (Wardell et al. 2008). Although reputation plays a critical role in determining procurement choices as well as perceptions about relative quality (Greenwood et al. 2005), the process through which PSFs project their reputations through pricing is not clear, particularly as they do not necessarily know, unlike their clients, what other PSFs charge.

13.6 CONCLUSIONS

This chapter has analyzed the research on marketing and reputation within PSFs. We have problematized the notion of marketing within PSFs and demonstrated that it is generally poorly understood and implemented. We also introduced the term reputation, which has often been conflated with other related terms such as identity and image, which has made it difficult to define and measure. We focused on the antecedents and consequences of reputation within PSFs, which is important because there are tangible positive and negative outcomes for organizations that hold particular reputations. Finally, we highlighted that marketing and reputation within PSFs are nascent areas of research and therefore remain poorly understood. Hence, we outlined in depth some potential avenues for future research which need greater scholarly attention.

REFERENCES

Aaker, D. A. (1996). "Measuring Brand Equity across Products and Markets," *California Management Review* 38(3): 102–120.

Albert, S. and Whetten, D. A. (1985) "Organizational Identity," in *Research in Organizational Behaviour*, ed. L. L. Cummings and B. M. Staw. Greenwich, CT: JAI Press, vol. 7, 263–295.

American Marketing Association (2013). "Definition of Marketing—American Marketing Association." <http://www.marketingpower.com/AboutAMA/Pages/Definitionof Marketing.aspx> (accessed January 30, 2014).

Amonini, C., McColl-Kennedy, J. R., Soutar, G. N., and Sweeney, J. C. (2010). "How Professional Service Firms Compete in the Market: An Exploratory Study," *Journal of Marketing Management* 26(1–2): 28–55.

Amorim, C. and Kipping, M. (1999). "Selling Consultancy Services: The Portuguese Case in Historical and Comparative Perspective," *Business and Economic History* 28(2): 45–56.

Bagdoniene, L. and Jakstaite, R. (2009). "Trust as Basis for Development of Relationships between Professional Service Providers and their Clients," *Economics & Management* 14: 360–366.

Barnett, M. L., Jermier, J. M., and Lafferty, B. A. (2006). "Corporate Reputation: The Definitional Landscape," *Corporate Reputation Review* 9(1): 26–38.

Beatty, R. P. and Ritter, J. R. (1986). "Investment Banking, Reputation, and the Underpricing of Initial Public Offerings," *Journal of Financial Economics* 15(1): 213–232.

Berry, L. L. (2000). "Cultivating Service Brand Equity," *Journal of the Academy of Marketing Science* 28(1): 128–137.

Berscheid, E. and Peplau L. A. (1983). "The Emerging Science of Relationships," in *Close Relationships*, ed. H. H. Kelley, E. Berscheid, A. Christensen, J. H. Harvey, T. L. Huston, G. Levinger, E. McClintock, L. A. Peplau, and D. R. Peterson. New York: Freeman, 1–19.

Bolton, R. N. (1998). "A Dynamic Model of the Duration of the Customer's Relationship with a Continuous Service Provider: The Role of Satisfaction," *Marketing Science* 17(1): 45–65.

Bromley, D. B. (2002). "Comparing Corporate Reputations: League Tables, Quotients, Benchmarks, or Case Studies," *Corporate Reputation Review* 5(1): 35–50.

Brown, T. J., Churchill Jr., G. A., and Peter, J. P. (1993). "Improving the Measurement of Service Quality," *Journal of Retailing* 69(1): 127–139.

Brown, T. J., Dacin, P. A., Pratt, M. G., and Whetten, D. A. (2006). "Identity, Intended Image, Construed Image, and Reputation: An Interdisciplinary Framework and Suggested Terminology," *Journal of the Academy of Marketing Science* 34: 99–106.

Cater, B. and Cater, T. (2009). "Emotional and Rational Motivations for Customer Motivations for Customer Loyalty in Business-to-Business Professional Services," *Service Industries Journal* 29(8): 1151–1169.

Cater, B. and Zabkar, V. (2009). "Antecedents and Consequences of Commitment in Marketing Services: The Client's Perspective," *Industrial Marketing Management* 38(7): 785–797.

Chambers, E. G., Foulon, M., Handfield-Jones, H., Hankin, S. M., and Michaels, E. G. (1998). "The War for Talent," *McKinsey Quarterly* 1(3): 44–57.

Chan, K. W., Yim, C. K., and Lam, S. S. K. (2010). "Is Customer Participation in Value Creation a Double-Edged Sword? Evidence from Professional Financial Services Across Cultures," *Journal of Marketing* 74(3): 48–64.

Chiou, J.-S. and Droge, C. (2006). "Service Quality, Trust, Specific Asset Investment, and Expertise: Direct and Indirect Effects in a Satisfaction-Loyalty Framework," *Journal of the Academy of Marketing Science* 34(4): 613–627.

Chun, R. (2005). "Corporate Reputation: Meaning and Measurement," *International Journal of Management Reviews* 7(2): 91–109.

Coleman, J. S. (1990). *Foundations of Social Theory*. Cambridge, MA: The Belknap Press of Harvard University Press.

Cronin Jr., J. J. and Taylor, S. A. (1994). "SERVPERF versus SERVQUAL: Reconciling Performance-Based and Perceptions-Minus-Expectations Measurement of Service Quality," *Journal of Marketing* 58(1): 125–131.

Dasgupta, P. (1988). "Trust as a Commodity," in *Trust: Making and Breaking Cooperative Relations*, ed. D. Gambetta. New York: Basil Blackwell, 47–72.

De Ruyter, K., Moorman, L., and Lemmink, J. (2001). "Antecedents of Commitment and Trust in Customer–Supplier Relationships in High Technology Markets," *Industrial Marketing Management* 30(3): 271–286.

Dwyer, F. R., Schurr, P. H., and Oh, S. (1987). "Developing Buyer–Seller Relationships," *Journal of Marketing* 51(2): 11–27.

Eisingerich, A. B. and Bell, S. J. (2007). "Maintaining Customer Relationships in High Credence Services," *Journal of Services Marketing* 21(4): 253–262.

Eriksson, C. B. and Lindvall, J. (2000). "Building Images." CRM2day. com Library. <http://www.crm2day.com/library/ap/ap0034.shtml/>.

Fang, L. H. (2005). "Investment Bank Reputation and the Price and Quality of Underwriting Services," *Journal of Finance* 60(6): 2729–2761.

Fombrun, C. J. (1996). *Reputation: Realizing Value from the Corporate Image*. Boston, MA: Harvard Business School Press.

Fombrun, C. J. (2012). "The Building Blocks of Corporate Reputation: Definitions, Antecedents, Consequences," in *The Oxford Handbook of Corporate Reputation*, ed. M. L. Barnett and T. G. Pollock. Oxford: Oxford University Press, 94–113.

Fombrun, C. J. and Shanley, M. (1990). "What's in a Name? Reputation Building and Corporate Strategy," *Academy of Management Journal* 33(2): 233–258.

Garry, T. (2007). "An Investigation into the Mediating Influence of Consumer Expertise on the Antecedents and Consequences of Affect within Professional Service Markets," *Journal of Marketing Management* 23(5–6): 461–481.

Geyskens, I., Steenkamp, J. B. E., Scheer, L. K., and Kumar, N. (1996). "The Effects of Trust and Interdependence on Relationship Commitment: A Trans-Atlantic Study," *International Journal of Research in Marketing* 13(4): 303–317.

Gillespie, N. A. and Mann, L. (2004). "Transformational Leadership and Shared Values: The Building Blocks of Trust," *Journal of Managerial Psychology* 19(6): 588–607.

Gilson, R. J. and Mnookin, R. H. (1989). "Coming of Age in a Corporate Law Firm: The Economics of Associate Career Patterns," *Stanford Law Review* 41(3): 567–595.

Glückler, J. and Armbrüster, T. (2003). "Bridging Uncertainty in Management Consulting: The Mechanisms of Trust and Networked Reputation," *Organization Studies* 24(2): 269–297.

Goleman, D. (1995). *Emotional Intelligence: Why It Can Matter More Than IQ*. London: Bloomsbury.

Gotsi, M. and Wilson, A. (2001). "Corporate Reputation Management: 'Living the Brand'," *Management Decision* 39(2): 99–104.

Gounaris, S. P. (2005). "Trust and Commitment Influences on Customer Retention: Insights from Business-to-Business Services," *Journal of Business Research* 58(2): 126–140.

Graffin, S. D., Bundy, J., Porac, J. F., Wade, J. B. and Quinn, D. P. (2013). "Falls from Grace and the Hazards of High Status: The 2009 British MP Expense Scandal and Its Impact on Parliamentary Elites," *Administrative Science Quarterly* 58(3): 313–345

Grandison, T. and Sloman, M. (2000). "A Survey of Trust in Internet Applications," *IEEE Communications Surveys & Tutorials* 3(4): 2–16.

Greenwood, R., Li, S. X., Prakesh, R., and Deephouse. D. L. (2005). "Reputation, Diversification, and Organizational Explanations of Performance in Professional Service Firms," *Organization Science* 16(6): 661–673.

Greyser, S. A. (1997). "Janus and Marketing: The Past, Present, and Prospective Future of Marketing," in *Reflections on the Futures of Marketing*, ed D. R. Lehmann and K. Jocz. Cambridge: Marketing Science Institute, 3–14.

Hacker, S., Willard, M., and Couturier, L. (2001). *The Trust Imperative: Performance Improvement Through Productive Relations*. Milwaukee, WI: Quality Press.

Hage, J. (1965). "An Axiomatic Theory of Organizations," *Administrative Science Quarterly* 10(3): 289–320.

Harste, R. and Richter, A. (2009). "Determinants of Client Loyalty for Consulting Services," *Academy of Management Proceedings* 1: 1–6.

Harvey, W. S. (2014). "Reputation in the International Context," in *International Human Resources Management*, ed. M. F. Özbilgin, D. Groutsis, and W. S. Harvey. Cambridge: Cambridge University Press, 165–178.

Harvey, W. S. and Morris T. (2012). "A Labor of Love? Understanding the Influence of Corporate Reputation in the Labor Market," in *The Oxford Handbook of Corporate Reputation*, ed. M. L. Barnett and T. G. Pollock. Oxford: Oxford University Press, 341–360.

Harvey, W. S., Morris, T., and Mueller, M. (2015). "Reaching for the Stars: Reputation Construction in Management Consulting" [Article under 2nd review].

Harvey, W. S., Morris, T., and Smets, M. (2013). "Corporate Reputation: Definitions and Dimensions," in *Law Firm Strategies for the 21st Century*, ed. C. H Vaagt. London: Globe Law and Business, 223–233.

Hayward, M. L., Rindova, V. P., and Pollock, T. G. (2004). "Believing One's Own Press: The Causes and Consequences of CEO Celebrity," *Strategic Management Journal* 25(7): 637–653.

Helm, S. (2007). "One Reputation or Many? Comparing Stakeholders' Perceptions of Corporate Reputation," *Corporate Communications: An International Journal* 12(3): 238–254.

Hitt, M. A., Bierman, L., Shimizu, K. and Kochhar, R. (2001). "Direct and Moderating Effects of Human Capital on Strategy and Performance in Professional Service Firms: A Resource-Based Perspective," *Academy of Management Journal* 44(1): 13–28.

Jøsang, A., Ismail, R., and Boyd, C. (2007). "A Survey of Trust and Reputation Systems for Online Service Provision," *Decision Support Systems* 43(2): 618–644.

Kaas, K. P. and Schade, C. (1995). "Unternehmensberater im Wettbewerb. Eine empirische Untersuchung aus der Perspektive der Neuen Institutionenlehre," *Zeitschrift für Betriebswirtschaft* 65(10): 1067–1089.

Kärreman, D. and Rylander, A. (2008). "Managing Meaning through Branding: The Case of a Consulting Firm," *Organization Studies* 29(1): 103–125.

Kidwell, B., Hardesty, D. M., Murtha, B. R., and Sheng, S. (2011). "Emotional Intelligence in Marketing Exchanges," *Journal of Marketing* 75(1): 78–95.

Kipping, M. (1999). "American Management Consulting Companies in Western Europe, 1920 to 1990: Products, Reputation, and Relationships," *Business History Review* 73(2): 190–220.

Kitay, J. and Wright, C. (2004). "Take the Money and Run? Organizational Boundaries and Consultants' Roles," *Service Industries Journal* 24(3): 1–18.

Klein, B. and Leffler, K. B. (1981). "The Role of Market Forces in Assuring Contractual Performance," *Journal of Political Economy* 89(4): 615–641.

Kumar, N., Scheer, L. K., and Steenkamp, J. B. E. (1995). "The Effects of Perceived Interdependence on Dealer Attitudes," *Journal of Marketing Research* 32(3): 348–356.

Kumar, V., Venkatesan, R., and Reinartz, W. (2008). "Performance Implications of Adopting a Customer-Focused Sales Campaign," *Journal of Marketing* 72(5): 50–68.

Lange, D., Lee, P. M., and Dai, Y. (2011). "Organizational Reputation: A Review," *Journal of Management* 37(1): 153–184.

Levy, D. S. and Lee, C. K. C. (2009). "Switching Behavior in Property Related Professional Services," *Journal of Property Research* 26(1): 87–103.

Lewicki, R. J., McAllister, D. J., and Bies, R. J. (1998). "Trust and Distrust: New Relationships and Realities," *Academy of Management Review* 23(3): 438–458.

Maister, D. H. (1997). *True Professionalism: The Courage to Care about Your People, Your Clients, and Your Career*. New York: Touchstone.

Malos, S. B. and Campion, M. A. (1995). "An Options-Based Model of Career Mobility in Professional Service Firms," *Academy of Management Review* 20(3): 611–644.

Maru, K. Cermak, D. S. P., and Prince, A. R. (1994). "Word-of-Mouth Effects in Professional Services Buyer Behaviour," *The Service Industries* 14(3): 301–314.

Mayer, J. D. and Salovey, P. (1995). "Emotional Intelligence and the Construction and Regulation of Feelings," *Applied and Preventive Psychology* 4(3): 197–208.

Mayer, R. C., Davis, J. H., and Schoorman, F. D. (1995). "An Integrative Model of Organization Trust," *Academy of Management Review* 20(3): 709–734.

Michaels, E., Handfield-Jones, H., and Axelrod, B. (2001). *The War for Talent*. Boston, MA: Harvard Business School Press.

Milgram, P. and Roberts, J. (1986). "Relying on the Information of Interested Buyers," *Rand Journal of Economics* 17(1): 18–32.

Morris, T. and Empson, L. (1998). "Organization and Expertise: An Exploration of Knowledge Bases and the Management of Accounting and Consulting Firms," *Accounting, Organizations and Society* 23(5–6): 609–624.

Nooteboom, B. (2000). *Learning and Innovation in Organizations and Economies*. Oxford: Oxford University Press.

Olorunniw, F. O. and Hsu, M. K. (2007). "An Investigation of Customer Experiences with Professional Services," *Marketing Quarterly* 29(2): 79–92.

Parasuraman, A., Zeithaml, V. A., and Berry, L. L. (1988). "Servqual," *Journal of Retailing* 64(1): 12–40.

Patterson, P. G., Johnson, L. W., and Spreng, R. A. (1997). "Modeling the Determinants of Customer Satisfaction for Business-to-Business Professional Services," *Journal of the Academy of Marketing Science* 25(1): 4–17.

Pfarrer, M. D., Pollock, T. G., and Rindova, V. P. (2010). "A Tale of Two Assets: The Effects of Firm Reputation and Celebrity on Earnings Surprises and Investors' Reactions," *Academy of Management Journal* 53(5): 1131–1152.

Podolny, J. M. (1993). "A Status-Based Model of Market Competition," *American Journal of Sociology* 98(4): 829–872.

Podolny, J. M. (1994). "Market Uncertainty and the Social Character of Economic Exchange," *Administrative Science Quarterly* 39(3): 458–483.

Pugh, D. S., Hickson, D. J., Hinings, C. R., and Turner, C. (1968). "Dimensions of Organization Structure," *Administrative Science Quarterly* 13(1): 65–105.

Putnam, R. D. (1995). "Bowling Alone: America's Declining Social Capital," *Journal of Democracy* 6(1): 65–78.

Rindova, V. P. and Fombrun, C. J. (1999). "Constructing Competitive Advantage: The Role of Firm-Constituent Interactions," *Strategic Management Journal* 20(8): 691–710.

Rindova, V. P., Petkova, A. P., and Kotha, S. (2006). "Standing Out: How New Firms in Emerging Markets Build Reputation," *Strategic Organization* 5(1): 31–70.

Rindova, V. P., Williamson, I. O., and Petkova, A. P. (2010). "Reputation as an Intangible Asset: Reflections on Theory and Methods in Two Empirical Studies of Business School Reputations," *Journal of Management* 36(3): 610–619.

Rindova, V. P., Williamson, I. O., Petkova, A. P., and Sever. J. M. (2005). "Being Good or Being Known: An Empirical Examination of the Dimensions, Antecedents, and Consequences of Organizational Reputation," *Academy of Management Journal* 48: 1033–1049.

Roberts, P. W. and Dowling, G. R. (2002). "Corporate Reputation and Sustained Superior Financial Performance," *Strategic Management Journal* 23(12): 1077–1093.

Rosenbaum, M. S., Massiah, C., and Jackson Jr., D. W. (2006). "An Investigation of Trust, Satisfaction, and Commitment on Repurchase Intentions in Professional Services," *Services Marketing Quarterly* 27(3): 115–135.

Ruekert, R. W., Walker Jr., O. C., and Roering, K. J. (1985). "The Organization of Marketing Activities: A Contingency Theory of Structure and Performance," *Journal of Marketing* 49(1): 13–25.

Scardino, L., Young, A., and Maurer, W. (2005). "Common Pricing Models and Best-Use Cases for IT Services and Outsourcing Contracts," *Gartner*, September.

Scott, S. G. and Lane, V. R. (2000). "A Stakeholder Approach to Organizational Identity," *Academy of Management Review* 25(1): 43–62.

Shapiro, C. (1982). "Optimal Pricing of Experience Goods," *The Bell Journal of Economics* 14(2): 497–507.

Sharma, N. and Patterson, P. (1999). "The Impact of Communication Effectiveness and Services Quality on Relationship Commitment in Consumer, Professional Services," *Journal of Service Marketing* 13(2): 151–170.

Sharma, N. and Patterson, P. (2000). "Switching Costs, Alternative Attractiveness and Experience as Moderators of Relationship Commitment in Professional, Consumer Services," *International Journal of Service Industry Management* 11(5): 470–490.

Sharp, B. (1996). "Brand Equity and Market-Based Assets of Professional Service Firms," *Journal of Professional Services Marketing* 13(1): 3–13.

Shostack, G. L. (1977). "Breaking Free from Product Marketing," *Journal of Marketing* 41(2): 73–80.

Sitkin, S. B. and Roth, N. L. (1993). "Explaining the Limited Effectiveness of Legalistic 'Remedies' for Trust/Distrust," *Organization Science* 4(3): 367–392.

Somaya, D., Williamson, I. O., and Lorinkova, N. (2008). "Gone But Not Lost: The Different Performance Impacts of Employee Mobility between Cooperators versus Competitors," *Academy of Management Journal* 51(5): 936–953.

Sonmez, M. and Moorhouse, A. (2010). "Purchasing Professional Services: Which Decision Criteria?" *Management Decision* 48(2): 189–206.

Stanton, N. (2014). 'Marketing Chiefs at City Law Firms Pocket Salaries of up to £477,000. *The Lawyer*. <http://www.thelawyer.com/analysis/the-lawyer-management/management-news/marketing-chiefs-at-city-law-firms-pocket-salaries-of-up-to-477000/3023839. article>.

Stigler, G. J. (1962). "Information in the Labor Market," *Journal of Political Economy* 70(5): 94–105.

Suk, K., Lee, J., and Lichtenstein, D. R. (2012). "The Influence of Price Presentation Order on Consumer Choice," *Journal of Marketing Research* 49(5): 708–717.

Swan, J. E., Trawick, I. F., and Silva, D. W. (1985). "How Industrial Salespeople Gain Customer Trust," *Industrial Marketing Management* 14(3): 203–211.

Tarique, I. and Schuler, R. S. (2010). "Global Talent Management: Literature Review, Integrative Framework, and Suggestions for Further Research," *Journal of World Business* 45(2): 122–133.

Varadarajan, P. R. (1992). "Marketing's Contribution to Strategy: The View from a Different Looking Glass," *Journal of the Academy of Marketing Science* 20(4): 335–343.

von Nordenflycht, A. (2010). "What is a Professional Service Firm? Toward a Theory and Taxonomy of Knowledge-Intensive Firms," *Academy of Management Review* 35(2): 155–174.

Walker, K. (2010). "A Systematic Review of the Corporate Reputation Literature: Definition, Measurement, and Theory," *Corporate Reputation Review* 12(4): 357–387.

Wardell, Clarence L. III., Wynter, L., and Helander, M. (2008). "Capacity and Value Based Pricing Model for Professional Services," *Journal of Revenue & Pricing* 7(4): 326–340.

Wartick, S. L. (2002). "Measuring Corporate Reputation: Definition and Data," *Business & Society* 41(4): 371–392.

Webster, F. E. (1997), "The Future Role of Marketing in the Organization," in *Reflections on the Futures of Marketing*, ed. D. R. Lehmann and K. E. Jocz. Cambridge, MA: Marketing Science Institute, 39–66.

Wetzels, M., De Ruyter, K., and Van Birgelen, M. (1998). "Marketing Service Relationships: The Role of Commitment," *Journal of Business & Industrial Marketing* 13(4/5): 406–423.

Whetten, D. A. (1997). "Part II: Where Do Reputations Come From? Theory Development and the Study of Corporate Reputation," *Corporate Reputation Review* 1(1): 25–34.

Workman, Jr., J. P., Homburg, C., and Gruner, K. (1998). "Marketing Organization: An Integrative Framework of Dimensions and Determinants," *Journal of Marketing* 63(2): 21–41.

CHAPTER 14

CLIENT RELATIONSHIPS IN PROFESSIONAL SERVICE FIRMS

JOSEPH P. BROSCHAK

14.1 INTRODUCTION

THE study of client relationships is central to scholarship on Professional Service Firms (PSFs). By definition, a PSF's very existence depends on having client relationships. Most researchers would agree that PSFs can be viewed as knowledge-intensive organizations, composed of individuals with prolonged and specialized training in an abstract body of knowledge, who customize their efforts for clients, exhibit a high degree of discretionary effort and exercise personal judgment in the delivery of their service, and who operate under the constraints of professional norms (Løwendahl 1997; Fosstenløkken et al. 2003; von Nordenflycht 2010). But this definition is incomplete and focusing on it alone would mistakenly lead one to believe it is possible to examine the structure and functioning of PSFs independent of any attention to client relationships.

PSFs have other important defining characteristics. The output of PSFs is intangible and impossible to hold in inventory (Mills and Margulies 1980; Sharma 1997), and professional services are co-produced through the coordinated efforts of professional service and client firms, often customized for individual clients (Bowen and Jones 1986; Larsson and Bowen 1989; Løwendahl 1997; Sharma 1997). Under the expanded definition, client relationships are essential to the activities and ongoing viability of PSFs. Understanding the nature and dynamics of client relationships is critical to developing in-depth knowledge about how PSFs are organized, are managed, and perform.

Client relationships are also important for PSFs because they are key strategic assets. The ability of PSFs to form and maintain client relationships is critical to maintaining these assets and ultimately to firm survival. The extent to which PSFs differ in their client relationship acquisition and management capabilities can be an important determinant of differential firm performance. Further, a PSF's portfolio of client relationships is an overall indicator of firm strategy. The number of client relationships and the distributional properties of a firm's portfolio of clients determine how PSFs compete and identify their market position relative to rivals in the competition for professional services (Baker et al. 1998).

Client relationships are significant for PSFs, yet surprisingly the amount of research focusing squarely on client relationships is modest. This reflects the general tendency among management scholars to cede the research domain of market relationships to marketing researchers and economists. Organizational scholars of professional services and PSFs are more likely to simply assume the existence of client relationships rather than make client relationships an explicit object of study.

The purpose of this chapter is to draw together the existing body of empirical research and conceptual thinking on relationships between PSFs and client firms and provide a comprehensive review of the research area. As a starting point I used von Nordenflycht's (2010) typology of professional services and identified research studies across a range of professional services that explicitly addressed client relationships. This process uncovered studies of accounting, advertising, architecture, engineering consulting, investment banking, law, management consulting, and public relations, with the majority focusing on client relationships in the areas of accounting, advertising, and law. Across all of the studies reviewed, researchers approached client relationships from one of two levels of analysis: the *dyadic level*, by examining relationships between a single PSF and client firm (Fichman and Goodman 1996), or the *portfolio level*, by emphasizing a PSF's set of client relationships (Baker et al. 1998; Broschak 2004). Most of the studies that were identified utilized data from either the United States or the United Kingdom, with a small number of studies set in other European countries, and few studies conducted elsewhere. In the concluding section of this chapter on future research, I address the implications of the sample's characteristics for furthering our knowledge and understanding of PSF–client relationships.

The chapter is organized around three themes. First, I examine the different ways that client relationships have been characterized in prior research. I highlight the different types of client relationships that have been identified or proposed and explain how these characterizations shape the attention of researchers; what aspects of client relationships are attended to and what assumptions researchers make about how client relationships should be studied and managed. Second, I organize the state of knowledge about client relationships around different phases of relationships, focusing on the three phenomena that are most widely studied: relationship formation, relationship performance and maintenance, and relationship dissolution. Third, building on the understanding that PSFs are not inert actors in client relationships, I review what has identified or proposed from existing research on how PSFs are affected and change as a result of the client relationships they maintain. I conclude the chapter by identifying some critical gaps in our knowledge of client relationships, and propose several promising directions for future research.

14.2 CHARACTERIZING CLIENT RELATIONSHIPS

14.2.1 Relational vs. Transactional Client Relationships

A number of researchers have identified different ways that PSF–client relationships can be characterized. How client relationships are characterized is important because it is an indicator of the attributes of firms and the behavior of professionals and managers that are likely related to the success of client relationships. The dominant perspective has long been that client relationships are inherently relational, particularly when compared to customer relationships involving manufactured products (Bowen and Jones 1986; Larsson and Bowen 1989; Maister 1993). The move to characterize PSF–client relationships as relational originated in the marketing literature where relational marketing was promoted as a way for marketers to differentiate the marketing of services from the marketing of products (Gronroos 1980; Berry 1983). Client relationships that are relational tend to be long term, involve regular and extensive interaction between the two firms, and are founded on attributes such as attraction, trust, and commitment (Halinen 1997).

The logic behind characterizing all client relationships as relational stems from the defining features of PSFs and professional services. Because the output of PSFs is co-produced through the coordinated efforts of the PSF and the client firm, close contact and ongoing communication between the two firms is necessary for the delivery of services to occur (Mills and Margulies 1980; Bowen and Jones 1986; Larsson and Bowen 1989; Sharma 1997). Due to the necessity for ongoing communication, client relationships logically need to be relational. PSFs are also knowledge-based organizations whose primary agents are individuals who have prolonged specialized training in a body of abstract knowledge and whose output is intangible and impossible to hold in inventory (Mills and Margulies 1980; Lowendhal 1997; Sharma 1997). Consequently, professionals have expertise that is outside the technical knowledge of their clients, while the work-related behaviors of professionals are difficult for clients to observe and assess. As a result, clients are often unable to evaluate or measure the output of a PSF (Bowen and Jones 1986; Larsson and Bowen 1989). These characteristics create information asymmetry and uncertainty, two conditions that are common to all PSF–client relationships (Mills and Moshavi 1999).

Information asymmetry in client relationships refers to how informed parties are about each other in a contractual relationship, to the differing amount of information clients and service providers have that must be shared for the professional service to be performed, and to the fact that clients and service providers may have different understandings of the information that needs to be shared (Mills and Moshavi 1999; Bagdoniene and Jakstaite 2009). Uncertainty refers to the number of behavioral contingencies that are available to professionals in the conduct of their service and to the inability of clients to predict those behaviors and their consequences in advance (Klein

1983). The existence of information asymmetry and uncertainty makes it difficult for clients to characterize problems to their professional service provider, to explain exactly what they want from their PSF, and to objectively evaluate any benefits they receive from the professional services provided (Bagdoniene and Jakstaite 2009). One way these problems can be mitigated is by being relational; taking a long-term perspective on the exchange and having relationships between client and PSFs that are based on trust and commitment (Halinen 1997).

Despite the convincing logic that client relationships work best when they are relational, other researchers have adopted a different perspective and argued that client relationships can be categorized as either relational or transactional. Whereas relational client relationships are long-lasting and involve considerable interaction between firms, transactional client relationships resemble the competitive markets of neo-classical economics where client firms are indifferent between suppliers. Transactional client relationships are short-lived and episodic, with clients keeping PSFs at arm's length, dispersing business among many competitors, limiting the amount and type of information that is shared, and letting price and profit, rather than commitment, drive relationships (Uzzi 1997). Baker (1990), in a study of investment banking services, found that corporations indeed developed long-term (relational) relationships with one or a few banks to take advantage of their trust in specific bankers and the relationship-working knowledge that developed between the two firms. But client firms also used other banks on a transactional basis, and rarely relied solely on relational service provider–client relationships for investment banking services.

Not only can dyadic client relationships be characterized as relational or transactional, but because firms may maintain portfolios of relationships, the characteristics of a firm's set of client relationships serve as an indicator of it having a relational or transactional orientation towards markets for professional services. Baker (1990) observed that the relative proportion of relational and transactional relationships maintained by client firms was an indicator of whether firms preferred long-term, stable relationships or short-term transactions with PSFs. Though this insight about a firm's portfolio of relationships indicating its market orientation was developed by studying client firms, the logic extends to PSFs. The extent to which a PSF is more relational or more transactional in their approach towards interacting with clients is reflected in the characteristics of its portfolio of client relationships.

A key issue with the dichotomous characterization is how one determines whether client relationships are relational or transactional. Most frequently, being relational is demarked by relationship duration. As Levinthal and Fichman (1988) first demonstrated, auditor–client relationships tend to become stronger over time. They argued this occurred because relationships become more relational due to the relationship-specific investments firms and individuals make over time. A firm's investments may be in the form of routines, proprietary software, or capital investments in facilities (Levinthal and Fichman 1988). Individuals separately make investments in relationship-specific skills, in-depth knowledge of their exchange partner's business, and personal relationships with their exchange partner counterparts (Uzzi 1996; Broschak 2004). The actual investments clients and PSFs make in client relationships are rarely, if ever assessed. Instead, duration is used as a proxy on the presumption that investments in client relationships grow over time, and client relationships become more and more embedded in social relationships (Granovetter 1985). To the extent that researchers have tried to quantify when client relationships are relational, relationship durations of as short as two years have been used to mark the threshold for the transactional–relational transition (Uzzi and Lancaster 2003, 2004). But there is little justification given for choosing a duration threshold, and more research is needed to better understand the point at which client relationships can no longer be considered transactional. Still, in general, one way of thinking about client relationships is that they progress from starting transactional when first formed and becoming relational over time.

Measurement issues also cloud how a firm's portfolio of client relationships is seen an indicator of a relational market orientation. Two measures tend to be prevalent in the literature: the number of client relationships a PSF maintains, and the average duration of a firm's portfolio of client relationships. No clear thresholds have been reported in the literature that distinguishes a relational from a transactional orientation towards markets for professional services; rather having qualitatively fewer client relationships or a qualitatively higher average duration among its client relationships indicates a more relational market orientation for PSFs (Broschak 2004).

While the relational–transactional dichotomy is prominent in the literature characterizing client relationships, Laing and Lian (2005) suggested that client relationships displayed greater variation than the simple dichotomy could capture. They classified client relationships into five different "ideal" types that were ordered to reflect being increasingly relational: elementary (similar to transactional relationships), interactive, embedded, partnering, and integration relationships. They established specific criteria (degree of trust, amount of relational closeness, and type of organizational policy) to facilitate discriminating one ideal-type relationship from another. But their key insight was that client relationships do not necessarily evolve from transactional to relational. Rather, client relationship type is a strategic choice that is made by clients, or made jointly by clients and PSFs.

14.2.2 Sources of Variation in Client Relationships

The extent to which client relationships are more or less relational may hinge on contingencies other than relationship duration or strategic choice. One such contingency is the type of professional services. Mills and Margulies's (1980: 260–264) typology of professional services is useful for understanding how different professional services have different demands for the extent of information sharing, the level of interaction between the PSF and client, and the extent to which clients are able to define problems and evaluate solutions. Auditing and investment banking conform to "maintenance-interactive" services in which client relationships tend to involve cosmetic, continuous interactions; auditors' and bankers' technical expertise is applied to solving discrete problems which clients typically understand and are aware of, and for which they can evaluate whether the professionals are solving the problems appropriately. Advertising, engineering, and management consulting are examples of "task-interactive" services, in which client relationships are slightly more complex. Clients are often able to define the problems to be solved (i.e., declining sales), but the technical expertise of advertising agencies or consulting companies is used to devise novel and varied techniques to problem-solving, techniques which clients typically find difficult to fully evaluate. Finally, law is most closely related to "personal-interactive" services which involve complex and highly personal interactions between law firms and client firms. Clients in general may be unaware of, or unable to precisely define, what will best serve their interests or how to go about finding a solution to their needs. Client firms become highly dependent on law firms because each task and each client–service firm interaction may require novel solutions or complex decisions by their law firm. Mills and Margulies's (1980) typology suggests that task-interactive and personal-interactive professional services are more likely to face demands for relational client relationships than maintenance-interactive professional services.

Malhotra and Morris (2009) similarly argue that the nature of client relationships differs across different types of professional services. Comparing law, accounting, and engineering consulting, they propose that professional services differ in the frequency of face-to-face communication that is required between the client and service provider, and in the degree of client capture; the extent to which clients have control over, or can influence, the service production process. Frequency of face-to-face communication and degree of client capture likely vary with the complexity and demands of the professional service provided as well as the characteristics of the two firms (e.g., relative size), and are proposed to affect, in turn, the physical structure of professional services firms (e.g., the geographic dispersion of offices) and the structure of pricing for professional services.

Another contingency may be PSFs' strategy for customizing or commoditizing their services for clients (Hansen et al. 1999; Greenwood and Empson 2003). While definitions of PSFs often imply that professional services are customized for clients, PSFs in fields such as auditing and management consulting sometimes pursue strategies where they reuse existing solutions making only minor adjustments to align the solution with different situations for new clients (Hansen et al. 1999). And because customized solutions require more collegial interaction with clients than commoditized solutions (Greenwood and Empson 2003), a PSF's strategy may influence the extent to which client relationships are relational.

Even within any particular professional service, firms may choose to pursue different models for how they interact with clients. For instance, in the domain of consultant–client relationships, Nikolova et al. (2009) identified three different models that are commonly attributed to client–consulting firm interactions. An "expert model" is one in which consultants behave as experts who hold positions of power in the relationship due to their possessing knowledge that is unavailable to their clients. As content knowledge experts, consultants are best equipped to correctly interpret and decide upon a client's needs and develop effective solutions. The role of clients is primarily one of information supplier without being actively involved in the creative part of the problem-solving process. A "critical model" views consultant–client relationships skeptically as impression management exercises. Professionals' expert knowledge is socially constructed rather than objective, and is dependent on maintaining perceived legitimacy by articulating a specific, yet ambiguous, language to clients (Alvesson 1993). Consultants attempt to impress and persuade clients through the use of management rhetoric which substitutes for an ambiguous, vague knowledge base. Clients in turn are passive actors who neither completely understand nor are capable of evaluating the actions of consultants. Finally, a "social-learning" model views clients and consultants as jointly involved in the problem-solving process. Both parties have valuable knowledge to contribute to generating potential solutions to clients' problems, and the consultant–client interaction becomes an exercise in communicating effectively, and developing a shared meaning and understanding. Each model represents a different approach consultants take to interacting with clients. While they have traditionally been viewed as independent models of consultant–client relationships, Nikolova et al. (2009) suggest that most consultant–client relationships actually contain elements of all three. Consultant behaviors in client relationships are contingent on the extent to which one model dominates over the others.

The institutional context also acts as a contingency that influences the extent to which client relationships are relational or transactional. For instance, industry norms regarding the continuity of client relationships tend to vary over time. Eccles and Crane (1988) presented evidence that client relationships involving US investment banks were relational during the decade of the 1970s, but gave way to transactional norms during the 1980s. Baker et al. (1998), studying US advertising, found the opposite pattern. Client relationships behaved more as transactions during the 1970s and 1990s but were much more relational, and less likely to dissolve, in the decade of the 1980s. Though the temporal pattern of industry norms varies across professional services, the evidence suggests that client relationships may wax and wane over time in the extent to which they are relational or transactional. Other researchers have noted that norms regarding the extent to which client relationships are relational vary across national contexts. Studies of law firms (Muzio and Faulconbridge 2013) and global advertising agencies (McCormick et al. 2014) demonstrate that the tendency for client relationships to be relational, or the likelihood that client relationships dissolve, is stronger in some geographic regions than in others. Finally, a shift in institutional logics from a professional logic to a financial logic may lead to the diffusion of new business models that dictate firms focus on pursuing larger transactions in global markets at the expense of maintaining smaller, ongoing client relationships (Faulconbridge and Muzio 2009; Thornton et al. 2012). Regardless of the specific driver, the idea that institutional pressures affect the extent to which client relationships are relational suggests that researchers should exercise caution in generalizing empirical findings from one institutional context to another.

The review of research on characterizing client relationships illustrates that the long-held assumption that all client relationships are relational may not be valid. Client relationships exhibit considerable variation both within and across professional services. The nature of a client relationship determines how firms and individual professionals behave, and, as we will point out in the next section, the attributes of PSFs and client relationships that are deemed important to PSF success.

At least two research questions merit further investigation. First, must client relationships be relational in order for firms and client relationships to be successful? Or can firms and relationships achieve success by being transactional? Relatively little research has tried to link the characteristics of client relationships to the performance of PSFs. Second, does the nature of client relationships vary widely with contingencies as researchers have intimated or are there commonalities in client relationships across different strategies, types of professional services, and over time?

14.3 CLIENT RELATIONSHIP PHENOMENA

Like most social relationships, client relationships exhibit a life cycle pattern. Relationships are formed, relationships develop and are maintained, and relationships end. While researchers have proposed a variety of complicated models for depicting the life cycle of client relationships (see Halinen 1997 for a review), we utilize the simple formation–maintenance–dissolution framework to organize the existing body of research and assess the state of knowledge about the dynamics of PSF–client relationships.

14.3.1 Client Relationship Formation

The decision to form client relationships is an activity fraught with considerable uncertainty because there is a scarcity of information about potential exchange partners. Power is asymmetrically distributed in markets for PSFs. Clients generally have more power and incentive to form ties despite the fact that client relationships are typically more consequential for PSFs. Yet trying to assess and compare PSFs for the purpose of selecting an exchange partner is difficult. Because the output of PSFs is intangible and the work-related behaviors of professionals are difficult to directly observe, there is little objective data for clients to use in evaluating the output or processes of PSFs. Thus, clients face high uncertainty discerning differences in the performance or capabilities of rival PSFs, key attributes in successful client relationships.

Due to the high uncertainty, clients rely on social signals to infer the quality and attractiveness of PSFs as prospective partners. One signal that suggests quality and thus influences the formation of client relationships is PSF reputation (Greenwood and Empson 2003). In studies of law and accounting, having a positive reputation increases a PSF's ability to attract clients because reputation is a surrogate for quality (Greenwood et al. 2005; Kim 2009). Reputation can be inferred from several different sources.

Relationships with other high-status clients, third-party ties to high-reputation peer firms, and network ties to prominent professionals in one's field are all indicators of a positive reputation (Greenwood et al. 2005; Kim 2009). Similarly, being referred to clients by other high-status clients or competitors enhances a PSF's reputation (Kim 2009). Positive media coverage is yet another source of reputation that increases the likelihood of forming new client relationships (Greenwood et al. 2005).

Some client firms may attend to the demographic characteristics of PSFs in making decisions to form exchange relationships. For instance, in markets for advertising services, size and scope matching often drives the formation of client relationships as clients infer higher quality when advertising agencies are similar in size or geographic scope to the client or to the demands of a client's project (von Nordenflycht 2011). Han (1994) reported similar results regarding size-matching in auditor–client relationships. Clients of advertising services also tend to form relationships with advertising agencies that are similar in size or market orientation (relational vs. transactional) to a previous advertising agency the client had used because similarity to one's previous service providers reduces the uncertainty over exchange partner selection (Broschak and Niehans 2006). Firm size and scope are not the only demographic characteristics that influence client relationship formation. Heinz et al. (2001) and Ashley and Empson (2013) noted that corporate clients of law firms preferred dealing with law firms where lawyers resembled themselves, suggesting that homophily processes play a role in forming law firm–client relationships (McPherson et al. 2001).

In general, clients have a strong preference to deal with known others, what is often referred to as the principle of social embeddedness (Granovetter 1985). Because prior social relationships reduce uncertainty over an exchange and reduce the costs of monitoring one's exchange partners, managers and executives in client organizations prefer forming relationships with PSFs with whom they have had prior dealings or who employ professionals with whom they have personal relationships or know through other social settings (Broschak and Niehans 2006; Somaya et al. 2008; Block et al. 2014). But the extent to which clients prefer forming relationships with PSFs they know well may be contingent on the task to be performed. Richter and Niewiem (2009) found that clients preferred to involve consultants with whom they already had a close relationship only when client-specific or proprietary knowledge was involved. Clients were more likely to involve consultants with whom they had no relationship when projects required functional, industry-specific, or methodological knowledge. The implication of this is that consulting firms may pay a price for developing in-depth relationships with clients as they may no longer be perceived as functional or industry specialists.

Though the power to form client relationships often rests with clients, PSFs are not passive actors in the relationship formation process. Managers and executives of PSFs often solicit and develop relationships with clients of competitors because personal knowledge and experience with a potential service provider creates trust that can serve as the foundation for forming new client relationships (Macaulay 1963; Granovetter 1985). PSFs can actively signal to potential clients their legitimacy as a service provider by selecting appropriate persuasive rhetoric when they pitch themselves to try and win clients' business. For instance, a study of entrepreneurial firms in architecture demonstrated that firms presenting themselves to potential government clients using a "professional" rhetoric were more effective at winning new business than firms that used either a "business" or a "state" rhetoric to describe themselves (Jones et al. 2010). PSFs that understand how potential clients see themselves relative to the profession's domain, and utilize this knowledge in presenting themselves to clients, are likely to be more effective at signaling legitimacy and at securing new client relationships. Bettencourt et al. (2002) suggested that professional service terms take an active role in the client selection process by selecting clients on the basis of their cultural and goal compatibility with the PSF, which was likely to lead to a more successful client relationship. Because of asymmetrical power in PSF markets, this prescription may be best applied to the choice of clients PSFs pursue rather than those they select.

One last point is that the ability to form client relationships is not unbridled in all markets for professional services. Institutional forces governing the exclusivity of client relationships and the choice of clients vary across professional services. For instance, in the case of auditing in the US, the Securities Act of 1993 legally mandates that corporate clients acquire an audit for its financial statements from an independent CPA firm and restricts corporations from using more than one auditor at a time (Han 1994). In contrast, markets for advertising have no formal rules setting limits on the allowable number of client relationships, but do have norms about the allowable competitive overlap in the markets of an advertising agency's set of clients (Baker et al. 1998). Further, powerful institutional actors such as investors and financial analysts often exert influence over a client's choice of PSFs. For example, Mathur and Mathur (1996) reported that publicly-traded US clients experienced negative wealth effects when they announced the formation of new client relationships with small, young agencies because investors and analysts preferred clients work with larger, older agencies. Thus the extent to which PSFs are free to pursue particular client relationships appears to vary across professional services due to variations in institutional pressures. More research that explicitly considers the professional context in which client relationships are formed is needed to better develop a fine-grained understanding of how, when, and with whom client relationships are formed.

14.3.2 Client Relationship Maintenance and Performance

Studies that address the maintenance of client relationships tend to focus almost completely on dyadic client relationships and adopt the position that the continuity or renewal of client relationships is a primary goal for PSFs, regardless of whether PSFs have a relational or transactional market orientation. Researchers have identified a number of reasons why maintaining existing client relationships is an important outcome for PSFs. In some professional services existing client relationships are an important source of revenue, with Ram (1999) reporting that as much as 60–80% of management consulting contracts come from a PSF's secure business. Having long-term client relationships increases the level of trust between client and PSFs, reduces information asymmetries, promotes the sharing of private or fine-grained information, reduces uncertainty over the actions and behaviors of exchange partners, and lowers relationship monitoring costs (Uzzi 1999; Uzzi and Lancaster 2003, 2004; Lancaster and Uzzi 2012). Clients can benefit as well because PSFs such as banks and law firms that maintain larger proportions of relational client relationships tend to offer clients lower prices (Uzzi and Lancaster 2003; Lancaster and Uzzi 2012).

Some researchers have argued that there is a downside to PSFs maintaining close relationships with clients. Client managers whose firms are in close, long-term relationships with management consulting firms are reportedly more willing to challenge or criticize their service providers, to negotiate for lower prices, and to pressure consultants to provide politically correct recommendations (Ram 1999). These downsides may produce higher levels of conflict that puts stress on client relationships, and raises questions about whether clients behave as "partial employees" of PSFs in the co-production process as is commonly assumed (Mills and Morris 1986), or whether professionals in long-term client relationships are captured by clients. Because the tendency is for researchers to emphasize the benefits of long-term client relationships, research that examines both their costs and benefits is needed to more fairly assess the relative merits of relational vs. transactional client relationships.

Researchers generally attribute responsibility for maintaining client relationships to PSFs even though the power to make and break client relationships lies more clearly with client firms (Baker et al. 1998; Broschak and Block 2014). PSFs can strengthen client relationships through a number of pathways. Trust, which is reviewed in greater depth elsewhere in this volume (Harvey and Mitchell, Chapter 13) is fundamental to maintaining strong client relationships. Heightened trust in studies of client relationships is related to PSFs minimizing conflict with clients and fulfilling client's expectations of performance quality, which increases client commitment to the relationship (LaBahn and Kohli 1997; Gluckler 2005).

Conflict in client relationships often arises around concerns over knowing each other's businesses, contributing to a consistent communication flow (Bourland 1993). A number of tactics have been proposed by researchers to help PSFs minimize conflict and promote smooth working client relationships. Specifying the client's roles in the co-production of services can reduce role ambiguity and promote role clarity, thereby reducing conflict (Bettencourt et al. 2002). Mills and Moshavi (1999) proposed that professional concern, the paradox of getting close to but remaining detached from clients, was a key factor in managing client relationships, and they identified client role accountability as one important dimension of professional concern. But as Alvesson et al. (2009) cautioned, clients and their roles in client relationships are not monolithic. Clients are diverse and roles are socially constructed, varying across firms, industries, and time, in part due to changing interactions with PSFs. Therefore, client roles are best viewed as negotiated in an ongoing manner over the course of a relationship rather than as a fixed structure common to all client relationships.

Manning et al. (2011) argued that client relationships can be strengthened by making client-specific investments in infrastructure and training, by developing a high degree of interdependence with the client organization, and maintaining a high frequency of client interaction. Davies (2009), in a study of UK advertising, suggested that a high level of quality interaction with clients creates conditions where clients have greater tolerance for service quality shortfalls. Thus regular and detailed communication can help sustain client relationships.

Finally, in studies of management consulting, researchers have suggested that clients respond to the choice of rhetoric professionals use in communicating with clients. Consultants can help maintain existing client relationships by using rhetoric that assures clients they have purchased a high-quality service, and provides a sense of security to client managers about the consultant's expertise and the technical rationality of their proposed solutions (Sturdy 1997; Fincham 1999).

Surprisingly, there are few studies that have tried to link the structure or functioning of client relationships to PSF performance. Greenwood et al. (2005) found that an accounting firm's reputation was positively related to firm financial performance while Hitt et al. (2006) found that among American law firms having relational capital (e.g., long-term client relationships) is positively associated with positive financial performance. Somaya et al. (2008) found that the movement of human capital between law firms and clients, and into law firms from competitors, enhances firm performance. Elsewhere, Hui et al. (2008) demonstrated that sharing responsibility for engineering design work between a client and PSF rather than having it owned by one or the other firm, resulted in poorer performance on complex projects due to the difficulties of coordinating reciprocally independent work across the client–service firm boundary. But generally, the link between client relationships and performance outcomes for PSFs has not been studied in any depth.

One caveat to the research on maintaining client relationships is that a PSF's ability to promote longevity of client relationships may be contingent on institutional context. Several studies have reported that the duration of advertising agency–client relationships tended to be longer in developed countries and much shorter in developing countries such as Turkey (Gulsoy 2012) and China (Prendergast et al. 2001), and in countries where clients were more business- than relationship-oriented, such as the Netherlands (Verbeke 1988). Research that compares the tactics and longevity of client relationships across different national contexts may shed light on the widespread applicability of researchers' prescriptions to maintain client relationships.

14.3.3 Client Relationship Dissolution

An emerging area of research in the study of PSFs is on understanding why client relationships end. I use the word end rather than fail because the decision to terminate a client relationship may occur for reasons independent of the quality of PSF performance or any relationship dysfunction.

One factor in the dissolution of client relationships is time. New client relationships typically experience a honeymoon period immediately after forming during which an initial stock of assets (e.g., goodwill, financial resources, feelings of commitment) buffer the relationship from dissolution. As this stock of resources is drawn down, the likelihood of client relationships dissolving rises until trust and relationship-specific expertise, developed in these early years, becomes a powerful inertial force. Thus, the likelihood of client relationships ending initially rises with time but later decreases as relationship-specific investments made by clients and PSFs strengthen client relationships over time (Levinthal and Fichman 1988). Client relationships also become more fragile when clients' needs change and the fit between a client's resource needs and a PSF's capabilities to serve the client weakens (Seabright et al. 1992).

Another factor related to the dissolution of client ties is the amount and frequency of attention clients receive from their PSFs. Studies of US advertisers reveal that dissatisfaction with an advertising agency's execution, often evidenced by a decline in a client's market share, precedes client relationship dissolution (Henke 1995; Kulkarni et al. 2013), as well as dissatisfaction with the amount of attention clients receive from their agency (Henke 1995). Being inattentive to a client's needs could be caused by professionals' poor performance, but may also be related to attributes of PSFs, such as the number of clients with whom a PSF maintains ties and firm size (Baker et al. 1998; Heinz et al. 2001; Broschak 2004). Serving larger numbers of clients and increasing PSF size both tend to make client relationships impersonal, raising the possibility that clients will become dissatisfied and end the client relationship. The dissolution of client relationships is also more likely when PSFs merge, creating large amounts of competitive overlap between their pre-merger and post-merger client's businesses, with the most relational client relationships being the ones that are most vulnerable to dissolution (Rogan 2014a).

The factor that has attracted the most recent attention for understanding the dissolution of client relationships is the mobility of people in and between professional service and client organizations. Managers and executives make investments in client relationships in relationship-specific expertise, in-depth knowledge of their exchange partner's business, and personal relationships that help sustain client relationships. In general, having longer-tenured exchange managers in roles related to client relationships, and thus having made great relationship-specific investments, tends to strengthen those relationships. The promotion of exchange managers between positions in PSFs, or their exit out of client firms or PSFs, which reduces the level of relationship-specific investment, increases the likelihood that client relationships dissolve (Seabright et al. 1992; Kim and Uzzi 2002; Broschak 2004; Broschak and Niehans 2006; Biong and Ulvnes 2011; Broschak and Block 2014; Rogan 2014b). Thus, client relationships are held together both by firm- and individual-level relationship-specific investments and the loss of these investments puts client relationships at risk.

There are two key ongoing debates in this stream of research to which researchers are only beginning to attend. First, from which roles in the professional service and client firm does mobility seem to matter the most to the dissolution of client relationships? Researchers have only started examining the extent to which the mobility of exchange managers who are closest to client relationships or the mobility executives who set firm strategy and forge client–PSF relationships is most detrimental to client relationships. And further, from which firm, the client or PSF, and under what conditions is the mobility of exchange managers and executives likely to matter the most? Preliminary findings from studies of advertising agencies indicate that the exit of executives and exchange managers from client firms has a greater effect on dyadic client relationship dissolution than the exit of managers from PSFs (Broschak and Block 2014). This is somewhat unexpected since it is a reasonable assumption to expect that the loss of key personnel from PSFs would be detrimental to their capabilities to serve client firms. However, the effect of the exit of PSF executives on client relationships is most pronounced in new relationships when fewer relationship-specific investments have been made and client relationships are sustained by the existence of trust and goodwill of the PSF's executives. As client relationships age, the loss of executives has little effect on the likelihood of client relationship dissolution.

A second debate concerns whether client relationships are embedded in the resources of individuals or in the resources of firms. Client relationships seem to be more resilient to the loss of executives and exchange managers when there are multiple points of contact between the client and PSF. The multiplexity of ties between clients and PSFs could be multiple individuals who are each assigned as contacts to a client, as some law firms do routinely with new client relationships (Lazega and Pattison 1999). It could be multiple units of a PSF each establishing connections with a particular client (Rogan 2014b). Or it could be a PSF's investments in standard operating procedures, internal knowledge-sharing routines, or client-specific routines that act as complements to the connections clients make with specific exchange managers and buffer client relationships from dissolution when exchange managers exit their PSFs (Biong and Ulvnes 2011). Further exploration into the conditions under which the movement of managers and executives is detrimental to client relationships, and the actions PSFs can and do take to protect against the loss of human capital, is sorely needed.

14.4 EFFECTS OF CLIENT RELATIONSHIPS ON PROFESSIONAL SERVICE FIRMS

A small amount of research has investigated how PSFs can be affected by the client relationships they maintain or pursue. PSFs are not inert actors in client relationships, mechanically serving the needs and interests of clients. Rather through the co-production process PSFs are exposed and susceptible to influences from clients that may shape their structure and internal processes.

First, PSFs sometimes respond to client relationships by internationalizing to match the expansion efforts of their existing clients. Law, accounting, and advertising firms, in particular, have demonstrated the tendency to internationalize along with their clients, expanding their own operations into multiple countries to coordinate work for and better serve clients across geographies (Cooper et al. 1998; von Nordenflycht 2011). Failure to expand may result in a mismatch between client needs and PSF capabilities, which increases the likelihood of client relationship dissolution. The tendency to expand is higher when PSFs have long-term rather than new client relationships (Gluckler 2005), and when large, multinational rather than small clients expand (Spar 1997; Hitt et al. 2006). Law firms and advertising agencies also have been observed diversifying into new lines of business in order to provide one-stop shopping for clients who have complex professional service needs (Heinz et al. 2001; von Nordenflycht 2011).

Whether international expansion and strategic diversity driven by the changing needs of existing clients is beneficial or detrimental for professional service is rarely studied. On one hand an international presence can increase a PSF's reputation, and allow them to garner referrals from existing clients, both of which may aid in securing new clients (Gluckler 2005). But internationalization creates complexities for PSFs as client relationships in different national cultures or geographic regions can be subject to different institutional rules and cultural norms (Morgan and Quack 2006; Muzio and Faulconbridge 2013). This may explain the observation that corporate clients tend to only use the services of the strongest PSFs in international markets, and why high levels of human capital enhance the effect of internationalization on professional firm performance (Hitt et al. 2006).

A second and related way client relationships influence PSFs is through their effect on organizational structure and control systems. For instance, some accounting firms design employee training and socialization programs, structure work arrangements, and induce employees to work long hours around the ideal of providing superior service to existing clients (Anderson-Gough et al. 2000). PSFs also sometimes make substantive physical changes, matching the geographic diversification of their clients by dispersing their own structure geographically, opening local offices, and decentralizing decision-making. A dispersed organizational structure may be beneficial to PSFs for three reasons. First, it may better serve the needs of clients operating in different geographic locales when jurisdictional boundaries prevent the widespread practice of professional services, such as professionals who are barred by regulation or norms from practicing in certain geographical regions (Malhotra and Morris 2009). Second, a dispersed structure may be beneficial when clients have high needs for face-to-face interaction with their PSFs. For example, advertising agencies with clients who have a large number of regional offices, each having control over particular products and brands, may open local offices to better respond to clients, thereby increasing client satisfaction and reducing conflict. Third, a geographically dispersed structure is a relationship-specific investment in physical assets that signals a PSF's commitment to a long-term client relationship (Broschak 2004).

A third way client relationships can affect PSFs is through learning and the exchange of knowledge. Client relationships are an important source of knowledge development for PSFs; knowledge that can be incorporated into the PSF's own knowledge base (Fosstenløkken et al. 2003). Learning from clients can occur through interactions and meetings with clients, by working on interdisciplinary client teams, or through the movement of employees between the two firms. For instance, the transfer of employees between IT consulting firms and corporate clients is how knowledge about client problems and potential solutions flows to consulting firms (Grimshaw and Miozzo 2006). Similarly, the movement of lawyers between client firms and their law firms results in the transfer of social capital and knowledge about the clients' business and practices (Somaya et al. 2008). The tacit knowledge may allow law firms to more effectively deploy their resources and better serve the needs of existing clients.

The ability to learn in client relationships depends on the role professionals play in the relationship. For instance, Sturdy et al. (2009) distinguished between a management consultant's role as an innovator and a legitimater in client–consultant relationships. Whereas innovators introduce new ideas, practices, and terms into client organizations, legitimaters are outsiders who confirm client ideas and practices. Knowledge is more likely to flow between the two organizations when consultants act as innovators and are in a position to gauge the reaction to and results of their solutions, carrying that knowledge back to their own firm. What roles professionals play in client relationships, and the mechanisms that are in place to capture learning, are key for PSFs potentially learning from client relationships.

A fourth effect of client relationships is their effect on a PSF's human resource practices. For instance, Beckman and Phillips's (2005) study of Silicon Valley law firms demonstrated how corporate clients were able to influence promotion patterns in their law firms. Law firms that served corporate clients who had women in leadership positions (e.g., president, CEO, legal counsel) experienced a higher growth rate of women partners in the subsequent year. Large corporate clients, particularly in situations where law firms had few clients, served as a powerful institutional force that acted on law firms to modify their promotion practices to address issues with gender inequality. Similarly, Grimshaw and Miozzo (2006) demonstrated how client firms in IT consulting relationships were able to influence service providers' human resource practices around employee recruitment, skill development, and job security, to be better able to serve the needs of the client firm. Ashley and Empson (2013) reported that law firms tended to hire and promote lawyers of particular social classes to match the social class of executives in client firms. Briscoe and von Nordenflycht (2014) showed that in one law firm women and racial-minority lawyers were disadvantaged in their ability to build successful careers by following a strategy of inheriting client relationships from retiring male partners. Women and racial-minority partners fared better by developing their own book of business, suggesting that PSFs' existing sets of client relationships, and the professionals to whom these client relationships are attached, influence workplace inequality and the strategies that can be used for overcoming it.

These examples demonstrate that the effects of client relationships on PSFs transcend the service being provided and influence more ancillary PSF practices. This suggests a blurring of the boundaries between the client and PSFs particularly in situations where clients are powerful relative to the service providers. Future research might examine how other firm practices are influenced through client relationships in ways that make PSFs more similar to their clients.

Finally, our discussion of how client relationships affect PSFs has generally implied that firms are positively affected by their client relationships. There is some evidence that PSFs can be negatively affected by their association with tainted client firms. For instance, Jensen (2006) investigated the collapse of Arthur Andersen in the wake of the audit failure of their client Enron. Despite the fact that Arthur Andersen was a high-status audit firm, their role in the restatement of Enron earnings led powerful institutional actors such as financial analysts and large institutional investors to hold them accountable. As a result, other clients disassociated themselves from Arthur Andersen and defected to other auditors leading to the eventual demise of the firm.

This case suggests that in markets with high standards of quality for professional services, PSFs are in part evaluated not only by their actions but also by the clients with whom they have professional relationships. Scandals and disasters that involve client firms may produce spillover effects that, as in this case, cause re-evaluations of the status and reputation of even prestigious PSFs. Future research might question what other ways the misdeeds of client firms affect PSFs, and whether client firms are able to negatively influence the practices, culture, or ethicality of professional services to the same extent they can influence them positively.

14.5 CONCLUSIONS AND FUTURE DIRECTIONS

Client relationships are critical to the performance and viability of PSFs. And yet all too often they are largely downplayed or ignored in organizational research on professional services and PSFs. In organizing what we do know about client relationships this chapter focused on three themes. First, it highlighted different ways to conceptualize and categorize client relationships, which are important drivers of the assumptions and attention of researchers and practitioners alike. Second, it reported on the state of knowledge around three important phenomena that make up the life cycle of client relationships: relationship formation, relationship maintenance, and relationship dissolution. Lastly, it identified several key ways that client relationships are affecting, or can affect, PSFs. Throughout the course of this review I have tried to highlight those areas that have received the most attention from researchers and identify some questions that warrant further investigation. I'll conclude with some observations about the literature on client relationships in general and point to several promising areas for future research.

First, client relationships are diverse both within and across professional services. Yet the tendency to view all client relationships as relational and emphasize the need to develop strong, long-term dyadic relationships with clients has long dominated our thinking and our assumptions about PSF–client relationships. This is especially evident in research on the maintenance of client relationships. What is needed is research that challenges this assumption and asks questions about alternative ways of conceptualizing client relationships. Do all client relationships need to be relational to be successful? If PSFs adopt more transactional approaches to client relationships what capabilities do they need to be successful? How does a PSF's overall portfolio of relational and transactional client relationships affect how it behaves, how it forms and maintains other client relationships, and how it performs relative to competitors? Researchers are starting to explicitly consider how clients differ across firms, professional services, and across time (Alvesson et al. 2009). The same consideration should be applied to the variability in client relationships.

Second, I am surprised by the lack of attention to how the culture and structure of PSFs affects client relationships, both what clients a PSF forms relationships with and how those relationships are managed. The research reviewed here suggested that cultural compatibility could be an important factor in selecting client relationships and that the structure of PSFs was at times affected by the client relationships in place. In general issues of structure and culture in PSFs seem to be more readily applied to the management of professionals, and not to the management of client relationships. Research that integrates internal structure and cultural with external relationships may provide new insights into variability in the performance and behaviors of different PSFs.

Finally, researchers would be wise to investigate what PSFs do in client relationships and the different contexts within which these relationships exist. One can imagine that whether clients rely on PSFs to perform high-expertise, specialized tasks, or more rote, mundane tasks is an important factor in how relationships are formed, how and how much interaction occurs, and what constitutes good performance from a client's perspective (Sako 2009). Similarly, the few studies conducted outside of developed countries such as the US, UK, and Germany suggest that institutional context is an important factor in determining how client relationships are formed, how long they last, and what constitutes good relationship performance. Our understanding of both the causes of client relationship performance and the consequences of having portfolios of client relationships will be enriched when researchers take a broader perspective about the role of institutional environments.

References

Alvesson, M. (1993). "Organizations as Rhetoric: Knowledge-Intensive Firms and the Struggle with Ambiguity," *Journal of Management Studies* 30(6): 997–1022.

Alvesson, M., Karreman, D., Sturdy, A., and Handley, K. (2009). "Unpacking the Client(s): Constructions, Positions and Client–Consultant Dynamics," *Scandinavian Journal of Management* 25(3): 253–263.

Anderson-Gough, F., Grey, C., and Robson, K. (2000). "In the Name of the Client: The Service Ethic in Two Professional Services Firms," *Human Relations* 53(9): 1151–1174.

Ashley, L. and Empson, L. (2013). "Differentiation and Discrimination: Understanding Social Class and Social Exclusion in Leading Law Firms," *Human Relations* 66(2): 219–244.

Bagdoniene, L. and Jakstaite, R. (2009). "Trust as Basis for Development of Relationships between Professional Service Providers and their Clients," *Economics & Management* 14: 360–366.

Baker, W. E. (1990). "Market Networks and Corporate Behavior," *American Journal of Sociology* 96(3): 589–625.

Baker, W. E., Faulkner, R. R., and Fisher, G. (1998). "Hazards of the Market: The Continuity and Dissolution of Interorganizational Market Relationships," *American Sociological Review* 63(2): 147–177.

Beckman, C. M., and Phillips, D. J. (2005). "Interorganizational Determinants of Promotion: Client Leadership and the Attainment of Women Attorneys," *American Sociological Review* 70(4): 678–701.

Berry, L. L. (1983). "Relational Marketing," in *Emerging Perspectives on Services Marketing*, ed. L. L. Berry, G. L. Shostack, and G. Upah. Chicago, IL: American Marketing Association, 25–28.

Bettencourt, L. A., Ostrom, A. L., Brown, S. W., and Roundtree, R. I. (2002). "Client Co-Production in Knowledge-Intensive Business Services," *California Management Review* 44(4): 100–128.

Biong, H. and Ulvnes, A. M. (2011). "If the Supplier's Human Capital Walks Away, Where Would The Customer Go?" *Journal of Business-to-Business Marketing* 18(3): 223–252.

Block, E. S., Broschak, J. P., and Koppman, S. (2014). "Which Came First—The Client Or The Managers? Resource Acquisition Strategies and the Circulation of Client Ties in Professional Service Firms," Working Paper, Notre Dame University.

Bourland, P. G. (1993). "The Nature of Conflict in Firm–Client Relations: A Content Analysis of *Public Relations Journal*, 1980–89," *Public Relations Review* 19(4): 385–398.

Bowen, D. E. and Jones, G. R. (1986). "Transaction Cost Analysis of Service Organization–Customer Exchanges," *Academy of Management Review* 11(2): 428–441.

Briscoe, F. and von Nordenflycht, A. (2014). "Which Path to Power? Workplace Networks and the Relative Effectiveness of Inheritance and Rainmaking Strategies for Professional Partners," *Journal of Professions and Organizations* 1(1): 33–48.

Broschak, J. P. (2004). "Will They Miss You When You're Gone? The Effect of Managers' Career Mobility on the Dissolution of Market Ties," *Administrative Science Quarterly* 49: 608–640.

Broschak, J. P. and Block, E. S. (2014). "With or Without You: When Does Managerial Exit Matter for the Dissolution of Dyadic Market Ties?" *Academy of Management Journal* 57(3): 743–765.

Broschak, J. P. and Niehans, K. M. (2006). "Social Structure, Employee Mobility, and the Circulation of Client Ties," *Research in the Sociology of Organizations: Professional Service Firms* 24: 369–401.

Cooper, D. J., Greenwood, R., Hinings, B., and Brown, J. L. (1998). "Globalization and Nationalism in a Multinational Accounting Firm: The Case of Opening New Markets in Eastern Europe," *Accounting, Organizations and Society* 23(5–6): 531–548.

Davies, M. (2009). "Service Quality Tolerance in Creative Business Service Relationships," *Service Industries Journal* 29(1): 91–110.

Eccles, R. G. and Crane, D. B. (1988). *Doing Deals: Investment Banks at Work*. Boston, MA: Harvard Business School Press.

Faulconbridge, J. R. and Muzio, D. (2009). "The Financialization of Large Law Firms: Situated Discourses and Practices of Reorganization," *Journal of Economic Geography* 9(5): 641–661.

Fincham, R. (1999). "The Consultant–Client Relationship: Critical Perspectives on the Management of Organizational Change," *Journal of Management Studies* 36(3): 335–351.

Fichman, M. and Goodman, P. (1996). "Customer–Supplier Ties in Interorganizational Relations," in *Research in Organizational Behavior*, vol. 18, ed. B. M. Staw and L. L. Cummings. Greenwich, CT: JAI Press, 285–329.

Fosstenløkken, S. M., Løwendahl, B. R., and Revang, O. (2003). "Knowledge Development through Client Interaction: A Comparative Study," *Organization Studies* 24(6): 859–879.

Gluckler, J. (2005). "Making Embeddedness Work: Social Practice Institutions in Foreign Consulting Markets," *Environment and Planning A* 37(10): 1727–1750.

Granovetter, M. (1985) "Economic Action and Social Structure: The Problem of Embeddedness," *American Journal of Sociology* 91(3): 481–510.

Greenwood, R., and Empson, L. (2003). "The Professional Partnership: Relic or Exemplary Form of Governance?" *Organization Studies* 24(6): 909–933.

Greenwood, R., Li, S. X., Prakash, R., and Deephouse, D. (2005). "Reputation, Diversification and Reputational Explanations of Performance in Professional Service Firms," *Organization Science* 16(6): 661–673.

Grimshaw, D. and Miozzo, M. (2006). "Institutional Effects on the IT Outsourcing Market: Analyzing Clients, Suppliers and Staff Transfer in Germany and the UK," *Organization Studies* 27(9): 1229–1259.

Grimshaw, D. and Miozzo, M. (2009). "New Human Resource Management Practices in Knowledge-Intensive Business Services Firms: The Case of Outsourcing with Staff Transfer," *Human Relations* 62(10): 1521–1550.

Gronroos, C. (1980). "Designing a Long Range Marketing Strategy for Services," *Long Range Planning* 13(2): 36–42.

Gulsoy, T. (2012). "Managing a Strategic Business Relationship in an Emerging Market: Advertising Agency–Client Relationships in Turkey," *Procedia—Social and Behavioral Sciences* 58: 1386–1394.

Halinen, A. (1997). *Relationship Marketing in Professional Services: A Study of Agency-Client Dynamics in the Advertising Sector*. London: Routledge.

Han, S. K. (1994). "Mimetic Isomorphism and Its Effect on the Audit Service Market," *Social Forces* 73(2): 637–663.

Hansen, M. T., Nohria, N., and Tierney, T. (1999). "What's Your Strategy for Managing Knowledge?" *Harvard Business Review* 77(2): 106–116.

Heinz, J. P., Nelson, R. L., and Laumann, E. O. (2001). "The Scale of Justice: Observations on the Transformation of Urban Law Practice," *Annual Review of Sociology* 27: 337–362.

Henke, L. L. (1995). "A Longitudinal Analysis of the Ad Agency–Client Relationship: Predictors of an Agency Switch," *Journal of Advertising Research* 35(2): 24–30.

Hitt, M. A., Bierman, L., Uhlenbruck, K., and Shimizu, K. (2006). "The Importance of Resources in the Internationalization of Professional Service Firms: The Good, the Bad, and the Ugly," *Academy of Management Journal* 49(6): 1137–1157.

Hui, P. P., Davis-Blake, A., and Broschak, J. P. (2008). "Managing Interdependence: The Effects of Outsourcing Structure on the Performance of Complex Projects," *Decision Sciences* 39(1): 5–31.

Jensen, M. (2006). "Should We Stay or Should We Go? Accountability, Status Anxiety, and Client Defections," *Administrative Science Quarterly* 51(1): 97–128.

Jones, C., Livne-Tarandach, R., and Balachandra, L. (2010). "Rhetoric That Wins Clients: Entrepreneurial Firms' Use of Institutional Logics When Competing for Resources," *Research in the Sociology of Work: Institutions and Entrepreneurship* 21: 183–218.

Kim, H. H. (2009). "Market Uncertainty and Socially Embedded Reputation," *American Journal of Economics and Sociology* 68(3): 679–701.

Kim, H. H. and Uzzi, B. (2002). "Network Determinants of Interorganizational Tie Dissolution," Working Paper, Northwestern University.

Klein, B. (1983). "Contracting Costs and Residual Claims: The Separation of Ownership and Control," *Journal of Law and Economics* 26(2): 367–374.

Kulkarni, M. S., Vora, P. P., and Brown, T. A. (2013). "Firing Advertising Agencies: Possible Reasons and Managerial Implications," *Journal of Advertising* 32(3): 77–86.

LaBahn, D. W. and Kohli, C. (1997). "Maintaining Client Commitment in Advertising Agency–Client Relationships," *Industrial Marketing Management* 26(6): 497–508.

Laing, A. W. and Lian, P. C. S. (2005). "Inter-Organizational Relationships in Professional Services: Towards a Typology of Service Relationships," *Journal of Services Marketing* 19(2): 114–127.

Lancaster, R. and Uzzi, B. (2012). "Legally Charged: Embeddedness and Profit in Large Law Firm Legal Billings," *Sociological Focus* 45(1): 1–22.

Larsson, R. and Bowen, D. E. (1989). "Organization and Customer: Managing Design and Coordination of Services," *Academy of Management Review* 14(2): 213–233.

Lazega, E. and Pattison, P. E. (1999). "Multiplexity, Generalized Exchange, and Cooperation in Organizations: A Case Study," *Social Networks* 21(1): 67–90.

Levinthal, D. A. and Fichman, M. (1988). "Dynamics of Interorganizational Attachments: Auditor–Client Relationships," *Administrative Science Quarterly* 33(3): 345–369.

Løwendahl, B. R. (1997). *Strategic Management of Professional Service Firms*. Copenhagen: Copenhagen Business School Press.

Macaulay, S. (1963). "Non-Contractual Relations in Business: A Preliminary Study," *American Sociological Review* 28: 55–70.

McCormick, M., Aguilera, R. V., and Broschak, J. P. (2014). "Employee Mobility and Inter-Firm Ties: A Cross-National Study of Social Embeddedness in Advertising Agencies in Europe, Asia, and the Americas," Working Paper, Butler University.

McPherson, M., Smith-Lovin, L., and Cook, J. M. (2001). "Birds of a Feather: Homophily in Social Networks," *Annual Review of Sociology* 27: 415–444.

Maister, D. H. (1993). *Managing the Professional Service Firm*. New York: Free Press.

Malhotra, N. and Morris, T. (2009). "Heterogeneity in Professional Service Firms," *Journal of Management Studies* 46(6): 895–922.

Manning, S., Lewin, A. Y., and Schuerch, M. (2011). "The Stability of Offshore Outsourcing Relationships: The Role of Relation Specificity and Client Control," *Management International Review* 51(3): 381–406.

Mathur, L. K. and Mathur, I. (1996). "Is Value Associated with Initiating New Advertising Agency–Client Relations?" *Journal of Advertising* 25(3): 1–12.

Mills, P. K. and Margulies, N. (1980). "Toward a Core Typology Of Service Organizations," *Academy of Management Review* 5(2): 255–265.

Mills, P. K. and Morris, J. H. (1986). "Clients as 'Partial' Employees of Service Organizations: Role Development in client Participation," *Academy of Management Review* 11(4): 726–735.

Mills, P. K. and Moshavi, D. S. (1999). "Professional concern: Managing Knowledge-Based Service Relationships," *International Journal of Service Management* 10(1): 48–67.

Morgan, G. and Quack, S. (2006). "The Internationalization of Professional Service Firms: Global Convergence, National Path-Dependency, or Cross-Border Hybridization," *Research in the Sociology of Organizations: Professional Service Firms* 24: 403–431.

Muzio, D. and Faulconbridge, J. (2013). "The Global Professional Service Firm: 'One Firm' Models versus (Italian) Distant Institutionalized Practices," *Organization Studies* 34(7): 897–925.

Nikolova, N., Reihlen, M., and Schlapfner, J. F. (2009). "Client–Consultant Interaction: Capturing Social Practices of Professional Service Production," *Scandinavian Journal of Management* 25(3): 289–298.

Prendergast, G., Shi, Y., and West, D. (2001). "Organizational Buying and Advertising Agency–Client Relationships in China," *Journal of Advertising* 30(2): 61–71.

Ram, M. (1999). "Managing Consultants in a Small Firm: A Case Study," *Journal of Management Studies* 36(6): 875–897.

Richter, A. and Niewiem, S. (2009). "Knowledge Transfer across Permeable Boundaries: An Empirical Study of Clients' Decisions to Involve Management Consultants," *Scandinavian Journal of Management* 25(3): 275–288.

Rogan, M. (2014a). "Too Close for Comfort? The Effect of Embeddedness and Competitive Overlap on Client Relationship Retention Following an Acquisition," *Organization Science* 25(1): 185–203.

Rogan, M. (2014b). "Executive Departures Without Client Losses: The Role of Multiplex Ties in Exchange Partner Retention," *Academy of Management Journal* 57(2): 563–584.

Sako, M. (2009). "Globalization of Knowledge-Intensive Professional Services," *Communications of the ACM* 52(7): 31–33.

Seabright, M. A., Levinthal, D. A., and Fichman, M. (1992). "Role of Individual Attachments in the Dissolution of Interorganizational Relationships," *Academy of Management Journal* 35(1): 122–160.

Sharma, A. (1997). "Professional as Agent: Knowledge Asymmetry in Agency Exchange," *Academy of Management Review* 22: 758–798.

Somaya, D., Williamson, I. O., and Lorinkova, N. (2008). "Gone But Not Lost: The Different Performance Impacts of Employee Mobility between Cooperators versus Competitors," *Academy of Management Journal* 51(5): 936–953.

Spar, D. L. (1997). "Lawyers Abroad: The Internationalization of Legal Practice," *California Management Review* 39(3): 8–28.

Sturdy, A. (1997). "The Consultancy Process: An Insecure Business," *Journal of Management Studies* 34(3): 389–413.

Sturdy, A., Clark, T., Fincham, R., and Handley, K. (2009). "Between Innovation and Legitimation: Boundaries and Knowledge Flow in Management Consultancy," *Organization* 16(5): 627–653.

Thornton, P. H., Ocasio, W., and Lounsbury, M. (2012). *The Institutional Logics Perspective.* Oxford: Oxford University Press.

Uzzi, B. (1996). "The Sources and Consequences of Embeddedness for the Economic Performance of Organizations: The Network Effect," *American Sociological Review* 61(4): 674–698.

Uzzi, B. (1997). "Social Structure and Competition in Interfirm Networks: The Paradox of Embeddedness," *Administrative Science Quarterly* 42(1): 35–67.

Uzzi, B. (1999). "Social Embeddedness in the Creation of Financial Capital," *American Sociological Review* 64(4): 481–505.

Uzzi, B. and Lancaster, R. (2003). "Relational Embeddedness and Learning: The Case of Bank Loan Managers and their Clients," *Management Science* 49(4): 383–399.

Uzzi, B. and Lancaster, R. (2004). "Embeddedness and Price Formation in the Corporate Law Market," *American Sociological Review* 69(3): 319–344.

Verbeke, W. (1988). "Developing an Advertising Agency–Client Relationship in the Netherlands," *Journal of Advertising Research* 28(6): 19–27.

von Nordenflycht, A. (2010). "What is a Professional Service Firm? Toward a Theory and Taxonomy of Knowledge-Intensive Firms," *Academy of Management Review* 35(1): 155–174.

von Nordenflycht, A. (2011). "Firm Size and Industry Structure under Human Capital Intensity: Insights from the Evolution of the Global Advertising Industry," *Organization Science* 22(1): 141–157.

CHAPTER 15

OUTSOURCING AND OFFSHORING OF PROFESSIONAL SERVICES

MARI SAKO

15.1 INTRODUCTION

GLOBALIZATION, digitization, and pressures to reduce costs have given rise to the outsourcing and offshoring of professional services. Outsourcing and offshoring are two outcomes of the same strategic drivers triggering firms to reconfigure their activities organizationally and geographically. This chapter analyzes the causes and consequences of this phenomenon from the perspective of Professional Service Firms (PSFs).

In order to fully capture the drivers behind this phenomenon, the chapter is predicated on three framing assumptions. First, we position PSFs in a global value chain, mindful of strategic interactions for all actors in the value chain. Sandwiched between corporate clients and suppliers of outsourced services, PSFs are both outsourced providers and outsourcers of services. Given this positioning, PSFs are intermediaries competing against new entrants with alternative business models. New entrants are potentially disruptive, with ramifications for the governance of professional service firms and the ecology of professions.

Second, this broad scoping requires maintaining a porous boundary between professional services and non-professional business services. It adds complexity to analyzing professional services, a category with considerable heterogeneity. But it also enables us to investigate how the disaggregation of professional tasks is transforming the boundary between professional and non-professional work. In order to focus on this aspect, we examine what Porter (1980) refers to as primary activities, not support activities, in the value chain. PSFs outsource and offshore both their support activities and primary activities, the latter being legal work for law firms, financial modeling for investment banks, design services for architectural firms, or business research for strategy consulting firms. We focus on primary activities to test the analytical purchase of existing theories about outsourcing and offshoring, when applied to PSFs.

Third, our core concern in this chapter is PSFs' strategies for outsourcing and offshoring. Outsourcing and offshoring are conceptually distinct. A different set of factors determines each. But as strategic decisions, they need to be analyzed simultaneously (Contractor et al. 2010) because no decision is organizationally or geographically "neutral." PSFs, as other firms, are confronted with a combinatorial choice, for instance between captive offshoring and offshore outsourcing. Arriving at an optimal choice requires drawing on a number of theories, and gauging whether different determinants (e.g., proximity vs. ownership) are substitutes or complements.

The practice of outsourcing and offshoring in professional services is of recent origin compared to the practice in manufacturing and services at large. Moreover, business corporations, and not PSFs, initiated outsourcing and offshoring as part of their corporate restructuring drive. Corporations make outsourcing and offshoring decisions in a range of business functions, including information technology (Lacity et al. 2009; Willcocks and Lacity 1999), engineering services (NAE 2008), R&D (Manning et al. 2008), finance and accounting (Bangemann 2005), human resources (Adler 2003; Gospel and Sako 2010), customer relations (Holman et al. 2007), and legal services (Sako 2011b). Consequently, the approach taken in this chapter is to review theories developed largely for business corporations in manufacturing and services, and draw implications for PSFs.

The chapter is structured as follows. Section 15.2 reviews various theories that are relevant to outsourcing and offshoring, and makes links to professional services. Section 15.3 discusses digital technology and the production-line approach (Levitt 1972) as prerequisites for outsourcing and offshoring. Section 15.4, the core of this chapter, homes in on PSFs and analyzes the impact of governance structures on the outsourcing/offshoring decision. We identify in what ways partnerships make some PSFs reluctant outsourcers and offshorers. Section 15.5 discusses the consequences of outsourcing and offshoring by PSFs with specific reference to the ecology of professions and the potentially disruptive nature of new entrants in business services. Section 15.6 concludes with suggestions for future research directions.

15.2 Theories Relevant to Outsourcing and Offshoring

Although the terms "outsourcing" and "offshoring" have a contemporary ring, the phenomenon is as old as the hills in professional services. Historically some liberal professions, such as in accounting and law, predated the rise of the modern corporation. Other professionals were created by corporations to meet their business needs in marketing, human resources, procurement, and later information technology (Galambos

2010). These organizational professionals and earlier "liberal" professionals always had the choice between working in market or in hierarchy, i.e., choosing between working outside business corporations as sole practitioners or in PSFs, and working inside business corporations (Sako 2013).

In the twentieth century, corporations rather than PSFs initiated outsourcing and offshoring. The first corporate activities to be outsourced and offshored were software programming and information technology (IT), dating back to the 1980s. In the 1990s, so-called IT-enabled services spread from customer relationship management, in the form of call centers, to other corporate functions in human resources (e.g., payroll administration), finance and accounting (e.g., accounts payable), procurement and logistics, and legal services (e.g., contract review and litigation support). The timing coincided with the integration of low-cost locations into the world trading system, in India, China, Philippines, South Africa, Latin America, and Central Europe.

From the perspective of business corporations, outsourcing and offshoring of professional services are part and parcel of corporate restructuring involving the "unbundling of corporate functions" (Sako 2005, 2006). This is the separation of administrative business processes from divisional business units to create corporate-wide shared services in pursuit of cost reduction, risk mitigation, and process improvements. Shared services centers may then be outsourced and/or offshored.

Outsourcing is a decision to change the firm boundary, by choosing "buy" over "make." *Offshoring* refers to the decision to relocate from within domestic borders to overseas. They are conceptually distinct, each with a different set of determinants. But as strategic decisions, outsourcing and offshoring need to be analyzed simultaneously, as no decision can be organizationally or geographically "neutral." Combining the two dimensions in a two-by-two matrix, firms have a choice among being in one of four "boxes," namely onshore insourcing, onshore outsourcing, offshore insourcing, and offshore outsourcing (see Figure 15.1). Oftentimes, insourcing of business services is known as "shared services," and offshore insourcing is referred to as "captive" offshoring (McIvor 2010).

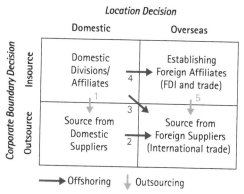

FIGURE 15.1 Defining outsourcing and offshoring.

Beyond these definitions, different social science theories use different levels of analysis to explain why outsourcing and offshoring occur. There are three types of theories, some addressing geography (i.e., for offshoring) only, others analyzing organizational boundary (i.e., for outsourcing) only, and yet another category dealing with both (see Table 15.1 for a summary).

Table 15.1 Theories relevant to outsourcing and offshoring

Subject area	Theories, concepts, frameworks	Outsourcing (firm boundary)	Offshoring (location)	Key implications
International trade	Comparative advantage	✗	✓	• Countries specialize in sectors which use a relatively abundant factor of production • Explains patterns of exports/imports and foreign direct investment
Economic geography	Agglomeration Clusters Global value chains	✗	✓	• Location or space continues to matter beyond claims of international economists, e.g., in the form of externalities that exist in export-oriented industrial clusters and cities • Offshoring might take the form of "deterritorialized" global commodity chains, but it might also create regional (sub-national) clusters
Theories of the firm	Transaction cost Resource-based view Dynamic capabilities	✓	✗	• Firms decide on their boundary giving regard to transaction costs, contracts, resources, and capabilities
International business	Internalization theory Location advantages	✓	✓	• Multinational firms choose to make overseas investment based on location advantages • Multinational firms also take advantage of "internalization" in the presence of market failure
Job characteristics	Job design	✓	✓	• Jobs with certain characteristics (no face-to-face or interactive tasks) are more offshoreable than others

Note: ✓ = theory addresses it; ✗ = theory does not address it.

First, with a focus on crossing national borders, international trade economists use the theory of comparative advantage to associate the concept of offshoring with international trade and foreign direct investment (FDI). In addition, economic geographers analyze locational and regional cluster advantages (Storper 2000). These disciplines have in common the national economy (or sub-national region) as the unit of analysis, without attributing much agency to firm-level decision-makers. Ownership structure of firms and make-or-buy decisions are not objects for analysis in identifying trade and FDI flows, nor in identifying global production networks and regional clusters.

In the past, manufacturing sectors dominated the empirical context for applying these theories. But more recently, previously non-tradable services have become increasingly tradable, resulting in services offshoring and "trade in tasks" (Baldwin 2006). Some of these services and tasks are in technical and administrative services (Kenny et al. 2009), a category that includes professional services. Services offshoring, identified as import (i.e., payment for services rendered overseas), was estimated to be in the range of $90–$100 billion in 2009, although the figure could be as high as $380 billion if intra-firm trading (i.e., captive offshoring) was taken into account (UNCTAD 2011). In a sub-category, "business, professional and technical services" offshoring activities are dominated by the US and EU, which both have a trade surplus (i.e., the supply of offshore services out of these locations outweighs their demand for offshore services) (see Figure 15.2).

A second set of theories, organization economics and managerial theories of the firm, focus on firm-level outsourcing decisions, relegating relocation decisions to be of secondary importance. Theories of the firm range from transaction cost economics, property rights theory, to the resource-based view and its various renditions involving knowledge and capabilities (Gibbons 2005; Grant 1996; Teece et al. 1997). Firms readjust their boundary by outsourcing or insourcing whenever changes occur in transaction costs, resources, or capabilities in market relative to hierarchy.

The dynamic aspect of firm boundary choice is important. In the professional services context, just as in the early days of adopting a new piece of technology, professional services may bias firms towards "make" because the underlying "knowledge is often tacit, that is, uncoded, non-verbalized, and often embedded in organizational routines" (Afuah 2001: 1212). However, professional services are not associated with fast rates of technological change. Perrons et al. (2004) found that "make" is preferred in industries with very fast or slow rates of technological change, while "buy" is more appropriate in industries with medium pace. Thus, the slow technological "clockspeed" in professional services might bias the firm's value chain design towards insourcing.

A third category of theories gives equal regard to offshoring and outsourcing, with certain assumptions made to make this possible. The eclectic paradigm in International Business (IB) represents a good example. Multinational corporations, as they expand internationally, leverage a combination of "location advantages" and "internalization advantages" (Dunning 1988). Location here embodies both costs, enabling arbitrage between locations, and benefits deriving from the quality of national institutions.

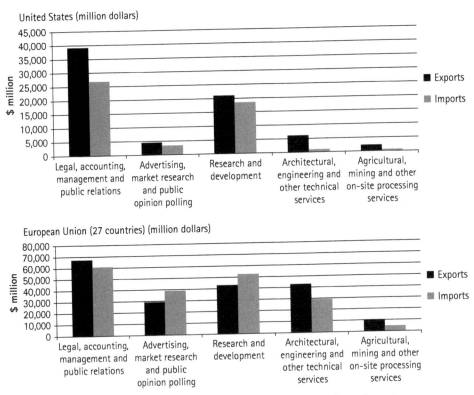

FIGURE 15.2 International trade in business, professional, and technical services, 2010.

Internalization, i.e., make rather than buy, derives from multinationals' attempt to avoid factor market failures in overseas locations.

Another approach, focusing on job characteristics, could address both offshoring and outsourcing, although studies were carried out primarily to address the fear of job loss due to offshoring. Blinder and colleagues make a distinction between "personal services" requiring face-to-face contact and "impersonal services" that do not and therefore can be delivered to, and from, remote locations. He also noted that both low-skilled jobs (e.g., hairdressers) and high-skilled jobs (e.g., court judges) require face-to-face interaction. Similarly, some low-skilled (e.g., typing) and high-skilled jobs (e.g., computer programming) may be in "impersonal services." Thus, jobs requiring higher skills are not necessarily less "offshoreable" than those with lower skill content (Blinder 2009; Blinder and Krueger 2009). By implication, professional jobs, while highly skilled, are "offshoreable" to a different degree, with some jobs (e.g., client-facing advisory work) containing greater elements of face-to-face interaction than other jobs (e.g., research).

Moreover, the underlying assumption that "impersonal services" are inherently offshoreable can be extended easily to the claim that they are also outsourceable. The reason for this ease of extension is that firm-level decisions are not theorized. Without decision-making agency, it is difficult to gauge under what conditions offshoreable jobs are actually offshored.

Eclectic combinations of the above theories would provide much insight into the outsourcing/offshoring decisions by PSFs. However, to date, outsourcing and offshoring tend to be treated separately in social science disciplines, privileging either the firm boundary decision or the relocation decision. The two need to be brought together more fully to analyze decisions by PSFs. For example, to what extent might geographic proximity replace or complement ownership as means of control? What is the impact of governance structures on the decision-making process?

15.3 UNDERSTANDING TRANSFORMATION IN PROFESSIONAL WORK

The nature of professional work has evolved over decades due to a complex set of factors, including digital technology, corporate strategy, and government regulation. In this context, outsourcing/offshoring is simultaneously a cause and a consequence of such transformation. It is a cause because outsourcing and offshoring require a certain degree of disaggregation, standardization, and modularization of tasks before services can be delivered from one legal entity to another at a geographic distance. It is a consequence also because the application of these operational techniques may be triggered by, and therefore follow, the decision to outsource or offshore.

A comparison with manufacturing highlights the challenges professionals and PSFs face in responding to offshoring. Offshoring in manufacturing, in the form of sourcing components and contract assembly from around the world, began in the middle of the twentieth century (Sturgeon 2002). But offshoring in services, particularly in professional services, is a relatively recent phenomenon. Trading at a distance requires the routinization and standardization of tasks. In manufacturing, modern technology and Taylorist principles of scientific management were applied to this end first, well before offshoring became prevalent (Gereffi et al. 2005; Sturgeon 2002; Thun 2010). In professional services, offshoring is on the rise at the same time that task standardization is spreading. In many cases, offshoring is a trigger to routinize tasks in professional jobs. In professional services, as in other sectors, offshoring is equivalent to turning an employment contract into a sales contract (Simon 1951).[1] This contractual shift, to an extent, necessitates codifying things that had been implicit prior to the shift (Davis-Blake and Broschak 2009).

Professional services are a subset of services. Services may, in turn, be categorized into high- and low-contact services, with contact defined as the physical presence of the customer in the service delivery system (Chase 1978). Another related distinction often made is between back-office and front-office operations. In a PSF context, law firms' front office provides legal advice to clients, while their back office includes managing billing and payment processes. Back-office operations require low or no customer contact and lend themselves to what Levitt called a production-line approach to services (Levitt 1972). By this, he meant that services could significantly improve their performance in both productivity and quality, if managers adopted the manufacturing principles of task standardization, clear division of labor, and process flows. By contrast, it is more challenging to apply the production-line approach to front-office services that require high levels of customer contact and inputs in the course of service delivery.[2]

A different kind of scholarship, led by economists interested in the impact of computer technology on skills, has developed a typology that sheds light on the substantive nature of professional skills. Building on cognitive and behavioral sciences, Levy and Murnane (2004) draw a distinction between "rule-based" tasks (for which information processing can be fully described in rules) and "pattern recognition" tasks. In the latter, rule-based solutions are not possible, and people solve problems through case-based reasoning, a type of pattern recognition, constructing analogies between the new problem and past problems. Computers change the task composition of human work. They substitute for workers carrying out routine "rule-based" tasks, while they complement workers carrying out non-routine problem-solving tasks (Autor et al. 2003) thus preserving a high level of discretion in professional work (e.g., use of video links in courts or digital images in open heart surgery).

The task analysis lens leads to a realization that the balance between routine and non-routine tasks varies across different profession work. This avoids the blanket application of "digital Taylorism" to describe the trend towards standardization in all professional jobs (Brown et al. 2011). Task disaggregation and routinization occur in part due to digital technology, automating manually intensive tasks. But we expect automation to happen less at PSFs with a partnership structure, which do not allocate or raise large sums for non-human capital investment (Greenwood and Empson 2003). Equally important is the brake on task disaggregation placed by self-regulating professions, who regard it as a threat to their professional identity and ethics.

Last but not least, the deregulation of some professional services markets (e.g., Legal Services Act 2007 in England and Wales) facilitates task disaggregation. Such policy puts pressure on professionals to justify the esoteric nature of their work that only fully qualified professionals are permitted to undertake. Deregulation facilitates the decomposition of professional work into tasks some of which may be carried out by semi-professionals and non-professionals. The more disaggregated the tasks the easier it is for non-professionals to carry out those tasks. Contract specialists who draft and review contracts (e.g., in derivatives) in financial services are one such example.

In short, professional services are receiving transformational pressures simultaneously from the "production-line approach" (Levitt 1972), digitization, and deregulation. All these forces have contributed towards disaggregating professional work into constituent tasks and standardizing some of those tasks. Disaggregation and standardization are a prerequisite for the efficient and effective outsourcing and offshoring of professional services. However, the extent to which they are adopted depends on the governance of PSFs, a topic to which we turn next.

15.4 OUTSOURCING AND OFFSHORING BY PROFESSIONAL SERVICE FIRMS

A central concern of this volume lies in understanding the nature of PSFs and their strategic management processes. The nature of an organization inevitably influences such processes (Greenwood et al. 1990). This section draws out the implications of different governance structures of PSFs for their outsourcing/offshoring decisions. Since PSFs are governed in different ways across sectors and over time, we identify enablers of, and barriers to, outsourcing and offshoring in each governance type—the public corporation, professional partnership, and managed professional business. In particular, consulting firms and investment banks practiced offshoring and outsourcing earlier and more widely than law firms because some of them adopted ownership structures other than partnerships (Greenwood and Empson 2003).

15.4.1 Evidence of Outsourcing and Offshoring by PSFs

Gary Senior, Managing Partner of Baker and McKenzie in London, defines offshoring as "teaming with people in another country in the provision of services, whether it is through the back office or the direct provision to clients."[3] He further states that offshoring is a technique to be efficient. Three things are of note about this particular perspective on offshoring. First, offshoring is regarded as an operational technique for enhancing efficiency, remote from strategic concerns of value creation. This implies that decentralized organization units can make offshoring decisions. Second, offshoring involves teamwork that crosses geographic boundaries. Although perhaps not fully intended, the term "teaming" implies an ambiguous division of labor with workflows that may go back and forth between locations. Third, offshoring applies equally to the back office and the front office. In fact, the same set of providers may supply to both offices.

Accounting firms, investment banks, and management consulting firms are seen as pioneers in creating captive offshore units in low cost locations such as India. For example, Ernst & Young established captive offshore units to prepare client tax returns, and other large accounting firms offshore non-judgmental audit procedures (Deloitte 2007). Similarly, investment banks have set up offshore units to undertake financial modeling and analytics, while strategy consulting firms have captive offshore "knowledge centers" to support onshore teams that undertake PowerPoint documentation and market research.

More recently, law firms have joined in to create "shared services" for back-office functions, and "knowledge centers" to deliver legal support work. Table 15.2 provides some examples of outsourcing and offshoring by law firms. For example, Clifford Chance and Allen & Overy have their knowledge centers in India and Northern Ireland respectively.

Table 15.2 Outsourcing and offshoring by law firms

Firm	What	Provider, location, outcomes
Allen & Overy	Litigation document review	Transaction-specific outsourcing to Integreon in New York, US and Mumbai, India. 30–50% cost saving
Clarke Willmott	Support functions	Secretarial (typing) work at its Birmingham office to Exigent in South Africa
Clifford Chance	Document review and due diligence. Support function: IT and document production	Legal services offshored to CC wholly-owned subsidiary in Gurgaon, India. Support function is delivered with Integreon from the same location
Eversheds	Support—document production	UK-wide secretarial work to be outsourced offshore to Exigent
Linklaters	Support—finance, leisure, accounting	Looking to outsource an onshore picture administration center and knowledge process outsourcing
Lovells	Litigation document review Real estate document production	Transaction specific. Exigent in South Africa Unnamed provider in India
Osborne Clarke	Non-strategic support functions	Onshore—£1m saved annually. Plans to extend
Pinsent Masons	Secretarial work, document review, and due diligence	Estimated 50% saving on low-level legal work. Dedicated team of qualified lawyers employed by Exigent in Cape Town
Simmons & Simmons	Document review, due diligence, and research	Dedicated outsourced team of five lawyers employed in Mumbai.
Slaughter and May	Document review and due diligence	Triggered by request from specific client

Source: Based on Luke McLeod-Roberts "A&O signs outsourcing deal with LPO provider Integreon," *The Lawyer*, 18 November 2009.

As shown, support functions (such as secretarial work) are listed alongside tasks that are closer to professional legal work such as litigation document review, due diligence, and legal research. Several mentions of cost savings in the table reveal the efficiency focus of offshoring. So why have PSFs come to take this particular approach to offshoring and outsourcing?

15.4.2 Public Corporations

In the absence of systematic evidence from PSFs which are public corporations, we draw on the experience of publicly quoted business corporations first. Hierarchical managerial control and centralized decision-making are clear facilitators of strategic outsourcing.

Outsourcing and offshoring at business corporations used to be about factory-level decisions to close down in-house production and to source from third-party suppliers.

The firm (or plant) boundary was affected, but not much else. More recently, however, business services outsourcing combines internal corporate restructuring of the administrative hierarchy and a make-or-buy decision (Gospel and Sako 2010). Distinct from vertical disintegration, the unbundling of corporate functions occurs when business processes at divisions in a multidivisional corporation are brought together into a company-wide shared services (SS) center before it is outsourced to a third party.

The creation and outsourcing of shared services by business corporations amount to the centralization of corporate functions at the headquarter level. Much of the cost savings and efficiency gains arise from corporate-wide standardization of business processes that such centralization enables. For instance, the corporation might decide to adopt a single accounting standard and a uniform enterprise software system. But existing corporate structures affect the process of implementation. For example, the more centralized structure led Procter & Gamble to create a central shared service first before outsourcing (Gospel and Sako 2010). By contrast, a more decentralized structure at Unilever meant outsourcing initiatives at the regional level first before diffusing such practices gradually within the corporation.

Thus, publicly listed corporations (PLCs) exercise hierarchical managerial control to make outsourcing and offshoring decisions. But some PLCs are more centralized than others, and centralized firms are better positioned to reap the benefits of outsourcing and offshoring more quickly as they can move decisively towards company-wide shared services.

15.4.3 Professional Partnerships

Compared to public corporations, traditional professional partnerships are characterized by peer control rather than hierarchical control (Empson and Chapman 2006). Professional partnerships, with partners combining the role of owner, manager, and producer, have multiple benefits, including low costs of monitoring complex non-routine activities, high incentives for sharing proprietary knowledge, and superior career progression incentives resulting in higher effort and productivity (Greenwood and Empson 2003). However, constraint on managerial authority and protection of professional autonomy imply that it is difficult to get all partners to cooperate with a specific management initiative (Empson and Chapman 2006). An initiative such as outsourcing and offshoring is no exception.

The configuration of controls for large professional partnerships articulated by Greenwood et al. (1990) provides a useful framework to analyze the consequences of the P^2 Form for outsourcing and offshoring. Compared to the public corporation, professional partnerships are characterized by the decentralization of operating control, the use of general (rather than specific) financial control, and a consensus-building approach to strategic control.

First, professional autonomy implies extreme decentralization of operational control, with individuals deciding what to do and how to do it. Therefore, actual decisions on what to outsource or offshore are left up to individual practice areas, or to individual partners or associates. Professionals are also reluctant to let go of their own work. Applying professional knowledge to complex problems requires one professional to have purview of the entire picture. Professionals also lack trust in the competence of semi-professionals and lay people, and therefore are bad at delegating tasks without close supervision. This makes it challenging to manage a clear division of labor and geographically dispersed teamwork.

Second, the use of general financial targets with low-powered incentives and accountability may hinder the use of outsourcing and offshoring. In professional partnerships, financial incentives for offshoring or outsourcing are opaque, absent, or adverse. For captive offshore operations, professional partnerships might have a profit share arrangement between the onshore and offshore operations, but this is not common practice. Given weak internal drivers to outsource or offshore, meeting client demand (e.g., for cost savings) is often the main reason why professional partnerships implement outsourcing and offshoring. Putting the client interests first is psychologically wired into some professionals (Moorhead, forthcoming), and is used in their outsourcing/offshoring decisions.

Last, but not least, a consensus-building approach to strategic control implies that outsourcing and offshoring decisions are not only decentralized, but are also given a status of operational trial-and-error in response to client demand. Outsourcing and offshoring is not a topic of strategic importance for managing partners in professional partnerships, in the way that it might be for members of the boards of public corporations. Moreover, as professionals dominate decision-making, non-professional business managers are subjugated in the outsourcing/offshoring decisions.

15.4.4 Managed Professional Business

Managed professional business (MPB) involves the introduction of a corporate style (replacing collegial control by hierarchical control) in managing PSFs. This adaptation in governance emerges as PSFs grow in size and geographic reach. Such growth pressurizes MPBs to introduce a degree of heterogeneity inside the firm, while attempting to commoditize client-specific bespoke services (Greenwood and Empson 2003). Thus, work handled by MPBs makes outsourcing and offshoring attractive.

In MPBs, non-professional business managers increase proportionately. Those managers led by a Chief Operating Officer are seen to lead the outsourcing/offshoring initiative at PSFs, distancing it from strategic control by professionals. This contributes to a tendency for outsourcing/offshoring to be side-lined in terms of strategic importance. Thus, with the rise of "organizational professionals" (i.e., non-professional managers) to manage PSFs (DiMaggio and Powell 1983), MPBs have to deal with the tension between professionals who own the PSF and non-owner managers.

As PSFs go global, Faulconbridge and Muzio argue in favor of bringing the professionals back in, that is to make the autonomy professionals normally expect and demand a central plank in understanding decision-making (Faulconbridge and Muzio 2007). In this context, outsourcing and offshoring decisions by globalizing MPBs are likely to continue to respect the autonomy of professionals. Consequently, the dominance of professionals in decision-making in MPBs leads to decentralized outsourcing and offshoring. Or else, if non-professional managers are given a seat at the table, they would most likely focus on centralizing the outsourcing and offshoring of back-office services, away from direct control by professionals.

To summarize, PSFs have different ownership structures, ranging from partnership to privately held and publicly listed company. Governance structures of PSFs, the institutional arrangements that legitimize how decisions are made, influence the pattern of outsourcing and offshoring. This section detailed the various reasons why PLCs tend to have a governance structure that predisposes them to make more decisive (strategic) moves towards outsourcing and offshoring than MPBs, and MPBs than traditional professional partnerships. However, within each ownership mode, the more centralized the decision-making, the more quickly and decisively PSFs can implement firm-wide outsourcing and offshoring. By contrast, preserving the autonomy of professionals in both traditional partnerships and MPBs contributes towards decentralized, case-by-case applications of outsourcing or offshoring. Consequently, efficiency gains resulting from discrete changes in workflow and project management are hard to garner.

15.5 CONSEQUENCES OF OFFSHORING AND OUTSOURCING IN A GLOBAL CONTEXT

What are the key consequences of the offshoring and outsourcing of professional services? Perhaps the most topical aspect is the impact on job loss and the resulting international division of labor. This section also reviews two further significant consequences, namely the impact on the ecology of professions and the structure of the professional services industry.

15.5.1 Impact on the Ecology of Professions

How many jobs are displaced by offshoring? McKinsey (2005) provided an estimate for service jobs in eight sectors (namely packaged software, IT services, banking, insurance, pharmaceutical, automotive, healthcare, and retailing).[4] The study calculated that 18.3 million jobs in these sectors could be done by people located anywhere in the world in 2003. They estimated that by 2008, 160 million jobs, or about 11% of total global service jobs, could be carried out remotely, but only 4.1 million of those would actually be offshored. This modest projected take-up was attributed to company-specific barriers rather than regulatory barriers. Such barriers were said to include operational issues, hostile management attitudes to offshoring, and insufficient scale.

The McKinsey study assumed that the nature of jobs that existed in the sectors they examined would remain unchanged as a result of offshoring. The same limitation is reflected in any analysis that is based on official employment statistics. However, the mix of tasks within jobs changes over time. There is evidence that such task changes within jobs have been quite large (Levy and Murnane 2004: 52). For example, in financial services, exceptions processing clerks in banks might have specialized in handling a single kind of exception, e.g., overdrafts. With digitization of checks, clerks' task scope has expanded to handle all types of exception—overdrafts, stop payments, address changes, etc. (Autor and Levy 2002).

Thus, outsourcing and offshoring, just like digital technology, may bring about a change in the mix of tasks in jobs. In fact, it is fully intended that with outsourcing and offshoring of professional services, the onshore in-house professionals allocate more of their time to essential tasks that require professional expertise and judgment, leaving photocopying, document drafting, and contract review to semi-professionals and non-professionals. As already noted in section 15.3, the disaggregation of professional work into constituent tasks enhances the domain of tasks that could be done by those other than fully qualified professionals.

In this way, outsourcing and offshoring may be regarded as a trigger in disturbing the ecology of professions, along with other exogenous and endogenous forces identified by Abbott (1988). Each professional is part of a broader system competing with others for the exclusive right to solve the public's and the state's problems. But if semi-professionals and non-professionals are deemed competent to provide disaggregated services in competition with professionals, clients now have a choice. Obtaining the same service from alternative sources potentially undermines the legitimacy of professionals' claim and pushes back their jurisdictional boundary.

15.5.2 Impact on the Structure of the Professional Services Industry

Outsourcing and offshoring of professional services have led to an industry structure in which incumbent PSFs source from, and compete with, new entrants. These new entrants are suppliers of business services, known as knowledge process outsourcing (KPO) providers. They are typically limited liability corporations (LLCs), funded in part by private equity or venture capital. KPO processes include business research, R&D, engineering services, financial research, patent filing, and legal research. Some KPO providers had been captive offshore units which were spun off (for example, Genpact had been part of GE). Others are start-ups founded by entrepreneurial professionals who had worked for PSFs as consultants, accountants, financial analysts, or lawyers.

Some new entrants have also bought captive offshore units established by investment banks, accounting firms, and consulting firms.

These new players in the globalizing professional services markets start with providing low-end, low-value support work for business corporations and PSFs. In the medium to long term, they intend to accumulate capabilities to create and capture value in global value chains, by pursuing three types of strategies, namely climbing up, scaling up, and broadening out (Sako 2011a).

First, just as contract manufacturers evolved into original design manufacturers, KPO providers have climbed up the value chain by providing higher value-adding services. This may involve writing an entire research report on the basis of business research for a consulting client or on the basis of the analysis of a valuation model for an investment-banking client. The clients then put their own brand onto the report and make recommendations. In legal services, KPO providers are not permitted to practice law, but may accumulate broader capabilities over time, so that a request to do prior art search initially may evolve into undertaking all necessary steps to file a patent short of prosecuting it.

Second, some KPO suppliers have scaled up their operations, investing heavily not only in IT infrastructure but also in process and quality improvements for their information processing factories. The LLC ownership structure of KPO providers enables them to make swift technology investment decisions, with ambitious growth targets that come from their private equity investors. The growth potential of offshore outsourcers is predicated not only on low labor costs, but also on investment in software tools and process improvement, regarded as a more sustainable source of competitive advantage.

Third, some KPO suppliers have pursued a diversification strategy by bundling different professional support services, for example by pulling together business, financial, and legal research under one roof. These KPO providers seek to work closely with functional heads of global business corporations, rather than with PSFs.

The "pure strategies" described above are combined in different ways by KPO providers which have an edge over PSFs (especially traditional partnerships) in pursuing these strategies. Table 15.3 summarizes the contrast between KPO providers and partnership PSFs (to make the contrast stark). First, the ownership structure is different. As a consequence of this difference, the nature of strategic control is different with a KPO provider having more top-down hierarchical control than a PSF. At the same time, operating control is different, with the KPO provider able to standardize tasks more easily than PSFs. These contrasting dimensions result in differential sources of competitive advantage. KPO providers can leverage their global delivery model with more standardized services, while PSFs excel in bespoke customized services delivered to clients face-to-face. Last but not least, KPO providers are subjected to explicit performance metrics in the form of service level agreements. By contrast, performance contracts remain implicit and taken on trust for PSFs, even as corporate clients attempt to introduce alternative billing arrangements to replace the billable hour.

What is the significance of KPO entry for the structure of the industry and the capabilities of PSFs? Given the importance of intangibles such as brand and reputation in

Table 15.3 Comparing PSF partnerships and KPO providers

	PSF partnerships	KPO providers
Ownership form	Limited liability partnership (LLP) with professionals as owners	Limited liability corporation (LLC) with investment from outside capital
Strategic control	Consensus/collegial	Hierarchical
Operating control	Via standardization of skills training	Via standardization of routines and tasks
Competitive advantage based on:	Bespoke, customized services	Process efficiency from standardization and economies of scale
Service delivery model	A federation of practice areas/ regional offices, with higher elements of need for proximity to clients	Global service model, with higher elements of remote delivery
Performance contract with clients	Implicit and taken on trust	Explicit, with performance metrics specified in service level agreements

driving power in global value chains in professional services, can KPO providers capture value away from PSFs, just as component suppliers such as Intel and Microsoft took away value from IBM?

The future structure of the professional services industry depends on interactions between the strategies of PSFs and those of new entrants. In this context, the pure cost drivers of outsourcing and offshoring should hold little long-term strategic interest for any firm, be it a PSF or an outsourcing provider. Cost savings in themselves do not provide sustainable competitive advantage, and will be superseded by other capabilities in the dynamics of competitive interaction within the industry (Kenny et al. 2009).

In response to KPO providers scaling up and excelling in delivering services more efficiently, PSFs have a choice between competing (by adopting the same strategy) or cooperating (by outsourcing more heavily to KPO providers for the sort of tasks that require volume). The latter might be an attractive division of labor for PSFs, but would lead to wiping out the in-house training grounds for junior professionals expected to experience some "grunt work" as part of their apprenticeship.

In response to KPO suppliers broadening out to provide a one-stop shop for business corporations, PSFs have to consider diversification within, by setting up a multidisciplinary practice, or across by forming alliances with PSFs in different domains. This puts further pressure on traditional professional partnerships, and gives an incentive to adopt different governance structures (as facilitated, for example, by the Alternative Business Structure in England and Wales). A failure to adapt heightens the threat of disintermediation of PSFs, as corporate clients go direct to alternative providers.

KPO providers' strategy to climb up the value chain should be understood in the context of disruptive innovation. Just as other industries were disrupted by new entrants that started by addressing low market segments ignored by incumbents (Christensen 1997), KPO providers begin with satisfying latent demand for clients who could not afford the service previously. Consulting is arguably on the cusp of such disruption (Christensen et al. 2013). Here, the fact that McKinsey has set up McKinsey Solutions to leverage analytics and rely less on human capital, indicates that PSF response is likely to take the form of a captive (rather than an outsourced) solution. This underpins the importance of brand and reputation in many areas of professional services.

In short, KPO providers pose both a threat and an opportunity for PSFs as they attempt to align their geographic presence with a target client base of global corporations and financial institutions. It poses a threat because KPO providers have been accumulating deeper skills and experience in global service delivery. It creates an opportunity for PSFs because KPO providers are at best potential joint venture partners, or else provide a template for transforming the governance of PSFs themselves in a globalizing world.

15.6 CONCLUSIONS AND FURTHER RESEARCH DIRECTIONS

Professional service firms play a dual role in the broad canvas of outsourcing and offshoring. They are, first and foremost, outsourcing providers, increasingly subjected to metrics (customer satisfaction, responsiveness, etc.) by which they are judged. They are also users of outsourced services, provided either by captive units or third party suppliers. Sandwiched between these two roles in increasingly globalizing value chains, PSFs may end up with a larger or a smaller segment of the pie depending on how they play their intermediary role.

This chapter began by defining outsourcing and offshoring, and reviewing relevant theories in international trade, economic geography, organization economics, managerial theories of the firm, international business, and job characteristics. By comparing with manufacturing, the chapter also noted the challenges professional services face in adopting a production-line approach at the same time that the industry is globalizing via offshoring and outsourcing. The chapter then examined the impact of governance structures at PSFs on their outsourcing and offshoring decisions. Lastly, we compared PSFs and outsourcing providers, their capabilities and sources of competitive advantage, in order to delineate possible future scenarios in professional services industry.

The need to draw on a variety of theories and empirical contexts from manufacturing and business corporations is a reflection of how nascent the research on outsourcing and offshoring by PSFs is. Thus, there is no shortage of topics for future research, as follows.

(a) *Governance and decision-making.* What is the impact of different governance structures on the outsourcing/offshoring decision by PSFs? What is the relation between professionals and non-professional managers when making outsourc-ing and offshoring decisions in MPBs? How does it differ from profession to pro-fession? What design principles are effective in using outsourcing and offshoring as part of restructuring PSFs with a global presence? Answering these questions is important, particularly as decision-making is the mediating factor that links the characteristics of jobs to the outsourcing/offshoring of those jobs. Much more work needs to be done to analyze what turns offshoreable jobs into actually offshore jobs.

(b) *Job quality, training, and careers.* How are the job quality and work team dynam-ics of professionals changing at PSFs implementing outsourcing and offshoring? What is the evolving job quality at providers of outsourced and offshore profes-sional services? What is the impact of professional identity as task disaggregation changes the boundary between professional and non-professional work? How is career progression and work–life balance being reconfigured for professionals working in sectors with outsourcing and offshoring? Answers to these questions touch on the very survival of professions, and address in what ways professional work might follow a path that is similar or different from that for manufacturing and clerical work. Such comparison is important for testing the generalizabil-ity of existing theories on job quality, deskilling, and career development when applied to under-explored contexts.

(c) *Globalization and comparative national systems.* Outsourcing and offshor-ing is part and parcel of the globalization of professional services markets. Further research on international comparisons would also give much trac-tion (Allsop et al. 2009) Offshoring in particular provides a good context for inquiring whether or not the dominance of the Anglo-American pattern of professionalization increases or decreases with globalization. In particular, in what ways are PSFs' outsourcing and offshoring decisions influenced by the varieties of capitalism (Hall and Soskice 2001)? For example, if German law-yers are less entrepreneurial and more business oriented (Morgan and Quack 2005), what does this imply for the geography of development of outsourcing and offshored markets? Would the globalization of PSFs, facilitated by out-sourcing and offshoring, lead to more dispersed nationalities amongst the top PSFs?

(d) *New entrant strategies and industry evolution.* Outsourcing and offshoring are not just about shifting the location of professional jobs. It is important to empha-size that they have also created new markets for business services, attracting new entrants with a different governance structure and business models from incumbent PSFs. From this industry evolution perspective, what are plausible scenarios for competitive dynamics between PSFs and new entrants in devel-oped economies? What are the possible scenarios in emerging markets? And what are the long-term implications for the international division of labor in professional work?

Notes

1. I thank John Forth for this insight.
2. In reality, both front-office work and back-office work can be decomposed into tasks, some of which are more routine than others. In considering employees who work within any corporate function, firms often make a distinction between "strategic partners" who make judgments (e.g., a finance manager involved in devising investment decisions) and "administrative experts" whose primary concern is to make routine business processes (e.g., accounts payable, non-judgmental audit procedure) more efficient.
3. <http://www.youtube.com/watch?v=_uVpSoNIkoo> (accessed August 7, 2013).
4. A similar approach for IT jobs is taken by ACM. 2006. Globalization and Offshoring of Software: A Report of the ACM Job Migration Task Force. New York: Association of Computing Machinery.

References

Abbott, A. (1988). *The System of Professions: An Essay on the Division of Expert Labor.* Chicago, IL: University of Chicago Press.

ACM (2006). *Globalization and Offshoring of Software: A Report of the ACM Job Migration Task Force.* New York: Association of Computing Machinery.

Adler, P. S. (2003). "Making the HR Outsourcing Decision," *Sloan Management Review,* October 15.

Afuah, A. (2001). "Dynamic Boundaries of the Firm: Are Firms Better Off Being Vertically Integrated in the Face of a Technological Change?" *Academy of Management Journal* 44(6): 1211–1228.

Allsop, J., Bourgeault, I. L., Evetts, J., Bianic, T. L., Jones, K., and Wrede, S. (2009). "Encountering Globalization: Professional Groups in an International Context," *Current Sociology* 57(4): 487–510.

Autor, D. H. and Levy, F. (2002). "Upstairs, Downstairs: Computers and Skills on Two Floors of a Large Bank," *Industrial and Labor Relations Review* 55: 432–447.

Autor, D. H., Levy, F., and Murnane, R. J. (2003). "The Skill Content of Recent Technological Change: An Empirical Exploration," *Quarterly Journal of Economics* 118(4): 1279–1333.

Baldwin, R. (2006). *Globalization: The Great Unbundling(s).* Helsinki: Economic Council of Finland.

Bangemann, T. O. (2005). *Shared Services in Finance and Accounting.* Aldershot: Gower.

Blinder, A. S. (2009). "How Many US Jobs Might Be Offshoreable?" *World Economics* 10(2): 41–78.

Blinder, A. S. and Krueger, A. B. (2009). "Alternative Measures of Offshorability: A Survey Approach," *NBER Working Paper 15287.* Cambridge, MA: National Bureau of Economic Research.

Brown, P., Lauder, H., and Ashton, D. (2011). *The Global Auction: The Broken Promises of Education, Jobs, and Incomes.* Oxford: Oxford University Press.

Chase, R. B. (1978). "Where Does the Customer Fit into Service Operation?" *Harvard Business Review* 56: 137–142.

Christensen, C. M. (1997). *The Innovator's Dilemma.* Boston, MA: Harvard Business School Press.

Christensen, C. M., Wang, D., and van Bever, D. (2013). "Consulting on the Cusp of Disruption," *Harvard Business Review*, October.

Contractor, F. J., Kumar, V., Kundu, S. K., and Pedersen, T. (2010). "Reconceptualizing the Firm in a World of Outsourcing and Offshoring: The Organizational and Geographical Relocation of High-Value Company Functions," *Journal of Management Studies* 47(8): 1417–1433.

Davis-Blake, A. and Broschak, J. P. (2009). "Outsourcing and the Changing Nature of Work," *Annual Review of Sociology* 35: 321–340.

Deloitte (2007). *Global Financial Services Offshoring Report 2007*. London: Deloitte.

DiMaggio, P. J. and Powell, W. W. (1983). "The Iron Cage Revisited: Institutional Isomorphism and Collective Rationality in Organizational Fields," *American Sociological Review* 48(2): 147–160.

Dunning, J. (1988). "The Eclectic Paradigm of International Production: A Restatement and Some Possible Extensions," *Journal of International Business Studies* 19(1): 1–31.

Empson, L. and Chapman, C. (2006). "Partnership versus Corporation: Implications of Alternative Forms of Governance in Professional Service Firms," *Research in the Sociology of Organizations* 24: 139–170.

Faulconbridge, J. R. and Muzio, D. (2007). "Reinserting the Professional into the Study of Globalizing Professional Service Firms: The Case of Law," *Global Networks* 7(3): 249–270.

Galambos, L. (2010). "The Role of Professionals in the Chandler Paradigm," *Industrial and Corporate Change* 19(2): 377–398.

Gereffi, G., Humphrey, J., and Sturgeon, T. (2005). "The Governance of Global Value Chains," *Review of International Political Economy* 12(1): 78–104.

Gibbons, R. (2005). "Four Formal(izable) Theories of the Firm," *Journal of Economic Behavior and Organization* 58(2): 200–245.

Gospel, H. and Sako, M. (2010). "Unbundling of Corporate Functions: The Evolution of Shared Services and Outsourcing in Human Resource Management," *Industrial and Corporate Change* 19(5): 1–30.

Grant, R. M. (1996). "Toward a Knowledge-Based Theory of the Firm," *Strategic Management Journal* 17(10): 109–122.

Greenwood, R. and Empson, L. (2003). "The Professional Partnership: Relic or Exemplary Form of Governance?" *Organization Studies* 24(6): 909–933.

Greenwood, R., Hinings, C. R., and Brown, J. (1990). "'P2-Form' Strategic Management: Corporate Practices in Professional Partnerships," *Academy of Management Journal* 33(4): 725–755.

Hall, P. and Soskice, D. (eds.) (2001). *Varieties of Capitalism*. Oxford: Oxford University Press.

Holman, D., Batt, R., and Holtgrewe, U. (2007). "Global Call Center Report: International Perspectives on Management and Employment," Ithaca: Cornell University.

Kenny, M., Massini, S., and Murtha, T. P. (2009). "Offshoring Administrative and Technical Work: New Fields for Understanding the Global Enterprise," *Journal of International Business Studies* 40(6): 887–900.

Lacity, M. C., Khan, S. A., and Willcocks, L. P. (2009). "A Review of the IT Outsourcing Literature: Insights for Practice," *Journal of Strategic Information Systems* 18(3): 130–146.

Levitt, T. (1972). "Production-Line Approach to Service," *Harvard Business Review*, September–October: 41–52.

Levy, F. and Murnane, R. J. (2004). *The New Division of Labor: How Computers are Creating the Next Job Market*. Princeton, NJ: Princeton University Press.

McIvor, R. (2010). *Global Services Outsourcing*. Cambridge: Cambridge University Press.

McKinsey (2005). *The Emerging Global Labor Market*. Washington, DC: McKinsey Global Institute.

Manning, S., Massini, S., and Lewin, A. Y. (2008). "A Dynamic Perspective on Next-Generation Offshoring: The Global Sourcing of Science and Engineering Talent," *Academy of Management Perspectives* 22(3): 35–54.

Moorhead, R. (forthcoming). "Precarious Professionalism: Some Empirical and Behavioural Perspectives on Lawyers," *Current Legal Problems*.

Morgan, G. and Quack, S. (2005). "Institutional Legacies and Firm Dynamics: The Growth and Internationalization of UK and German Law Firms," *Organization Studies* 26(12): 1765–1785.

NAE (2008). "The Off-shoring of Engineering: Facts, Unknowns, and Potential Implications," Washington, DC: National Academy of Engineering.

Perrons, R. K., Richards, M. G., and Platts, K. (2004). "The Effect of Industry Clockspeed on Make-Buy Decisions in the Face of Radical Innovations: An Empirical Test," *International Journal of Technology Management* 8(4).

Porter, M. E. (1980). *Competitive Strategy*. New York: Free Press.

Sako, M. (2005). "Outsourcing and Offshoring: Key Trends and Issues," *Emerging Markets Forum*. Oxford.

Sako, M. (2006). "Outsourcing and Offshoring: Implications for Productivity of Business Services," *Oxford Review of Economic Policy* 22(4): 499–512.

Sako, M. (2011a). "Driving Power in Global Supply Chains," *Communications of the ACM* 54(7): 23–25.

Sako, M. (2011b). "General Counsel with Power?" *Insight Series No.7*, Novak Druce Centre for Professional Service Firms, University of Oxford.

Sako, M. (2013). "Professionals between Market and Hierarchy: A Comparative Political Economy Perspective," *Socio-Economic Review* 11(1): 1–28.

Simon, H. A. (1951). "A Formal Theory of the Employment Relationship," *Econometrica* 19(3): 293–305.

Storper, M. (2000). "Globalization, Localization, and Trade," in *The Oxford Handbook of Economic Geography*, ed. G. L. Clark, M. P. Feldman, and M. S. Gertler. Oxford: Oxford University Press, 146–165.

Sturgeon, T. J. (2002). "Modular Production Networks: A New American Model of Industrial Organization," *Industrial and Corporate Change* 11(3): 451–496.

Teece, D. J., Pisano, G., and Shuen, A. (1997). "Dynamic Capabilities and Strategic Management," *Strategic Management Journal* 18(7): 509–533.

Thun, E. (2010). "The Globalization of Production," in *Global Political Economy*, ed. S. Ravenhill. New York: Oxford University Press, 283–304.

UNCTAD (2011). *World Investment Report: Non-Equity Modes of Production and Development*. New York and Geneva: United Nations Conference on Trade and Development.

Willcocks, L. P. and Lacity, M. C. (1999). "IT Outsourcing in Insurance Services: Risk, Creative Contracting and Business Advantage," *Information Systems Journal* 9(3): 163–180.

PART III

PROFESSIONAL SERVICE FIRMS: INDIVIDUALS AND INTERACTIONS

CHAPTER 16

INTERPLAY OF PROFESSIONAL, BUREAUCRATIC, AND ENTREPRENEURIAL CAREER FORMS IN PROFESSIONAL SERVICE FIRMS

LAURIE COHEN

16.1 INTRODUCTION

IT is easy to imagine careers in bureaucracies, unfolding systematically over time as individuals navigate through their organizations in pursuit of hierarchical advancement. Scholars have argued that bureaucracy is at the heart of the career concept itself (Gowler and Legge 1989). But what of careers in Professional Service Firms (PSFs)? Can we assume the same onwards and upwards logic? Of course this is a somewhat crude caricature. We know that career-making is more complex than this, even in large, M-form organizations, and that in both theory and practice careers have been decoupled from the bureaucracies to which they were once seen to be inextricably linked. This greater variety is vividly illustrated in the metaphors of boundaryless (Arthur and Rousseau 1996), protean (Hall 2004), kaleidoscope (Mainiero and Sullivan 2005), and portfolio (Mallon and Cohen 2001) careers that have been introduced in the literature in the past two decades. Nevertheless, mindful of this diversity, bureaucracies continue to provide an organizing principle which bestows a sense of legitimacy, a reference point against which we gauge our aspirations and measure our success. Notwithstanding dissenting voices and unsettling experiences, metaphors of onward and upward die hard.

However, when we consider the implications of macro changes for the careers of individuals in different sectors and types of organization, our understandings appear fragmented. Although much careers research focuses on highly skilled actors, often working in PSFs, this context itself has received limited concerted attention—more often as a setting in which the "career action" takes place rather than as part of the action itself. How firms attempt to manage their incumbents' careers and how individuals themselves consider and enact their careers within these settings remain open questions. Drawing on some well-established conceptualizations and tapping into current debates, this chapter seeks to offer new insights into our understandings of careers in PSFs.

The chapter consists of four broad sections. Section 16.2 draws on Kanter's (1989) typology of career forms as bureaucratic, professional, and entrepreneurial, suggesting that in the contemporary PSF these forms overlap, sometimes peacefully coexisting and sometimes competing. Section 16.3 focuses on specific career management practices (more or less institutionalized) that can be associated with these forms. Transecting all three is the client—a figure whose role remains a shadowy presence in the extant literature but whose significance for people's career-making is critical. Section 16.4 turns to the individual, considering how the literature depicts the professional's engagement with the practices identified. A central issue here is that of control—who is in charge of individuals' careers and how people position themselves within the rules of the game. Section 16.5 proposes that a useful way of depicting careers in PSFs is as contested arenas, characterized by residual, dominant, and emergent meaning systems and practices (Williams 1977), working in dynamic hierarchies of prestige and legitimacy. The chapter concludes with some possible avenues for further research.

16.2 Bureaucratic, Professional, and Entrepreneurial Career Forms in the Professional Service Firm

PSFs are characterized by highly skilled professionals who provide specialist knowledge to clients' often complex problems (Empson 2007). Because of the importance of autonomy and self-determination, bureaucratic forms of organizing are assumed to be unsuitable for the practice of professional work and development of professional careers. Instead partnerships, based on principles of collegiality and self-monitoring, have been adopted as the most appropriate structures (Greenwood and Empson 2003). However, as PSFs have grown, an ideology of managerialism has become pervasive in late twentieth- and early twenty-first-century workplaces, regulatory changes have led to increasingly competitive markets for professional work, and as some professionals are rethinking how they want to live their lives (Galanter and Henderson 2008; Malhotra et al. 2010; Mueller et al. 2011), traditional forms of governance are arguably giving way to alternative arrangements.

Empson suggests that in contemporary PSFs there is a growing tension between the "twin ideals of professionalism and partnership" and the "increasing emphasis on commercialism and corporatism" (Empson 2007: 1314), with significant implications for forms of governance and dimensions of work organization, such as the basis of authority, division of labor, and management approaches. But what of the career implications of these changes? Although it is now 25 years old, Kanter's (1989) contribution to the first *Handbook of Career Theory* (Arthur et al. 1989) provides a useful framework for thinking about this question.

Kanter bemoans the narrowness of the careers literature (as it was in 1989), criticizing its neglect of the macro contexts in which careers are situated. She proposes three macro "forms of opportunity from which career patterns derive" (1989: 508): bureaucratic, professional, and entrepreneurial. The careers literature has certainly moved on apace on since 1989. However, this chapter returns to Kanter's three forms and considers their relevance to career-making in PSFs. Although we might expect them to fall squarely into Kanter's professional form, in fact we can observe elements of all three. Indeed, at the level of the career, the tension Empson predicts is partly played out in the coexistence of these different structures of opportunity and constraint.

16.2.1 The Professional Career Form

The logic underpinning Kanter's professional career form "is defined by craft or skill, with monopolization of socially valued knowledge the key determinant of occupational status, and 'reputation' the key resource for the individual" (1989: 510). Individuals operating within this form often have the same job title, and do more or less the same job, for many years. Opportunity and advancement involve taking on ever more complex, creative, or high-status cases—and conversely, being "stuck" is a consequence of limited challenge. Central to this form are principles of autonomy and self-determination. In Kanter's words, "[the professional form] creates a community of nominal peers with a broad range of skills who decide among themselves how best to deploy those skills. Gone are the trappings of hierarchy, from job classifications to grading systems to stacks of supervisors" (1989: 514). Instead it is professionals themselves who decide how work is distributed, and who gets the most complex (and most lucrative) cases.

However, this does not suggest that across a particular sector skills and expertise are necessarily given equal value or that individuals are always judged on their merits. Rather, within the professions there are hierarchies of prestige that determine how specific areas of expertise are accorded value. For example, in the legal field some specialisms, such as commercial and property law, enjoy higher status than immigration or family law, with resulting differences in reputational and material rewards (Schultz 2003).

Professional reputation also has a significant moral dimension that is unmentioned in Kanter's analysis. Abbott (1988) notes the importance of "character" to the image of the traditional professional. McKinlay develops this issue in his (2002) study of nineteenth-century bankers, portraying career as a moral project in which advancement was based on conformity to socially ratified rules. Although both Abbott and Galanter and Henderson (2008) depict the concept of professional reputation as continuously evolving, with its moral dimension fading in and out of view, the idea of the professional as charged with upholding society's moral values has persisted. This is apparent in the ways in which professionals present themselves to the outside world and in the public imagination. Significantly, in light of recent scandals, Faulconbridge and Muzio (2009) point to a certain skepticism with which professionals' commitment to the public good has come to be viewed. In spite of its continued (though contested) salience, the issue of morality in developing a career in PSFs has received very little research attention (see Dinovitzer et al., Chapter 6, this volume).

Within the professional career form, advancement is partly symbolic, linked to how one is viewed by stakeholder communities, within the firm and externally. For instance, in the UK a personal injury lawyer's reputation would be developed and performed within the firm, externally within the Association of Personal Injury Lawyers and other stakeholders with whom they interact, and of course through relationships with clients. While some professionals are deeply embedded within their organizations, others are less so (Pinnington 2011). Where mobility between PSFs is prevalent, reputation in this wider sense is even more important. Here computer software developers, who O'Riain (2010) characterizes as typically moving between producer and client firms, are a good example. The key point here is that within Kanter's professional career form it is above all reputation (variously construed) that drives material rewards, enabling high-status professionals to charge higher hourly rates than their lesser-known colleagues.

16.2.2 The Bureaucratic Career Form

In the bureaucratic form the individual's connection with the organization is fundamental. For Kanter, bureaucratic careers are characterized by a "logic of advancement" (1989: 509). Set within a hierarchical structure, progress consists of upward movement over an established timeframe. Opportunity is not only equated with material rewards, but also with learning, greater responsibility, and influence. These are closely tied to rank—the higher you are, the more and better you get. Some scholars, such as Malos and Campion (1995), suggest that bureaucratic principles are at odds with PSFs which exhibit few formal hierarchies and where autonomy and freedom to exercise one's professional judgment are prized over conformity to established rules. However, I would argue that although hierarchies do tend to be quite flat, this is not to suggest that the principle of advancement has no salience. Rather, as Greenwood and Empson (2003) show, junior recruits are enticed by the prospect of partnership and are willing to work hard for modest levels of remuneration in return for possible opportunities for vertical progress and greater material rewards. While aspects of this model are arguably being reconfigured (Galanter and Henderson 2008), in their empirical work scholars such as Malhotra et al. (2010) found that many individuals working in PSFs perceive that its basic tenets remain intact. Furthermore, Alvehus and Empson (2014) suggest that although in these settings specific hierarchical arrangements and the distinctions between "leaders" and "follow-ers" are much fuzzier than in traditional bureaucracies, managerial authority remains a crucial feature.

In the bureaucratic career form it is not the accrual of expert knowledge that is most valued, but long-term commitment to and steady progress within the organiza-tion. Kanter maintains that the bureaucratic type thereby creates weak task loyalty, but strong loyalties to the organization, "since ultimate financial and political rewards will only come with sticking it out long enough" (1989: 509). The traditional partnership structure still dominant in PSFs can be seen as a particular expression of this long-term affiliation—although recent research indicates that cracks have begun to emerge in this expectation of permanence (Galanter and Henderson 2008).

In their contribution to the *Handbook of Career Theory*, Gowler and Legge (1989) explain that the concept of career itself is inseparable from the bureaucratic forms of organization that emerged in the late nineteenth and twentieth centuries. Central to both is a type of control based on interlinked principles of accountability, hierarchy, achievement, and membership (1989). They suggest that it is through the rhetoric of career that these control mechanisms are internalized and enacted. This might appear to be at odds with the emphasis on autonomy and self-determination within the profes-sional career. However, in his analysis of careers in a Big Four accountancy firm, Grey (1994) proposes that in the PSF career development is a vehicle through which bureau-cratic control is embedded. This position will be further considered as the chapter pro-gresses. The issue here is that although these bureaucratic elements might seem to be inconsistent with Kanter's notion of the professional career form as an ideal type, and indeed some scholars downplay their relevance, others depict them as salient (indeed, increasingly prominent) features of individuals' career-making in PSFs.

With respect to reputation, Kanter's and Gowler and Legge's views diverge. Kanter associates it exclusively with the professional career form, arguing that: "The profession-al's reliance on reputation stands in great contrast with the anonymity of the bureau-crat" (1989: 512). Conversely, Gowler and Legge see reputation as fundamental to the bureaucratic career because hierarchical advancement depends on superiors' sponsor-ship: "Managing a career . . . involves the development of a 'high profile' and 'targeting' it at those with the authority to 'ease one's way up the ladder.' In other words, it involves the construction of a reputation that will further one's career" (1989: 446). The difference between reputation in the professional and the bureaucratic types is that for the former it is a proxy for expertise, moral virtue, and individual discretion, while in the latter it is an outcome of strict adherence to bureaucratic control mechanisms. Developing one's career in light of these conflicting but related imperatives is not always straightforward.

16.2.3 The Entrepreneurial Career Form

Kanter's third form is the entrepreneurial career. Although typically associated with the establishment of new, high-growth business ventures, her view is wider, extending to a career "in which growth occurs through the creation of new value or new organizational capacity . . . the key resource in an entrepreneurial career is the capacity to create valued outputs" (1989: 516). In the entrepreneurial form one's title might not change from year to year and the idea of hierarchical progress can be irrelevant. So advancement is growth in the domain over which one is responsible. In the PSF this idea of "growing territory" is most apparent in cases where an individual is charged with developing a new area of work, their remuneration is based on profits generated from this venture, and in some instances where one's tenure within the firm is dependent on the success of the initiative (see Reihlen and Werr, Chapter 12, and Barrett and Hinings, Chapter 11, this volume). The entrepreneurial career form, in which the individual is most exposed to the market, is the riskiest of Kanter's three.

Just as it promises least security, the entrepreneurial career is also characterized by the lowest levels of organizational embeddedness. Having developed a territory, the entrepreneurial professional becomes highly mobile, less dependent on the firm than on external affiliations, and with a reputation based more on clients' perceptions than the judgments of senior colleagues (Galanter and Henderson 2008). Within this form the professional's stock of knowledge extends beyond explicit, codified professional skills to include more general business competencies. Thus the entrepreneurial career most fully embraces the commercial imperative highlighted by Empson (2007).

Another take on the notion of the entrepreneurial career form is highlighted by Grey (1994). Drawing on Rose's (1989) Foucauldian analysis, he suggests that within the contemporary labor process individuals are increasingly construed as "entrepreneurs of the self": self-governing entities, self-contained and in charge of their own career development. From this perspective, the "enterprise" is not a new business venture; instead, the enterprise is the *self*, and the career is the vehicle through which the self is realized (Grey 1994). Grey argues that success involves a rigorous process of self-discipline and self-surveillance, including aspects of life outside of work that likewise must be "contained." Because the entrepreneurial project is the self, individuals' embeddedness within their organizations is not inevitable. Grey proposes that although professionals appear to be autonomous, they are in fact tightly bound and subject to their firms—internalizing their rules in the name of career.

16.2.4 Mixed Career Patterns

Of Kanter's three macro career forms the professional one is most obviously equated with PSFs. However, within these organizations are elements of all three. Kanter herself acknowledges that in practice they intersect in a range of ways: "mixed patterns" where aspects of the three forms combine; in transitions which in some cases can be seen as a move from one form to another; and as collective change resulting from larger ideological shifts, such as the advent of managerialism in the professional service context. It is at this level that we notice the potential clash between the ideals of professionalism, commercialism, and managerialism noted earlier. At the level of the organization, because of their differing priorities, required skill sets, and conceptualizations of success, the presence of all aspects of all three forms could engender greater inclusivity, thus enabling a wider diversity of people to be successful. Alternatively, the challenge that bureaucratic and entrepreneurial forms pose to the established professional career could ultimately lead to an erosion of professional ideologies of autonomy, self-determination, moral responsibility, and long-term commitment to the partnership which have been seen as important stabilizing, legitimating mechanisms. At the level of the individual the interplay of professional, bureaucratic, and entrepreneurial forms could pose challenges as people attempt to enact their careers amidst these sometimes incompatible imperatives, or conversely create spaces for them to steer their careers in accordance with their own priorities and aspirations. In the sections that follow I will first consider how, at the level of the firm, these career forms can be seen as (strongly or weakly) institutionalized through specific career practices. I will then consider how individuals enact their careers in light of these imperatives.

16.3 Career Forms in Practice

Kanter pitches her analysis at a macro level and does not examine how professional, bureaucratic, and entrepreneurial forms play out in people's career-making in PSFs. This section considers how they are institutionalized through specific career practices. It is an apt time to examine this issue. Traditionally PSFs paid little heed to career issues. Time-honored approaches prevailed and there was an implicit assumption that what was good for the firm was good for the people working within it. However, as Malhotra et al. (2010) highlight, operating in increasingly crowded fields where regulations are changing to include new entrants whose modes of behavior can be different from the established players', firms have begun to pay greater attention to issues of career development and engagement.

Here a few points must be noted. First, the scope of this chapter does not intend to be an exhaustive review of firms' practices. Rather, I have selected examples that have been identified as significant within the extant literature and my own research, and that exemplify key differences between Kanter's types. Second, there is a danger that we consider PSFs operating out of major cosmopolitan centers as the norm (an example being the prevalence of the Big Four firms in the literature on careers in accounting). Of course this is not the case and many, if not most professionals work outside of these settings. Third, as Chapter 1 of this volume emphasizes (Empson et al.) PSFs are a moving picture. With rapid changes afoot, existing career practices are likely to change in the coming years.

16.3.1 Career Practices in the Professional Form

Unsurprisingly, within PSFs the professional career form is the most strongly institutionalized, illustrated in the persistence of two related practices: an apprenticeship system and a "tournament" (Galanter and Palay 1991) or "up-and-out" promotion system (Greenwood and Empson 2003). As Malos and Campion (1995) explain, a unique feature of these firms is that when recruiting junior staff, senior members are not only looking for short-term productivity, but also future partners. To support this arrangement, systems are needed that enable newly qualified members to develop requisite skills and expertise, and also the tacit knowledge necessary to be productive and to develop their (and ultimately the firm's) reputation—in other words, that teach these new recruits the rules of the game. Second, it is necessary to have a progression model that ensures the continued stability and robustness of the partnership. Originating in elite New York City law firms in the early twentieth century (Galanter and Palay 1991), over the course of the century the tournament model moved from the US to the UK and extended to other sectors, including management consultancy and accounting, to become the dominant approach (Malhotra et al. 2010).

Following up Galanter and Palay's important work more than a decade-and-a-half later, Galanter and Henderson (2008) consider what happened to the tournament career system in the intervening period. Their conclusion is that although the robustness of the equity partnership model endured, other aspects of the tournament had changed significantly. They suggest that this new "elastic" tournament is characterized by a proliferation of non-partner roles, an increasingly complex promotion structure, and the geographical dispersion (in some cases disaggregation) of firms, not only across the United States, but also internationally. Galanter and Henderson argue that this structural transformation has had a significant influence on firms' cultural processes and practices, sense of affiliation, and community. With opportunities embodied in a range of alternative roles and positions, new prospects of mobility, and the chance to work in more entrepreneurial ways, one might assume that these changes would ultimately have profound implications for career-making in PSFs. However, despite allegations that the tournament is increasingly anachronistic, exclusive, and high risk (Pinnington and Sandberg 2013), in one form or another (Malhotra et al. 2010) it continues to feature in PSFs' career landscape, although operating more or less flexibly depending on the sector, firm, and geographical setting.

Within apprenticeship and tournament systems, new recruits work under the close guidance (or in Grey's (1994) view, under the close surveillance and control) of more senior colleagues. They progress through a limited number of hierarchical levels until they are invited to join the partnership, initially salaried and later buying in as equity partners. Individuals who fail to progress are asked to leave, or upon recognizing their limited prospects, might choose to go. Attrition can happen at any progression threshold, but a typical stage is between salaried and equity partnership, where a professional is given the nominal status of partner, but is not invited to share the profits—thus capping not only their earning potential, but also their influence. A significant aspect of this system is that at the outset compensation packages tend to be modest, with more generous remuneration opportunities coming later. Another is that the most interesting, challenging, and creative work is reserved for most experience, senior partners (Sang et al. 2014). It is the promise of such rewards that serves to align the interests of associates and partners within PSFs (Greenwood and Empson 2003).

Although this established model is based on principles of stability and continuity with the traditional expectation that partnerships are long-term arrangements, there is an in-built anomaly. Associates who are not invited to join their firms' partnerships (or earlier on who are not invited to progress on from one stage to another) typically leave, creating a market of professionals who are more or less experienced, but who have failed in the tournament model. Although less strongly institutionalized and less talked about than the tournament, firms develop recruitment practices which target these middle-ranking professionals, sometimes taking them on to cover staffing shortfalls or to develop new areas of work, with the expectation that if successful they can return to the partnership track. Significantly, this group of professional workers has received very little research attention.

16.3.2 Career Practices in the Bureaucratic Form

The career practices associated with the bureaucratic form are less strongly institutionalized than the professional ones. That said, there are three points to mention: first are bureaucratic elements within the tournament model; second are opportunities for senior professionals to focus on firm management; and third, scholars such as Galanter and Henderson (2008), Malhotra et al. (2010), and Mueller et al. (2011) argue that with the steady entrenchment of managerialist ideologies and recent regulatory changes in many sectors, tournament models in their various guises are starting to give way to more corporate approaches.

Regarding the first point, although the ideology of autonomy and the emphasis on expertise appear to drive the up-and-out model, underpinning this is a regime of management control: clearly enforced rules, surveillance, hierarchical distribution of roles and responsibilities, and an element of "serving time" as associates' progression movements are carefully monitored and managed according to strict timescales. As Grey (1994) suggests, the paradox is that within the PSF such is the motivation to progress that these mechanisms are internalized and thus rendered almost invisible, becoming forms of self-discipline imperative for career success. This effectively serves to perpetuate the ideology long associated with professional work.

Second, it is of course erroneous to think that development is only a matter for professionals at the start of their careers. At more senior levels there are opportunities for senior people to follow a more managerial trajectory—either out of interest or when the retirement of a current managing partner leaves a gap that needs filling. Although these routes are not strongly institutionalized, across professional sectors continuing professional development programs (CPD) provide pathways for those who choose these more bureaucratic trajectories. For example, CPD provided by the Royal Institute of British Architects includes courses on topics such as strategic management, and building and managing a business. Notably, partners who pursue management routes usually do them in combination with fee earning work, although over time some decide to focus exclusively on their management roles (Empson et al. 2013). In both cases, this non-fee earning work is compensated for within firms' profit sharing arrangements.

Third, although this position is not universally accepted (see Malos and Campion 1995 for a critique) Mueller and his colleagues (2011) argue there is an emerging consensus that the professional services sector is transforming from a model based on professionalism and partnership to a "managed professional business" emphasizing corporate and commercial values. According to Malhotra et al. (2010), the career practices resulting from this shift include a wider range of professional roles, such as "Of Council," a senior consultancy-type role (more prevalent in the US than the UK), the formalization of permanent associate positions, and professional support staff (sometimes termed paralegals, or in the UK, legal executives). Furthermore, firms have begun to develop their professional service functions, establishing human resource, finance, and accounts departments. Whereas these roles were traditionally undertaken by partners, in some firms they have now been shifted to specialists (Empson et al. 2013).

With some exceptions (Malhotra et al. 2010; Mueller et al. 2011), as yet there has been little research into these emerging forms. However, on the basis of conversations with informal contacts, I would suggest a number of ways in which these changes might impact on firms' career practices. Rather than the hybrid professional/managerial roles that senior partners often assume in a more or less serendipitous ways, in some firms these management positions could become more formalized and, as a consequence, acquire greater legitimacy as alternatives to production-oriented roles. Conversely, the recruitment of non-professional managers in functional areas could limit the potential for professionals to move across professional/managerial boundaries, restricting them to production trajectories. For example, in the legal sector the emergence of Alternative Business Structures (ABS) in which professionals and non-professionals share in firm ownership and management are likely to lead to new career practices that overlap with existing models. A particularly interesting case is that of Slater and Gordon, the Australian firm that has taken over UK firms to the extent that in November 2013 it was reported as holding 5% of the UK personal injury market, and was in number one or two position in other consumer law areas (Legal Futures website). In this ABS organization not only is there a very clear demarcation between professionals and non-professionals, but given that the firm is headquartered in Australia, senior partners are increasingly distanced from the firm's decision-making processes, potentially leading to the erosion of the ideology of autonomy and self-determination, and the established moral codes which have long underpinned professional work (Faulconbridge and Muzio 2009).

16.3.3 Career Practices in the Entrepreneurial Form

Finally, with regard to the entrepreneurial career form I will briefly consider two sets of practices. The first relates to the development of new business, while the second is linked to the concept of the professional as an "entrepreneur of the self" and the career as the vehicle through which this is realized. Within the entrepreneurial form professionals are explicitly positioned as service providers and the market has a presence in their career development. For individual career-making, this has important implications. As noted earlier, middle, and senior ranking professionals who are well established within their client markets and who have a "following," such that they can bring work with them or develop new territories, are seen as desirable commodities and can expect generous remuneration packages and progression prospects. These "rainmakers," often targeted by head-hunters, experience high levels of inter-firm mobility (Galanter and Henderson 2008; Sang et al. 2014)—arguably adding an element of dynamism and impermanence to sectors which have long been characterized by their stability and security. In his research into software developers, O'Riain (2010) found another form of career mobility to be between PSFs and client organizations. For his IT specialists it was not necessarily partnership within a specialist firm that was seen as the pinnacle of success; rather, they moved back and forth between producer and client organizations searching for the best career opportunities.

Clearly, different sectors will engage with aspects of the market in diverse ways: while software developers might be exceptional amongst professional sectors in their exposure to the market, for others such as architects or solicitors its effects will play out in other ways. The point here is not to catalogue the many and varied forms that market engagement might take, but rather to highlight its significance for career-making in PSFs, in particular the challenge it poses both to dominant professional career practices and also to less explicit bureaucratic ones that frequently operate under the radar. One might argue that through the entrepreneurial form residual ideologies of professional autonomy and self-determination are being re-inscribed and renegotiated, but with a strong orientation to the environment beyond the firm itself. This is likely to have significant implications for organizational embeddedness and for the long-termism traditionally associated with PSFs.

With respect to careers, the notion of the entrepreneur of the self can be linked, first, to the long-established tournament model and second, to more weakly institutionalized practices associated with career self-management. I previously referred to the tournament promotion model as a deeply institutionalized example of the professional career form with its focus on skills and expertise, but based on the bureaucratic principle of advancement and underpinned by (largely invisible) management control mechanisms. However, by placing responsibility for career advancement squarely at the feet of the individual professional worker, it is also strongly entrepreneurial.

The conviction that individuals are now in charge of their own career development coupled with organizations' increasing tendency to divest themselves of career management responsibilities have led careers researchers to take an interest in career self-management. Here King's (2004) typology of career self-management practices is a notable example. Although in most cases the practices she identifies are not strongly institutionalized, they are nevertheless in evidence in PSFs. King proposes that career self-management consists of three co-occurring behaviors. Through *positioning* people ensure that they have the right contacts, skills, and knowledge to advance, while *influencing* is about developing relationships with gatekeepers who actively promote the individual. Although strongly associated with the professional career form, the apprenticeship model can be seen to powerfully facilitate both. King's third strategy, *boundary management*, concerns the management of home and work spheres in order that they become mutually enhancing, or at least so that they don't clash. This practice is the most weakly institutionalized of King's three. Given its social salience, the issue of home/work harmonization is notable for its absence in the literature on careers in PSFs.

16.4 CLIENTS AND CAREER PRACTICES IN PROFESSIONAL SERVICE FIRMS

PSFs operate simultaneously in two markets: the market for clients and the market for staff. As Maister (1982) points out, these are inextricably linked, kept in balance via firms' economic and organizational structures. Both have a profound impact not only on elements of governance, structure, and firm design, but also on the ways in which work is carried out on a day-to-day basis. With respect to clients, although fundamental to individuals' career advancement, with a few notable exceptions (see, for example, O'Riain 2010) it is a missing dimension in analyses of careers in PSFs (see also Broschak, Chapter 14, this volume).

In career terms the development of relationships with clients is most obviously associated with the entrepreneurial form, in particular with middle and senior level career transitions where having a client following is often seen as a condition of progression (Sang et al. 2014). In some sectors, like IT, it can also lead to mobility between PSFs and client organizations. Indeed in my own research I have interviewed architects, solicitors, and accountants who have used their extensive contacts with clients to move from professional to non-professional organizations, such as banks, local authorities, and non-governmental organizations (NGOs).

However, the importance of the client for careers in PSFs extends beyond the practices associated with the entrepreneurial form. First, in the UK legal sector, firms have been allowed to advertise since 1986, with the practice moving on apace in the past decade following the passing of the Legal Services Act 2007. Coming into force in 2011, this opened up the legal field to non-lawyers, leading to intense competition and a whole new approach to advertising as lawyers and non-lawyers vie for market share. At firm level, one consequence has been the expansion of marketing activities. Although its ultimate impact on career practices is yet to be resolved, in some firms it has already led to the inclusion of marketing positions as an element of solicitors' progression and an increasing sense that this is a legitimate way for legal professionals to develop their career.

Second, although somewhat obscured in the ideal type, in practice the client is at center stage in the professional career form. Indeed it is to a large extent in relation to the client (individually or collectively) that a professional's reputation is made. Taking architecture, for example, Cohen et al. (2005) revealed the ways in which firms and individual architects established their reputations with respect to their client constituencies: visionary clients who look to their architects for artistic and design innovation; contractors who emphasize economies of scale; public sector clients who prioritize social function; ecclesiastical clients interested in historical preservation and the development of community; and homeowners seeking to extend their living space and add value to their property. Importantly, we found that architects did not enjoy the same degree of power or influence with these different types of clients: the starkest examples being at one extreme clients who accepted and deferred to the architect's creativity and expertise, and at the other contractors who saw the architect as in their employ and working to their agenda. Furthermore, professionals' reputations are formally codified in sector-specific rankings and league labels. In law, guides such as the Legal 500 and Chambers rank lawyers and firms based on feedback from peers and significantly, clients. As Alvehus and Empson (2014) point out, in order to be seen as a credible leader within the firm, an individual's success within the client market is essential. These rankings therefore play a crucial role in the establishment of reputation and thus they are critical in the process of career advancement.

There is another, more insidious way in which Ashley and Empson (2013) and Sang et al. (2014) found the client to impact on careers in PSFs. As noted earlier, there is a symbolic element to reputation that cannot be reduced to a person's skillfulness or depth of knowledge. In their study of why leading law firms discriminate on the basis of class, Ashley and Empson argue that in an increasingly volatile and crowded marketplace, clients find it difficult to discern quality on the basis of traditional, knowledge-based measures or brand value. To differentiate themselves, elite firms thus turn to the social, human, and embodied capital of their staff, privileging white, middle-class people who typically attended top public schools and universities and who comport themselves in ways which make clients feel comfortable (see also Sommerlad and Ashley, Chapter 20, this volume). As a partner in one of their case study firms explained: "[Corporate finance lawyers] have to stand up in a room, command someone's attention and tell them what they're going to be doing [which means that] having somebody who is more polished . . . speaks in the correct accent, and looks the part is actually quite important" (Ashley and Empson 2013: 237). According to Ashley and Empson, in spheres where knowledge is complex and the meaning of quality ambiguous, clients rely on other signifiers, like professionals' education and demeanor, to assess their (and by association their firm's) credibility. In the elite legal sector, social class thus became an important component of reputation and people from working-class backgrounds and/or those who did not attend the most prestigious universities found it difficult to advance.

Sang and her colleagues (2014) applied a similar sort of argument to their research into women in architectural firms. They show how women are systematically excluded from key client networking activities (such as golf and drinking). This exclusion had two important effects: first, it meant that women's contributions were frequently ignored and second, it made it very difficult for them to develop new business. Importantly, both were seen as essential to career progression. While the scope of this chapter does not allow for an extended discussion of the important issue of occupational closure, of central concern here is the breadth of clients' influence on the structure of career opportunity and constraint in PSFs and its implications for processes of diversity and social mobility (see Sommerlad and Ashley, Chapter 20, this volume).

16.5 ENACTING CAREERS IN PROFESSIONAL SERVICE FIRMS

When it comes to individuals' career enactment, according to Pinnington (2011) the literature is narrow in its sampling and perspectives, typically focusing on people working in large, established firms based in metropolitan settings, while neglecting the spectrum of firms that exists and the diversity of people working within them. What literature there is, however, highlights some of the ways in which individuals engage with the professional, bureaucratic, and career practices operating within their firms and the logic behind their choices and trajectories. This section examines Kanter's typology in relation to individuals' lived experiences.

One way of relating professional, bureaucratic, and entrepreneurial forms to individuals' career-making is to consider professional sectors in terms of their dominant orientation. Devine et al.'s (2000) study of accountants, actuarial professionals, solicitors, and financial consultants found that after an initial period of professional training, there were significant differences. The corporate bankers and the actuaries were predominantly bureaucratic in their career focus, perhaps unsurprisingly venture capitalists adhered more strongly to Kanter's entrepreneurial form, and the solicitors and accountants oriented mainly to professional trajectories. In each of these cases it was not that Kanter's other forms were irrelevant, but rather that they were legitimated within what was seen to be the dominant imperative.

However, a single, overarching career orientation is not inevitable. Rather, the extant literature depicts firms as including elements of all three, but shows how individuals engage with them differentially, frequently as a function of career stage. In early career proving one's professional competence is a central career preoccupation (Devine et al. 2000; Anderson-Gough et al. 2001; Mueller et al. 2011; Pinnington 2011). For example, Devine and her colleagues found that respondents in their four sectors were initially put on training contracts and their uppermost concern was to gain the requisite professional qualifications. In the words of one interviewee: "the firm didn't look at you as a professional person until you had your professional qualification" (2000: 532–533). This was likewise the case in Pinnington's (2011) analysis of an Australian law firm, where junior members prioritized technical expertise above all else. As they progressed, the lawyers in their study added bureaucratic and entrepreneurial activities to their portfolios: training junior colleagues, marketing and developing new business, leading groups and departments. In addition to participation in various activities and responsibilities that relate to Kanter's three forms, career advancement involves the taking on of new occupational identities. In a classic study, Ibarra (1999) describes career progression as a process of socialization through which people experiment with these "provisional selves," over time coming to see themselves as partners, leaders, or indeed entrepreneurs. More critical perspectives (Anderson-Gough et al. 2001; Mueller et al. 2011; Costas and Grey 2014) likewise underline the formation of identity as an important aspect of career progression, although conceptualizing it as a powerful disciplinary mechanism rather than a space for the exercise of individual agency. They see early career as an important stage during which this process of "intensive 'identity regulation'" (Costas and Grey 2014: 910) begins and "the future is conceived of in terms of ongoing improvement and success within organizations in ways potentially consistent with organizational power structures" (Costas and Grey 2014: 910).

As individuals advance, the interplay of professional, bureaucratic, and entrepreneurial forms is perhaps most vividly depicted in the development of reputation (see also Harvey and Mitchell, Chapter 13, this volume). At once inward and outward facing, it is in the concept of reputation that Ibarra's diverse "selves" begin to crystallize. A quote from one of the respondents to Mueller et al. (2011) illustrates how elements of the three intermingle in this process:

> I think it is a combination of making sure that you sell yourself—that you market yourself to the right people, so that those that have the power to make decisions are aware of who you are; showing true dedication and commitment; and a passion for what you, is another; and having something that separates you from the others. But you still have to sell yourself. (2011: 557)

Having successfully passed through the initial professional apprenticeship, constructing one's reputation is not simply a matter of technical acumen, but rather is political and performative—necessitating an acute awareness of how the firm's hierarchy works, but also how to appeal to relevant stakeholders beyond the boundaries of the firm itself. As one's career advances, building a reputation thus involves attention to the rules of the game, and strategic maneuvering through these imperatives.

A central issue here is how professionals position themselves with respect to the rules and in light of this, how they engage with the game (Coffey 1994; Anderson-Gough et al. 2001). The respondents in Grey's (1994) study of careers in a Big Four accountancy firm seemed to uncritically accept the rules and whole-heartedly threw themselves into the game. As "entrepreneurs of the self," they took full responsibility for their career development, internalizing mechanisms of management control which Grey argues underpinned the various career management practices at work in that organization. However, because they were disguised by an ideology of professional autonomy and self-determination, these external control mechanisms were rendered invisible, translated into self-discipline and an unwavering belief that whatever happened was in their best career interests. Describing the rating process Grey argues that:

> Instead of being construed as an irksome, intrusive and threatening technique of management control, it becomes a benevolent process for the realization of this perfection, a technique to assist individuals to become their true selves and to realize their aspirations. Even the act of sacking is reconstituted through the personnel department as 'counseling out' a supposedly mutual career decision for the employee to leave the firm. (Grey 1994: 489)

Thus what was good for the firm appeared to be uniformly understood as good for the individual. What is so striking about Grey's analysis is that it appears to be so all-encompassing, including not only what happens at work but "disciplining" and effectively neutralizing other aspects of life as well: "If . . . this game comes to include all other forms of social relations, so much the better, since this renders the project of self-management ever more achievable" (Grey 1994: 495). It is also lacking in any resistant voices. In Grey's view, people have no wish to resist because it is simply not in their interests to do so.

In the intervening 20 years, however, such voices have started to resound. The literature emerging from this period conveys a stronger sense of individual agency, depicting individuals not as trapped by their firms' career structures, but as actively engaging with the varied imperatives at work in their firms and beyond. Focusing, like Grey, on Big Four accountancy firms, Kosmala and Herrbach (2006) show how people's sense of professional integrity was challenged by their firms' overarching emphasis on commercial gain. In true postmodern spirit, they describe how their respondents "played" with the rules of the game, maneuvering amongst the demands of the accountancy profession, their firm, colleagues, and peers in highly agentic ways that gave them a sense of freedom and autonomy, but at the same time ensuring their continued compliance, ultimately securing their career advancement. Five years later, writing once again about the same setting (albeit in Australia) and investigating the experience of women managers in particular, Mueller and his colleagues (2011) paint a darker and more ambivalent picture. Although recognizing the link between promotion, networking, and playing politics, many of the women in their study responded by becoming cynical and distancing themselves from the entrepreneurial imperatives which had become so pivotal to career advancement:

> Our respondents seemed to put a negative evaluation on exposure, visibility and marketing yourself: thus they do not seem to have become complicit in the management of the self as having effectively been handed over for the benefit of the firm. (Mueller et al. 2011: 558)

A more recent take on the exercise of agency and the possibility of resistance within PSFs is provided by Costas and Grey (2014). Through their study of management consultants, they examine the relationship between temporality and power. In addition to the two approaches discussed thus far (one which aligned the developing self with the organization, and a more cynical view in which respondents distanced themselves but ultimately capitulated for the sake of progression), they found that individuals construct imaginary "future selves" that reject corporate disciplinary regimes and their demand for constant improvement:

> These imaginary future selves express little faith in an improved future self by align-ing oneself to the disciplinary power regime—such a future self seems to be feared or disdained. Imaginary future selves entail an alternative future construction, one which appears less 'colonized' by the organizational power regimes. (Costas and Grey 2014: 925)

Here it was not the case of maneuvering between different career forms, but rather rejecting the corporate regime as a whole, together with its never-ending demands for people to become more and better. An important issue, left somewhat unresolved, is whether these imaginary futures effectively work as a coping mechanism that leaves the status quo intact, or constitute a challenge to existing arrangements.

This strand of research also raises questions about which professional workers are engaging in these alternative forms of identity work and why. As noted earlier, research into diversity and PSFs has highlighted processes of social closure and the restriction of opportunities for certain social groupings (Ashley and Empson 2013; Tomlinson et al. 2013; Sang et al. 2014). In this light, one might speculate that for the women in Mueller et al.'s study, the strategy of distancing themselves from the rules of the game was a response to such exclusionary mechanisms. This remains an open question.

However, it is not only through processes of identity construction that people inter-act with firm structures and career practices. Reminiscent of King's work on career self-management, research has highlighted the specific behavioral strategies through which individuals deal with exclusionary career practices. In a study of the careers of women professionals and managers in Sri Lanka (a third of whom worked in PSFs), Dulini Fernando and I (2011) identified eight strategies that women developed to over-come gender-related obstacles: adapting, compromising, explaining, manipulating, deceiving, networking, resisting, and opting out. Two years later this list was echoed, with some differences, in Tomlinson et al.'s (2013) research into black and minority eth-nic lawyers. Examples from both studies demonstrate individuals' skillfully navigat-ing between professional, bureaucratic, and entrepreneurial practices: where barriers were perceived in one form, they turned to opportunities in others. For example, in the Sri Lankan study, because established professional models of advancement sometimes eluded them, gaining sponsorship from superiors was essential to progression and respondents explained how they deployed strategies such as networking and manipulat-ing to secure their bosses' support. In Tomlinson et al.'s research, "rainmakers" sought to develop extensive networks of clients outside of their own firms, much like O'Riain's (2010) IT professionals. A notable but unsurprising element in both studies is that often women's strategies were aimed at enabling them to surreptitiously cope with roles and responsibilities at home that were seen to conflict with their work lives—a dimension that receives very little attention in the extant literature (apart from that which specifically focuses on gender). The exception here is Malhotra et al.'s (2010) human resources managers. It is interesting that although these respondents highlight the increasing importance of lifestyle issues in professionals' career thinking, it does not appear in the accounts of the professionals themselves.

Such studies highlight the scope for exercising individual agency in the enactment of careers in professional firms, the extent to which individuals who are constrained by the established career systems can find ways to advance and the way in which the existence of different career forms provides space for negotiation and navigation. However, it is notable that with only one exception, the deployment of these strategies left the prevailing order largely untouched, illustrating the robustness of existing arrangements. Notwithstanding the current emphasis on change and diversity, an overriding message from the extant research is the persistence of established notions of legitimacy, the reluctance of senior staff to ratify alternative approaches, and the collusion of associates in "policing" and thereby securing the status quo.

16.6 CONCLUSIONS

At the outset of this chapter I suggested that Kanter's macro framework could be applied to PSFs, capturing in an ideal-typical way the coexistence of three career logics: professional, bureaucratic, and entrepreneurial. It is thus a useful typology for understanding some of the tensions at play in the process of career-making: the focus on skill, expertise, and reputation in the professional form; on advancement and the adherence to formal rules and regulations in the bureaucratic one; and in the entrepreneurial form on business innovation and growth on one hand, and the development of the career as a project of the self on the other. The presence of these apparently contradictory forms within PSFs creates spaces for negotiation, contestation, and navigation.

As is the case with any ideal-typical framework, the precise ways in which these forms combine and play out in practice will differ between firms, sectors, geographical settings, etc. Significantly, the practices associated with these types are not "pure" in any sense, but rather contain aspects of the others, thus highlighting their inherent dynamism. While some practices such as the apprenticeship and the tournament are deeply institutionalized and remarkably resilient, they nevertheless operate within a rapidly changing environment, melding with new approaches that arise in the wake of these ongoing modifications. A useful way of thinking about the interplay of professional, bureaucratic, and entrepreneurial career forms (and their associated practices) in this dynamic setting is offered by Raymond Williams in *Marxism and Literature* (1977). Williams proposes a threefold framework for thinking about cultural systems and practices: dominant, residual, and emergent. Dominant meaning systems reflect the

interests of the most powerful actors in the setting and as such hold the greatest legitimacy; residual are those brought from the past but reconstituted in the present; and
emergent are those "new meanings and values, new practices, new relationships and
kinds of relationship [that] are continually being created" (Williams 1977: 123). None
of these modes is static, and in practice it can be difficult to discern one from the other.
However, as a heuristic device this framework is useful in highlighting how, over time,
patterns of meaning-making and practice intersect, sometimes working in parallel but
more often entangled and competing for prestige and legitimacy. Although Williams
was primarily interested in social class formation, reproduction, and transformation
his framework can be usefully applied to careers (Cohen 2006). Considering the interplay of professional, bureaucratic, and entrepreneurial career forms (and their related
practices) in terms of dominant, residual, and emergent patterns can provide valuable
insights into processes of reproduction, resistance, and transformation, and into the
ongoing negotiation of legitimacy within PSFs.

Turning to the individual, this chapter has considered the diverse ways in which individuals navigate through their complex settings in developing their careers. Central
here is the alignment of individuals' and firms' interests. While Grey's study presents
a view of management control as ubiquitous, later work reveals tears in his canvas and
the emergence of resistant voices and alternative identities, thus creating possibilities
for change. Studies of women and people from minority ethnic backgrounds highlight
subtle mechanisms of social closure, draw attention to non-work spheres that receive
very little coverage in the literature and identify strategies that individuals use to achieve
career progress. Although these strategies offer possibilities of resistance and challenge,
more typically they serve to reinforce existing arrangements.

As stated at the outset of this chapter, notwithstanding the social, economic, and cultural significance of PSFs, careers researchers have not yet fully investigated processes of
career-making within these settings. Portraying the PSF as a contested arena, this review
has identified some fruitful avenues for further research. First, it is important that
researchers continue to examine the complex relationship between management control
and individual autonomy, and the ways in which individuals make sense of and seek to
develop their careers in a setting characterized by these sometimes conflicting imperatives. Within the extant careers field this relationship has been examined using Giddens'
(1979) theory of structuration, applied to careers by Barley in 1989 and latterly further
developed by Duberley et al. (2006). Another tack is via Bourdieu's field theory (1977),
introduced to the careers field by Iellatchitch and his colleagues (2003) and applied
widely since then (Pinnington and Gray 2007; Doherty and Dickmann 2009; Duberley
and Cohen 2010). While both approaches posit an iterative, mutually constitutive interplay of structural contexts and individual action, scholars have in the main focused their
empirical work at the level of the individual, paying far less heed to how individuals'
career-making impacts back on their organizations and more widely on the institutions
in which they are situated. A further approach, therefore, would be the application of
current research into institutional work (transformation and maintenance) (Lawrence

et al. 2011) to consider how professionals' career-making behavior reverberates on these contexts.

Second, traversing the forms and impacting on career practices in a range of ways are the clients. A largely missing element from careers research generally and PSFs in particular, their influence is profound. It is with the client in mind that reputations are built—including not only established and expected aspects like skill, expertise, and moral integrity, but in some cases also subtler and more insidious elements like "pedigree," comportment, and appearance. Furthermore, the development of a client base is central to career mobility and advancement at middle and later career stages. These stages remain under-researched. This is an unfortunate gap because there is an implicit assumption that for professionals nothing much happens after early career. Not only is this erroneous with respect to established practices, but the turbulent context in which professional firms operate has led to far more movement at more senior levels, with significant implications for the concept of partnership and the increasingly divergent ways in which it is enacted.

Third, while this review has noted the headway that scholars have made into the implications of gender, ethnicity, and social class for career-making in PSFs, this could usefully be developed. In particular, current debates on intersectionality and its relevance to work and organization (Walby et al. 2012; Harding et al. 2013) could offer valuable insights into the reproduction of existing arrangements within PSFs, but also highlight their potential for change. In particular, intersectional perspectives could enhance our understandings of how diverse individuals proactively engage with and navigate through their work settings in their career-making activities.

Fourth, it is important that further research into careers in PSFs continues to address issues of change. Galanter and Henderson (2008) detailed the ways in which the tournament promotion model became increasingly "elastic" in the years following Galanter and Palay's 1991 analysis. As PSFs continue to respond to new regulatory arrangements, changing markets (both in terms of clients and the professional labor force) and constantly evolving social attitudes, values, and lifestyle preferences, careers research needs to track and examine the implications of such wide-ranging changes for firms, individuals, and their interplay. A significant aspect of this endeavor will be a consideration of the moral dimension of professional careers (Abbott 1988; McKinlay 2002) which, as noted earlier, has been largely neglected in the extant literature.

Finally, future work might pay greater heed to non-elite firms based in provincial towns and cities. In spite of the fact that the majority of people work in such places, their contribution to extant understandings remains marginal in a field dominated by research on the highest profile law firms and "Big Four" accountancy firms in important metropolitan centers. Although within the careers field there have long been calls for deeper engagement with context and some extremely valuable work at the level of the national and supranational context (Mayrhofer et al. 2004), in the main the significance of particular local settings for career building has been neglected. As Johns (2006: 389) argues, "The fruits of extant research on work context are often ignored unless they are a declared, substantive aspect of a particular research study. In addition, such contextual features are often studied in a piecemeal fashion, in isolation from each other." Indeed, it was this lack of contextualization that Kanter herself was responding to through the bureaucratic, professional, entrepreneurial typology. In a recent article, entrepreneurship scholars Gill and Larson (2014) take issue with the privileging of Silicon Valley in dominant understandings of entrepreneurship, highlighting instead the importance of local geographies in our sense-making and subsequent action. Likewise, academics studying how careers are constructed and enacted in PSFs might usefully turn their attention beyond our major cities and high-status firms to more ordinary local settings in which most professionals conduct their day-to-day working lives and, over time, build their careers.

REFERENCES

Abbott, A. (1988). *The System of Professions*. Chicago, IL: University of Chicago Press.

Alvehus, J. and Empson, L. (2014). "Leading Autonomous Followers: Indirect, Overt and Covert Leadership Practices in Professional Service Firms," Working Paper, CPSF-0012.

Anderson-Gough, F., Grey, C. and Robson, K. (2001). "Test of Time: Organizational Time-Reckoning and the Making of Accountants in two Multi-National Accounting Firms," *Accounting, Organizations and Society* 26(2): 99–122.

Arthur, M. B. and Rousseau, D. (eds.) (1996). *The Boundaryless Career: A New Employment Principle for a New Organizational Era*. Oxford: Oxford University Press.

Arthur, M. B., Hall, D. T., and Lawrence, B. S. (eds.) (1989). *Handbook of Career Theory*. Cambridge: Cambridge University Press.

Ashley, L. and Empson, L. (2013). "Differentiation and Discrimination: Understanding Social Class and Social Exclusion in Leading Law Firms," *Human Relations* 66(2): 219–244.

Barley, S. R. (1989). "Careers, Identities and Institutions," in *The Handbook of Career Theory*, ed. M. B. Arthur and B. S. Lawrence. Cambridge: Cambridge University Press, 41–61.

Bourdieu, P. (1977). *Outline of a Theory of Practice*, trans. R. Nice. Cambridge: Cambridge University Press.

Coffey, A. (1994). "'Timing is Everything': Graduate Accountants, Time and Organizational Commitment," *Sociology* 28(4): 943–956.

Cohen, L. (2006). "'Remembrance of Things Past': Cultural Process and Practice in the Analysis of Career Stories," *Journal of Vocational Behavior* 69(2): 189–201.

Cohen, L., Wilkinson, A., Arnold, J. and Finn, R. (2005). "'Remember I'm the Bloody Architect': Architects, Organizations and Discourses of Profession," *Work, Employment & Society* 19(4): 775–796

Costas, J. and Grey, C. (2014). "The Temporality of Power and the Power of Temporality: Imaginary Future Selves in Professional Service Firms," *Organization Studies* 35: 909–937.

Devine, F., Britton, J., Mellor, R., and Halfpenny, P. (2000). "Professional Work and Professional Careers in Manchester's Business and Financial Sector," *Work, Employment & Society* 14(3): 521–540.

Doherty, N. and Dickmann, M. (2009). "Exposing the Symbolic Capital of International Assignments," *International Journal of Human Resource Management* 20(2): 301–320.

Duberley, J. and Cohen, L. (2010). "Gendering Career Capital: An Investigation of Scientific Careers," *Journal of Vocational Behavior* 76(2): 187–197.

Duberley, J., Cohen, L., and Mallon, M. (2006). "Constructing Scientific Careers: Change, Continuity and Context," *Organization Studies* 27: 1131–1151.

Empson, L. (2007). "Professional Service Firms," in *International Encyclopedia of Organizational Studies*, ed. S. Clegg and J. Bailey. London: Sage, 1311–1315.

Empson, L., Cleaver, I., and Allen, J. (2013). "Managing Partners and Management Professionals: Institutional Work Dyads in Professional Partnerships," *Journal of Management Studies* 50: 808–844.

Faulconbridge, J. R. and Muzio, D. (2009). "The Financialization of Large Law Firms: Situated Discourses and Practices of Reorganization," *Journal of Economic Geography* 9(5): 641–661.

Fernando, D. and Cohen, L. (2011). "Exploring the Interplay between Gender, Organizational Context and Career: A Sri Lankan Perspective," *Career Development International* 16: 553–571.

Galanter, M. and Henderson, W. (2008). "The Elastic Tournament: A Second Transformation of the Big Law Firm," *Stanford Law Review* 60: 1867–1929.

Galanter, M. and Palay, T. (1991). *Tournament of Lawyers*. Chicago, IL: University of Chicago Press.

Giddens, A. (1979). *Central Problems in Social Theory*. Berkeley, CA: University of California Press.

Gill, R. and Larson, G. (2104). "Making the Ideal (Local) Entrepreneur: Place and the Regional Development of High-Tech Entrepreneurial Identity," *Human Relations* 67(5): 519–542.

Gowler, D. and Legge, K. (1989). "Rhetoric in Bureaucratic Careers: Managing the Meaning of Management Success," in *Handbook of Career Theory*, ed. M. B. Arthur, D. T. Hall, and B. S. Lawrence. Cambridge: Cambridge University Press, 437–453.

Greenwood, R. and Empson, L. (2003). "The Professional Partnership: Relic or Exemplary Form of Governance?" *Organization Studies* 24: 909–933.

Grey, C. (1994). "Career as Project of the Self and Labour Process Discipline," *Sociology* 28(2): 479–497.

Hall, D. T. (2004). "The Protean Career: A Quarter-Century Journey," *Journal of Vocational Behavior* 65(1): 1–13.

Harding, N., Ford, J., and Fotaki, M. (2013). "Is the 'F'-Word Still Dirty? A Past, Present and Future of/for Feminist and Gender Studies in *Organization*," *Organization* 20(1): 51–65.

Ibarra, H. (1999). "Provisional Selves: Experimenting with Image and Identity in Professional Adaptation," *Administrative Science Quarterly* 44(4): 764–791.

Iellatchitch, A., Mayrhofer, W., and Meyer, M. (2003). "Career Fields: A Small Step towards a Grand Theory?" *International Review of Human Resource Management* 14(5): 728–750.

Johns, G. (2006). "The Essential Impact of Context on Organizational Behaviour," *Academy of Management Review* 31(3): 386–408.

Kanter, R. M. (1989). "Career and the Wealth of Nations: A Macro-Perspective on the Structure and Implications of Career Forms," in *Handbook of Career Theory*, ed. M. B. Arthur, D. T. Hall, and B. S. Lawrence. Cambridge: Cambridge University Press, 506–521.

King, Z. (2004). "Career Self-Management: Its Nature, Causes and Consequences," *Journal of Vocational Behavior* 65(1): 112–133.

Kosmala, K. and Herrbach, O. (2006). "The Ambivalence of Professional Identity: On Cynicism and Jouissance," *Human Relations* 59(10): 1393–1428.

Lawrence, T. B., Suddaby, R., and Leca, B. (2011). "Institutional Work: Refocusing Institutional Studies of Organization," *Journal of Management Inquiry* 20(1): 52–58.

Legal Futures. <http://www.legalfutures.co.uk>, accessed February 24, 2014.

McKinlay, A. (2002). "Dead Selves: The Birth of the Modern Career," *Organization* 9(4): 594–614.

Mainiero, L. A. and Sullivan, S. E. (2005). "Kaleidoscope Careers: An Alternate Explanation for the 'Opt-Out' Revolution," *Academy of Management Executive* 19(1): 106–123.

Maister, D. (1982). "Balancing the Professional Service Firm," *Sloan Management Review* 24: 15–29.

Malhotra, N., Morris, T., and Smets, M. (2010). "New Career Models in UK Professional Service Firms: From Up-and-Out to Up-and-Going-Nowhere?" *International Journal of Human Resource Management* 21: 1396–1413.

Mallon, M. and Cohen, L. (2001). "Time for a Change? Women's Accounts of the Move from Organizational Careers to Self-Employment," *British Journal of Management* 12(3): 217–230.

Malos, S. and Campion, M. (1995). "An Options-Based Model of Career Mobility in Professional Service Firms," *Academy of Management Review* 20(3): 611–644.

Mayrhofer, W., Meyer, M., Iellatchitch, A., and Schiffinger, M. (2004). "Careers and Human Resource Management: A European Perspective," *Human Resource Management Review* 14(4): 473–498.

Mueller, F., Carter, C., and Ross-Smith, A. (2011). "Making Sense of Career in a Big Four Accounting Firm," *Current Sociology* 59(4): 551–567.

O'Riain, S. (2010). "The Missing Customer and the Ever-Present Market: Software Developers and the Service Economy," *Work & Occupations* 37(3): 320–348.

Pinnington, A. (2011). "Competence Development and Career Advancement in Professional Service Firms," *Personnel Review* 40(4): 443–465.

Pinnington, A. and Gray, J. (2007). "The Global Restructuring of Legal Services Work? A Study of the Internationalization of Australian Law Firms," *International Journal of the Legal Profession* 14: 147–172.

Pinnington, A. and Sandberg, J. (2013). "Lawyers' Professional Careers: Increasing Women's Inclusion in the Partnership of Law Firms," *Gender, Work & Organization* 20(6): 616–631.

Rose, N. (1989). *Governing the Soul: The Shaping of the Private Self.* London: Routledge.

Sang, K., Dainty, A., and Ison, S. (2014). "Gender in the UK Architectural Profession: (Re)producing and Challenging Hegemonic Masculinity," *Work, Employment and Society* 28(2): 247–264.

Schultz, U. (2003). "Women in the World's Legal Professions: Overview and Synthesis," in *Women in the World's Legal Professions*, ed. U. Schultz and G. Shaw. Oxford and Portland, OR: Hart Publishing, xxv–lix.

Tomlinson, J., Muzio, D., Sommerlad, H., Webley, L., and Duff, L. (2013). "Structure, Agency and Career Strategies of White Women and Black and Minority Ethnic Individuals in the Legal Profession," *Human Relations* 66(2): 245–270.

Walby, S., Armstrong, J., and Strid, S. (2012). "Intersectionality: Multiple Inequalities in Social Theory," *Sociology* 46(2): 224–240.

Williams, R. (1977). *Marxism and Literature.* Oxford: Oxford University Press.

CHAPTER 17

TEAMWORK AND COLLABORATION IN PROFESSIONAL SERVICE FIRMS

Evolution, Challenges, and Opportunities

HEIDI K. GARDNER

17.1 INTRODUCTION

KNOWLEDGE is the essential ingredient that enables Professional Service Firms (PSFs) to deliver services to their clients (Greenwood et al. 2005; Hitt et al. 2001; Morris et al. 2012), and teams are a primary vehicle for conducting work in these types of firms (Werr and Stjernberg 2003). PSF teams bring together members to undertake client work that is too large, complex, uncertain, and non-routine to be managed by a single person alone. Across a range of professional contexts, from consulting and accounting to engineering and software services, work has typically been delivered by fluid teams of knowledge workers who come together to execute a project before breaking up and moving on to the next project (Edmondson and Nembhard 2009; Huckman et al. 2009). Such project teams are usually structured hierarchically, with a designated team leader having formal authority over a small pyramid of team members who represent different levels of seniority. As such, these teams deliver the financial benefits of workforce leverage (Maister 2004) and provide the foundation of professional firms' classic apprenticeship-based professional development models by allowing junior team members to learn from directly interacting with more senior team members.

Increasingly, trends in the PSF arena, as will be explained below, have given rise to a new form of teamwork that involves more open-ended, fluid collaborations between senior-level peers or partners within firms. One common form of such collaboration involves senior professionals within a firm who form client service teams to manage relationships and coordinate business development with key accounts (see Broschak, Chapter 14, and Harvey and Mitchell, Chapter 13, this volume). Even in historically individualistic fields, such as law or executive search, more leading global firms are examining the ways in which collaborative working might result in better client service and create a lasting competitive edge (Adler et al. 2008).

The core premise of this chapter is that this evolution from traditional, highly structured project teams to more fluid, open-ended, peer-to-peer collaboration presents a number of fundamental challenges for professional firms. This shift is further complicated by some of the other trends in the PSF arena, which are elaborated below. Overall, however, these issues remain largely under-researched. The chapter therefore lays out a research agenda focusing on opportunities to better understand peer collaboration in PSFs, particularly with regard to senior-level collaboration such as between highly autonomous partners. In addition, the chapter identifies some ways that recent changes in the professional sector challenge our understanding of even traditional teamwork, and it identifies specific gaps that deserve scholarly attention.

To lay a foundation, the first section draws on existing literature to provide a brief analysis of the evolution teamwork in PSFs. At the outset, it examines the nature of traditional project-based teams in PSFs and contrasts them with the emerging forms of less bounded, partner-to-partner collaboration. Then it outlines the market and sector trends that are driving the need for firms to embrace new forms of teamwork. It concludes by summarizing the distinctive characteristics of PSFs that can pose challenges to working effectively in either traditional project teams or less-bounded collaborations in this setting.

Despite the shift towards looser forms of collaboration, professional firms' performance still depends in great part on the extent to which classic project teams are able to leverage the full complement of their diverse expertise (Gardner et al. 2012). The next section steps back to review what we know about these more traditionally-structured work groups. It focuses on three essential knowledge-related processes—(1) identifying member knowledge, (2) seeking and sharing knowledge, and (3) integrating and applying knowledge—and the challenges to doing them effectively in PSFs. To propose future directions for PSF-specific research, this section identifies gaps in our understanding about project teams in this setting and considers avenues to extend the ideas to more loosely bounded, dynamic, senior-level collaborations.

Organizational researchers, like the professional firms they study, are now working to understand the opportunities associated with evolving forms of teamwork, and much work remains to be done. The third section examines some nascent research focused on fluid, partner-to-partner collaborative working. Given that such research is in its early stages, this section focuses primarily on setting the stage for research going forward.

The chapter concludes by summarizing the core themes and integrating them to propose an overarching agenda for future research.

17.2 THE EVOLUTION OF TEAMWORK AND COLLABORATION IN PROFESSIONAL SERVICE FIRMS

Historically, PSFs have relied on project teams as the primary vehicle to deliver client work. Although their size and composition differed somewhat across firms and professional sectors, project teams nevertheless held many common features, outlined below, that corresponded roughly to what Hackman (1990) called a "real team." Recent research suggests, though, the nature of interdependent working is evolving in PSFs. This section reviews literature to explain how the new forms of collaboration contrast with traditional project teams and to suggest why those shifts are occurring. It also draws on existing research to define characteristics of PSFs that make both classic and newer forms of teamwork especially challenging compared to many other organizational settings.

17.2.1 Traditional, Structured Project Teams versus Dynamic, Partner-to-Partner Collaboration

A large literature on project-based organizations (e.g., Hobday 2000; Sydow et al. 2004) indicates that classic project teams in PSFs share two broad structural features. First, project teams' boundaries are typically clearly delineated in terms of their membership, time, and responsibility. That is, a defined group of teammates work together for a set period of time to achieve a certain goal or carry out a specific task (Sydow et al. 2004). When the given task is accomplished, traditional project teams disband before each member is assigned to another project (Edmondson and Nembhard 2009). Second, project teams typically have a hierarchical structure, including a formal leader and junior members occupying roles aligned to their organizational tenure. In PSFs, team members are usually either selected by the partners in charge or assigned by a firm's staffing director in an attempt to match each member's knowledge and skills with the requirements of the project, given availability constraints.

Both these aspects of project teams—the boundaries and the hierarchy—are becoming more fluid in contemporary PSFs, following trends in the broader environment (for general reviews, see Tannenbaum et al. 2012; Wageman et al. 2012). For example, professionals increasingly work on multiple projects simultaneously (O'Leary et al. 2011), which may blur the boundaries of membership. Cummings and Haas (2012: 334–335) note, "The [professional services] organization we studied provides one illustration of how stable, bounded teams might be a relic of the past: not a single team in our dataset had all members allocate 100 percent of their time to the team." Further, PSF project teams often experience membership changes because of staff turnover or transfers, or changing project requirements (Huckman et al. 2009). In addition, advances in communication technology that allow teams with geographically distributed members to work together more efficiently have given rise to more "virtual" teams (McDonough et al. 2001), and this trend is similarly observable in contemporary PSFs. Finally, professional work that would historically have been conducted by a single team in one firm is increasingly broken into parts that are each done by specialized providers who can perform them better or more cost-effectively (see Sako, Chapter 15, this volume). In sum, studies have identified multi-team membership, frequent compositional changes, geographic distribution, and disaggregation as aspects of teamwork in contemporary PSFs that mean team boundaries are fuzzier and less stable than the literature on project teams has generally acknowledged.

It stands to reason that all four of these factors would be amplified when senior professionals (e.g., partners, senior-level content experts, PSF executives) work together. For example, partners might collaborate to develop business with a new set of clients, and this effort would likely stretch over time and across clients; meanwhile each partner would need to devote time to serving his or her existing clients. Multi-team membership is therefore likely to be the norm for most senior-level collaborations. The group composition will typically change repeatedly because most partners will be involved only in the parts of the initiative that directly relate to their area of expertise. Furthermore, client service teams comprise professionals from various practice groups across a firm who work together to develop a coordinated approach for handling the client's needs and to generate additional business through cross-selling others' specialty services. Overall, then, collaboration among senior professionals is likely to be considerably more dynamic and distributed, and the boundaries less clear than in traditional project team structures.

Research also suggests that the associated power dynamics are another important difference between project teams and senior-level collaboration. Unlike associates, who are typically assigned to a project team, participants in peer collaboration have a much greater degree of choice about getting involved in a given project (see Lazega 2001: 127–131 for a discussion of associates' low power; also Galanter and Palay 1991). They also work together more as equivalents. As Bedwell et al. (2012: 134) write in their definition of collaboration:

> One party dictating and controlling another party [as in the case of a partner and his/her subordinate associates] cannot be considered collaboration as this type of interaction would be better defined as delegation of work ... Although the engagement or participation from each party [in a collaboration] does not need to be equal, it is critical that all involved entities work interdependently and contribute sufficiently toward reaching their joint aims.

Although partners may differ in status (e.g., "rainmakers" have greater prestige than "service partners," see Maister 1993), they often have similar formal authority (see Empson and Langley, Chapter 8, this volume). Lazega (2001: 5) notes, however, that just because people who collaborate are peers, scholars must carefully consider the political aspects of their interactions because their social relations help to form the basis for informal power by giving them access to and control over valued resources such as knowledge and access. He writes, "collegial is not a synonym for congenial and nice. Partners can manage their interdependencies in informal but truly Machiavellian ways."

Thus, in contrast to traditional project teams that often have a defined leader and relatively clear hierarchy to facilitate smooth working, senior-level collaboration requires peers from different practice groups with different sub-cultures to establish task allocation, credit recognition, and decision-making norms. These working arrangements need to be continually renegotiated as people who lead one engagement may need to defer to their former followers on the next. Reordering the status hierarchy is often a difficult, politically charged act (Sutton and Hargadon 1996). Further, integrating highly specialized expertise is not only cognitively complex (Dougherty 1992), but can generate competition and conflict when experts represent different organizational units (Lawrence and Lorsch 1967).

In short, existing research highlights some core differences between traditional teams and dynamic, senior-level collaboration in PSFs; the remainder of this chapter builds on these distinctions to develop insights about avenues for scholarly research that would deepen our insights about how professionals work together effectively.

17.2.2 Drivers of Change towards Less Structured, More Senior, Peer-to-Peer Collaboration

The literature reveals a number of trends in the professional services sector that are shaping PSFs' moves towards this new form, looser, less hierarchical teamwork. First, in recent decades, many PSFs have focused on expertise *specialization*, creating narrowly defined practice areas and rewarding professionals for developing reputations in increasingly narrow, atomized professional niches (Ariens 1993; Hia 2002). As Hazard (1997: 387) wrote, "In all professional fields research and practical experimentation yield new knowledge and new methodologies by the minute . . . there are limits to the depth of knowledge and skill that can be achieved by anyone, except an occasional Renaissance Man, so that we all must specialize to stay abreast." The collective expertise in such firms has therefore become distributed between partners.

Second, the growing *complexity* of client issues demands that professionals collaborate with others throughout the firm and often around the world who have the complementary specialist expertise necessary to develop and serve clients. According to a 2010 study of 1,500 chief executive officers (Palmisano 2010), their biggest challenge was a rapid escalation in the complexity of problems that their companies faced. They expected this complexity to continue and accelerate over time, and attributed it to an increasingly interconnected and interdependent global economy. PSF teams must therefore bring together members to undertake projects that are too complex, uncertain, and non-routine to be managed by a single, specialist expert.

Third, the continuing *globalization* of business means that the clients are demanding seamless, multinational service (see Boussebaa and Morgan, Chapter 4, this volume). Providing this requires coordination across many jurisdictions because professionals with deep pockets of functional or sector expertise are usually concentrated in a firm's key markets whereas those who can tailor the project based on local markets, regulatory regimes, cultural considerations, and so on are based in outlying offices. Partners who have multinational clients must therefore develop collaborative relationships with their partners across multiple international offices (Rose and Hinings 1999).

With increased *competition*, firms must find exceptional ways to integrate and apply their diverse and distributed knowledge resources as a source of competitive advantage. By bringing together professionals with different types of expertise, a collaborative approach to serving clients has the potential to develop outcomes that are customized to the specific needs of the client, thereby increasing satisfaction and repeat business (Adler et al. 2008). Cross-discipline collaboration also promotes innovation, such as novel services that attract new clients and increase their satisfaction and loyalty (Gardner 2012a; Maister 1993). Finally, collaboration allows firms to take on increasingly sophisticated client work, which in turn lets them charge higher prices (Gardner 2013). Competitive pressures thus increase the demands for professionals to collaborate with peer experts.

17.2.3 Challenges for Effective Teamwork and Collaboration in PSFs

Analysis of literature concerning professional firms and the professions reveals five fundamental reasons that make teamwork—both bounded project teams and dynamic collaboration—especially challenging in PSFs.

First, *the diversity and distribution of expertise* in PSF teams often arises from team members who have widely varying knowledge bases and experience associated with the problem they are working on (Gardner 2012a). For example, one member may have relevant functional experience, another industry knowledge, and so on. In addition, PSF projects typically involve a divide-and-conquer approach to data gathering and problem solving; that is, after the team clarifies the project's focus, each member typically takes responsibility for a piece of the puzzle and collects data and conducts analysis on this sub-issue. This division of labor exacerbates the divide between members' knowledge bases. It may lead to divergent perspectives about the preferred solution, members' capabilities, or other task- and team-related variables, ultimately undermining team performance (Gardner and Kwan 2012; Mathieu et al. 2000).

Second, many PSFs have *talent management that induce competition* rather than foster interdependence. An especially salient feature of many professional firms is the human resource practice widely known as the "up-or-out" system (Maister 1982). Employees are brought in at the bottom rungs of the hierarchy; they are expected either to progress up the hierarchy or will be dismissed out of the organization if they fail to get promoted (Sherer and Lee 2002). Professionals pitted against each other for promotion in their firm's "tournament system" (Galanter and Palay 1991) might find it hard to see the immediate value in using another's expertise, which would require them to share both intellectual and perhaps financial credit. Throughout their careers, professionals must continue to cultivate a reputation for their mastery of professional expertise and client service (Løwendahl 2005) and many sectors have competitions or ranking systems to commend their most well-known professionals. Further, many PSFs celebrate individual achievement through their "star culture" (Groysberg 2010; Lorsch and Tierney 2002), where professionals can operate as "chieftains" (Maister and Walker 2006) in territories defined by their particular expertise.

Third, notions of *professional autonomy* may hinder teamwork. Professionals typically place great value on having autonomy over their work and have tremendous latitude to carry out their work the way they choose (von Nordenflycht 2010). Although junior professionals may have relatively little input into their assignments to projects and teams, their autonomy increases with career progression. At senior levels, for example among partners, the diffuse power structures within PSFs make collaboration difficult to foster and even harder to demand. Typically partners hold a much stronger bargaining position relative to the firm than do employees in a standard corporation (von Nordenflycht 2010) based on their relationships with clients that are vital to the firm (Greenwood et al. 1990). Further, directive decision-making runs counter to most PSFs' prevailing culture, making it prohibitively difficult to "mandate" collaboration at senior levels (Løwendahl 2005; see also Empson and Langley, Chapter 8, this volume).

Fourth, several features of contemporary PSFs may *reduce interpersonal familiarity and trust*, which are essential for high-functioning teams and collaboration. In many professions the career path for juniors often involves rapid moves up the ladder (see Cohen, Chapter 16, this volume); lower-level consultants and accountants, for example, tend to assume new roles every 12–24 months. This fluidity can make it difficult to keep track of rising experts within the firm and to efficiently form teams. Further, in some firms, especially in the consulting arena, a typical career path also includes a two-year leave for graduate business school, which further disrupts continuity. For more senior professionals, their firms' rapidly expanding size—often accomplished through mergers, acquisitions, and extensive lateral hiring—also decreases the opportunity for professionals to get to know and trust each other (Henderson and Bierman 2009). Trust is essential for teamwork and collaboration because it allows one to take a "leap of faith" when interacting with others (Rousseau et al. 1998). In particular, research suggests that collaboration in PSFs would require two kinds of trust (Empson 2001)—both a deep respect for a colleague's competence ("I trust you not to make a blunder") and a belief in their integrity ("I trust you won't undermine my relationship with my client"). To the extent that lateral hires come from firms with significantly different norms and cultures, trust may be even harder to establish. Although partners will be applauded for bringing their books of business to a new firm, their new colleagues may think twice about introducing them to key clients when they consider the newcomers' deftness at transporting critical relationships. Research also shows that the more tightly intertwined a group of lawyers were in their legacy firm or practice—as measured by the amount of business they referred to one another—the less integrated they are likely to become in a merged firm (Briscoe and Tsai 2011).

Finally, contemporary professional firms face an *increasingly competitive market*, with individuals held to ever more stringent financial and productivity metrics (Adler et al. 2008). Two kinds of pressure emerge that can both undermine effective teamwork. First, competitive intensity can generate an acute sense of time pressure. Professionals, especially those like lawyers who bill their time by the hour, develop a strong economic orientation towards the value of time that makes the opportunity costs of their time chronically salient (Pfeffer and DeVoe 2012). Consequently, they tend to focus almost exclusively on tasks that they believe are core to their professional success, such as responding to client requests or generating client materials, rather than on managerial tasks that they see as a cost, such as providing feedback, coaching juniors, or communicating a coherent team strategy. In short, time pressure makes them even more likely to focus on "taskwork" rather than "teamwork" (Janz et al. 1997), thus depriving their team of essential support. Second, performance pressure arises when a client demands extraordinarily high-quality performance on a high-stakes issue—for example, when the client faces a hostile takeover or a damaging lawsuit, or when the PSF is in direct competition to win a high-value project (Gardner 2012b). Teams facing performance pressure generally have the required time and the resources for their important project, but members are so anxious and stressed that they engage in counter-productive team processes that undermine their ability to effectively use these resources—especially team members' knowledge (Gardner 2012a).

17.3 Core Knowledge-Based Processes for Project Teams in PSFs

Knowledge and learning are foundational to the functioning of PSFs (see Faulconbridge, Chapter 19, this volume). The performance of teams engaging in knowledge-based projects depends on members' abilities to (1) identify each other's specialized knowledge, (2) access it by seeking it out and sharing it whenever necessary, and (3) integrate diverse knowledge so that they can apply it to the task at hand (see Lewis 2004). In reviewing the literature on those three knowledge-related team processes, this section reveals that some recent changes in the professional sector challenge our knowledge about how traditional project teams operate. Extending the analysis suggests how the processes would change for less-bounded, senior-level collaboration and exposes opportunities for research to deepen our understanding of interdependent working in PSFs.

17.3.1 Identifying Intra-Team Member Knowledge

Teams in PSFs typically include members with complementary, rather than redundant, knowledge that is essential for superior client service. To leverage that distributed knowledge team members must first identify each other's area of expertise. In the teams' literature, the ability to "know who knows what" is called a transactive memory system (TMS). A TMS is all the more important when each person's intellectual resources are discrete, necessary for project completion, and novel to the other team members, as is likely to be common in PSFs. A TMS facilitates the cognitive division of labor necessary for complex problem-solving through the encoding, storage, and retrieval of knowledge (for a review, see Ren and Argote 2011). Lewis (2004) investigated TMS with consulting teams tackling complex and ambiguous tasks that required members to apply specialized knowledge such as marketing, accounting, and information systems. She found that team member familiarity at the outset and open communication during the project predicted that team's ability to develop an effective TMS, in turn leading to higher team performance.

Prior research shows that team member familiarity increases transactive memory systems because past experiences together provide a more accurate view on the content, credibility, and depth of each other's expertise (Moreland 1999), and allow members to access, evaluate, communicate, and make use of their collective knowledge better than they would be able to with strangers (Hollingshead et al. 2010). As a consequence, the fluidity versus stability of team membership affects members' ability to know who knows what (Moreland et al. 1996). Huckman et al. (2009) studied the effects of changes in composition of software development teams solving complex, client-related problems. They found that both familiarity of team members with each other and their experience in a team role increased team performance. Lewis and colleagues (2007) showed that actions and assumptions of both the incumbent team members and newly joining member make expertise use difficult when the team composition changes: when a new member replaces a departing one, a team's remaining members typically continue to use previously established cues for identifying the newcomer's knowledge, which may or may not be represent his or her actual expertise. Further, new members further undermine TMS efficiency by adapting their specialization to the old members' positions in the TMS structure, regardless of their own expertise.

These tendencies of both incumbents and newcomers are likely be especially problematic in PSFs where professionals' expertise is (1) increasingly specialized and non-fungible and (2) less tangible and more subject to quality interpretation than output such as software. But so far we have little empirical research to understand TMS functioning in such firms. The issue of how interpersonal familiarity and team stability affect TMS will provide an increasingly fruitful avenue of research in PSFs, given that firms' rapid growth, industry consolidation, and professional mobility all make it harder for professionals to know their own colleagues and make it more likely that the composition of a team shifts even in the course of a project.

Additionally, changes in a team's task—for example, entry of a new competitor or technology, shifting client demands or preferences—are likely to make at least some team knowledge obsolete, thus altering the effectiveness of established TMS (Akgun et al. 2006). The more volatile the environment (e.g., tasks change rapidly, knowledge value decays quickly), the more important it is for members to rapidly update their TMS through effective ongoing communication, and the more valuable TMS becomes for team performance outcomes (Ren et al. 2006).

Research that considers PSF-specific characteristics could provide a deeper, more nuanced view of TMS. For example, research could explore whether these effects change based on variability in the nature of the task and the degree of face-to-face interaction required between professionals and their clients (Malhotra and Morris 2009). In sectors such as law and advertising, for example, clients typically define a problem and then the PSF team resolves it primarily on its own; in contrast many consulting projects include clients as members of the team. Are these mixed teams subject to greater team and task volatility that affects TMS development and functioning? Do team members use more stereotypical assumptions about out-group members (e.g., clients, colleagues from a far-off office) who join the team, or do the newcomers' differences remind team members to reflect more closely on their actual expertise?

Beyond these questions, research outside the PSF domain highlights a fundamental relationship between TMS and time pressure. Laboratory studies show that time pressure can produce acute stress that diminishes a team's transactive memory processes such as directory updating, information allocation, and retrieval coordination (Ellis 2006). These effects arise because members focus simply on getting the job done rather than locating the ideal knowledge for the problem (Janz et al. 1997). As reviewed above, time pressure is especially salient for professionals like lawyers and engineers who often bill their time by the hour. Future research could focus specifically on the ways that professionals' beliefs about opportunity costs and their perceived value of time affect, for instance, their propensity to turn to colleagues whom they know and like but who are not ideal for the task (Casciaro and Lobo 2008). Studies could assess whether this tendency affects not only their ability to accurately understand who knows what but also to use that knowledge when required.

Taken together, TMS research suggests that team fluidity, task fluctuations, and time pressure all present challenges to the way that teams effectively identify their members' expertise and draw on it when necessary. Extending these insights to the realm of less bounded collaboration that stretches over time and across projects, as is typical of many types of joint working for partners in PSFs, suggests that developing and using TMS will be especially challenging during those tasks and raises interesting directions for possible research. For example, through experience, do partners develop a capability of moving into and out of collaborative work more effectively? Is that capability transferable to new sets of collaborators? Do partners' professional reputations that help to signal their expertise make it easier for senior teams to develop a TMS directory, but harder for them to adjust their perceptions as teammates' knowledge bases change or the tasks shift? Each of these questions presents an opportunity for both theoretical development and empirical exploration that would help us to understand knowledge processes in PSFs.

17.3.2 Seeking and Sharing Knowledge

After team members recognize each other's knowledge bases and develop an ability to draw on that expertise effectively, they often need to look beyond their team boundaries for additional information. From a very broad set of literatures spanning disciplines such as sociology, organizational behavior, and psychology, this section draws on some of the more recent research that addresses specific areas of challenge for teams' seeking and sharing knowledge in present-day PSFs.

Peripheral team members. The rapid growth and increasing diversity of contemporary PSFs present a situation where some organizational members may be relatively disadvantaged in their search for important task-related information. Singh et al. (2010) conducted a field experiment in a multinational management consulting firm to understand the effects of team members' characteristics on their ability to carry out efficient knowledge searches. They theorized that a person's ability to locate colleagues with project-crucial expertise depended on how closely connected the seeker was to the organization's social structure. Specifically, long-tenured employees were likely to have a more central network position than short-tenured ones because they had more time to build network connections in the organization. They also reasoned that women would be disadvantaged in PSFs because they were excluded from social activities that strengthen interpersonal ties, or they were outside the typically male dominant coalition that includes knowledge experts and information about them. Consistent with their theorizing, peripheral members of a firm, including women and those with short tenure, had a difficult time accessing these experts because (1) they did not know whom to contact, and (2) their own contacts were also on the organizational periphery and could not provide the introductions. Singh et al. (2010: 21) note that their findings help explain some of the more subtle and implicit forms of inequity that persist in PSFs: "Because the consultants worked under severe time pressure and needed information at the beginning of a project task, locating an expert, quickly, likely explained the ability to assimilate high-quality information, leading to different work performances."

Future research in PSFs could connect these findings to a growing stream of networks-in-teams research (e.g., Chung and Jackson 2013; Katz et al. 2004) to deepen our understanding of how PSF team members' peripheral status contributes to effective knowledge seeking and sharing. For example, can a team with peripheral leaders but well-connected members still access information efficiently? Do peripheral team members also receive less of experts' attention, and therefore have trouble obtaining crucial knowledge even after locating the expert? Researchers could investigate how firms' different patterns of globalization (see Boussebaa and Morgan, Chapter 4, this volume) affect professionals' connection to others within their firm, and the way that their centrality affects knowledge flows, knowledge seeking behaviors, and related outcomes.

Multiple team membership. Professionals are increasingly called upon to work in multiple teams simultaneously (O'Leary et al. 2011). For example, lawyers generally work on multiple client matters each day, depending on their specialty, requiring frequent switching between tasks, clients, and team members' needs (Gardner and Lobb 2013). Theory suggests that being a member of multiple teams at once can lead individuals to seek out more efficient work practices and to prioritize better, but team members may experience heightened time pressure that reduces activities like knowledge seeking and sharing that are essential for learning and problem-solving (O'Leary et al. 2011).

Cummings and Haas (2012) investigated team virtuality and multiple team membership in a study of 285 knowledge-worker teams. They found that especially in geographically distributed teams, performance was higher for teams whose members allocate a greater proportion of their time to that focal team than to the other concurrent project teams. Such "virtual" teams demand extra effort and attention for handling increased coordination needs and information about other far-flung members' priorities, constraints, and contexts. Further, higher ranking, more experienced team members allocated less time to the focal team because they were in great demand from many teams at once. The implication for PSFs is that partners may undermine team performance—especially that of virtual teams—if they fail to devote enough attention to each project; future research exploring this relationship would be important for both theory and practice.

Members' motivation to seek and share (versus retreat and withhold). In some teams, knowledge flow may be limited because professionals are hesitant to share their unique information and expertise. Research shows that this motivated process occurs because valuable information is a source of status within the group and a way to impress others (Bendersky and Hays 2012), but relinquishing information reduces the holder's relative status within the group. If professional firms' up-or-out systems heighten the sense of competition between team members, as suggested above, then a resulting implication that researchers could investigate is whether people are less likely to share their expertise with peers whom they see as a threat to their own advancement.

Understanding senior professionals' motivation to share or withhold knowledge requires a more nuanced approach. Lazega (2001) argues that partner-level collaborations are an arena for professionals to play out status competitions, meaning that they share knowledge as a way to enhance their standing. In the time since his study was conducted in the early 1990s, increased mobility of partners between competitor firms may have made professionals more guarded in their knowledge sharing. At the same time, partners who move into a new firm may be highly motivated to share knowledge in order to build a reputation and attract work from their new partners. Research could contribute significantly to the literature on knowledge sharing by investigating the effect of these trends in PSFs. More generally, research that connects PSF teams' seeking and sharing behaviors with the PSFs' reward systems would be highly valuable.

Amabile et al. (2014) studied the design firm IDEO to understand how to encourage employees to share their expertise and provide timely project feedback. Their research confirmed that employees sometimes failed to exchange knowledge, even when their project would have benefited. Those who might have sought help were worried about looking weak, and potential knowledge sources were hindered by their competitive impulse. The authors found that trust and accessibility were the most important factors when deciding to see colleagues' help, although others' competence was also considered. Organizational slack allowed employees to work with each other in unplanned ways and to cultivate relationships that allowed for improved long-term efficiency. Future research could build on this finding about slack to study team members' motivation to seek and share knowledge in PSFs that use time-related performance metrics (e.g., hourly-billing targets) versus broader contribution objectives.

Finally, Gardner and Bunderson (2014) conducted a two-year study of knowledge seeking and sharing during planned organizational change at a global consulting firm. They found that professionals' motivation to engage in communication processes not only affected how much information was shared but also how recipients reacted to what they learned. Specifically, the study showed that organizational members were generally nervous about the planned change, and therefore sought out three kinds of information sources for knowledge that would help them resolve their uncertainty: formal leaders, organizational "stars" (i.e., high revenue generators), and professionals who were most closely affected by the change itself.

Results demonstrated that the more motivated the formal leaders were about the change—that is, the more they believed it would benefit the firm and themselves—the more they proactively shared their knowledge. In contrast, other sought-after experts were more focused on client service than on knowledge sharing; even if they agreed with the firm's plans, their concerns about spending time on change-related conversations instead of generating revenue dampened their motivation to share information. More surprisingly, the authors found that experts' motivation to share could backfire: whereas positive change-related information from an organizational star increased the recipient's confidence in the initiative, similar information from an enthusiastic professional who was seen as potentially benefiting from the change decreased a recipient's support for the change. Future research could connect findings from this chapter with those from Amabile et al. (2014) for a deeper investigation into the effects of time pressure (or its opposite, slack) and performance pressure on professionals' motivation to engage in seeking and sharing knowledge.

17.3.3 Integrating and Applying Knowledge

Most of the studies on knowledge processes in teams have focused on seeking and sharing, even though the mere sharing of information does not mean that it will be used effectively by other team members. In fact, research shows that project teams' success depends more on information use than information exchange (Toma and Butera 2009). The emphasis in the literature may reflect the empirical reality that it is easier to collect data on either information sharing behaviors or outcomes (reported by team members or captured in archival systems like knowledge-management databases) than it is to operationalize and measure the use of knowledge. This section reviews four streams of research that each address a different factor that affect PSF teams' ability to integrate and apply their knowledge. Each stream uses a different approach to measure teams' knowledge integration and use, and the review highlights ways that future research could build on both the findings and the empirical approach in order to make important contributions to our nascent understanding of this phenomenon in professional settings.

Team knowledge-integration capability. As suggested above, PSFs face an increasingly complex and rapidly changing set of demands. Teams in this setting must therefore develop the ability to dynamically integrate members' expertise in response to volatility.

In a global accounting firm, Gardner and colleagues (2012) examined teams' success in building a dynamic knowledge-integration capability (KIC), which they defined as *a reliable pattern of team communication that generates joint contributions to the understanding of complex problems*. The authors measured KIC with a new ten-item survey scale that captured team members' perceptions of their collective ability to discuss, evaluate, and apply each other's ideas.

Results showed that intra-team familiarity—either a small number of very deep dyadic relationships between team members or a greater number of more shallow ones—enhanced the development of KIC, especially for teams that were facing ambiguous tasks. The authors theorized that in such teams, familiarity gave teams more accurate expectations about each other's knowledge, which lowered the stress associated with uncertain tasks and allowed them to more effectively use others' contributions. In contrast, the study found that teams with highly experienced, long-tenured members typically failed to effectively integrate their members' knowledge, especially when facing heightened uncertainty. The authors reasoned that these teams' prior experience became what prior literature had identified as a "core rigidity" (Levitt and March 1988) that limited their ability to integrate members' knowledge in order to address ambiguous or changing client demands.

A follow-on study using Gardner et al.'s KIC scale found that knowledge-integration capability was associated with higher team innovation and allowed teams to productively harness the contributions that emerged during task-related debates and conflict (Xie et al. 2014). Further, Resick et al. (2014) found that a knowledge-integration capability allowed functionally diverse teams, similar to typical PSF teams, to transform their breadth of knowledge resources into actionable solutions to complex problems, and that this ability was especially valuable for teams facing environmental turbulence.

These studies began to highlight the factors such as environmental dynamism that make teamwork especially challenging in PSFs, but further research on knowledge-integration capability is needed to gain a better understanding of the social and psychological mechanisms underlying it. For example, more field-based research on project teams facing uncertainty would help to deepen our understanding of the processes that link members' familiarity and professional experience with, respectively, higher or lower ability to integrate members' knowledge. In addition, research has yet to examine knowledge-integration capability during peer-to-peer collaborations. The finding that members' greater professional experience makes it harder for teams to effectively adapt to external changes suggests that this arena could be especially problematic, but studies could investigate, for example, whether familiarity among collaborating partners mitigates this risk.

Status effects on knowledge integration. As discussed above, many PSFs are characterized by an internally competitive environment enhanced by their tournament-style promotion systems. Research on client service teams has confirmed that PSF project work is a key site for negotiating status; team members often engage in overt or subtle status conflict during which they jockey to attain valuable resources such as power, credit, and reputational benefits (Bendersky and Hays 2012; Haas 2005). Studies show that status contests are bad for teams because they reduce information sharing and may lead members to misallocate resources away from performance improvement in order to resolve problems between members (e.g., Bendersky and Shah 2012). Even without explicit status contests, research suggests that when team members privately—even unconsciously—disagree about one another's relative expertise or status, the team suffers from poor coordination, heightened task conflict, and lower performance (Gardner and Kwan 2012). Additional research shows that teams with too many "stars" focused in one area are unproductively competitive whereas teams whose members have complementary but only lightly overlapping expertise tend to perform better (Groysberg et al. 2011). One implication across these studies is that collaboration amongst peers can be problematic because they will compete, unless their knowledge provides boundaries that allow each of them to shine in their own specialized domain. Scholars could specifically investigate this proposition by studying senior-level collaboration in PSFs.

Further, research on knowledge-based teams shows that status affects the way that information gets interpreted and applied—or ignored—in the development of a team's recommendations (Hackman 2011). Team members with socially valued demographic attributes, longer tenure in the firm, or more dominant behavioral styles tend to have influence over their team's outcome that is disproportionate to the actual level of expertise (Bunderson 2003). Research in PSF teams shows how this tendency undermines group performance: it leads teams to over-rely on suggestions coming from more senior members at the expense of marginalizing relevant, "hands-on" knowledge about the client that junior members glean from their day-to-day interactions with client liaisons—knowledge that would have been essential for increasing client satisfaction (Gardner 2012a). This challenge may be especially acute in PSFs because they attract individualistic, high-achievement-oriented individuals who tend to be sensitive to status concerns (Lorsch and Tierney 2002). More empirical research in the PSF setting would help us to identify conditions under which both project teams and senior-level collaborations are best able to integrate and apply their members' expertise without improperly using member status as the determinant of whose contributions to use.

Across the status-related studies, researchers have tended to measure inputs such as team characteristics (e.g., status hierarchy, composition, member attributes), processes (e.g., status-related behaviors, conflict) and performance-related outputs, but have only theorized and inferred the mechanism as teams' knowledge use. Future research that directly measures knowledge integration and empirically links it to these antecedents and outcomes would be especially valuable.

Codified versus personalized knowledge. In a large global accounting firm, Haas and Hansen (2005, 2007) investigated temporary, ad hoc sales teams that were assembled to develop bid proposals for new client contracts. Such teams benefit from codified knowledge, in the form of electronic documents, that helps them assess the client's general commercial environment, and from personal knowledge, in the form of advice from expert colleagues, that helps them develop a customized solution. Using surveys to capture the extent of teams' use of these two types of knowledge, the papers examine the effects on the team's ability to win their bid (2005), and on three further outcome

variables: time saved by leveraging the firm's knowledge resources, enhanced work quality, and the ability to signal competence to potential clients (2007).

The authors found that for all teams—even very inexperienced ones—using codified
knowledge was at best useless for increasing performance, and for highly experienced
teams it was harmful. Indeed, the costs and risks of obtaining and using knowledge were
further amplified when a team was operating under intense time pressure because the
team likely devoted too little effort differentiating itself from competitors. In contrast,
they found that inexperienced sales teams benefited from personal advice gained by
talking to knowledgeable colleagues outside the team. Surprisingly, experienced teams'
use of personal knowledge lowered their chance of winning the bid, perhaps because
they wasted precious time by seeking knowledge that they already possessed, rather
than spending that time applying what they already knew. This study, like Gardner et al.
(2012) reviewed above, highlights some of the challenges that senior-level professionals
face when they are attempting to integrate their deep, specialized knowledge with peers'.
The implication for future research on senior-level collaboration is that researchers
must carefully consider the ways that participants' experience level affects their choices
and the effectiveness of their knowledge use.

Performance pressure. Gardner's (2012a) study of two global professional firms' teams
showed that even when motivated to successfully deliver a high-stakes project, pressured teams engaged in performance-detracting behaviors that led them to ignore some
of their members' important knowledge. The paper identified performance pressure as a
set of three interrelated factors that increase the importance of a team delivering a superior outcome, including shared outcome accountability, heightened scrutiny and evaluation of its work, and significant consequences associated with the team's performance.
This study is one of the few that attempts to directly measure a team's use of member
expertise, rather than inferring it as a linking mechanism. Specifically, the measure
of expertise use was calculated as the team-level deviation between each member's
actual expertise (as indicated by data such as their level of professional/technical qualifications and professional tenure) and the amount of influence that each member had on
the team's final report (a score given to her or him by teammates).

Results showed that as performance pressure increased, team members privileged
the use of general expertise (that which is gained through formal training or "typical" client experiences and is applicable across a range of projects) at the expense of
using domain-specific expertise (that which is relevant only to a particular client such
as knowledge of the internal politics, systems, data integrity, etc.). Drawing on prior
research about accountability's effects on knowledge processing (Lerner and Tetlock
1999), Gardner theorized that teams used general knowledge because it was perceived as
safer, more easily proven than domain-specific expertise. Results showed, however, that
teams' over-reliance on general expertise lowered performance because clients expected
teams to develop customized—rather than robust but generic—solutions.

Two further insights from this paper about team knowledge use under high pressure
have important implications for future research, especially on senior-level, peer-to-peer
collaboration. First, the implicit coercion to employ seemingly safe options came neither

strictly from overly controlling team leaders nor from meek juniors who deferred unnecessarily to authority; instead, other mid-level teammates were equally likely to engage in behaviors that ultimately privileged general experts and silenced people with domain-specific expertise. The repressive effect of peers' actions on team knowledge use deserves further research attention, especially because PSF partners are most likely to collaborate with colleagues on high-stakes projects where performance pressure is prevalent. Second, Gardner's study found that even the most senior team members suffered from the dysfunctional effects of performance pressure: they refrained from introducing ideas that were perceived as risky, and oftentimes their novel contributions were ignored by the team. Given that peer collaboration is itself seen as risky and politically charged (Gardner and Valentine 2014; Lazega 2001), partners may be even more apprehensive to offer innovative ideas in peer collaborations than when leading a hierarchical project team.

Future field-based studies that employ Gardner's (2012a) empirical approach to directly measure knowledge use would be especially valuable in understanding this crucial process in both project teams and broader collaborations. Such research could provide a more nuanced and specific understanding of how PSF teams do their core work: integrating and applying knowledge to solve client issues.

17.4 PARTNER-TO-PARTNER COLLABORATION IN PSFs

The topic of collaboration (broadly defined) has received considerable attention in disciplines including management, organizational behavior, sociology, anthropology, and medicine (see Bedwell et al. 2012 for a review). The sociological literature in particular has tended to study professional settings such as investment banks, advertising firms, and corporate law firms, primarily from the angle of collaboration as a means of reconciling the tension between professional expertise and bureaucratic or hierarchical control (e.g., Eccles and Crane 1988; Ibarra 1992; Nelson 1988). Nevertheless, the literature is still characterized, in the words of Lazega (2001: 2), by a "relative lack of progress in the study of specific social mechanisms that underlie cooperation among peers." This section reviews the nascent literature about the social processes underlying senior-level, peer collaboration in PSFs and identifies opportunities for deepening our understanding in this particular context.

Motivation to collaborate. In explaining why the neo-Weberian approach in sociology falls short of helping to explain collaborative social processes, Lazega (2001: 3) pointed out the "obvious conflicts between the individual and the collective interest." On the one hand, he outlined why partners in a professional firm would be motivated to develop a subset of colleagues with whom they repeatedly collaborate to serve clients: such a group "offers its members resources at a low cost, a sense of identity and of long-term common interests, and the stimulation that is needed to work productively together. Its multiplex exchange system sustains cohesive and durable work relationships in contexts often dominated by flexibility and short-term calculations." His empirical analysis and interpretation, however, focused mostly on the constraints that such collaborative systems place on individual workers (both partners and associates): professional performance resulted from the pressure peers apply to get their colleagues to work longer hours. Although the greater effort may have resulted in higher compensation, the main benefits in Lazega's analysis flowed to the firm as a whole. Individual professionals' motivation to collaborate remained empirically unspecified. Similarly, prior research on collaboration had found that greater collaboration produced performance benefits for professional firms and their sub-units (e.g., Hansen 2013), but had yet to explain the motivation of individual professionals who considered the collaboration vis-à-vis more independent working.

A parallel gap exists in the traditional teams' literature, which tends to take small group interactions as a given starting point, rather than questioning the circumstances that lead people to work interdependently versus alone (see Wageman et al. 2012 for more on this critique). To begin understanding individuals' motivation to collaborate among peers, Gardner and Valentine (2014) conducted a multi-method field study to investigate why highly autonomous professionals—who have traditionally been rewarded for specialized expertise and individual achievement—chose to collaborate, and to what benefit. Interviews revealed that professionals' motivation to collaborate hinged primarily on their beliefs about the relative costs and benefits to them personally (i.e., instrumentality beliefs: Vroom 1964). In terms of benefits, professionals across the four firms in the study identified common hazards that they faced from collaborating with peers, and these risks were widely perceived to threaten individual reputation and success. Most professionals were skeptical that collaboration would benefit them personally.

In contrast, a minority of professionals in the study had developed strategies to mitigate the risks and maximize the benefits, and the authors found that collaboration—especially when it spanned practice groups—resulted in two kinds of reputational benefits. First, those who collaborated more frequently on more complex, multidisciplinary work achieved better individual performance in the subsequent year because they could charge a premium for their client service work, which is a clear indication of a professional's external reputation. Second, the authors found that the more peers that partners collaborated with in their firm, the more colleagues referred work to them in the next year, which signals an enhanced internal, firm-wide reputation.

Briscoe and Tsai's (2011) work takes a more structural approach to understanding partners' motivation and ability to collaborate, specifically the degree to which they refer work to one another. In examining a law firm formed by a recent three-way merger of existing firms, the authors found that partners' pre-merger collaboration patterns affected their willingness to refer work to colleagues in the new, larger firm. Specifically, partners who previously collaborated with colleagues in other practice groups in the legacy firm were more likely to share work across units in the new firm because they were attuned to spotting collaboration opportunities and because they were less beholden to same-practice colleagues. Their willingness to invite diverse experts to collaborate on their client work enhanced their revenue generation, a finding that echoes Gardner and Valentine's results showing the performance benefits of multidisciplinary collaboration.

Overall, this research begins to unpack the motivational underpinnings and associated outcomes of collaboration between high-status, autonomous knowledge workers who have the latitude to decide how they work. Future research could build on the findings of Gardner and Valentine (2014) to examine whether and how firms' collective benefits are affected when professionals are motivated to use collaboration to enhance their personal performance. Further, scholars could draw on Lazega's (2001) arguments to examine the ways in which collaboration structures may curb individuals' ability to self-enhance by creating a balance of power among strong individuals and between those partners and the firm. And given the continued consolidation and globalization trends in the professional sector, research opportunities exist to use Briscoe and Tsai's (2011) approach to deepen our understanding of the ways that firms' structural changes affect professionals' motivation to collaborate with unfamiliar colleagues.

A host of unanswered questions link a firm's organizational design and structures to professionals' motivation to collaborate: How does the compensation system affect propensity to collaborate? What sorts of performance management systems foster collaboration and which ones undermine it? Are partners more collaborative if they have had certain experiences (training, mentoring, business development opportunities, etc.) as associates? How does a firm's hiring policy and processes (e.g., interviewing, onboarding) for lateral partners affect the newly joined professionals' and the incumbents' willingness to collaborate together? Bedwell et al. (2012) offer a useful general framework for studying human resource processes such as selection, staffing, training, and appraisals that provides the architecture for fostering collaboration within organizations. This framework could be applied in PSF-specific research to study specific contextual features that affect professional's enthusiasm and ability to collaborate.

Transition towards peer collaboration PSFs. General research outlining the way that teamwork is shifting hints that the transition from traditional project team structures to less bounded collaboration will be a ripe area for study (e.g., Wageman et al. 2012). In PSFs, this transition is perhaps more extreme and provides an especially interesting direction for future research. In traditional PSFs that have historically celebrated individual achievement through their culture and formal systems like compensation and promotion, fostering a change towards more collaborative working is a significant challenge. A few case studies delve into the transition from individualistic to collaborative working between highly autonomous professional knowledge workers. Gardner and Herman (2011) examined the crucial role of compensation in motivating professional workers to adopt more interdependent working within a public relations firm. This case study illustrates the prior research finding (summarized in Bedwell et al. 2012: 141) that "team reward contingencies have been found to be the strongest predictor of collaborative success," but it also showed that incentives must be tightly coupled with other organizational processes (e.g., performance metrics) in order to affect professionals' behaviors. Another case study (Gardner et al. 2011) examined how leaders can use structural interventions to encourage highly autonomous professionals to collaborate across traditional organizational silos. Institutionally prohibited from altering either the compensation or promotion systems, the leader implemented project management processes (e.g., planning, budgeting, staffing), administrative support structures, and resource allocation to motivate individuals to shift some of their efforts from individual to joint projects with peers. This study also revealed the significant challenges associated with such attempts, and highlighted the crucial role of leadership in making such organizational changes (see Empson and Langley, Chapter 8, this volume). A similar set of structural and process interventions were explored in the arena of investment banking (Groysberg and Vargas 2005), where the transition from individualistic to collaborative work was equally challenging but important for client service.

Future work in this arena could address a more robust empirical examination of the ways that PSF-specific talent management systems (e.g., performance appraisals and feedback, promotion criteria and processes, compensation and other incentives) help or hinder a firm's move towards fostering partner-to-partner collaboration. In addition, robust comparative case studies could examine the leadership behaviors involved in this change process, including not only formal leaders but also other high-status or knowledgeable experts (see Gardner and Bunderson 2014, reviewed above).

Additional future research directions about collaboration. Beyond the suggested research directions offered above, the topic of peer collaboration between highly autonomous professionals offers a rich set of opportunities for future research. Especially valuable will be rigorous empirical (qualitative or quantitative) studies that move beyond conceptualizing collaboration to examine its inputs, enabling and constraining conditions, detailed processes, and individual- and collective-level outcomes (see Bedwell et al. 2012 for a conceptual framework delineating these different aspects of collaboration). As an example of studying *inputs*, small groups' research suggests that when entities differ in meaningful ways, it can often be difficult for them to work together effectively (for a review, see Van Knippenberg and Schippers 2007). Researchers could link this work on team diversity with knowledge about professionals' characteristics (e.g., differences in terms of status, gender or ethnicity, social capital) to study how these factors affect collaboration and shape professional interactions. Although Lazega (2001) found that people choose strong work ties with colleagues in the same specialty and office, and of a similar status, he found that personal characteristics such as gender and law school did not make a difference in selecting whom to collaborate with. Future research could build on these findings to examine how collaboration partners' diverse characteristics affect not only their mutual selection, but also their ability to work together once committed. In addition, teams' research shows that differences in terms of language, knowledge, and backgrounds can lead to a lack of common understanding (Cronin and Weingart 2007). Given the strong trends towards increased professional specialization, covered above, research could investigate how partners' different areas of focus affect their ability to develop a shared approach and mutually agreeable goals for a joint collaboration.

A rich opportunity also exists to study the *outputs* of professional, senior-level collaboration. The Briscoe and Tsai (2011) and Gardner and Valentine (2014) papers outlined above both provide examples of the way collaboration affects individual performance outcomes such as revenue, billed hours, and hourly rates. At the collective level, Gardner (2013) shows how cross-practice collaboration affects revenue for both participating practice groups and the firm overall. She argues that this effect occurs in part because collaboration can result in higher value and more sophisticated work that is less likely to become commoditized, and it commands higher prices. Hansen's (2013) approach takes into consideration not only a firm's financial benefits of collaboration but also the direct costs of collaboration (e.g., additional efforts to coordinate across units) and the opportunity costs (i.e., gains that could have been captured had the professionals used their efforts to improve solo work).

Much scope remains for future research to examine the commercial outcomes associated with collaboration, especially through longitudinal research designs to capture the effects that are likely to accrue only over the long-term. For example, collaborating with a colleague increases the chances that he or she will refer work in the following year because the joint working builds trust and familiarity (Gardner and Valentine 2014); but even if teammates want to refer work, they must wait until the opportunity arises in their client to bring in additional resources, and it might take multiple years to develop that chance. Research tracing the long-term impact of collaboration on work referrals could answer questions about how reciprocity—both generalized and direct—plays out over time, how the trust-building effects of collaboration spread and whether they decay after a certain amount of time, how the costs of maintaining a collaborative tie relate to the long-term benefits, and so on.

Beyond the financial outcomes, however, collaboration is likely to have less tangible effects that are nonetheless important to consider. Lazega (2001), for example, examines collaboration as a means of negotiating power dynamics inside professional firms, and argues that the exchange mechanism associated with collaboration "helps collegial organization to solve the problems of endless deliberation about norms and values, and thus about firm management policies regarding issues such as work intake and assignment, compensation, marketing and peer review. [. . .] In effect, regulatory decisions are also made from within the organizational exchange system" (2001: 15). Given that Lazega based his research on a mid-sized US domestic firm in the early 1990s, additional exploration in contemporary firms could help us to understand how these effects change with firms' rapid growth where the effects of collaborative exchange might be diminished or unevenly distributed, or in merged firms where political coalitions might cross-cut the collaborative network to result in less efficient negotiation of firm-level issues.

In addition, Gardner (2013) argues that collaboration is likely to increase retention of both senior and junior professional staff because the more that professionals work in teams, the more they come to identify with the firm and the less they see themselves as individual contributors. Stronger organizational identification means that professionals are more likely not only to stay at their firm but also to engage in pro-social, firm-building activities such as mentoring junior lawyers. These activities, in turn, enhance the desirable retention of high-performing associates. Future empirical research could test these claims and seek to identify the social and psychological mechanisms that link collaboration with employee retention and similar outcomes.

In fields outside PSFs, collaboration has been linked to higher levels of innovation. For example, in academia, teams are becoming not only more prominent in the production of knowledge but also achieving greater impact than individual researchers (Wuchty et al. 2007). A similar finding applies to scientific research, where the sole "Renaissance Man" inventor is now inferior to a team of specialists collaborating on research initiatives (Gardner et al. 2011; Jones 2009). Like academics and scientists, professionals have become increasingly specialized in their domain of expertise, and it stands to reason that they will also produce greater innovation through collaboration. Process research examining how collaboration affects innovation in PSFs could help build a much deeper understanding of the behaviors, personal motivation, contextual factors, and other influences that may be unique in a professional setting. Research focused on the innovative outcomes of collaboration could help to specify and quantify the magnitude of the effects, identify boundary conditions, and uncover more precise mechanisms that link a collaborative approach to specific kinds of innovation (e.g., novel delivery channels versus creative solutions).

Overall, then, future research could provide significant contributions for both the scholarly and practitioner audiences to deepen our understanding of collaboration among highly autonomous professionals.

17.5 CONCLUSIONS

This chapter has demonstrated that the nature of teamwork in PSFs is evolving from traditional, highly structured project teams to more fluid, open-ended, peer-to-peer collaboration, and it analyzes the way that these shifts challenge our notions of effective teamwork and offer opportunities for future research. Whereas project teams have long been a primary way for PSFs to do core client-facing tasks such as conduct an annual financial audit, develop an advertising campaign, or generate a consulting report, this chapter identifies four important trends that make firms increasingly reliant on partner-level collaboration to serve clients. As in other knowledge-based fields like science or academia, professionals must concentrate their expertise in progressively narrower domains in order to stay abreast of rapidly changing knowledge. This expertise specialization presents a critical tension, however, because the growing complexity and global nature of clients' problems demand broad, multidisciplinary, multinational solutions. Consequently, very senior, specialized professionals must increasingly work with equally powerful, expert peers to generate and deliver client work. Heightened competitive pressures means that firms have little option but to move towards this mode of senior-level collaboration as a way to leverage the knowledge of their most valuable partners. Yet, this chapter also reviews work showing how peer collaboration—especially among powerful, high-autonomy professionals—involves additional obstacles that tend not to arise in hierarchical project teams with clear leaders, well-defined goals, and dedicated team members.

Even for traditional, project-based teams in PSFs, important questions remain about how some recent changes in the professional sector affect their functioning and outcomes. By focusing on three essential knowledge-related processes—(1) identifying team members' knowledge, (2) seeking and sharing knowledge beyond the team, and (3) integrating and applying knowledge—this chapter identifies how gaps in our understanding about project teams in this setting have arisen from developments in the PSF arena. The analysis presented here suggests that the rapid growth and increasing diversity of the professional workforce challenge teams' ability to operate across the three processes. What we lack, for example, is a deep understanding of how professionals' status, affiliation with the firm's dominant national culture, or recent tenure in a firm (e.g., for laterally hired professionals or those belonging to a newly merged entity) may make them relatively disadvantaged in their ability to access and get help from experts who neither know nor necessarily trust them. Scholars could conduct rich, multi-level studies to examine the effects on teams and their individual members when such barriers arise, and findings would enrich the teams' and the professional firms' literature. Another important issue that affects all three knowledge-related processes in project teams involves the effects of PSFs' talent management systems. Lab-based studies that replicate, for instance, the tournament-style promotion processes or "eat what you kill" incentive schemes could examine the mechanisms through which these structures affect teams' motivation to seek, share, and use their teammates' and the wider firm's existing knowledge or to generate innovative solutions to complex problems. Field-based studies would add nuance and richer understanding of how professionals react to such systems, and how changes in the talent management systems over time affect professionals' engagement in knowledge-based teamwork. Finally, the study of project teams responding to their rapidly changing environment presents opportunities for methodological innovation in the study of PSF teams. For example, the chapter highlights the paucity of studies that have included direct measures of teams' knowledge integration, instead of simply inferring this process as the mechanism linking assessed income and output variables. Given that one of the main reasons for using project teams in PSFs is to leverage members' different knowledge bases, finding more ways to accurately measure teams' effectiveness in doing so would be a major advancement.

A second major avenue for future research that this chapter identified relates to more loosely bounded, dynamic, senior-level collaborations. Section 17.4 offers a host of unanswered questions concerning this phenomenon in PSFs, including those that extend existing research and those that apply Bedwell et al.'s (2012) conceptual framework of collaboration. Given the interdisciplinary nature of studying collaboration, scholars can draw on a wide set of theoretical bases including sociology, psychology, economics, and organizational behavior in order to develop and test predictions about how senior-level professionals work interdependently on complex problems. Further, scholars interested in this phenomenon can turn to research in other knowledge-intensive environments that have parallels to PSFs: for example, research in healthcare (e.g., Bartunek 2011), open-source innovation (e.g., Boudreau et al. 2014), science (Salazar et al. 2012), or academia (Wuchty et al. 2007). Finally, research on multi-team systems examines how networks of teams integrate their efforts to succeed collectively (Marks et al. 2005), and this line of research could be applied to understand the firm-level effects of multiple senior-level collaborations. Any of these approaches will require sufficient consideration of the power and politics involved in collaboration among highly autonomous professional peers.

Cutting across both of these directions for future research are issues that link teamwork—both traditional project teams and especially partner-level collaboration—to PSF-specific antecedents and outcomes at other levels of analysis. For example, this chapter highlighted many aspects of teamwork that are likely to be affected by a firm's talent management processes; in particular, the increased hiring of partners from competitor firms decreases interpersonal familiarity and may erode trust, which were both shown to be important precursors to effective teaming. Compensation and rewards are other firm-level factors that will likely affect teamwork, perhaps especially for partners whose pay is likely to be more variable and performance-based than junior colleagues'. In parallel, teamwork in PSFs is likely to affect outcomes at both more micro and more macro levels. The chapter identified numerous paths for fruitful research about collaboration's effects on individual-level outcomes like financial rewards, career outcomes, and professional identity and on firm-level outcomes like client loyalty, staff retention, and firm culture. Given these unanswered research questions, it is essential for scholars to develop and pursue a research agenda that captures the multi-level aspects of teamwork and collaboration, rather than studying them only with traditional group-level approaches.

In conclusion, teamwork is evolving in contemporary PSFs in response to numerous changes in the external environment. Many aspects of this shift challenge our understanding of how teams operate effectively in PSFs and what effect teams have on their members and the firms. A promising research agenda offers scholars the opportunity to apply multi-level theorizing and analysis, methodological innovations, and consideration of informal, political, and motivational aspects of teamwork in order to better understand the complex and nuanced aspects of collaboration in contemporary professional service firms.

REFERENCES

Adler, P. S., Kwon, S. W., and Heckscher, C. (2008). "Professional Work: The Emergence of Collaborative Community," *Organization Science* 19(2): 359–376.

Akgun, A. E., Byrne, J. C., Keskin, H., and Lynn, G. S. (2006). "Transactive Memory System in New Product Development Teams," *Engineering Management, IEEE Transactions* 53(1): 95–111.

Amabile, T., Fisher C. M., and Pillemer, J. (2014). "IDEO's Culture of Helping," *Harvard Business Review* 92: 54–61.

Ariens, M. (1993). "Know the Law: A History of Legal Specialization," *South Carolina Law Review* 45: 1003–1061.

Bartunek, J. M. (2011). "Intergroup Relationships and Quality Improvement in Health Care," *BMJ: Quality and Safety* 20 (Suppl. 1): i62—i66.

Bedwell, W. L., Wildman, J. L., DiazGranados, D., Salazar, M., Kramer, W. S., and Salas E. (2012). "Collaboration at Work: An Integrative Multilevel Conceptualization," *Human Resource Management Review* 22(2): 128–145.

Bendersky, C. and Hays, N. (2012). "Status Conflict in Groups," *Organization Science* 23(2): 323–340.

Bendersky, C. and Shah, N. P. (2012). "The Cost of Status Enhancement: Performance Effects of Individuals' Status Mobility in Task Groups," *Organization Science* 23(2): 308–322.

Boudreau, K., Gaule, P., Lakhani, K. R., Riedl, C., and Woolley, A. W. (2014). "From Crowds to Collaborators: Initiating Effort and Catalyzing Interactions Among Online Creative Workers," *Harvard Business School Working Paper*, No. 14–060.

Briscoe, F. and Tsai, W. (2011). "Overcoming Relational Inertia: How Organizational Members Respond to Acquisition Events in a Law Firm," *Administrative Science Quarterly* 56(3): 408–440.

Bunderson, J. S. (2003). "Recognizing and Utilizing Expertise in Work Groups: A Status Characteristics Perspective," *Administrative Science Quarterly* 48(4): 557–591.

Casciaro, T. and Lobo, M. S. (2008). "When Competence is Irrelevant: The Role of Interpersonal Affect in Task-Related Ties," *Administrative Science Quarterly* 53(4): 655–684.

Chung, Y. and Jackson, S. E. (2013). "The Internal and External Networks of Knowledge-Intensive Teams: The Role of Task Routineness," *Journal of Management* 39(2): 442–468.

Cronin, M. A. and Weingart, L. R. (2007). "Representational Gaps, Information Processing, and Conflict in Functionally Diverse Teams," *Academy of Management Review* 32(3): 761–773.

Cummings, J. N. and Haas, M. (2012). "So Many Teams, So Little Time: Time Allocation Matters in Geographically Dispersed Teams," *Journal of Organizational Behavior* 33(3): 316–341.

Dougherty, D. (1992). "Interpretive Barriers to Successful Product Innovation in Large Firms," *Organization Science* 3(2): 179–202.

Eccles, R. and Crane, D. (1988) *Doing Deals: Investment Banks at Work*. Boston, MA: Harvard Business School Press.

Edmondson, A. and Nembhard, I. (2009). "Product Development and Learning in Project Teams: The Challenges are the Benefits," *Journal of Product Innovation Management* 26(2): 123–138.

Ellis, A. P. J. (2006). "System Breakdown: The Role of Mental Models and Transactive Memory in the Relationship between Acute Stress and Team Performance," *Academy of Management Journal* 49(3): 576–589.

Empson, L. (2001). "Fear of Exploitation and Fear of Contamination: Impediments to Knowledge Transfer in Mergers between Professional Service Firms," *Human Relations* 54(7): 839–862.

Galanter, M. and Palay, T. (1991). *Tournament of Lawyers*. Chicago, IL: University of Chicago Press.

Gardner, H. K. (2012a). "Performance Pressure as a Double-edged Sword: Enhancing Team Motivation but Undermining the Use of Team Knowledge," *Administrative Science Quarterly* 57(1): 1–46.

Gardner, H. K. (2012b). "Coming Through When It Matters Most: How Great Teams Do Their Best Work Under Pressure," *Harvard Business Review* 90(4): 82–91.

Gardner, H. K. (2013). "Rewarding Partnerships," *Financial Times*, October 4.

Gardner, H. K. and Bunderson, J. S. (2014). "Informal Conversations and the Diffusion of Buy-in to Planned Organizational Change: Insights from a Professional Service Firm," Harvard Business School Working Paper.

Gardner, H. K. and Herman, K. (2011). "Marshall and Gordon: Designing an Effective Compensation System (A)," Harvard Business School Case 411–038.

Gardner, H. K. and Kwan, L. (2012). "Expertise Dissensus: A Multi-level Model of Teams' Differing Perceptions about Member Expertise," Harvard Business School Working Paper No. 12–070.

Gardner, H. K. and Lobb, A. (2013). "Collaborating for Growth: Duane Morris in a Turbulent Legal Sector," Harvard Business School Case 414–022.

Gardner, H. K. and McFee, E. (2012). "Marshall and Gordon: Designing an Effective Compensation System (TN) (A) and (B)," Harvard Business School Teaching Note 412–077.

Gardner, H. K. and Valentine, M. A. (2014). "Instrumental Collaboration: Why Autonomous Professionals Collaborate and How They Benefit," Harvard Business School Working Paper.

Gardner, H. K., Bedzra, E. K. S., and Elnahal, S. M. (2011) "Ganging up on Cancer: Integrative Research Centers at Dana-Farber Cancer Institute (A)," Harvard Business School Case 412–029 and Teaching Note 412–112.

Gardner, H. K., Gino, F., and Staats, B. (2012). "Dynamically Integrating Knowledge in Teams: Transforming Resources into Performance," *Academy of Management Journal* 55(4): 998–1022.

Greenwood, R., Hinings, C. R., and Brown, J. (1990). "'P2-Form' Strategic Management: Corporate Practices in Professional Partnerships," *Academy of Management Journal* 33(4): 725–755.

Greenwood, R., Li, S. X., Prakash, R., and Deephouse, D. L. (2005). "Reputation, Diversification, and Organizational Explanations of Performance in Professional Service Firms," *Organization Science* 16(6): 661–673.

Groysberg, B. (2010). *Chasing Stars: The Myth of Talent and the Portability of Performance.* Princeton, NJ: Princeton University Press.

Groysberg, B. and Vargas, I. (2005). "Innovation and Collaboration at Merrill Lynch," Harvard Business School Case 406–081.

Groysberg, B., Polzer, J. T., and Elfenbein, H. A. (2011). "Too Many Cooks Spoil the Broth: How High-Status Individuals Decrease Group Effectiveness," *Organization Science* 22(3): 722–737.

Haas, M. R. (2005). "Cosmopolitans and Locals: Status Rivalries, Deference, and Knowledge in International Teams," *Research on Managing Groups and Teams* 7: 201–227.

Haas, M. R. and Hansen, M. T. (2005). "When Using Knowledge Can Hurt Performance: The Value of Organizational Capabilities in a Management Consulting Company," *Strategic Management Journal* 26(1): 1–24.

Haas, M. R. and Hansen, M. T. (2007). "Different Knowledge, Different Benefits: Towards a Productivity Perspective on Knowledge Sharing in Organizations," *Strategic Management Journal* 28(11): 1133–1153.

Hackman, J. R. (1990). *Groups That Work (and Those That Don't).* San Francisco, CA: Jossey-Bass.

Hackman, J. R. (2011). *Collaborative Intelligence: Using Teams to Solve Hard Problems.* San Francisco, CA: Berrett-Koehler Publishers.

Hansen, M. (2013). *Collaboration: How Leaders Avoid the Traps, Build Common Ground, and Reap Big Results.* Boston, MA: Harvard Business Press.

Hazard Jr, G. C. (1997). "Practice in Law and Other Professions," *Arizona Law Review* 39: 387–399.

Henderson, W. D. and Bierman, L. (2009). "Empirical Analysis of Lateral Lawyer Trends from 2000 to 2007: The Emerging Equilibrium for Corporate Law Firms," *Georgetown Journal of Legal Ethics* 22: 1395–1430.

Hia, T. (2002). "Que Sera, Sera: The Future of Specialization in Large Law Firms," *Columbia Business Law Review* 102(2): 541–572.

Hitt, M. A., Bierman, L., Shimizu, K., and Kochhar, R. (2001). "Direct and Moderating Effects of Human Capital on Strategy and Performance in Professional Service Firms: A Resource-Based Perspective," *Academy of Management Journal* 44(1): 13–28.

Hobday, M. (2000). "The Project-Based Organisation: An Ideal Form for Managing Complex Products and Systems?" *Research Policy* 29: 871–893.

Hollingshead, A. B., Brandon, D. P., Yoon, K., and Gupta, N. (2010). "Communication and Knowledge-Sharing Errors in Groups: A Transactive Memory Perspective," in *Communication and Organizational Knowledge: Contemporary Issues for Theory and Practice*, ed. H. Canary and R. McPhee. New York: Taylor & Francis, 113–151.

Huckman, R. S., Staats, B. R., and Upton, D. M. (2009). "Team Familiarity, Role Experience, and Performance: Evidence from Indian Software Services," *Management Science* 55(1): 85–100.

Ibarra, H. (1992). "Homophily and Differential Returns: Sex Differences in Network Structure and Access in an Advertising Firm," *Administrative Science Quarterly* 37(3): 422–427.

Janz, B. D., Colquitt, J. A., and Noe, R. A. (1997). "Knowledge Worker Team Effectiveness: The Role of Autonomy, Interdependence, Team Development, and Contextual Support Variables," *Personnel Psychology* 50(4): 877–904.

Jones, B. F. (2009). "The Burden of Knowledge and the 'Death of the Renaissance Man': Is Innovation Getting Harder?" *Review of Economics and Statistics* 76: 283–317.

Katz, N., Lazer, D., Arrow, H., and Contractor, N. (2004). "Network Theory and Small Groups," *Small Group Research* 35(3): 307–332.

Lawrence, P. R. and Lorsch, J. W. (1967). *Organization and Environment*. Boston, MA: Harvard Business School, Division of Research (reissued by Harvard Business School Press, 1986).

Lazega, E. (2001) *The Collegial Phenomenon: The Social Mechanisms of Cooperation among Peers in a Corporate Law Partnership*. Oxford: Oxford University Press.

Lerner, J. S. and Tetlock, P. E. (1999). "Accounting for the Effects of Accountability," *Psychological Bulletin* 125(2): 255–275.

Levitt, B. and March, J. G. 1988. "Organizational Learning," in *Annual Review of Sociology*, ed. W. R. Scott. Palo Alto, CA: Annual Reviews, 319–340.

Lewis, K. (2004). "Knowledge and Performance in Knowledge-Worker Teams: A Longitudinal Study of Transactive Memory Systems," *Management Science* 50(11): 1519–1533.

Lewis, K., Belliveau, M., Herndon, B., and Keller, J. (2007). "Group Cognition, Membership Change, and Performance: Investigating the Benefits and Detriments of Collective Knowledge," *Organizational Behavior and Human Decision Processes* 103(2): 159–178.

Lorsch, J. W. and Tierney, T. J. (2002). *Aligning the Stars: How to Succeed When Professionals Drive Results*. Boston, MA: Harvard Business Press.

Løwendahl. B. (2005). *Strategic Management of Professional Service Firms*. Copenhagen: Copenhagen Business School Press.

McDonough, E. F. III, Kahn, K. B., and Barczak, G. (2001). "An Investigation of the Use of Global, Virtual, and Colocated New Product Development Teams," *Journal of Product Innovation Management* 18(2): 110–120.

Maister, D. H. (1982). "Balancing the Professional Service Firm," *Sloan Management Review* 24(1): 15–29.

Maister, D. H. (1993). *Managing the Professional Service Firm*. New York: Free Press.

Maister, D. H. (2004). "The Anatomy of a Consulting Firm," in *The Advice Business: Essential Tools and Models for Managing Consulting*, ed. C. J. Fombrun and M. D. Nevins. Upper Saddle River, NJ: Pearson Prentice-Hall, 17–31.

Maister, D. H. and Walker, J. (2006). "The One-Firm Firm Revisited." <http://davidmaister.com/articles/the-one-firm-firm-revisited/>.

Malhotra, N. and Morris, T. (2009). "Heterogeneity in Professional Service Firms," *Journal of Management Studies* 46(6): 895–922.

Marks, M. A., DeChurch, L. A., Mathieu, J. E., Panzer, F. J., and Alonso, A. (2005). "Teamwork in Multiteam Systems," *Journal of Applied Psychology* 90(5): 964–971.

Mathieu, J. E., Heffner, T. S., Goodwin, G. F., Salas, E., and Cannon-Bowers, J. A. (2000). "The Influence of Shared Mental Models on Team Process and Performance," *Journal of Applied Psychology* 85(2): 273–283.

Moreland, R. L. (1999). "Transactive Memory: Learning Who Knows What in Work Groups and Organizations," in *Shared Cognition in Organizations: The Management of Knowledge*, ed. L. Thompson, D. Messick, and J. Levine. Mahwah, NJ: Erlbaum, 3–31.

Moreland, R. L., Argote, L., and Krishnan (1996). "Socially Shared Cognition at Work: Transactive Memory and Group Performance," in *What's Social About Social Cognition? Research on Socially Shared Cognition in Small Groups*, ed. J. L. Nye and A. M. Brower. Thousand Oaks, CA: Sage, 57–84.

Morris, T., Gardner, H. K., and Anand, N. (2012). "Structuring Consulting Firms," in *The Oxford Handbook of Management Consulting*, ed. M. Kipping and T. Clark. Oxford: Oxford University Press, 285–302.

Nelson, R. (1988). *Partners with Power: The Social Transformation of the Large Law Firm*. Berkeley, CA: University of California Press.

O'Leary, M. B., Mortensen, M., and Woolley, A. W. (2011). "Multiple Team Membership: A Theoretical Model of its Effects on Productivity and Learning for Individuals and Teams," *Academy of Management Review* 36(3): 461–478.

Palmisano, S. J. (2010). *The 2010 IBM Global CEO Study—Capitalizing on Complexity*. <http://www-935.ibm.com/services/us/ceo/ceostudy2010/index.html>.

Pfeffer, J. and DeVoe, S. E. (2012). "The Economic Evaluation of Time: Organizational Causes and Individual Consequences," *Research in Organizational Behavior* 32: 47–62.

Ren, Y. and Argote, L. (2011). "Transactive Memory Systems 1985–2010: An Integrative Framework of Key Dimensions, Antecedents, and Consequences," *Academy of Management Annals* 5(1): 189–229.

Ren, Y., Carley, K., and Argote, L. (2006). "The Contingent Effects of Transactive Memory: When is It More Beneficial to Know What Others Know?" *Management Science* 52(5): 671–682.

Resick, C. J., Murase, T., Randall, K. R., and DeChurch, L. A. (2014). "Information Elaboration and Team Performance: Examining the Psychological Origins and Environmental Contingencies," *Organizational Behavior and Human Decision Processes* 124(2): 165–176

Rose, T. and Hinings, B. (1999). "Global Clients' Demands Driving Change in Global Business Advisory Firms," in *Restructuring the Professional Organization: Accounting, Health Care and Law*, ed. D. M. Brock, M. J. Powell, and C. R. Hinings. London: Routledge, 41–67.

Rousseau, D. M., Sitkin, S. B., Burt, R., and Camerer, C. (1998). "Not So Different After All: A Cross-Disciplinary View of Trust," *Academy of Management Review* 23(3): 393–404.

Salazar, M. R., Lant, T. K., Fiore, S. M., and Salas, E. (2012). "Facilitating Innovation in Diverse Science Teams Through Integrative Capacity," *Small Group Research* 43(5): 527–558.

Sherer, P. D. and Lee, K. (2002). "Institutional Change in Large Law Firms: A Resource Dependency and Institutional Perspective," *Academy of Management Journal* 45(1): 102–119.

Singh, J., Hansen, M. T., and Podolny, J. M. (2010). "The World is Not Small for Everyone: Inequity in Searching for Knowledge in Organizations," *Management Science* 56(9): 1415–1438.

Sutton, R. I. and Hargadon, A. (1996). "Brainstorming Groups in Context: Effectiveness in a Product Design Firm," *Administrative Science Quarterly* 41(4): 685–718.

Sydow, J., Lindkvist, L. and DeFillippi, R. (2004). "Project-Based Organizations, Embeddedness and Repositories of Knowledge: Editorial," *Organization Studies* 25(9): 1475–1489.

Tannenbaum, S. I., Mathieu, J. E, Salas, E., and Cohen, D. (2012). "Teams are Changing: Are Research and Practice Evolving Fast Enough?" *Industrial and Organizational Psychology* 5: 2–24.

Toma, C. and Butera, F. (2009). "Hidden Profiles and Concealed Information: Strategic Information Sharing and Use in Group Decision Making," *Personality and Social Psychology Bulletin* 35(6): 793–806.

Van Knippenberg, D. and Schippers, M. C. (2007). "Work Group Diversity," *Annual Review of Psychology* 58: 515–541.

von Nordenflycht, A. (2010). "What is a Professional Service Firm? Towards a Theory and Taxonomy of Knowledge Intensive Firms," *Academy of Management Review* 35(1): 155–174.

Vroom, V. H. (1964). *Work and Motivation*. New York: John Wiley.

Wageman, R., Gardner, H., and Mortensen, M. (2012). "The Changing Ecology of teams: New Directions for Teams Research," *Journal of Organizational Behavior* 33(3): 301–315.

Werr, A. and Stjernberg, T. (2003). "Exploring Management Consulting Firms as Knowledge Systems," *Organization Studies* 24(6): 881–908.

Wuchty, S., Jones, B. F., and Uzzi, B. (2007). "The Increasing Dominance of Teams in Production of Knowledge," *Science* 316: 1036–1039.

Xie, X., Wang, W., and Luan, K. (2014). "It is Not What We Have, But How We Use It: Reexploring the Relationship between Conflict and Team Innovation from the Resource-Based View," *Group Processes Intergroup Relations* 17(2): 240–251.

CHAPTER 18

....

PROFESSIONAL SERVICE FIRMS AND IDENTITY

....

MATS ALVESSON, DAN KÄRREMAN, AND KATE SULLIVAN

18.1 INTRODUCTION

....

IDENTITY is presumed to reveal key elements of individuals or groups. The term can be used in many different ways and to depict various levels of analysis, such as personal, national, occupational, professional, or organizational (Albert and Whetten 1985; Alvesson et al. 2008; Ashforth and Mael 1989; Dutton and Dukerich 1991; Ravasi and Schultz 2006). For example, organizational identity is typically defined as "the set of beliefs shared by top managers and stakeholders about the central, enduring, and distinctive characteristics of an organization" (Scott and Lane 2000: 44). Individual identity concerns how individuals construct particular versions of themselves.

Yet, as of late, scholars acknowledge that identity is complex, diffuse, and levels of analysis overlap. Therefore, apart from some work exclusively focusing on organizational identity, identity studies typically explore the intersections between individual and organizational identities, focusing on how Professional Service Firms (PSFs) seek to construct and maintain a particular identity and how professionals seek to uphold, maintain, or challenge these identities (Alvesson and Empson 2008; Kärreman and Rylander 2008).

Identity provides clues for action, interpretation, and conduct. It is broadly seen as a crucial theme for understanding how people relate to their work and how organizations function (Alvesson 2001; Kärreman and Alvesson 2004). Therefore, it may operate as a proxy for organizational control in that it stands in as a substitute or surrogate for rules, procedures, and other forms of behavioral control. This chapter accounts for the concept of identity, including its significance in PSFs and its role with regard to management control more broadly. In all identity research it is important to distinguish between levels of identity, although it is widely acknowledged that various levels intersect and influence one another. In this chapter, we pay particular attention to the level of the individual and the level of the organization and how they relate. This chapter concludes with an overview of how the management of identity themes is carried out in PSFs. Although there is considerable variation among PSFs, they each have an impact on identity and benefit from efforts to control identity.

We begin by examining the relationship between individual and organizational identity in general before going on to examine the nature of identity in PSFs and the tenuous nature of elite identity in this context. We identify four main issues for management control in PSFs and three main modes of identity-focused control in PSFs. We examine contemporary challenges to elite identities and the critique of concepts of professionalism in this context. We conclude by examining the implications for future research.

18.2 INDIVIDUAL AND ORGANIZATIONAL IDENTITY

Identity is a construction of one's self, group, or organization, typically in a favorable light (Dutton et al. 2011), in terms of key orientations, distinctiveness, and some degree of continuity and coherence (Albert and Whetten 1985). Put shortly, identity provides answers to the questions "Who am I?", "Who are we?", and "What does this organization stand for?" As a multi-level concept, identity can be organizational, professional, social group, or individual. The levels are sometimes supposed to be linked, such as when organizational or other social identities are seen as fueling the identities of individuals (Ashforth and Mael 1989; Dutton et al. 1994; Elsbach 1999; Ladge et al. 2012). Hence, people may associate themselves with their organizations and define themselves as organizational members.

Although it was once common to conceptualize identity as essential traits or stable characteristics or essences (Albert and Whetten 1985), contemporary studies often acknowledge the constructed and processual nature of identity (Gioia et al. 2000; Ibarra 1999; Pratt 2000). Here, identity is not a mere reflection of psychological or social "objective reality," but instead it is constructed, multiple, varying, and maintained from within systems of power, control, and resistance (Alvesson and Willmott 2002). Constructions involve an element of invention and the use of a vocabulary that creates a particular version of who and how an individual or a group (or an organization) views him/her- or themselves (Ibarra and Barbulescu 2010).

This shift—from viewing identity as a stable reflection to conceptualizing it as socially constructed and fluid—enables scholarship that pays close attention to the ways in which individual and organizational identities are uncertain and multi-leveled. In dynamic contexts—such as many parts of contemporary social and working life—identities are changing, making it more reasonable to talk about temporary forms of coherence rather than something fixed and stable. At the same time, identity studies also allow us to question that which is considered coherent and distinct. Not all identity constructions swing or are plural, so it may be wise to consider both possibilities for inertia and for people sticking to favored narratives of oneself or organization (Alvesson 2010).

Individual identity concerns how a person constructs a particular version of him- or herself and addresses the questions, "Who am I?" and—by implication—"How should I act?" The answers to these questions provide cues as to how an individual is situated within cultural contexts. They also have consequences for how an individual thinks, acts, prioritizes, and experiences motivation. Individual identity is not fixed, but is to some extent an open question and highly related to one's organizational context and social interactions. For instance, individual identity is constituted through comparisons and interactions with other people and groups, meaning that how others relate to us is crucial for how we see ourselves (Beech et al. 2008). For example, a person who sees herself as a consultant does so in part because clients confirm her position. Her self-evaluation is contingent upon the negotiations of meaning around social and client relations and the specifics of her labor. Therefore, even individual identities are constituted, negotiated, reproduced, and threatened in social interaction, in the form of narratives, and also in material practices. An important element of individual identity is its public, interactive, and confirming or disconfirming nature (Pratt 2000). At the same time, there is typically an element of "narcissism" in identity constructions, as individuals and collectives often construct very positive, sometimes fantasy-inspired versions of who and how they are, sometimes disregarding or reinterpreting, or being highly selective in incorporating, the views of the environment.

Organizational identity refers to how people in an organization more or less share an understanding of what the organization stands for. Organizations, such as PSFs, are often a source of a shared social identity that employees draw upon to define who they are. In the organizational and work context it is often social, rather than highly individualized, identities that are of greatest relevance. A social identity refers to the group category that the individual identifies with: company, division, occupation, gender, nationality, ethnicity, and age (Ashforth and Mael 1989; Haslam 2004). It is important to avoid confusing the concept of social identity with other issues such as internalization of values and norms and commitment to a certain issue. Social identity refers to self-categorizations as a point of departure for thinking and relating. It does not necessarily imply a set of sentiments and should not be equated with corporate, or any other, culture. One may feel like a corporate member, a woman, or a Frenchman without necessarily internalizing all or most of the values, emotions, and meanings assumed to be typical for the category (Turner 1984). For example, two groups may have similar values and beliefs but still perceive differences and exaggerate their distinctiveness. Often, however, a specific social identity increases the likelihood that certain ideas, values, and norms associated with the group or organization are internalized.

Taken together, individual and organizational identity formation and maintenance are rooted in the context of power relations (Foucault 1982; Knights and Willmott 1989). Individuals are regulated through defining who they are—or believe they should be. Power is exercised as individuals seek to avoid deviations from the ideal. Certainly, the degree to which power relations subject individuals is dependent upon several factors, such as one's willingness to be regulated or to accept definitions and norms. Yet in order to craft personal and social identities that feel more secure, people in organizations routinely engage in identity work, which can be defined as the processes of "forming, repairing, maintaining, strengthening or revising the constructions that are productive of a sense of coherence and distinctiveness" (Sveningsson and Alvesson 2003: 1165). Identity work, if successful, creates a feeling of coherence and allows one to share their identity with others, which in turn is necessary for coping with work tasks and social interactions (Alvesson 1994; Alvesson and Willmott 2002; Watson 2008).

18.3 PSFs AND TENUOUS ELITE IDENTITIES

Turning our attention to PSFs in particular highlights that issues of identity are of special significance for several reasons, including the importance of securing a base for control, image management, loyalty, and existential security. Although there does not appear to be a shared definition of PSFs, they are commonly characterized as having knowledge intensity that is put to use in the service of clients, low capital intensity, meaning that most broker in immaterial and ambiguous rather than material labor, a (homogenized) professionalized workforce, and the desire to be "elite" (Alvesson 2004; von Nordenflycht 2010). These characteristics are evident in the PSF industries which tend to dominate the literature such as accounting, law, management consulting, advertising, architecture, and investment banking (von Nordenflycht 2010).

A key component in constructing and maintaining an elite identity rests on PSFs' abilities to claim knowledge intensity (Blackler 1995; Morris and Empson 1998; Newell et al. 2009). Faulconbridge (Chapter 19, this volume) explores knowledge in PSFs and notes that management research frequently contrasts the knowledge intensity present in PSFs with bureaucracy and industrial set-ups, the latter of which are associated with tedious, repetitive, and monotonous labor. Knowledge work differs from this, as here value is created through knowledge and knowledge workers rather than labor or capital.

The emphasis on the knowledge workers themselves is key to understanding elite identity constructions in PSFs. These professionals share a common framing in the literature as highly competent knowledge-intensive individuals (von Nordenflycht 2010) who have "esoteric expertise" (Starbuck 1993), namely of specific, rare, and abstruse knowledge in their work practices (Kärreman 2010). Instead of routines and standardized work processes, creativity, problem solving, and task complexity largely characterize their work (Løwendahl 1997). As Newell et al. (2009: 127) note, "knowledge workers typically expect to be given interesting and varied work rather than follow a prescribed routine." The nature of knowledge work requires that professionals are granted a high degree of self-organization and work in relatively loose team structures outside the direct supervision of management.

This autonomous structure, alongside the fact that "knowledge" as a product of labor is highly ambiguous (Alvesson 2004) and important to most PSFs (Schreyögg and Geiger 2007) highlights the tenuous nature of retaining an elite identity. An individual and a firm are only as secure as their ability to convince others of their value. Three characteristics of knowledge in organizations can be singled out. First, knowledge is a resource. It is trivial to point out that knowledge is perhaps the most important resource available to many organizations—although the exact meaning of this is often unclear. It is not trivial to highlight that it is only in its esoteric and rare forms that knowledge can have a decisive influence on the form and competitiveness of firms—and by extension its identity. Second, knowledge is associated with expertise and has high status and is related to asymmetries and politics. Knowledge and expertise are often contested terrain. Third, and related to the first two points, knowledge is about persuasion and perceptions. Claiming expertise and knowledge necessarily includes engaging in plays of persuasion (Alvesson 2004; Contu and Willmott 2003)—of which the professionals' conceptualization of their own and their firm's identity will play a role. Outsiders are not going to grant some people exclusive license to control a particular field of expertise without having been convinced that this expertise is reliable and superior. In a crowded market clients have to be consistently moved and convinced by the knowledge workers themselves. The latter also need to convince themselves about their unique qualities and superiority in relationship to competitors and clients within the targeted domain of expertise (all of which relate back to their conceptualization of identity with regard to their competitors and clients).

Perhaps due to perceptions that these workers have unique expertise, characterizations of elite professionals in PSFs tend to be presented alongside discussions of the managerial challenges of retaining and directing them (von Nordenflycht 2010). The fear that sophisticated knowledge is, per definition, scarce means that organizations are always under threat of key employees going elsewhere or having coercive bargaining power.

Yet it would be a mistake to assume that knowledge workers fall outside of managerial control. Profitability and working hours debited can sometimes be measured on a group or individual level. At the same time as traditional forms of bureaucratic and technological control, such as strict formal protocols, behavioral regulations and the monitoring of outputs in terms of knowledge contributions are arguably more difficult to execute in PSFs, cultural control, namely managerial attempts to regulate individuals' ideas, values, and selves, assumes significance (Grey 1994; Kunda 1992). Although control takes on a more subtle form (and relates specifically to identity as discussed below) it also highlights the ways in which workers struggle to balance ambiguities and instabilities while maintaining an image of elite professionals. For these reasons we next outline four issues that tend to stand in the way of the development of a positive and stable identity for many elite professionals.

18.4 FOUR ISSUES SURROUNDING KNOWLEDGE WORKERS' IDENTITIES

Management in general, and even more so in professional service firms, is partly about trying to control identity (Alvesson and Willmott 2002). This means that the target of control is not so much behavior or the measurement of output as it is how employees define themselves (see also Empson and Langley, Chapter 8, this volume). This is not to deny the centrality of behavioral control or output measurement in PSFs, as sometimes there is a strong focus on the profitability of individuals and projects (Empson 2004). Nevertheless, studies show that when hierarchical and technical means cannot prescribe behavior in detail due to the complexity and organic nature of the work tasks, the self-image and social group(s) through which workers define themselves gain in significance (Alvesson 2004).

Many firms engage in subtle forms of control through the development of a strong corporate image or brand that knowledge workers are expected to "live" through a set of orientations that make people able to communicate the image both in specific, image-selling situations such as presentations and in everyday work situations (Alvesson 1995; Covaleski et al. 1998). It is not necessary, nor perhaps possible or profitable, to produce identities that perfectly match the aspired elite image, but if the discrepancy is too strong, the image may be compromised and subsequently control measures are intensified around identity.

18.4.1 Issue 1: PSFs Appear to Support and Provide Worker Autonomy yet Require Employees to Live a Particular Image

In PSFs, notable issues arise around the possible tensions between professional autonomy and more traditional bureaucratic control. Professional work normally is seen as based on a high level of autonomy, although often performed in highly institutionalized settings (Chreim et al. 2007), making individuality and collective belonging complex. Even though most people doing "professional" work in the PSF sector(s) do not belong to the classical professions and are typically oriented to commercial work in a corporate context, there are still anticipations of a fairly high level of autonomy and individuality.

The consequences for how we understand the links between identity and autonomy and control in PSFs are manifold, but two stand out. First, the importance of social-ideological (Alvesson and Kärreman 2004; Kärreman and Alvesson 2004) forms of control are emphasized over bureaucratic forms of control. Thus, significant managerial activity may be focused on affecting meanings and interpretations of the symbolic environment organizational members operate in. Second, an emphasis on qualified individuals to perform professional work puts the individual in focus and problematizes traditional bureaucratic organizational forms and management practices. In PSFs it is common to see an upgrading of the professionals, at least in theory, and some down-grading of management and organizational structures, systems, and procedures.

18.4.2 Issue 2: Knowledge-Intensive Employees both Seek Autonomy and Struggle for Stability in an Environment where Work is Ambiguous

Issue 1 shows that PSFs often engender competing options for workers to be autonomous and still regimented. Turning our attention to the knowledge workers themselves makes clear that being "loosely autonomous" in this manner comes with dilemmas. Contemporary social life has many features that threaten a strong sense of self-identity, including a massive circulation of idealized, grandiose images of excellent firms, consumption, careers, and happiness, and recipes for the optimal life, leading to uncertainty, anxiety, and a low or fluctuating self-esteem (Alvesson 2012; Lasch 1978; Sennett 1998). Current trends towards flexible organizations place an exceptional amount of uncertainty and stress on the contemporary worker. Whereas traditional workplaces and professional roles emphasized symbolic values of education and offered stable templates of work identity (see Faulconbridge, Chapter 19, this volume), modern workplaces are far less stable arenas and often present challenges to the worker attempting to uphold traditional work and career roles (Sennett 1998). Performing knowledge work, and living up to the image of the knowledge worker demands a work-self that does not fail and is always in control (Sturdy 1997). While a rigid adherence to a particular construction of identity may lead to all sorts of problems in a society calling for flexibility and change, some integration, coherence, and stability around identity is necessary for mental well-being and a sense of direction.

PSFs often require workers to navigate in an arena that is consummately ambiguous. For instance, living up to the image of "expertise" requires project leaders to be relatively autonomous in order to adequately service clients. Not only would the image of "expertise" crumble if a knowledge worker, such as a lawyer or accountant, had to seek permission before acting, it would also prove detrimental to the overall functioning PSFs as lean and efficient instead of bureaucratic and hierarchical. Yet, the degree to which autonomy exists is suspect, as part of the job is also adhering to the identity of the firm.

For employees, identity represents the integration of a sense of self and thus ontological security in a destabilized working world (Knights and Willmott 1989). For most people in PSFs much is at stake. In many PSFs there is a blurring of boundaries between self and work and sometimes also self and organization. As Kunda (1992: 91) observes in a large high tech company, "members are expected to invest heavily not only their time and effort, but also their thoughts, feelings, and conceptions of themselves." In work and organizational contexts weak on "substance" and where assessment of work quality frequently is difficult, some vital sources of the stabilization and reinforcement of identity that work well in other job contexts, are only modestly helpful in PSFs. Often lacking are practical mastery of physical objects, direct feedback from people receiving services, and a stable social environment. The presence of alternative sources of identification and loyalty tensions as addressed in the previous sections also adds to the ambiguities and vulnerabilities of identity in many PSFs.

18.4.3 Issue 3: Client Relations are Paramount to Success, yet Close Identification with Client Needs Creates Loyalty Divisions

The ambiguities that knowledge workers face are exacerbated with the introduction of a third party such as clients (see Broschak, Chapter 14, this volume). PSFs encourage workers to appeal to and service a wide array of clients (Ashforth and Mael 1989). Yet, from an organizational loyalty perspective there may be significant negative consequences should employees identify more with their clients than with the firm. Client relationships are often long-term and complex, which increases the chances that workers will identify with the client—and possibly change employment or give priority to the client's interest. Consultants in long-term projects sometimes say that they know the client's organization better than their own (Alvesson 1995). For instance, Deetz's (1995) study of an IT consultancy unit found that some people occasionally under-reported the (chargeable) time they worked for clients, thus favoring the client at the expense of the employing organization, when services are perceived as suboptimal or the client manager has a difficult time keeping the budget, and so on. Certain versions of "client orientation" can thus undermine loyalty to the employer—at the same time as it is often vague what is exactly in the interest of the employer in terms of (short-term) maximizing revenues or making the client satisfied.

This leaves workers in a position to navigate multiple loyalties, in working conditions that do not lend themselves to simple choices. For instance, "client" is not a uniform category in a PSF context, as it might be for physicians or lawyers working for an individual. Within a firm "clients" might refer to top management, project managers, or personnel. Professionals working in PSFs must navigate those in their direct contact as well as the people who are directly affected—for better or worse—by the systems, procedures, practices, or downsizing following from the PSF's operations (Alvesson et al. 2009).

18.4.4 Issue 4: The Ambiguous and Client-Based Nature of PSFs Puts Employees at Greater Risk for Critical External Evaluation and Therefore Requires Employees to have Heightened Sensitivity to Identity

Knowledge workers in PSFs are often thought to be privileged and autonomous (see Suddaby and Muzio, Chapter 2, this volume). Yet the issues brought forth in this chapter acknowledge that the ambiguous nature of knowledge as well as the sometimes tricky loyalties between firms and clients mean that knowledge workers are subject to multiple outside evaluations that may or may not correspond with their actual work. A special feature in PSFs, largely due to the difficulty in evaluating the results of knowledge-intensive work, is the strong contingency upon the opinion of the clients, where there may be elements of randomness, arbitrariness, and politics in their evaluation of professionals. Therefore, despite the comparatively high status of knowledge workers, their self-esteem is not always easy to safeguard in comparison with workers whose competence and results are more materially grounded or based on the mastery of routines.

Economic health and social stability certainly mediate the degree to which clients engage in more critical questioning and scrutiny of both the outcome of labor in PSFs and its value. The market for many PSFs, most notably management consultancy services, has increased rapidly and steadily over a number of years and this may be seen as a sign that these services provide outstanding quality and value. But the market is a very imperfect evaluator. Clients typically have mixed feelings about the PSFs they hire (Clark 1995). More broadly, there is often considerable distrust and skepticism, or at least the absence of full confirmation of knowledge workers' claims to having a superior and effective problem-solving knowledge base. Such is the case in both general public discussions (O'Shea and Madigan 1998) and in specific client settings (Alvesson and Sveningsson 2011). Despite—or perhaps because of—the high status and high fees of many professionals, there are widespread mixed impressions and the reputations of these professionals and companies are called into question. The combination of being highly paid and questioned may be a source of confusion and bewilderment for many workers.

Overall, knowledge workers' external value appears to be subject to change at a project's notice. In a study of a public relations company, a vice president spoke favorably about a young man in the company but when asked if he will be promoted, the interviewee responded:

> Well, just because he is great today does not mean he will be great tomorrow. Anything can happen. He has to keep his clients happy if he wants us to stay happy with him. (Jackall 1988: 172)

This quote shows an oscillation between an ideal, glamorous, high-status professional and a less satisfying, more subservient positioning as an overpaid service worker. This chronic uncertainty around one's competence may threaten a sense of identity and stability in life. Sometimes individuals can act out their preferred identity but sometimes they need to take a much more humble role positioning, potentially undermining their self-esteem.

These four issues together show that compared to many other groups, professional workers have had access to highly powerful symbolic resources in their construction of a positive work identity. Education, status, high pay, and interesting work tasks facilitate identity work and create a strong advantage in developing and maintaining a positive work identity. For this group, status building in order to uphold a certain reputation has been an important way to do identity work. However, the traditional mystique and exclusiveness of knowledge-intensive work is fading away as a consequence of the rapid increase of higher education and consequent inflationary tendency in the symbolic value of professional qualifications. More and more groups are claiming to be professionals, leading to intra- and inter-occupational competition and a devaluation of claims of being a "professional" (Alvesson 2013). Those claiming expertise are often questioned and engage increasingly in efforts to convince others of their value (Alvesson 2004). Many work in large organizations with a fairly high level of hierarchy and bureaucracy. The unpredictable, relationship-dependent, and fluctuating character of work in PSFs can make it difficult for workers to accomplish and sustain a stable feeling of competence and respect. Self-esteem and a coherent sense of self is instead vulnerable, calling for intensive identity work.

Here, organizational and individual identities must be treated as interrelated as PSFs actively engage in crafting particular organizational identities by managing individual workers' identities (Alvesson and Empson 2008). Visions, branding, corporate cultures, and other organizational identity-defining devices are here crucial internal resources—at the same time as these are difficult to get to work as intended. Herein lies the double-edge sword that many PSFs experience: controlling employee identity is treated as paramount yet difficult to accomplish and maintain without strategic interventions. In section 18.5, we label these interventions as three modes of identity-focused control that PSFs may engage in to respond to the difficulties of retaining and managing knowledge workers: mode 1: crafting an image of being an elite firm; mode 2: homogenization of the workforce; and mode 3: anxiety-regulation.

18.5 Three Modes of Identity-Focused Control

18.5.1 Mode 1: Crafting an Image of Being an Elite Firm

Being elite is important to many knowledge workers and the high status of many large knowledge-intensive organizations lends itself to employee identification (Alvesson and Robertson 2006; Empson 2004). Therefore, constructing an organizational identity that is attractive to current and potential employees is often a priority in PSFs. Exceptions to this include instances where the organization wishes for employees to leave, such as downsizing, or in individual cases where people are not chosen for promotion (in up-or-out systems).

Employees often attach personal value to being a successful member of a specific institution (Selznick 1957). Therefore, PSFs often seek to foster employee identification via a combination of internal corporate pride and the conferred status of being affiliated with a prestigious organization. For instance, in a study of branding and organizational identification in a management consulting firm, Kärreman and Rylander (2008) found a surprisingly coherent discourse among organizational members about "who they are" as consultants and the organization's "central and distinctive" characteristics—i.e., its organizational identity. Notably, respondents emphasized that they were part of an elite team, professional, and superior at supporting each other and never turning down a request for help—no matter how late in the day. Yet during lean times, the overall branding shifted from emphasizing the strength of the collective to highlighting the extraordinary and elite character of the firm, explicitly by associating the firm with a prominent sports star.

Alvesson and Empson (2008) found a similarly strong and coherent identity discourse within the consulting firms they studied. Within elite consulting firms professionals described themselves and their firms as "classy and sexy" and made liberal reference to identity markers, such as "Clint Eastwood types," or "as good as McKinsey but more interesting." Within highly successful consulting firms involved in lower status, though nevertheless highly profitable work, identity markers included reference to themselves as " 'The McDonald's of consulting" and "not 'architects' but 'first-rate plumbers.'"

This study suggests that the more distinctive, well known, and well respected the organization, the more likely employees are to define themselves as members (Ashforth and Mael 1989; Dutton et al. 1994, 2010). Further, when organizations fall on hard times or have less access to prestigious claims, managers may engage in great efforts to construct an appealing corporate identity to support identification with it. Efforts include elaborate rhetoric and image management signaling the claimed unique characteristics and excellence of the company such as in Robertson's (1999) study which describes how a small law consultancy firm uses status symbols such as office location and quality, choice of bank, and a company limousine for local and regional traveling to appear grander. What remains unclear is the fate of the professional workers during these lean times.

18.5.2 Mode 2: Homogenization of the Workforce

Hiring is another powerful way in which PSFs shape their identities. The people in an organization can stand in as powerful markers of what the firm represents. Therefore, it stands to reason that PSFs pay close attention to designing a workforce that supports its carefully crafted, typically elite, identity (Alvesson 2004; Covaleski et al. 1998; Hatch and Schultz 2013; Kärreman and Rylander 2008).

Achieving a relatively homogeneous organizational identity is made easier through the recruitment of people with similar class and education backgrounds and personal attributes and orientations (see Sommerlad and Ashley, Chapter 20, this volume). On the one hand, the creation of fairly homogeneous groups associated with the firm lends numerical strength to the organization as a source of identity and is touted as a strategic advantage. Employees are thought to gain from belonging to a collective, which gives strong symbolic support for self-definition and may counteract the fragmentation and mixed messages that the rest of the world produces. Regardless of the perceived organizational and individual benefits, the end result of strategic hiring is a strong homogenization of both employees and organizational identity (Alvesson and Kärreman 2011). On the other hand, scholars are turning their attention to the problematic nature of hiring for fit by recognizing that homogenization commonly occurs around race, class, gender, and sexuality as well as values and work orientations. Ashcraft's (2013) collective-associative view of professional identity addresses the complexity of relationships between PSFs and knowledge workers by arguing that often the nature of work is tightly associated with the social identities, or more simply the bodies, aligned with it.

Rivera's (2012) study of elite PSFs illustrates this argument as she notes that in this case employers base their hiring decisions on how well candidates match their own and their firm's personalities. Cultural matching in terms of leisure pursuits (such as an interest in lacrosse or squash), experiences, and self-presentation mattered deeply to hiring agents who often searched candidates' profiles for non-work-related interests. Hiring managers deemed cultural similarities important because elite professionals are expected to spend so much time at work and with co-workers and being similar might benefit organizational and interpersonal well-being. Yet cultural matching also suggests that evaluators are looking at candidates to see if they match (perceptions of) the firm, going beyond both perceived skills and demographic characteristics such as gender and race, yet closely related to one's embodied identity and class markers. A firm's composition of a certain type of employee enabled evaluators to explain who they are as a collective by putting forth succinct descriptors such as, " 'white-shoe' or 'country club' " (Rivera 2012: 1008). Hiring for fit assisted hiring managers in maintaining the status quo rather than disrupting it.

This makes hiring practices consequential from an organizational as well as an individual identity standpoint, as Ashley and Empson (2013) discovered in their study of how leading law firms reduce risk and enhance their image by differentiating and discriminating based on social class. Specifically, findings suggest that law firms preferred to hire lawyers who embodied an "upmarket" image in order to verify claims that what the firm is offering is elite. The desire to hire employees who embody social class increased in firms where objectively assessing the knowledge-based products and outcomes proved more challenging. In other words, the more ambiguous the firm's offering, the more important hiring people who "live" and present the preferred identity becomes (Alvesson 2004; Covaleski et al. 1998).

Ashcraft (2013), Ashley and Empson (2013), and Rivera (2012) argue that one's body and embodied presentation can keep one out of an elite profession or encourage one to modify themselves to fit in. For instance, Hayne's (2012) study of women in accounting and law firms shows that professional embodiment in these PSFs remains tied to masculinity, regardless of the presence of female associates. PSFs maintain elite status in part through hiring and promotions. In other instances, employees are encouraged to quit, whether for cultural or embodied matching, rigid gatekeeping, or control-based socializing. Such gatekeeping mechanisms ensure homogenization, differentiation, exclusion, and ill-defined inclusion (Ashcraft et al. 2012) at the same time that they appear to aid PSFs in their aims of crafting an elite identity for employees to mirror.

18.5.3 Mode 3: Anxiety-Regulation

The personnel policy of professional service firms with a partnership system such as "up-or-out" contains a contradictory mix of various elements that can lead to high employee anxiety (see Cohen, Chapter 16, this volume). This is particularly pronounced in larger and more prestigious PSFs in fields such as management consultancy and accounting, which tend to dominate. Employees, the core of the firm's success, regularly hear that they are replaceable and that there are limited spots for promotion in the hierarchy, suggesting that many will be forced to resign. This breeds uncertainty between feeling important and proud and feeling anxious about receiving negative feedback about poor performance (Bergström 1998; Kärreman and Alvesson 2004). Given the value attached to being employed by prestigious companies and this group's tendency to be career-oriented, believing that one must improve in order to continue in the company, many find it difficult to relax and be satisfied with the status quo. It is either up or out.

Studies such as Kunda's (1992) on cultural management in a high tech corporation provide a vivid rendering how identity regulation may affect organizational members' anxieties. Here, intense efforts to streamline the organizational membership role and the scripts to identify with the role increased the levels of ambiguity in a workplace already rife with ambiguity and anxiety. On balance, Kunda's study highlights that high-intensity identity regulation through enforced ideology leads to cynical and opportunistic conduct that distorts and disrupts social relations, and, ultimately, it may undermine organizational members' capacity to craft selves that are not colonized or co-opted by organizational ideology.

Kunda's account is compelling, but it is important to remember that most organizations do not engage in creating that kind of idiosyncratic and intense ideology. PSFs in particular are more likely to exploit collective identities already at hand, rather than create them wholesale. One way such exploitation may happen is by engaging in aspirational control (Alvesson and Kärreman 2007; see also Thornborrow and Brown 2009 and Costas and Kärreman 2013). This type of control is exercised through tying a specific identity to a particular career/employment idea and prospect. It involves a mix of encouraging employees to identify with a perceived attractive identity, to acquire a recognized skill set, opportunities to realize objectives and rewards, and the facilitation of compliance with a specific normative order.

Living up to the standard of a good organizational member is a fairly strong driving force: the aspirations are less about linking identity with a future state of being, a possible self, or sense of one's self in the context of the aspired identity (see Markus and Nurius 1986), but more about fitting in and being a full member of the corporate collective. Therefore, aspirational control is likely to increase employee anxieties because it emerges whenever distinct and clear-cut career trajectories are articulated, encouraging the occurrence of provisional selves (Ibarra 1999). It shifts agency to the target of control (i.e., employees), thus converting individuals to accomplices, through confession-like mechanisms such as self-evaluations and career coaching.

18.6 DEMYSTIFYING PROFESSIONALISM

These three modes of control illustrate the strategic ways in which PSFs seek to construct and maintain a particular organizational identity by ignoring and sometimes inviting the anxieties of elite workers. In part, these strategies are in response to the tensions (perceived or otherwise) that PSFs face in managing knowledge-intensive workers who spend a significant amount of time developing external loyalties to clients. Along with the fear that these elite workers could leave and take their knowledge with them, firms face pressures to "utilize" their workforce as part of developing an appealing brand. A common engagement when knowledge workers feel threatened or anxious is to seek to comply with the organization's identity. Minus anxiety, if people see themselves as professionals claiming a very high degree of autonomy and expertise, they will likely meet hierarchical control with resistance. They might also view their client's attempts to control with resistance, as "true professionals" may be disinclined to accept that the customer knows best. Compliance and obedience call for the right kind of subordinate identity that includes calls for discipline and a high degree of uniformity amongst employees.

As noted above, compared to many other groups, knowledge workers have access to some powerful symbolic resources in the construction of a positive work identity such as education, status, high pay, and interesting work tasks. Yet it is a mistake to assume that knowledge workers have the upper hand. They too face dilemmas that leave them hyper aware of the high standards they must reach in an ambitious and shifting market. The traditional mystique and exclusiveness of professional and other knowledge-intensive work is fading away as a consequence of the rapid increase of more people seeking higher education in general and the expansion of occupations claiming expertise and status, in particular. The "massification" of many forms of professional services and increasing numbers of people working in large, well-branded, hierarchical, and bureaucratic firms leave many people feeling at odds with the traditional notion of the autonomous and authoritative professional.

These pressures are not only from within. People are increasingly aware of broad social critiques of professions and expertise (see Dinovitzer et al., Chapter 6, this volume). There is an expanded skepticism and reflexivity about social institutions and experts' claims (Giddens 1991), meaning many professions are facing losses in status. Given the centrality of work and work-related identities to people in PSFs, a lack of confirmation of their valued identity is consequential. Identity then becomes more salient as a problem and a theme for knowledge workers to engage with.

18.7 CONCLUSIONS

This chapter has primarily outlined the challenges and incredible pressures facing knowledge workers in PSFs as consequences of operating in an image-sensitive terrain increasingly focused on image, branding, and persuasion. Many of these challenges are shared across industries and can be located within (post-) affluent societies, where the economy is largely based on persuasion, or "sweet talk" (Alvesson 2013). For PSFs in particular, given the absence of a clear material base and a product demonstrating value, a credible appearance becomes crucial. This is well documented, but the identity implications are not so carefully researched.

With an eye towards future studies and interesting discoveries, this chapter suggests that scholars take a highly contextual view to address how the construction of work identities affects the self.

18.7.1 Not all PSFs are Created Equal

It is perhaps appealing to rely on a "traits view" of PSFs, relying on our knowledge of their typical characteristics. Within the PSF domains there is considerable diversity and more systematic comparative work is needed (see von Nordenflycht et al., Chapter 7, this volume). This vision takes seriously the notion that not all PSFs are created equal in terms of status and identity, nor do they wish to be. Three important distinctions around type of PSF, status, and size could be considered. First, there are various types of PSFs, which have different access to claims of professionalism. For instance, there are PSFs with strong links to institutionalized professions, primarily law and accounting firms, and fields dominated by occupations which are not characterized by homogeneous education, strong professional associations, or certification like management, IT, and communication consultancies. There is also great diversity around firms' access to claims of status. Elite firms can make different claims from those at the lower ends of the market and this distinction may have a telling impact on how firms manage their workforce. For instance, elite firms are prestigious and attractive as employers but also quite demanding, often putting heavy pressure on people, in particular younger people, to conform and comply. Non-elite firms are easily seen as secondary but may offer less of pressure, competition, and anxiety and allow for more space. Of course, the meaning of "elite" varies and sometimes firms not broadly seen as "elite" may construct themselves in such a way (Alvesson and Empson 2008; Alvesson and Robertson 2006). A third important dimension concerns size. Large PSFs typically involve both public recognition—whether as viewed as elite or not—but include the need for management control and thus reduce the significance of the role of the autonomous professional. Small firms are often less reliant on organizational resources such as systems, structures, and images. These three distinctions are not absolute but still have identity implications and signify important themes for further research on organizational identity, identification, and self-identity work issues. Perhaps most importantly, taking seriously the need to explore PSFs as contextual and varied will enable scholars to engage in the tensions that workers face.

18.7.2 Not all Workers are Considered Equal

As this chapter notes, one of the ways in which PSFs seek to manage and control identity is via the homogenization of their workforce, typically around status and cultural markers. A key question that emerges from the idea that organizational identities intersect with individual identities is whether and how image-based struggles are transferred onto the "real person."

Taking seriously the idea that firms hire for fit means looking at identity as both collective and associative. Instead of viewing work and firms as "above" or "untouched" by affiliations with those doing the work or looking at how workers navigate their own identities in relation to their firm, scholars can to look at how PSFs are constituted as much by who they hire as they are by the nature or structure of the organization (Ashcraft 2013; see also Kärreman and Alvesson 2004).

18.7.3 Coping Mechanisms both Create and Respond to Identity Challenges

In many ways, challenging traditional notions of PSFs as necessarily elite opens the door to studies that dig into the specific identity challenges firms and employees face. In this chapter we have noted several issues that complicate identity such as autonomy as necessary yet tenuous, the anxieties around limited advancement, and the often challenging realities of client satisfaction and retention. Certainly, the potential is there for employees to experience a distressed state should their identity struggles be inconsistent or even a failure. But overall, scholars can explore how modern knowledge workers regulate identity, or "cope," so that they are in harmony with the projected organizational identity. Exploring how workers cope when organizational practice and organizational image contradict each other is one means of addressing identity challenges. For instance, topics such hypocrisy (Brunsson 1993), cynicism (Fleming and Spicer 2003), and resistance (Contu 2008; Fleming and Sewell 2002; Kärreman and Alvesson 2009) can be explored alongside an open curiosity around coping mechanisms as constitutive parts of the modern workplace identity.

18.7.4 Multiple Actors Affect Identity in PSFs

Clients have a strong part to play in the ongoing negotiation of identity in PSFs. They are not passive consumers; instead they often select providers for various reasons, including how a firm or consultant might affect the identity claims that client firms can make. Yet clients are often under-explored in studies concerned with individual and occupational identity. Certainly, clients are central as evidenced by the fact that PSFs often contain rhetoric around "client orientation" understood as "doing whatever is necessary to make the client happy." This comes with the notion that those striving for professional standing must convince stakeholders such as clients, governmental agencies, and other professions of their credentials. Professionals are often at the same time superior, well-paid experts, assumed to have authority, *and* client-oriented, servants of power, dependent on clients, which may make them feel like corporate slaves rather than the privileged elite. How clients are centered in PSFs is, again, complicated and perhaps not well understood and more attention is needed beyond individualized contexts. Scholars can take a client-centered approach to the study of PSFs, drawing on the various expectations that clients hold and how PSFs and knowledge workers are part of their ongoing identity projects. Taking the audience into account brings added understanding to the efficacy of identity work and highlights the importance of contexts such as workers' subjectivities and the nature of the task at hand.

18.7.5 Depth of Identity Construction

A very important general theme for consideration but also a topic for particular studies concerns issues of the depth of identity construction. Arguably, there can be superficial and deep identity issues, perhaps relating to the different identity reference points. There may for example be deep professional identity and surface organizational identity or the opposite. This can be related to how strong a specific occupation is in terms of socialization, source of status, homogenization, the relevance and salience of occupational communities (associations), etc. Elite firms, with long internal careers and various markers of uniqueness and status may lead to strong identification and possibly depth identity. But temporary identification and deeper identities are not the same so this issue, also related to competition between various social identities, may be complicated.

An additional key issue around depth is the importance of reserving the concept of identity for themes that have a certain durability or richness and intensity in terms of personal meaning and commitment. Very often scholars and others seem to (mis)use the term identity as referring to almost everything, including social category, role, preference, or even behavior. Careful exploration of whether these are identity-related or not is vital. Many issues may preferably be understood in other ways than through references to identity.

The relationship between the individual and the organization is of fundamental importance in PSFs, yet in this chapter we advocate the need to explore identity as complex and multifaceted.

Identity has particular relevance for organizational activities in this context, as it provides clues for action, interpretation, and conduct. In this sense, it may operate as a proxy for organizational control; for instance as a substitute or surrogate for rules, procedures, and other forms of behavioral control. At the same time, it is important to not ascribe too much significance to identity; there are many other aspects of significance, including many dimensions of organizational culture not really captured by concepts of individual, professional, or organizational identity.

In this chapter we have identified four main issues for management control in PSFs: autonomy/conformity tensions, the client conundrum, ambiguity saturation, and intangibility; and three main modes of identity-focused control in PSFs: positive image, homogenization of the workforce, and anxiety-regulation.

Identity regulation has a sinister subtext of indoctrination and manipulation, and there are certainly reasons to take this seriously (e.g., Kunda 1992; Willmott 1993), but there are also mixed or positive stories about identity regulation bringing about a better match between individuals and their work organizations, more smooth working relationships, and, thereby, better work results (Alvesson and Kärreman 2011; Empson 2004). Generally speaking we think that the reliance on indirect forms of control in PSFs does not necessarily mean that professionals experience more effective control. Identity is complex and indirect forms of control are often difficult to accomplish.

REFERENCES

Albert, S. and Whetten, D. A. (1985). "Organizational Identity," *Research in Organizational Behavior* 17: 263–295.

Alvesson, M. (1994). "Talking in Organizations: Managing Identity and Image in an Advertising Agency," *Organization Studies* 15(4): 535–563.

Alvesson, M. (1995). *Management of Knowledge-Intensive Companies*. Berlin and New York: de Gruyter.

Alvesson, M. (2001). "Knowledge Work: Ambiguity, Image and Identity," *Human Relations* 54(7): 863–886.

Alvesson, M. (2004). *Knowledge Work and Knowledge-Intensive Firms*. Oxford: Oxford University Press.

Alvesson, M. (2010). "Self-Doubters, Strugglers, Story-Tellers, Surfers and Others: Images of Self-Identity in Organization Studies," *Human Relations* 63(2): 193–217.

Alvesson, M. (2012). "Managing Consultants: Control and Identity," in *The Oxford Handbook of Management Consultancy*, ed. T. Clark and M. Kipping. Oxford: Oxford University Press, 303–324.

Alvesson, M. (2013). *The Triumph of Emptiness: Consumption, Higher Education & Work Organization*. Oxford: Oxford University Press.

Alvesson, M. and Empson, L. (2008). "The Construction of Organizational Identity: Comparative Case Studies of Consulting Firms," *Scandinavian Journal of Management* 24(1): 1–16.

Alvesson, M. and Kärreman, D. (2004). "Interfaces of Control: Technocratic and Socio-Ideological Control in a Global Management Consultancy Firm," *Accounting, Organizations and Society* 29(3–4): 423–444.

Alvesson, M. and Kärreman, D. (2007). "Unraveling HRM: Identity, Ceremony, and Control in a Management Consultancy Firm," *Organization Science* 18(4): 711–723.

Alvesson, M. and Kärreman, D. (2011). "Meritocracy Versus Sociocracy: Personnel Concepts and HR Themes in Two IT/Management Consulting Firms," in *Managing Modernity: Beyond Bureaucracy*, ed. S. Clegg, M. Harris, and H. Höpfl. Oxford: Oxford University Press, 154–175.

Alvesson, M. and Robertson, M. (2006). "The Brightest and the Best: The Role of Elite Identity in Knowledge Intensive Companies," *Organization* 13(2): 195–224.

Alvesson, M. and Sveningsson, S. (2011). "Identity Work in Consultancy Projects: Ambiguity and Distribution of Credit and Blame," in *Discourses of Deficit*, ed. C. Candlin and J. Crichton. Basingstoke: Palgrave Macmillan, 159–174.

Alvesson, M. and Willmott, H. (2002). "Identity Regulation as Organizational Control," *Journal of Management Studies* 39(5): 619–644.

Alvesson, M., Ashcraft, K. L., and Thomas, R. (2008). "Identity Matters: Reflections on the Construction of Identity Scholarship in Organization Studies," *Organization* 15(1): 5–28.

Alvesson, M., Kärreman, D., Sturdy, A., and Handley, K. (2009). "Unpacking the Client(s): Constructions, Positions and Client–Consultant Dynamics," *Scandinavian Journal of Management* 25(3): 253–263.

Ashcraft, K. L. (2013). "The Glass Slipper: 'Incorporating' Occupational Identity in Management Studies," *Academy of Management Review* 38(1): 6–31.

Ashcraft, K. L., Muhr, S. L., Rennstam, J., and Sullivan, K. (2012). "Professionalization as a Branding Activity: Occupational Identity and the Dialectic of Inclusivity-Exclusivity," *Gender, Work and Organization* 19(5): 467–488.

Ashforth, B. and Mael, F. (1989). "Social Identity Theory and the Organization," *Academy of Management Review* 14(1): 20–39.

Ashley, L. and Empson, L. (2013). "Differentiation and Discrimination: Understanding Social Class and Social Exclusion in Leading Law Firms," *Human Relations* 66(2): 219–244.

Beech, N., MacIntosh, R., and McInnes, P. (2008). "Identity Work: Processes and Dynamics of Identity Formation," *International Journal of Public Administration* 31(9): 957–970.

Bergström, O. (1998). *Att passa in. Rekryteringsarbete i ett kunskapsintensivt företag*. Göteborg: BAS.

Blackler, F. (1995). "Knowledge, Knowledge Work and Organizations: An Overview and Interpretation," *Organization Studies* 16(6): 1021–1046.

Brunsson, N. (1993). "Ideas and Actions: Justification and Hypocrisy as Alternatives to Control," *Accounting, Organizations and Society* 18(6): 489–506.

Chreim, S., Williams, B. B., and Hinings, C. B. (2007). "Interlevel Influences on the Reconstruction of Professional Role Identity," *Academy of Management Journal* 50(6): 1515–1539.

Clark. T. (1995). *Managing Consultants*. Milton Keynes: Open University Press.

Contu, A. (2008). "Decaf Resistance on Misbehavior, Cynicism, and Desire in Liberal Workplaces," *Management Communication Quarterly* 21(3): 364–379.

Contu, A. and Willmott, H. (2003). "Re-embedding Situatedness: The Importance of Power Relations in Learning Theory," *Organization Science* 14(3): 283–296.

Costas, J. and Kärreman, D. (2013). "Conscience as Control: Managing Employees through CSR," *Organization* 20(3): 394–415.

Covaleski, M. A., Dirsmith, M. W., Heian, J. B., and Samuel, S. (1998). "The Calculated and the Avowed: Techniques of Discipline and Struggles over Identity in Big Six Public Accounting Firms," *Administrative Science Quarterly* 43(2): 293–327.

Deetz, S. (1995). *Transforming Communication, Transforming Business: Building Responsive and Responsible Workplaces.* Cresskill, NJ: Hampton Press.

Dutton, J. E. and Dukerich, J. M. (1991). "Keeping an Eye on the Mirror: Image and Identity in Organizational Adaptation," *Academy of Management Journal* 34(3): 517–554.

Dutton, J. E., Dukerich, J. M., and Harquail, C. V. (1994). "Organizational Images and Member Identification," *Administrative Science Quarterly* 39(2): 239–263.

Dutton, J. E., Roberts, L. M., and Bednar, J. (2010). "Pathways for Positive Identity Construction at Work: Four Types of Positive Identity and the Building of Social Resources," *Academy of Management Review* 35(2): 265–293.

Dutton, J., Roberts, L. M., and Bednar, J. (2011). "Using a Positive Lens to Complicate the Positive in Identity Research," *Academy of Management Review* 36(2): 427–431.

Elsbach, K. D. (1999). "An Expanded Model of Organizational Identification," in *Research in Organizational Behavior*, ed. R. Sutton and B. Staw. Amsterdam: Elsevier Science Press, 163–200.

Empson, L. (2004). "Organizational Identity Change: Managerial Regulation and Member Identification in an Accounting Firm Acquisition," *Accounting, Organizations and Society* 29(8): 759–781.

Fleming, P. and Sewell, G. (2002). "Looking for the Good Soldier, Švejk Alternative Modalities of Resistance in the Contemporary Workplace," *Sociology* 36(4): 857–873.

Fleming, P. and Spicer, A. (2003). "Working at a Cynical Distance: Implications for Power, Subjectivity and Resistance," *Organization* 10(1): 157–179.

Foucault, M. (1982). "The Subject and Power," *Critical Inquiry* 8(4): 777–795.

Giddens, A. (1991). *Modernity and Self-Identity: Self and Society in the Late Modern Age.* Stanford, CA: Stanford University Press.

Gioia, D. A., Schultz, M., and Corley, K. G. (2000). "Organizational Identity, Image, and Adaptive Instability," *Academy of Management Review* 25(1): 63–81.

Grey, C. (1994). "Career as a Project of the Self and Labor Process Discipline," *Sociology* 28(2): 479–497.

Haslam, A. (2004). *Psychology of Organizations*, 2nd edn. London: Sage.

Hatch, M. J. and Shultz. M. (2013). "The Dynamics of Corporate Brand Charisma: Routinization and Activation at Carlsberg IT," *Scandinavian Journal of Management* 29(2): 147–162.

Hayne, K. (2012). "Body Beautiful? Gender, Identity and the Body in Professional Services Firms," *Gender, Work & Organization* 19(5): 489–507.

Ibarra, H. (1999). "Provisional Selves: Experimenting with Image and Identity in Professional Adaptation," *Administrative Science Quarterly* 44(4): 764–791.

Ibarra H. and Barbulescu, I. (2010). "Identity as Narrative: Prevalence, Effectiveness, and Consequences of Narrative Identity Work in Macro Work Role Transitions," *Academy of Management Review* 35(1): 135–154.

Jackall, R. (1988). *Moral Mazes: The World of Corporate Managers.* New York: Oxford University Press.

Kärreman, D. (2010). "The Power of Knowledge: Learning from 'Learning by Knowledge-Intensive Firm," *Journal of Management Studies* 47(7): 1405–1416.

Kärreman, D. and Alvesson, M. (2004). "Cages in Tandem: Management Control, Social Identity, and Identification in a Knowledge-Intensive Firm," *Organization* 11(1): 149–175.

Kärreman, D. and Alvesson, M. (2009). "Resisting Resistance: Counter-Resistance, Consent and Compliance in a Consultancy Firm," *Human Relations* 62(8): 1115–1144.

Kärreman, D. and Rylander, A. (2008). "Managing Meaning through Branding: The Case of a Consulting Firm," *Organization Studies* 29(1): 103–125.

Knights, D. and Willmott, H. (1989). "Power and Subjectivity at Work: From Degradation to Subjugation in Social Relations," *Sociology* 23(4): 535–558.

Kunda, G. (1992). *Engineering Culture: Control and Commitment in a High-Tech Organization.* Philadelphia: Temple University Press.

Ladge, J. J., Clair, J. A., and Greenberg, D. (2012). "Cross-Domain Identity Transition during Liminal Periods: Constructing Multiple Selves as Professional and Mother during Pregnancy," *Academy of Management Journal* 55(6): 1449–1471.

Lasch, C. (1978). *The Culture of Narcissism.* New York: W. W. Norton.

Løwendahl, B. R. (1997). *Strategic Management of Professional Service Firms.* Copenhagen: Copenhagen Business School Press.

Markus, H. and Nurius, P. (1986). "Possible Selves," *American Psychologist* 41(9): 954–969.

Morris, T. and Empson, L. (1998). "Organization and Expertise: An Exploration of Knowledge Bases and the Management of Accounting and Consulting Firms," *Accounting, Organizations and Society* 23(5–6): 609–624.

Newell, S., Robertson, M., Scarbrough, H., and Swan, J. (2009). *Managing Knowledge Work and Innovation.* Basingstoke: Palgrave Macmillan.

O'Shea, J. and Madigan, C. (1998). *Dangerous Company: Management Consultants and the Businesses They Save and Ruin.* New York: Penguin.

Pratt, M. G. (2000). "The Good, the Bad, and the Ambivalent: Managing Identification among Amway Distributors," *Administrative Science Quarterly* 45(3): 456–493.

Ravasi, D. and Schultz, M. (2006). "Responding to Organizational Identity Threats: Exploring the Role of Organizational Culture," *Academy of Management Journal* 49(3): 433–458.

Rivera, L. A. (2012). "Hiring as Cultural Matching: The Case of Elite Professional Service Firms," *American Sociological Review* 77(6): 999–1022.

Robertson, M. (1999). "Sustaining Knowledge Creation within Knowledge-Intensive Firms," dissertation, Warwick Business School.

Schreyögg, G. and Geiger, D. (2007). "The Significance of Distinctiveness: A Proposal for Rethinking Organizational Knowledge," *Organization* 14(1): 77–100.

Scott, S. G. and Lane, V. R. (2000). "A Stakeholder Approach to Organizational Identity," *Academy of Management Review* 25(1): 43–62.

Selznick, P. (1957). *Leadership in Administration: A Sociological Interpretation.* New York: Harper & Row.

Sennett, R. (1998). *The Corrosion of Character.* New York: W. W. Norton.

Starbuck, W. H. (1993). "Keeping a Butterfly and an Elephant in a House of Cards: The Elements of Exceptional Success*," *Journal of Management Studies* 30(6): 885–921.

Sturdy, A. (1997). "The Consultancy Process: An Insecure Business," *Journal of Management Studies* 34(3): 389–414.

Sveningsson, S. and Alvesson, M. (2003). "Managing Managerial Identities: Organizational Fragmentation, Discourse and Identity Struggle," *Human Relations* 56(10): 1163–1193.

Thornborrow, T. and Brown, A. D. (2009). "'Being Regimented': Aspiration, Discipline and Identity Work in the British Parachute Regime," *Organization Studies* 30(4): 355–376.

Turner, J. (1984). "Social Identification and Psychological Group Formation," in *The Social Dimension*, vol. 2, ed. H. Tajfel. Cambridge: Cambridge University Press, 518–538.

von Nordenflycht, A. (2010). "What is a Professional Service Firm? Toward a Theory and Taxonomy of Knowledge-Intensive Firms," *Academy of Management Review* 35(1): 155–174.

Watson, T. (2008). "Managing Identity, Identity Work, Personal Predicaments and Structured Circumstances," *Organization* 15: 121–143.

Willmott, H. (1993). "Strength is Ignorance; Slavery is Freedom: Managing Culture in Modern Organizations," *Journal of Management Studies* 30(4): 515–552.

CHAPTER 19

KNOWLEDGE AND LEARNING IN PROFESSIONAL SERVICE FIRMS

JAMES FAULCONBRIDGE

19.1 INTRODUCTION

FROM Mintzberg's (1979) early work on professional adhocracies and bureaucracies, through to more recent work on strategic management (Løwendahl 2005) and internationalization (Hitt et al. 2006; Malhotra and Morris 2009), questions about knowledge base, knowledge management, and learning have been at the center of analyses of Professional Service Firms (PSFs). Indeed, the main argument of this chapter is that it is difficult to understand the form, management, markets, and ultimately the services produced by PSFs without analysis of the characteristics of knowledge and learning in such organizations. To develop this argument, the chapter begins by exploring the way issues of knowledge and learning in PSFs have been examined in literature emerging from work on the sociology of the professions and from management studies. This leads into the second substantive part of the chapter in which the implications of knowledge's centrality in PSFs are considered in relation to three distinctive issues, as outlined below.

First, impacts on organizational form are explored. Comparisons are made within and between both the "old" (e.g., accountancy and law) and the new (e.g., advertising and management consultancy) PSFs (see von Nordenflycht et al., Chapter 7, this volume) to reveal the way knowledge base influences organizational form. This relates also to issues of governance (see Greenwood and Empson 2003; Leblebici and Sherer, Chapter 9, this volume) and team structure (see Gardner, Chapter 17, this volume; Malhotra and Morris 2009). Second, issues surrounding knowledge management and learning are unpacked. From explicit knowledge management and the database (Swart and Kinnie 2003), to tacit knowledge and the community of practice (Faulconbridge 2006, 2010a), tactics adopted in professional services to enhance and leverage the expertise of workers are explored and the reasons for variable levels of success and failure analyzed (on such issues see especially Empson 2001a). The role of training in PSFs is used to illustrate such concerns. Finally, the embedded jurisdictional nature of knowledge in professional service firms is examined. Here questions about both the forces regulating the market capture of particular professions and firms (Abel 1988; Larson 1977; Suddaby and Greenwood 2001), as well as the local–global dynamics of expertise (Evetts 1998; Faulconbridge and Muzio 2012; Quack and Schüßler, Chapter 3, this volume), are outlined so as to reveal the way jurisdictionally structured knowledge prescribes in temporally fluid ways the domain of operation of PSFs.

The chapter concludes by outlining a schema that characterizes the relationships between knowledge and learning and different dimensions of the organization, management, and jurisdiction of PSFs, and by reflecting on the future directions for research demanded by the uncertainties and conundrums that persist. The discussion draws attention, in particular, to the trajectory of change in the increasingly managed PSFs, the increasing role of technology, the growing transnationality of professional jurisdictions, and the implications of all of these for client services.

19.2 Sociologies of the Professions

The starting point for analyzing the significance of issues of knowledge and learning in PSFs is an extensive body of work that can be broadly badged as studies of the sociology of the professions (Abbott 1988; Burrage et al. 1990; Evetts 2003; Johnson 1972; Larson 1977; Macdonald 1995; Parsons 1963). In this work, the primary preoccupation has been unpacking the way that the definition, protection, and maintenance of a knowledge base, tied to a particular professional grouping, has allowed the carving out of a protected space of service production and delivery.

Suddaby and Muzio (Chapter 2, this volume) offer a comprehensive review of the way the literature on the sociology of the professions has come to influence research on PSFs. It is, nonetheless, worth briefly returning to and interrogating further some of the issues they raise because of their importance to the topic of this chapter. As outlined below, the sociology of the professions literature highlights two fundamental themes associated with a codified and widely recognized core knowledge base. Firstly, the "traditional" professions which emerged in the early twentieth century or before (the likes of architecture, law, medicine, and more recently accounting) exemplify the relationship between a codified knowledge base and the protection, through state-supported monopolies, of certain types of service work. For instance, fundamental to some of the earliest work on the professions (e.g., Parsons 1963) was analysis of the way that doctors and lawyers used recourse to the importance of their core knowledge in protecting the public good to justify restrictions on who could join the profession and deliver services. Such restrictions were, and continue to be, at the heart of closure regimes through which a limited set of eligibles become members of a profession. Only those with the credentials that confirm possession of a defined body of expertise (which in the present era are predominantly represented by a university degree) have the right to be part of a profession and in turn be a practitioner in a PSF.

A second body of work documents attempts by aspiring professions to mimic the approach of "traditional" professions and define a core knowledge base. For example, over the past 50 years, management consultants have made several attempts through various professional bodies to define the core knowledge base of consultants. The underlying motivation has been to give legitimacy to and secure a market for services (McKenna 2006). Similar trends can be seen in executive search and project management (Beaverstock et al. 2010; Hodgson 2007; Muzio et al. 2011).

The fact that both the "traditional" and the aspiring "new" professions see fit to turn to definitions of knowledge base as a tool to justify claims to professional status confirms tight connections between knowledge and the professions. This is despite powerful critiques of the fundamental logic that such knowledge is the basis for public protection (Johnson 1972; Larson 1977). There is, however, still much to be done to connect the understanding generated by the sociology of the professions literature to work on PSFs. Most fundamentally this is because the literature does not explicitly consider organizations and specifically PSFs in its analysis—a well-recognized shortcoming (Faulconbridge and Muzio 2012; Muzio et al. 2011). The next section of the chapter considers why recent efforts to rectify this shortcoming are so important for understandings of knowledge and learning in PSFs.

19.3 What is "Knowledge" and "Learning" in Professional Service Firms?

The fundamental idea that the professions are associated with specialist expertise, and that in turn professional work and practitioners are in some way "unique" (compared to non-professional service work or manufacturing work) penetrates to the heart of the organization and management of PSFs in a variety of ways. Yet, what exactly is meant by the term "knowledge" is often unclear. Skirting around the edges of definitions of knowledge in PSFs is a widely recognized problem in the existing literature (see Alvesson 2004; Morris and Empson 1998). Ambiguity plagues discussions of exactly what the knowledge base of a PSF is, and in turn how firms should organize to leverage this knowledge (Alvesson 2001). Perhaps most problematically, ambiguity surrounds understanding of what PSFs deliver in terms of knowledge to their increasingly savvy clients (see Broschak, Chapter 14, this volume; Empson 2001a; Løwendahl 2005).

The sociology of the professions literature would suggest that the focus for analysis should be the value-added clients accrue when professional practitioners apply their formally defined knowledge bases to a particular business problem. This insight raises, however, as many questions as it provides answers. For instance, it tells us very little about what "applying" knowledge means, or about what the value-added of the deployment of the knowledge might be from the client's perspective. Indeed, some have even suggested that, when unpacked, the work of PSFs is far less knowledge-intensive than we might expect (Alvesson 2001; Blackler 1995). Such arguments question the meaning and discursive construction of expertise in relation to the professions and PSFs. As such, there is a risk that ambiguity is reinforced by an exclusive focus on formally defined knowledge bases. It is, therefore, necessary to consider how fundamental debates about knowledge and learning that are emerging from broadly defined management studies might help overcome this impasse.

Amin and Cohendet (2004) and Newell et al. (2002) provide useful overviews of debates about the nature of knowledge and learning. In the case of PSFs, three core questions framing these debates are of special relevance. What form does knowledge take in PSFs? What is the relationship in PSFs between individual and organizational knowledges? And how can PSFs generate the conditions for new expertise to emerge?

First, this literature forces us to ask a question that takes us back to and beyond work on the sociology of the professions: *what form does knowledge take in PSFs?* At its most fundamental this requires attention to debates about the relationship between data, information and knowledge so as to develop a clearer sense of the different ways knowledge might exist and be deployed and developed in PSFs. Burton-Jones (1999: 5) provides us with a useful conceptualization in this regard, suggesting that:

> data are defined as signals which can be sent by an originator to a recipient—human or otherwise. Information is defined as data that is intelligible to the recipient. Finally, knowledge is defined as the cumulative stock of skills derived from the use of information by the recipient.

Such differentiation matters because it reveals the centrality in the production of knowledge of "cognitive structures which can assimilate information" (Howells 2000: 53). Recognizing the role of cognitive structures is important in the context of PSFs because it draws attention to the fact that the individual and their cognitive abilities needs to be a fundamental concern. The highly relevant distinction between "know what" and "know how" reiterates this point. In the case of PSFs the former is often associated with the knowledge new graduates bring to their employers via their accredited qualifications; in other words, the defined knowledge base that work on the sociology of the professions puts so much emphasis on. The latter "know how" form of knowledge most closely corresponds with the expertise or "gray hair" accrued through years of experience of producing and delivering services (Maister 2003; Marchant and Robinson 1999). The distinction between "know what" and "know how" also corresponds broadly with the differences between explicit and tacit knowledge long ago identified by Polanyi (1966), with the tacit dimension and "knowing more than you can tell" being shown to be at the heart of the production process in PSF (Faulconbridge 2006, 2007a; Marchant and Robinson 1999). Indeed, as Alvesson (2004: 50) notes, it is impossible to develop a handbook for a knowledge worker. Instead, judgment and the ability to use tacit "know how," alongside the fundamental "know what" knowledge base associated with a profession, is the key determinant for successful service production and delivery.

In sum, what this work tells us is that the answer to the question "what form does knowledge take in PSFs?" requires appreciation of a dialectical relationship between individuals and their explicit (formalized and profession specific) and tacit (individualized expertise) forms of knowledge. The latter type is arguably the most crucial in terms of generating value-adding and innovative services, but is insufficient if not coupled to the former type (see Barrett and Hinings, Chapter 11, and Swart et al., Chapter 21, this volume). This in turn means that a consideration of learning in a professional context must involve the different processes involved in developing both explicit and tacit knowledge.

A second relevant question framing debates about knowledge and learning builds on the previous point about the role of individualized tacit knowledge in PSFs. Specifically, the importance of the individual leads to the question: *what is the relationship in PSFs between individual and organizational knowledges?* At the heart of questions about knowledge that is more or less tacit or explicit are concerns about the extent to which an organization can capture, commoditize, and reuse knowledge to gain competitive advantage in a market. This in effect is organizational as distinct from individual learning, "the vehicle for utilizing past experiences, adapting to environmental changes and enabling future options" (Berends et al. 2003: 1036).

Nonaka and Takeuchi (1995) in their influential book *The Knowledge-Creating Company* addressed this dilemma by examining the extent to which "know how" can be captured through forms of database or other mechanism and then leveraged and combined in future projects. In particular, they consider how processes of externalization might be used to extract tacit understanding from employees, render it explicit, and in turn maximize the knowledge assets possessed by the organization. For PSFs such a concern is very real. The familiar metaphor that the assets of the professional service firm leave via the elevator at the end of the day very much captures the way that a heavy reliance on "know how" renders PSFs fragile organizations, dependent on the retention of key individuals and their tacit knowledge (Løwendahl 2005; Maister 2003). To reduce this fragility, the creation of organizational assets out of individualized expertise would seem important. But, how realistic is such an externalization process?

Many have suggested that externalization attempts are likely to have only limited success (Empson 2001b; Horvath 1999). Some have even suggested that "tacit knowledge, though rare, non-substitutable, immutable and valuable (when used to advance corporate goals), does not satisfy the ex-post conditions of a strategic asset" (Meso and Smith 2000: 232–233, emphasis removed). It is important to note, therefore, that when questions about the relationship between individualized and organizational knowledges are raised in relation to PSFs, answers tend to focus on the significant uncertainties that exist about whether firms can ever develop organizational knowledge-based competencies.

The challenge of managing a firm heavily reliant on tacit expertise, and potentially having few organizational knowledge assets, brings us to a final key question about knowledge and learning: *how can PSFs generate the conditions for new expertise to emerge?* (see Barrett and Hinings, Chapter 11, this volume, for a detailed overview of innovation in this context). Of particular significance when seeking to address this question are epistemological debates that distinguish between learning as a process of information acquisition and learning in practice (see Amin and Cohendet 2004; Brown and Duguid 2000).

On the one hand, there are those who view learning as a process that requires knowledge to be transferred between individuals—this literature tends to emphasize knowledge management as a technical challenge (e.g., Skyrme 1999; Teece 2000). On the other hand, a more sociologically informed camp argue that learning is a social process that occurs as part of everyday practice. The implication of this strand of literature is that, rather than concerning ourselves with knowledge being transferred from one individual to another, focus needs to fall on "knowledgeability of action, this is on knowing (a verb connoting action, doing, practice) rather than knowledge (a noun connoting things, elements, facts, processes, descriptions)" (Orlikowski 2002: 250–251). Associated with work on communities of practice (Lave and Wenger 1991; Wenger 1998), the practice perspective conceives of learning as involving processes of continual sense-making by individuals as they develop their own tacit understandings through interacting with those around them.

Such distinctions matter for PSFs because they cut to the heart of questions about how firms might engage in knowledge management and create a context in which collective learning and innovation can happen through more or less technological or social systems (Faulconbridge 2010a; Gottschalk 2000; Terrett 1998). Specifically, these literatures suggest that responses to the question "how can PSFs generate the conditions for new expertise to emerge?" need to explore how the optimum organizational environment that facilitates forms of both explicit and tacit learning might be created.

19.4 KNOWLEDGE AND ITS IMPACTS ON THE ORGANIZATION OF PROFESSIONAL SERVICE FIRMS

At first glance, the issues discussed in the previous section might be seen as a concern only to those charged with knowledge management. However, the existing literature shows that such factors have much wider and fundamental implications. In particular, organizational theorists have explained through reference to issues associated with knowledge the apparently peculiar organizational form of PSFs. Two issues are important in this regard. Firstly, the direct implications of employing professionals—i.e., individuals who have gained membership of an exclusive occupational field with its own closure regime. Secondly, the effects on organizational form and control of reliance on the explicit and tacit knowledge of professionals. Both discussions reveal that having knowledge as the main input into the production process (the employment of knowledgeable individuals) and as the main output (advice that addresses a client's needs) poses some unique challenges.

19.4.1 Defined, Protected, and Maintained Knowledge Bases: Implications for Practice and Governance

The fact that professions not only have defined knowledge bases but also actively protect and maintain their knowledge bases has, according to the sociology of the profession literatures, several implications for PSFs. Most fundamentally, the "traditional" professions (and in some cases also the "new" professions) have well-established institutions that ensure connections between knowledge base and closure are upheld. They also ensure that the core defined knowledge base evolves in appropriate ways over time (see Suddaby and Muzio, Chapter 2, this volume). The role of professional associations in protection and maintenance work exemplifies such issues.

As Burrage et al. (1990) highlighted in their seminal analysis of key actors in professional projects, in many contexts protection and maintenance work involves professional associations acting as quasi-autonomous bodies that regulate the professions on behalf of the state. In so doing they become the agents that control the boundaries of the professional knowledge base, the policing of closure regimes, and the evolution in definitions of knowledge. Professional associations exert such control through regulative institutions, targeted both at individual professionals and the organizations that employ them. They enforce these controls through punishments ranging from fines to expulsion from a profession. For PSFs, because of their direct employment of professionals, the way knowledge bases are protected and maintained has several implications (on the implications see also Reihlen and Werr, Chapter 12, this volume). Most fundamentally, by connecting to definitions of the core knowledge base of a profession (and often the ethical principles that go back to the public protection logics originally associated with the professions) associations create and police a set of rules which delimit the market jurisdiction of a PSF.

This influence of associations has been demonstrated most notably through work on accountancy PSFs and the way changes to the jurisdiction of accountants' professional expertise had to be negotiated by, in particular, Big Four firms seeking to also provide consultancy services (Greenwood et al. 2002). This demonstrates how ties between knowledge bases, professional jurisdictions, and the role of professional associations in defining and policing jurisdictional boundaries directly affect what PSFs can and cannot provide in terms of services.

Table 19.1 provides other examples of how the relationship between knowledge and the policing work of associations impacts upon the PSF. The first three examples of "knowledge-related issues" in the table reveal the control that professional associations

Table 19.1 How knowledge's centrality to the professions shapes the work of professional associations and in turn impacts on Professional Service Firms

Knowledge-related issue	Key regulative governance issues	Examples of impacts on PSFs
Regulation of core competencies professionals must possess, and in turn definition of jurisdiction of a professional group	To uphold claims of monopoly over particular jurisdiction, links made between knowledge and the types of work a professional can and cannot do	Certain types of work protected, along with fee income for such work, but other types of work also designated out of bounds, potentially restricting service provision that can be offered
Regulation of context for employment of professionals	To ensure professionals are able to effectively deploy their knowledge for the benefit of clients, rules set about the contexts in which professionals can work	On a country-by-country or state-by-state basis, certain organizational forms (e.g., the limited liability partnership) or types of employment contract are rendered impossible (e.g., in Italy rules limit the possibilities for salaried employment in a law firm)
Mandatory forms of continuing professional development	To guarantee that throughout their careers individuals maintain the core knowledge base of the profession, certain forms of ongoing training are defined and monitored	Firms compelled to provide certain forms of learning and development opportunities, impinging on time for fee-earning activities and autonomy of corporate training programmes
Regulation of standards of professional competency	Definition and policing of standards used to ensure clients receive benefits of professional's expertise and logics of public protection maintained	Standards of employee and firm performance defined by associations as well as employing firms; firm-level systems must be put in place to monitor externally imposed standards so as to protect corporate reputation

exert over PSFs. The fourth example reveals how the importance of knowledge leads to PSFs also being co-opted as regulators of professionals, their knowledge, and the way this knowledge is exercised in practice. Combined, the examples reveal that there are significant effects of the association between professions and knowledge on the activities and also on the responsibilities and necessary organizational forms of PSFs. Further understanding these effects is the purpose of the next sub-section of the chapter.

19.4.2 Individuals and Their Knowledge: Producing the Aberrant PSF Organizational Form

Cutting across studies of the organizational form of PSFs is a common theme: the many aberrations that mark such firms out as distinctive compared to their non-professional service or manufacturing peers. The starting point for such studies was the seminal work of Henry Mintzberg (1979) in which he identified the distinctive features of the professional bureaucracy and adhocracy. Specifically, he pointed to the significance of professional standards as the main means of defining quality in both organizational forms, but also to differences between the two forms in terms of systems of control. In the bureaucracy, attempts are made to organize production through the pigeonholing of client problems and solutions into categories of knowledge. A techno structure with managerial responsibilities also appears; its role in part being to manage the pigeonholing process. In contrast, in the adhocracy, problem identification and solution development are left entirely in the hands of professionals so as to be sensitive to the importance of the tacit knowledge of individuals in the professional production and delivery process. There are dedicated managers in the bureaucracy but in the adhocracy professionals take on managerial responsibilities, usually while continuing to also be involved in professional practice. The distinctiveness of the two forms of organization compared to manufacturing is usually explained as a product of the knowledge intensity of professional service work; this intensity meaning all organizational forms must place questions of how to manage knowledge at the forefront (Empson 2001a).

Mintzberg's insights were confirmed and developed by contributions from Freidson (1983) and Raelin (1991). For Freidson, professionalism acts a distinctive work logic in which the value of the knowledge of the individual practitioner is recognized through organizational arrangements designed to grant high degrees of autonomy. Reflecting Mintzberg's professional adhocracy, this means that in organizations in which logics of professionalism dominate, control over the entire production process is placed in the hands of the professional. At the same time the quality of work is judged by peers against widely recognized professional knowledge-based standards, rather than organizationally-specific standards. Meanwhile, quality and ethical practice rather than efficiency are deemed to be the main priority in the design of organizational forms and control mechanisms.

Raelin (1991) offered a subtly different but complementary take, highlighting the way that the underlying logic of professionalism produces unique management arrangements in PSFs. Specifically, for Raelin, the idiosyncrasies of PSFs and their reliance on individuals and their knowledge means that management without managers is typical. This involves the peer review control process which Freidson identified, but also a participative and consultative form of management whereby those in positions of authority represent (often following elections) their peers' views and priorities rather than commanding and controlling the labor force (see Empson and Langley, Chapter 8, this volume, for a more detailed analysis of this dynamic). Lazega (2001) more recently has referred to this as the "collegial phenomenon" based on insights from his study of legal PSFs. Such an approach to management is a response to the combined need, first, to maintain the autonomy and discretion of individuals to use their tacit knowledge to develop high quality services, and second, to maintain individuals' commitment to the organization (so as not to lose their tacit knowledge through exit). Giving professionals a sense of control over their own destiny is seen as important in this regard.

The most important outcome of the work of Mintzberg, Freidson, and Raelin was recognition that PSFs are distinctive organizational forms. This recognition spurred an important body of work on their specificities, a significant concern being the extent to which the organizational characteristics of PSFs are universal or variegated across the broad range of sectors subsumed under the category (for more on this see von Nordenflycht et al., Chapter 7, this volume). Mintzberg (1979) problematized the homogeneous category by distinguishing between the bureaucracy and the adhocracy, but others have since gone further and pointed out how "Professional service firms differ substantially on a number of key dimensions, and these differences exist even if we compare firms from a single industry" (Løwendahl 2005: 118).

The several attempts made over the years to desegregate the PSF category are useful in furthering our discussion here of the centrality of knowledge to organizational form—Table 19.2 gives five examples of studies attempting this task. Significantly for this chapter, in all of the cases detailed in Table 19.2, the nature of the knowledge needed to deliver the service in question is at the heart of the differentiations made. Specifically, important variations are shown in the extent to which the tacit knowledge of individuals is crucial to the work of the PSF in question, and the importance of autonomy, peer-control, and professional standards driven forms of governance highlighted by Mintzberg, Freidson, and Raelin. There are, however, also important variations in how these literatures understand the role of knowledge that are worth reflecting on.

For instance, in Table 19.2 the work of Løwendahl, von Nordenflycht, and Hansen et al. suggests that knowledge matters because of its implications for intra-firm organizational issues. By contrast, Winch and Schneider and Morris and Empson suggest the implications reach more widely, in terms of client experiences and benefits, and professional labor markets. This highlights potential questions about the extent to which knowledge, its nature and management is a concern simply for PSFs, or whether studying knowledge in PSFs is also insightful in relation to questions about the professions

Table 19.2 Three approaches to disaggregating the Professional Service Firm category, and the knowledge-based explanation of the differentiations

	Løwendahl (2005)	Von Nordenflycht (2010)	Winch and Schneider (1993)	Hansen, Nohria, and Tierney (1999)	Morris and Empson (1998)
Key knowledge-based differentiator	Dependence on individually controlled assets, and hence significance of loyalty of individuals and provision of autonomy to encourage this	Degree to which knowledge is embodied in individuals or in products and routines	The intangibility of the expertise provided and variations in substantive benefits for clients	Whether knowledge is viewed as something that should be individualized and deeply tacit or collective and codified into systems and products	Characteristics of knowledge determine firm's economic and organizational structure, the market which professional workers firms operate in, and the nature of services
Category differentiations	*Client relation based*: the expertise of individuals in relation to a particular client and their industry is key *Solution or output based*: particular service products are the basis of competitive advantage, with individuals and their expertise less significant as their role is to adapt and recycle organizational knowledges *Problem solving or creativity*: individual ability to innovate and solve problems using experience and insight crucial	*Technology developers*: Reliance on combination of individual expertise and capital assets (e.g., equipment in a biotech research firm) *Neo-PSFs*: high reliance on individual expertise but some ability to engage in limited bureaucracy due to non-professionalized workforce (e.g., management consultants) *Professional campuses*: high reliance of individual expertise of multiple professions (e.g. hospitals) *Classic (or regulated) PSFs*: high reliance on individual expertise of single profession	*Probity*: ability of individuals to provide neutral and expertise-based advice *Creativity*: use of autonomy in employing organization by individual professionals allows unrivalled creativity and innovativeness *Technology*: specialist expertise of individuals relating to a particular technical challenge	*Reuse*: the expertise of individuals used to develop products that with small adaptations can be sold to many clients *Personalization*: the tacit expertise of an individual is used to develop bespoke client advice	*Expertise/training (embrained)*: reliance on individuals and their unique knowledge of a technical issue *Precedent/system/process (encoded)*: reliance on collectively held and accessible codified knowledge *Experience/wisdom and technique (embodied)*: reliance on experience of how things are done in particular markets and client groups *Embedded in routines and relationships (encultured)*: organizationally specific and collectively understood ways of producing and delivering services

more widely and their relationships with other constituencies, including clients and regulators.

Similarly, in Table 19.2 the category distinctions made by different authors also vary in terms of the extent to which the production process or product distinguishes between types of PSF; Løwendahl, von Nordenflycht, and Morris and Empson emphasizing more the former, Hansen et al. the latter, and Winch and Schneider a combination of the two. This suggests that different approaches might be taken in the management of PSFs depending on whether ideals about the process or product of professional work determine organizational form. The questions raised by Table 19. 2 are returned to in the conclusions section of the chapter.

In addition to the differentiations outlined in Table 19.2, existing research also highlights several other fundamental relationships between understandings of knowledge in PSFs and in turn the organizational forms used. Greenwood and Empson (2003) compared law, accounting, architecture, advertising, and management consultancy PSFs in order to analyze the varying role for professional partnership, private, and public corporate forms. Results indicated variations ranging from 100% use of the partnership model in law firms, to 100% corporate form in advertising (77% private, 23% public), and a mix of all three forms in accounting. Of most significance here are the explanations of such variations. Knowledge was identified as a crucial factor in all cases, though not the only explanation (for example, regulation demanded partnership structures in law firms while issues of liability can encourage use of corporate forms). For instance, partnership becomes more likely as the reliance on individuals and their tacit knowledge increases, the logic being that partnership provides the autonomy and collegial management that professionals value. Meanwhile, the more homogeneous and commodifiable the knowledge needed to produce services, the less bespoke the services provided to clients, and the more reliance on assets such as equipment instead of or as well as individual expertise, the more likely corporate forms become. This confirms, then, the close relationship between the nature and role of knowledge in PSFs and organizational forms.

Demonstrating similarly strong connections, Malhotra and Morris (2009) reveal that (in addition to macro-scale structural differences such as between partnership and corporate forms) micro-scale diversity, such as the use of more or less hierarchical and sequential team-working arrangements, is connected to the effects of knowledge. By focusing on the degree to which individualized tacit knowledge matters—by differentiating between PSFs that rely on normative (value related), technical, and syncretic (both normative and technical) knowledges—Malhotra and Morris (2009) suggest that tendencies towards bureaucracy, hierarchy, and sequential teams increase as reliance on technical knowledge decreases.

It is important to also note, however, that the kinds of variations noted by Malhotra and Morris (2009) are not just inter-sectoral. Several studies demonstrate that variations can be as significant within a professional sector. For example Winch and Schneider (1993) distinguish between "strong delivery," "strong experience," "strong ideas," and "strong ambition" firms in the case of architecture. Faulconbridge (2010b) differentiates City of London and regional law firms in England along the lines of degrees of commoditized work. Suddaby et al. (2009) reveal distinctive priorities and practices between high-profile large corporate accounting firms in Canada and their smaller counterparts. All these studies indicate that the nature of knowledge and associated organizational forms vary within a PSF category.

19.5 KNOWLEDGE MANAGEMENT IN PROFESSIONAL SERVICE FIRMS?

Embedded within the organization of most PSFs, whether more or less bureaucratic and hierarchical, are structures designed to facilitate the production of new and the leverage of existing knowledge, when possible rendering it an organizational asset. However, as noted in the introductory section to the chapter, such knowledge management tactics are far from straightforward and many uncertainties exist about the likelihood of success.

It is usually assumed that the explicit knowledge base of workers has its foundations laid and tested through the education needed to negotiate the closure process associated with becoming a professional. This means the activities of universities impact upon PSFs; universities having the role, according to the literature on the sociology of the professions, of instilling in new recruits to the profession the core knowledge base needed (Burrage et al. 1990; Macdonald 1995). But, the role of universities relates to more than the core (more explicit) knowledge base of new professionals. Learning about how to deploy knowledge in practice is also a fundamental part of the education process, something which relates to everything from professional ethics, research, and analysis processes, to expectations of autonomy, behavior towards colleagues, and legitimate forms of client relationships. Such a role for universities in learning about practice is demonstrated by the distinctively different understandings of professional practice that are instilled by universities operating in common and civil law jurisdictions and the management challenges this poses global firms operating across the distinctively different professional worlds (Faulconbridge and Muzio 2007; Morgan and Quack 2005; Muzio and Faulconbridge 2013).

The baseline knowledge defined by the universities within a firm's jurisdiction defines the starting point for any efforts to train and enhance the knowledgeability of new recruits. Indeed, as Table 19.1 notes, PSFs are required to provide opportunities for their employees to maintain their professional knowledge bases, for instance through continuing professional development training. In sum, PSFs face some unique knowledge management related challenges because of their employment of professionals who rely on a defined explicit knowledge base.

Moreover, PSFs also face the challenge, experienced by all organizations, of leveraging knowledge assets and seeding opportunities for new knowledge to emerge, the latter being intimately related to innovation processes (on which see Barrett and Hinings, Chapter 11, this volume). Specifically a common conundrum is how to balance the use of technocratic modes of knowledge management, which usually involve computer database systems, alongside "softer" social processes of learning. The rest of this section of the chapter considers these knowledge management challenges. It highlights how two starkly contrasting responses to these challenges exist, corresponding with the distinction outlined earlier between learning as a process of information acquisition and learning in practice.

19.5.1 Knowledge Networking: The Knowledge Management Database

In PSFs, as in many organizations, the 1990s saw an exponential growth in interest in knowledge management and, in particular, in the role of computer databases in transforming firms' abilities to leverage the expertise of employees (Swart and Kinnie 2003; Terrett 1998). As Alvesson (2004) notes, this triggered a knowledge exploitation epidemic in which the knowledge management department in PSFs was (re)invented and took on a key strategic role. Morris (2001) associates such moves with a desire to generate organizational assets out of the previously hard to commoditize tacit expertise of employees.

Knowledge management database approaches involve attempts at knowledge preservation. Efforts to render visible individualized expertise grew, reflecting the fact that if an individual resigns, the PSF in question risks losing significant assets. Kaiser and Ringlstetter (2011) note that this often involves a "people to document" strategy as databases are populated with texts that are supposed to reflect the insights of individual professionals. These texts can relate to profession-specific technical issues, often in the form of case studies of a project structured using "lessons learned" templates, but also to insights specific to a particular client. Both Løwendahl (2005) and Terrett (1998) point out that in PSFs exploiting expertise that allows client relations to be best leveraged is as important as technical knowledge.

Brivot (2011), using a study of law firms, notes how knowledge management databases are used by professionals, often as a starting point for the production of services. Databases, as well as providing ready-made solutions on occasions, can provide "leads for developing answers to new questions of law" and the opportunity to "observe and monitor peers' work" (Brivot 2011: 497). However, resistance to databases was also observed because of the control they seek to exert over knowledge. The lawyers studied held a variety of opinions about the merits of the databases and displayed varying levels of willingness to contribute and use the databases. Such uncertainties are a result of the fundamental irony of knowledge management efforts in PSFs: that they seek to render redundant the very assets—individuals and their judgment—that are widely recognized to form the basis of the competitive advantage of PSFs.

To some extent, the rise of knowledge management databases has been a fundamental feature differentiating between commoditized and bespoke service providers. The former have tended to use computer-based systems more heavily to deliver quick and low-cost advice to clients in relation to common matters. The latter are more likely to continue to rely more heavily upon tailored advice produced using the individual expertise of a practitioner. Yet the existence of databases in both commoditized and bespoke service-providing firms brings into view critical questions about how much of the work of PSFs is actually knowledge intensive. Indeed, Blackler (1995) pointed out some time ago that the discourse of knowledge is as important as the actual knowledge that exists and is produced in professional and other supposedly knowledge-intensive firms. Perhaps, then, thanks to the affordances of technological change, individual expertise is increasingly the icing on the cake offered by bespoke PSFs, with the fundamental process of baking the cake increasingly reliant on more explicit and commoditized forms of knowledge, managed by databases and other systems?

This does not mean individuals and their tacit expertise are completely devalued. For instance, Newell et al. (2002) point out that the written form used in databases is probably the least appropriate way to capture insights from knowledge-intensive workers, the risk being that the process is the reverse of learning and reduces knowledge to information. Such difficulties are exaggerated if professionals are guarded in what they reveal in the documentation process, although as Morris (2001) notes such issues are often mitigated by the fact that many professionals realize that the decay that occurs as part of documentation devalues what they share with the organization and renders it of limited value.

It would seem, then, that a nuanced view of the coexistence of explicit and tacit knowledge and associated management techniques in the work of PSFs is needed. Indeed, Kaiser and Ringlstetter (2011) suggest that one way of balancing the need for both explicit and tacit knowledge is the use of databases to allow forms of personalization; this being an approach that uses the database to put individuals who could benefit from one another's expertise into contact (see also Brivot 2011). Such an approach is significant because it potentially acts as a way of seeding the kinds of knowledge management and learning associated with tacit knowledge.

19.5.2 Knowing in Action: The Community of Practice

Alvesson (2004) proposes knowledge exploration as an alternative and distinct approach to knowledge management. In such an approach, questions about whether knowledge can ever actually be managed because of the importance of its tacit dimensions are recognized and responded to through strategies designed to seed social processes of learning. Heavily influenced by work on communities of practice (Lave and Wenger 1991; Wenger 1998) and more recently wider ideas about learning in practice (Brown and Duguid 2000; Gherardi and Nicolini 2006), knowledge exploration approaches emphasize the importance of forms of social interaction that allow individual and collective sense-making, something which helps develop tacit understandings.

Practically, the knowledge exploration approach promotes management strategies that focus on generating organizational conditions conducive to the kinds of social interaction that allow learning in practice. The personalization approach described by Kaiser and Ringlstetter (2011) can play a part in generating such conditions, creating social networks that act as the basis for collective learning. However, as if not more important are organizational mechanisms that help ensure the kinds of social interaction that allow learning occur regularly and that the organizational cultures that maximize the value of such interactions exist.

In terms of mechanisms for ensuring that social interactions occur, efforts tend to focus on seeding more or less formal interactions between professionals, whether that be the water cooler conversation, everyday mentoring relationships between senior and junior professionals (Marchant and Robinson 1999), the project team meeting, or the practice group conference (Faulconbridge 2007a). This can be a logistical and resource challenge, but also a challenge because of the difficulties in ensuring such interactions are valued. Illustrating this, Faulconbridge (2006, 2010a) shows that in PSFs the key to effective forms of learning in practice is the existence of a sense of mutual engagement (in a common task), joint enterprise (a common way of working), and shared repertoire (similar approaches to work); these being the basis for the emergence of a community of practice. While such phenomena exist naturally in most PSFs thanks to the common professional background of workers, effort still has to be made to reinforce the bonds and provide a shared focus of attention. Tactics to do so can include the production of a common corporate "language" and the sharing of newsletters that act as boundary spanners between individuals who may interact infrequently (whether that be due to office layouts, segregated projects, or being based in offices in different parts of the country or world).

Importantly, though, mechanisms that ensure social interactions are only useful if supportive cultures exist in the organization. Seeding the conditions for learning in practice is, then, more than a logistical challenge. It also involves promoting a culture of sharing; something Swart and Kinnie (2003) suggest may be aided by the alignment of remuneration with the success of the overall firm. Such a culture matters because, as Empson (2001b) notes, professionals can feel exploited if their knowledge is "managed" in a way they see as inappropriate. Indeed, maintaining a sense of informality in the mechanisms used to manage learning in practice can be especially important in maximizing effectiveness.

In addition, a growing literature suggests that in PSFs the community of practice needs to be conceptualized as also including clients, regulators, and competitors. Clients can act as co-innovators because of their ability to bring industry-specific understanding into the service production process, thus problematizing a linear understanding which conceives of PSFs working alone to produce and then deliver services to client (see Broschak, Chapter 14, this volume; Gallouj and Weinstein 1997). Regulators and competitors are important because of their role in shaping markets for PSFs. Interactions with regulators allow learning about and the influencing of regulatory priorities and perspectives that could affect a firm and its services (Greenwood and Suddaby 2006).

Meanwhile, interactions with competitors provide insights into both how current market conditions and future trends are understood and responded to (Grabher 2001), with the caveat of course that competitors will always to some degree be guarded about what they share with their rivals. The professional association often acts as an important forum where both regulators and competitors come together, interact, and learn from one another (Faulconbridge 2007b; Greenwood et al. 2002).

The learning in practice approach highlights, then, how any attempt to manage knowledge and learning has to operate in a way that reflects the particular nature of knowledge in PSFs. Hence "hard" knowledge management database solutions alone are insufficient given the importance of tacit expertise and the difficulty of capturing such expertise in documents. This does not mean databases are of no value; they can help build the explicit knowledge of professionals and may play a role in seeding the informal interactions that allow learning in practice. But a technocratic approach to knowledge management must exist alongside a "softer" social approach that is generative of the conditions of learning in practice. Training and professional development practices in PSFs exemplify such a balancing act.

19.5.3 Training as Knowledge Management

As noted above, PSFs are often compelled to provide training for their staff because of requirements imposed by regulators. Consequently, at one level training in PSFs might be seen as a strategy tied to the explicit knowledge associated with a profession, and as such may be seen as an information and fact transfer process. Indeed, technical briefings are common in many PSFs and serve just such a function.

In addition, though, a body of literature has emerged which identifies the more tacit learning role that training can fulfill, following the logic of ideas about learning in practice (Anderson-Gough et al. 1998; Covaleski et al. 1998; Faulconbridge et al. 2012; Grey 1998). At one level this relates to training that allows practical skill to be developed. One example would be simulation sessions in which junior professionals work alongside their seniors on an imaginary project, the idea being that in the process they develop the tacit expertise needed to handle the complexities of client problem solving through observation and direct experience (Faulconbridge and Hall 2014). In such scenarios, training provides the opportunities for social interaction that allow learning in practice. At another level, however, this literature highlights how learning in practice is as much about how to perform the role of a professional as it is about the technical expertise required to effectively advise clients. Specifically, studies have revealed that learning about legitimate ways of dressing, behaving, talking, and approaching clients is a crucial component of training in PSFs (Anderson-Gough et al. 1998; Grey 1998).

Closely associated with idea of socialization, such insights begin to peel back the veneer which presents knowledge in PSFs as purely associated with profession-specific expertise. For instance, Faulconbridge et al. (2012) reveal that in law firms training has two streams, one associated with the technical knowledge of "the law," another associated with the skills needed to be an effective practitioner in the eyes of the employing organization. Meanwhile, Anderson-Gough et al. (2002: 47) argue that "For the trainees in our study [of accountancy firms], the significance of professional behavior as a way of presenting activity rather than determining the content or quality of that activity was clearly dominant."

The insights gained from studies of training in PSFs are important, then, because they not only confirm the challenge of managing the more or less explicit and tacit knowledge base of professionals, but also because they help to further demystify the tacit dimension to expertise, in the process problematizing the idea that all knowledge in PSFs relates to solving technical problems. The insights thus also further highlight the importance of questions about the ambiguity of knowledge and the apparently questionable discourse of knowledge intensity in PSFs discussed previously.

19.4 KNOWLEDGE, JURISDICTIONS, AND THE GEOGRAPHIES OF PROFESSIONAL SERVICE FIRMS

The final implication of the particularities of the knowledge base of PSFs relates to the market reach of any organization. Two issues are important in this regard.

Firstly, the spatial jurisdiction in which any PSF is authorized to operate is intimately related to knowledge bases. PSFs, through their professionals, lay claim to monopoly rights over certain markets. Because such claims are based on ideas about the expertise needed to serve clients in a market, and this expertise is regulated by professional associations (see Table 19.1), barriers to the operation of PSFs emerge. For instance, German law firms were until 1989 restricted to operating in one Länder (region) as a result of rules that only recognized the expertise of professionals in the Länder in which they qualified (Morgan and Quack 2005; Schultz 2005). This meant a law firm in Frankfurt was prohibited from advising clients outside of the Hesse Länder, and could not, for example, have clients in Munich. While such barriers have now been removed, the example is indicative of the intimate relationship between knowledge and spatial jurisdiction (Krause 1996). Indeed, such issues continue to be highly significant for firms when new countries are entered.

Both Scott-Kennel and von Batenburg (2012) and Malhotra and Morris (2009) highlight how the internationalization strategies of PSFs are intimately related to the characteristics of the knowledge base of the professionals employed by the firm (on internationalization generally see Boussebaa and Morgan, Chapter 4, this volume). This means that firms offering more commoditized types of service that have less normative (public protection) dimensions, in many cases these being firms more reliant on explicit knowledge in service production, are more likely to internationalize due to less regulatory controls on their practice. Underlying the greater likelihood of these firms internationalizing is the fundamental logic that overseas operations should leverage existing assets (Muzio and Faulconbridge 2013; Segal-Horn and Dean 2009), something only possible if regulatory constraints do not prevent the replication of home-country practices and models in a new market. When regulation of the jurisdiction of the knowledge base of the firm is strict (usually when more normative and tacit issues are central to the work of the PSF in question) internationalization becomes in some cases impossible—for example the barring of foreign lawyers and firms from India. In other cases internationalization is simply more challenging as rafts of locally qualified professionals have to be employed due to the multiple layers of adaptation required to reflect local knowledge and practice—for example, law firms in China.

The second significant effect of knowledge–jurisdiction relationships concerns attempts to establish new transnational jurisdictions. Most extensively documented in relation to the accountancy profession (Arnold 2005; Suddaby et al. 2007), but also being relevant to law (Morgan 2006; Quack 2007) and to a lesser extent architecture (Faulconbridge 2009), some important developments have characterized the early years of the new millennium. PSFs, both independently and through the extension of existing national or the formation of new transnational bodies (Evetts 1998; Faulconbridge and Muzio 2012), have sought to dis-embed expertise from regional or national jurisdictional boundaries. The exploitation of World Trade Organization rules associated with the General Agreement on Trade in Services has been a key mechanism for such developments. Most fundamentally this has involved seeking and establishing mobility rights for professionals which allow an individual educated and registered in one jurisdiction (usually a country) to move to another jurisdiction. This creates a transnational class of mobile, cosmopolitan professionals (Smets et al. 2012) who, with limited re-training and re-registration, can deploy their expertise in new jurisdictions.

Relatedly, PSFs have also sought to create and institutionalize new bodies of transnational knowledge (Suddaby and Greenwood 2001). Associated with attempts to create new jurisdictions in which the largest global PSFs can colonize profitable markets, new regulatory regimes can create markets that transcend the historically national jurisdictions discussed above (see Quack and Schüßler, Chapter 3, this volume). Examples include the International Financial Reporting Standards that global accounting PSFs have been integral to developing (Cooper and Robson 2006), and legal regimes associated with antitrust (competition) (Morgan 2006) and bankruptcy (Halliday and Carruthers 2009) that global law firms have helped engineer.

Such bodies of knowledge locate key global PSFs at the heart of the production and maintenance of neo-liberal capitalism (Faulconbridge et al. 2008), as well as at the center of state-making projects in post-socialist and emerging economies (Halliday and Carruthers 2009). Such developments are significant not only because they transform the historically national fix of professional activity (Faulconbridge and Muzio 2012), but because they also further challenge the idea that professional knowledge is associated primarily with fiduciary and safeguarding activities. Being complicit in neo-liberal capitalism also means being complicit with the agendas of transnational corporations and a central role in the furthering of their economic projects. The global financial crisis and the centrality of accountancy and law PSFs in the production of the products that undermined the global financial system is illustrative of how a central role in the co-production of transnational capitalist regimes further problematizes the earlier discussed historical interpretations of professional projects as being in the public interest.

Intimately coupled to the development of transnational jurisdictions and the complicity of PSFs in neo-liberal globalization is also the related expansion of the functional jurisdiction of PSFs. Such an issue emerged at the turn of the new millennium as the multidisciplinary partnership gained hold, particularly in accountancy firms, as part of efforts to develop cross-profession organizations, for instance providing accounting but also legal and consultancy advice. To some extent curtailed by regulatory barriers, and by the fallout from the collapse of Arthur Anderson, there remain nonetheless ongoing efforts to redefine the functional jurisdiction of PSFs through the reworking of definitions of expertise. This is mostly clearly illustrated in relation to accounting PSFs who have sought to engage in strategic negotiations about the functional expertise of accountants, this being part of efforts to redraw the boundaries of work to encompass more and more domains that are not limited to audit (Suddaby and Greenwood 2005).

19.5 CONCLUSIONS

This chapter has demonstrated that intimate connections between PSFs and knowledge are crucial for explaining some of the most fundamental features of the organization, management, and market reach of firms. Figure 19.1 captures these insights and the heuristic lens that the chapter has developed by placing questions of knowledge at the center of the analysis of PSFs.

As Figure 19.1 reveals, the nature of knowledge is important in a series of crucial debates in existing literatures about PSFs, and also frames key future research questions. These future research questions relate primarily to the constant dynamics that define both the nature of knowledge in PSFs, and its influence on questions of organization and management. Figure 19.1 highlights three core areas in this regard.

First, important questions exist about the extent to which in general PSFs are becoming increasingly bureaucratic and managerialist, this having implications for the ability of professionals to deploy their tacit expertise for client benefit. In many ways this is not a new trend; Cooper et al. (1996) long ago reported on the growing trend towards managed professional businesses. However, the 2000s have seen such developments take on new trajectories. For instance, the financialization of PSFs (Alvehus and Spicer 2012; Faulconbridge and Muzio 2009), with increased emphasis on both the financial performance of individuals and of the organization as a whole, has created new imperatives for bureaucracy and managerialism. Yet, the implications of this for the exercise of tacit expertise have been little considered. This matters for two reasons. First, because any such trend would potentially indicate an ever greater differentiation between bespoke

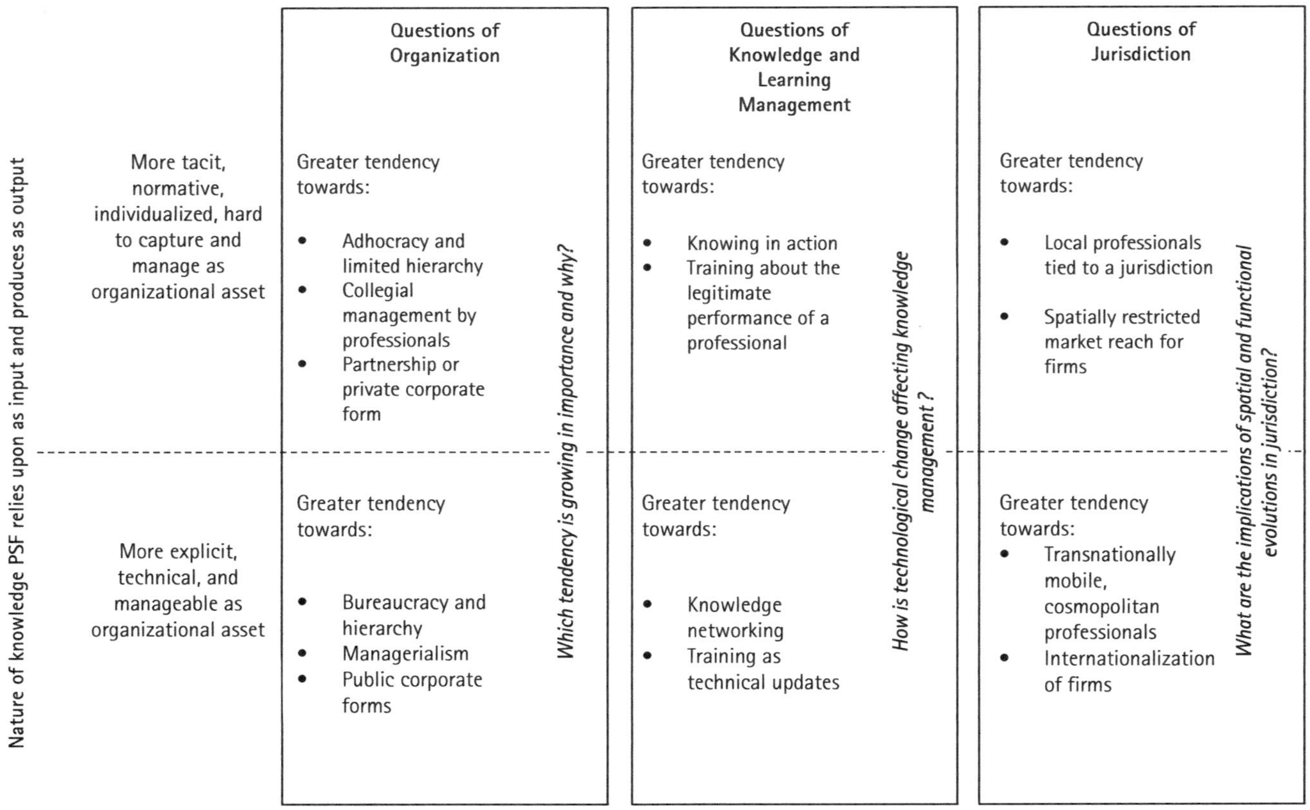

Nature of knowledge PSF relies upon as input and produces as output

More tacit, normative, individualized, hard to capture and manage as organizational asset

More explicit, technical, and manageable as organizational asset

Questions of Organization

Which tendency is growing in importance and why?

Greater tendency towards:
- Adhocracy and limited hierarchy
- Collegial management by professionals
- Partnership or private corporate form

Greater tendency towards:
- Bureaucracy and hierarchy
- Managerialism
- Public corporate forms

Questions of Knowledge and Learning Management

How is technological change affecting knowledge management?

Greater tendency towards:
- Knowing in action
- Training about the legitimate performance of a professional

Greater tendency towards:
- Knowledge networking
- Training as technical updates

Questions of Jurisdiction

What are the implications of spatial and functional evolutions in jurisdiction?

Greater tendency towards:
- Local professionals tied to a jurisdiction
- Spatially restricted market reach for firms

Greater tendency towards:
- Transnationally mobile, cosmopolitan professionals
- Internationalization of firms

FIGURE 19.1 The impacts of knowledge and learning on the characteristics of and future agendas for research on Professional Service Firms.

and commoditized PSFs, with those in the former category becoming potentially more and more unique and niche in the kind of work they do. Or, put another way, this trend could mean that it is increasingly difficult to identify a PSF that does not in some way seek to commoditize knowledge. Second, because new innovative techniques of organization are potentially needed to ensure that even in the most bureaucratized and managerialist PSFs spaces for autonomy still exist. How this might be achieved alongside the fundamental efficiency and control logics underlying more bureaucratic forms is not clear, and thus is an important research agenda.

A second major future theme relates to the way technology is changing the production of services within PSFs. This has particular implications for the way knowledge is managed. For instance, the extent to which increased use of technology is associated with greater codification of knowledge, or might allow new ways of learning in communities of practice to occur is unclear. It is tempting to assume that the former rather than the latter scenario is most likely. But, research should investigate this more thoroughly. After all, in the web 2.0 era this is not a foregone conclusion.

Third, the evolution of the jurisdiction of PSFs, along spatial and functional lines, poses fundamental challenges to theoretical conceptions. It is now less of a question of whether change has occurred compared with the situation when the literature on the professions and PSFs was born in the twentieth century, and more a question of the effects of change for how we understand the claims of PSFs over particular markets. There seems to be a crucial need to examine how the increasingly transnational domain of professional work reconfigures our understanding of the role of professions and PSFs in state projects, how attempts to expand the functional reach of firms into new domains challenges assumptions about these firms as sites of the exercise of defined bodies of distinctive professional knowledge, and in turn how all of this matters for the organization and management of the firms themselves.

Cutting across all three of the previously mentioned areas for future research are also questions about the way the knowledge-based advice PSFs produce is consumed and valued by clients. This matters in terms of the impacts on clients of different organizational forms and knowledge management strategies, and in terms of the way redefined professional jurisdictions bring PSFs into interaction with changing client bases. In part such questions return us to the perennial difficulties of assessing the quality of the work of PSFs, as discussed in the first half of this chapter. Nonetheless, it seems crucial to develop a research agenda and associated theoretical framing that allows the contribution of PSFs to clients' activities to be more effectively revealed. In part the challenge this raises is further capturing, methodologically as well as theoretically, the knowledge that PSFs produce and deploy on behalf of their clients. But it also means thinking about more tangible effects, in terms of the development of new products, markets and capabilities. Developing such research would help close the loop. Existing research can tell us a lot about the knowledge raw materials that act as the inputs into the activities of PSFs, so it follows that future research should seek to develop a better understanding of the outputs of professional work, and more specifically how knowledge is applied and created in the process.

ACKNOWLEDGMENTS

Some of the ideas outlined in this chapter were developed as part of work funded by the UK's Economic and Social Research Council through grant RES-000-22-2957. Feedback on an earlier version of the chapter from Laura Empson helped refine the ideas presented.

REFERENCES

Abbott, A. (1988). *The System of Professions: An Essay on the Division of Expert Labor*. Chicago, IL: University of Chicago Press.

Abel, R. L. (1988). *The Legal Profession in England and Wales*. Oxford: Blackwell.

Alvehus, J. and Spicer, A. (2012). "Financialization as a Strategy of Workplace Control in Professional Service Firms," *Critical Perspectives on Accounting* 23(7): 497–510.

Alvesson, M. (2001). "Knowledge Work: Ambiguity, Image and Identity," *Human Relations* 54(7): 863–886.

Alvesson, M. (2004). *Knowledge Work and Knowledge-Intensive Firms*. Oxford: Oxford University Press.

Amin, A. and Cohendet, P. (2004). *Architectures of Knowledge: Firms, Capabilities, and Communities*. Oxford: Oxford University Press.

Anderson-Gough, F., Grey, C., and Robson, K. (1998). *Making up Accountants: The Professional and Organizational Socialization of Trainee Chartered Accountants*. Aldershot: Ashgate/ICAEW.

Anderson-Gough, F., Grey, C., and Robson, K. (2002). "Accounting Professionals and the Accounting Profession: Linking Conduct and Context," *Accounting and Business Research* 32(1): 41–56.

Arnold, P. (2005). "Disciplining Domestic Regulation: The World Trade Organization and the Market for Professional Services," *Accounting, Organizations and Society* 30(4): 299–330.

Beaverstock, J. V., Faulconbridge, J. R., and Hall, S. J. E. (2010). "Professionalization, Legitimization and the Creation of Executive Search Markets in Europe," *Journal of Economic Geography* 10(6): 825–843.

Berends, H., Boersma, K., and Weggeman, M. (2003). "The Structuration of Organizational Learning," *Human Relations* 56(9): 1035–1056.

Blackler, F. (1995). "Knowledge, Knowledge Work and Organizations: An Overview and Interpretation," *Organization Studies* 16(6): 1021–1046.

Brivot, M. (2011). "Controls of Knowledge Production, Sharing and Use in Bureaucratized Professional Service Firms," *Organization Studies* 32(4): 489–508.

Brown, J. S. and Duguid, P. (2000). *The Social Life of Information*. Boston, MA: Harvard Business School Press.

Burrage, M., Jarausch, K., and Sigrist, H. (1990). "An Actor-Based Framework for the Study of the Professions," in *Professions in Theory and History*, ed. M. Burrage, and R. Torstendahl. London: Sage, 203–255.

Burton-Jones, A. (1999). *Knowledge Capitalism: Business, Work, and Learning in the New Economy*. Oxford: Oxford University Press.

Cooper, D. J. and Robson, K. (2006). "Accounting, Professions and Regulation: Locating the Sites of Professionalization," *Accounting, Organizations and Society* 31(4–5): 415–444.

Cooper, D., Hinings, C. R., Greenwood, R., and Brown, J. L. (1996). "Sedimentation and Transformation in Organizational Change: The Case of Canadian Law Firms," *Organization Studies* 17(4): 623–647.

Covaleski, M. A., Dirsmith, M. W., Heian, J. B., and Samuel, S. (1998). "The Calculated and the Avowed: Techniques of Discipline and Struggle over Identity in Big Six Public Accounting Firms," *Administrative Science Quarterly* 43(2): 293–327.

Empson, L. (2001a). "Fear of Exploitation and Fear of Contamination: Impediments to Knowledge Transfer in Mergers between Professional Service Firms," *Human Relations* 54(7): 839–862.

Empson, L. (2001b). "Introduction: Knowledge Management in Professional Service Firms," *Human Relations* 54(7): 811–817.

Evetts, J. (1998). "Professionalism Beyond the Nation-State: International Systems of Professional Regulation in Europe," *International Journal of Sociology and Social Policy* 18(12): 47–64.

Evetts, J. (2003). "The Sociological Analysis of Professionalism: Occupational Change in the Modern World," *International Sociology* 18(2): 395–415.

Faulconbridge, J. R. (2006). "Stretching Tacit Knowledge beyond a Local Fix? Global Spaces of Learning in Advertising Professional Service Firms," *Journal of Economic Geography* 6(4): 517–540.

Faulconbridge, J. R. (2007a). "Relational Spaces of Knowledge Production in Transnational Law Firms," *Geoforum* 38: 925–940.

Faulconbridge, J. R. (2007b). "Exploring the Role of Professional Associations in Collective Learning in London and New York's Advertising and Law Professional Service Firm Clusters," *Environment and Planning A* 39(4): 965–984.

Faulconbridge, J. R. (2009). "The Regulation of Design in Architecture Firms: Embedding and Emplacing Buildings," *Urban Studies* 46(12): 2537–2554.

Faulconbridge, J. R. (2010a). "Global Architects: Learning and Innovation through Communities and Constellations of Practice," *Environment and Planning A* 42(12): 2842–2858.

Faulconbridge, J. R. (2010b). "Business Services: Driving the Knowledge-Based Economy in the UK?," in *The Economic Geography of the UK*, ed. N. M. Coe and A. Jones. London: Sage, 153–165.

Faulconbridge, J. R. and Hall, S. (2014). "Reproducing the City of London's Institutional Landscape: The Role of Education and the Learning of Situated Practices by Early Career Elites," *Environment and Planning A* 46(7): 1682–1698.

Faulconbridge, J. R. and Muzio, D. (2007). "Reinserting the Professional into the Study of Professional Service Firms: The Case of Law," *Global Networks* 7(3): 249–270.

Faulconbridge, J. R. and Muzio, D. (2009). "The Financialization of Large Law Firms: Situated Discourses and Practices of Reorganization," *Journal of Economic Geography* 9: 641–661.

Faulconbridge, J. and Muzio, D. (2012). "The Rescaling of the Professions: Towards a Transnational Sociology of the Professions," *International Sociology* 27(1): 109–125.

Faulconbridge, J. R., Beaverstock, J. V., Muzio, D., and Taylor, P. J. (2008). "Global Law Firms: Globalization and Organizational Spaces of Cross-Border Legal Work," *Northwestern Journal of International Law and Business* 28(3): 455–488.

Faulconbridge, J. R., Muzio, D., and Cook, A. (2012). "Institutional Legacies in TNCs and their Management through Training Academies: The Case of Transnational Law Firms in Italy," *Global Networks* 12(1): 48–70.

Freidson, E. (1983). *Structures in Fives: Designing Effective Organizations*. Englewood Cliffs, NJ: Prentice-Hall.

Gallouj, F. and Weinstein, O. (1997). "Innovation in Services," *Research Policy* 26(4–5): 537–556.

Gherardi, S. and Nicolini, D. (2006). *Organizational Knowledge: The Texture of Workplace Learning*. Malden, MA: Blackwell Publishing.

Gottschalk, P. (2000). "Predictors of IT Support for Knowledge Management in the Professions: An Empirical Study of Law Firms in Norway," *Journal of Information Technology* 15: 69–78.

Grabher, G. (2001). "Ecologies of Creativity: The Village, the Group and the Heterarchic Organisation of the British Advertising Industry," *Environment and Planning A* 33(2): 351–374.

Greenwood, R. and Empson, L. (2003). "The Professional Partnership: Relic or Exemplary Form of Governance?" *Organization Studies* 24(6): 909–933.

Greenwood, R. and Suddaby, R. (2006). "Institutional Entrepreneurship in Mature Fields: The Big Five Accounting Firms," *Academy of Management Journal* 49(1): 27–48.

Greenwood, R., Suddaby, R., and Hinings, C. R. (2002). "Theorizing Change: The Role of Professional Associations in the Transformation of Institutionalized Fields," *Academy of Management Journal* 45(1): 58–80.

Grey, C. (1998). "On Being a Professional in a 'Big Six' Firm," *Accounting, Organizations and Society* 23(5–6): 569–587.

Halliday, T. C. and Carruthers, B. G. (2009). *Bankrupt: Global Lawmaking and Systemic Financial Crisis*. Stanford, CA: Stanford University Press.

Hansen, M. T., Nohria, N., and Tierney, T. (1999). "What's Your Strategy for Managing Knowledge?," in *The Knowledge Management Yearbook 2000–2001*, ed. J. Woods and J. Cortada. Woburn, MA: Butterworth-Heinemann, 55–69.

Hitt, M. A., Bierman, L., Uhlenbruch, K., and Shimizu, K. (2006). "The Importance of Resources in the Internationalization of Professional Service Firms: The Good, the Bad, and the Ugly," *Academy of Management Journal* 49(6): 1137–1157.

Hodgson, D. (2007). "The New Professionals; Professionalisation and the Struggle for Occupational Control in the Field of Project Management," in *Redirections in the Study of Expert Labour: Medicine, Law and Management Consultancy*, ed. D. Muzio, S. Ackroyd, and J. F. Chanlat. Basingstoke: Palgrave Macmillan, 217–235.

Horvath, J. A. (1999). "Preface: Tacit Knowledge in the Profession," in *Tacit Knowledge in Professional Practice: Researcher and Practitioner Perspectives*, ed. R. J. Sternberg and J. A. Horvath. London: Lawrence Erlbaum Associates, ix–xii.

Howells, J. (2000). "Knowledge, Innovation and Location," in *Knowledge, Space, Economy*, ed. J. Bryson, P. W. Daniels, N. Henry, and J. Pollard. London: Routledge, 50–62.

Johnson, T. (1972). *Professions and Power*. London: Macmillan.

Kaiser, S. and Ringlstetter, M. (2011). *Strategic Management of Professional Service Firms*. Berlin: Springer Verlag.

Krause, E. A. (1996). *Death of the Guilds*. New Haven, CT: Yale University Press.

Larson, M. S. (1977). *The Rise of Professionalism: A Sociological Analysis*. Berkeley, CA: University of California Press.

Lave, J. and Wenger, E. (1991). *Situated Learning: Legitimate Peripheral Participation*. Cambridge: Cambridge University Press.

Lazega, E. (2001). *The Collegial Phenomenon: The Social Mechanisms of Cooperation among Peers in a Corporate Law Partnership*. Oxford: Oxford University Press.

Løwendahl, B. (2005). *Strategic Management of Professional Service Firms*, 3rd edn. Copenhagen: Copenhagen Business School Press.

Macdonald, K. M. (1995). *The Sociology of the Professions*. London: Sage.

McKenna, C. D. (2006). *The World's Newest Profession: Management Consulting in the Twentieth Century*. Cambridge: Cambridge University Press.

Maister, D. (2003). *Managing the Professional Service Firm*. London: Simon Schuster.

Malhotra, N. and Morris, T. (2009). "Heterogeneity in Professional Service Firms," *Journal of Management Studies* 46(6): 895–922.

Marchant, G. and Robinson, J. (1999). "Is Knowing the Tax Code All It Takes to be a Tax Expert? On the Development of Legal Expertise," in *Tacit Knowledge in Professional Practice: Researcher and Practitioner Perspectives*, ed. R. J. Sternberg and J. A. Horvath. London: Lawrence Erlbaum Associates, 3–20.

Meso, P. and Smith, R. (2000). "A Resource-Based View of Organizational Knowledge Management Systems," *Journal of Knowledge Management* 4(3): 224–234.

Mintzberg, H. (1979). *The Structuring of Organizations*. London: Prentice-Hall.

Morgan, G. (2006). "Transnational Actors, Transnational Institutions, Transnational Spaces: The Role of Law Firms in the Internationalization of Competition Regulation," in *Transnational Governance: Institutional Dynamics of Regulation*, ed. M.-L. Djelic and K. Sahlin-Andersson. Cambridge: Cambridge University Press, 139–160.

Morgan, G. and Quack, S. (2005). "Institutional Legacies and Firm Dynamics: The Growth and Internationalization of UK and German Law Firms," *Organization Studies* 26(12): 1765–1785.

Morris, C. and Empson, L. (1998). "Organisation and Expertise: An Exploration of Knowledge Bases and the Management and Consulting Firms," *Accounting, Organizations and Society* 23(5–6): 609–624.

Morris, T. (2001). "Asserting Property Rights: Knowledge Codification in the Professional Service Firm," *Human Relations* 54(7): 819–838.

Muzio, D. and Faulconbridge, J. R. (2013). "The Global Professional Service Firm: 'One Firm' Models versus (Italian) Distant Institutionalised Practices," *Organization Studies* 34: 897–925.

Muzio, D., Hodgson, D., Faulconbridge, J., Beaverstock, J., and Hall, S. (2011). "Towards Corporate Professionalization: The Case of Project Management, Management Consultancy and Executive Search," *Current Sociology* 59(4): 443–464.

Newell, S., Robertson, M., Scarborough, H., and Swan, J. (2002). *Managing Knowledge Work*. New York: Palgrave Macmillan.

Nonaka, I. and Takeuchi, H. (1995). *The Knowledge-Creating Company*. Oxford: Oxford University Press.

Orlikowski, W. (2002). "Knowing in Practice: Enacting a Collective Capability in Distributed Organizing," *Organization Science* 13(1): 249–273.

Parsons, T. (1963). "On the Concept of Political Power," *Proceedings of the American Philosophical Society* 107(3): 232–262.

Polanyi, M. (1966). *The Tacit Dimension*. London: Routledge & Kegan Paul.

Quack, S. (2007). "Legal Professionals and Transnational Law-Making: A Case of Distributed Agency," *Organization* 14(5): 643–666.

Raelin, J. A. (1991). *The Clash of Cultures: Managers Managing Professionals*. Boston, MA: Harvard Business School Press.

Schultz, U. (2005). "Germany, Regulated Deregulation: The Case of the German Legal Profession," in *Reorganisation and Resistance: Legal Professions Confront a Changing World*, ed. W. L. Felstiner. Oxford and Portland, OR: Hart Publishing, 93–130.

Scott-Kennel, J. and von Batenburg, Z. (2012). "The Role of Knowledge and Learning in the Internationalisation of Professional Service Firms," *Service Industries Journal* 32(10): 1667–1690.

Segal-Horn, S. and Dean, A. (2009). "Delivering 'Effortless Experience' across Borders: Managing Internal Consistency in Professional Service Firms," *Journal of World Business* 44(1): 41–50.

Skyrme D. J. (1999). *Knowledge Networking: Creating the Collaborative Enterprise*. Oxford: Butterworth-Heinemann.

Smets, M., Morris, T., and Greenwood, R. (2012). "From Practice to Field: A Multilevel Model of Practice-Driven Institutional Change," *Academy of Management Journal* 55(4): 877–904.

Suddaby, R. and Greenwood, R. (2001). "Colonizing Knowledge: Commodification as a Dynamic of Jurisdictional Expansion in Professional Service Firms," *Human Relations* 54(7): 933–953.

Suddaby, R. and Greenwood, R. (2005). "Rhetorical Strategies of Legitimacy," *Administrative Science Quarterly* 50(1): 35–67.

Suddaby, R., Cooper, D. J., and Greenwood, R. (2007). "Transnational Regulation of Professional Services: Governance Dynamics of Field Level Organizational Change," *Accounting, Organizations and Society* 32(4–5): 333–362.

Suddaby, R., Gendron, Y., and Lam, H. (2009). "The Organizational Context of Professionalism in Accounting," *Accounting, Organizations and Society* 34(3–4): 409–427.

Swart, J. and Kinnie, N. (2003). "Sharing Knowledge in Knowledge-Intensive Firms," *Human Resource Management Journal* 13(2): 60–75.

Teece, D. (2000). *Managing Intellectual Capital*. Oxford: Oxford University Press.

Terrett, A. (1998). "Knowledge Management and the Law Firm," *Journal of Knowledge Management* 2(1): 67–76.

Wenger, E. (1998). *Communities of Practice: Learning, Meaning, and Identity*. Cambridge: Cambridge University Press.

Winch, G. and Schneider, E. (1993). "Managing the knowledge-Based Organization: The Case of Architectural Practice," *Journal of Management Studies* 30(6): 923–936.

....

CHAPTER 20

DIVERSITY AND INCLUSION IN PROFESSIONAL SERVICE FIRMS

....

HILARY SOMMERLAD AND LOUISE ASHLEY

20.1 INTRODUCTION

....

DURING the past 25 years the dramatic expansion of the global professional services market has been facilitated by increasing numbers of female and Black, Asian, and Minority Ethnic (BAME) professionals. Today, in many professions and in many countries, the entry rates of women are either similar to or exceed those of their male counterparts. For instance, in England and Wales women comprised 47.7% of solicitors with practicing certificates in 2013 (Law Society 2014), and 34.8% of barristers and 53% of those called to the Bar in 2009/2010 (Sauboorah 2011). In the US, women comprise almost half (44.8%) the associates in private law firms (ABA 2014) and half of newly hired accounting graduates at certified public accountant (CPA) firms (Moore et al. 2011). In England and Wales women comprise 42% of all Institute of Chartered Accountants accounting students and between 30% and 40% of the intake in management consultancy firms (Kumra and Vinnicombe 2008).

The growth in the proportion of BAME professionals has been similarly exponential. For instance, between 2000 and 2010 the percentage of BAME solicitors with practicing certificates in England and Wales rose by over 80% (Cole 2000; Fletcher and Muratova 2010). By 2013 BAME professionals made up just over 13% of solicitors with practicing certificates (Law Society 2014) and in 2009, just over 20% of trainee solicitors of known ethnicity were drawn from minority ethnic groups in England and Wales (Cole et al. 2009). A similar story is evident in other countries and professions. Within the US legal sector, minority enrollment stood at 24.5% of J.D. students in 2011/2012 (ABA 2012) and were drawn from minority ethnic groups.

However, although contemporary professions are numerically diverse, statistics show that women and minorities are overwhelmingly clustered in lower grade roles or sectors. For example, women comprised 43% of lawyers in private practice in England and Wales in 2009 overall. However, just 21.5% of women were partners, compared with 49.1% of men, within an overall total of 37.2% (Cole et al. 2009). Further, the more prestigious the firm, the smaller the percentage of female partners: less than 10% of equity partners in the top 100 law firms by turnover are women (Burton 2012). Similarly, according to one survey, the average percentage of BAME partners in leading firms is just over 5% (Chambers 2014). In 2013 women represented just over 20% of US law firm partners (ABA 2014) and in 2014 minorities accounted for 7.33% of partners in major firms (NALP 2015). Other professions are similarly stratified. For instance in the UK accountancy sector just six firms in the top 50 by turnover had more than 20% female partners in 2013 and several had none at all (Accountancy Age 2014). Ethnic minorities account for 6% of partners in UK accountancy firms, and this figure falls to 3% in the UK's "Big Four" firms (Business in the Community 2009). Under-representation of women accountants has also been documented in societies as diverse as China (Song and Liu 2007) and Sweden (Collin et al. 2007), and of ethnic minorities in New Zealand (Kim 2004) and South Africa (Hammond et al. 2009). Even in more ostensibly feminized professions such as public relations, relatively few women hold senior level positions (Chartered Institute of Public Relations 2013).

Although statistics for other diversity strands (such as sexual orientation) are less available, there is some evidence of the barriers posed by class and disability. For instance it has become increasingly difficult for individuals from lower socio-economic groups to enter the professions in the UK (Cabinet Office 2009). The ABA reports that approximately 6.87% of its members identify as having a disability (ABA 2011), which compares with one in five in the US population as a whole.

The purpose of this chapter is to draw on theoretical and empirical work to explore the causes of these patterns of inequality and discrimination, and to consider whether the diversity approach to workplace equality, widely adopted over the course of the last two to three decades, has the potential to produce a more equitable and inclusive sector. The issue is significant for four main reasons. First, diversification has been integral to the transformation of the professions, and also to Professional Service Firms' (PSFs) expansion and profitability (Hagan and Kay 1995; Sommerlad 2011, 2012b). Second, as the above statistical snapshot suggests, the form which diversification has taken confounds the claims of the professions to neutrality and rationality and of firms to engage in meritocratic practices, making the question of diversity an important feature of workplace politics and human resource practices (see also Swart et al., Chapter 21, this volume). On the other hand, the ubiquity of category-based segregation and subordination in corporate life has provoked suggestions that there is nothing "special" about professionalism which justifies its treatment as a separate field (Crompton and Sanderson 1990). The close resemblance of the contemporary PSF to a business corporation (Muzio et al. 2013) offers support for this argument. However, the professions *do* still exercise key socio-economic and political functions and enjoy especially high status. Furthermore, the correspondence between the division of labor and status hierarchies in PSFs and macro-level social arrangements suggests that these divisions are rational thereby naturalizing pre-existing ideas about, for instance, male and white authority and in this sense act as brakes on social modernization. A final reason for focusing on diversity is its neglect in much of the mainstream literature, which continues to treat PSFs as neutral or homogeneous entities.

We aim to highlight these various aspects of diversity by situating our discussion within the sweeping socio-economic changes of the last few decades, frequently summarized by the portmanteau term "neo-liberal" (Harvey 2005). In addition to the dramatic expansion and diversification of professions' supply bases and the mainstreaming of ideas of equality and diversity, these changes include the revival of individualizing, free market ideologies; globalization; the commercialization and marketization of the professions; and displacement of the power of professional bodies to the PSF. As a result of these changes, the key terms of the debate over professionalism and diversity are now highly ambiguous.

We begin the chapter by reflecting on these ambiguities. We then provide a brief review of relevant theory which, again fueled by wider social changes, includes major shifts in both theories of the professions and the sociology of subordination. This section is followed by a critical outline of the transition from Equal Opportunities (EO) to Diversity and Inclusion (D&I) policy and practice, which leads us to focus on the "myth of merit" (Young 1990). We use this critique to highlight the context-dependent nature of merit, and the operation of power relations and discourses in society generally, and also in most classical professions. We conclude with some suggestions for future research.

20.2 Profession, Social Categories, and Diversity: Conceptual Confusion

Even within the Anglo-American field, the meaning of profession has been contested (Larson 1977; Saks 2012), although its association with a specific historical era and function as an intermediary between early capitalism and the state lent the term some precision. The moral and intellectual authority implicit in this function was delineated in the interlinked "traits" which professions claimed as their hallmarks (Carr-Saunders and Wilson 1933; see also Suddaby and Muzio, Chapter 2, this volume). These included a monopoly of specialist knowledge and a distinctive ethical code and provided the grounds for professions' high status, rewards, and market power (Freidson 1970, 1994). These privileges were achieved and retained through social closure (Larson 1977), where professions maintain an artificial skill scarcity and maximize rewards by limiting access and opportunities "to a restricted number of eligibles" (Parkin 1974: 44). However, the shift in power from professional associations and the displacement of the pre-capitalist professional partnership (Burrage 1996) by the capitalist PSF has entailed changes in these forms of closure. For example, while PSFs' need for large numbers of "technicians" has eroded the barriers for some groups (such as women), it has also entailed restricting them to PSFs' lower tiers, thereby marking them out as "lesser" professionals (Bolton and Muzio 2007; Sommerlad 2012a, 2012b).

Thus the inclusion of outsiders has significantly contributed to the dissolution of the traditional meaning of profession, a process compounded by the application of the term to a vast range of occupations (Fournier 1999). Today, the discourse of professionalism is used in connection with occupations characterized by few or none of the classical traits, as well as traditional professions, such as law, which are so transformed that they too now differ dramatically from the classical model (Derber 1982). However, an additional conceptual complexity stems from the fact that the elite sectors of these classical professions retain vestiges of their nineteenth-century form and draw on trait professionalism discourse to justify their exclusionary practices, which protect the generally white, upper-middle-class male professionals whose working conditions continue to resemble those of the traditional, autonomous practitioner. It is vital to bear in mind both this variability between and within professions and complex fusion of continuity and change when analyzing the discourse and materiality of diversity in PSFs today.

Two further complexities present themselves. First, finding precise descriptors for those who should be beneficiaries of D&I is also problematic. For example, the concepts of both class and race have long been subject to a range of interpretations, and this variability has been compounded by the claim that the macro-level socio-economic changes referred to above have effectively rendered them meaningless "zombie categories" (Beck 1992). This theoretical position is reinforced by the rise of identity politics and echoed in claims that contemporary society is post-social category. However it is important to note that the increasingly complex classifications required to capture the contemporary multiplicity and fluidity of identity have undermined the validity of any synoptic analysis of social life (Carrier 2012). The problem is exemplified by the term "BAME," commonly used in official statistics and yet encompassing the entire range of non-white identities. Partly as a result, all social commentators on diversity are locked into a number of contradictions due to the simultaneous continuing salience of category and fluidity of contemporary identities. Second, this fluidity extends our conceptual difficulties to the term "diversity" itself, which has been described as an "ambiguous transnational signifier" (Titley and Lentin 2008: 14), a "broad discursive space" (Cooper 2004: 5), and diversity discourse as ambiguous, multivocal, and banal (Vertovec 2012).

We take up these themes throughout the remainder of this chapter. Given the size of the extant literature on this subject, we have restricted ourselves to the Anglo-American professional model, and primarily the legal profession since law was a paradigmatic profession, of pivotal social and institutional importance, making inequalities here particularly significant (Brint 1994; see also Dinovitzer et al., Chapter 6, this volume). In terms of categories of diversity, we focus on gender and, to a lesser extent, "race"/ethnicity. Our argument that discussion of the professions and diversity must be contextualized is underlined by the changes in how patterns of exclusion and inclusion have been theorized over the past four decades. In the next section of this chapter, we provide an overview of these shifting perspectives and underline the reflexive relationship between wider macro-social developments and dominant strands of academic thought. An important dimension of the debate is provided by the contrast between a concern with the supply side of the labor market (represented by aspirant professionals) as opposed to the demand side (represented by the public and private sector organizations which might employ them), and it is here that we start.

20.3 STRUCTURE, SOCIAL CLASS, AND STRATIFICATION THEORY

The mainstream vision of professional labor markets is as meritocratic arenas and their gendered and raced segmentation is consequently largely attributed to the characteristics or attitudes of non-normative groups. The academic version of this supply-side perspective is human capital theory (Becker 1985), which views the labor market as a level playing field and its segmentation as the result of the domestic division of labor and individual agency. Hakim (2000) has developed a variant of this perspective termed rational preference theory, arguing that women's under-representation in "top jobs" is not indicative of a discriminatory work environment but rather caused by men and women's different values, life goals, and hence labor market behavior, leading her to conclude that men disproportionately occupy the top jobs because they "will fight much harder to get there" (Hakim 2006: 290). Adopting a similar approach, Richard Sander (2006) attributes white men's dominance of US law firm partnerships to women's choices and to black lawyers' human capital deficit.

This "deficit model" interpretation of labor market subordination has been widely critiqued (Crompton and Lyonette 2011; Sommerlad 2012b). Empirical evidence contradicts its generalized claim that white men's investment in their careers exceeds that of females (certainly at career entry level), and that black male professionals' human capital is deficient. Consequently, demand-side explanations tend to dominate the academic literature on professional exclusion. Working in this tradition, neo-Weberian scholars, in contrast to functionalist, trait theorists, saw professionalism as a status project to constitute and control a market (Freidson 1970). This approach posits that one of the professions' defining features is their claim to jurisdictional exclusivity, which generates social closure practices. Building a "monopoly of expertise" by making "theoretically inexhaustible knowledge resources . . . socially finite" (Larson 1977: 223) is fundamental to these practices, which serve both to frustrate attempted encroachments on a profession's market by other professions and to restrict entry to those whom it deems fit and proper persons. The location of these projects within "the structural and historical parameters of patriarchal-capitalism" of the nineteenth century meant that only white males could be such persons (Witz 1990: 675).

Building this synergy with macro-level social values (Freidson 1970: 73), vital to creating and sustaining professional markets, is an ongoing task. Social modernization entailed the increasing public presence of women and other outsiders and related delegitimation of male monopolies, reducing the professions' capacity for closure, ultimately weakening the neo-Weberian perspective. Nevertheless, closure has continued to be a valuable explanatory tool for interpreting PSFs' response to the professional bodies' loss of control over their supply base following the move to graduate entry. For example, the confinement of "outsider" groups to lower professional strata has been achieved by mobilizing informal criteria, often based on archaic, class-based notions of merit, thereby simultaneously containing the threat they pose to PSFs' status and white male hegemony, while boosting firms' profitability (the following discuss this development in the legal profession: Abel 2003; Ackroyd and Muzio 2007; Faulconbridge and Muzio 2009; Sommerlad 2012a, 2012b).

However, the organizational fragmentation and differentiation of professional work produced by the erosion of state support for market shelters also generated new theorizations of the professions. For instance, Abbott's work on the system of professions and professional ecologies (1988, 2005) explores not only how individual professional markets are controlled, but also how restricting access to these and raising the price of services can open up new, lower priced markets for other groups, which may or may not be regulated. More recently, neo-institutional theory has drawn on this work to analyze contemporary patterns of professionalization within an organizational rather than solely occupational context, in order to address the apparent "blind spots" associated with neo-Weberian theory (Muzio et al. 2013).

20.4 POST-STRUCTURALISM, GENDER, AND RACE

As our summary of neo-Weberian theory indicates, outsiders' claims to professionalism and their usurpationary strategies (Witz 1992) formed part of the new intellectual and cultural currents which were major dimensions and also engines of the macro-level socio-economic change process which began in the 1960s. These claims generated new theories, including reconceptualizations of stratification theory, which rejected the exclusive focus on class as the primary form of inequality, and expanded the meaning and location of injustice (Fraser 2013: 214). Gender stratification theorists focused on the nexus between private and public patriarchy (Walby 1990) which was held to perpetuate women's (unpaid and devalued) responsibility for social reproduction, their subordination in both the private and public spheres, and male labor market dominance. These injustices were viewed as systemic: in their analysis of the labor market, they highlighted the structural barriers which either exclude women or position them in strata or segments characterized by inferior rewards and status, in spite of any act of will on their part (see e.g.,Tomaskovic-Devey 1993). Thus the relationship between the gendered domestic division of labor and "on-demand" character of professional practice was argued to present practical problems for women (Brockman 2001; Reichman and Sterling 2004: 949; Smithson et al. 2004) and ground assumptions about their commitment, confining them to the "mommy track" (Korzec 1997) even when they delay motherhood to reduce conflict with their career progression (Blair-Loy and DeHart 2003).

Gender stratification theorists therefore attributed the barriers to women's full inclusion in professional labor markets to their structures and also cultures, grounded in essentialist conceptions of female "nature." Bureaucratic processes are consequently perceived as indirectly discriminatory in favor of the dominant occupational group, often in ways that are taken for granted (Kanter 1977; Spencer and Podmore 1982, 1987). Building on these insights, Acker (1990) wrote of "gendered" organizations, in which terms such as "task" or "performance" are not neutral but rather social constructs. This recognition of the significance of symbols and images supported further investigations of the specifics of gender relations at work and underlined the role of micro-organizational processes in reproducing and reworking inequalities (Anderson-Gough et al. 2005; Kornberger et al. 2010).

This engagement with the symbolic order and organizational cultures formed part of a wider theoretical turn, while the shift from class and macro-level structure was mirrored in the concern with neglected subordinated identities and intersections between identities. For instance, the early 1980s saw the development of Critical Race Theory (CRT) (e.g., Crenshaw 1991; Hooks 1989; Lorde 1984). Much CRT writing, like gender stratification scholarship, addressed structural barriers. CRT studies of the US legal profession have therefore emphasized the role of external, structural constraints and organizational practices in determining the outcomes of BAME individuals' careers (Payne-Pikus et al. 2010; Wilkins and Gulati 1996).

However CRT scholarship, again echoing broader theoretical developments, also came to embrace post-structural insights about the role language, symbolism, and culture play in exclusionary processes. Fundamental to this perspective is the view that "race" is a socially constructed and therefore dynamic category (Gilroy 2000; Miles and Brown 1989; Omi and Winant 1994; Ramji 2009); the discussion is therefore of racializing processes and racial formations. Race is seen as constructed in daily interactions, and CRT's focus on the role of micro practices in this process and in particular the "psychic harms" these practices inflict (a concern too of much feminist scholarship) has meant that the "language of psychology has broadly come to replace a grammar of exploitation" in the academic literature (Lawler 2005: 799). Correspondingly, the contemporary assertion that society is race-free (and labor markets, therefore, level playing fields) is viewed as false, individualizing the effects of systemic discrimination and thus representing a form of modern racism (Dalal 2008; Miles and Brown 1989). For instance, studies of accountancy speak of an "everyday racism" underlying the surface neutrality, making the non-white subject simultaneously invisible in terms of recognition of merit and hyper visible (Kyriacou and Johnston 2006, 2011).

20.5 Embodiment, Identity, and Performance

The shift in focus outlined above, towards an understanding of identity as socially constructed and consequently fluid and intersectional has come to dominate critical social theory (West and Fenstermaker 1995; on this theme see also Alvesson et al., Chapter 18, this volume). The social context for this development is the identity politics which emerged during the 1980s and 1990s across the globe, which articulated new claims to social justice through cultural recognition, and as such was a direct reaction to the particularisms that were typically presented as universal in radical and liberal politics (Cooper 2004). For some scholars (e.g., Beck 1992; Giddens 1994), this fluidity of contemporary identities creates the potential for individual agency and is therefore emancipatory. Other critical scholars view the emphasis on agency as both an aspect, and stimulus, of neo-liberalism, one of the core intellectual components of which is the Hayekian reduction of society to individuals operating in free markets (Fraser 2013).

This less optimistic approach also characterizes post-structuralist work which focuses on regulation, discipline, and control. For Foucault (1977) hierarchical social relations are produced and reinforced through the creation of norms and structures which sanction particular ways of being, central to which is self-surveillance. This interpretation of the operation of processes of normalization and subjectification has been deployed in a range of studies on occupational socialization (Hodgson 2005; Kosmala and Herrbach 2006) which engage with themes of identity, embodiment, and discipline to consider the production of the "ideal practitioner" who looks "right" (Nickson et al. 2003) and possesses the correct (gendered, classed, and raced) technical and behavioral attributes (Anderson-Gough et al. 2000, 2001, 2005; Coffey 1994; Cooper and Robson 2006; Covaleski et al. 1998; Fournier 1999; Grey 1994; Sommerlad 2007). The emphasis in these studies is therefore on the workplace as a site "where professional identities are mediated, formed and transformed" (Cooper and Robson 2006: 416), so that, while the construction of the normative professional continues to take place at the occupational level (Cook et al. 2012), social closure and control is exercised at the individual and organizational level. Again drawing on Foucault, professionalism is thus conceptualized as a discursive strategy deployed to motivate and control staff, realigning individual identities with organizational priorities (Fournier 1999; Muzio and Tomlinson 2012; Tomlinson et al. 2013). These priorities include efficiency and responsibility and extend to a strong client service ethic, requiring "total commitment" (Sommerlad and Sanderson 1998) and engagement in emotional labor (Hochschild 1983), requirements which impact the participation and progress of non-normative groups within PSFs (Anderson-Gough et al. 2000; Evetts 2003; Fournier 1999; Grey 1998; Kornberger et al. 2010).

A lens for investigating the reproduction of workplace hierarchies which seeks to overcome the dichotomy between structure and culture hinted at above is offered by the sociology of Pierre Bourdieu (1977a, 1977b, 1984, 1994). Bourdieu's explanatory framework for the reproduction of disadvantage is grounded in his conceptualization of the social world as comprising fields organized around behaviors and practices which are strongly patterned by traditions. These traditions form part of a field's doxa (or common sense) which produce its distinctive habitual dispositions (habitus) and determine its cultural practices. Success in a field requires internalization of its habitus and doxa, and the possession of those symbolic goods—forms of capital—which are regarded as the attributes of excellence; however, these are shaped by the interests of the dominating class (Bourdieu 1984) and consequently, the participation of outsiders has failed to displace toxic understandings of what is excellence, or what it is to be either a lawyer or a woman, having instead produced a "fictitious universalism" (Bourdieu 2001: 116).

Bourdieu's focus on the relationship between cultural capital and class has informed a number of studies of the professions (Ashley 2010; Ashley and Empson 2013; Faulconbridge and Muzio 2012; Jacobs 2003; Jewel 2008; Sommerlad 2012b; Sommerlad and Sanderson 1998), and his emphasis on the significance of embodied practices in demonstrating cultural capital has generated the concept of "physical capital" (Haynes 2012). Haynes draws too on neo-Weberian theory, arguing with reference to the accountancy sector, that embodiment practices constitute a "professional closure" mechanism, marginalizing those, including fertile women, whose body image is dissimilar to that of the accepted professional body image (Haynes 2012; see also Sommerlad 2007). In the next section, we consider the implications of these theoretical approaches in relation to policy and practice.

20.6 POLICY AND PRACTICE

As with the development of theoretical perspectives, there is a relationship between the types of policies and practices designed to address inequalities and macro-social structure. The equal opportunity (EO)/affirmative action approach of the interventionist state sought primarily to address material inequalities through structural change, generating legal sanctions and policy interventions designed to guarantee equal treatment of first women and subsequently also BAME individuals and to prevent discrimination. However, other diversity strands were not recognized and claims could only be brought by individuals, with success dependent on establishing that their treatment had differed from a comparable norm—thereby, as gender stratification work argued, reinforcing a normative standard generally based on a male worker (Acker 1990: 149). Consequently, EO mounted little real challenge to organizations' structure and culture (Fredman 2011; Liff and Wajcman 1996).

From the 1980s and into the 1990s the transition in countries across the world from the Keynesian economic model to one grounded in a neo-liberal logic resulted in the widespread displacement of these policies by the diversity and inclusion (D&I) approach to equality. Mirroring the theoretical developments discussed above, this tends to emphasize culture above structure; it also suggests that by treating people in the same way, without consideration for their specific circumstances or context, existing inequalities may be deepened rather than reduced, the implication being that in some cases, equality is only achieved by treating different people differently (Tomei 2003). D&I is characterized by voluntarism, reflecting the general move towards deregulation, and by the argument that its adoption will bring business benefits. This suggests that recognizing and rewarding difference brings commercial benefits, including within the professions the ability to serve new markets, improved managerial skills, and enhanced problem-solving capabilities (Wilkins 2007).

This synergy between neo-liberal policies and the business case for diversity approach has made D&I pervasive across the professional services sector, particularly in Anglo-Saxon contexts. For example, by 2004, 86% of the UK's top accountancy firms had a formal diversity policy in place (Fielding 2004). Similarly, 80% of respondents to the InterLaw Diversity Forum's 2012 survey of 1,700 legal professionals in the UK said that their firm had a well-publicized diversity strategy. However, the statistical evidence suggests that these policies have been relatively ineffective in generating more equal outcomes (Chadderton 2012).

This situation is not the result of inactivity. In contrast to the EO concern to eliminate direct discrimination, D&I has addressed aspects of organizational culture which could constitute indirect discrimination. This has led for example to "diversity audits," as firms have deployed questionnaire surveys and qualitative research, to identify and understand those features of organizational structure and culture which impede equity both in terms of access and also career progression. Audits have informed policy development, the objective of which is to sensitize individuals responsible for recruitment, selection, and promotion decisions towards difference and unconscious bias, and to reduce stereotypical thinking, often through the provision of diversity training. A major aim of this training is to erode "cultural matching" (the tendency of senior members of PSFs to recruit in their own image: Rivera 2012) and the allocation of work on the basis of essentialist assumptions about men and women's aptitudes and skills, or cultural fit (Epstein 1992; Heilman 2001; Kay and Hagan 2003; Kay et al. 2009; McCracken 1999). For instance, following the introduction of unconscious bias training, the Head of Diversity at UK headquartered law firm Freshfields, Bruckhaus and Deringer stated that it would "encourage people to think a bit more carefully about the reasons behind their decisions" (Ring 2011). A further objective is to highlight the informal practices which prioritize stereotypically male traits, and can foster male bonding, excluding women (Sommerlad et al. 2010). Many firms have employed organizational psychologists to enhance understanding of how hidden biases shape views both of appropriate skills and attributes for promotion, and who is likely to have these.

However, another aspect of D&I is its emphasis on supply-side weaknesses, or "deficits"—such as a reluctance to apply for high-profile positions. Therefore networking, affinity, or employee or business resource groups have been introduced, particularly by larger PSFs. These groups often have a dual purpose: first to provide a supportive space in which minority groups can share their experiences and second (underlining the significance of commercial drivers in D&I policies), to leverage marketing opportunities with similar groups in client organizations. Thus US headquartered international firm Weil, Gotshal and Manges LLP offers Women@Weil which is said to "embrace the talents and energy of women across Weil Gotshal, focusing on mentoring and networking, recruiting and retention, pro bono initiatives, and business development and outreach."[1] In the financial services sector, the Interbank LGBT Forum aims to create an open and inclusive space for LGBT employees from its 15 member institutions to share best practices between network groups and promote and encourage networking opportunities.

Firms such as Ernst & Young report that they work in partnership with their networks to develop their ethnic minority employees, alongside a formal leadership program, which entails identifying and developing high potential employees from diverse backgrounds. Indeed, over the last five years all the major accountancy firms in the UK and US and many leading law firms have developed either mentoring and/or sponsorship programs for women and ethnic minorities. These programs acknowledge, for example, that women are less likely than men to take credit for their achievements and more likely to avoid self-promoting behaviors rather than risk social censure for transgressing gender stereotypical norms (Eagly 1995; Gorman and Kmec 2009; Kumra and Vinnicombe 2010). Recognizing also that promotion to partner requires not just technical skills but significant social and cultural capital (Sommerlad 2011) such programs aim to help women and other minorities improve their visibility at senior levels, and provide specific individuals with those opportunities for career development which their white, male peers more regularly receive. Some programs are tailored to address cultural differences identified as preventing professionals from certain ethnic and cultural backgrounds responding positively to feedback or displaying "initiative."

As this discussion of D&I policies indicates, these have historically focused on characteristics which are protected in law, primarily gender, encouraged by the high rates and associated costs of female attrition, and more recently, ethnicity. However, D&I's individualized approach means that it encompasses a wider set of diversity strands including sexual orientation, and to a lesser extent, disability and, more recently, class. The growing recognition of the significance of socio-economic background in producing disadvantage within the professions (Cabinet Office 2009) has generated the development, in partnership with charitable and educational foundations, of a range of outreach programs, mentoring opportunities, and internships with the aim of helping less privileged students to build social and cultural capital (Ashley and Empson 2013). These programs, such as the Sutton Trust's Pathways to Law and the Social Mobility Foundation's Aspiring Professionals Programme, also aim to help widen access to elite universities, since most PSFs, particularly the largest and most prestigious, continue to recruit predominantly from those institutions (Ashley 2010). A primary focus of such programs is therefore on addressing "deficits" in the supply side, such as lack of aspiration (Cabinet Office 2009) and perceptions that the professions are only open to the more privileged, which a 2007 report on entry to the Bar suggested were self-fulfilling (Neuberger Report 2007). However, some firms now also aim to address demand-side attitudes and assumptions linked to socio-economic background. For example, Clifford Chance has implemented a "CV blind" approach to final interviews with graduate applicants, whereby staff are not informed about either the university or school which the candidate attended (Garner 2014). During its first year the firm appointed graduate trainees educated at 41 different educational insitutions, a rise of nearly 30% on the number represented in the previous year using the previous recruitment system.

Whether the D&I approach necessarily delivers such positive outcomes is, though, debatable, as we discuss next.

20.7 DIVERSITY AND INCLUSION IN PRACTICE

There has then been a raft of activity within the professional service sector aimed at becoming (quantitatively) more diverse and (qualitatively) more inclusive. Yet, as our introductory statistical snapshot revealed, women and minorities remain seriously under-represented in leadership positions throughout the professions, while individuals from less privileged backgrounds are increasingly excluded from the elite professions altogether (Cabinet Office 2009).

One explanation for the relative failure of D&I to achieve transformational change is that, though expressed in terms of a business case, PSFs are motivated more by a desire to achieve social legitimacy (Süss and Kleiner 2008) than by a commitment to competitive advantage via progressive employment practices. Consequently, measures introduced to support minorities are presented not as rights but as favors, requiring individual negotiation (Mossman 1994). As Liff (1999: 68) points out, a genuinely progressive diversity agenda would entail a fundamental rethink of organizational structures, cultures, and policies, whereas in practice the change generated by the diversity approach tends to be cosmetic and superficial. Ahmed (2007), writing about diversity in higher education, describes this gestural approach as "doing the document," and argues that the dissatisfaction it produces amongst non-normative professionals results in institutions seeing them as "trouble-makers," such that they, rather than the organization, are perceived as the "problem."

As a result, many D&I policies are underpinned by the conceptualization of the non-normative professional as deficient in terms of, for instance, skill or assertiveness, so that it is s/he, not the firm, that must change. Policies intended to support women and minorities can generate additional barriers since, while they give an impression of change, in practice they are premised on outsiders' need to assimilate to a culture within which they may never quite "fit" (Rhode 2011). The alien and entrenched nature of organizational cultures is exemplified by Kumra and Vinnicombe's (2008) study of promotion to partnership in a management consultancy, which reveals how the self-promotion this requires entails extensive networking (usually with male colleagues) and conformity to a prevailing masculine model of success. Their findings chime with those of other studies focused on gender, which suggest that female professionals' lack of fit with the dominant culture produces a "double-bind" such that they risk constantly appearing either too soft or too strident, too aggressive or not aggressive enough (Heilman et al. 1989; Rhode 2011).

D&I policies may also be criticized for their failure to address the problems flowing from the intersection of multiple identities within a professional environment. For example, one research study in the US (Bagati 2008) found that women of color at law firms were more likely than any other group to experience exclusion and racial and gender stereotyping and therefore most likely to feel it necessary to make adjustments to fit in, and to report a lack of constructive feedback as a barrier to advancement. A similar study of the accountancy sector found that people of color report a very significant disconnect between a firm's commitment to diversity and the execution of the practices that support that commitment (Bagati 2007).

A range of researchers note this disjuncture between what D&I policies *say* and what they *do*. Their analysis tends to support the insights of much of the theoretical work discussed earlier, such as that of CRT and gender stratification scholars and Bourdieu. As Leblebici (2007) has pointed out, PSFs are "connected systems," making it difficult to change any particular practice without effecting a more general transformation of their structures, cultures, and practices. Formal policies which attempt to change organizational cultures are therefore unlikely to succeed unless they also challenge the informal practices that reflect and sustain a professional order dominated by men, who are usually white and able-bodied (Ely and Meyerson 2000). Thus the coexistence of unconscious bias training with "no fault" discrimination, which posits that once sensitivity training has alerted managers to their discriminatory behavior, they will take action and disadvantage will be eradicated, fails to address the deep-rooted biases underpinning organizational culture, and hence to produce real and lasting transformation (Sommerlad 2002).

"Flexible work" exemplifies both this problem and the distinction between D&I policies which deploy a language of choice and EO discourses of positive discrimination (Smithson et al. 2004). Originally an EO policy which aimed to create more family friendly working environments, flexible work today is understood as any working pattern adapted to suit the needs of the individual (Johnson et al. 2008). Thus, although it has been widely adopted by PSFs as a means of making work–life issues central to organizational policy (Kandola and Fullerton 1998), it has been presented in gender-neutral terms. In practice, however, without other simultaneous changes—for instance to the way the working day is structured and charged to clients—it can have little impact on PSF culture. In fact, the ongoing intensification of work means that far from resulting in recognition and reward for "difference" (Ransome 2007), those working flexibly tend to be viewed as lacking in "commitment" (Crompton and Lyonette 2011; Kornberger et al. 2010; Sommerlad and Sanderson 1998; Wald 2009), and to experience a competitive pressure to maximize their productivity within those hours when they are present (Epstein et al. 1999). At the same time, the emphasis within the business case on profitability naturalizes the "need" for organizations to differentiate between the more and less "committed." The virtually exclusive use of flexible working arrangements by women then legitimates both female marginalization and the construction of this marginalization as the result of their choices rather than of unequal structures and practices (Hakim 2000, 2006). Far from producing a more equitable working environment these policies have therefore been viewed as reinforcing an essentialist, socio-biological view of women which pathologizes them (Thornton and Bagust 2007).

These reflections feed into consideration of one of the most problematic issues in the debate over diversity and the professions, namely merit, a construct which has played a central role in recent social modernizing processes (Sommerlad 2015). Merit's centrality parallels and verifies the claimed neutrality of labor markets and the concomitant claim that wider society is post-category and is therefore a foundational concept for D&I policies. As a core component of "common sense" it may be described, following Foucault, as a technology, for in practice its indeterminacy makes it capable of legitimating differential treatment in recruitment and career progression by embracing any qualities that distinguish the successful from the unsuccessful candidate and elevating these to be the determining factors in a decision—this circularity lending it a teleological quality.

The key role of "merit" (or talent) in reproducing and legitimating exclusionary practices is illustrated in a number of empirical studies, which show how context-specific conceptualizations of merit inform and naturalize the informal cultural practices of PSFs (Kumra 2014). Again, these studies underline the argument in much of the theoretical and empirical work we have discussed that cultural practices represent more significant barriers to the capacity of non-normative professionals to configure themselves as merit-worthy professionals, than such tangible obstacles as long hours (Smithson et al. 2004). As in the era of classical professionalism, these practices revolve around the making and sustaining of personal bonds (re-)producing a homosocial culture (Sommerlad et al. 2010) which generates a range of further practices, many of which may be directly traced to the (white) male legacy of the majority of elite professions, that serve to naturalize the stereotypes which perpetuate difference (Thornton 1996).

In summary, although the way in which the diversity agenda is interpreted and applied is of course context-specific it has several overarching features which reduce its capacity to counter exclusion. First, it is generally predicated on the assumption that the PSF is a neutral arena, whose culture and HR practices are inherently rational, leaving no room either for recognition of the ubiquitous practice of homosocial reproduction or, therefore, of residual and historical bias based on category (Liff and Wajcman 1996). Second, it is built on an ideal-typical (entrepreneurial) worker with sufficient resources to engage in a successful career project (Sommerlad 2011; see also Cohen, Chapter 16, this volume), and cannot support the worker with "potential" but whose material background does not equip them with such resources (Skeggs 2004). Third, its explicitly business-based rationale privileges economistic values over those based on equity or social justice (Litvin 2006; Lorbiecki and Jack 2000). This is problematic because as Wilkins (2007) points out, where diversity is valued primarily for the advantages it offers to business, but achieving these advantages is considered costly, firms may persist with the long-standing concerns, routines, and assumptions that define the current status quo and achieve only a "cosmetic" form of diversity. In common with many scholars of diversity and of the professions, he suggests that attention to the ethical case for diversity would ensure that the agenda is not hostage to the "changing winds of self-interest of both law firm leaders and their corporate clients" (Wilkins 2007: 54; see also Dinovitzer et al., Chapter 6, this volume).

Currently therefore, the relationship between the business case rationale, the workplace policies and practices it generates, and neo-liberal macro-social processes would appear to represent a major barrier to achieving the inclusion of disadvantaged groups on more equal terms. For, as we argued at the beginning of this chapter, disadvantaged groups have been included within the professions as lesser professionals, to carry out routine tasks, thus playing central roles in the transformation of traditional professional firms into capitalist PSFs (Hagan and Kay 1995). It is perhaps not surprising therefore that progress towards more equal outcomes has been slow. Nevertheless, the broader understanding of diversity and emphasis on agency of recent theoretical work is potentially liberatory for some groups and individuals. It has for example supported contestation by women and minorities of their subordination, a project with which academic work can and should engage. With this in mind we use our conclusion to discuss the suggestions for future research generated by our analysis.

20.8 Conclusions

As noted at the beginning of this chapter, while the profession's high status is dependent in part on its exclusionary practices, these also threaten their social legitimacy. The significance of social legitimacy echoes the neo-Weberian view that the professional project depends on retaining a connection with lay culture, which today requires labor markets to be meritocratic, and key institutions such as PSFs to be (at least relatively) representative. However, in order to explore the relationship between professional legitimacy and diversity in further depth, we suggest first a study of the views of key stakeholders such as regulators and clients on diversity in PSFs. Another under-researched theme is the relationship between D&I and merit or "talent management" within the professions (Lewis and Heckman 2006), and our second recommendation is therefore for research into how key personnel drawn from functional departments such as human resources, as well as partners and heads of departments in a range of PSFs, interpret, identify, and define talent, and the impact on both individuals and organizations.

Third, there is a need for research into the impact on diversity of PSFs' patterning into increasingly complex hierarchies, and in particular the growing divide between a "knowledge" and "administrative elite" (Freidson 1994, 2001; Hanlon 1998; Muzio and Kirkpatrick 2011). As our introductory statistical outline of the professions demonstrates, the latter group is largely comprised of non-normative workers who carry out the routinized, commoditized, and low-paid work, including an emerging group whose casualized working conditions suggest that they may be described as a precariat (Sommerlad 2012a, 2015; Standing 2011). Fourth, we encourage the growing focus within the sociology of the professions on organizations and institutions (Muzio et al. 2013), alongside the traditional concern with occupations (Larson 1977). One framework seeking to achieve this is neo-institutional theory (Muzio et al. 2013; Suddaby and Viale 2011). Like CRT scholarship, this approach identifies the mundane but conscious actions of individual and collective actors, and may be deployed to provide new insights into the maintenance of institutionalized disadvantage within the professions, and how this may be disrupted.

Fifth, the significance of intersectionality, which we have sought to highlight in this chapter, calls out for research which engages with questions of essentialism and which might thus help overcome the determinism of previous ways of thinking about identities that often classified individuals into fixed categories, as either oppressed or oppressor (Valentine 2007). Sixth, we suggest a more general attention to neglected diversity axes such as religion, disability, and indeed masculinity (Collier 2009), while the multinational character of many PSFs indicates a need for comparative studies of organizational cultures and diversity practices, including the cross-national transfer of diversity practice between contrasting locations (Terjesen and Singh 2008). Our recommendation is that all these studies should be informed by an inter-disciplinary approach, and also that there is a place for small-scale qualitative research alongside projects based on large-scale quantitative data.

The objective behind these suggestions is to assist stakeholders within the professional services sector to interrogate and engage with their organizational cultures in order to facilitate more genuinely inclusive recruitment and promotion strategies, and support the agency of "outsiders." Though often subverted by long-standing workplace practices and cultural barriers, the identity politics from which D&I originates does have an emancipatory potential. A common feature of academic work based in this tradition is its challenge to the belief that identity is singular or fixed, generating attention to positionality and context. We welcome this commitment to the creation of situated knowledge, and the emphasis on reflexivity and the conditions which would support it, and suggest that this approach should extend to academia's own status as a profession and its role as a body which creates knowledge and belief systems (Thornton 2002: 83).

NOTE

1. <http://www.weil.com/about-weil/diversity-and-inclusion/women-weil>   (accessed February 11, 2015).

REFERENCES

Abbott, A. (1988). *The System of Professions: An Essay on the Division of Expert Labor*. Chicago, IL: University of Chicago Press.

Abbott, A. (2005). "Linked Ecologies: States and Universities as Environments for Professions," *Sociological Theory* 23(3): 245–274.

Abel, R. L. (2003). *English Lawyers between Market and State: The Politics of Professionalism*. Oxford: Oxford University Press.

Accountancy Age (2014). Top 50 Survey of Firms. <http://www.accountancyage.com/digital_assets/7572/Top_50_chart_2013.pdf> (accessed April 7, 2014).

Acker, J. (1990). "Hierarchies, Jobs, Bodies: A Theory of Gendered Organizations," *Gender and Society* 4(2): 139–158.

Ackroyd, S. and Muzio, D. (2007). "The Reconstructed Professional Firm: Explaining Change in English Legal Practices," *Organization Studies* 28(5): 729–747.

Ahmed, S. (2007). " 'You End Up Doing the Document rather than Doing the Doing': Diversity, Race Equality and the Politics of Documentation," *Ethnic and Racial Studies* 30(4): 590–609.

American Bar Association (2011). *ABA Disability Statistics Report*. Chicago, IL: ABA.

American Bar Association (2012). *Lawyer Demographics*. Chicago, IL: ABA.

American Bar Association (2014). *A Current Glance at Women in the Law*. Chicago, IL: ABA.

Anderson-Gough, F., Grey, C., and Robson, K. (2000). "In the Name of the Client: The Service Ethic in Two Professional Services Firms," *Human Relations* 53(9): 1151–1174.

Anderson-Gough, F., Grey, C., and Robson, K. (2001). "Tests of Time: Organizational Time-Reckoning and the Making of Accountants in Two Multi-National Accounting Firms," *Accounting, Organizations and Society* 26(2): 99–122.

Anderson-Gough, F., Grey, C., and Robson, K., (2005). " 'Helping them to Forget': The Organizational Embedding of Gender Relations in Public Audit Firms," *Accounting, Organizations and Society* 30(5): 469–490.

Ashley, L. (2010). "Making a Difference? The Use (and Abuse) of Diversity Management at the UK's Elite Law Firms," *Work, Employment & Society* 24(4): 711–727.

Ashley, L. and Empson, L. (2013). "Differentiation and Discrimination: Understanding Social Class and Social Exclusion in Leading Law Firms," *Human Relations* 66(2): 219–244.

Bagati, D. (2007). *Retaining People of Color: What Accounting Firms Need to Know*. New York: Catalyst.

Bagati, D. (2008). *Women of Color in U.S. Law Firms*. New York: Catalyst.

Beck, U. (1992). *Risk Society: Towards a New Modernity*. London: Sage.

Becker, G. S. (1985). "Human Capital, Effort, and the Sexual Division of Labor," *Journal of Labor Economics* 3(1): S33–S58.

Blair-Loy, M. and DeHart, G. (2003). "Family and Career Trajectories among African American Female Attorneys," *Journal of Family Issues* 24(7): 908–933.

Bolton, S. and Muzio, D (2007). "Can't Live with 'em, Can't Live without 'em: Gendered Segmentation in the Legal Profession," *Sociology* 41(2): 47–64.

Bourdieu, P. (1977a) *Outline of a Theory of Practice*. Cambridge: Cambridge University Press.

Bourdieu, P. (1977b). "Cultural Reproduction and Social Reproduction," in *Power and Ideology in Education*, ed. J. M. Karabel and H. Halsey. New York: Oxford University Press, 487–511.

Bourdieu, P. (1984). *Distinction: A Social Critique of the Judgment of Taste*. Cambridge, MA: Harvard University Press.

Bourdieu, P. (1994). "Structures, Habitus, Power: Basis for a Theory of Symbolic Power," in *Culture/Power/History: A Reader in Contemporary Social Theory*, ed. N. B. Dirks, G. Eley, and S. B. Ortner. Princeton, NJ: Princeton University Press, 155–199.

Bourdieu, P. (2001). *Masculine Domination*, trans. R. Nice. Stanford, CA: Stanford University Press.

Brint, S. (1994). *In an Age of Experts: The Changing Role of Professionals in Politics and Public Life*. Princeton, NJ: Princeton University Press.

Brockman, J. (2001). *Gender in the Legal Profession: Fitting or Breaking the Mould*. Vancouver: UBC Press.

Burrage, M. (1996). "From a Gentlemen's to a Public Profession: Status and Politics in the History of English Solicitors," *International Journal of the Legal Profession* 3(1–2): 45–80.

Burton, L. (2012). "Revealed: Females Make Up Less than 10 per cent of top 100's Equity Partner Ranks," *Legal Week*, October. <http://www.thelawyer.com/revealed-females-make-up-less-than-10-per-cent-of-top-100s-equity-partner-ranks/1015190.article> (accessed April 10, 2014).

Business in the Community (2009). "Ethnic Minorities in Business, Finance Administration and Mathmatics." <http://raceforopportunity.bitc.org.uk/research_insight/ethnic_minority_sector_factsheets> (accessed February 13, 2015).

Cabinet Office (2009). *Unleashing Aspirations: The Final Report of the Panel on Fair Access to the Professions*. London: Cabinet Office.

Carr-Saunders, A. M. and Wilson, P. A. (1933). *The Professions*. London: Oxford University Press.

Carrier, J. (2012). "The Trouble with Class," *European Journal of Sociology* 53(3): 263–284.

Chadderton, S. (2012). "Firms have well-Publicized Diversity Strategies—But They Are Not Working InterLaw Finds," *The Lawyer*. <http://www.thelawyer.com/firms-have-well-publicised-diversity-programmes-but-theyre-not-working-interlaw-finds/1013321.article> (accessed April 10, 2014).

Chambers (2014). *Ethnicity in the Law Survey*. <http://www.chambersstudent.co.uk/where-to-start/newsletter/2014-ethnicity-in-the-law-survey> (accessed February 13, 2015).

Chartered Institute of Public Relations (2013). *State of the Profession Annual Benchmarking Survey 2012/13*. London: CIPR.

Coffey, A. J. (1994). "Timing is Everything; Graduate Accountants, Time and Organizational Commitment," *Sociology* 28(4): 943–956.

Cole, B. (2000). *Trends in the Solicitors' Profession*. London: Law Society.

Cole, B., Fletcher, N., Chittenden, T., and Cox, J. (2009). *Trends in the Solicitors' Profession*. London: Law Society.

Collier, R. (2009). *Men, Law and Gender: Essays on the "Man" of Law*. London: Routledge-Cavendish.

Collin, S.-O. Y., Jonnergård, K., Qvick, P., Silfverberg, B., and Zabit, S. (2007). "Gendered Career Rein: A Gendered Analysis of the Certification Process of Auditors in Sweden," *International Journal of Auditing* 11(1): 17–39.

Cook, A. C., Faulconbridge, J. R., and Muzio, D. (2012). "London's Legal Elite: Recruitment through Cultural Capital and the Reproduction of Social Exclusivity in City Professional Service Fields," *Environment and Planning A* 44(7): 1744–1762.

Cooper, D. (2004). *Challenging Diversity: Rethinking Equality and the Value of Difference*. Cambridge: Cambridge University Press.

Cooper, D. J. and Robson, K. (2006). "Accounting, Professions and Regulation: Locating the Sites of Professionalization," *Accounting, Organizations and Society* 31(4): 415–444.

Covaleski, M. A., Dirsmith, M. W., Heian, J. B., and Samuel, S. (1998). "The Calculated and the Avowed: Techniques of Discipline and Struggles over Identity in Big Six Public Accounting Firms," *Administrative Science Quarterly* 43(2): 293–327.

Crenshaw, K. (1991). "Mapping the Margins: Intersectionality, Identity Politics, and Violence against Women of Color," *Stanford Law Review* 43(6): 1241–1299.

Crompton, R. and Lyonette, C. (2011). "Women's Career Success and Work–Life Adaptations in the Accountancy and Medical Professions in Britain," *Gender, Work and Organization* 18(2): 231–254.

Crompton, R. and Sanderson, K. (1990). *Gendered Jobs and Social Change*. London: Routledge.

Dalal, F. (2008). "Against the Celebration of Diversity," *British Journal of Psychotherapy* 24: 4–19.

Derber, C. (1982) "Managing Professionals: Ideological Proletarianization and Mental Labor," in *Professionals as Workers: Mental Labor in Advanced Capitalism*, ed. C. Derber, Boston, MA: G. K. Hall, 167–190.

Eagly, A. H. (1995). "The Science and Politics of Comparing Women and Men," *American Psychologist* 50(3): 145–158.

Ely, R. J. and Meyerson, D. E. (2000). "Theories of Gender in Organizations: A New Approach to Organizational Analysis and Change," *Research in Organizational Behavior* 22: 103–151.

Epstein, C., Seron, C., Oglensky, B., and Saute, R. (1999). *The Part-Time Paradox: Time Norms, Professional Life, Family and Gender*. New York and London: Routledge

Epstein, R. A. (1992). "Legal Education and the Politics of Exclusion," *Stanford Law Review* 45: 1607–1626.

Evetts, J. (2003). "The Construction of Professionalism in New and Existing Occupational Contexts: Promoting and Facilitating Occupational Change," *International Journal of Sociology and Social Policy* 23(4–5): 22–35.

Faulconbridge, J. R. and Muzio, D. (2009). "The Financialization of Large Law Firms: Situated Discourses and Practices of Reorganization," *Journal of Economic Geography* 9(5): 641–661.

Faulconbridge, J. R. and Muzio, D. (2012). "Professions in a Globalizing World: Towards a Transnational Sociology of the Professions," *International Sociology* 27(1): 136–152.

Fielding, R. (2004). "Top 50: Your Perfect Partners," *Accountancy Age*. <http://www.accoun-tancyage.com/aa/feature/1762120/top-your-perfect-partners> (accessed April 10, 2014).

Fletcher, N. and Muratova, Y. (2010). *Trends in the Solicitors' Profession*. London: Law Society.

Foucault, M. (1977). *Discipline and Punish*. London: Random House.

Fournier, V. (1999). "The Appeal to 'Professionalism' as a Disciplinary Mechanism," *Sociological Review* 47(2): 280–307.

Fraser, N. (2013). *Fortunes of Feminism: From State-Managed Capitalism to Neoliberal Crisis*. London: Verso.

Fredman, S. (2011). *Discrimination Law*. Oxford: Oxford University Press.

Freidson, E. (1970). *Professional Dominance: The Social Structure of Medical Care*. New Brunswick, NJ: Transaction Books.

Freidson, E. (1994). *Professionalism Reborn: Theory, Prophecy, and Policy*. Chicago, IL: University of Chicago Press.

Freidson, E. (2001) *Professionalism: The Third Logic*. Cambridge: Polity Press.

Garner, R. (2014). "Law Firm Clifford Chance Adopts 'CV Blind' Policy to Break Oxbridge Recruitment Bias," *The Independent*, January 9.

Giddens, A. (1994). "Replies and Critiques: Risk, Trust, Reflexivity," in U. Beck, A. Giddens, and S. Lash, *Reflexive Modernization: Politics, Tradition and Aesthetics in the Modern Social Order*. Stanford, CA: Stanford University Press, 184–197.

Gilroy, P. (2000). *Against Race: Imagining Political Culture beyond the Color Line*. Cambridge, MA: Harvard University Press.

Gorman, E. H. and Kmec, J. A. (2009). "Hierarchical Rank and Women's Organizational Mobility: Glass Ceilings in Corporate Law Firms," *American Journal of Sociology* 114(5): 1428–1474.

Grey, C. (1994). "Career as a Project of the Self and Labor Process Discipline," *Sociology* 28(2): 479–497.

Grey, C. (1998). "On Being a Professional in a 'Big Six' Firm," *Accounting, Organizations and Society* 23(5–6): 569–587.

Hagan, J. and Kay, F. (1995) *Gender in Practice: A Study of Lawyers' Lives*. New York: Oxford University Press.

Hakim, C. (2000). *Work-Lifestyle Choices in the 21st Century: Preference Theory*. Oxford: Oxford University Press.

Hakim, C. (2006). "Women, Careers, and Work–Life Preferences," *British Journal of Guidance and Counselling* 34(3): 279–294.

Hammond T., Clayton, B. A., and Arnold, P. J. (2009). "South Africa's Transition from Apartheid: The Role of Professional Closure in the Experience of Black Chartered Accountants," *Accounting, Organizations and Society* 34(6–7): 705–721.

Hanlon, G. (1998). "Professionalism as Enterprise: Service Class Politics and the Redefinition of Professionalism," *Sociology* 32(1): 43–63.

Harvey, D. (2005). *A Brief History of Neoliberalism*. Oxford: Oxford University Press.

Haynes, K. (2012). "Body Beautiful? Gender, Identity and the Body in Professional Services Firms," *Gender, Work and Organization* 19(5): 489–507.

Heilman, M. E. (2001). "Description and Prescription: How Gender Stereotypes Prevent Women's Ascent Up the Organizational Ladder," *Journal of Social Issues* 57(4): 657–674.

Heilman, M. E., Block, C. J., Martell, R. F., and Simon, M. C. (1989). "Has Anything Changed? Current Characterizations of Men, Women, and Managers," *Journal of Applied Psychology* 74(6): 935–942.

Hochschild, A. R. (1983). *The Managed Heart: Commercialization of Human Feeling*. Berkeley, CA: University of California Press.

Hodgson, D. (2005). "Putting on a Professional Performance': Performativity, Subversion and Project Management," *Organization* 12(1): 51–68.

Hooks, B. (1989). *Talking Back: Thinking Feminist, Thinking Black*. Boston, MA: South End Press.

Jacobs, K. (2003). "Class Reproduction in Professional Recruitment: Examining the Accounting Profession," *Critical Perspectives on Accounting* 14(5): 569–596.

Jewel, L. (2008). "Bourdieu and American Legal Education: How Law Schools Reproduce Social Stratification and Class Hierarchy," *Buffalo Law Review* 56: 1155–1224.

Johnson, E. N., Lowe, D. J., and Reckers, P. M. (2008). "Alternative Work Arrangements and Perceived Career Success: Current Evidence from the Big Four Firms in the US," *Accounting, Organizations and Society* 33(1): 48–72.

Kandola, R. S. and Fullerton, J. (1998). *Diversity in Action: Managing the Mosaic*. London: CIPD Publishing.

Kanter, R. M. (1977). *Men and Women of the Corporation*. New York: Basic Books.

Kay, F. M. and Hagan, J. (2003). "Building Trust: Social Capital, Distributive Justice, and Loyalty to the Firm," *Law and Social Inquiry* 28(2): 483–519.

Kay, F. M., Hagan, J., and Parker, P. (2009). "Principals in Practice: The Importance of Mentorship in the Early Stages of Career Development," *Law and Policy* 31(1): 69–110.

Kim, S. N. (2004). "Racialized Gendering on the Accountancy Profession: Toward an Understanding of Chinese Women's Experiences in Accountancy in New Zealand," *Critical Perspectives on Accounting* 15(3): 400–428.

Kornberger, M., Carter, C., and Ross-Smith, A. (2010). "Changing Gender Domination in a Big Four Accounting Firm: Flexibility, Performance and Client Service in Practice," *Accounting, Organizations and Society* 35(8): 775–791.

Korzec, R. (1997). "Working on The Mommy-Track: Motherhood and Women Lawyers," *Hastings Women's Legal Journal* 8: 117–140.

Kosmala, K. and Herrbach, O. (2006). "The Ambivalence of Professional Identity: On Cynicism and Jouissance in Audit Firms," *Human Relations* 59(10): 1393–1428.

Kumra, S. (2014). "Gendered Constructions of Merit and Impression Management within Professional Service Firms," in *The Oxford Handbook of Gender in Organizations*, ed. S. Kumra, R. Simpson, and R. J. Burke. Oxford: Oxford University Press, 269–290.

Kumra, S. and Vinnicombe, S. (2008). "A Study of the Promotion to Partner Process in a Professional Services Firm: How Women are Disadvantaged," *British Journal of Management* 19(s1): S65–S74.

Kumra, S. and Vinnicombe, S. (2010). "Impressing for Success: A Gendered Analysis of a Key Social Capital Accumulation Strategy," *Gender, Work and Organization* 17(5): 521–546.

Kyriacou, O. and Johnston, R. (2006). "Accounting for (in)Visibilities: Resistance, Gender and Control," *Accountancy Business and the Public Interest* 5(2): 54–88.

Kyriacou, O. and Johnston, R. (2011). "Exploring Inclusion, Exclusion and Ethnicities in the Institutional Structures of UK Accountancy," *Equality, Diversity and Inclusion: An International Journal* 30(6): 482–497.

Larson, M. S. (1977). *The Rise of Professionalism: A Sociological Analysis*. Berkeley, CA: University of California Press.

Law Society (2014). "Diversity Profile of the Profession: A Short Synopsis," April. <http://www.lawsociety.org.uk/support-services/advice/articles/diversity-in-the-profession/> (accessed February 11, 2015).

Lawler, S. (2005). "Introduction: Class, Culture and Identity," *Sociology* 39(5): 797–806.

Leblebici, H. (2007). "Determining the Value of Legal Knowledge: Billing and Compensation Practices in Law Firms," in *Managing the Modern Law Firm*, ed. L. Empson. Oxford: Oxford University Press, 117–140.

Lewis, R. E. and Heckman, R. J. (2006). "Talent Management: A Critical Review," *Human Resource Management Review* 16(2): 139–154.

Liff, S. (1999). "Diversity and Equal Opportunities: Room for a Constructive Compromise?" *Human Resources Management Journal* 9(1): 65–75.

Liff, S. and Wajcman, J. (1996). " 'Sameness' and 'Difference' Revisited: Which Way Forward for Equal Opportunities Initiatives?" *Journal of Management Studies* 33(1): 79–94.

Litvin, D. R. (2006). "Making Space for a Better Case," in *Handbook of Workplace Diversity*, ed. A. M. Konrad and J. Pringle. London: Sage, 75–94.

Lorbiecki, A. and Jack, G. (2000). "Critical Turns in the Evolution of Diversity Management," *British Journal of Management* 11 (Special Issue): S17–S31.

Lorde, A. (1984). *Sister Outsider: Essays and Speeches by Audre Lorde.* Freedom, CA: Crossing.

McCracken, D. M. (1999). "Winning the Talent War for Women. Sometimes It Takes a Revolution," *Harvard Business Review* 78(6): 159–160.

Miles, R. and Brown, M. (1989). *Racism.* London: Routledge.

Moore, S., Mahler, R., and Ashton, R. (2011). *Trends in the Supply of Accounting Graduates and the Demand for Public Accounting Recruits.* Durham, NC: American Institute of Chartered Public Accountants.

Mossman, M. J. (1994). "Gender Equality, Family Law and Access to Justice," *International Journal of Law, Policy and the Family* 8(3): 357–373.

Muzio, D. and Kirkpatrick, I. (2011). "Introduction: Professions and Organizations: A Conceptual Framework," *Current Sociology* 59(4): 389–405.

Muzio, D. and Tomlinson, J. (2012). "Editorial: Researching Gender, Inclusion and Diversity in Contemporary Professions and Professional Organizations," *Gender, Work and Organization* 19(5): 455–466.

Muzio, D., Brock, D. M., and Suddaby, R. (2013). "Professions and Institutional Change: Towards an Institutionalist Sociology of the Professions," *Journal of Management Studies* 50(5): 699–721.

National Association for Law Placement (2015). Diversity Numbers at Law Firms Eke Out Small Gains. <http://www.nalp.org/lawfirmdiversity_feb2015> (accessed April 20 2015).

Neuberger Report (2007). *Entry to the Bar Working Party: Final Report.* London: Bar Council.

Nickson, D., Warhurst, C., Cullen, A., and Watt, A. (2003). "Bringing in the Excluded? Aesthetic Labor, Skills and Training in the 'New' Economy," *Journal of Education and Work* 16(2): 185–203.

Omi, M. and Winant, H. (1994). *Racial Formation in the United States: From the 1960s to the 1990s.* New York: Routledge.

Parkin, F. (1974). *The Social Analysis of Class Structure.* London: Tavistock Press.

Payne-Pikus, M., Hagan, J., and Nelson, R. (2010). "Experiencing Discrimination: Race and Retention in America's Largest Law Firms," *Law and Society Review* 44(3): 553–583.

Ramji, H. (2009). *Researching Race: Theory, Methods and Analysis.* Milton Keynes: Open University Press.

Ransome, P. (2007). "Conceptualizing Boundaries between 'Life' and 'Work'," *International Journal of Human Resource Management* 18(3): 374–386.

Reichman, N. J. and Sterling, J. S. (2004). "Sticky Floors, Broken Steps, and Concrete Ceilings in Legal Careers," *Texan Journal of Women and Law* 14: 26–76.

Rhode, D. L. (2011). "From Platitudes to Priorities: Diversity and Gender Equity in Law Firms," *Georgetown Journal of Legal Ethics* 24: 1041–1070.

Ring, S. (2011) "Freshfields Rolls Out Unconscious Bias Training in Diversity Push," *Legal Week*, April. <http://www.legalweek.com/legal-week/news/2040932/freshfields-rolls-unconscious-bias-training-diversity-push> (accessed March 17, 2014).

Rivera, L. A. (2012). "Hiring as Cultural Matching The Case of Elite Professional Service Firms," *American Sociological Review* 77(6): 999–1022.

Saks, M. (2012). "Defining a Profession: The Role of Knowledge and Expertise," *Professions and Professionalism* 2(1): 1–10.

Sander, R. H. (2006). "Racial Paradox of the Corporate Law Firm," *National Carolina Law Review* 84: 1755–1822.

Sauboorah, J. (2011). *Bar Barometer: Trends in the Profile of the Bar.* London: Bar Council.

Skeggs, B. (2004). *Class, Self, Culture.* London: Routledge.

Smithson, J., Lewis, S., Cooper, C., and Dyer, J. (2004). "Flexible Working and the Gender Pay Gap in the Accountancy Profession," *Work, Employment and Society* 18(1): 115–135.

Sommerlad, H. (2002). "Women Solicitors in a Fractured Profession: Intersections of Gender and Professionalism in England and Wales," *International Journal of the Legal Profession* 9(3): 213–234.

Sommerlad, H. (2007). "Researching and Theorizing the Processes of Professional Identity Formation," *Journal of Law and Society* 34(2): 190–217.

Sommerlad, H. (2011). "The Commercialization of Law and the Enterprising Legal Practitioner: Continuity and Change," *International Journal of the Legal Profession* 18(1–2): 73–108.

Sommerlad, H. (2012a). "The Professional Precariat: The Case of Law," keynote to Propel Inaugural Conference: Professions and Professional Learning in Turbulent Times: Emergent Practices and Transgressive Knowledges, Stirling University, May 11. <http://www.propel. stir.ac.uk/downloads/HilarySommerlad-FullPaper.pdf>.

Sommerlad, H. (2012b). "Minorities, Merit, and Misrecognition in the Globalized Profession," *Fordham Law Review* 80: 2481–2512.

Sommerlad, H. (2015). "The 'Social Magic' of Merit: Diversity, Equity and Inclusion in the English and Welsh Legal Profession," *Fordham Law Review* 83: 101–124.

Sommerlad, H. and Sanderson, P. (1998). *Gender, Choice, and Commitment: Women Solicitors in England and Wales and the Struggle for Equal Status*. Aldershot: Ashgate.

Sommerlad, H., Webley, L., Duff, L., Muzio, D., Tomlinson, J., and Parnham, R. (2010). *Diversity in the Legal Profession in England and Wales: A Qualitative Study of Barriers and Individual Choices*. London: Legal Service Board.

Song, S. J. and Liu, L. (2007). "Research on Gender Structure of Accounting Profession in China," *Journal of Modern Accounting & Auditing* 3(11): 7–13.

Spencer, A. and Podmore, D. (1982). "Women Lawyers in England: The Experience of Inequality," *Work and Occupations* 9(3): 337–357.

Spencer, A. and Podmore, D. B. (eds.) (1987). *In a Man's World: Essays on Women in Male-Dominated Professions*. London: Taylor & Francis.

Standing, G. (2011). *The Precariat: The New Dangerous Class*. London: Bloomsbury Academic.

Suddaby, R. and Viale, T. (2011). "Professionals and Field-Level Change: Institutional Work and the Professional Project," *Current Sociology* 59(4): 423–442.

Süss, S. and Kleiner, M. (2008). "Dissemination of Diversity Management in Germany: A New Institutionalist Approach," *European Management Journal* 26(1): 35–47.

Terjesen, S. and Singh, V. (2008). "Female Presence on Corporate Boards: A Multi-Country Study of Environmental Context," *Journal of Business Ethics* 83(1): 55–63.

Thornton, M. (1996). *Dissonance and Distrust: Women in the Legal Profession*. Oxford: Oxford University Press.

Thornton, M. (2002). *Romancing the Tomes: Popular Culture, Law and Feminism*. London: Cavendish Publishing.

Thornton, M. and Bagust, J. (2007). "The Gender Trap: Flexible Work in Corporate Legal Practice," *Osgoode Hall Law Journal* 45: 773–811.

Titley, G. and Lentin, A. (eds.) (2008). *The Politics of Diversity in Europe*. Strasbourg: Council of Europe Publishing.

Tomaskovic-Devey, D. (1993). *Gender and Racial Inequality at Work: The Sources and Consequences of Job Segregation (No. 27)*. New York: Cornell University Press.

Tomei, M. (2003). "Discrimination and Equality at Work: A Review of the Concepts," *International Labor Review* 142(4): 401–418.

Tomlinson, J., Muzio, D., Sommerlad, H., Webley, L., and Duff, L. (2013). "Structure, Agency and Career Strategies of White Women and Black and Minority Ethnic Individuals in the Legal Profession," *Human Relations* 66(2): 245–269.

Valentine, G. (2007). "Theorizing and Researching Intersectionality: A Challenge for Feminist Geography," *Professional Geographer* 59(1): 10–21.

Vertovec, S. (2012). "Diversity and the Social Imaginary," *European Journal of Sociology* 53(3): 287–312.

Walby, S. (1990). *Theorizing Patriarchy*. Oxford: Blackwell.

Wald, E. (2009). "Glass Ceilings and Dead Ends: Professional Ideologies, Gender Stereotypes, and the Future of Women Lawyers at Large Law Firms," *Fordham Law Review* 78: 2245–2288.

West, C. and Fenstermaker, S. (1995). "Doing Difference," *Gender and Society* 9(1): 8–37.

Wilkins, D. B. (2007). "Valuing Diversity: Some Cautionary Lessons from the American Experience," in *Managing the Modern Law Firm*, ed. L. Empson. Oxford: Oxford University Press, 37–63.

Wilkins, D. B. and Gulati, G. M. (1996). "Why are There So Few Black Lawyers in Corporate Law Firms? An Institutional Analysis," *California Law Review* 84: 501–614.

Witz, A. (1990). "Patriarchy and Professions: The Gendered Politics of Occupational Closure," *Sociology* 24(4): 675–690.

Witz, A. (1992). *Professions and Patriarchy*. London: Routledge.

Young, I. M. (1990). *Justice and the Politics of Difference*. Princeton, NJ: Princeton University Press.

CHAPTER 21

STRATEGIC HUMAN RESOURCE MANAGEMENT AND PERFORMANCE MANAGEMENT IN PROFESSIONAL SERVICE FIRMS

JUANI SWART, NINA KATRIN HANSEN, AND NICHOLAS KINNIE

21.1 INTRODUCTION

THE performance of Professional Service Firms (PSFs) can be defined in several ways: financial outputs, achievement of individual targets, new business growth, and, more recently, the value of the firm's reputational capital as expressed in their brand. These diverse perspectives on performance mean there is a plethora of approaches to performance management within the PSF. Our emphasis in this chapter is on performance management in the context of strategic Human Resource Management (HRM) practices which are often dominated by a focus on the individual, or human capital, to generate firm-level performance. However, contemporary research and practice highlights two important issues to consider in order understand the performance management and performance outputs of PSFs:

(i) the firm relies predominantly on knowledge, in particular deeply specialist know-how, to generate performance;

(ii) the ability to sustain superior performance is determined by more than just the management of the professional's knowledge and is reliant upon the complex interplay between relationships, processes, and technologies.

We therefore adopt a perspective that enables us to take into account the multi-dimensionality of knowledge resources (inputs) as well as a knowledge-centric view of firm performance (outputs).

All knowledge-intensive firms, and PSFs in particular, rely on the skills and experience of their employees to generate valuable output for clients and customers (Alvesson 2004; Lepak et al. 2011; Sherer 1995; Swart and Kinnie 2010). It is clear therefore that human capital plays a central role in determining the performance of the PSF and should consequently be the focus of the HRM practices. This view has strong support in the literature and there is an established body of research on the management of human capital (Lepak et al. 2006; Lopez et al. 2006; Youndt and Snell 2004; Youndt et al. 2004).

Most of the research has adopted the micro-perspective which emphasizes the use of individual HRM practices to manage human capital, i.e., jobs and individuals (Jackson et al. 2003; Lepak and Snell 2003, 2007; Minbaeva et al. 2009). For example, Davis-Blake and Hui (2003) studied the use of contractors while Pulakos et al. (2003) examined recruiting "stars." The impact of HR practices in knowledge transfer has examined training and development of staff (Kase et al. 2009) and the support for developing creative practitioners (Oldham 2003), while Lawler (2003) studied the impact of managing and rewarding human capital. Other research has looked at the implementation of these practices, such as Zupan and Kase (2007) who considered the role of line managers.

Research has also adopted a strategic HR perspective (Jackson et al. 2003: 424) and develops the earlier classic strategic research on the configurations of HR practices (Delery and Doty 1996; Hitt et al. 2001; Lepak and Snell 1999). Delery and Doty (1996) recognized the internal and market type configurations of knowledge assets, while Doorewaard and Meihuizen (2000) identified two knowledge-based strategies (efficiency and expertise) and then explained how HRM practices supported these. Lopez et al. (2006) identified the positive relationships between selective hiring, strategic development, and employee participation and organizational learning. More recently Kang et al. (2007) and Kang and Snell (2009) have proposed close ties between specific HRM practices and particular types of knowledge assets. In particular they drew attention to the need to consider social and organizational capital as well as human capital.

In this chapter, therefore, we draw on previous research to consider how HRM practices are used to manage human and social capital to generate superior performance. Initially we outline the research on human and social capital and then consider existing studies of HRM practices in PSFs. We then draw on our own research to outline two models of HRM practices which are used to manage human and social capital and discuss the link to innovation.[1] Finally, in a conclusion we consider the implications for further research.

21.2 HUMAN AND SOCIAL CAPITAL IN PROFESSIONAL SERVICE FIRMS

Given the knowledge intensity of the resource-base of PSFs we focus on *capital* which is not financial or physical but is knowledge-based and creates outcomes which have value in the marketplace. The interplay between the various forms of capital is necessary to create intellectual capital, defined here as outputs, which takes the form of products or services produced for clients, for example consulting or legal advice (Swart 2007).

Human capital theory (Becker 1964) typically uses economic logic to study individual decisions dealing with investments in productivity-enhancing skills and knowledge (schooling, training, firm-specific knowledge investment), career choices (decision to work, switching employment, labor mobility), and other work characteristics (wages, reservation wages, hours of work) (Gimeno et al. 1997). Lepak and Snell (1999) argue that human capital theory emphasizes the labor cost relative to the return on investment (i.e., future productivity) for developing employee skills and knowledge. Most definitions of human capital emphasize that it comprises knowledge, skills, intellect, and talent of individuals (Davenport 1999; Lepak and Snell 1999; Pennings et al. 1998). For example, Pennings et al. (1998: 426) state that the human capital of a PSF is the knowledge and skills of its professionals that can be used to produce professional services. In a similar vein Davenport (1999) argues that employees take a rent on time, energy, and intelligence invested in the form of compensation, development, and an enjoyable work environment.

Typically, and extremely relevant to the performance of the PSF, human capital is categorized according to its specificity (see Table 21.1) (Lepak and Snell 1999; Swart 2007; see also Mawdsley and Somaya, Chapter 10, this volume). Occupation-specific human capital is at the heart of the PSF as it is focused on the deep technical expertise in a particular profession whereas industry-specific human capital can be transferred between firms within a particular industry (Kang et al. 2012). Firm-specific human capital is valuable because the knowledge held by employees provides the firm with a unique product or service and cannot easily be transferred to its competitors (Kim and Gong 2009). Unique skills are often developed when employees engage in the solution of firm-specific problems or when unique operating procedures are followed. This method of skill development is also widely known as a strategy to retain key knowledge workers by erecting mobility barriers (Coff 1997; Swart and Kinnie 2003).

Individuals use not only their own knowledge and skills but also rely on vibrant, creative, and trusting relationships (social capital) in order to produce professional services (Wright et al. 2001). We define social capital as the value created by leveraging knowledge that is embedded within social networks and interrelationships (Leana and van Buren 1999; Nahapiet and Ghoshal 1998; Taylor 2007). The current research on social capital is dominated by a *within-firm* unit of analysis which includes the individual level, e.g., advancing one's own career or educational opportunities (Burt 1992), the business-unit

Table 21.1 Individual and collective knowledge resources: forms of capital

Knowledge types and measures	Categorization	Characteristic
Human capital	Occupation-/profession-specific	Developed through professional qualifications
		Individual investment
		Transferable within professions
	Industry-specific	Developed through the application of a professional skill within a particular industry or client
		Individual and organizational investment
		Transferable within a particular industry across PSFs
	Firm-specific	Developed through working within firm-focused processes and systems
		Firm (PSF) investment
		Transferable only within the firm across client projects
Social capital	Entrepreneurial	Loosely connected networks where the actors rely on direct contact and detailed knowledge of one another to build trust
	Cooperative	Tightly coupled, dense networks and trust that is developed via institutional norms

level (Snell 2002), and the organizational level (Nahapiet and Ghoshal 1998). In addition to professional work that takes place within organizations professionals also continually work across the firm boundaries, with clients and collaborators such as contract workers and associates, to produce firm-level outputs. The unit of analysis therefore needs to be extended beyond the boundaries of the firm to include external social capital which includes the client/customer and network level relationships (Pennings et al. 1998).

The nature of the social capital varies according to the *type of network* within which the relationships are situated and the subsequent *trust* associated with these relationships (Youndt and Snell 2004). In the literature on social capital in PSFs (Kang and Snell 2009; Kang et al. 2012) two main types of relationships have been identified, i.e., *entrepreneurial* and *cooperative* (see Table 21.1). Entrepreneurial social capital is based on loosely connected networks where the actors rely on direct contact and detailed knowledge of one another to build trust. Cooperative social capital involves tightly coupled, dense networks and trust that is developed via institutional norms.

These forms of social capital play a very important role in the performance of the PSF. Firstly, their main function is to provide access to resources (Nahapiet and Ghoshal

1998). In other words, it is seen as the medium through which other "desired" resources can be made available. In the PSF the individual will be able to access prior experience, know-how, and often mentoring, which develops their professional skills, through his/her relationships.

Secondly, social capital is regarded as a means of enforcing norms of behavior among individuals or corporate actors (Walker et al. 1997) and therefore builds identity (Alvesson 2004; Alvesson and Empson 2008; Empson 2001) or a "sense of belonging." The trust generated by social capital also acts as an important enabler of knowledge sharing (Wilkesmann 2009) which is central to the generation of performance outputs.

Thirdly, social capital has been associated with the generation of commitment (Postmes et al. 2001). As professionals develop strong trusting relationships with clients, colleagues, and other network partners, they become more committed to that relevant party. This may, however, present a challenge for the PSF given that the various agents, i.e., the client, the firm, the team, and the profession, may compete for the commitment of the individual (Becker 2009; Kinnie and Swart 2012; Swart and Kinnie 2013; Vandenberghe and Bentein 2009). Importantly, recent research also establishes a clear link between commitment and performance-generating behaviors, often described as discretionary behaviors (Bentein et al. 2002).

In summary, previous research indicates that in order to sustain successful performance at the level of the firm, PSFs focus on the management of human capital; i.e., how it recruits, develops, and retains its employees as well as social relationships with clients and other network partners. There is, however, relatively little empirical research into the ways in which HRM practices can enable the management of both human and social capital (Kang and Snell 2009; Kang et al. 2007; Lopez et al. 2006) in order to generate superior performance. In the section that follows we review the previous research on strategic HRM systems in PSFs.

21.3 STRATEGIC HRM PRACTICES IN PSFs

In the strategic human resource management literature, research on HRM systems has a long-standing tradition (e.g., Delery and Doty 1996; Huselid 1995; Lepak and Snell 1999, 2002; Lepak et al. 2006; for an overview see Alewell and Hansen 2012). Following a configurational approach (e.g., Baron and Kreps 1999; Youndt et al. 2004), most authors have focused on issues of internal fit and the coherent configuration of HR practices in HRM systems. From this "holistic" perspective, the internally aligned and synergistic HRM systems are seen as the source of a firm's sustained competitive advantage. Consistent bundles of HRM practices are thereby considered to exhibit nonlinear synergistic effects and higher-order interactions (Delery and Doty 1996: 808). Therefore, the firm-specific combination of complementary and interdependent HR practices is suggested to constitute a strategic resource that meets the necessary conditions stated by Barney (1991) (see also Wright et al. 2001).

Table 21.2 Human resource management practices in Professional Service Firms

HR practices	Expertise-oriented	Efficiency-oriented
PSF type	Traditional	Neo-classic
Resourcing	Authenticity	Junior orientated
	Senior orientated	
Training and development	Coaching and mentoring	Firm-specific training
	General training	On-the-job training
Performance management	Grow to go	Senior retention
Reward	Profession specific, e.g., time and billing	Firm-specific targets

Following Doorewaard and Meihuizen (2000), two central strategic HRM systems can be identified in the context of PSFs: an efficiency- and an expertise-oriented HRM system which resemble the ideal or archetypes of internal labor markets and high-commitment work systems with PSF-specific features (see Table 21.2) (Hansen and Alewell 2013). Overall, most PSFs will exhibit an HR architecture as a combination of an efficiency and an expertise orientation. However, on the level of the business unit or the HRM subsystem, PSFs may lean towards one or the other archetype and one tendency may dominate (Doorewaard and Meihuizen 2000; Hansen and Alewell 2013). In the following section we will outline how the main HR practice areas are differently shaped in efficiency- and expertise-oriented PSFs.

21.3.1 Resourcing in Efficiency- and Expertise-Oriented PSFs

PSFs that rely on an efficiency-orientated HRM system are based on an HR approach of a bureaucratic regulation of their employees. It is characterized by a pyramid structure that resembles Maister's experience-based "gray hair" organization model (Maister 1993). The strategic focus of efficiency-oriented PSFs lies on organizationally controlled resources, ready-made solutions, and the delivery of high-quality but standard products. In efficiency-oriented organizations professionals are expected to express their loyalty to the firm by performing in accordance with the organizational standard procedures and intervention techniques and to solve unexpected client problems in terms of established concepts (Doorewaard and Meihuizen 2000). On the basis of ingrained patterns of behavior and interdependence, this enables an efficient coordination within the PSFs and the control of the employees' responses to a wide range of tasks and problems (Kang and Snell 2009).

The focus lies on the constitution and maintenance of a strong organizational reputation and an organizational culture of group autonomy. The production of professional services is based on relatively stable functional teams that perform specialized tasks in different client organizations. This work organization leads to cooperative internal relationships with strong social ties and facilitates the identification and exchange of the professionals' job-related in-depth knowledge (Kang and Snell 2009; Kang et al. 2007).

In efficiency-oriented PSFs the management of the personnel flow is based on a classic pyramid structure with a greater number of junior professionals on the bottom and a smaller group of senior professionals at the top of the hierarchy. Selective and formal recruiting practices (e.g., standardized selection and assessment tests) and an intensive initial screening ensure an individual–organization fit and a strong identification with the firm. The focus of the recruiting practices lies on junior professionals such as high-potential graduate students who can be quickly trained in the firm's standardized procedures (Doorewaard and Meihuizen 2000). The aim is to acquaint and retain professionals with firm-specific skills and knowledge that correspond to the firm's idiosyncratic production model. Due to the development of firm-specific skills, positions in the firm's internal labor market are more attractive for the professionals and firms offer "senior plus jobs" and alternative positions to the traditional partnership (Doorewaard and Meihuizen 2000; Malhotra et al. 2010; Smets et al. 2012).

In contrast, PSFs that have implemented an expertise-oriented HRM system rely on a HR approach of mobilizing their employees and on a corresponding "diamond" structure that can be associated to Maister's "brains" organizational model (Maister 1993). The focus lies on individually controlled resources and the professionals' personal client relationships. Although an expertise organization's corporate culture is an important selling point in the labor market as well as in the output market, professionals are encouraged to develop a significant personal reputation and an individual approach in dealing with new and unfamiliar client problems (Doorewaard and Meihuizen 2000).

Based on a flat hierarchy, a small group of junior professionals supports a relatively large group of senior professionals. In performing their jobs and tasks in flexible project teams, professionals have a high degree of individual autonomy to deliver customized products for their clients. The professionals are motivated by a stimulating working atmosphere and challenging job characteristics that bind them towards the organization. The organizational policy is not to define any formal rules or procedures which serve the professionals' preference for autonomy thereby fostering individual freedom of decision-making and entrepreneurial attitudes (Dooreward and Meihuizen 2000). So the professionals are able to develop spontaneous interactions (Swart and Kinnie 2010) that facilitate fast cycles of knowledge exchange and transfer based on simple and dense networks (Xiao and Tsui 2007).

Recruiting practices in expertise PSFs in the form of formal and informal talent assessment, e.g., creativity tests or personal references, are thereby more senior-oriented than in efficiency-oriented PSFs. Based on explicit networking strategies, the aim is to win the best experienced professionals from clients or small independent PSFs operating in different industries and sectors.

21.3.2 Training and Development in Efficiency- and Expertise-Oriented PSFs

Training and development practices in efficiency-oriented PSFs are based on firm-specific training. Employees learn the established procedures and standards on the basis of on-the-job training and mentoring as well as additional firm-specific formal training courses to accomplish the required level of efficiency and information on specific professional services. The young professionals develop competencies that allow an outstanding performance in the application of leading standard procedures to familiar client problems. Professionals in efficiency-oriented PSFs are specialists in a certain function and exhibit a combination of expert knowledge, accuracy, and craftsmanship which enables them to give their clients in-depth customized advice in specialized fields (Doorewaard and Meihuizen 2000).

The result is a job- and task-focused development of the professionals' specific human capital and the improvement and deepening of existing organizational knowledge stocks. On the basis of an "exploitative" learning mode (Kang and Snell 2009; March 1991), knowledge development focuses on the efficient reproduction, implementation, and successful execution of approved processes and established routines which allow efficiency-oriented PSFs to perform two specific exploitative learning modes: a short-term refinement and adaptation of existing solutions as well as a long-term application of expert solutions (Swart and Kinnie 2010).

In contrast, the training and development practices in expertise-oriented HRM systems are primarily based on general training programs such as regular internal "eye-opener courses" which are complemented by individual coaching and mentoring of juniors by senior professionals. Professionals are thereby introduced to a wide range of tasks and assignments so that they are broadly trained in their specific professional domain. This enables the professionals to develop a "helicopter view" and become creative generalists who constantly explore new areas of knowledge. The aim is to continuously widen and deepen the professionals' knowledge base in order to meet current and changing market demands and to deliver tailor-made solutions for extraordinary client problems. On the basis of a mutual learning process, on the one hand the junior professionals learn the "tricks of the trade" from their senior mentors. On the other hand, the senior professionals also benefit from the mentoring relationship due to an exchange of fresh ideas and different experiences and perspectives (Doorewaard and Meihuizen 2000).

The expertise-oriented HRM system facilitates the development of general human capital on the basis of a broad and generalized collective search for novel ideas and cutting-edge professional knowledge. This enables a rapid absorption of new knowledge into existing processes and a proactive approach to find customized solutions for unfamiliar client problems and new environmental challenges (Kang and Snell 2009; Swart and Kinnie 2010). The result is an "exploratory" learning mode which constitutes organizational flexibility and innovation capability.

21.3.3 Performance and Reward Systems in Efficiency- and Expertise-Oriented PSFs

As efficiency-oriented PSFs rely on the specific knowledge of their professionals, the HRM systems offer senior retention to preserve valuable expert knowledge and experience in specific areas of practice (Doorewaard and Meihuizen 2000; Malhotra et al. 2010; Sherer and Lee 2002; Smets et al. 2012). Senior alternative positions to the traditional partner track may be created for associates who do not make it to the partner level (Sherer and Lee 2002) but have shown a high professional performance which has a high value to the firm. From an option-based theoretical perspective, this is a rational decision of the employer: a professional's specific human capital may have a high project value so it is the employer's aim to keep the experienced professionals who provide valued professional services. However, due to the generation of only modest revenues and the professional's related low option value—his or her potential to generate growth in client relationships—he or she is not going to be offered a partner position in the firm (Malos and Campion 1995). This extension and flexibilization of the original Cravath model has been a successful adaption of existing professional promotion and career models to new market and institutional pressures while retaining the benefits of the traditional up-or-out tournament (Malhotra et al. 2010; Sherer and Lee 2002).

The performance management system is closely linked to the development of firm-specific knowledge and skills and the professionals' contribution to collective values, standard procedures, cooperative knowledge sharing, and the generation of new business opportunities. The reward system is based on firm-specific target achievements, firm- and group-wide incentives and tenure-based rewards. Several variations of the traditional "lock-step" compensation model are conceivable.

In contrast, expertise-oriented PSFs do not rely on long-term employment relationships with a senior retention model (Doorewaard and Meihuizen 2000). However, the focus lies on a strict "grow or go" principle also known as the traditional "up-or-out" career model, which only leaves room for top expertise and plays a crucial role in institutionalizing performance standards (Malhotra et al. 2010; Malos and Campion 1995, 2000; Morris and Pinnington 1998; Sherer and Lee 2002; Smets et al. 2012). In particular, the implemented up-or-out principle in expertise-oriented PSFs addresses the often discussed "cat-herding problem" in PSFs. As an alternative incentive mechanism, the up-or-out principle serves as an effective monitoring device to control the performance and productiveness of the professionals and to ensure their extraordinary performance and superior motivation. In a professional context, where the relationship between knowledge-based inputs and outputs are complex and the professionals' effort, as well as the quality of the professional services, is hard to measure, this monitoring and motivation mechanism is of central importance (Sherer and Lee 2002; von Nordenflycht 2010).

The corresponding individually focused reward system is profession-specific and often based on time and billing targets as a central incentive device (Sherer 1995; Smets et al. 2012). The reward system in the efficiency-oriented HRM system will have more aspects of a tournament-based, "eat what you kill" system than within the efficiency-oriented HRM system. The individuals' focus will lie on the maximization of billable hours and the generation of new business opportunities to increase their option value and to reach the desired partner level.

We have thus far identified the key HRM practices which are adopted in different types of PSFs. Traditional PSFs are associated with the expertise-oriented system and "neo"-PSFs (von Nordenflycht 2010) with the efficiency-oriented system. In the next section we develop this approach by adopting a knowledge-based perspective on performance. In particular we focus on how strategic HRM practices are used to manage human and social capital both inside and outside the firm.

21.4 PROMINENT HRM MODELS IN PROFESSIONAL SERVICE FIRMS: EVIDENCE FROM PRACTICE

The knowledge-based perspective to performance emphasizes the delivery of superior products and services and the subsequent ability of the firm to appropriate value from the rents generated by the intellectual capital outputs (Coff 1997). This perspective allows us to draw on empirical research, to identify two prominent HRM models within PSFs used for managing human and social capital: *centripetal* and *centrifugal* (see Table 21.3).

In the *centripetal* model the PSF seeks to retain its valuable human capital by adopting a values-driven approach to managing performance, and therefore carefully manages the permeability of the boundary between the firm and the client. The focal point for the HRM practices is therefore *within* the boundaries of the firm (Youndt et al. 2004). The aim of the PSF is to develop firm-specific human capital by encouraging employees to adopt PSF-centric methodologies and practices. The professionals' experience may therefore become less transportable to other firms as it is more intertwined with the processes and practices of the particular PSF. This in turn will enable the firm to retain its human capital, due to the mobility barriers that are erected via the firm-specificity of the skills developed. Alongside the practices that are used to develop firm-specific skills, discussed below, the firm also develops its employees through strong socialization practices driven by the values of the firm, and it buffers more junior members of staff from over-demanding clients in the network (Swart and Kinnie 2014). The main client contact is therefore between the more senior levels of the PSF and the client. Given the way in which client relationships are managed the centripetal model is associated with cooperative internal social capital and entrepreneurial external social capital (client relationships). The PSF emphasizes organizational culture and values to develop firm-specific know-how and tacit routines. This enables the PSF to further embed its

Table 21.3 Human resource management models

Centripetal HRM model

	Resourcing	T&D	Pay and reward
Human capital: firm-specific	Values-driven Broad job designs Rotation of roles between projects	Firm-specific skills	Profession-focused
Social capital: Cooperative internal Entrepreneurial external	Fluid project-team boundaries Multiplicity of team membership	T-shaped professionals Informal knowledge-sharing events	Balance score-card: individual and social is important Objectives set with limited involvement from client Longer term organization (rather than just individual) objectives are set

Centrifugal HRM model

	Resourcing	T&D	Pay and reward
Human capital: client-specific	Professional expertise, technical skill and abilities which can immediately be applied to superior client services	Profession and industry-related	Profession or industry and client tend to use target-based reward systems Individual Competitive
Social capital: Entrepreneurial internal Cooperative external	Client contact at all levels in client project team Work with limited number of client teams Limited rotation between teams	Client involved in development processes Limited internal mentoring that is not client/industry-specific	Client becomes involved in objective setting Client influence on tournament-based reward system

collective knowledge in the fabric of the organization. In addition, and importantly for the renewal of the knowledge base in the firm, it allows for creativity where newer members of staff can also influence how things are done in the organization.

In the second, *centrifugal* model, the PSF seeks to develop human capital that is client- and industry-specific and the HRM practices are more client-focused. The PSF becomes almost client dominated. For example, a law firm may recruit an employment lawyer who specializes in the energy sector. The professionals would also often see themselves as having a more direct relationship with their clients. The combination of the type of professional knowledge and how this impacts on the client relationship results in the much more fluid boundaries between the PSF and the client. These close client relationships, together with the loosely connected team or department relationships, lead to entrepreneurial internal and cooperative external social capital.

We have outlined the purpose of each of the HRM models. In the section that follows we adopt a well-known categorization system (Lepak and Snell 2003) to discuss the two prominent HRM models in PSFs, i.e., we group the HRM practices into:

(i) resourcing (i.e., job design, recruitment and selection, as well as internal resourcing of client project teams);

(ii) development (i.e., formal training, as well as informal learning and knowledge sharing;

(iii) performance and reward (i.e., the performance management system and reward structures).

21.4.1 Centripetal/Firm-Centered Human Resource Management Practices

In order to generate firm-specific human capital, *resourcing* is values-driven and focused on the professional's potential as well as previous expertise and credentials. This ensures a fit between the professional skill and the firm-specific approach to, for example, delivering consulting solutions. The combination of broad job designs and selection criteria which emphasize future development (Malos and Campion 1995) also encourages experimentation, e.g., moving outside one's domain knowledge (Kang et al. 2012), and in turn can stimulate innovation. This approach is also reflected in the way in which client project teams are resourced. Roles in these teams are typically designed to encourage rotation between client teams, thereby supporting cooperation between professional teams and support staff and the development of dense organizational rather than team-based networks.

The focus on organizational values during the resourcing process, on the one hand, and the penumbrated professional, team, and client boundaries, on the other, enable the firm to anchor the professional's commitment to the firm. This in turn provides an infrastructure for employees to share knowledge between teams, thereby generating cooperative internal social capital (Swart et al. 2013). In this HRM model internal social capital is often seen as *the* most important criterion for staff allocation to teams. The values-driven resourcing model has a direct impact upon external social capital insofar as the client does not have a direct influence on which professionals will be working on their client accounts. Hence, resourcing practices are more firm- than client-focused. Some professionals find this attractive as it provides them with an opportunity to develop flexible skills across a variety of client work. This internal fluidity, combined with client contact at more senior levels in the PSF, results in more loosely connected relationship networks between the PSF and the client, which supports the development of entrepreneurial external social capital.

The *development practices* in this model are aimed at honing firm-specific skills. It is therefore important not to lock experience into professional silos but to ensure the development of T-shaped professionals (Swart and Harvey 2011) who maintain both generalist and architectural knowledge (Kang et al. 2012) as well as specific domain knowledge, such as consulting. In this context mentoring is often used as a powerful vehicle to convey firm-specific practices, which connect various professions to one another. The mentoring or apprenticeship approach also embeds occupation- or profession-specific tacit know-how within the firm. In practice, this means that the professional is part of a client project team, a community of practice, and has access to a dedicated mentoring or coaching relationship. The multiplicity of team membership has a direct impact on cooperative internal social capital. In this model it is, for example, common practice to implement formal training programs that are attended by employees from different parts of the business with the aim of developing strong organization-wide relational networks.

Another prominent development practice is the use of informal knowledge-sharing events such as brown-bag lunches, where professionals openly discuss client experiences and professional skill development. This builds institutional trust through the specific cross-specialist-boundary processes. These processes seek to build organizational networks which create the right environment to build firm-specific human capital and cooperative internal social capital. In addition the development model is aligned with the way in which the PSF interacts with its clients. Given that client contact is at the more senior levels of the firm, advanced career professionals have access to client relationship management training, which is often housed internally in the firm, to promote firm-specific engagement processes with the client. The way in which training and development impacts on the boundaries and relationships between the PSF and the client ensures that valuable but loosely connected client relationships are developed.

Performance management and reward systems play a key role in the development of human capital and give very powerful messages on what is valued, which in turn impacts on both internal and external social capital (Swart 2007). In the centripetal model the PSF continues to focus on firm-specific human capital by linking the performance management systems to the culture and values of the firm. This is often done via a scorecard, or multiple objectives, approach which not only emphasizes the achievement of performance objectives but also assesses the way in which these objectives are achieved, i.e., the firm-specificity of the behavior. The balanced-scorecard approach uses broadly defined criteria and collects data from a variety of sources. The collective aspects of performance are also encouraged via the performance management system by setting client team as well departmental objectives. This encourages the professional to engage in discretionary behavior and to act beyond the confines of their professional or client boundary. Some PSFs will, for example, have explicit performance objectives that relate to knowledge sharing and new business development. All of which encourages the formation of cooperative internal social capital. These types of performance objectives also tend to encourage creativity and experimentation, or put differently, exploratory learning (Kang and Snell 2009: 81). The capability of the firm takes preference over "standard individual objectives" which in turn enables the firm to respond flexibly within a changing market. The performance management system is also used to influence the boundary between the PSF and the client. In particular, firm-specific performance objectives are set with limited involvement from the client. These objectives are carefully crafted by senior staff to meet client expectations; however, the client will seldom dictate these objectives given the professional respect that is entrusted with the firm.

Reward structures are aligned with the focus of the performance management system insofar as their emphasis is on the PSF's values, collective behavior, and long-term involvement in the firm-specific processes. This behavior is frequently encouraged by firm-wide incentives rather than individually driven targets. A further prominent method of reward adopted in the centripetal model is that of tenure-based pay structures which reward service in and contribution to the firm rather than short-term individual performance. This will appeal to early career employees who are prepared to build up experience and eventually gain promotion to partner (Malos and Campion 1995). The emphasis on behaving in a way that is of benefit to both the individual and the firm, for example by engaging in discretionary behaviors such as knowledge sharing, encourages the development of the rich firm-wide networks that are so characteristic of cooperative internal social capital.

These reward structures also contribute to informal aspects of organizational life. Research indicates that professionals who believe that the investment of their valuable, income-generating time in their team and firm will be rewarded, feel a sense of belonging and identification with the firm (Postmes et al. 2001). They will therefore be more likely to display organizational commitment, for example by putting in extra effort contributing to firm-relevant processes such as new business development. This also strengthens the institutionally based trust which is so central to cooperative internal social capital. This approach is in sharp contrast with the more traditional industry practice which often forces competition between professionals for client contacts which may strengthen their individual power base within the firm.

21.4.2 Centrifugal/Client-Centered Human Resource Management Practices

In this model the PSF adopts *resourcing practices* which are client-focused and the emphasis is on professional expertise and abilities which can immediately be applied to superior client services. This is evidenced by in-depth prior experience, often in a narrowly defined profession, for example as a particular branch of a discipline such as naval engineering. In addition, the resourcing process seeks to attract professionals with industry- or client-specific knowledge. This is because the very nature of the development of professional expertise means that profession-specific human capital becomes intertwined with industry and client knowledge. The profession- and client-specific approach to resourcing also means that staff cannot easily be rotated between client project teams because the know-how becomes so client-specific. The blending of these factors may ultimately result in the loss of the employee as s/he becomes very valuable to the client and may begin to identify more with the client than the employing organization.

The emphasis on explicit knowledge, evident in skills often governed by professional bodies (Kirkpatrick et al. 2011) during the recruitment process, does not contribute to the development of firm-specific procedures. This has a direct impact on the network of relationships in the firm, which are associated with looser intra-firm networks based on professional respect, i.e., entrepreneurial internal social capital (Kang and Snell 2009). It is also because of the specialized nature of the knowledge that the professional can interact directly with the client which results in strong, dense networks and professionally driven values (Swart and Kinnie 2010).

The firm's skill base of deep and narrow expertise impacts on the way in which client projects are resourced. Here it is often the case that employees will work with a limited number of clients in a specific industry, thereby reducing the capability to rotate between client work. There is also an increasing trend to adopt this model between PSFs where professionals with complementary skill sets, such as an aerodynamicist and a transonic engineer, will work together on large Integrated Project Teams (IPTs) for very long periods of time, often spanning decades. Other examples are found in consulting (Nikolova et al. 2009) and the National Health Service (Marchington et al. 2011). The resourcing model is driven by what the professional can offer to the wider client project needs (Swart and Kinnie 2014). Given that the IPT is often resourced and housed at a location that is physically removed from the organization there is a further incentive for the professionals to develop cooperative client relationships which goes hand-in-hand with more fluid within-firm relationships, i.e., entrepreneurial internal social capital.

The notion of resourcing in accordance with profession-specific and industry-related standards is also associated with more formal organizational systems which need to adhere to these governing standards. As professionals draw on their specialized experience they also develop guidelines—heuristics which codify and represent their tacit knowledge. There is also a need to develop this more formal aspect of organizational processes as it acts as an infrastructure which knits the formal and professional practices in the organization together. That is to say, if the boundaries between the firm and the client become very permeable and knowledge is bound up in client- and industry-specific processes then it becomes essential to hold the explicit components, such as operating procedures and best practices, within the firm via organizational structures, systems, databases, manuals, and patents.

The *training and development practices* in this model are profession- and industry-related and tend to be formalized and governed by professional bodies. In cases where informal development is adopted via mentoring schemes, for example, the mentor will shape the profession-specific tacit know-how of the young professional. The very nature of the professional skill means that this has to be done in the client- or industry-specific context, thereby strengthening the client-specific human capital. There are very limited opportunities to develop firm-specific human capital precisely due to the strong influence of professional standards. The necessity to adopt a more formalized and profession-targeted approach to development has an impact on the capability of the firm to generate learning across boundaries. PSFs tend to structure their development into communities of practice that share a similar knowledge base. For example, marine biologists would learn from one another as they conducted research together and likewise naval engineers may not work closely with structural engineers. This has an impact on relationships between vocational/professional groups insofar as groups with heterogeneous knowledge become loosely connected, i.e., they develop entrepreneurial internal social capital. Conversely the professional knowledge development becomes intertwined with client-specific needs and processes, thereby creating greater homogeneity of knowledge outside the firm, which strengthens the cooperative external social capital.

There is also a clear link between the development system adopted in this model and the establishment of more formal organizational processes. In law firms some practice groups, for example employment law, rely on professional, industry-specific knowledge which tends to be communicated by formal training programs and stored in data management systems. In this context, professional knowledge is "bought" rather than "made" and the emphasis is on using this knowledge effectively within streamlined organizational systems.

PSFs that link their *performance and reward systems* to the profession or industry and client tend to use target-based reward systems (Sherer 1995). Many firms following this model set utilization targets for their employees as part of the performance management system. In law firms this is typically referred to as green (billable) time and red (non-billable) time, which can be closely monitored in fractions of an hour. The professional knowledge that is used to meet these targets tends to be similar across the profession.

The target-based systems are individually focused and can encourage competition amongst professionals, for example, to generate new business or maximize billable time. This can subsequently dilute the social cohesion within the firm and can lead to more loosely connected networks, i.e., entrepreneurial internal social capital where the "rainmakers" are respected and admired (Maister 1993) at the cost of developing strong internal social networks. The very nature of the client relationship in this context impacts on the performance objectives in the firm (see Broschak, Chapter 14, this volume). The client will often be directly involved in the setting of performance standards and will monitor outputs (i.e., the standard of professional products and services) very closely. This is linked to the high fee-rates which can be charged and the need of the client to see a visible impact in their firms, measured for example in increased revenues, cost savings, or improved efficiencies. The close interrelationship between the client's performance expectations and the deliverables set by the firm in the performance management system supports the development of strong client relationships.

This holds a strategic challenge for the PSF as the employee may engage in extra role behaviors that benefit the client at the expense of the firm; they may begin to identify closely with the client and become focused on achieving their individual client-performance objectives in order to advance their career within the firm. For example, an emphasis on individual results and billable hours may encourage employees to feel more attached to their profession and their client than their firm. This creates an incentive to hoard rather than share knowledge because it enhances their individual value (Hislop 2009). To the extent that knowledge is shared it is usually on the basis of some kind of reward being received in return rather than some general good (Zagenczyk and Murrell 2009).

The target-based approach also strengthens mechanistic organizational processes by highlighting the formalized and individually focused performance objectives. The achievement of the target can therefore become the central focus for the professional as they seek to develop their careers. It becomes the currency with which they trade for promotion, be that internally or externally with other competitors who will have similar professionally focused promotion systems.

Rewards that are based on the achievement of the client- and profession-driven targets are also therefore role-based. As with the performance management system these tend to recognize the achievement of individual rather than group-based targets. These tournament-based pay structures encourage professionals, typically at the mid and senior career stages, to compete for professional recognition and financial rewards which may take the form of becoming a partner, earning a higher salary or bonuses. Highly experienced lawyers, for example, are able to demonstrate both their past value, through well-recognized measures such as annual billings, and their potential for future earnings, through their clients and the fee income they bring with them. Once established, the partner can move between firms, demanding high rewards.

The client will also influence the tournament-based reward system in both direct and indirect ways. Direct impact is linked to the fee which the client pays for the achievement of project-specific objectives and which, once appropriated by the firm, can be reflected in the employee's reward. Indirect impact of the client can also be seen where there is a drive to work with a client on a retainer basis. This results from long-term, strong, trusting client relationships.

The tournament-based reward structures are also used to strengthen more formal HRM practices. This can be reflected in the career progression system within the PSF which is aligned with the salary bands within the firm. There is typically a high dispersion between the highest and lowest paid employees. This in turn manages the motivational contract (Swart and Kinnie 2014) as younger career professionals admire successful, higher earning, and well-respected senior professionals and seek to gain success or partnership within a given firm. The characteristic steep hierarchical differentials are also designed to attract talented performers to join, stay, and perform well within the firm.

21.5 HRM Models and Performance Outputs: An Innovation Perspective

We define the performance of PSFs in terms of the ability to generate innovative products and services (Kimberly and Evanisko 1981) which hold value in the market. The focus is on the ability of the firm to appropriate value from the innovative outputs generated, i.e., products sold or professional services delivered. In the processes of generating innovative performance outputs the firm will draw on human and social capital as discussed in the first section of this chapter. Following the logic of the chapter, the PSF would therefore draw predominantly on either the centripetal or the centrifugal HRM models to attract, develop, and strengthen its knowledge resource-base. It would be naïve to assume that the PSF will adopt only one of these HRM models. In practice the achievement of high performance will result from the ability of the firm to adopt the most appropriate HRM model while managing the innovation challenges that it may present.

The centripetal model emphasizes firm-specificity: strong intra-organizational relationships and more loosely connected inter-firm networks. This has a direct impact on the capability of the firm to innovate. We identify three key challenges. Firstly, the firm may develop highly innovative outputs but because of its loosely connected external networks, these innovations may not be in high demand in the client market. Secondly, the PSF may become overly focused on the refinement of its existing skill base. This can clearly be seen in advertising agencies which specialize in developing creative and expensive campaigns based around TV commercials, only to find that clients are not willing to pay a premium price for these outputs because they want more targeted multiple platform digital solutions to market their products and services. The third challenge pertains to the way in which the PSF manages the boundary between the firm and the client; i.e., client contact is mainly at senior levels and often driven by client relationship experts rather than technical experts. It is because of this structure that the client relationship expert needs to translate the innovation demands of the client to the technical/professional skill base in the PSF. This presents several "translation traps" as the client contact aims to translate market demands into technical innovation specifications.

The central mechanisms which manage innovation challenges in the centripetal model include:

(i) the development of connective structures between the PSF and the client market; and

(ii) the implementation of processes which support the translation of innovation demands into professional/technical solutions.

In the context of the centripetal HRM model the PSF would also need to ensure that their innovative outputs are connected to the client market. This is most easily achieved by working within networks of collaborators and competitors where innovative products and services can be co-developed, tested, and shaped to ensure value appropriation.

The centrifugal HRM model, which is characterized by a client-focused development of human capital and densely connected inter-firm networks—and consequently more loosely structured intra-firm networks—also holds very real challenges for the production of innovative outputs. Firstly, the professional works directly with the client, as opposed to solely through a client engagement manager, which results in fluid boundaries between the PSF and the client. This may result in radical innovations that are so client-specific that they are not able to be integrated and leveraged within the PSF for other client services. The challenge is therefore to establish a communicative infrastructure that will connect client-specific innovation with firm-specific process.

PSFs use a variety of practices to support the integration of innovative services and products and ultimately enable high performance outputs. The first of these is linked to reward structures in the form of showcasing award-winning innovations. It is by encouraging the start of intra-firm projects through the creation of awareness of client-specific innovations that intra-firm interest is sparked, knowledge sharing facilitated, and adaptations of specific innovations to diverse client markets encouraged. For example, a marketing agency developed advanced satellite tracking systems for a fast food outlet to ensure that their customers were able to order and receive goods while being remote—for example, at a music festival. The output and results of this innovation were then shared internally which enabled re-engineering and adaptation to other client segments. Secondly, the firm can balance the dominant client focus with firm-specific processes such as membership of intra-firm project teams, which create a sense of belonging and contribute to the success of the firm. In this context a research organization involved chemists in the development of its performance appraisal system, thereby strengthening the organizational capital and ensuring its successful implementation.

A further challenge that is inherent in the centrifugal model is the need to maintain the motivational contract of the professional in situations where the client demands incremental innovation. The individual may be working for several months or years on a client account where opportunities to engage in variation, risk taking, experimentation, and discovery (March 1991: 71) are limited. This is often combined with long-term trusting client relationships where the client can demand that a particular individual work with them. In this context the PSFs adopt a career management perspective. For example, a more senior professional would be involved in mentoring a mid-career specialist in the same profession and industry. Then, as the client confidence and professional respect (characteristic of cooperative external social capital) develops, the more senior professional can be given the opportunity to leverage the client experience internally in the firm by working on new product development. This is often the case in financial modeling or pitching for new business in, for example, advertising agencies. Alternatively, the individual would work on different client accounts within the same sector.

21.6 CONCLUSIONS AND IMPLICATIONS

In this chapter we have adopted a knowledge-based perspective on HRM and performance in PSFs. We have defined performance as innovative outputs and have illustrated how multidimensional knowledge assets need to be managed to sustain the success of the PSF. Our emphasis was on performance management in the context of strategic Human Resource Management (HRM) practices and we sought to be appreciative of:

(i) The importance of *knowledge* in generating firm-level performance. This enables us to look beyond mere financial, growth, or target-based approaches to performance and we therefore adopted a view which paid attention to inputs (knowledge resources), processes and practices (HRM models), and outputs (innovation).

(ii) The *multidimensionality of knowledge resources* which enable performance (innovative outputs). We include *human capital* (knowledge and skills) *and social capital* (relationships inside and outside the PSF).

(iii) The *variation in approaches* to managing these various knowledge resources. We identified two prominent HRM models, i.e., *centripetal and centrifugal*. Each HRM model varied according to the focus of its HRM practices (firm-centric or client-centric) and the way in which the PSF seeks to manage the permeability of the boundaries with its clients.

The identification of the two HRM models which can be used to manage human and social capital in PSFs has important theoretical implications. Firstly, it demonstrates how HRM can play a strategic role in the generation of competitive advantage where firms rely on their individual and collective knowledge assets. This provides the opportunity for HR to demonstrate its legitimacy and the potential contribution of their role in professional firms. Secondly, we have a greater understanding of how the context of the firm, in particular its client relationships, influences the adoption of particular HRM models needed to manage diverse knowledge assets. Some insights have also been provided into the HRM practices used in firms which rely on their expertise or efficiency to generate their competitive advantage. Thirdly, we add to the work of Lepak and Snell (2007), Kang and Snell (2009), and Hitt et al. (2001) by providing empirical evidence of the links between HRM and the maximization of competitive advantage in knowledge-based firms.

Further research in this area might consider the particular role that HRM might play in this context to maximize its contribution to competitive advantage. In particular, there is a need to understand how HRM practices can extend beyond the boundaries of the firm to manage not only a diverse range of client relationships but also other stakeholders such as professional bodies, suppliers, and collaborators. This would allow the benefits of the cross-boundary or network-based perspective on HRM to be exploited fully whereas the current HRM approaches tend to be dominated by an intra-organizational perspective.

A second future research avenue includes a more systematic consideration of the HRM models identified here in a heterogeneous range of PSFs. These considerations would benefit from a focus on a variety of governance structures and knowledge characteristics as well as the nature of the professional service provided. Moreover, we also need to consider internal heterogeneity and the impact of the pace of external and internal change on the adoption of specific HRM practices. Developments in external market conditions may lead to changes in the knowledge required and client relations leading to adaptations to these HRM models.

The final area for future research could consider the impact of these models on employee commitment and turnover and the subsequent effect on firm performance. In particular, future work can consider whether a centripetal model would be associated with high levels of organizational commitment while a centrifugal model would be associated with higher levels of commitment to the client. The wider implications of the network-based perspective on HRM for performance might also be usefully explored. Indeed, this perspective poses a challenge to measures based solely within the firm and encourages the development of both firm- and network-based performance evaluation.

In conclusion, the management of professionals and PSFs using HRM practices and, specifically, performance management is complex and needs to be sensitive to the multiplicity of knowledge resources, the inherent personal and political processes, and the need to achieve the golden mean which enables innovative outputs. In particular, the identification and resolution of tensions associated with the management of diverse human and social capital inside and outside the firm within heterogeneous and fast-changing environments presents a fascinating challenge for those seeking to understand the links between HRM and performance in PSFs.

NOTE

1. We are thankful to the Chartered Institute of Personnel and Development (CIPD) who funded the research on HRM practices in Professional Services Firms that we present here. Our research was carried out in a range of PSFs including consulting, software, law, and creative organizations.

REFERENCES

Alewell, D. and Hansen, N. K. (2012). "Human Resource Management Systems: A Structured Review of Research Contributions and Open Questions," *German Journal of Industrial Relations* 19: 90–123.

Alvesson, M. (2004). *Knowledge Work and Knowledge-Intensive Firms*. Oxford: Oxford University Press.

Alvesson, M. and Empson, L. (2008). "The Construction of Organizational Identity: Comparative Case Studies of Consulting Firms," *Scandinavian Journal of Management* 24(1): 1–16.

Barney, J. B. (1991). "Firm Resources and Sustained Competitive Advantage," *Journal of Management* 17(1): 99–120.

Baron, J. N. and Kreps, D. M. (1999). *Strategic Human Resources: Frameworks for General Managers.* New York: John Wiley.

Becker, G. (1964). *Human Capital.* New York: Columbia University Press.

Becker, T. E. (2009). "Interpersonal Commitments," in *Commitment in Organizations: Accumulated Wisdom and New Directions*, ed. H. J. Klein, T. E. Becker, and J. P. Meyer. New York: Routledge, 137–178.

Bentein, K., Stinglhamber, F., and Vandenberghe, C. (2002). "Organization, Supervisor, and Workgroup Directed Commitments and Citizenship Behaviours: A Comparison of Models," *European Journal of Work and Organizational Psychology* 11: 341–362.

Burt, G. (1992). *Structural Holes.* Cambridge, MA: Harvard University Press.

Coff, R. W. (1997). "Human Assets and Management Dilemmas: Coping with Hazards on the Road to Resource Based Theory," *Academy of Management Review* 22(2): 374–402.

Davenport, T. (1999) *Human Capital.* San Francisco, CA: Jossey-Bass.

Davis-Blake, A. and Hui, P. P. (2003). "Contracting Talent for Knowledge-Based Competition," in *Managing Knowledge for Sustained Competitive Advantage*, ed. S. E. Jackson, M. A. Hitt, and A. S. DeNisi. San Francisco, CA: Jossey-Bass, 178–206.

Delery, J. and Doty, D. (1996). "Modes of Theorizing in Strategic Human Resource Management: Tests of Universalistic, Contingency and Configurational Performance Predictions," *Academy of Management Journal* 39(4): 165–197.

Doorewaard, H. and Meihuizen, H. (2000). "Strategic Performance Options in Professional Service Organizations," *Human Resource Management Journal* 10(2): 37–57.

Empson, L. (2001). "Introduction: Knowledge Management in Professional Service Firms," *Human Relations* 54(7): 811–817.

Gimeno, J., Folta, T., B., Cooper, A. C., and Woo, C. Y. (1997). "Survival of the Fittest? Entrepreneurial Human Capital and the Persistence of Underperforming Firms," *Administrative Science Quarterly* 42(4): 750–783.

Hansen, N. K. and Alewell, D. (2013). "Employment Systems as Governance Mechanisms of Human Capital and Capability Development," *International Journal of Human Resource Management* 24(11): 2131–2153.

Hislop, D. (2003). "Linking Human Resource Management and Knowledge Management via Commitment: A Review and Research Agenda," *Employee Relations* 25(2): 182–202.

Hislop, D. (2009). *Knowledge Management in Organizations: A Critical Introduction*, 2nd edn. Oxford: Oxford University Press.

Hitt, M., Bierman, L., Shimizu, K., and Kochhar, R. (2001). "Direct and Moderating Effects of Human Capital on Strategy Performance in Professional Service Firms: A Resource-Based Perspective," *Academy of Management Journal* 44(1): 13–28.

Huselid, M. A. (1995). "The Impact of Human Resource Management Practices on Turnover, Productivity, and Corporate Financial Performance," *Academy of Management Journal* 38(3): 635–672.

Jackson, S. E., Hitt, M. A., and DeNisi, A. (eds.) (2003). *Managing Knowledge for Sustained Competitive Advantage.* San Francisco, CA: Jossey-Bass.

Kang, S. C. and Snell, S. (2009). "Intellectual Capital Architectures and Ambidextrous Learning: A Framework for Human Resource Management," *Journal of Management Studies* 46(1): 65–92.

Kang, S. C., Morris, S., and Snell, S. (2007). "Relational Archetypes, Organizational Learning and Value Creation: Extending the Human Resource Architecture," *Academy of Management Review* 32(1): 236–256.

Kang, S., Snell, S., and Swart, J., (2012). "Options-Based HRM, Intellectual Capital and Exploratory and Exploitive Learning in Law Firms' Practice Groups," *Human Resource Management* 51(4): 461–485.

Kase, R., Paauwe, J., and Zupan, N. (2009). "HR Practices, Interpersonal Relations and Intra-Firm Knowledge Transfer in Knowledge-Intensive Firms: A Social Network Perspective," *Human Resource Management* 48(4): 615–639.

Kim, H. and Gong, Y. (2009). "The Roles of Tacit Knowledge and OCB in the Relationship between Group-Based Pay and Firm Performance," *Human Resource Management Journal* 19(2): 120–139.

Kimberly, J. and Evanisko, M. J. (1981). "Organizational Innovation: The Influence of Individual, Organizational and Contextual Factors on Hospital Adoption of Technological Administrative Innovations," *Academy of Management Journal* 24(4): 689–713.

Kinnie, N. and Swart J. (2012). "Committed to Whom? Professional Knowledge Worker Commitment in Cross-Boundary Organizations," *Human Resource Management Journal* 22(1): 21–38.

Kirkpatrick, I., Muzio, D., and Ackroyd, S. (2011). "Professions and Professionalism in Management Consulting," in *The Oxford Handbook of Management Consulting*, ed. M. Kipping and T. Clark. Oxford: Oxford University Press, 187–206.

Lawler, E. E. (2003). "Reward Systems in Knowledge-Based Organizations," in *Managing Knowledge for Sustained Competitive Advantage*, ed. S. E. Jackson, M. A. Hitt, and A. S. DeNisi. San Francisco, CA: Jossey-Bass, 274–302.

Leana, C. R. and Van Buren, H. J. (1999). "Organizational Social Capital and Employment Practices," *Academy of Management Review* 24(3): 538–555.

Lepak, D. and Snell, S. A. (1999). "The Strategic Management of Human Capital: Determinants and Implications of Different Relationships," *Academy of Management Review* 24(1): 1–18.

Lepak, D. and Snell, S. A. (2002). "Examining the Human Resource Architecture: The Relationship among Human Capital, Employment, and Human Resource Configurations," *Journal of Management* 28(4): 517–543.

Lepak, D. P. and Snell, S. A. (2003). "Managing the Human Resource Architecture for Knowledge Based Competition," in *Managing Knowledge for Sustained Competitive Advantage*, ed. S. E. Jackson, M. A. Hitt, and A. S. DeNisi. San Francisco, CA: Jossey-Bass, 127–154.

Lepak, D. P. and Snell, S. A. (2007). "Employment Subsystems and the 'HR Architecture'," in *The Oxford Handbook of Human Resource Management*, ed. P. Boxall, J. Purcell, and P. Wright. Oxford: Oxford University Press, 201–230.

Lepak, D. P., Liao, H., Chung, Y., and Harden, E. (2006). "A Conceptual Review of Human Resource Management Systems in Strategic Human Resource Management Research," *Research in Personnel and Human Resource Management* 25: 217–271.

Lepak, D., Takeuchi, R., and Swart, J. (2011). "How Organizations Evaluate and Maintain Fit of Human Capital with Their Needs," in *The Oxford Handbook of Human Capital*, ed. A. Burton-Jones and J.-C. Spender. Oxford: Oxford University Press, 333–358.

Lopez, S. P., Peon, J. M., and Ordas, C. M. (2006). "Human Resource Management as a Determining Factor in Organizational Learning," *Management Learning* 37(2): 215–239.

Maister, D. (1993). *Managing the Professional Service Firm*. New York: Free Press.

Malhotra, N., Morris, T., and Smets, M. (2010). "New Career Models in UK Professional Service Firms: From Up-or-Out to Up-and-Going-Nowhere?" *International Journal of Human Resource Management* 21(9): 1396–1414.

Malos, S. B. and Campion, M. A. (1995). "An Options-Based Model of Career Mobility in Professional Service Firms," *Academy of Management Review* 20(3): 611–644.

Malos, S. B. and Campion, M. A. (2000): "Human Resource Strategy and Career Mobility in Professional Service Firms: A Test of an Options-Based Model," *Academy of Management Journal* 43(4): 749–760.

March, J. G. (1991). "Exploration and Exploitation in Organizational Learning," *Organization Science* 2(1): 71–87.

Marchington, M., Rubery, J., and Grimshaw, D. (2011). "Alignment Integration and Consistency in HRM across Multi-Employer Networks," *Human Resource Management* 50(3): 313–339.

Minbaeva, D., Foss, N., and Snell, S. (2009). "Bringing the Knowledge Perspective into HRM," *Human Resource Management* 48(4): 477–483.

Morris, T. and Pinnington, A. (1998). "Promotion to Partner in Professional Service Firms," *Human Relations* 51(1): 3–23.

Nahapiet, J. and Ghoshal, S. (1998). "Social Capital, Intellectual Capital, and the Organizational Advantage," *Academy of Management Review* 23(2): 242–266.

Nikolova, N., Reihlen, M., and Schlapfner, J.-F. (2009). "Client-Consultant Interaction: Capturing Social Practices of Professional Service Production," *Scandinavian Journal of Management* 25(3): 289–298.

Oldham, G. R. (2003). "Stimulating and Supporting Creativity in Organizations," in *Managing Knowledge for Sustained Competitive Advantage*, ed. S. E. Jackson, M. A. Hitt, and A. S. DeNisi. San Francisco, CA: Jossey-Bass, 243–273.

Pennings, J. M., Lee, K., and Van Witteloostuijn, A. (1998). "Human Capital, Social Capital and Firm Dissolution," *Academy of Management Journal* 41(4): 425–440.

Postmes, T., Tanis, M., and de Wit, B. (2001). "Communication and Commitment in Organizations: A Social Identity Approach," *Group Processes and Intergroup Relations* 4(3): 227–246.

Pulakos, E. D., Dorsey, D. W., and Borman, W.C. (2003). "Hiring for Knowledge-Based Competition," in *Managing Knowledge for Sustained Competitive Advantage*, ed. S. E. Jackson, M. A. Hitt, and A. S. DeNisi. San Francisco, CA: Jossey-Bass, 155–177.

Sherer, P. (1995). "Leveraging Human Assets in Law Firms: Human Capital Structures and Organizational Capabilities," *Industrial and Labor Relations Review* 48(4): 671–691.

Sherer, P. D. and Lee, K. (2002). "Institutional Change in Large Law Firms: A Resource Dependency and Institutional Perspective," *Academy of Management Journal* 45(1): 102–119.

Smets, M., Morris, T., and Malhotra, N. (2012). "Changing Career Models and Capacity for Innovation in Professional Services," in *Handbook of Research on Entrepreneurship in Professional Services*, ed. M. Rheilen and A. Werr. Cheltenham: Edward Elgar, 127–147.

Snell, S. A. (2002). "Social Capital and Strategic HRM: It's Who You Know," *Human Resource Planning* 22(1): 62–65.

Storey, J. and Quintas, P. (2001). "Knowledge Management and HRM," in *Human Resource Management: A Critical Text*, ed. J. Storey. London: Thompson Learning, 339–363.

Swart, J. (2006). "Intellectual Capital: Disentangling an Enigmatic Concept," *Journal of Intellectual Capital* 7(2): 136–159.

Swart, J. (2007). "HRM and Knowledge Workers," in *The Oxford Handbook of Human Resource Management*, ed. P. Boxall, J. Purcell, and P. Wright. Oxford: Oxford University Press, 450–468.

Swart, J. (2011). "That's Why It Matters: The Value Generating Properties of Knowledge," *Management Learning* 49(3): 319–332.

Swart, J. and Harvey, P. (2011). "Identifying Knowledge Boundaries: The Case of Networked Projects," *Journal of Knowledge Management* 15(5): 703–721.

Swart, J. and Kinnie, N. (2003). "HR Systems in Growing Knowledge Intensive Firms: The Impact of Client Relationships," *Human Resource Management Journal* 13(3): 37–55.

Swart, J. and Kinnie, N. (2010). "Organisational Learning, Knowledge Assets and HR Practices in Professional Service Firms," *Human Resource Management Journal* 20(1): 64–79.

Swart, J. and Kinnie, N. (2013). "Managing Multi-Dimensional Knowledge Assets: HR Configurations in Professional Service Firms," *Human Resource Management Journal* 23(2): 160–179.

Swart, J. and Kinnie, N. (2014). "Re-considering Boundaries: Human Resource Management in a Networked World," *Human Resource Management* 53(2): 291–310.

Swart, J., Kinnie, N., and Van Rossenberg, Y. (2013). "With Whom Do I Share My Knowledge? Commitment Profiles and Knowledge Sharing Behaviour," paper presented at the Organizational Learning, Knowledge and Capability conference. Washington, April 23–25.

Taylor, S. (2007). "Creating Social Capital in MNCs: The International Human Resource Management Challenge," *Human Resource Management Journal* 17(4): 336–354.

Tsui, A. S. and Wang, D. (2002). "Employment Relationships from the Employer's Perspective: Current Research and Future Directions," *International Review of Industrial and Organizational Psychology* 17: 77–114.

Tsui, A. S., Pearce, J. L., Porter, L. W., and Hite, J. P. (1995). "Choice of Employee-Organization Relationship: Influence of External and Internal Organizational Factors," in *Research in Personal and Human Resources Management*, vol. 13, ed. G. R. Ferris. Greenwich, CT: JAI Press, 117–151.

Vandenberghe, C. and Bentein, K. (2009). "A Closer Look at the Relationship between Affective Commitment to Supervisors and Organizations and Turnover," *Journal of Occupational and Organizational Psychology* 82(2): 331–348.

von Nordenflycht, A. (2010). "What is A Professional Service Firm? Toward a Theory and Taxonomy of Knowledge-Intensive Firms," *Academy of Management Review* 35(1): 155–175.

Walker, G., Kogut, B., and Shan, W. (1997). "Social Capital, Structural Holes and the Formation of an Industry Network," *Organization Science* 8(2): 109–125.

Wilkesmann, U. (2009). "Cultural Characteristics of Knowledge Transfer," *Journal of Knowledge Management* 13(6): 464–477.

Wright, P., Dunford, B., and Snell, S. A. (2001). "Human Resources and the Resource-Based View of the Firm," *Journal of Management* 27(6): 701–721.

Xiao, Z. and Tsui, A. S. (2007). "When Brokers May Not Work: The Cultural Contingency of Social Capital in Chinese High-Tech Firms," *Administrative Science Quarterly* 52(1): 1–31.

Youndt, M. A. and Snell, S. (2004). "Human Resource Configurations, Intellectual Capital and Organizational Performance," *Journal of Management Issues* 16(3): 337–360.

Youndt, M. A., Subramanian, O., and Snell, S. A. (2004). "Intellectual Capital Profiles: An Examination of Investment and Returns," *Journal of Management Studies* 41(2): 335–361.

Zagenczyk, T. J. and Murrell, A. M (2009). "It Is Better to Receive than to Give: Advice Network Effect on Job and Work-Unit," *Journal of Business and Psychology* 24(2): 139–152.

Zupan, N. and Kase, R. (2007). "The Role of HR Actors in Knowledge Networks," *International Journal of Manpower* 28(3–4): 243–259.

Index